Against All Hope

RESISTANCE IN THE NAZI
CONCENTRATION CAMPS
1938–1945

Against All Hope

RESISTANCE IN THE NAZI
CONCENTRATION CAMPS
1938–1945

By Hermann Langbein

TRANSLATED BY HARRY ZOHN

Paragon House / New York

First American edition, 1994

Published in the United States by

Paragon House
370 Lexington Ave.
New York, New York 10017

Copyright © 1994 by Paragon House

Originally published in German under the title . . . *nicht wie
die Schafe zur Schlachtbank: Widerstand in den
nationalsozialistischen Konzentrationslagern 1938–1945.*
Copyright © Fischer Taschenbuch Verlag, 1980.

Manufactured in the United States of America

Library of Congress Cataloging-in-Publication Data

Langbein, Hermann, 1912–
[—nicht wie die Schafe zur Schlachtbank. English]
Against all hope : resistance in the Nazi concentration camps,
1938–1945 / by Hermann Langbein ;
translated from the German by Harry Zohn.—1st U.S. ed.
p.   cm.
Includes bibliographical references and index.
ISBN 1-55778-363-2
1. Anti-Nazi movements—Germany.   2. Concentration camps—
Germany.   3. Germany—Politics and government—1933–1945.   4. World
War, 1939–1945—Concentration camps.   I. Title.
DD256.3.L3313   1994
943.086—dc20   93-16247
                                                        CIP

Contents

The Actions

The End

Appendix

1

INTRODUCTION

There already exists an extensive bibliography of writings about the Nazi concentration camps. Many books, however, have not been translated into other languages, and a considerable number are not to be found even in specialized libraries, for in the early years after the defeat of National Socialism, international communication was still difficult, and the paper shortage of those days permitted only small editions. Moreover, even experts cannot be familiar with what literature is accessible, and despite innumerable publications, the subject has not been exhausted.

More than anything else, the Nazi concentration camps teach us how the ideology of German National Socialism was to be translated into action, for in this area Nazism was able to put its plans into practice without being inhibited by traditions, where it was necessary to build upon existing institutions. The National Socialists created their concentration camps from scratch, and operated them with people selected and specially trained. In these camps they carried their theory about a master race to its logical conclusion: the extermination of human beings whom their ideology equated, on the basis of their descent, with vermin that could be destroyed without qualms. Those who had been trained to pour the poison gas Zyklon B (hydrocyanic or prussic acid) into the gas chambers of Auschwitz were officially called "disinfectors."

The mass murder of concentration-camp inmates did not begin until 1941, when disabled and "racially inferior" prisoners were transferred to "euthanasia" institutions and there butchered. Nevertheless, these camps were equipped from the beginning in such a way that they could later—without regard for laws still in force—safely serve as sites for mass murder. No other fascist or totalitarian system has so ideologically motivated and prepared genocide and so utilized the institutions of the state for this purpose. This differentiates German National Socialism from all other fascist regimes, and that is why its concentration camps, the sites of this

1

mass extermination, are not comparable to those that were—or still are—in use in other countries. It is for this reason that not only survivors of those camps but also modern historians, psychologists, sociologists, writers, and artists have repeatedly concerned themselves with the conditions in those camps. David Rousset has described them as *"l'univers concentrationnaire"* and Eugen Kogon as "the SS state"—a world all its own from which the natural laws of any human community were banished.

Any caprice or whim could mean the death of a prisoner, and nobody asked why this prisoner had been killed. Those concentration-camp inmates who were allowed to live were turned into numbers, deprived of the last vestige of human dignity, and transformed into the totally submissive objects of the SS men running the camps.

This is reflected in numerous reports published after the liberation of the camps, when survivors felt a need to cry out about the torments they had suffered. For the succeeding generations this created a distorted stereotype of the concentration camp victim. When younger people meet survivors, they often cry out in bewilderment: "Why did you let yourself be led to slaughter like sheep?"

It is too little known that there was resistance in the camps—in defiance of an inconceivably brutal and totally effective system of terror—resistance to the killing of human beings and of everything human, and not just individual resistance, but organized resistance. In view of the dimensions of the crimes committed by the SS, some may regard this activity as insignificant. However, in all camps many people did try to resist and were not discouraged by repeated disappointments or life-and-death decisions that such activities required. As a rule only a small number of people could be helped, and selecting some meant deciding not to help others. Such resistance is convincing proof that an inhumane regime, although it can murder people, cannot completely stamp out human impulses on the part of others. This experience fills me with optimism, and thus I feel that all the difficulties and problems connected with these actions should be better known than they are. This is why I have chosen, as the subject of my final study of the Nazi concentration camps, the resistance in those camps.

Many episodes of resistance have already been written up, but so far there has been no comprehensive critical presentation that faces up to the problems this resistance involved. There are many obstacles to such a presentation, many problems that someone who has never experienced the world of the Nazi camps cannot understand. On the other hand, a former inmate of a camp finds it difficult to muster the necessary scholarly detachment. Furthermore, everyone experienced the camps differently, and therefore the reports and stories differ from one another. Whereas one person relates episodes of a resistance movement from personal experience, another inmate of the same camp at the same time reports that there was no organized resistance of any kind. When an incident of resistance is described to such a person, he is apt to call it an ex post facto fabrication, for he never heard about secret activities. Then, too, there are different reports about many actions—not the result of faulty recollection but of personal, political, or national conflicts in the camps, and most frequently as the result of revisionist efforts to give credit to a political ideology or a nation. It therefore seemed best to attempt a comprehensive critical presentation, while eyewitnesses are still alive. If there are contradictions in the description of individual episodes, such eyewitnesses can be consulted. On more than one occasion it was brought home to me how short time is. There are quite a few people whom I can no longer thank for sharing their experiences with me, for they died while I was working on this book.

If this work is to meet scholarly standards, there can be no whitewash for the sake of any person or party, and no negative comments must be suppressed. An author must decide whether critical voices should be disregarded because the people criticized were murdered by the SS as a result of their resistance activities. I do not believe that negative facts or opinions should be ignored, and thus I have cited these complaints. This certainly does not diminish one's respect for those who deliberately, in addition to all the perils of life in a concentration camp, courted the dangers of resistance activity. From a historian's viewpoint such voices are important, too. If an author balked at reproducing criticisms of the martyred, then no one could point out the errors of those German officers who consciously risked their privileged positions, their lives, and the lives of their families in an attempt to assassinate Hitler. If criticism of the dead were taboo, important chapters of modern history, which could teach us a great deal, would remain unwritten.

The present study delimits its subject by beginning its description of the resistance with the arrival of foreigners—the time when the character of the camps was changed. This is not meant to suggest that there was no resistance prior to that, or that this resistance was of less value. However, when only Germans were detained in the concentration camps, resistance was different in nature. In those years the camps were still relatively small and more easily managed by the SS men, who did not need to consolidate their control by playing the members of various nations off against one another.

April 2, 1938, marked the arrival of Austrians, the first foreigners in the concentration camps. To be sure, this did not yet alter the character of those camps, for the National Socialists regarded them as Germans and treated them as such in the camps. However, following the occupation of Czechoslovakia (March 15, 1939), and especially after the beginning of the war, there was an influx of all those nations that the Nazis' military victories brought under their control. The numbers of these foreigners increased steadily and shaped the specific character of the concentration camps, and this in turn determined all resistance activity that followed— in the worst, and therefore most decisive, years.

This study deals only with the concentration camps under the central camp administration, and it does not include ghettos and special camps, like Theresienstadt or Hinzert, and such transit camps as Drancy or Westerbork. In these special areas, organizers created conditions far different from those in the real concentration camps, and hence resistance activity faced different conditions as well. An analysis of such camps would have led us too far afield.

I have made one exception, however, by including the camps devoted entirely to extermination, primarily Treblinka and Sobibor, though these were not under the above-mentioned central management. The small number of prisoners—people who were allowed to live there only for as long as the camp management could use them to work in the gas chambers and crematoria—lived under the same extreme conditions as the members of similar special units at Auschwitz. Thus the uprisings at Treblinka and Sobibor had to be prepared under conditions analogous to those at Auschwitz, and their activity had to be described in the same context. In the final analysis, if the activities in the extermination camps were not discussed in this work, it would be hard for me to rectify the misconception "Why did you let yourself be led to slaughter like sheep?"

So much for the definition of my subject. To avoid the constant repetition of elaborate circumlocutions, I have resorted to some of the lingo of the camps. For example, prisoners are described in accordance with the triangular insignia they had to wear next to or under their camp numbers. Thus the political prisoners are designated as Reds (wearing a red triangle) and those with a criminal record as Greens (with a green marking). With few exceptions the Greens were Germans (or Austrians, who were regarded as Germans). Irrespective of the reason for their imprisonment, foreigners usually wore a red marking plus an initial indicating their nationality. Some categories of inmates wore triangles of different colors, but these hardly figured in resistance activities—with the exception of Jehovah's Witnesses, who were designated by a violet triangle. Those sent to a concentration camp for "racial" reasons were given special markings and treatment. Under their marking Jews wore two yellow triangles sewn on in such a way that a Star of David was formed. Gypsies had to wear the black triangle of the "antisocials"; when they were concentrated in Auschwitz, starting in February 1943, they were given special numbers that started with a Z (for *Zigeuner*, "Gypsy").

In the camps people usually called fellow inmates by their first names, frequently the usual short form—for instance, Rudi for Rudolf, Sepp for Joseph, Schorsch for Georg, Gustl for August, Edek for Edward, and Zbyszek for Zbigniew (the last two being Polish names). Such forms are found in later reports quoted in this study.

A number of family names appear in different versions because the authors had only heard and not read them. Russian names are variously transliterated. I have consistently used either the version that is proved correct by existing documents, or in the absence of documents, the one most frequently encountered. Transliterations from the Cyrillic alphabet are given in the phonetically most logical version (in the present edition, American phonetics—ed.).

Finally, I beg my readers' indulgence for the bulk of the apparatus, but it appeared necessary to cite every source that I used. To minimize references to notes, the publications listed in the bibliography have been entered according to the author/date system—author's name plus the date of the publication quoted and the page number (e.g., Bayle 1950, 142).

This book had a gestation period of seven years, and I spent the first half of this period collecting documents, comparing sources, and submitting available records to eyewitnesses. This work would have been impossible without the support and exceptional patience of the Ludwig Boltzmann Institute for the History of the Workers' Movement at the University of Linz, the assistance of numerous institutes devoted to modern history, and especially the readiness of many survivors to share their memories and give me access to their notes. I hope these informants will forgive me for not expressing my gratitude individually, but readers will find the names of those helpful persons and institutes in the notes and bibliography.

Many of those who in defiance of all impediments and perils mustered the strength for resistance in a Nazi concentration camp are mentioned by name, but others had to remain unnamed. There was no one to bear witness to their efforts and deeds, and their names have not come down to us. It is to them in particular that this book is dedicated.

The Conditions

2

THE CONCENTRATION CAMPS
FROM 1938 TO 1945

Living conditions in the concentration camps changed materially in the course of the years, and so did the conditions for resistance activity. Such activities were, of course, also decisively influenced by developments at the front. There is no need to discuss the course of the war here. The changes in the camps will be discussed to the extent that they were significant for resistance activity, but first I must briefly cover the period from 1933 to 1938.

Unlike some institutions in other countries that gave the Nazi concentration camps their name, the latter were not a concomitant of the war. From the outset they constituted a major component of the terrorism on which National Socialism was based. In other areas Nazism continued certain traditions, but in the special field of terrorism, it was inventive and struck out in new directions.

At an early stage, various internment camps for political opponents—spontaneously established after Hitler's appointment as Reich chancellor—were placed under the central administration of the SS. This laid the foundation for the SS state. The first concentration camp was Dachau, and the central administration always regarded it as a model camp whose institutions were copied by the other camps. At the beginning of the period under discussion here, before April 2, 1938, Buchenwald and Sachsenhausen were in operation as well.

Since Sachsenhausen was established under circumstances that differed from those of the other concentration camps, a brief history of that camp is in order here. In the summer of 1938 prisoners from the Esterwegen camp—which, like many others, was later disbanded—were assigned to build a camp at Sachsenhausen. There were an equal number of political prisoners (Reds) and convicts (Greens) who had been equally oppressed by the very brutal terror in Esterwegen and had thus "acquired solidarity," as one of them put it. "We tolerated one another," Harry Naujoks wrote by way of characterizing this shared period—a time before the SS men had begun to play one group off against another.[1] Heinz Junge, who was sent to Sachsenhausen at a later date, even speaks of a "good collaboration" between the Reds and the Greens,[2] a description unique to that camp. For instance, on November 28, 1942, eighteen German Reds were punitively transferred from Sachsenhausen to the Flossenbürg concentration camp and marked for being "done in." The camp administration at Flossenbürg instructed the Greens, who were holding a key position in the so-called inmate self-operation, to keep the new arrivals in strict isolation. Nevertheless, the Greens protected the eighteen men, for they had known them from Sachsenhausen. Franz Ahrens cites a statement by the senior inmate of that camp, whom he describes as a "gentleman thief": "In Sachsenhausen you treated us like comrades, and you can be sure that we shall treat you the same way here" (Ahrens 1968, 94). Naujoks, one of the eighteen, emphasizes that "the help of the Greens was most extraordinary," and it was effective, for despite the particularly harsh measures of the SS—actions then no longer being taken against German prisoners—they stayed alive. The only exceptions were Hans Guckenham and Rudi Grosse, who were killed by the SS in a quarry that was part of the camp (Lienau 1949, 85).[3]

The extraordinary nature of this comradeship is underlined by comparison with the treatment suffered at Flossenbürg by political prisoners transferred from Dachau more than two years earlier. According to a report by Alfred Hübsch, they were given a spiteful reception by Green capos (trusties) who knew them from Dachau and now gloated over having the Reds under their control.[4] Karl Ludwig Schecher, who was sent to Flossenbürg at that time, speaks of convicts taking revenge on Reds: "They did what we had done in Dachau"—that is, they kept the Reds from holding any office.[5]

Fritz Selbmann, one of the eighteen men transferred from Sachsenhausen, cites a statement by the prominent Greens in the camp: In the event of a "revolution," the Communists would be important people, and then it would be helpful to be in their good graces (Selbmann, 1961, 281). By this he means that the Reds from Dachau arrived in Flossenbürg right after the beginning of the war, whereas those from Sachsenhausen did not come until a German defeat at Stalingrad was looming. However, as Selbmann has confirmed, the extraordinary atmosphere to which sixteen men from Sachsenhausen owed their lives was surely a result of the time the political prisoners and criminals had shared in Esterwegen.[6] This special relationship between the Reds and the Greens made itself felt at Sachsenhausen in other ways as well.

After April 2, 1938, but before the outbreak of the war, the Flossenbürg, Mauthausen, and Ravensbrück camps were established. The last-named was the first camp for women, and Mauthausen the first in an occupied country (Austria). Neuengamme was built in 1938 as well; it functioned as a satellite camp of Sachsenhausen at first and did not become an independent camp until June 1940.

The establishment of these new concentration camps on the eve of Hitler's war was the central camp administration's way of preparing for the conflict, for the only discernible reason for such expansion was to make room for prisoners from conquered countries.

After the beginning of the war, additional camps were established in the captured areas. On May 20, 1940, Auschwitz was built in the part of Poland that was added to Upper Silesia, and on August 2 of the same year a camp was established at Gross–Rosen, near Breslau (now Wrocław), that was also primarily intended for Polish prisoners. It was initially a satellite camp of Sachsenhausen, but on May 1, 1941, it was given the status of an independent concentration camp. On the same day, following the fall of France, the Natzweiler camp was established in Alsace,[7] and the camp at Stutthof near Danzig (now Gdansk), which had hitherto housed civilians, was added to the list of camps administered by the central office at Oranienburg.

Whether these new camps started out as satellites of existing camps or were independent from the beginning, their SS personnel brought along prisoners who, they knew from experience in other camps, had performed certain functions satisfactorily.[8]

"The first inmates of Neuengamme," writes Albin Lüdke, "were hundreds of Greens. Things were wild in those days."[9] Further transfers from Sachsenhausen in the first part of 1940 included political prisoners, Lüdke among them. Neuengamme and Gross–Rosen, originally satellite camps, received from the Sachsenhausen camp thirty inmates who were to be used to intensify the SS terror—hence the choice by SS Roll-call Officer (Rapportführer) Palitzsch of Greens. They were brutal murderers, who could easily clash with the Polish new arrivals because several of them came from the multilingual area of Silesia, where national conflicts were virulent—or so the SS thought. But among them was a Green who was not minded to lord it over his Polish fellow prisoners. Instead, he befriended many Poles and eventually played a major part in the resistance movement of Auschwitz.

At Natzweiler, the cadre of approximately 150 men also came from Sachsenhausen and consisted predominantly of Greens. This group included the Austrian Karl Haas, who wore red markings (his unusual story, a special episode in the resistance at Natzweiler, will be told at a later point), and it was soon followed by a second group. Other German prisoners, predominantly Greens, were transferred from Sachsenhausen to

Auschwitz to take over certain roles in that fast-growing camp. Three hundred criminals were sent from Dachau to build Mauthausen, and as already mentioned, Greens from Sachsenhausen were transferred to Flossenbürg.

For simplicity's sake, those camps that had been established as satellite camps and did not become independent until a later date are here discussed as regular camps. This applies to Dora, which was years later established as a subsidiary camp of Buchenwald, before it achieved sorry celebrity as the Dora–Mittelbau concentration camp.

Prior to September 1939 large numbers of prisoners were occasionally released. In April 1939, in honor of the Führer's birthday, 2,300 prisoners were released from Buchenwald and 1,200 from Sachsenhausen. Those from Buchenwald were mostly "antisocials," and among those from Sachsenhausen were 250 or 300 political prisoners, including prominent Communists who had performed important functions in the camp. They had also occupied positions in the clandestine Communist organization, and thus their release necessitated its reorganization.[10] At that time the Communist underground in Buchenwald went through a particularly critical phase, for shortly before Theo Neubauer's April release, another leader, the Communist Reichstag delegate Walter Stoecker, died. Hasso Grabner may be exaggerating when he says that "the camp was like an orphaned child whose beloved father has died," but his statement does graphically illustrate the importance of these two Communist functionaries in the early period.[11]

At that time around 400 prisoners were released from Dachau—"a mixture of political prisoners and criminals," as Karl Röder put it, "including both well-known and unknown people, high officers of political parties as well as little fellow travelers." This strange mix caused this action to be called "journeyman amnesty."[12] After the outbreak of the war, large numbers of German anti-Fascists were arrested again, with 500 being sent to Sachsenhausen alone. Thereafter major release actions were limited to Buchenwald; these involved mainly Germans, but some Dutchmen, who had been arrested as hostages, were also released.[13] These actions were not resumed until the SS was recruiting Germans, at first convicts and later political prisoners, for the special SS unit named after its commander, Oskar Dirlewanger (a penal arm of the SS, to which other branches of the SS sent their delinquent members for punishment—ed.). There are statistics to indicate that the stop of releases was due to a desire to keep events in the camp from becoming public knowledge. In the first half of 1942, 952 prisoners were released from Auschwitz, but in the second half there were only twenty-six. In the middle of that year, the machinery of extermination was started at Auschwitz (Gutman/Rothkirchen 1976, 309).

A few figures may illustrate the size of the camps and the composition of the prisoners in that period. Before September 1938, Buchenwald had fewer than 8,000 inmates; then a large number of foreigners were brought in for the first time—Jews from Austria. On November 9–10, 1938, the infamous pogrom known as *Kristallnacht* (the Night of Broken Glass) took place [so called from the many plate glass windows of Jewish shopkeepers that were smashed and synagogues that were burned—ed.]. Mass arrests were carried out all over Germany, and the number of prisoners was raised to almost 20,000. But deaths, releases of rounded-up Jews, and transfers of Greens to Mauthausen and Flossenbürg reduced Buchenwald to less than 5,400. The camp reached this lowest point just before the outbreak of the war; then Germans "unfit to bear arms," the first Czechs, and soon thereafter Poles arrived. The first Dutchmen came in July 1940, but most of these were later transferred to the Herzogenbusch concentration camp in the Netherlands. Around the middle of August 1941, there were 6,700 prisoners in Buchenwald.[14]

The statistics for Dachau indicate a similar development. When the first Austrians arrived on April 2, 1938, there were 2,600 prisoners; that fall the Jewish roundup caused the number to rise to almost 15,000 (11,199 Jews arrived in November alone),[15] but by the beginning of the war, it decreased to fewer than 4,000. Between September 1939 and March 1940, the camp was evacuated; most of the prisoners were transferred to Flossenbürg, Mauthausen, and Buchenwald, and only a small command post remained. After the prisoners who were still alive had been returned, the camp had fewer than 3,000 inmates in late March 1940, but by March of 1941, the number had risen to more than 10,000, and this did not change much during the following year.[16]

By the end of 1939, Sachsenhausen, which had housed a little over 6,500 inmates before the outbreak of the war, had more than 12,000. The new arrivals included more than 2,000 Czechs.[17]

In late 1938, around 1,000 people were imprisoned at Mauthausen, and these were primarily Austrian and German convicts. Political prisoners did not arrive until May 1939, when the first Czechs were also sent to this camp. They were followed in May 1940 by Poles and in August of that year by Spaniards who had gone to France after Franco's victory in the Spanish Civil War. Since these people had fought together in Spain and knew one another from French labor batallions and subsequent internment camps in France, there developed a solidarity among them that greatly impressed everyone and established these men's special position in the concentration camp (Bernadac 1974, 75 ff). Despite enormous losses, there was a great increase in the number of Spaniards. By the end of 1940, more than 8,000 people were imprisoned in Mauthausen and its big satellite camp Gusen (Maršàlek 1974, 92 ff).

By the middle of 1941, more than 17,000 prison numbers had been issued in Auschwitz (Czech 1959–64). This does not indicate the number of people in the camp at that time; transfers to other camps, deaths, and some releases had reduced the total number considerably. The overwhelming majority were Poles, the first arrivals in that camp who were under the supervision of the few Germans, usually convicts, requisitioned from other camps to fill the main positions. An even smaller number of Germans, including some political prisoners, arrived later in group transports; they were assigned roles on all the important details, and this assured them of some influence. In June 1941, Czechs arrived in Auschwitz as the first homogeneous group of members of another nation (Czech 1959–64).

The women's camp, Ravensbrück, housed political prisoners and criminals—Germans and Austrians—as well as a considerable number of prostitutes, "antisocials," who were required to wear a black triangle. The first Polish women, deported shortly after the occupation of their homeland, were at first kept in isolation. The lack of contact made it easier for the camp management to play the others off against them. In 1940 and later, when the number of Poles steadily increased and all prisoners were supposed to do labor, it was impossible to maintain this isolation. Contacts among politically conscious women of different nationalities helped to thwart some maneuvers of the SS.[18]

Neuengamme, which had between 4,500 and 5,000 inmates in the fall of 1940, received its first transports from Holland and Belgium in the fall of the following year. A small group of Czechs had arrived there earlier.[19]

The German attack on the Soviet Union in June 1941 marked the beginning of a new phase in the development of the concentration camps. For one thing, systematic mass murder of Soviet prisoners of war soon took place there. This mass murder was differently organized in the various camps, but it was evidently managed by a central authority, and this had a great impact on all the camps. Those who were allowed to live shared the fate of every wave of new arrivals—that is, they bore the brunt of the terror. That period also marked the beginning of the most extensive butchery, the killing of people whom the Nazis denied the right to live on "racial" grounds—namely, Jews and Gypsies. At first, extermination camps were established for this purpose in the East. Chelmno was the first of these camps, and mass killings began there in late 1941; this was followed by Belzec in mid-March 1942, then Sobibor and Treblinka, where mass murders were initiated in early May and late July respectively (Arndt 1976).[20]

The capacity of these extermination camps was not sufficient, and therefore Himmler ordered the construction of a central extermination facility of hitherto unimaginable dimensions—in the Auschwitz concentration camp. Soon the transports of Jews were directed there in increasing numbers. In the fall of 1942, all Jewish prisoners were, in accordance with a central order, transferred to Auschwitz from other concentration camps.[21] The killing of Gypsies declared to be "unfit to live" was concentrated in Auschwitz as well. A section of Birkenau, the compound bigger than all camps erected next to Auschwitz, was established as a Gypsy camp.

In the winter of 1941–42, when hopes for a rapid victory in the East had been dashed, a further reorganization of the concentration camps began, and this had as great an effect in the succeeding years as the construction of the machinery of extermination did. As early as the latter part of January 1942, Himmler announced that the next weeks would bring "great economic tasks" for the concentration camps. To ensure the performance of these tasks, 100,000 Jewish men and up to 50,000 Jewish women would be sent to those camps, since "Russian prisoners of war are not expected in the near future."[22] In accordance with this plan, the central administration of the concentration camps was reorganized in March 1942. All camps were placed under the direction of the newly founded SS Main Economic and Administrative Office (Wirtschafts-Verwaltungshauptamt). As its first measure, its head, SS Lieutenant General (Obergruppenführer) Oswald Pohl, decreed that henceforth emphasis should be placed on the mobilization of all the manpower in the camps for military purposes.[23]

The prisoners had always been obliged to work, and they had been organized in labor units. Since work was intended as punishment, many of them performed meaningless tasks, the kind that really wears a person down. Only members of units that were charged with maintaining the operation of the camp and its workshops escaped such demoralizing activities as swiftly carrying rocks to a certain place and then carrying them back the same way.

To be sure, to the end, many an SS officer relapsed into his favorite pastime of tormenting prisoners by ordering them to perform meaningless tasks, but for the growing number of inmates who were placed at the disposal of the armaments industry, the nature of the work did change.

This reorganization was pursued vigorously after the defeat at Stalingrad in the winter of 1942–43, and it was stepped up as the fortunes of war declined for the Third Reich. As a result, it was necessary for each concentration camp to establish subsidiary camps at nearby arms factories. The number of such camps grew by leaps and bounds.

The reorganization produced an ambivalent attitude among the central leadership. On the one hand, the greatest possible number of "racial" prisoners were to be exterminated. On the other hand, as Himmler was to tell his Führer, a growing number of prisoners were placed at the disposal of the armaments industry.

This ambivalence made itself felt most strongly at Auschwitz, the camp of choice for those destined for immediate gassing. Auschwitz's four rapidly erected crematories with built-in gas chambers made such killing possible with the smallest expenditure of guards and service personnel. But because the arms industry required ever more workers, those destined for extermination were subjected to a selection process, something that was not done in the extermination camps of eastern Poland. Those who appeared to be capable of working were not immediately escorted to one of the gas chambers, but the young and strong became inmates of the camp, where they were prepared for "extermination through labor"—an expression taken from the record of a discussion between Himmler and Minister of Justice Otto Thierack in late September 1942. This record also contains the classification of the various groups of people. The purpose of the conference was to arrange for the penal system to provide as many people as possible for this "extermination through labor." This agreement obligated the German courts to supply to Himmler—in addition to Jews and Gypsies, who were first on the list—Russians, Ukrainians, and Poles with sentences of more than three years, Czechs and Germans with sentences of more than eight years, and finally the "worst antisocial elements among the last-named."[24]

By concentrating all the extermination measures in Auschwitz and using the system of selections, this concentration camp became the largest by far. The number of Jews classified as fit for work at the admissions selections, together with other newly admitted prisoners, exceeded the number of those "exterminated through labor." This necessitated the establishment of a women's camp at Auschwitz for the female deportees who were designated as fit for work. In accordance with general practice, in March 1942 female inmates of Ravensbrück were sent to Auschwitz, together with female SS guards, to help build the camp. As a consequence of conflicting tendencies in the management of the concentration camps, one side—the Main Security Office of the Reich (*Reichssicherheitshauptamt*), the central office in which Eichmann was active—pushed the deportation of Jews, and as a result crematories repeatedly broke down because of overuse. The other side—sections of the SS Main Economic and Administrative Office—instructed all camp commandants to lower the mortality rate substantially, as a directive dated December 28, 1942, put it. On January 20, 1943, this directive was repeated with the following admonition: "I shall hold the camp commandant personally responsible for doing everything possible to preserve the manpower of the prisoners."[25]

These conflicting instructions did not escape the attention of those inmates who had been detailed to work in offices. (Having a job in the administration office enabled a prisoner to become familiar with administrative matters, and such people were useful for throwing a monkey wrench into the works of the SS extermination machinery when it became possible.) Since the instructions to lower the mortality rate were primarily directed at the SS doctors, some of whom could, on the basis of their profession, more easily be persuaded at least to limit the mass murders, the resistance movement of the prisoners in several camps attempted to influence physicians who were on duty there in SS uniforms.

The above-mentioned directives from the central office at Oranienburg were a reaction to a hitherto unknown death rate. It rose most horrendously in Auschwitz, where the Jews who had been allowed to live were concentrated. In the latter part of 1942, more than one fifth of all prisoners died each month, and this 20 percent death rate does not include those who were gassed immediately. There was a drastic decline in the death rate, for in Auschwitz the attitude of the senior SS physician, Dr. Eduard Wirth, enabled the resistance movement to utilize the contradictory directives of the central office most effectively. In July and August 1943, the mortality rate declined to 3.5 percent in each of these months, and only to a minor extent was this due to the more favorable weather.[26]

For August 1943, we have mortality figures for other camps as well, and this enables us to make a comparison of living conditions. In Stutthof and Flossenbürg, the percentage of deaths was about as high as in Auschwitz at that time. In Mauthausen, more than 1.3 percent died, and in Sachsenhausen and Buchenwald, the percentage of those who died in August 1943 was 0.73 percent and 0.67 percent respectively. The rate was lowest in Ravensbrück (0.27 percent) and in Dachau (0.23 percent) (Arndt 1970, 121; Maršàlek 1974, 128 ff). Even though the mortality rate had not been anywhere near as high in any camp as it was in Auschwitz (with the possible exception of Majdanek, for which there are no statistics), the general mortality before August 1943 was higher. This is indicated by the following figures: In February 1943, 8.14 percent of the prisoners in all camps died, but by May of that year the rate had gone down to 2.8 percent.[27] This decline was due in large measure to the lower death rate in Auschwitz, the largest camp (5.2 percent in May as compared to 25.5 percent in February),[28] but to a lesser extent the same trend probably obtained in other camps as well. The favorable spring weather cannot be the sole explanation. Statistics collected by Michel de Bouard on the basis of the preserved death records of Mauthausen and Gusen indicate that the mortality in these two camps (Gusen was listed separately) was relatively smallest between June 1943 and September 1944; despite the fact that both camps had more inmates, it was clearly lower than in the two preceding years. October 1944, however, marked the beginning of an unprecedented rise in both Mauthausen and Gusen.[29]

Lowering the mortality rate was not nearly as important to the Economic Office as sending more and more prisoners to the camps in order to have sufficient manpower. There was an explosive rise in the number of inmates. There were about 25,000 prisoners in all camps at the outbreak of the war, but their number increased to 88,000 by December 1942 and to 224,000 by August 1943—this despite the high mortality rate (Broszat 1965, 158). This tremendous growth of the camps not only produced overcrowding, a worsening of hygienic conditions, and epidemics, but it also caused those in charge of the camps to lose track of things. The internal self-operation of the inmates became increasingly important, and this broadened the opportunities for those prisoners who were prepared to work against the SS.

New camps were established; in addition to Herzogenbusch in Holland, camps were built in the Baltic region near Riga, at Kauen, and in Vaivara. These camps remained relatively small, and there is little information about them, but another camp became well known. On April 9, 1943, Lublin–Majdanek, originally built as a camp for Russian prisoners of war, was placed under the jurisdiction of the central office at Oranienburg. It did not have the dimensions of Auschwitz, but like Auschwitz it was both a concentration camp and an extermination camp. In April 1943 Bergen–Belsen was placed under the control of the Economic Office, but initially it had the status of a transit camp. At first it housed Jews who were to be available to be exchanged for Germans interned by the Allies, and thus they were not treated as badly as Jews in Auschwitz or Majdanek. In the course of time, this special character steadily eroded and was lost entirely in the final phase.[30]

The number of subsidiary camps near arms factories increased markedly. In 1941 only Dachau had more than ten satellite camps, not all of which were located near factories producing war materials, but by the middle of 1943 there were more than twenty. At that time Ravensbrück, Sachsenhausen, Buchenwald, and Mauthausen already had more than ten subsidiary camps as well.[31] The biggest satellite camp of Auschwitz was constructed in the fall of 1942 at the Buna Works of I. G. Farben at Monowitz.

The camp complex at Auschwitz, which at that time housed about one third of all concentration-camp inmates, had grown to such an extent that the administration was about to lose control of it. Therefore, in November 1943, Auschwitz was divided into three parts: The base camp was designated as Auschwitz I, the Birkenau complex with its extermination facilities became known as Auschwitz II, and Monowitz was listed as Auschwitz III. Auschwitz was put in charge of all other subsidiary camps established at arms factories. This partition was not complete, however; all three camps shared the political division and the camp doctor. Thus contacts in the administrative structure permitted the resistance movement to continue to have a unified leadership.

In August 1943, Dora was founded as a subsidiary camp of Buchenwald. There, prisoners had to work in subterranean tunnels on the production of V-1 and V-2 rockets, which had been shifted after the bombardment of Peenemünde. On October 28, 1944, Dora, which had grown from 4,400 prisoners at the beginning of the year to over 32,000 (Mader 1963, 288), was proclaimed an independent concentration camp, and a number of subsidiary camps with similar work were added to it. However, the resistance movement of this camp, where working and living conditions were probably even worse than in the other camps of that time, was able to maintain contact with the earlier base camp Buchenwald.

The concentration on work in the arms industry was accompanied by a number of new camp commandants, whom the central office regarded as better suited for this task than those who had become specialists in the unleashing of unrestrained terror.

For instance, in the model camp Dachau, on September 1, 1942, Martin Weiss was appointed as commandant, and he remained in that position for fourteen months. Pater Lenz writes that this man modified the sadism of the camp administration and the omnipotence of the camp bigwigs (Lenz 1956, 170). Provost Heinrich Grüber believes that the new camp commandant Weiss "showed his human side" (Grüber 1968, 186), and Arthur Haulot and Ali Kuci, who compiled a kind of camp chronicle immediately after the liberation of Dachau, write: "Dachau has changed. . . . For the people in the labor details, living conditions have become almost bearable."[32] In early 1942, the commandant of Buchenwald, Karl Koch, was replaced because he had engaged so blatantly in corrupt practices that it could no longer be hushed up, and his removal brought some relief. Eugen Kogon has characterized the new commandant, Hermann Pister, as the type of bureaucrat who likes to procrastinate (Kogon 1946, 335). In Ernst Thape's Buchenwald diary we read: "After Pister's arrival the senseless sadistic executions greatly diminished and after some time stopped almost entirely."[33] Krzystof Dunin-Wasowicz reports that in Stutthof the terror declined in 1943 and that the general situation improved (Dunin-Wasowicz 1972, 192). Even in Auschwitz the prisoners at that time registered a similar development, and the above-mentioned decrease in the number of deaths does confirm this. They believed they knew the reasons for it. Marie-Claude Vaillant-Couturier testified at the Nuremberg trial that the improvement of conditions—according to her recollection, from 1943 on—was due to British radio broadcasts about what was happening in Auschwitz (Seweryn 1965). On November 11, 1943, the notorious commandant Rudolf Höss was replaced by Arthur Liebehenschel. This brought about a change in the atmosphere, though this made itself felt primarily in the base camp Auschwitz I, where Liebehenschel became commandant. On July 5, 1945, the well-informed SS noncommissioned officer, Senior Squad Leader Wilhelm Boger, who had been captured by the Americans, stated that Höss had been unable to stay in Auschwitz "for reasons of foreign policy." "When the mass murder of Auschwitz became known to the world in the fall of 1943, there suddenly were changes in the camp leadership."[34] At that time the resistance movement already had an international organization, and it was able to influence Liebehenschel. The information it sent to the Polish resistance movement at Cracow was broadcast by the BBC and had the effect described by Vaillant-Couturier and Boger. This would undoubtedly not have happened if the military situation had been more favorable for Hitler at that time.

At around the same time there was a change of commandants in Majdanek. The Pole Zacheusz Pawlak writes about it as follows: "After the camp commandant Florstedt had been arrested for embezzlement of Jewish property, the behavior of the SS toward the prisoners improved. He was replaced after November 3 [1943] by SS Lieutenant Colonel (*Obersturmbannführer*) Martin Weiss, who saw to it that the bestiality of the SS was somewhat reduced" (Pawlak 1979, 148 ff).

The unfavorable developments on all fronts and the destruction caused by the increasingly intensive bombardments of the German hinterland prompted Himmler to have more and more people sent to the camps. Between August 1943 and August 1944, the number of inmates in all the camps more than doubled. In the last summer of the war, it already amounted to 524,000, and despite an increase in the number of deaths (through epidemics caused by overcrowding as well as hitherto unprecedented starvation), it rose to 714,000 by January 1945.[35] Thus the number of inmates at Buchenwald increased from 9,500 to more than 63,000 between late 1942 and late 1944 (the latter figure does not include the inmates of Dora, because this camp had already become independent) (*Buchenwald* 1960, 86), and in the same period the number at Mauthausen rose from 14,000 to 72,400. These figures include all subsidiary camps (Maršàlek 1974, 106 ff).

Since the new arrivals were almost exclusively foreigners, the percentage of German prisoners decreased radically. At that time, Ravensbrück had the largest number of Germans (as with all SS statistics, Austrian women were listed as Germans), an estimated 20 percent, counting all

those with red, green, or black markings.[36] After the liberation of Buchenwald, 12 percent of the inmates were identified as Germans, almost a third
of these being Austrians.[37] In Mauthausen, there were about 9 percent
Germans in March 1945,[38] and on April 1 of that year 8 percent Germans
were registered in Dora and its subsidiary camps.[39] According to a report
written by twelve inmates of Sachsenhausen immediately after that
camp's liberation, Germans constituted a minority of 8 to 10 percent from
1942 on, and only a small number of these were political prisoners.[40] On
the day of the liberation, 3.7 percent Germans and 0.8 percent Austrians
were counted in Dachau,[41] some Germans having been evacuated a short
time previously. Andrzej Kamiński believes that about 2.5 percent of Germans were interned in Gross–Rosen and all its subsidiary camps, "most of
them Greens."[42] Toni Siegert estimates that as of February 28, 1942, 5.5
percent Germans were detained at Flossenbürg and its numerous satellite
camps, while two years previously 37.5 percent of all prisoners had been
Germans, more than half with green insignia (Siegert 1979, 461). The
number of Germans interned at Neuengamme was so diminished by three
transports to the Dirlewanger Unit of the SS that by late November 1944,
there were fewer than a thousand of them.[43] At Ebensee, the large subsidiary camp of Mauthausen, Germans amounted to a mere 1 percent a few
days after the liberation.[44] Even in Auschwitz the percentage of Germans
was below average: 2.7 percent in May 1943 and 1.9 by August 1944.[45]

With the marked increase in the camp population the number of subsidiary camps rose tremendously. In Dachau there were more than 130, plus
fifteen satellite camps for female prisoners. In Buchenwald and Gross–
Rosen there were around a hundred, and almost the same number in
Flossenbürg.[46] A dense network of camps of all sizes stretched across
Germany and the countries occupied by it, and these camps ranged from
some with a small number of prisoners to compounds housing several
thousand. It stands to reason that this made the originally intended her-
metic isolation of prisoners utterly impossible.

An excerpt from the testimony of Karl Sommer, the deputy head of the
Economic office, at the Nuremberg trial graphically illustrates how the
use of prisoners in the arms industry evolved: "At the urging of the Ministry of War it began in August–September 1942.... As I remember it,
concentration-camp inmates worked in almost all German industrial
firms that could use such a mass of laborers.... As many as 500,000
prisoners worked in German industry" (Antoni 1979, 126).

As the concentration-camp system expanded, the increasingly unfavorable situation at the front caused an ever more insistent demand for
soldiers. This produced a change in the composition of the guards, one
that the prisoners were able to utilize. The original staff, which had been

trained at Dachau to regard inmates as a kind of vermin, had long occupied key positions in all concentration camps. They did continue to set the tone, but could not be effective everywhere. Willi Bleicher, a longtime inmate of Buchenwald, describes the change: "After Stalingrad the terror abated, and we had greater privileges." The most brutal SS guards had been replaced by older men [47] and an ever-increasing number of ethnic Germans. The latter, as citizens of nominally independent states like Hungary or Romania, could not be conscripted for service in the Wehrmacht but were able to join the SS on a more or less voluntary basis. The leadership saw to it that enough of them did (Langbein 1972, 317 ff). Once indoctrinated, many ethnic Germans proved to be docile students, and yet, for the camp leaders, they constituted an element of uncertainty. Since they were themselves not regarded as equals, some of them sympathized with harshly treated "inferior" prisoners. After all, the mother tongue of many a guard was the same as that of the person he was guarding. In May 1944, when even the recruitment of ethnic Germans had failed to supply enough guards, Hitler ordered that members of the Wehrmacht who were no longer fit for service at the front be placed under the command of the SS and detailed for guard duty in the camps.[48]

This development, too, worked in the prisoners' favor. According to a report by Andrzej Kamiński, the guards in the subsidiary camp Brief an der Oder, where 1,000 prisoners from Gross–Rosen had been transferred in August 1944, were members of the Luftwaffe [airforce], as were the officer-in-charge and the roll-call officer. Since the senior camp inmate, a German Green named August Schneider, was also a decent man, an atmosphere quite unusual for a concentration camp developed. This is evidenced by the fact that in two months only one prisoner died there.[49] However, such relatively idyllic conditions were hardly typical of all places where members of the Wehrmacht were on duty. For one thing, the camp commandants customarily placed an SS man with camp experience in at least one key position; for another, a considerable number of army men accepted the SS's harsh attitude toward the prisoners.

The final and most disastrous period in the history of the concentration camps began with the evacuation of the camps necessitated by the advance of the Allied armies. On July 22, 1944, Majdanek became the first large camp to be evacuated—after its population had been reduced by mass killings, particularly of Jews, and by transfers. The thousand remaining prisoners were taken to Auschwitz. This first evacuation on foot signalled the procedure of the succeeding ones. Six days later, 698 persons arrived in Auschwitz; the other 302 had been shot as too feeble to march (Czech

1959–64). The survivors' description of the liquidation of Majdanek was a clear warning to those inmates of Auschwitz who were considering resistance, just as the subsequent fate of other evacuation transports showed the inmates of the receiving camps what fate threatened every evacuee. On September 2, 1944, three months after the landing of the Allies in Normandy, the inmates of Natzweiler (located on the Rhine) were transferred to Dachau and its subsidiary camps,[50] and around that time the Herzogenbusch camp (in the Netherlands) was cleared as well.

In the course of 1944, a growing number of prisoners were transferred from Auschwitz to camps that were still far in the rear. These were primarily Russians and Poles, whom the SS feared the most because of the Polish resistance movement and the approaching Russian front. In November, Himmler ordered the dismantling of the extermination camps, and on January 17, 1945, the commandant of Auschwitz received orders to evacuate the camp (Czech 1959–64), whereupon more than 60,000 persons were driven out into the street. These processions, which were soon followed by others, have entered the history of the concentration camps as death marches. In accordance with a central order, no prisoner was to fall into the hands of the Allies alive. At that time there began the evacuation of Stutthof and a few weeks later that of Gross–Rosen and all its satellite camps. These transports overcrowded the camps inside Germany to a hitherto unknown extent.

Even as the Allies were closing in on the German heartland from East and West, the SS did not stop driving prisoners from one camp to another. The closer the end of the war came and the more demoralized the SS grew, the fewer the chances at evacuation became and the more drastically the death transports acted as a warning. In this way, the inmates of the camps not yet evacuated clearly perceived the need—the opportunity—to delay the evacuation of their own camps.

In early April 1945 Dora and its subsidiary camps were evacuated. On April 11, the inmates of Buchenwald, which had only been evacuated partially, were liberated (see Chapter 24).

Bergen–Belsen in its final weeks was flooded with an immense number of half-starved persons, and no attempt at evacuation was made. It was liberated on April 15. One week later the remaining 3,000 prisoners of Sachsenhausen were freed from the yoke of the SS.[51] Flossenbürg began to be evacuated on April 20 and Ravensbrück one day later. The liberation of Dachau followed on April 29, after the SS had been able to take only a small part of the inmates to an unknown destination. The commandant of Neuengamme found a special way of carrying out the order to let no prisoner fall into the hands of the Allies alive: Since no road was open for an evacuation march, the prisoners were put on ships (in nearby Lübeck Bay—ed.) and these were bombed and sunk by Allied planes on May 3, 1945. The way in which the last concentration camp, Mauthausen, was liberated is part of the history of the resistance movement in that camp and will be described in connection with it.

3

THE SELF-GOVERNMENT OF
THE INMATES

National Socialism replaced democratic institutions with a system of command and obedience, the so-called Führer principle, and it was this system that the Nazis installed in their concentration camps. It goes without saying that any command by a member of the SS had to be unconditionally carried out by all prisoners. Refusal or hesitation was liable to lead to a cruel death. The camp administration not only saw to it that every command was carried out, but also held inmates assigned to certain jobs responsible for completing them. In this way it facilitated its own work and was also able to play one prisoner off against another. This system was already working when the first foreigners arrived at the camps in 1938. Each unit housing prisoners, whether a barrack or a brick building, was called a block. The camp administration held a senior block inmate (*Blockältester*) responsible for enforcing discipline, keeping order, and carrying out all commands. If a dwelling unit was divided into rooms, a senior block inmate was assisted by senior barracks inmates and their staff. A senior camp inmate (*Lagerältester*) was responsible for the operation of the entire camp, and it was he who proposed the appointment of senior block inmates to the officer-in-charge. After the expansion of the camps, several senior camp inmates were appointed in a number of the camps, and they divided the tasks among them. Each labor detail was headed by a capo (trusty), and if the size of the detail required it, he had assistant capos or foremen under him. The capo himself was exempted from work, but he had to see to it that the required work was done by his underlings. Capos, senior block inmates, and senior camp inmates were identified by an armband with the appropriate inscription. These armband wearers, as they were generally called, were under the protection of the camp administration, often enjoyed extensive privileges, and as a rule had unlimited power over those under them. This is to be taken literally, for if an armband wearer killed an underling, he did not (with a few exceptions) have to answer to anyone, provided a timely report of the death was made and the roll call was corrected. An ordinary prisoner was completely at the mercy of his capo and senior block inmate.

As a rule the SS bestowed armbands on prisoners they could expect to be willing tools in return for their privileged status. As soon as German convicts arrived in the camps—that is, before 1938—the SS preferred them to morally stable men. Thus, having been despised as outsiders by society all their lives, they now wielded immense power over others by virtue of a simple armband. If one of these men earned the hatred of his fellow prisoners by misusing this power, he was utterly at the mercy of the SS, for armband wearers with blood on their hands, once they lost their jobs and thus the protection of the SS, were fair game for a vengeful camp. A number of fallen capos were gang-murdered. In a conversation with generals in the summer of 1944, Himmler characterized this system with cynical frankness: "These approximately 40,000 German political and professional criminals . . . are my 'noncommissioned officer corps' for this whole kit and caboodle. We have appointed so-called capos here; one of these is the supervisor responsible for thirty, forty, or a hundred other prisoners. The moment he is made a capo, he no longer sleeps where they do. He is responsible for getting the work done, for making sure that there is no sabotage, that people are clean and the beds are of good construction. . . . So he has to spur his men on. The minute we're dissatisfied with him, he is no longer a capo and bunks with his men again. He knows that they will then kill him during the first night. . . . Of course, we can't do it with Germans alone, and so we use a Frenchman as a capo in charge of Poles, a Pole as a capo over Russians, playing one nation off against another."[1]

With years of practice behind them, many camp commandants were virtuosos at running this system. Since it was aimed at completely destroying the human dignity of anti-Nazis, a hardened criminal was able to order an anti-Nazi around as he saw fit. Such people were at the criminal's mercy when there was no SS man in the camp. Anyone who wanted to fight this system had to reduce or, if possible, abolish the effectiveness of this Führer principle, as it applied to the inmates. Occasionally even some SS leaders assisted in this endeavor.

On a number of occasions, commandants and officers-in-charge could be persuaded to entrust the self-government of the inmates to prisoners without a criminal past. On the basis of his experiences in Buchenwald, Walter Poller writes: "Even some SS henchmen in the concentration camp who tried very hard to treat political prisoners in accordance with instructions [that is, as harshly as possible—H.L.] could not conceal the fact that this demand of their leadership and ideology [that is, to assess political offenses as criminal ones—H.L.] did not make complete sense to them" (Poller 1960, 183). As already mentioned, according to the camp chronicle written by Arthur Haulot and Ali Kuci immediately after the liberation of Dachau, the change of commandants there in the fall of 1942 had a favorable effect: "The majority of capos, senior block inmates, and other people in responsible positions have been replaced; their newly appointed successors, all of them political prisoners, are generally behaving better."[2]

The last commandant of Buchenwald, Hermann Pister, also tended to give jobs to German political rather than criminal prisoners, and Otto Fröschner, who was transferred from there to Dora to become the commandant of that new camp (originally a subsidiary camp of Buchenwald), followed Pister's example (Bornemann/Broszat 1970, 170). One reason for this may have been the fact that the labor details of that camp, which had been established exclusively for what was then the most important area of the arms industry, the production of V-1 and V-2 rockets, required specialized training that was more likely to be found among political prisoners. Thus the German Communist Albert Kuntz, an expert who headed the construction office at Dora, managed to convince both Commandant Fröschner and the director of the Sawatzki Works (where prisoners had to do forced labor), that political prisoners could manage the camp better than criminals. A description of resistance activities is relevant here: "An attempt was made to displace the BVs [for *Berufsverbrecher*, professional criminals—H.L.] gradually. July 1944 brought a favorable opportunity for this: The SS Major General Pister from Buchenwald inspected the camp. With the active participation of Albert Kuntz, the anti-Fascists managed to persuade Pister, via the SS Major Fröschner, to transfer two new senior camp inmates from Buchenwald to Dora. These were the comrades Christl Beham and Jupp Gamisch. The BVs were relieved of their duties..." (Češpiva/Giessner Pelny 1964, 47). To be sure, at that time the Greens could no longer be pushed out definitively, and the two Reds did not remain in office for long. In this connection J. B. Krokowski asks whether this shift promoted production or furthered its sabotage.[3]

The resistance organization in Auschwitz was able to induce Arthur Liebehenschel, the new commandant appointed in November 1943, to replace the Green senior camp inmate in the base camp with a Red (Langbein 1949, 150 ff). In this they were aided by the SS camp doctor Eduard Wirths, who had earlier replaced convicts with political prisoners in the camp hospitals of which he was in charge.

The prisoners who were put to work in the hospital (called infirmary or sick bay, *Revier*, in some camps) had considerable influence. The *Revier* could either offer protection or serve as the antechamber of death. The head of this important labor detail was called *Revier* capo or senior inmate of the prison hospital [*Häftlingskrankenbau*, HKB]. He was under the supervision of the SS doctor and the medical officer [*Sanitätsdienstgrad*, SDG] under him, but as a rule this capo was able to exercise his authority for good or ill. Other SS doctors could also be influenced by the prisoners, as in the above-mentioned case of Wirths in Auschwitz. Eugen Kogon reports that Dr. Waldemar Hoven was partial to political prisoners. Dr. Ding-Schuler too, whom Kogon served as a secretary in Buchenwald, just as I worked for Wirths in Auschwitz, was so accessible to the arguments of politically conscious prisoners that after Kogon had been in his employ for two months, "there was no political and military event about which he did not ask me my opinion" (Kogon 1946, 319). It stands to reason that this kind of relationship enabled a prisoner to have some input in the filling of offices in the prisoners' self-operation. Otto Horn goes even further in his characterization of Dr. Hoven, writing immediately after the liberation that "he took an active part in the struggle between the political prisoners and the Greens." Benedikt Kautsky has testified that in the struggle between the political prisoners and the criminals, Dr. Hoven was clearly on the side of the former and even acted as executor of secret judgments against criminals. On the other hand, he had no scruples about killing inmates (Kautsky 1961, 122). This is confirmed by the Czech physician Paul Schnabel, who worked in the *Revier* and thus had a chance to observe Dr. Hoven.[4] Horn writes in his report that Dr. Hoven demanded a quid pro quo from the Reds for his help.[5] Wirths, on the other hand, gave preferential treatment to political prisoners without expecting anything in return, such as the procurement of items from camp workshops. He was the only man who broke a taboo observed in all camps and gave jobs to imprisoned doctors, finally even installing Polish doctors as senior inmates in prison hospitals, which made them the superiors of German medics.[6] It was one of the peculiarities of the "SS state" that, with the exception of what Wirths did at Auschwitz in August 1943, prisoners who were not medical men were entrusted with the running of hospitals, even though the prison population, once the camps were filled with non-Germans, included many doctors. The SS men's dislike of intellectuals may have been responsible for this. Thus the chief hospital capo in Buchenwald was a printer and his successor—a political prisoner who did a great deal for his fellow sufferers—a metalsmith. The latter was shot when his knowledge of internal affairs at the camp began to be a threat to the commandant, and he was not succeeded by a physician but by the Communist Reichstag delegate Ernst Busse, who, as Kogon writes on the basis of his close observation of these conditions, "contributed a great deal to the further consolidation of the situation." He goes on to say in this connection that "a medical expert in the top position in the hospital would have inevitably precipitated a crisis, since he could not possibly have been equal to the far-flung network of intrigues that frequently had a fatal outcome" (Kogon 1946, 144 f). Things evidently were different in Sachsenhausen, as witnessed by a diary entry of the Norwegian Odd Nansen, who noted on December 13, 1943, that the "chief medical officer" August, an electrician by profession, had the lives of many fellow prisoners on his conscience (Nansen 1949, 128).[7]

The SS also employed prisoners for administrative tasks, since these became increasingly complex with the growth of the camps and frequently exceeded the intellectual capacity of the SS men. The concern of overweening importance in each camp was the accuracy of the roll call, which was conducted every morning and evening. An inmate had to keep a record of the numbers of prisoners in each block and to make a timely report of all transfers, admissions to and discharges from the infirmary, and every "departure through death." All these reports were gathered in a central office, where prisoners had to put together a report before every roll call. This report was then simply checked by the SS.

In another central office—called Work Assignments [*Arbeitseinsatz*] in some camps and Labor Records [*Arbeitsstatistik*] in others—the assignment of prisoners to labor details was handled on the basis of a file listing their occupations. That office also kept transfer lists of prisoners, often specialists, who were requisitioned for a subsidiary camp. The clerks on duty usually received blanket orders for a specific number of prisoners to be made available for one detail or another and were responsible for making assignments and transfers and for keeping a card index that could be used at any time to ascertain where a prisoner had been assigned to work. To be sure, the opportunities and power of those who worked in the roll-call office and in the Work Assignments were not as evident as those of a capo or senior block inmate—men who often flaunted their power cudgel in hand. This power was, however, greater than that of armband wearers. The following episode from Sachsenhausen illustrates the extent to which the position of a writer of reports could be expanded.

A special commission had come to the camp to investigate irregularities, and for its research it used numerous prisoners as informers. Since the political prisoners were providing these informers with incorrect information, this led the camp administration (also under investigation by the commission) to sabotage this project. It rendered the inmates appointed by the commission incapable of assuring an orderly management of affairs, and the commission finally found itself obliged to make the following proposal:

"The office, which is staffed exclusively by prisoners, is causing Kuhnke, a senior camp inmate and the V-man [*Vertrauensmann*, confidante, in this case an informer] appointed by the commission, considerable difficulty in the preparation of the morning roll call, and of course this also materially impedes the political investigation. The difficulties caused to Kuhnke derive from the fact that the writers of the report, all of them Communists and opponents of V-man Kuhnke, deliberately supply false information. This cannot be proved, however, because the writers can always claim that they have misheard something or made a clerical error. Given the present circumstances, and in order to safeguard the further investigation by the V-man, the removal of the deputy report-writer Ernst Harter is absolutely necessary. This cannot be done immediately, because his replacement will have to be trained first, and this can only be done by Harter. If Harter finds out that he is to be replaced, it may be regarded as certain that he will not train his successor sufficiently and impede him in other ways as well. Under these circumstances it would be appropriate to release Harter from protective custody and notify him of this well in advance, so that he can instruct his successor properly."[8]

This grotesque situation could arise only because the SS camp administration also did its best to obstruct the commission's work and because in July 1944 Sachsenhausen was already so large that it was hard to know what was going on. Nevertheless, this story illustrates the great power that a writer of reports could attain with the connivance of other prisoners with special assignments.

In most roll-call offices the red insignia of the political prisoners predominated, for these were most likely to have the qualifications needed for this work (organizing ability, accuracy, typing skills, linguistic ability). There were exceptions, to be sure. Otto Küsel, a Berliner who until his escape from Auschwitz at Christmastime 1942 ran the Work Assignments office there in rare exemplary fashion and whom inmates of Sachsenhausen remembered fondly because he had helped many people on labor details,[9] wore the green triangle. So did the Viennese Rudi Meixner, about whom the Pole Stanisław Nogaj wrote a positive report. Meixner performed the function of chief camp clerk in Gusen for the benefit of the Poles interned there, whereas his successor, also a Green, raged against them.[10] In the Mauthausen main camp, the replacement of the chief camp clerk, a dreaded Green, with a Czech political prisoner ushered in a new period that clearly affected the entire atmosphere of the camp in a positive way.[11] Kurt Schreiber, a German Green who was capo of the roll-call office in Dora for about two months, has been described by Krokowski as one of the most fair-minded and helpful inmates he ever met. As a bookkeeper he had the proper training for his complicated activity.[12] Tadeusz Patzer also emphasized Schreiber's willingness to help.[13]

In this book, I must frequently report on the cruelty of Greens who abused their position to assure themselves of a good life at the expense of their fellow prisoners and to give free rein to their desires as members of the "master race." So, it is only fair to remember that, as Eugen Kogon has pointed out, it was basically the system of the SS leadership that must be held responsible for the terrible conditions (Kogon 1946, 66). Not every camp inmate realized this. Many a prisoner remembered very clearly the person who had beaten him or killed his friend, but he saw no farther into the system that allowed this to occur. It is due to the untrammeled application of the Führer principle, under the most extreme conditions that, as Benedikt Kautsky puts it, "violent men were able to beat others to their heart's content, thieves and cheats could steal their comrades' food, and even sex fiends could run riot" (Kautsky n.d., 3). In fairness, it must be recorded here that the SS managed to corrupt many of those with red triangles by making little Führers out of them, too. Like their Green colleagues, these armband wearers strutted around the camp, and even their attire—breeches and boots were their status symbol—indicated that they endeavored to adapt to their masters.

This was true not only of inmates who were listed as political prisoners but also of those who had been sent to the camps for other reasons than as opponents of the National Socialist regime. It stands to reason that such "quasi-political prisoners," men who were not accepted as equals by the interned anti-Nazis, were most likely to adapt to the Greens.

The repeatedly cited report that was written in Sachsenhausen after the liberation speaks of "imprisoned members of the SS and other Fascist organizations" whom the camp management installed in "important positions (senior camp inmates, senior block inmates, foremen)" and who used their power to join the SS in terrorizing the foreign inmates—that is, those at the bottom of the camp hierarchy.[14] The Norwegian Odd Nansen was evidently referring to these when he wrote in his diary on May 6, 1944, that German senior block inmates with red triangles were bullies and brutes, and that one of them had beaten him (Nansen 1949, 160).

There are similar statements in the report written by Otto Horn immediately after the liberation of Buchenwald about the history of that camp: "In the camp were hundreds of former members of the SS or SA [storm troopers] who had committed crimes." They were listed as Reds, but after they realized that nothing could be expected from the political prisoners, they joined the Greens. The most notorious person in this group was the former cavalry captain Wolff, a German nationalist who had been sent to Buchenwald because of a sex crime and quickly rose to the position of senior camp inmate. He became a V-man "not only of the SS but of certain groups of prisoners as well. He appointed as senior block inmates former members of the Wehrmacht who had been sent to the camp because of antisocial activities." Horn closes by remarking that Wolff finally became "one of the most bitter enemies of all political prisoners."[15] At a later point, we shall relate how these deposed him in order to safeguard resistance activities.

With the growth of the camps, the self-government of the prisoners assumed increased importance, though not always proportionately. Karl Ludwig Schecher, who was transferred from Dachau to Flossenbürg in late September 1939, noted that this self-government was more developed and more influential in Flossenbürg than in Dachau.[16] The greater the number of labor details that were sent to arms factories, the greater the chances for Reds to become capos. For excavations or other unskilled labor, the ideal capo was, in the eyes of the camp administration, the man who used a club most effectively as a spur, but the foreman of a labor detail in an arms factory was supposed to know something about production. A stick is not a very suitable tool for getting a skilled laborer to work at maximum efficiency. When David Rousset notes that, in Buchenwald, the Greens were good at terrorizing people but proved incapable of organized work in a factory for which many Communist specialists were available, this only indicates a trend, but his observation does have general validity.[17] Albin Lüdke points to exceptions to this rule: In Neuengamme it was never possible to eliminate Green capos entirely, because there were specialists among them, too, who were capable of heading details required to do skilled labor.[18] The steady decline in the percentage of Germans in the concentration camps finally forced the management to give even foreigners a capo's armband. Although the SS endeavored to keep the Germans in the camps because they were needed "to perform those tasks of administration and organization that really should have been assumed by the SS," as Gerhard Harig and Max Mayr put it,[19] it was not possible to keep non-Germans from moving into privileged positions as well.

Mieczysław Mołdawa reports that from 1943 on, when more and more labor details were required in arms factories, non-Germans were installed as capos in Gross–Rosen (Mołdowa 1967, 110, 141). According to Kornelis Hofman, in Herzogenbusch there was another reason for replacing prominent German Greens, a factor that played a part in other camps as well: The convicts had abused their privileges and stolen things too brazenly whenever they had a chance, and this finally prompted the camp administration to replace them with Dutchmen.[20] Karl Ludwig Schecher has given a graphic description of this development in Dachau: "In addition to the old German prisoners, the Austrians, the Sudeten Germans, the Czechs, the inmates taken to Auschwitz from the North German camps, and the people from the first transports of Poles had long been numbered among the 'old prisoners.' [Apart from nationality, an important factor in the assignment of a function was the time the candidate for an armband had spent in the camp—H.L.] Since at the same time a large number of prisoners, particularly Germans, were either transferred to other camps [for purposes of construction or expansion—H.L.] or released, the Germans increasingly found themselves in the minority. Even influential positions were filled with foreigners." Schecher modifies this statement when he writes: "In general, Germans in the widest sense—that is, those from the Reich as well as Austrians and Sudeten Germans, and even some Poles and Czechs—were still used as senior block inmates and block clerks."[21]

Foreigners were most likely to be used as block clerks or in the offices, for there were too few German prisoners without functions who were able to do this increasingly complex work. Knowledge of the German language was, of course, a prerequisite. For example, in Auschwitz numerous Polish students who had grown up in a bilingual area and thus knew German were employed in offices. The German inmates in administrative positions could always obtain foreigners by arguing that the offices needed people who knew other languages and could keep all lists and files in order. Heinz Junge, who worked in the office at Sachsenhausen, states that from early 1943 on, this detail was international in nature, for it was claimed that interpreters were needed for every language. "Thus the office was turned into a European parliament," he writes.[22]

There was a similar development in other camps as well. Hans Maršálek, who served as an assistant clerk at Mauthausen, sums up the result of the efforts to make the office staff as international as possible, as follows: "It was easier and safer to push through Germans, Austrians, or Luxembourgers—in Mauthausen, Spaniards as well [this first major group of non-German inmates in that camp had gradually managed to improve its position—H.L.] than Poles, Soviet Russians, Greeks, or Yugoslavs, not to mention Jews." The camp administration did not begin to consider Jews for desirable details until the winter of 1944–45. Maršálek remembers the national composition of this detail in the last phase: The office staff consisted of two Germans, two Austrians, two Czechs, one Spaniard, one Frenchman, and one Pole.[23] Non-Germans were more likely to be given positions in subsidiaries of Mauthausen and other camps, for there were very few German prisoners in those places. Thus the commandant of the satellite camp Loiblpass made those French or Polish prisoners capos whom he regarded as the best workers (Lacaze 1978, 295). The Frenchman Pierre de Froment remembers that, at the Heinkel Works at Mödling, those Poles were preferred for barracks duty who eagerly did the bidding of their German masters (Bernadac 1975, 57 ff).

According to Krokowski, the labor office of Dora, which was staffed by Reds, also employed Frenchmen.[24] This was of great importance to the numerous Frenchmen in that camp.

In an anonymous report written on May 14, 1945, immediately after the liberation of Sachsenhausen, we read: "In the last phase the workforce consisted of a group of forty or fifty prisoners." The importance of the writers of reports is underlined: "At times the writer of reports had greater influence than the senior camp inmate." Given the complexity of a camp compound at a time of overcrowding and a steady growth in the number of subsidiary camps, such a writer was indispensable: "Since the completion of a report presupposed a great deal of experience, it was impossible to dismiss or replace this writer overnight."[25] Georg Buch, who worked in this office in the final phase, remembers that it was staffed almost exclusively with Reds.[26] Pierre Gregoire, from Luxembourg, was part of this detail as well and characterizes this center of the camp administration as an "omnipotent office" (Stein 1946, 171). Fritz Selbmann has described the activity of the Sachsenhausen camp clerk, the Berlin Communist Rudi Kleine, as "just as indispensable to the camp administration as it was beneficial for the camp community. . . . He is the soul of the bureaucratic red tape of camp life."[27]

The prisoners employed in Buchenwald managed to enlarge the Labor Records detail as much as possible. The ethnic composition of this detail, which was headed by the German Communist Willi Seifert, indicates the positions that members of the various nations were able to fill: In 1944, this detail included twenty-eight Czechs (many Czechs spoke German fluently and had been in the camp for a long time), twenty-four Germans, seven Russians, seven Poles, three Frenchmen, two Austrians, one Dutchman, one Belgian, and one Spaniard (Drobisch 1968, 97 ff).

In the final phase, the SS was no longer able to exclude the Jews, the group of prisoners that it had always vigorously pushed to the lowest level of the camp hierarchy, thus keeping them out of details with bearable working conditions, from positions that were necessary to keep the camp going. From the fall of 1942 on, the Jews were concentrated in Auschwitz and Majdanek. Beginning with the spring of 1944, they were permitted to be transferred to concentration camps within the German Reich, because more and more workers were needed for the subsidiary camps there and because, at a time when the German armies were retreating on all fronts, the Jews were the only major group of prisoners left. For this reason it was necessary to provide Jews with the authority of an armband, and this was first done in Auschwitz, where many subsidiary camps housed Jews almost exclusively. The Auschwitz main camp no longer had sufficient Germans for even the top jobs in all these camps, and thus the SS had to resort to Jews. When another subsidiary camp had to be built, at Fürstengrube in late June 1943, all important positions, from the senior camp inmate down, were initially filled with German Jews. Later the officer-in-charge sent for German convicts from Birkenau, who in his judgment were experienced and efficient workers and now replaced many Jewish armband wearers.[28] A report from the commandant's office dated October 6, 1943, shows that this was already common practice, for it prohibits the use of Jewish capos in labor details where German prisoners would be subjected to their authority.[29] In subsidiary camps that housed only Jews, however, Jews continued to hold top positions. Thus the German Jew Karl Demerer wore the armband of a senior camp inmate in Blechhammer when that camp became part of Auschwitz in the spring of 1944. His skill in the performance of this very sensitive function and his humaneness were appreciated by all his fellow sufferers (Langbein 1972, 197 ff).

Coal-mine Inspector Bergmann, of the subsidiary camp Jaworzno, paid an unintended compliment to Jewish capos when he asked, in a letter to the commandant of Auschwitz dated June 28, 1944, that Jewish capos be replaced with "Aryan" ones, because such a change would result in greater productivity (Piper 1970, 103). In August 1944, the management of the refinery at Trzebinia, the location of a subsidiary camp of Auschwitz, replaced Jewish capos with German ones, and according to a report, this "improved the efficiency of the prisoners' work" (Piper 1978, 116 ff). When Zacheusz Pawlak arrived at Majdanek in early 1943, the prisoners holding jobs consisted of "German criminals as well as Czech, Slovak, and Polish Jews. . . . The highest positions, such as senior camp inmate or capo, were of course held by the Hitler Germans, the lower ones—senior block inmate, block clerk, foreman—by Jews." Jews also worked in the kitchen, in the office, and in the hospital. Pawlak remembers Jewish senior block inmates, particularly two from Warsaw, who beat and kicked people— often "only to demonstrate their power." He describes the Jewish attendants in the hospital, with some exceptions, as "antisocial types" (Pawlak 1979, 12, 18, 64).

Jewish prisoners were sent to the Württemberg subsidiary camps that were part of the Natzweiler concentration camp—transferred from Radom to Vaihingen, which was built in the summer of 1944, and from Stutthof to Echterdingen, which was constructed in the fall of that year. The Jewish senior camp inmate of Radom performed the same function in Vaihingen (Keuerleber-Siegle 1978, 139). The Dutchman Floris B. Bakels describes the young Polish Jews who held the most important positions in the camp as "good-hearted" and "helpful toward the Dutch" (Bakels 1979, 279). A fellow prisoner has described the conduct of the Jew who wore the armband of a senior camp inmate in Echterdingen as "disagreeable" (Böckle 1978, 139). In Bergen–Belsen Jewish officials were replaced with "Aryan" ones when Kramer became commandant there in December 1944. The Jewish armband wearers have been described as corrupt, first and foremost the senior camp inmate Jacques Albala (Hanna Lévy-Hass characterizes them as "totally ruthless and unscrupulous," though the judgment of Eberhard Kolb, the chronicler of that camp, is less harsh), but the newly appointed top officials ruled "cynically, cruelly, and sadistically." A German criminal who functioned as senior camp inmate and two Polish capos are singled out for special mention because they terrorized the camp with clubs and whips (Lévy-Hass 1979, 28, 44; Kolb 1962, 76, 125). In Buchenwald there was just one Jewish senior block inmate immediately before the liberation—Emil Carlebach[30]—but several German Jews had been entrusted with that function previously.[31]

Several preserved reports illustrate the shifts in the ethnic composition of the camp leadership in the final phase of the concentration camps. Krokowski reports that, of the fifty-six senior block inmates in Dora, fifteen were Czechs, three or four Poles (including one Jew), and one French; all the others were Germans. Among the block clerks the number of Germans was smaller. Krokowski remembers that about half were Czechs (many Czechs spoke German); there were also five Poles, four Frenchmen, three Russians, and a Yugoslav; the rest were Germans. Krokowski lists no Germans among those doing barracks duty; the majority were Russians, followed by Czechs, Frenchmen, and Poles.[32] In other camps, too, there were few Germans assisting the senior block inmates with the work in the barracks. Götz Dieckmann details the composition of the German senior block inmates in Dora before the evacuation. Sixteen were criminals, one wore the black insignia of the "antisocials," one the pink triangle of the homosexuals, and eight a red marking. Hans Maršálek has published a list containing the composition of the camp officials in Mauthausen as of February 23, 1945. In those days inmates were permitted to wear watches—one of the privileges the camp management granted to functionaries. The Germans clearly dominate this list with 134, including 114 convicts. They are followed by nineteen Czechs, eighteen Poles, eight Spaniards, and five Yugoslavs (Maršálek 1974, 40).

In the prison hospitals it was easier for Red inmates and foreigners to attain influential positions. As early as January 1938 political prisoners replaced the Greens, who had dominated this detail, in the infirmary at Buchenwald.[33] In Dachau, too, there were no Green functionaries in the infirmary. Thanks to capo Mathias Mai, the Reds also were in charge of the hospital at Neuengamme.[34] In Herzogenbusch the infirmary already constituted a center of the Dutch resistance organization when that camp was still run by German convicts.[35]

Although Poles were able to occupy influential positions in the Auschwitz hospital from the beginning, Polish physicians did not manage to hold important positions at the Gross–Rosen infirmary until 1943 (Mołdowa

1967, 148); this facility continued to be run by Greens. The staffing of the hospital at Dora is known. Nine physicians, four of them Frenchmen, worked under the supervision of a German capo, who wore a red triangle and was not a doctor. According to a report dated February 26, 1944, the attendants comprised eleven Czechs, eight Germans, seven Frenchmen, six Poles, six Russians, and two Dutchmen (Dieckmann/Hochmuth n.d., 43). The following list gives the ethnic composition of this detail at the end of 1944 and the beginning of 1945 and indicates how those working in the Buchenwald prison hospital managed to induce the SS doctors to expand this important detail. The staff of the hospital at that time included 201 Germans, fifty-five Czechs, forty-four Russians, thirty-nine Frenchmen, twenty-seven Poles, nineteen Dutchmen, seven Austrians, two Yugoslavs, two Luxembourgers, and one Belgian. Most of the forty or forty-five physicians there must have been foreigners (Drobisch 1962, 94). When Ebensee, the big subsidiary camp of Mauthausen, was liberated, there were twenty-five doctors in the hospital, seven of them Hungarians (evidently Jews), six Poles, six Frenchmen, two Belgians, one Dutchman, one German, and one Russian. (Le Chêne 1971, 239).

With the enormous growth of the camps, which made them hard to control, the system of self-government by the prisoners—originally created as an extension of the SS to carry its terrorism to every nook and cranny of the camp—now offered chances to work against the SS's system of terror. In Leitmeritz, the big subsidiary camp of Flossenbürg, only spot checks were made of the capos in the winter of 1944–45. It has been reported that, due to lack of supervision and thanks to the comradely attitude of the capos, such a tightly knit community was created that effective help could be given to the sick and the exhausted (Trhlínová 1974). A similar situation obtained in other camps as well, and thus the actions of the prisoners' self-government were a matter of life and death for innumerable people. The fight for key positions was far more than a struggle for privileged posts. In every camp its outcome determined the chances to organize effective resistance.

4

THE BATTLE BETWEEN REDS
AND GREENS

Before describing this battle, I must once more refer to the numerous exceptions to generalizations about a contest between the Reds and the Greens. These exceptions derive in part from the arbitrariness with which the Gestapo sometimes assigned the color of the triangles to its victims. I have already pointed out that not every wearer of a red insignia was actually an opponent of National Socialism. With reference to Sachsenhausen, Heinz Junge says that the greatest bandits and stool pigeons wore red markings.[1] There are similar, though not so crass, reports about other camps, but it would be just as erroneous to assume that all Reds were bandits and informers.

Additional confusion arose from the fact that in some cases prominent criminals used their influence with the camp administration to exchange their markings for red ones. A case in point is Hessel, the notorious camp clerk of Majdanek.[2] Bruno Brodniewicz, whose heinous deeds are remembered all too well by "old" inmates of Auschwitz, was exempted from wearing an insignia next to his inmate number 1, and thus his criminal past was evident only from his demeanor.[3] Otto Küsel, who worked in the labor-records office at Auschwitz and wore number 2, was probably the most striking exception, though not the only one, from the Greens' practice of trying to use the power connected with their function for their own benefit and at the expense of the other prisoners. There are many descriptions of the ruthless behavior of the Green capos at Dora. Franz Fox, who wore a green triangle, worked in the crematorium there. When the SS was informed that inmates were planning to build a radio transmitter, the people involved asked Fox to destroy the components before the SS had a chance to conduct a search—a clear indication of the political prisoners' confidence in Fox. Informers told the SS about this request as well, and when components of the transmitter were found in the crematorium and

38

Fox refused to divulge who had brought them to him, he was incarcerated in a bunker. All they were able to get out of him, however, were statements like this one: "I am not a Communist and don't concern myself with politics. I am an old BV [professional criminal—H.L.] and the word betrayal isn't in my vocabulary." This is confirmed by the Pole Tadeusz Patzer, who shared Fox's bunker cell for a time.[4] Patzer also mentions Peter Schröder, who enjoyed special privileges in the tunnel, where prisoners were forced to work on rockets, and "didn't deny me anything." Patzer repeatedly asked him to help his fellow countrymen.[5]

Stanisław Nogaj reports that at Gusen "there were bloodthirsty murderers among both the Greens and the Reds," but he also mentions that one of the five successive senior camp inmates, Karl Rohrbacher, acted "for the benefit of the prisoners."[6] Erwin Gostner characterizes this man, who also wore a green triangle, as a "fourflusher," but he also emphasizes that Rohrbacher strengthened the sense of solidarity among the inmates. According to Gostner, there were many among the younger BVs who extended this sense of solidarity to political prisoners as well.[7]

A punishment meted out by the commandant's office at Flossenbürg indicates that on August 2, 1943, the German capo Fritz Born permitted the inmates under his command to hide during working hours and get some sleep while he kept watch. Born did wear the black triangle of the "antisocials," but as a rule the Blacks were hardly different from the Greens, to whom they had to adapt if they wanted to obtain positions and privileges in a camp ruled by convicts.[8] The Frenchman Jacques Lusseyran had to get a taste of the "little camp," which probably was the worst place in Buchenwald in its last year. In that place a fellow Frenchman and "honorable citizen" secretly stole the bread of his comrades at night, but the German criminal Dietrich, who had served a seven-year jail term for murdering his mother and his wife and evidently had a position in that block, shared his bread with others "courageously and magnanimously." Lusseyran concludes that "after a year in Buchenwald I comprehended that life was not at all the way I had been taught—neither life nor society" (Lusseyran 1963, 213).

Walter Poller has summarized his pertinent Buchenwald experiences in these words: "It is true that I encountered wonderful people among the criminals—strange though this may sound, even some of great moral character, men whose behavior in every situation was unreservedly comradely. The majority of the criminals, however, were a dirty, unprincipled, vigilante-like bunch" (Poller 1960, 182).

Many additional examples could be adduced by way of cautioning against a generalization. Nevertheless, we shall have to continue speaking of a "battle between Reds and Greens," for history will record the struggle for internal power in the camps under this designation. It was essentially a battle between unscrupulous egotists, morally unstable opportunists, and demoralized men on one side, the majority of whom were Greens or those Reds who had adapted to them, and on the other side politically conscious men and those with a stable character who regarded the privileges conferred by positions as an obligation. The latter were primarily political opponents of the Nazis who continued their struggle against Nazism even behind the electrically charged barbed wire and had their morality strengthened by the feeling that they were able to do something useful even in such a place. Sticking together and keeping a check on one another guarded many against the temptations that the assumption of a Führer's role in a concentration camp involved.

In the concentration camps that were in existence before 1938 this battle was already waged when only Germans were interned. This was most evident in Dachau, the oldest camp, which at first housed political prisoners exclusively. Thus these prisoners occupied all key positions in the camp self-operation. "When I came to Dachau in early 1937," writes Gustl Gattinger, "it was a Red camp," but he adds immediately that not all Reds were in fact political prisoners and that even inmates who had clearly been imprisoned for political reasons became willing tools of the SS. This applies both to individual capos and to a senior camp inmate.[9]

The situation was different in Buchenwald. "At first Buchenwald was dominated by the Greens," writes Eugen Kogon (Kogon 1946, 312). Walter Poller, another connoisseur of conditions in that era, writes: "When the Buchenwald camp was built, two Greens became senior camp inmates, and that is why convicts occupied almost all positions as informers and capos as the camp expanded" (Poller 1960, 184).

The result is indicated by the number of deaths. In 1937 and 1938, Buchenwald had a higher death rate than any other camp in existence (Pingel 1978, 80 ff). Robert Leibbrand has pointed out that the struggle against the abuses that had so palpably worsened conditions in the camps was a matter of life and death (Leibbrand 1945, 10). The domination of the Greens had to be ended. The first successes came in September 1937, when senior barracks inmates were able to occupy political positions. In January 1938, Reds were added to the hospital staff (*Buchenwald* 1960, 582). Otto Horn states that capo positions in the administrative details (that is, in the laundry, the storage rooms, etc.) were in the hands of the political prisoners from the beginning. He characterizes these positions as oases in the struggle.[10] Benedikt Kautsky was transferred from Dachau to Buchenwald and thus had a basis for comparison: "We owed a great deal to the fact that the administration of the camp, to the extent that it was carried on by inmates [in Dachau—H.L.], was entirely in the hands of political prisoners. I did not appreciate this until we Dachau Jews were transferred to Buchenwald on September 23, 1938. There the Greens were in charge, and thus there was corruption, torture, starvation, and maltreatment of prisoners by prisoners."[11]

We have already seen why the struggle between Greens and Reds in Sachsenhausen was not as bitter as it was in Buchenwald, but this should lead no one to conclude that there was no struggle. Fritz Selbmann writes that "the battle between Reds and Greens, this constant struggle for the leadership in the camp, never ceased. . . . The German prisoners became a minority, and this minority was strictly divided into two large groups whose most active forces constantly struggled for power in the camp— Reds and Greens, on one side political prisoners headed by Communists, on the other side habitual criminals and antisocials of all kinds headed by the Green bigwigs, the chiefs of the crime rings from the outside" (Selbmann 1961, 221). Pierre Gregoire has this to say about the same subject: "The Red tactics did not fully carry the day, nor was the Green infamy vanquished entirely" (Stein 1946, 168). Neither in Buchenwald nor in Sachsenhausen were the positions of the Reds as unchallenged as they were for a considerable period in Dachau, though for a time the Greens threatened the Red-dominated prisoner self-operation in Dachau. In Sachsenhausen Greens managed to have top Red officials replaced, arrested, and even transferred by accusing them of arranging help for companions in misfortune.[12] On June 8, 1944, the Norwegian Odd Nansen described the consequences of this change: "The Communist block chiefs were certainly brutal and insensitive—most of them, anyway—but these [the professional criminals—H.L.] are much worse" (Nansen 1949, 169).

An examination of Buchenwald can illustrate the way in which the political prisoners managed to end the dominance of the Greens in several camps. There as elsewhere the SS had deliberately organized and fomented a bitter fight between the Reds and the Greens.[13] A general indication of the tactics of the SS was given by Rudolf Höss, the commandant of Auschwitz, when he said that, as far as running the camp was concerned, ten Green prisoner functionaries were better than a hundred SS men. Like many of his colleagues, Höss was a product of the Dachau school, and he summarized the further experience he gained in Sachsenhausen as follows: "In the concentration camps these antitheses [between opposing groups of inmates—H.L.] were eagerly preserved and fostered by the leadership in order to prevent a tight organization of all prisoners. Political differences, but especially those of color [evidently referring to those between the Reds and the Greens—H.L.] played a major part in this. Without the aid of these differences even the strongest camp administration would not have been able to control and manage thousands of prisoners" (Höss 1958, 101 ff). About Sachsenhausen Höss has this to say: "The two main colors (red and green) fought bitterly, and thus the camp management found it easy to exploit this for its purposes and play the two sides off against each other" (Höss 1958, 83). Those in charge of Buchenwald employed these tactics as well. Bruno Heilig, who, like Kautsky, was transferred there from Dachau, writes: "They [the Greens] played the same role in Buchenwald that the political prisoners played in Dachau" (Heilig 1948, 145). This role, to be sure, soon came to an end, for after the assassination of Ernst vom Rath, the German legation counselor in Paris [which prompted the *Kristallnacht* pogrom—ed.], all concentration camps were crowded with Jews. In those days Jews were still allowed to take their money with them. The SS found ever new pretexts for relieving them of it, and soon the convicts vied with the SS in this pursuit. These shady activities assumed such dimensions that, when the schemes failed, the criminals' methods of skimming off funds became public knowledge. That was the reason for the removal of the Green senior camp inmate Richter, a former member of the SA, whom Kogon has characterized as a man of incredible brutality (Kogon 1946, 64). At that time numerous Greens were transferred to Flossenbürg and Mauthausen, where "proven" prisoner functionaries were needed for the camp then under construction (Heilig 1948, 243).

Other newly founded camps, too, were initially staffed by German convicts who had compromised themselves excessively and knew too much about the shady dealings of the camp administration. There the SS further benefited from their camp experience and their willingness to be integrated into the mechanism of terror. Neuengamme and later Auschwitz, Gross–Rosen, and Natzweiler were established in accordance with this practice. These camps lacked a large number of German political prisoners who were able to end the domination of the Greens in Dachau, Buchenwald, and Sachsenhausen, though there were some setbacks. Individual political prisoners who arrived in a camp dominated by Greens did not have any chance to do this. The Green bigwigs in the camps did not allow any Red to advance who was not prepared to accommodate them, for they had been forewarned by the defeats dealt them by prisoners in other camps. Thus the Pole Józef Kret remembers an Austrian Communist named Hirsch, the only German with a red triangle in his group: "As a political prisoner, he not only did not advance to the position of a capo but was fair game for the malice and chicanery of the Greens" (Kret 1973). Only where there were politically conscious men of various nationalities who had not yet been broken physically and morally was there a chance to end the terror of the Greens. When a struggle between Reds and Greens in these camps gave rise to a more or less active resistance movement, it soon became international in nature. By contrast, the German political prisoners clearly set the tone in the leadership of resistance organizations in the old camps Dachau, Buchenwald, and Sachsenhausen even when the steady growth in the number of foreigners made an internationalization unavoidable.

Nevertheless, Germans (including Austrians) played a part in the newly created camps even when a group with distinctively political experience arrived there. A case in point is the transfer, in August 1942, of seventeen political prisoners from the Dachau hospital staff to the Auschwitz hospital. They had been requisitioned to help combat an epidemic of typhus, and thus they were spared the initial difficulties that did in many a new arrival. These men were immediately given positions in the infirmary, and thus they remained capable of acting as a group. Since they had worked together in Dachau, everyone knew what he could expect from the next fellow (Langbein 1949, 62 ff; 1972, 48). Albert Hommel reports that when Egon Zill was transferred from Dachau to become commandant of Natzweiler, he brought along Reds, who later ended the dominance of the Greens. To be sure, Hommel adds that the worst Reds were then being transferred from Dachau.[14] Louis Maury, a Frenchman whose employment in the roll-call office at Neuengamme in December 1944 and January 1945 gave him a good chance to observe the conditions there, writes that in those days the Green criminals and the "false Reds" set the tone in that camp (Maury 1955, 48).

The struggle between the Reds and the Greens produced a momentous dilemma. If someone was successfully deprived of a key position, it was necessary to try to remove him from the camp entirely, for otherwise there was a risk that he would utilize his connections with the SS to regain power and take revenge. Often the only logical way was to shunt the deposed man off to a subsidiary camp or another concentration camp. Since more and more satellite camps were established and inmates were often shifted from one camp to another, this was not too difficult, provided those who had engineered the removal had a good relationship with the Work Assignments. The SS knew that the transferred men had experience in filling camp positions, and the man also reminded them of that fact. Thus, while Reds repeatedly rid their camp of willing tools of the SS, such men were frequently able to regain authority in another camp. Julius Freund has described the battle against the Greens in Buchenwald that ended with Karl Barthel being made senior camp inmate, which consolidated the rule of the Reds: "A defense team was organized that was ready to confront Green capos who had attacked inmates and to give them a whipping in isolated places. Slowly but surely the rug was pulled out from under the Greens. Deaths were blamed on them and one strike followed another, so that after a few months the camp administration put the

Greens in empty barracks overnight and thus completely isolated them from the other inmates. A closed transport then took all Greens to the quarry of Mauthausen. . . . This marked the end of the battle between the Reds and the Greens" (Freund 1945, 104ff).

All inmates of Mauthausen can testify to the savagery of the Greens there. Aimé Bonifas points out that, owing to the predominance of German political prisoners in Buchenwald, there was a certain rule of law there, in contrast to the majority of the subsidiary camps, where a Green mafia tyrannized the other prisoners (Bonifas 1968, 54). Similar conditions developed in other camps. The most discredited Greens were often transferred from Mauthausen to nearby Gusen, and many a Green capo found a new sphere of activity in Birkenau after he had been "busted" in the Auschwitz main camp.

The inmates of Majdanek can also tell a tale of woe about the effects of such transfers of German convicts. The Pole Zacheusz Pawlak adds this to his description of the general chicanery: "The terror increased even further when in July [1943] fifty German criminals arrived from Buchenwald and were appointed capos. They vied with the SS in killing prisoners. The ones who suffered the most were the Jews, for they were treated far worse than the others" (Pawlak 1978, 122).

In Mauthausen a key position could be attained only by means of a veritable intrigue in which members of various nations participated. The chief camp clerk, a Viennese con man named Josef Leitzinger, had so consolidated his position that he was called King of Mauthausen. He not only behaved like an oriental potentate, strutting around the camp wearing white gloves, but, according to Hans Maršàlek, the chronicler of Mauthausen, he "outdid many an SS man in brutality" (Maršàlek 1974, 39). Leitzinger was a morphine addict, and his adversaries made use of this addiction by supplying him with increasing doses of drugs from the hospital. Under the influence of these drugs Leitzinger became so presumptuous that he thought even the commandant could not touch him. At an auspicious time, inmates called the camp administration's attention to his abnormal behavior. There was a confrontation that resulted in Leitzinger's deposal, punishment, and transfer to Gusen.[15] There he was not given a good reception by Green capos, who had not forgotten his reign of terror among them. Leitzinger finally shared the fate of many whose positions had given too deep an insight into what the camp administration did behind the scenes. In January 1945, he was "shot while trying to escape" (Maršàlek 1974, 40). As a consequence of the international nature of this action, after Leitzinger's departure a Czech, an Austrian, and a Spaniard were able to work together in the office for the good of the camp.

Not every intrigue produced such a good result. In Gross–Rosen, Hans

Dick, a German, used his position as an orderly of the commandant to get his master to oppose the sadistic practices of Kurt Vogel, a Green. Since Vogel had mistreated and "done in" some Red Germans, he incurred their vengeance. The commandant relieved him of his armband, but the roll-call officer, who had come to appreciate Vogel's terrorism and did not mind his sadistic excesses, soon made him senior block inmate of the penal company, where Vogel found a fertile field of activity. Mieczysław Mołdawa explains why no general improvement could be effected in this fashion: "The officer-in-charge Anton Thumann [the immediate superior of the roll-call officer—H.L.] did not permit German Reds to perform any functions in the camp" (Mołdawa 1967, 89). Mołdawa describes the special conditions created by the camp administration of Gross–Rosen: "Where positions were occupied by the Greens, the Reds were invariably 'done in' and soon liquidated by the Greens with the clear agreement of the Hitlerites, who had filled all positions with Greens in Gross–Rosen. From 1940 to 1943, 90 percent of the functionaries were Greens, but between 1943 and 1945 there were only 75 percent" (Hessel 1954, 62).

The attempt by political prisoners to overthrow the senior camp inmate of Flossenbürg, a convict, was also unsuccessful. They wanted to inform the camp administration of his homosexuality, for the Nazis regarded sexual intercourse between men as a serious crime. The attempt failed because the senior camp inmate's lover refused to testify against him. Thus that man retained his position to the end (Heger 1972, 65).

The conditions under which the battle between Reds and Greens was waged in the various camps differed radically and produced a basically different quality of life. The inmates of Dachau who were transferred to other camps in late September 1939 were the most likely to have a basis for comparison when they were sent back to Dachau in March 1940. I have already referred to the difference between the "red" Dachau and the "green" Flossenbürg that Karl Ludwig Schecher experienced. When his comrades from Mauthausen returned as well, the difference between Mauthausen and Flossenbürg was brought home to him in graphic terms: "We had thought we had lived through particularly difficult times, but now we were horrified to learn about conditions in Mauthausen. There the SS men and Green prisoner functionaries had banded together into a gang of criminals that shrank from nothing. Murdering an inmate to obtain a gold tooth from his mouth was nothing unusual there."[16]

Alfred Hübsch, the gatekeeper of Dachau, describes in his diary the terrible condition of the prisoners who had been transferred from Gross–Rosen to Dachau in 1942: "Everyone is complaining about the crimes of the Green capos, those criminals."[17] After Leitzinger's fall, things improved in Mauthausen, but "it was not possible to push out the entire staff

of convicts and fill their posts with political prisoners." On the contrary,
"the criminals ruled in Gusen and Mauthausen to the end." Two men who
were acquainted with conditions in Mauthausen report that "Mauthausen
was a Green camp to the end, only the hospital was Red."[18] The Frenchman Michel de Bouard has given a graphic description of the effects of
the convicts' domination in Mauthausen: "The deportees who joined us
from Buchenwald [in February 1944] and later [in February 1945] from
Sachsenhausen realized how much harder their lot became. A large number of packages arrived in Buchenwald, and because the internal administration of the camp was in the hands of political prisoners rather than
convicts, the food situation was clearly better there than in Mauthausen"
(Bernadac 1974, 273). The food was distributed by the senior block inmates, and it was up to them to decide whether they should strive for
fairness or whether they wanted to retain portions for deals. The amount of
pilferage from the parcels depended to a certain degree on the prisoners
who handled them. If they were ready to help themselves to the contents in
concert with the SS, very little remained for the recipients. If, however, the
SS was not able to corrupt those inmates to become their companions in
pilferage, their opportunities for theft were limited.

The foreigners who arrived in the camps in increasing numbers were
drawn into the fight between the Reds and the Greens—more quickly
where it was not carried on by a strong organization of German political
prisoners than in the "old" camps. It should not come as a surprise that
many inmates adapted to the convicts in charge. Given the terrorism of
the camp that always raged most horrendously against the most recent
arrivals, many people saw no other way out but to curry favor with their
superiors, German convicts—either by granting them sexual favors (if
they were young lads) or by sharing their packages with them (provided
they received any). Only those who were able to accommodate themselves
to the group of bigwigs were given an opportunity to occupy positions and
enjoy the attendant privileges. When Manuel Razola, a Spaniard, was sent
to Mauthausen in April 1941, the camp was in the hands of German
convicts. Only a few Poles occupied positions, "but they were reactionaries
and displayed great political hostility toward us Spaniards" (Razola 1969,
57). Political opposition was added to ethnic aversion, which was constantly fomented by the fact that earlier national groups were somewhat
better off after newcomers arrived and were pushed to the lowest level of
the camp hierarchy, thus inheriting the older group's suffering. Poles with
a strong religious and conservative orientation felt uneasy about the fight
of the Spanish republicans against Franco, because this struggle was supported by the Communists, while the clergy was on the side of the Fascists.
Brother Birin reports that in Dora all positions were occupied by Greens,

mostly Germans and Poles, and that the latter acted in particularly cynical fashion, as evidenced by beatings administered by Poles on barracks duty (Birin 1947, 49 ff). The Belgian Leon Halkin describes similar conditions in Gross–Rosen; he too names Germans and Poles who terrorized the new arrivals under the leadership of the SS (Halkin 1965, 101 ff). Aimé Spitz writes that Dutch assistant capos gave beatings in the subsidiary camp of Natzweiler and that one of these, a man with the first name Gert, "spritzed" patients (Spitz 1970, 30)—the camp term for killing by injections of poison, a practice for which the SS often enough employed members of the hospital staff. Such statements are, of course, not meant to indicate that in Green camps only Poles or Dutchmen succumbed to the temptation to improve their own position by adapting to the behavior of the bigwigs, for there are examples of this kind involving members of every nationality. It should not be overlooked, however, that Poles have been most often criticized in this connection, and it cannot be a coincidence that both the Czech Jan Češpiva and the Dutchman Anton van Velsen mention the chauvinism of Polish prisoner functionaries in Birkenau.[19]

It must be borne in mind, however, that it was far more difficult for a foreigner to occupy a position than it was for a German. In accordance with its ideology, even behind barbed wire the SS classified German prisoners as members of the "master race"—not only criminals but even political adversaries—and SS men attempted to corrupt them by making this plain to everyone. A foreign armband wearer could not dare to treat a German under his authority too badly, for this German might find his way to the camp administration and denounce his superior as anti-German. It was hard for German political prisoners to resist the temptation to let the SS incite them and play them off against foreigners.

Members of various nationalities who participated in the struggle between Reds and Greens had different starting positions. Those who had been in the camps the longest knew the conditions best. To a certain degree, "old boys" were respected even by the camp administration. Inmates who could communicate in German had a big advantage, and members of nations that the German Nazis had classified as "racially valuable"—for example, Scandinavians or Dutchmen—were in a more favorable position than Slavs, particularly Russians, not to mention Jews and Gypsies. And last but not least, recipients of packages—and such receipt was permitted after late 1942 or early 1943[20]—had a chance to get into the good graces of their superiors. Thus Edouard Barbel reports that their packages enabled the Luxembourgers to end the dominance of the Greens in Natzweiler,[21] and the Norwegian Odd Nansen calls the fact that the Norwegians received packages in Sachsenhausen "of immeasurable significance" (Nansen 1949, 66).

In the final phase, the position of the Greens was weakened by another development. After May 1943, and much more intensely after spring 1944, criminal prisoners were recruited for a special SS unit that was named for its leader, Oskar Dirlewanger. This "recruitment" (a very problematic term under the conditions of a concentration camp) did not extend to political prisoners until autumn 1944.[22] Arthur Hansen, a Luxembourger, remembers that after the "recruitment" for the Dirlewanger unit only a few older Greens remained in Flossenbürg, though these included the Green senior camp inmate. This ended their absolute dominance.[23] Some other statements paint a different picture, however. Thus Bruno Furch, one of eight political prisoners transferred from Dachau to Flossenbürg on July 10, 1944, reports that "every position was filled by German professional criminals" who, with some exceptions, exercised "a horrendous reign of terror, with constant beatings and killings."[24] Manuel Razola and Mariano Constante write that in Mauthausen political prisoners were able to occupy important positions after many Greens had left the camp in the course of this process (Razola/Constante 1969, 136).

The inhuman methods of the SS imposed cruel forms upon the internal struggle for dominance in the camp self-government. Many political prisoners lost their lives in that struggle after they had been denounced or "done in" as members of a bad detail. The Reds, too, sometimes used the harshest methods. Robert Leibbrand concludes his description of the battle between Reds and Greens in Buchenwald as follows: "Every means was used to sabotage and discredit the Green senior camp inmates. In the long run, their own corruption and incompetence rendered them useless to the SS as well, and so they were pushed out by the Reds again. . . . The Green senior camp inmate Ohles and five of his infamous informers were beaten to death by prisoners within a few weeks" (Leibbrand 1945, 26). Otto Horn confirms this when he writes that "Ohles & Co. were ruthlessly exterminated along with their Red associates."[25] Arthur Ullrich has described (Buchenwald 1960, 360) how Armin Walther, a man characterized by Eugen Kogon as an astute Social Democrat who did a lot for the camp (Kogon 1946, 194), was able to foil Ohles's intrigues, which were responsible for the transfer of more than seventy known German political prisoners to a penal company (Drobisch 1968, 55 ff.). The brutality imposed on this struggle for internal power by the camp administration often made it very difficult for an individual who attained power to decide what was permitted by the unwritten laws of the camp, and having been infected by the bloody atmosphere in the camps, to determine at what point he might succumb to the temptation to abuse his power against others without compelling necessity. Many lives would have been in danger if a person hired by the SS as a mass murderer had been given a chance to take revenge for his removal from a position of power. Heinrich Christian Meier re-members the bitter self-reproaches of political prisoners that he heard in Neuengamme. They had thought they had to become agents of the SS if they wanted to be able to help others (Meier 1948, 108).

Many Reds who had exposed themselves in the fight for the leadership of the prisoners' self-government were later accused. Only someone ac-quainted with conditions in the camps and the concrete circumstances of specific cases can judge whether such accusations were justified. There were political prisoners who were mindful of the dilemmas in which armband wearers might find themselves in the camps and thus were not prepared to accept positions they might have obtained. Eugen Kogon writes that in critical situations an armband wearer had "only a choice between active assistance and a shirking of responsibility which, as expe-rience proved, gave rise to far worse things" (Kogon 1946, 371). In rare instances even Jews were confronted with this problem. Vera Alexander, who was deported from Slovakia to Auschwitz with one of the first women's transports, reports that when she was already an "old inmate," a roll-call clerk named Katja Singer, also a Slovak Jew, asked her to become block clerk: "I replied that I couldn't do that. She asked me to assume that responsibility, for she thought such positions should, as far as possible, be filled by good people." Alexander accepted, and she describes the oppor-tunities this position afforded her. It was possible to "see to it that every-one actually received the few things allotted to her. . . . Sometimes I was able to conceal in the block women who had been sentenced to death in a selection. . . . At other times I was able to hide sick women so that they escaped the selection" (Hausner 1967, 253).

I remember that I once vainly urged a Dutch naval officer in Lerbeck, a small subsidiary camp of Neuengamme, to accept a capo's armband. The guards had no camp experience and thus were unable to organize the usual terror. However, the senior camp inmate, a German with a red triangle, acted in their stead and demanded that the capos behave as brutally as he. It would have been important for the prisoners, and a matter of life and death for some of them, to get a morally unobjectionable and responsible capo who was impervious to the influence of the senior camp inmate. As roll-call clerk I had a chance to propose the Dutchman for this position, and he did have the qualifications for it (a knowledge of languages, self-assurance, an unbroken intelligence). To this day I believe that the Dutch-man's refusal made things easier for him but was against the interests of the camp.

Stanisław Nogaj has described the same difficulties, though in a far more complicated situation. When the opportunity arose to depose murderous capos and senior block inmates in Gusen, it was impossible to find anyone who was prepared to take their places, "for the prisoners were very prejudiced against fellow inmates who occupied such positions" (Nogaj 1967, 166).

Finally, I shall let witnesses who cannot be suspected of speaking out of personal bias confirm that the Reds had to carry on the struggle against the Greens despite all the problems this entailed. At the Majdanek trial in Düsseldorf, the former SS senior squad leader (Oberscharführer) and field leader (Feldführer) in that camp, Heinz Petrick, testified that "the political capos were more humane than the BVs, who did all they could to torment the inmates." Petrick had no reason to depict political prisoners as better than they were.[26] The French chronicler of the *"univers concentrationnaire,"* David Rousset, says that the victory of the Reds over the Greens in Buchenwald was to everyone's advantage.[27] His judgment carries all the more weight because this struggle was carried on primarily by German Communists, to whom Rousset was opposed, and the German bigwigs in the camps transferred comrades of his to the infamous Dora camp precisely because of this anti-Communism. This also applies to the Dutchman Floris B. Bakels, a very religious man, who sums up his experiences in Natzweiler as follows: "In the camps it was literally a matter of life and death whether the leadership of the camp was composed of ordinary criminals or of political prisoners (especially Communists). The latter was, of course, preferable to the former. . . . In some camps the fight for leadership was a life-and-death struggle between the Greens and the Communists, and no intrigue was too underhand for them. The SS was the gloating bystander" (Bakels 1979, 77 ff).

To conclude this chapter, here is a summary by Eugen Kogon: "The struggle for the self-government of the anti-Fascist forces was based on the premise that the power in the camp was under all circumstances clearly in the hands of the political prisoners. The SS principle of mixing categories, fostering natural differences, and creating artificial ones had to be thwarted and rendered ineffective in a constant struggle. The only groups that ever made an attempt to gain control of the internal leadership of the camps were the political prisoners and the BVs" (Kogon 1946, 312).

Only by restricting or eliminating the domination of criminal prisoners—a dominance deliberately fostered by the camp management— could the inmates lay the foundation for an organized resistance. As a rule, individual acts of resistance were bound to remain ineffective, for they had no chance against the all-powerful machinery of the camp administration.

5

WHAT IS MEANT BY
RESISTANCE?

No definition of "resistance in the concentration camps" is universally valid. Narrowly defined, it means only active resistance to guards. Interpreted in the widest sense it encompasses everything that was done or planned to subvert the aims of the camp administration. Here we shall use the concept of resistance neither in the narrowest nor in the widest sense.

Prisoners were in the camps to be morally broken and even physically destroyed. Hence any act that could restore morale or help save lives was in direct opposition to the masters of the camps. If someone obtained a better detail for a companion in misfortune, that could mean the saving of a life. If someone shared his bread with a person who suffered from chronic hunger more severely than others, this meant physical and spiritual help. If someone saw a spontaneous opportunity to escape and succeeded in getting away, then a life had been snatched from the clutches of the SS.

Such resistance should never be underestimated. To share one's bread, when one suffered constant hunger pangs oneself, was not an easy decision. To buoy up a demoralized person required iron self-discipline, for under the conditions of the concentration camps lack of courage was infectious. To attempt an escape took energy and resolution and, above all, suppression of a feeling that was systematically fostered by the camp administration—namely, that the SS was all-powerful, that there was no hope of escaping its control, and that its punishments for evading orders were to be feared more than death.

Nevertheless, in this context such actions are not defined as resistance. This is certainly not intended as a disparagement of those who mustered enough strength for personal heroism. On the contrary, anyone who was forced to live in a concentration camp knows how to value such feats. Nevertheless, in this context the aid given to a friend and spontaneous actions are not included in our definition of active resistance. By resistance we mean an organized activity with far-reaching goals.

Our definition of resistance encompasses actions, or preparations for actions, that were undertaken in order to thwart or mitigate management campaigns directed against all inmates or a group of them. This includes the tendency of the SS to split up the army of inmates and play groups off against each another, its methods of systematic demoralization of the prisoners, and finally its intention to exterminate them. Naturally, all actions aimed at improving the general conditions in the camps also fall within this definition. It also includes all efforts to diminish the exploitation of the workforce for Nazi war aims and to inform the outside world about the camps—a method that eventually slowed the Nazis' program of extermination once they had begun to lose the war. Escapes are included in this definition if they were planned and organized, and especially if they were undertaken to bring news about the crimes committed by the SS to the outside world.

It goes without saying that the limits of this definition of resistance cannot be rigid. In many instances individual initiatives went hand in hand with the organized action of a group.

Considering the far-reaching opportunities offered by the prisoners' self-operating system, one would think it relatively easy to organize resistance activity. Self-operation could be utilized, of course, but there were numerous factors that thwarted activity of that sort—and even the very thought of it.

One such factor has been described by Wanda Kiedrzyńska: "The community of prisoners . . . was basically different from a community that is subject to normal laws of development. It was an artificial and accidental structure. The abnormal camp regime brought about an abnormal restructuring of the community of prisoners." Another experience gained by Kiedrzyńska in Ravensbrück has general validity: "The political prisoners in the camp did not constitute a unified block. Not all of them had the strength to offer resistance to the crushing system of the concentration camps."[1]

The central goal of camp life was demoralization. Those who found themselves in the power of the SS were fodder for total demoralization, and this demoralization had to be overcome before there could be any thought of resistance. A prisoner's human dignity began to be shattered the moment he or she arrived at a concentration camp, and this amounted to an object lesson in the omnipotence of the SS and the impotence of the prisoners in zebra-striped rags. If a prisoner as much as lifted a hand to ward off the blows of an SS man, this was considered resistance, and the unfortunate person had to pay a heavy price for it. Whenever an SS man set out to beat a prisoner, the latter had to take the beating while standing at attention with his hands on his trouser seams. Anyone who was drilled in

this discipline and constantly received object lessons in the lethal consequences of not remaining servile toward his masters did not even think of
offering resistance to a man with a death's head on his uniform cap.

Karl Röder, an inmate of a concentration camp from 1933 on, writes:
"During the years of my imprisonment I saw only two instances of physical resistance, and each one involved new arrivals. After just one day in the
camp, it became clear that such resistance was pointless." Röder cites each
of these cases: A peasant who had just arrived in Dachau struck back when
his face was slapped, and he was shot on the spot. Another new arrival, a
Jew, was also beaten, but instead of moaning and whining, he promptly
displayed to his tormentors a decoration from World War I. That man
disappeared from the camp.[2]

Acts of resistance that are customary in prisons and camps, such as a
hunger strike, were inconceivable in the Nazi concentration camps. There
was no hope of scaring a camp management with the consequences of a
hunger strike, nor could such a strike mobilize help from the outside. The
inmates were made drastically aware of their complete isolation from the
world.

Such an atmosphere was demoralizing enough, but the prisoners' sense
of helplessness was exacerbated by the same threat, heard over and over
again when new people were admitted and on numerous other occasions:
"There is only one way out of here: through the chimney." After the
beginning of the war, no one could reasonably count on being released, and
in the period of Hitler's lightning victories, this thought severely undermined morale. Many of those who were able to obtain more favorable
positions concentrated their entire energy on getting through the day
and declined to think of the morrow. Those whose outlook for the future
was the bleakest were, of course, affected the most. The Jews, who had to
wear the yellow badge in the camps, carried a far greater emotional burden
than the Germans, who were given preferential treatment over "racially
inferior" persons. In the early years of the war, the slogan about the
"Thousand-Year Reich" darkened hopes of an eventual return to normal
life. But in the course of time propaganda about the invincibility of the
system lost much of its inhibiting effect.

It should also be borne in mind that people are more likely to transcend
themselves if they know that the public will be informed of their actions.
In the hermetically sealed world of the concentration camps, no one could
count on posterity being informed about them. The camps were not a
suitable soil for heroes and martyrs.

In addition to all these factors weighing on the psyche of the inmates,
there was the permanent terrorism of the SS. In every camp, there was a
political department—as the camp secret police was designated—with a

hired or blackmailed army of informers. This "Gestapo" saw to it that there was no talk of resistance and that no cell of a prisoners' organization came into being. In all too many cases, an unproved denunciation or a mild suspicion was enough to kill a prisoner. Even more momentously, when it was a matter of tracking down a group that plotted resistance, the SS resorted to indescribably cruel tortures. Many a man who had the noblest intention of never informing on anyone broke down under these tortures. Does anyone who has not himself survived such tortures have a right to condemn such a person? A number of prisoners who were active in a secret organization committed suicide when they faced the threat of capture by the political department, thus avoiding the risk of betraying comrades.

This department was dreaded in every camp, but its power was greatest in Auschwitz, because there the SS was most afraid of secret activity on the part of prisoners. For one thing, Polish escapees could easily establish contact with the surrounding population, and for another, everything had to be done to keep the world from learning about the mass extermination of human beings that was concentrated in Auschwitz.

Chronic malnutrition inhibited any thought of action against the SS. The people who had to get through the dark days in the camps without any glimmer of hope, foraging for food and trying to escape beatings, were in no condition, psychically and physically, to defy the apparently all-powerful machinery.

Thus anyone who would so much as think of resisting had to have attained a position that enabled him to overcome the most oppressive problems. If such a person wanted to enlist like-minded people, he had to change their living conditions in such a way that they no longer suffered the pangs of chronic hunger. Smuggling a comrade-in-arms into a better detail was a prerequisite for group activity in every camp.

Resistance groups have sometimes been criticized on such grounds. They have been accused of having helped only one another and later boasted that they had engaged in resistance activity. Undoubtedly there were such cases. A differentiation between an instance of resistance activity and mutual aid among friends and like-minded people depends on whether this aid was an end in itself or the foundation of an activity intended to transcend this group.

I fear that even a recital of all the obstacles to any thought of resistance will not prevent readers from underestimating these difficulties. Nevertheless, they were surmounted by many people, and that is due to the fact that, as Lucie Adelsberger has put it, "it is one of the worst things in the world to have to stand by helplessly and watch another person being tortured" (Adelsberger 1956, 64). Another reason, one mentioned by Tadeusz Patzer,[3] is that if a person has no hope of staying alive, he at least does not want to die in vain. Both Adelsberger and Patzer derived their insights from the extreme situation at Auschwitz.

Finally, everyone who occupied a position within the framework of the prisoner self-government had a powerful motivation for incurring the risk of resistance activity. If he engaged in this activity only to keep his privileged position, then he became a tool of the camp administration. Only when such a person used his opportunities to oppose the administration could he clear his conscience of the charge that he was acting as an extension of the SS.

6

SOURCES AND CRITIQUE
OF SOURCES

Any history of the resistance offered by prisoners in the Nazi concentration camps must remain incomplete, for nobody knows how many acts of resistance or plans for such resistance remained unknown because the actors and witnesses did not survive.

Even an objective presentation of acts attested to by survivors bristles with difficulties, for every report is given from a different point of view. To prevent the SS from finding out too much from a single prisoner under torture, resistance organizations observed the conspiracy rules that a person should know only what was absolutely necessary for his own duties. For this reason later statements about the same episode can differ substantially; in fact, some persons participated in acts of resistance without ever learning that they were acting in behalf of an organization. A friend might ask such a person to do a favor for him, and a good prisoner with camp experience did not ask a lot of questions. Even in camps where a resistance organization was active for years, the overwhelming majority of prisoners knew nothing about it. Only when the conspiracy became less tight, in the final phase of the camps, did outsiders notice an organized activity in some camps. Even persons who survived because of something a particular group had done often had no idea to whom they owed their lives. Most prisoners did not learn of organized acts of resistance until later. It will come as no surprise that some reports were received skeptically or that in some others the merits of the writer, and even more frequently of the political group to which he belonged, were emphasized and often overemphasized.

In addition, the forms of organization in the camps varied according to the intensity of the terror of the political department and the number of political prisoners who knew one another well from years of shared imprisonment. Thus, for the final phase, it is possible to give the number of active resistance fighters in the old camps—those with a steady, strong complement of German Reds. The German Communist Harry Kuhn, who was responsible for the military organization of Buchenwald in the camp's last days, states that in late March 1945 there were about 850 active fighters organized in 178 groups (*Buchenwald* 1960, 489). In Auschwitz, however, where the terror was strongest and the number of political prisoners much smaller, the Combat Group probably had only a solid nucleus. Each member had more or less numerous contacts with friends, who might have suspected that there was some organized activity but frequently knew nothing about it. Thus any later attempt to calculate numbers would be merely speculative.

The most unambiguous documents of resistance activity on the part of the inmates are those written while the camps were still in existence. Understandably enough, there are only a few of these, for every organization was careful not to preserve written records. In most instances nothing was written down, for in the overcrowded quarters there were a host of informers, and no one could foresee who else might be pressured into acting as a stool pigeon. Nevertheless, a few documents have been preserved, and these do demonstrate the activity of resistance organizations.

The organizations in Auschwitz probably had the closest contact with the outside—that is, the Polish resistance movement—and because the Cracow group of the latter dared to preserve this correspondence, we do have convincing documentation. In its initial phase the Auschwitz resistance organization was comprised exclusively of Poles. At a later date an international organization was created, and it called itself Combat Group (*Kampfgruppe*) Auschwitz (Langbein 1949, 115 ff.). Its Polish leaders were able to maintain contact with the outside, for they were known to the leaders of the Polish resistance organization and in the best position to establish contact with the Polish civilians who worked in the camp area and were in charge of the mail. Mail arriving at the camp was quickly destroyed, but in Cracow 350 letters from Auschwitz were preserved—impressive evidence of the intensity of this contact, which was established by Polish prisoners as early as 1940, i.e., in the first year of the camp's existence.[1] It is extremely regrettable that thus far only a portion of these valuable documents has been published.

Of course, a major part of this correspondence was for purposes of publicity, for the Polish organization in Cracow was supposed to do its best to inform the public about what was going on at Auschwitz. News about Auschwitz was also sent to Czechoslovakia by Czech prisoners and to Vienna by Austrian inmates.[2] However, the regular information sent to Cracow was most important, because the Polish organization was able to transmit this news to the Allies in London.

The surviving documents contain many details about the activities of the Combat Group Auschwitz. For example, on September 4, 1944, "two rolls of metal film for camera 6:9" were urgently requested, and photos were sent out showing the bodies of gassed people being burned in the open air next to one of the crematories. These photos were intended to dispel any doubt about reports of the mass extermination of human beings. The machinery of mass murder produced such unbelievable results that the Combat Group took the risk of documenting its reports with photographs (Smoleń 1960–67, 36, 84).

Since this correspondence also served to specify how escapees could be aided on the outside, the activity of the Combat Group has been documented in this area as well (Smoleń 1960–67, 36).

A letter written by this group in November 1942, when it consisted only of Poles, demonstrates the importance of giving the resistance movement in Auschwitz an international character. That letter confirms the receipt of medicines (which were regularly sent) and emphasizes their value: "The largest percentage of our patients [in the infirmary of the base camp— H.L.] are Poles, about 50 percent, and we are helping only these."[3] Before an international front against the murderous terror could be formed, it was necessary to counteract the narrow chauvinism of some Poles who had attained key positions in the hospital. Without the active intervention of the Pole Jósef Cyrankiewicz, who before his arrest had been a leader in the Socialist Party in Cracow and thus was supported by the organization that maintained contact with the camp, this national selfishness could not have been curbed (Langbein 1949, 116; Kłodziński 1970, II/2, 79). The result of these persistent efforts may be found in a declaration of the Combat Group dated summer 1944: "Only solidarity, international cooperation, and the fight for freedom give us the right to regard ourselves as fellow fighters against the misfortune that Hitler's Fascism has brought over the world."[4]

The information sent by the Combat Group Auschwitz reached London via Cracow and was disseminated over the radio there. This is well documented. When the leaders of the group noticed that the SS itself had begun to be demoralized they decided that this demoralization could be utilized and in early 1944 they sent out the names and personal data of those SS men who were operating the machinery of extermination. The BBC in London put those persons on notice that they would be held responsible for their atrocities, and the effect of this broadcast was clearly noticeable in the camp. Years later former members of the SS testified before a Frankfurt jury that the BBC broadcast caused a particularly notorious member of the political department to make a hasty name change, and a new paybook was issued to him under it (Langbein 1949, 154; 1965, 120 ff). When Roland Freisler, the presiding judge of the so-called People's Court, asserted in the trial of officers who had plotted to eliminate Hitler on July 20, 1944 that only criminals were being detained in the concentration camps, Combat Group Auschwitz issued a declaration protesting this statement and "informed the free world about our existence and our unequal struggle for the rights of all political prisoners" (Smoleń 1978, 93).

Other letters had no concrete effect. Thus a note sent on June 24, 1943, contains this statement: "Next to our blocks in the camp area an enormous factory is being built and the machines are already being installed. I believe the birds ought to fly to this target in a month's time. As regards us, don't hold back because we are living here. The firm of Krupp must be destroyed and razed to the ground."[5] The Krupp building, however, was not bombed [in June 1943, the Allies had not yet invaded Sicily, southern Poland was nearly 1,000 miles away and out of range for precision bombing—ed.] any more than were the crematories and gas chambers at Auschwitz, which the Combat Group Auschwitz urged be targeted at a later date.

A letter dated March 25, 1944, contains information about the Katowice airport and the building of hospitals in the immediate vicinity or at some distance. The Combat Group was able to secure details about this, and by disseminating this information it evidently wished to improve the knowledge of the Polish underground organizations.[6]

When the victories of the Russian army caused the SS to make preparations for the liquidation of Auschwitz, the Combat Group feared that the inmates would be destroyed along with the camp in an effort to deprive the Allies of witnesses to Nazi crimes. Thus the Combat Group on September 6, 1944, informed its contacts in Cracow of this apprehension and requested that the British radio be informed as soon as possible. This was done, and when the Polish government-in-exile in London called for a protest against this threatening mass murder, the British government replied that if this plan for destruction was carried out, those responsible would face the most severe punishment (Seweryn 1965, 152 ff). This statement was made public, and in the end the SS abandoned its plan to liquidate Auschwitz.

In addition to this proof of the effectiveness of resistance activities in Auschwitz, a document preserved in Cracow sheds light on the problems faced by the Austrians, who headed the Combat Group together with the Poles. Alfred Klahr, a member of the central committee of the Austrian Communist Party, who was interned in Auschwitz under the name Lokmanis and was the author of pioneering theoretical works on the Austrian national question, wrote in German a detailed study of the German question, the shared responsibility of the German people for the crimes of National Socialism, and the necessity for the German working class to overcome "the heritage of Fascism, including its ideology." After analyzing the recent history of Germany, Klahr comes to this conclusion: "No wonder that in the national question the [German Communist] Party was taken in tow by the Fascists." He called on the German Communists to examine themselves critically, particularly their attitude toward the question of nationality.[7]

The fact that the Austrian members of the Combat Group risked discussing this subject in writing indicates the difficulties they encountered in collaborating with German Communists. The Austrian Josef Meisel remembers heated, almost venomous discussions with the German Communist Bruno Baum, discussions that were partly responsible for the production of the above-mentioned document.[8] This lack of unity among the Communists weakened their resistance.

Resistance groups of other camps were not able to maintain an equally intensive contact with secret organizations outside the camp, and thus we must rely on postwar statements about their activities to an even greater extent than in the case of Auschwitz.

There were a few exceptions. Thus Polish women in Ravensbrück managed to send out messages from the adjacent subsidiary camps, which were also eventually transmitted to the Allies by the outside Polish secret organization. Urszula Wińska writes that, in February 1943, 700 women were scheduled to be gassed. The British radio is said to have broadcast this information, and this led the SS to change its plans and to transfer these women to Auschwitz and Majdanek, from which some of them were sent back to Ravensbrück at a later date.[9] Maria Kurcyuszowa reports that the Allies were also sent information about medical experiments on healthy inmates, the kind performed on Polish women in Ravensbrück. When the end of the camps approached, the SS wanted to eliminate witnesses to its most heinous crimes, and the lives of the "guinea pigs" were threatened; but these women were reportedly able to persuade the SS not to execute them by pointing out that the Allies already knew about the operations that had been performed on them.[10]

Since the Herzogenbusch concentration camp, like the one at Auschwitz, was located in a German-occupied country, the Dutchmen interned there were able to consolidate their contacts with the Dutch population so effectively that, for example, Cornelis Fels managed to smuggle out an article about the crimes committed by the camp administration; this article was published in a special issue of the illegal Dutch newspaper *De Waarheid*, The Truth.[11] Cornelis Hofman reported from the same camp that Ben Meyering, who worked in the post office, procured a censor's stamp and used it for uncensored communications to the outside world. In fact, he wrote about the camp to the International Red Cross in Geneva on the letterhead of the German Wehrmacht, and this letter is said to have arrived.[12]

Although German prisoners found it much harder than foreign ones to use contacts to inform the outside world about their endeavors, pertinent documents have been preserved or could be reconstructed.

At the initiative of Hermann Brill, an official of the German Social Democratic Party, a popular-front committee was formed at Buchenwald in February 1944. Its leadership consisted of four Germans (two officers of the Socialist Party, one from the Communist Party, and one from the Catholic camp), and on May 1 of that year, it published the demands of the political prisoners for the time after the defeat of Nazism. However, the underground nature of this committee limited the dissemination of this document. Since at a later date all written documents in the camp had to be destroyed, the four leaders of the committee reconstructed these demands in Buchenwald shortly after the liberation of that camp. In addition to calling for a peace "without annexations and imposts," "recognition of the Germans' duty to pay reparations," and "no forced labor by Germans," this document demands a "withdrawal of German troops behind the boundaries of 1938," which meant that the annexation [*Anschluss*] of Austria was not to be rescinded. This program was adopted by representatives of Communist and Socialist parties from ten nations. The German members also included representatives of the Christian Democrats and the Scholl students' group of Munich, and the French ones representatives of the Radical Socialist Party (Brill 1946, 94). The document includes a report about the activities of this committee (Brill 1946, 88 ff). In contrast to the attitude of the Austrian Communists in Auschwitz, which is pointedly mentioned by Klahr in the above-mentioned theoretical work, the representatives of the Austrian Communists and Socialists at Buchenwald evidently had no objections to remaining annexed.

An organization of German Communists in the Sachsenhausen camp was able to establish contact with Communist groups illegally operating in Berlin. They got members appointed to outside details, which were assigned to do work in nearby Berlin, and these men managed to make contact with civilians. With the aid of these contacts, in the spring of 1944, this group organized the escape of several Communists, who afterward worked in the illegal organization in Berlin.[13] However, on March 27, 1944, the camp administration caught a prisoner listening to news on a radio installed in a workshop at the Sachsenhausen base camp. An immediate search uncovered leaflets containing instructions for illegal work in the Ruhr region. This triggered lengthy investigations, a wave of arrests of Communist prison functionaries, and finally executions and transfers to other camps. As a result these contacts were destroyed.[14]

It probably was possible to smuggle an occasional letter out of any camp. Some that have been preserved contain references to underground activity in the camps. Thus Heinz Schmidt was evidently referring to the above-mentioned episode when he stated in a letter written in a satellite camp of Sachsenhausen on August 31, 1944: "In the big camp we had an underground political leadership, and these comrades were betrayed by informers and professional criminals." Elsewhere in this letter he writes: "The potential anti-Fascist forces in this camp ought to have been mobilized in good time."[15]

In the concentration camps located outside Germany, there were more favorable conditions for contact with the outside world, and thus it was possible to document many actions of the resistance groups. The "old" camps in Germany permitted some prisoners in particularly favorable positions to make and preserve notes. There, the camp Gestapo did not work as intensively as it did in places like Auschwitz, and the network of political prisoners was tighter, thus affording better protection. In some extant documents, there are also references to resistance activity.

Thus Emil Büge, who was assigned to the political department of Sachsenhausen as an interpreter, managed to continue working late, after the closing of the official workday, and to use the lack of supervision in the office to keep a diary. Since the political department was the first to know when a prisoner was about to be released, he pasted his notes in old eyeglass cases and gave them to reliable comrades who were leaving. When he found out that he was himself scheduled to be released on April 20, 1943 (the Führer's birthday), he prepared more cases with the rest of his notes (Lienan 1949, 158 ff). These have been preserved, and some of them contain information not only about resistance activities but also about their evaluation by other prisoners. Here are some of Büge's notes: "On July 21, '42, two Poles, 28275 Johann Piotrowski and 21353 Josef Rukowski, were hanged [Büge was following the usual SS practice of preceding the names of prisoners with their numbers—H.L.]. . . . What was their crime? They were using sandblasts to remove the paint from steel helmets about to be repainted, and jokingly said to their Polish coworkers that a steel helmet could be made much thinner if the jet was kept on it a bit longer. An SS man had their remarks translated and denounced them."[16] In documents of the camp administration that have been preserved the names of the two Poles appear with this note: "Order to hang them carried out on July 21, 1942, at 6:10."[17]

Here is another revealing note: "In 1942 the Ukrainians planned a conspiracy. When a number of them in the Speer labor detail were examined, around seventy-five sharpened pocket knives and daggers were found. Two ringleaders confessed that they had been preparing for an attack since

Christmas. They were hanged and others followed. In the forest detail, which is made up chiefly of workers from the East, a secret radio was found buried in the forest soil. There can be no doubt that the Ukrainians are endangering us all. Quite apart from their rebellious intentions, which put all of us at risk, they are behaving badly in the camp. . . ."[18] This last remark refers to an additional difficulty of resistance actions: The SS system of taking reprisals against everyone, as soon as individual breaches of discipline or an attempted rebellion were discovered, had some success.

Heinrich Lienau, who worked together with Büge in a Sachsenhausen detail, continued Büge's notes after the latter's release. Lienau writes that these notes and the ones smuggled out of the camp by Büge helped him fashion his book of memoirs, *Zwölf Jahre Nacht*, Twelve Years of Night (Lienau 1949, 160). It is regrettable that Lienau did not publish the notes made in the camp verbatim, for an adaptation made after the fact does not have the same documentary value. This also applies to the diary kept in Gusen by the Pole Stanisław Nogaj. He concealed his notes under the floor of a barracks, and after the liberation they were retrieved from there, whereupon he made changes and additions.[19] Unfortunately these were not identified as such. It appears that Alfred Hübsch also later revised the notes he took from 1938 on as gatekeeper of Dachau and was able to hide.[20]

Edgar Kupfer-Koberwitz also had the unusual opportunity of noting his experiences and impressions during his internment in Dachau. He stresses the fact that normally it was impossible to do any secret writing in Dachau, let alone keep such writing hidden. However, he was working in the office of the Präzifix screw factory on the camp grounds, and because of a typhus epidemic, the inmates in this detail slept in barracks next to the factory to keep the epidemic from spreading to civilian employees. This gave Kupfer-Koberwitz, like Büge in Sachsenhausen, a chance to stay in his office after the normal working hours. Two factors worked in his favor: He was known as a writer of occasional verse, and a number of civilians hired him to write poems for them. Thus he was able to write things unrelated to his office work without attracting attention. In addition, the documents of the arms factory were classified information, and even the SS guards did not have access to the papers in the office. With the aid of discreet friends, Kupfer-Koberwitz buried his manuscript in the storeroom. When it was dug up after the liberation of Dachau, it was damaged, but most of it was decipherable. The first part was written from memory, but from December 8, 1942, to the liberation it is in diary form (Kupfer-Koberwitz 1957/1960, 7 ff).

Since Kupfer-Koberwitz lived away from the big camp, life there is reflected in this diary only distantly, and only rumors of acts of resistance reached the diarist. When four young Russians escaped from the Präzifix detail on July 16, 1943, he remarked that for them it was easier to escape than for Germans, for there were Russian and Polish forced laborers everywhere. Like so many others, Kupfer-Koberwitz knew that a German escapee could not count on assistance from the German population. Even though the Russians had prepared their escape well and in collaboration with others, three of them were captured and returned to the camp (Kupfer-Koberwitz 1957/1960, 142 ff).

The German Communist Karl Barthel had a job in Buchenwald that afforded him unusual freedom of movement. He used his position in the SS officers' mess to write down what happened in that camp and sent these accounts to his wife with the assistance of German civilians and two SS group leaders. During this entire period, Czech fellow sufferers helped him by supplying him with information (Arndt 1970, 5). With literary embellishments, Barthel describes an episode that does not appear elsewhere in the literature on Buchenwald, which is probably more extensive than that about any other concentration camp. Vladimir Mikhaelich Kovalenko, a young Russian who had escaped from the camp together with other of his countrymen, had been caught and sent to the bunker. On June 3, 1944, when he was being taken from his cell to be executed, he stabbed an SS guard to death with a knife that had been smuggled into his cell and was shot to death (Bartel 1946, 79 ff.).

The Belgian Arthur Haulot did not give the notes he was able to make in Dachau any literary treatment. Since he played an important part in the last phase of the international resistance organization, his recollections of the last weeks and days of Dachau have particular historical value.[21] This also applies to the diary of Ernst Thape, one of the leaders of the Popular Front committee in Buchenwald, which he was able to keep in the chaotic days after April 1, 1945.[22] Both documents are indispensable as descriptions of the liberation of the two camps.

When Hanna Lévy-Hass was deported to the Bergen–Belsen concentration camp in summer 1944, she did not find it very hard to keep a diary, and this diary reflects the atmosphere in that camp more vividly than accounts written later.[23] The Norwegian Odd Nansen had started a diary in Norwegian prisons and faced no insuperable obstacles in continuing it in Sachsenhausen, where he was transferred in the fall of 1943 (Nansen 1949). In keeping her diary, Lévy-Hass may have been aided by the chaotic conditions in Bergen–Belsen, and Nansen was presumably helped by the privileged position of the Norwegians. The diary that the Dutchman Floris B. Bakels was able to keep in various prisons and later at Natzweiler and its subsidiary camps contains "almost no detailed description of the horrible deeds he witnessed; these are only hinted at." Nevertheless, this diary, which was later incorporated in his book, does give a graphic picture of the atmosphere and of the author's attitude (Bakels 1979, 16). The Spanish photographer Francisco Boix-Campos, who was at Mauthausen from January 1941 on and worked in the police records department there, procured negatives of photos that captured such important events as a visit by Himmler or the procession to the gallows (with musical accompaniment) of a recaptured fugitive. Acting at the request of a Spanish youth organization that had been formed in the camp, Boix-Campos hid these negatives and thus was able to transmit them to posterity.[24]

The description of the preparation and implementation of the uprising of Jewish prisoners in Sobibor is the work of Aleksandr Pečerskii, one of the initiators of this heroic struggle, and it is based on notes that he systematically made about the most important events since his arrival and took with him at the breakout (Nirenstein n. d., 308).

In camps that could no longer be completely evacuated before their liberation by Allied armies, notes about the camp were made immediately afterward; some of these represent collaborative efforts. The historical value of such documents is particularly high when the authors held different political views and belonged to different nationalities.[25]

These remarks do not mean that any memoir written down later should be dismissed out of hand as one-sided, glorifying, or biased in some other way. It seems appropriate, however, to compare such descriptions, whenever possible, with documents written while the camp was still in existence or immediately after its liberation.

We also have some SS documents that permit us to infer acts of resistance by inmates. Thus a memorandum to all camp commandants dated September 15, 1943, states that, according to information from the Security Office, prisoners were passing on news that they had heard over enemy radio stations while repairing radios. An investigation of such opportunities was ordered.[26] This news source was used more or less systematically by prisoners in virtually all camps. Extant telexes to Gestapo offices and reports about the number of people in the camps give the numbers and names of escapees. From the camp administration of Auschwitz alone, we have 139 telegrams of this kind with the names of 206 escapees for the period from January 7, 1943, to June 15, 1944 (with a gap between November 30, 1943, and February 24, 1944). Lists of wanted persons, guard books, and commandants' orders are an additional source of information for escapes from Auschwitz (Iwaszko 1964, 44).

Because of what appeared to be especially dangerous circumstances, the SS investigated certain escapes more thoroughly than was the norm. Thus a special SS detail that was originally charged with investigating corruption in Sachsenhausen extended its activity to presumed acts of resistance. On June 12, 1944, this detail wrote a report that begins with a reference to the successful escape, on February 2, 1944, of one French and one Lux-embourgian prisoner from the outside detail Fichtengrund and goes on to say: "In the course of our investigation of Communist activities in the Sachsenhausen concentration camp, we were able to establish that the escaped prisoners had contact with Gerassimow, who provided these pris-oners with important plans of Heinkel [an arms factory that employed inmates—H.L.], the Sachsenhausen base camp, and notes about important outside details of Sachsenhausen. The majority of these plans were de-signed to give, in particular, enemy bombers precise information about important factories or other institutions of the armaments industry. The aforementioned Gerassimow was also a prisoner in Sachsenhausen, and in view of our investigation and for reasons of expediency he was for the time being placed in the main prison of the Security Office. Gerassimow him-self intended to escape together with another Russian by the name of Vasilenko, but certain circumstances foiled their plans. Hence he gave the papers (plans) and notes in his possession to the prisoners who were escap-ing and also provided them with the Berlin contacts known to him. It is characteristic of Gerassimow's activities that he also gave Feiler, a prisoner who escaped from the balloon building outside detail on July 14, 1943, notes as well as the address of his contact, which proves that he utilized every opportunity to get important information to the outside deliberately and in line with his special orders from the Soviet Union" (Damals in Sachsenhausen, Those Days in Sachsenhausen 1967, 96).

The two fugitives mentioned above at first hid out in a prisoner-of-war camp for French officers in Berlin. Paul Müller later confided in his fellow Luxembourger René Trauffler: "All plans relating to the Heinkel Works, the motor vehicle depot, and the entire camp with all surrounding workshops were copied here in order to keep them from falling into the hands of the Germans again if one of us were nabbed." Together with a French friend he was able to traverse Germany and reach Luxembourg. Müller also told his fellow countryman that they had bribed a guard to help them escape and that this guard was soon thereafter arrested, tortured, and shot. Thus it is reasonable to assume that the special SS detail was able to extort from this man some of the facts in the above-mentioned report.[27]

Another letter written by the same SS detail, one dated July 11, 1944, also refers to resistance activity. It requests that the French prisoner Bertrand Gauchet be made available for "intensive questioning" [the offi-cial euphemism for torture—H.L.], since he was arrested because of his "membership in a Communist cell in Block 38 and sabotage at the forest motor depot," though he denied everything and called the witnesses liars (Damals in Sachsenhausen 1967, 96).

A number of documents contain information about acts of sabotage by inmates who were employed in arms factories. Those responsible for the production of rockets were most concerned about this sabotage. A special directive issued by the management of the Mittelwerke Ltd. on January 8, 1944, begins with this statement: "We have reason to point out that our installations are damaged repeatedly, deliberately, and maliciously by disruption, destruction, and theft." It goes on to order measures against attempts at sabotage. Inmates of the Dora camp were doing forced labor in this factory. On March 21 of that year a man named Schumacher, who was in charge of security in a department, complained to the SS Work Assignments that "the big furnace . . . has evidently been damaged through sabotage" and that a number of other acts of sabotage "constantly hamper production" (Drobisch 1968, 127; Mader 1963, 311).

In a memorandum dated April 11, 1944, SS Lieutenant Colonel Maurer of the Economic Office calls the attention of all camp commandants to the increasing reports of sabotage and writes: "In future demonstrable cases of sabotage, please request death by hanging. The execution is to take place in the presence of all prisoners who are members of the labor detail" (Female Concentration Camp Ravensbrück 1973, 205). This order resulted in an even greater number of mass executions for suspected or actual sabotage in the concentration camps.

Between May 6, 1944, and March 11, 1945, sixty-five Russian women were executed in Ravensbrück (*Frauen-KZ Ravensbrück*, Female Concentration Camp Ravensbrück 1973, 201). The greatest number of executions took place in Dora, where they were promoted by an extensive network of informers, mass arrests, and torture. On March 10, 1945, fifty-eight inmates were executed in the roll-call area and thirty each on March 20 and 21.[28] These were the most extensive mass executions in that period, but by no means the only ones. Here, too, Russians were the primary victims. Of those hanged in 1945, SS statistics show that 133 were Russians, twenty-five Poles, three Czechs, and one Lithuanian (Bornemann/Borszat 1970, 194).

As the end of the National Socialist dictatorship approached, the camp administrations became visibly nervous. In Dachau, where political prisoners had predominated for the longest period of time, the SS believed it had detected a Communist conspiracy. Following arrests and the obligatory tortures—which, however, did not produce the demanded confessions and denunciations—the camp administration reported to the central office as follows: "In the Dachau camp there is a whole group of Communist functionaries who have not changed their old orientation after ten or eleven years of imprisonment in houses of correction and concentration camps. Although it has not been possible to determine organized preparations for a rebellion, it may be regarded as certain that these men have had a subversive influence on the positions they have occupied in the camp: Work Assignments, records office, capos, block personnel, and hospital personnel. This has resulted in a general slackening of discipline, absenteeism, and increasing acts of sabotage in the arms industry. Their amicable relationship with foreigners and the solidarity among the German political prisoners give us reason to fear that law and order in the camp can no longer be ensured." To this call for help, which gives a more positive picture of the German Reds than any after-the-fact description could have done, the central office responded with its usual order that suspects be transferred to other camps (Schatzle 1946, 34 ff.). On June 19, 1944, nine inmates were transferred from Dachau to Mauthausen (Maršàlek n.d., 22), among them the Austrian Josef Lauscher, whose escape will be described later. This was followed by transfers to other camps,[29] and the camp administration filled the vacant positions with Greens. Walter Vielhauer has described the consequences of these transfers as follows: "The core of the organization was crushed and its fabric torn."[30]

On March 23, 1945, the head of the Buchenwald outside detail at Bad Salzungen reported that the senior camp inmate, a German political prisoner, and the camp doctor, a Russian prisoner, had been returned to their original camp because the senior camp inmate was "absolutely unreliable" and the doctor had sabotaged the labor assignments by putting numerous men on the sick list (Drobisch 1962, 122).

A report monitored by the London radio gives impressive evidence of the good connection that the Combat Group Auschwitz had with London by way of Cracow: "According to a report received in London, the German authorities have ordered the killing of 3,000 Czech Jews in the gas chambers of Birkenau on or about June 20. These Jews were taken to Birkenau from the concentration camp Theresienstadt on the Elbe river last December. Four thousand Czech Jews who had been transported to Birkenau from Theresienstadt in December 1943 were murdered in the gas chambers on March 7. The German authorities in Czechoslovakia and those in responsible positions under them are hereby informed that London has detailed reports about the mass murders in Birkenau. All those responsible for these mass murders, from those giving commands to those who carry them out, will be taken to account." This announcement was monitored by the Germans on June 15, 1944 (Obóz Koncentracyzny Oświęcim 1968, 157), and a confidential report by the Foreign Office in Berlin, dated June 18, 1944 refers to it.

The Combat Group had hoped that this announcement would prevent the murder of the inmates of the Theresienstadt family camp, but this murder did take place. On July 11, 1944, around 3,000 women and children from this section of the Birkenau camp were killed in the gas chambers, and during the following night the other Jews were gassed (Czech 1959–64). Thus the Auschwitz resistance organization had known about the preparations for this murder for a long time.

We have a letter written by Jozef Cyrankiewicz, one of two Poles in the leadership of the Combat Group Auschwitz, in which he warns against rash publications of situation reports and adds: "However, we should make optimal use of those statements that are especially useful for propaganda purposes—for example, the recent information about the gassing of the 3,000, the entire first transport from Theresienstadt, including the doctors. This sort of thing must be sent abroad forcefully. Theresienstadt, in the protectorate, must be warned, for they are planning to send further transports from there. Let these people offer resistance!"[31]

The strength of this organization, which to the very end, the SS felt without being able to get it in its grip, is convincingly demonstrated by a report from Oswald Pohl, the head of the Economic Office, dated April 5, 1944. Responding to Himmler's query about security measures for Auschwitz, Pohl estimated that, not counting sick people and those employed in subsidiary camps, around 34,000 prisoners "could constitute a menace to Auschwitz in the A-case." Elsewhere in this report Pohl speaks of the "endangerment of Upper Silesia by a possible uprising or breakout of the prisoners," thus indicating what is meant by A-case. At that time the Economic Office, in addition to taking military security measures, ordered the transfer to other camps of the prisoners it regarded as the most dangerous, primarily Poles and Russians.[32]

That the Combat Group nevertheless managed to keep its most important Polish collaborators out of these transports is documented by a report from the head of the security police in Katowice dated December 18, 1944. In late September, this outfit arrested an officer of the Polish underground organization and found papers that proved that this organization had contact with inmates of Auschwitz. Here is an excerpt from this report: "The captured material shows that the concentration camp Auschwitz is under the purview of the AK [Armja Krajowa, a Polish military underground organization—H.L.] and is serviced through the WRO [Wojskowa Rada Obozu, military council of the camp—H.L.] A number of persons maintain contact with the camp, particularly the Danuta area commanders and the PPS man Kostka [PPS, the Socialist Party of Poland—H.L.] A certain Rot [code name of Cyrankiewicz—H.L.] has been appointed AK commandant of the camp. He concerns himself especially with making reports about the camp and transmits these to the area via a certain Urban. These reports about Auschwitz include information about arrivals and departures of prisoners, the structure of the camp, personnel, evaluation of SS leaders, organization of the inmates, and plans for the future. Among the tasks of the WRO are preparations for prisoners' escapes, and their further flight is handled by an especially created organization, *Bojowka* [War], which has connections with Cracow via various contacts" (Czech 1959–64).

Only a brief notice in the minutes of a fighter pilots' staff meeting at the Reich Ministry of Aviation on May 2, 1944, refers to the attempted uprising of prisoners assigned to work at the St. Micheln Erla Works at Mülsen (erroneously given as Moesel) near Zwickau, in a subsidiary camp of Flossenbürg: "They piled up their pallets etc. and set them on fire. Most of the factory burned down, and the flames and the collapse of the building are said to have totally destroyed 100 to 300 pairs of [airplane] wings. The police sprang into action and shot 200 prisoners during the rebellion. Eighty were seriously wounded and twenty escaped." Concerning this, Hans Kammler, an SS major general (*Gruppenführer*), remarked: "As always, this happened because the people noticed that they were no longer being treated harshly enough. By way of giving them special treatment, I had thirty people hanged. Since these hangings order has been pretty much restored."[33] In the specialized literature, there are no reports about this rebellion, which was organized by Russian prisoners of war. Evidently no eyewitnesses have survived.

Another uprising is documented by more than the following matter-of-fact account in a report by the head of the police in the Lublin district: "On October 14, 1943, around 5 P.M., uprising of the Jews in the SS camp Sobibor, 40 kilometers north of Cholm. They overpowered the guards, cleaned out the arms depot, and after a gun fight with the other SS personnel, they fled in an unknown direction. Nine SS men were killed, one SS man wounded, two foreign guards shot. Around 300 Jews escaped; the others were shot or are in the camp" (Sauer 1974). Survivors of this breakout are able to give further details about the preparation and implementation of this uprising, the greatest success of inmates in open resistance.

After the liberation of the concentration camps, an enormous number of descriptions came into being, for numerous authors owe their strength to survive to their ardent desire to inform the world about all the incredible things that they had had to suffer and witness. A considerable number of them had promised friends who had been marked for death to bear witness after the liberation and now kept that promise. The paper shortage in the early postwar period forced publishers to print only small editions, and this made it even harder to keep abreast of a literature that is as dissimilar as it is comprehensive. Many reports contain references to resistance activity on the part of the prisoners, but frequently there is only cursory mention of such activities, for many authors have only vague information about it.

The most comprehensive documentation about resistance activity is by inmates of Buchenwald—for one thing, because the organization there was especially strong, and for another, because the liberated prisoners had to stay in the camp for a while longer and thus began to write down the facts right then and there, utilizing documents of the camp administration that had escaped destruction. Then, too, the three standard works written immediately after the liberation—David Rousset's *L'univers concentrationnaire*, Benedikt Kautsky's *Teufel und Verdammte*, and especially Eugen Kogon's *The Theory and Practice of Hell* analyze the system of the Nazi concentration camps on the basis of Buchenwald, where all three authors were interned.[34]

The topic "Resistance in Buchenwald" probably produced the most heated discussions. The dramatic events of April 11, 1945, the day of liberation, demonstrate the difficulties of an after-the-fact reconstruction. Albert Beffort, a Luxembourger who experienced that day in Buchenwald, even speaks of a deliberate falsification of history with reference to exaggerated accounts of a struggle for liberation that appeared in East German publications. Beffort believes this was done because "the uprising was led largely by Communists" and "the bad Americans were to be pushed into the background." At the same time, however, Beffort justifiably warns against writing off everything derived from sources that can be shown to have been given occasional political coloration after the fact.[35] Anyone who wishes to separate facts from legends must simply use all sources, compare and critically examine them, if possible secure the judgment of eyewitnesses about the truth content of a publication, and above all guard against all prejudices.

In a critical examination of the essays in the collection entitled *Buchenwald . . .*, one cannot ignore a notice at the end of some of them: "Written in 1945, revised" [at a much later date–H.L.]. Considering that this volume was published in East Germany under the auspices of the Communist-dominated Fédération Internationale des Résistants (FIR), the possibility that in such a revision party politics was given priority over historical truth cannot be ruled out. In the various editions of this collection, there are not only minor alterations but also omitted paragraphs. (*Buchenwald* 1960).[36]

In some cases there is nothing to indicate that such revisions have been made. For example, in a pamphlet titled *Damals in Sachsenhausen* and published in 1967 by the Deutscher Verlag der Wissenschaften in East Berlin, there is a report by political prisoners who remained in the camp in which some facts and figures were tacitly changed. One small correction is particularly striking. In the original report, a description of the arrival of the first Russian troops in Sachsenhausen is followed by this sentence:

"The men of the Red Army are not staying here; they are moving on." In the 1967 publication we read instead: "The Red Army men are in a great hurry and have to move on."[37] The reason for this change may become clear if one is acquainted with the Communist criticism of the conduct of the first American troops at the liberation of Buchenwald: They also moved on after the SS had fled upon their approach.

When Julius Mader published his book *Sepp Plieseis, Partisan der Berge* in East Berlin in 1971, he leads his readers to believe that he found Plieseis's autobiographical account after his death in 1966. But in fact it was published in Linz in 1946 under the title *Vom Ebro zum Dachstein* and, a little political retouching is in evidence in the republication. The original states that in Dachau Plieseis was "taken into the big organization that included all political prisoners, especially the Austrians," but Mader omitted the reference to the Austrians (Pliesei's 1946, 7, 187; 1971, 147). Evidently he did not wish to convey the impression that the leading forces in the Dachau resistance were not Germans.

Likewise, different references to the formation of an international organization in Mauthausen, in the weeks before the liberation, assign different roles to the German Communist functionary Franz Dahlem. The Spaniard Juan de Diego, whose work in the office made him independent of rumors or accounts by others, believes that Dahlem's part is documented.[38] In the pamphlet *Mauthausen mahnt* issued in Vienna shortly after the end of the war, Dahlem's name is included among those who formed the international inmates' committee in early March 1945. Hans Maršàlek, who compiled this brochure, admitted when interviewed recently that Dahlem did not actually join it until some weeks later.[39] (At the time of the pamphlet's publication, Dahlem was an important party official in the German Democratic Republic.) In this pamphlet we also read paeans like this one: "The prisoners were absolutely convinced that, if they were free today, this would be primarily the work of the Union of Soviet Socialist Republics and its glorious Red Army" (Maršàlek n.d., 42). It is evident that such a generalization could not possibly have represented the conviction of all prisoners. Later Maršàlek found the courage to tell the full truth: "Such formulations were suggested to me by the publishing house," he wrote me, "which was under the direction of Communists."[40] Thanks to Maršàlek's complete honesty, the historical value of his most important publication, *Die Geschichte des Konzentrationslagers Mauthausen* (Maršàlek 1974), is beyond doubt. It is food for thought for all those who want to write off all Communist authors as one-sided.

Details of an incident differ from one account to another. For example, according to Jakob Boulanger, the Austrian Social Democrat Leopold Mayer informed the illegal organization in Auschwitz that the political department had a list of seventy-eight functionaries who were scheduled to be killed. Since he was on cleaning duty in that department, Mayer could have seen this list, and he was finally able to destroy it in mid-April, when the SS was already in a state of panic (Boulanger 1957, 127). Mayer himself remembers this occasion somewhat differently. He did see a sheaf of documents in the political department, but he did not know the people whose ID numbers were on the list (he recognized only the ID numbers of three Germans of his acquaintance), nor did he know whether the listed inmates were actually destined for destruction, although this was to be presumed. He notified one of the three Germans, and that man asked Mayer to dispose of the documents, which he was able to do.[41]

Even publications of respected institutions cannot be accepted uncritically. This is true even of the Auschwitz Museum, which deservedly enjoys a good reputation among experts. In a study of the prisoner hospital in Monowitz (Auschwitz III), Antoni Makowski gives an entirely positive picture of the Polish senior inmate, Stefan Budiaszek, without making any reference to the serious charges brought against him by numerous fellow prisoners (Makowski 1975, 127 ff.). In Germany, where Budiaszek lived after the war, legal proceedings were brought against him for complicity in numerous murders, and this action was not dropped until many years later.[42] These facts are certainly known to the staff of the museum. It is true that Budiaszek's great initiative in the expansion of the hospital did benefit the patients and he did use his position to help Poles. His attitude toward Jewish patients, however, which is the source of most charges against him, is another matter, and it seems like dubious scholarship to name him uncritically in connection with resistance activity. In her study of the Birkenau hospital, even a historian as well-informed and scholarly as Danuta Czech does mention that the Polish physician Dr. Roman Zenkteller, himself a prisoner, "was not especially loved by the inmates" but in her detailed characterization of that key figure she ignores the serious charges against him that have been documented for years. (Czech 1975, 78 ff.; Langbein 1972, 251 ff.)

The first few instances of retouching detailed above were evidently intended to emphasize the glories of the Communist Party; omissions from the Budiaszek story were probably to cover up the anti-Semitism of some Polish prisoners. The Pole Jozef Gárliński, who published after emigrating to London, is a case in point. In his book *Fighting Auschwitz*, he details the resistance organization of Polish officers but minimizes the familiar charges that important members of this circle were active anti-Semites in the camp. Even though a moral judgment was made for that very reason against Dr. Władysław Dering in a trial that created a sensation in London, Gárliński represents the charges against Dering as products of a personal controversy (Gárliński 1975, 220, 273 ff.).[43] Gárliński also denies that another leading member of the organization of Polish officers, Alfred Stössel, was among the prisoners who, on orders from the SS, killed sick or weak people by injecting poison into their hearts (Gárliński 1975, 272).[44]

Some authors, apparently for reasons of party politics, minimized the role in the resistance movement of persons whose attitude after the liberation they disapproved of. Gárliński does this when he seeks to downplay the importance of Jósef Cyrankiewicz and the Combat Group Auschwitz—obviously because as the Polish prime minister Cyrankiewicz shared responsibility for many things that Gárliński (justifiably) condemns (Gárliński 1975, 200).[45]

Bruno Baum eliminated the names of Hermann Langbein and Heinz Brandt from later editions of his little book *Widerstand in Auschwitz* (Resistance in Auschwitz) because both men had broken with the Communist Party.[46] When the Russian M. S. Sobochenii listed the names of those who founded Combat Group Auschwitz in the spring of 1943, he replaced Langbein with Bruno Baum (Sobochenii 1965), even though Baum himself, who was then a recent arrival in Auschwitz, has stated that he did not become active in that group until summer 1944.

The Belgian André Mandryckxs was ill used even after his death. This young Communist functionary did outstanding work in the Work Service in Auschwitz. His courageous advocacy of his fellow sufferers netted him a punitive transfer, and he did not survive the camps. Despite this, some of his fellow countrymen claimed afterward that he had used his office only to help Russians and Communists,[47] though this is unanimously contradicted by former prisoners who are not themselves Communists. Emil Peters, a Luxembourger, emphasizes that André (as he was generally called in the camp) was very kind to the (politically unaffiliated) Luxembourg policemen who were interned in Neuengamme,[48] and his fellow countryman Pierre Schneider has stated that André was "a fine lad" who was never observed giving preferential treatment to his fellow Communists.[49] David Rousset calls Mandryckxs "a remarkable human being" who made a very good impression,[50] and Heinrich Christian Meier writes that he was "venerated by the poor and feared by the bigwigs," that he had, in fact, become a symbol of solidarity.[51] In a comprehensive presentation of the Neuengamme camp community, this statement appears in connection with the big transports of foreigners that arrived in 1943: "Now the already existing small circle of active political prisoners, including André Mandryckxs, was able to set about introducing a somewhat more humane atmosphere."[52] Elsewhere Mandryckxs is described as "a truly great person," and a poem entitled "André" hails him as "the conscience of woe" (*So ging es zu Ende* 32).

There is another source of error to consider. As Maršàlek puts it, eyewitness accounts "not infrequently give an idealized picture of the atmosphere and the solidarity in the camp" (Maršàlek 1974, 245), and Franz Danimann writes: "The battle against the SS and its henchmen, the criminal prisoners, was waged across all ideological boundaries on an absolutely nonpartisan basis." In the international cooperation, "there were no differences regarding the common goal, and in the shared suffering the political prisoners became brothers, no matter what part of Europe they were from" (Danimann 1960/67, 64). It is likely that a camaraderie did develop in the camps that transcended national and political boundary lines, and this camaraderie is one of the survivors' finest memories. In every camp, however, there were heated disputes on political and national grounds.

Even among former prisoners who belonged to the same party, the differences outlasted the camps. This is confirmed by Heinz Junge, a Communist who has served as secretary of the association of Sachsenhausen inmates in the Federal Republic of Germany. To reconstruct the history of that camp, a committee was formed in the German Democratic Republic and another one in the Federal Republic. Junge has explained this dual-track situation by saying that political differences have prevented any joint publication.[53]

It is self-evident that books cannot be used as sources if their authors not only describe things they heard in the camp incorrectly (a frequent occurrence, because there were numerous rumors in every concentration camp) or give wrong dates (the most common mistake in firsthand accounts), but also describe as personal experiences events that cannot possibly have taken place. Thus Paul Rassinier describes in detail how Thälmann punched him with his fist in Buchenwald and how Breitscheid shoved him around (Rassinier 1959, 68). It is a known fact, however, that Thälmann never was interned in Buchenwald, though the SS announced after the bombing of Buchenwald on August 24, 1944, that Thälmann had been a victim. As for Breitscheid, he was kept in solitary confinement and had no contact with any of the other prisoners (Kogon 1946, 193, 279).[54]

If one makes allowance for such problems, then all sources for resistance in the Nazi concentration camps are useful. As synopsized, supplemented, and in many cases corrected by former inmates whom it was possible to question, they form a mosaic that enables one to derive a graphic total picture. Even though it will never be possible to reconstruct the complete truth, such a picture probably comes closest to it.

7

DIFFERENT CONDITIONS AND CHANGED GOALS

In the concentration camps that already had a history when the first foreigners arrived, German political prisoners found the most favorable preconditions for resistance activity. They were very numerous there, had camp experience, and in many cases knew one another from years of shared imprisonment. Since most of them were Communists—a result of the bitter fights between Communists and National Socialists before Hitler's assumption of power—familiar with the hierarchic structure of that party and the discipline it had instilled in its members, they were equipped to play an outstanding role in the resistance movement. Eugen Kogon, a close observer, writes: "In contrast to men of liberal views, they [the Communists] were used to absolute party discipline and were almost the only ones who were the enemy's match as far as means and methods were concerned" (Kogon 1946, 310). Benedikt Kautsky has characterized them as follows: "The majority of those who had been in the camps for many years were Communists. By virtue of their youth, their working-class origin, the courage they had demonstrated in street fights, and the toughness they had acquired (or displayed) there, they made an excellent adjustment to camp life" (Kautsky 1961, 131). Bruno Heilig, who was sent to Dachau after the occupation of Austria, estimates that nine tenths of the positions there were held by Communists. "The others were Social Democrats, and very few came from other circles" (Heilig 1948, 133). This estimate is for the prewar period.

Middle class anti-Nazis did not arrive in the concentration camps in considerable numbers until after the occupation of Austria, and most of them were sent to Dachau. "Our advantage was our discipline and organization," writes Harry Naujoks, an official of the KPD (*Kommunistische Partei Deutschlands*, the German Communist Party). He was installed as senior camp inmate in Sachsenhausen in spring 1939 at the behest of the influential Communist organization, after his predecessor, also a German Communist, had been dismissed. Afterward Naujoks made this comment: "I had to abide by this decision, but I did so reluctantly." He also stated that this stark Communist discipline made a catastrophic impression on outsiders.[1]

In the three "old" camps, Dachau, Sachsenhausen, and Buchenwald, groups formed on a regional basis. Thus Dachau had Communist groups of Bavarians, Swabians, and Franconians. Swabian Hans Gasparitsch describes Swabians of the early period as quite homogeneous,[2] and Walter Vielhauer speaks in this connection of ancient regional conflicts.[3] With reference to Buchenwald, Robert Leibbrand writes: "Of course, comrades from the same city or the same district knew one another best and could most easily get together without arousing suspicion. The first illegal groups consisted almost entirely of Communists" (Leibbrand 1945, 27). The Pole Wacław Czarnecki observed that the Germans in Buchenwald formed nineteen regional associations that existed until the end of the camp. "At first there were some groups of two or three persons who came from the same towns or provinces and knew each other well. In the course of time the members of groups from various provinces were placed under a certain leader" (Czarnecki 1968). According to Ernst von Salomon, groups of five and later of three were formed, and by virtue of their discipline, the Communists were the first to demonstrate their ability to do battle with the Greens for key positions and thus lay the foundation for organized activity (Salomon 1960, 149, 154). When Walter Poller arrived in Buchenwald in December 1938 he immediately gained the impression "that there was some organization among the prisoners," with the Communists as its backbone (Poller 1960, 32). Robert Leibbrand has described the "Red core," mostly Communists who had been behind barbed wire since 1933. "These constituted a sworn community in which comradeship was the supreme law. Any member of this community was supported by his comrades at all times and with all means" (Leibbrand 1945, 11). This cliquishness was the object of criticism by outsiders, and Eugen Kogon has formulated it as follows: "The main reproach to be leveled at the Communist Party in the concentration camps involves its reluctance to purge its own ranks. Only in very rare cases did it eliminate outright criminal types, Communists who served as senior block inmates or capos, in any other way but by transferring them to outside labor details, where they were able to do their dirty work with even less control." However, Kogon emphasizes that the positive achievement of the Communists "can hardly be overestimated" (Kogon 1946, 311).

In the camps that were not founded until shortly before the outbreak of the war or afterward, Germans did not constitute the same solid core of resistance that they did in Buchenwald and Sachsenhausen—until the end, or in Dachau, until the camp administration struck a decisive blow against them a short time before liberation.

Conditions in Ravensbrück were somewhat similar, for German women who had been arrested for political reasons were concentrated there as soon as that camp was established, and thus they managed to form the cadre of a resistance group. The first considerable transports of foreign women arrived there from Czechoslovakia, and these women also soon played a special role. In those concentration camps that the SS filled with German criminals and that never housed a comparable number of German political prisoners, conditions caused a resistance movement to develop in a different form—to the extent that they permitted organized resistance at all.

In the early period of Auschwitz, Poles were the only political prisoners. Kazimierz Smoleń writes that "as early as 1940 [the year in which Auschwitz was built—H.L.] there was a wide-ranging underground cooperation" (Smoleń 1960–67, 34). Communists predominated in resistance activities in the old camps, but in Auschwitz their place was taken by Polish officers. Józef Gárliński describes as its organizer Witold Pilecki, an officer who had himself arrested during a raid in Warsaw in September 1940 with the intention of establishing a secret military organization in Auschwitz. Since he had been provided with false papers, he was listed under the name Tomasz Serafinński (Gárliński 1975, 34). He immediately started to form groups of five; its members had to take an oath, and the designation was "Union of the military organization" (Gárliński 1975, 35). Its first report reached the Polish government-in-exile in London as early as March 18, 1941 (Lenz 1956, 55). Parallel groups of Polish officers came into being. To achieve collaboration among them it was necessary to overcome questions of prestige (Gárliński 1975, 73, 109). Pilecki had been a mere captain in the Polish army whereas others had held a higher rank, and this caused difficulties. Barbara Jarosz has named various groups and their leaders (Jarosz 1978, 146 ff.). Kazimierz Smoleń remembers that Polish officers on potato-peeling duty—a detail with light work which the organization managed to staff especially with older members—addressed one another by their military rank.[4] In Auschwitz this was not merely grotesque but exceedingly dangerous, for the political department was searching primarily for Polish prisoners who were officers. In point of fact, virtually none of the cadres of this group lived to see the end of Auschwitz. A few organized their escape, but most were shot to death by the political department.

In January 1943 this department caught a Polish block clerk with notes that led to extensive arrests and executions. On September 16 of that year, a denunciation triggered another wave of terror that ended with the shooting of numerous Polish officers and intellectuals (Brol 1959, 35, 37). Józef

Gárliński has named seventy-four Poles whom the political department sent to the bunker between that day and September 29. According to Gárliński, of the forty-seven who were finally shot, twenty-eight were leading members of the Polish military organization. Tadeusz Hołuj, a man well acquainted with the activities of the Polish underground movement of Auschwitz, believes that this denunciation and the bloody terror was not the only reason for the breakup of the military organization. The formation of an international organization in which numerous Poles were active eliminated its field of activity. Holuj feels that "all they cared about were their own interests" (Friedman/Hołuj 1946, 145).

It was probably Gárliński's one-sided overemphasis on the importance of the Polish military organization that prompted Kazimierz Smoleń to mention in a later publication that as early as 1940 resistance actions were directed "not only by the military but also by Polish political groups" and to document this by listing many names (Smoleń 1978, 86).

The Majdanek resistance organization had a comparable origin, though it never became as strong as the Auschwitz one. Polish officers were its backbone, and they too managed to establish an enduring contact with Poles outside the camp who were in touch with partisan groups (Kroiatkowsky 1966, 248 ff.; Gryń/Murawska n.d., 63 ff.).

In Mauthausen the first group of Spanish anti-Nazis was formed. Its forte was its marked unity, which derived from these men's joint service in the army of the Spanish Republic against Franco's Fascists and their shared internment in French camps after the defeat. There they had formed an organization with conspiracy rules, and they continued this organization after the Germans occupied France and deported them to Mauthausen. In those days the Greens were in total control of Mauthausen, and hence the living conditions there were much more unfavorable than in other camps. The canniest men managed to form a nucleus that could later be expanded to become the center of a resistance organization.[5] One day made a strong impression on all Spaniards who have described the formation of this organization: The Sunday that Hitler attacked the Soviet Union (June 22, 1941), there was a general disinfection in Mauthausen, and all inmates were forced to strip and wait all day out in the open until the lodgings and the clothes had been disinfected. In the meantime information about the invasion came over the loudspeaker, the blaring of which enabled the Spaniards to talk to one another, something that the average prisoner ordinarily had little chance to do. They used this opportunity to organize the leadership of an organization (Razola/Constante 1969, 86). Knowledge of the language and, to an even greater extent, the same ideology and common experiences soon facilitated contact between the Spanish group and other Civil War veterans interned in Mauthausen. They constituted a link between the Spanish national resistance organization and other national groups (Razola/Constante 1969, 71 ff.). Mariano Constante mentions, in addition to Czech, German, and Austrian veterans of the Spanish Civil War, Frenchmen, Russians, Romanians, Italians, and Hungarians (Razola/Constante 1969, 86). The Russian Valentin Sakharov reports that these groups were able to place his fellow countryman, Major Ivan Alekseyevich Panfilov, also a fighter in Spain, in the laundry-drying detail, a good place for observing things. Sakharov remembers that this man "had many friends among the Spaniards" (Sakharov 1961, 198). Hans Maršàlek, the chronicler of Mauthausen, also emphasizes the pioneering work of the Spaniards: "The Spanish republicans were the first to display solidarity within an international framework. They made contact with the former members of the international brigade in the camp and supported them" (Kogon 1946, 257). The Frenchman Michel de Bouard also emphasizes their cohesion and their courage and points out that they were the first national group to build a solid organization both in the Mauthausen base camp and in Gusen (Bouard 1954, 57, 68; 1962, 54). Despite special difficulties, Spanish Communists soon established a firm organization in the subsidiary camp Steyr Works (Bernadac 1976, 208).

As soon as international cohesion could be achieved, Austrian prisoners, large numbers of whom had by then arrived in Mauthausen, were entrusted with important tasks, for as "Germans" they were in a more favorable situation and, because Mauthausen is in Austria, they had a better chance to establish contact with the outside (Kogon 1946, 259).[6] The first contact with the Spaniards was made by Josef Kohl, a man who is repeatedly praised by Spanish Communists, while others are divided about his role (Razola/Constante 1969, 106).[7] Juan de Diego remembers that, as in Auschwitz, Germans initially played only a subordinate role.[8]

It was only natural that all resistance activities in Herzogenbusch were carried on by Dutchmen, for they were the only ones in the camp, apart from German criminals, who held positions there.

In Natzweiler, Frenchmen played much the same role that Poles played in Auschwitz or Spaniards in Mauthausen—particularly Alsatians, who were the first arrivals in the camp and spoke German.

As for those concentration camps where German criminals set the tone from the very beginning, the politically aware Germans had their best chance of gaining power in Neuengamme. Since Neuengamme was initially operated as a subsidiary camp of Sachsenhausen, the Reds transferred there from Sachsenhausen benefited from their contact with their original camp, where they had had experience with conspiracy. However, in Neuengamme the political element among the foreigners played a more important part than it did in Dachau or Buchenwald in the early war years.

We have already mentioned the importance of the Belgian André Mandryckxs in the resistance activity at Neuengamme. Although only 870 of the 2,800 Germans in Neuengamme wore red markings,[9] the camp was firmly under the control of political prisoners.[10] A declaration of the international prisoner committee issued immediately after the liberation emphasizes that the German anti-Fascists managed "to give us significant aid." The specific mention of the Work Assignments and Albin Lüdke constitutes a distinction that not many Germans received at the time (Meier 1948, 118).

The Pole Urbonas has described what happened in Stutthof because it had never been possible to break the complete dominance of the Greens there. A very small number of people did make plans, but no organized resistance was possible in that camp.[11] Krzysztof Dunin-Wąsowicz does mention active groups—Polish officers and boy scouts, Russian prisoners of war, a very cohesive Danish group, and German Communists—but he too speaks of a lack of contacts, particularly between Poles and Germans. The camp administration was repeatedly able to smash resistance cells by transferring men to other camps or executing them (Dunin-Wąsowicz 1970, I ff., 13).

There are even more unfavorable reports about the situation in Gross–Rosen. To the very end, whippings were administered in that camp not only by the SS but by Greens as well.[12] Every Green or Black senior block inmate was a potential informer, and according to Mieczysław Mołdawa, anyone who attracted the attention of such an informer was in danger of being placed in a killer detail. This was brought about by several factors. When the camp was under construction, and prisoner labor was requested, particularly notorious German criminals were transferred there from Buchenwald, where the Reds had been able to prevail after hard fights against the Greens.[13] As a matter of principle, Thümann, the officer-in-charge, did not permit any political prisoner to hold a position in Gross–Rosen. Moreover, the number of German criminals there greatly exceeded the number of positions, and so these organized a "killing contest" in order to curry favor with the SS and obtain the privileges of VIPs (Mołdawa 1967, 63 ff. 140). Even in the last year of the war, the atmosphere was grimmer in Gross–Rosen than in any other camp; this is evidenced by an order dated August 26, 1944: "It has recently been observed that prisoners are discussing the war more than seems necessary. I interpret this as "forbidden political activity . . . and remind every prisoner that he must immediately report any statements made by his fellow prisoners" (Mołdawa 1967, 140 ff).[14]

In their fight against political prisoners, Greens were able to make excellent use of orders of this kind. But where political prisoners constituted a major factor in the prisoner self-governing such orders were meaningless, for anyone who made such a report would have been subject to severe retaliation from the Reds working in the camp administration. In such camps, the SS staked out informers, and such men were used in Gross–Rosen as well. The Pole Andrzej Kamiński has pointed out that some of the small number of Germans with a red triangle were "political" in name only,[15] and the Belgian Leon Halkin has given us a portrait of his senior block inmate, who really was imprisoned for political reasons: "He has been in the camp for seven years and has all but forgotten what it means to live in freedom. This prisoner may have been an excellent resistance fighter, but he did not cease to disappoint and discourage us" (Halkin 1965, 105). Under such conditions it was possible to form a group here or there—Mołdawa mentions some Polish ones—but, unlike the situation in other camps, it was impossible to organize a resistance center (Mołdawa 1967, 140).[16] In her diary Hanna Lévy-Hass, a Jewish Communist who was deported from Montenegro to Bergen–Belsen in the summer of 1944, describes the atmosphere that rendered organized resistance impossible more vividly and graphically than could have been accomplished by an account written later: "People from different social strata are crowded together here, but the petit-bourgeois type predominates. . . . If only some clearly defined common consciousness bound us together! But this is not the case. . . . Shared misery unites human beings who can barely stand one another." And she goes on to say: "Everyone is highly irritable and always ready to regard his fellow man as a personal enemy. . . . Everything human is reduced to zero. . . . We are still alive, but we are dead men and women" (Lévy-Hass 1979, 8, 18, 37).

Conditions for prisoner activity could not develop uniformly in the large concentration camps. In the Mauthausen base camp, for example, the political prisoners eventually constituted an important factor in the camp hierarchy, which greatly benefited the resistance organization—in fact, it made it possible. However, in neighboring Gusen the prisoners' attempt, in the final phase before the liberation, to create "the embryo of an organization," as Sim Kessel put it, was doomed to failure (Kessel 1970, 226). The Spaniards Manuel Razola and Mariano Constante, who were able to observe conditions in Gusen longer than Kessel, also testify that the tremendous terror of the SS, which was supplemented by Green prisoner functionaries, made an organization there impossible (Razola 1969, 166). When Fritz Kleinmann was transferred to Gusen II in February 1945, he had had experience with underground activities in Buchenwald and Monowitz. "There was no organization," he writes. "To the very end Greens killed people. I was utterly demolished there." Kleinmann's words illustrate the difference between Gusen and the above-mentioned camps.[17]

In Birkenau the pressure of the camp administration was also stronger than it was in Auschwitz base camp, and the domination of the Greens remained unbroken there. However, since the big complex was divided into independent sections, the makings of an organization could develop in some of them, particularly in the women's camp. There a group of French-women who had been arrested for political reasons played a major role alongside German Communists, who had been transferred from Ravensbrück together with antisocials and criminals in order to help build the camp. In addition, Combat Group Auschwitz kept in touch with contact people in Birkenau; in fact, it was instrumental in getting reliable and experienced people transferred there to strengthen the organization. Thus the German Communist Adolf Schilling and the Austrian veteran of the Spanish Civil War Sioma Lechtmann could be placed in positions at Birkenau that enabled them to function effectively (Langbein 1949, 12 ff., 160 ff.).

The central administration of the concentration camps was in the habit of transferring inmates from one camp to another for a variety of reasons: to obtain experienced workers for building a camp; for a special task (for example, the transfer of male nurses from Dachau to Auschwitz when an epidemic of typhus broke out there); or to get rid of dangerous elements (predominantly Germans, for suspicious foreigners were all too often shot on the spot). The punitive transfer of eighteen German Red prisoner functionaries from Sachsenhausen to Flossenbürg has already been mentioned, as has the transfer, from Dachau to other camps, of German armband wearers whom the SS suspected of engaging in secret political activities. When secret activities of political prisoners were to be stopped in Sachsenhausen, there were not merely executions. On October 20, 1944, 103 German, French, Czech, Luxembourgian, and Russian prisoners were sent to Mauthausen.[18] One of these, the German Hans Seigewasser, writes that there they were promptly placed under the protection of the camp committee, and the punitive measures that had been ordered against them were soon set aside (literally: punched full of holes) (Sacharov 1961, 235 ff.). Finally, requisitions of skilled workers for arms factories repeatedly led to transfers. The lively traffic among the various camps facilitated an orientation about the situation in other camps and an exchange of experiences and often of information as well.

When whole groups were transferred at once, it was possible to shift political activities from one camp to another. Thus Franz Graczoll reports how a group transferred from Auschwitz undermined the harsh discipline in Gross–Rosen. When, for instance, a Green capo whipped one of theirs, there was a chorus of "No beatings!" The men from Auschwitz filled the Greens with great fury, but the transferred men were helped by their camp experience and solidarity.[19] Mołdawa too has given an account of the solidarity of a group that came to Gross–Rosen (Mołdawa 1967, 146).

When, in the fall of 1942, Jews from all camps were concentrated in Auschwitz, a group of Jewish Communists from Buchenwald arrived at Monowitz, a camp then being built. Thanks to their unity and camp experience, they managed to form the nucleus of an underground movement in the hospital, and they were soon able to establish contact with the Combat Group in the Auschwitz main camp.[20] Janez Ranzinger, a Yugoslav, was a member of the Combat Group, and when he was transferred to Buchenwald in the summer of 1943, he formed a group among the Yugoslav inmates on the pattern of Auschwitz. This group then operated within the framework of the international organization in Buchenwald (Buchenwald 1960, 429 ff.).

Because Dora was initially administered as a subsidiary camp of Buchenwald, the close contacts between these two camps could be maintained when Dora became independent. The Czech physician Jan Češpiva gathered his first experiences in conspiracy in Birkenau (Kraus/Kulka 1957, 219). When he was transferred to Buchenwald in August 1943, together with most other Czechs, he was assigned to the Dora prison hospital. Even though Dora was especially sealed off in order to prevent any information about the production of the V-rockets from leaking out, the prisoners were able to develop a special news service. The inmates of Buchenwald concealed letters in medicines that were being sent to Dora, and those employed in the Dora infirmary hid their messages under the bandages wrapped around corpses. When there was no crematorium in Dora, the bodies of prisoners were taken to Buchenwald to be cremated (Češpiva/Giessner/Pelný 1964, 48 ff.; "Dora" 1967, 30; Dieckmann Hochmuth n.d., 69 ff.).[21] Thanks to the close contact between camps it was sometimes possible for the secret organization to be informed about a transfer before it happened. Toni Lehr and two female friends were deported to Auschwitz for two reasons: They were Jews and had been arrested in Austria because of underground activities for the Communist Party. Past experience led them to believe that their death sentence would be sent along with them. However, when they were transferred to Ravensbrück, evidently with a note about their special status, the resistance organization in that women's camp had already been informed about their dangerous situation, immediately took charge of the three women, and successfully protected them.[22] Similar reports have been given by Walter Vielhauer and Karl Wagner after their punitive transfer from Dachau to Buchenwald.[23] When I was transferred from Dachau to Auschwitz in August 1942, Josef Lauscher, a Viennese with a leading position in the Dachau organization, gave me the name of a fellow Austrian, Ernst Burger.

I sought him out as soon as possible, and we developed an organization in Auschwitz, on the basis of our Dachau experience (Langheim 1949, 60, 67).

When the camps were evacuated toward the end of the war, contacts and acquaintances, whether from political life in freedom or from shared camp experience, also came in handy. After the evacuation of Auschwitz, those leading members of the Combat Group who were still alive and had stayed in the camp until the end were integrated into the illegal organization of Mauthausen (Maršàlek n.d., 27; Baum 1965, 56). The experienced Russian Pirogov, who had been transferred to that camp from Sachsenhausen, was immediately used for underground activities (Sakharov 1967, 174 ff., 236). By virtue of his contacts with the secret organization in Birkenau, the Dutchman Antonius van Velsen was immediately made senior block inmate at Melk, a subsidiary camp of Mauthausen.[24]

The exchange of experiences between one camp and another facilitated a parallel development of resistance activity. This activity was stepped up as the military situation changed, and this also led to changes in organization goals.

In the early period in Buchenwald, the resistance groups were small and ethnically organized. (Apart from self-evident mutual aid), Robert Leibbrand has named their three main tasks information from the outside, warning against informers, and preparation for imminent interrogations by the Gestapo (Leibbrand 1945, 27). The last-named task soon became unnecessary, for in early days the Gestapo dealt summarily with foreign prisoners, whereas most Germans, who arrived at a later date, had already been interrogated. Robert Siewert, who is repeatedly mentioned among the leading Communists of the Buchenwald resistance, has described the tasks of the early period in similar fashion: "to constantly influence a group of sympathizers, to put the struggle against the SS, its henchmen, and all critical elements on a broad basis, to help sick and weak comrades in every way, and to assure a fair distribution of foodstuffs. It was, above all, a matter of opposing those prisoners who exploited their position in the camp to have a better life at the expense of other inmates." With the words "mutual aid became a firm principle" Siewert sums up the goals set by the first groups of Germans, organized by region, whom he also mentions (Siewert 1960–67, 46). In a report written immediately after the liberation of Buchenwald, Otto Horn confirms that the Germans in the international resistance organization remained organized on a regional basis until the middle of 1944 and then reorganized themselves by blocks.[25] In a "Preliminary Report about the Military Organization in the Buchenwald Concentration Camp," it is also stated that the German section "was organized on a regional basis until mid-September 1944" in that area as well.[26] Karl Wagner remembers that he became a member of the Württemberg group when he was transferred from Dachau to Buchenwald on July 20, 1944.[27]

Ernst Busse, whose name is always linked with that of Siewert in the development of the Buchenwald resistance, has summarized the tasks of that period as follows: "It was the goal of this activity to preserve our active fighters against Nazism and to protect them from the terror of the SS." In addition Busse points to preparations for future activity: "It was one of the main tasks to create effective fighting groups that would be able to protect the lives of all prisoners and gain their freedom in the inevitable contests at the collapse of the Nazis." The tasks he mentions are passive in nature, though it is possible that Busse's remarks, which appeared in a collective newspaper, have been abridged. Busse can no longer be consulted; he did become a minister in Thuringia (German Democratic Republic), but later the Russians dragged him off to one of their camps, and he did not live to see his rehabilitation. Klaus Masse has described the goals of the Buchenwald organization in similar terms: "To fill the positions held by career criminals . . . with responsible prisoners. To protect endangered prisoners and strengthen their moral power of resistance." His remarks refer to the year 1940.[28] The correspondence of these statements entitles them to general validity.

Max Heinl indicates that a similar situation existed in Dachau at that time when he describes the activities as "less a policy of resistance than mutual aid given to improve personal protection against all the horrors in the camp." However, Heinl admits that his judgment can refer only to actions that came to his attention and that there also were "real resistance groups" whose members, armband wearers, also strove to protect nameless comrades from the despotism of the SS,—at risk of being punished themselves.[29] One of these prisoners, the German Schorsch Scherer, who is favorably remembered for his activity as senior camp inmate of Dachau, speaks less of belonging to an organization than of discussing the essential goal of his activities with comrades.[30]

Ernst Platz, a Berlin Social Democratic journalist who was sent to Buchenwald in the spring of 1938, reports that German Communists immediately placed him under their protection and admitted him to their secret nocturnal meetings. Platz had been interned as a Jew, and since, before the outbreak of the war, Jews could be released if they could demonstrate an opportunity to emigrate, the comrades made him promise that if he was released he would tell the world what was going on in Buchenwald. After only five days they got him out of the penal company that all Jews were placed in and saw to it that he was released from the killing work in a gravel pit—"something that had never before happened," as Platz put it. After thirteen months in Buchenwald, Platz, who had, in accordance with his instructions, trained his memory, was actually released and was able to emigrate.[31] This episode points to one task of the resistance that was to be of much greater significance later on—namely, to inform the world about what was happening in the concentration camps.

This task is particularly emphasized by foreigners who took the initiative in the resistance movements in the early period. Witold Pilecki has named the following aims of the Polish officers in Auschwitz: raising morale by disseminating news from the outside, procuring additional food and clothing for the members of the organization, sending information to the outside, and creating battle-ready groups (Gárliński 1975, 24). Once the machinery of extermination was built into the concentration camps and prisoners were employed in the production of secret weapons, the search for ways of informing the world became more urgent. Such efforts are like a red thread running through the history of the resistance movement, and it is easy to understand how desperate they must have seemed to the inmates of Auschwitz.

The extension of the war to the Soviet Union in June 1941 created a new driving force for actions against the regime. In Auschwitz it was less strong, for the Polish officers then predominant felt the historically based animosity of their people against the Russians, which exacerbated by Stalin's pact with Hitler and the subsequent partition of Poland. Among the Spaniards, however, who constituted the first cell of a resistance movement in Auschwitz, the attack on the Soviet Union produced ardent feelings of solidarity. Many of them had learned to appreciate the Soviet Union during the Spanish Civil War, and numerous leaders of this group were Communists themselves.

The Spanish organization, created on the day of the invasion of the Soviet Union and comprised of members of leftist groups, added the following to the tasks already named: to place trusted people in positions where they could gather information and observe the SS; to seek contacts with political prisoners of other nationalities; and particularly to strengthen confidence in the powers of the nations and of democracy and to stifle all doubt about the final victory. Sabotage and lying down on the job are mentioned as forms of fighting the Nazis even at a time when prisoners were as yet not detailed to work in the arms industry (Razola 1969, 87 ff.).

Shortly after the German invasion, the first Russian prisoners of war were sent to the camps, and those who were not immediately murdered were subjected to treatment that was unusually harsh even by concentration-camp standards. Their arrival produced a wave of active sympathy, particularly in the old camps. German Communists with armbands risked a great deal to show the Russians that they were ready to help them.

The 2,000 prisoners of war who arrived at Buchenwald on October 18, 1941, were supposed to be kept in strict isolation. However, "the SS was not able to prevent the camp inmates from giving the prisoners of war an enthusiastic reception and providing them with bread, food, cigarettes, and the like. Punishment was meted out to the entire camp and to individuals (the responsible senior block inmates) who had attracted particular attention."[32] The Austrian Communist Otto Horn has described this episode as follows: "The first Russians who arrived at the camp, so-called Ukrainians, were given a very friendly reception by the camp, but their uncooperative conduct soon caused them to be snubbed. The situation changed when . . . the first transports of Soviet prisoners of war arrived. The entire camp, all nations, displayed solidarity with the prisoners of war."[33] In Sachsenhausen, too, there were demonstrations of solidarity with the remaining prisoners of war who arrived in the camp; in mid-November 1941, only 2,500 of more than 20,000 were still alive.[34]

Even earlier a spontaneous demonstration of solidarity in Dachau showed the strength of the political prisoners. After the occupation of France by German armies, the veterans of the international brigades in the Spanish Civil War, who were interned there, fell into the hands of the Gestapo. The Germans were taken to prisons in their homeland and then sent individually to concentration camps; the Austrians—including myself—arrived in Dachau as a group on May 1, 1941. Since we had taken up arms against Spanish fascism and thus also against Hitler, who had vigorously supported it—something that the foes of National Socialism who had been imprisoned before the beginning of the Civil War had not been able to do—our arrival produced friendly feelings among the inmates, and this helped us in the early period, the most difficult one in any concentration camp.

On the basis of her experience in Ravensbrück, the Pole Wanda Kiedrzyńska includes among the tasks of the resistance groups, in addition to "biological protection" and "preservation of human dignity"—constant aims of any activity—the organization of educational work. The Polish girls who had been deported to Ravensbrück were secretly given instruction. Among the goals set by her group Kiedrzyńska mentions, in addition to the development of artistic and religious life as well as "sabotage of work for the Germans," was escape from the camp. She guards against the exaggerations that are apt to occur in from-memory descriptions by admitting that the struggle assumed organized form "at times" (Kiedrzyński 1960, 95 ff.).

The thought of flight occurred to foreigners more easily than to Germans, usually coupled with a desire to join an active group of partisan fighters. Since this desire was most likely to be realized in Auschwitz and Majdanek—where conditions made even a very great risk attractive—the organization of escapes played a greater role in those camps than elsewhere. In the area around Auschwitz, partisan units came into being that were composed to a large extent of Poles who had been able to flee from the camp—for example, a partisan group that called itself "Sosieski" and operated in the vicinity of the camp. "One of the aims of this outfit was the organization of escapes from the camp and the care of the fugitives."[35] An account of several flights from Majdanek is followed by this summarizing conclusion: "All fugitives immediately joined the partisans" (Gryń/Murawska n.d., 67). Inmates of Loiblpass, a subsidiary camp of Mauthausen that was located in Slovenia, also utilized the opportunity to flee and join the partisans operating in the immediate vicinity.

In other camps, resistance groups initially declined to organize escapes, and not only because of the great difficulties and the small chances, but because of the murderous reprisals of the camp administration. "The camp never liked a fugitive"—this is how Bruno Apitz characterizes the general mood in Buchenwald. Emil Carlebach has pointed out that the severe reprisals against everyone by the SS after every escape caused the German-led Buchenwald resistance organization to plan no escapes. This attitude did not change until the fall of 1944.[36] Walter Poller confirms that not a single escape was attempted in Buchenwald between December 1938 and May 1940; it would, in any case, have been "tantamount to certain death" (Poller 1960, 222).

The harshest reprisals after flights were ordered by Rudolf Höss, the commandant of Auschwitz. At first he ordered ten prisoners from the escapee's block to be locked up in a dark cell of the bunker and left without food and water until the fugitive had been captured or the prisoners had died. Later he had the family members of a fugitive, Poles, brought to the camp and displayed to everyone (Iwaszko 1964). Despite this there were repeated escape attempts. According to Witold Pilecki, in the early period, the murderous consequences for a fugitive's comrades caused the group of Polish officers to refuse to organize escapes and even to condemn all attempts of that kind. When the reprisals became less severe in early 1942, the Polish officers changed their attitude, and two of their members escaped in May of that year (Gárliński 1975, 66, 101 ff.)

With the growing confidence of prisoners and the increasing demoralization of the SS—both developments promoted by the course of the war—a further task came to the fore: attempts to corrupt the SS. Eugen Kogon, who gathered ample experience in this area in Buchenwald, writes that

"the basic tendency of the SS toward corruption was very shrewdly fostered and exploited by the political prisoners in the camp. . . . On occasion
it was possible to turn higher SS officers into tools of the prisoners' self-
assertion, not only through corruption but also through direct political
influence. These cases were extremely rare and fraught with great danger"
(Kogon 1946, 317 ff.). The resistance organizations were able to develop
this opportunity systematically in Buchenwald and Auschwitz in particular.

Wherever prisoners were employed in arms factories, the thought of
sabotage arose. Apart from its efforts to prevent escapes, the SS concentrated most intensively on forestalling opportunities to commit
sabotage. Despite all its brutality, this effort failed in many cases. To be
sure, the resistance organizations in Buchenwald and, under their influence, in Dora, concluded in consideration of the bloody terror, that
they should try to prevent individual acts of sabotage and direct sabotage
in arms factories, for individual actions usually had no great effect on
production but all too often led to executions. A well-thought-out sabotage plan, on the other hand, was harder to trace.[37] This shift was anything but easy. Emil Carlebach has written that it was "enormously
difficult" to make the Russians, who were especially inclined to commit
individual acts of sabotage, understand how the production could be
sabotaged more effectively and with less risk.[38] Otto Horn has pointed
out an additional difficulty that he observed among prisoners who were
skilled workers and had been imprisoned for many years. They felt a need
to exercise their skills again at long last, and it was "not always very easy
to find the exact line between the danger of being killed as a saboteur
lying down on the job on the one hand and keeping a worker's professional pride in check on the other.[39] The Pole Krzysztof Dunin-Wąsowicz,
a keen observer at Stutthof, does not deny that every act of sabotage had
no more effect than a tiny grain, but he points out that a prisoner's
psyche was visibly influenced by knowing that he was doing his part to
weaken the military power of German National Socialism (Dunin-
Wąsowicz 1972, 15). The moral component of all acts of resistance, attempted and accomplished, should not be underestimated, for it prevented the SS from completely destroying the prisoners' sense of self-
worth.

The tremendous increase in the use of prisoners in the arms industry
brought an additional problem: Should a resistance group keep its cadres
together in the main camp, where it could best care for and control everyone, or should it send reliable and experienced workers, with initiative, to
the ever more numerous and important satellite camps in order to make a
difference there? Robert Leibbrand addressed this dilemma when

he wrote: "The halfway tolerable conditions in the Buchenwald arms factories were an exception [to the normal conditions in concentration camps—ed.] that [we were obliged to retain only for] our active in-house organization.... In the outside details the situation was much more difficult. We tried to create a core of active anti-Fascists in all of those as well, and there were a number of relatively good outside details in which active sabotage was carried out. However, it was not possible to send a sufficiently strong and dependable cadre into each of the sixty outside details. Thus working conditions in most details of the outside arms factories were considerably more severe, with maltreatment and punishment as the order of the day. Conditions were worst where new arms factories were being built" (Leibbrand n.d., 43). The most important of these were Dora and other factories located in subterranean tunnels.

Heinrich Christian Meier has described the same problem as seen from Neuengamme in the fall of 1944: "Our political comrades cannot be saved from being transported [to the subsidiary camps, which rapidly increased in number there as well—H.L.], and so the only thing that can be done is to make them perform their functions and send them off with an assignment. Yes, the best men must sacrifice themselves; more is at stake than comfortable positions" (Meier 1949, 449).

As Karl Wagner has testified, the Dachau resistance organization had a different motivation when it had reliable political prisoners transferred to subsidiary camps. These men were to establish contacts with the population and help open its eyes to the situation and the prospects of the war. When a new small satellite camp was established in the Stubai Valley (Tyrol) in the fall of 1942, the organization saw to it that Wagner was sent there as a construction foreman and that this detail included "eight experienced, proven comrades who had fought with the international brigades in Spain and had experience with partisan fighting," for the intentions even went beyond this: "We wanted to try to make contact with the partisans in the Tyrolean mountains" (Wagner 1979, 11 ff.).

Since numerous small subsidiary camps were guarded by members of the SS (and sometimes of the Wehrmacht) who had no camp experience and hence had to leave the running of the camps, more or less, to the prisoner functionaries, such a person could make an important difference there. Józef Gárliński, who was transferred to the Neuengamme subsidiary camp Wittenberge in early 1944, emphasizes this succinctly: "There was a good senior camp inmate, and therefore the camp was good."[40] In late 1944 I myself observed in Lerbeck, another satellite camp, how a vicious senior camp inmate could poison the atmosphere in a small camp. Conditions in Lerbeck might otherwise have been relatively good, because the hopeless traffic situation repeatedly brought work to a halt in the factory to which we had been assigned (Langbein 1949, 200).

When the Allied armies were approaching the camps, the resistance-minded men faced the task of preparing for the liquidation of their camp. This could mean either an evacuation or mass destruction, but no one knew which. In Majdanek, the SS combined the two methods; most of the inmates, especially the Jews, were murdered, and the rest—Germans and some Poles—were forced to march to Auschwitz.

According to the "Preliminary Report About the Military Organization in the Buchenwald Concentration Camp," which was evidently written immediately after the liberation, preparations for the final phase began early in Buchenwald. This report begins with these words: "In the summer of 1942, the organization of the military cadres was started, initially only in the German section. In early 1943 Russian prisoners of war, Russian civilians, and Czechs were included, and in late 1943 the cadres of the French, Spanish, Italian, and Belgian sections were added. In the middle of the following year the cadres of the Yugoslavs and Poles were organized."[41] This order not only reveals when major contingents of the various nationalities (for example, Frenchmen and Italians) had arrived in the camp, but it also documents the pace at which the contact between the leading German group and national groups that had arrived earlier (for instance, the Poles) developed. The specialized literature gives different dates,[42] for evidently it is possible to interpret the concept "beginning of the organization of military cadres" in different ways.

In Majdanek, plans were made to achieve the liberation of the camp, in concert with partisan groups, at the end of 1944, and the military organization set December 31, 1943, as the date. Setting fire to the barracks was to be the signal, but the action had to be canceled. Jerzy Kwiatkowski believes that the reasons were fear of reprisals against the people of Lublin and disagreements in the outside organizations about what should be done with the liberated inmates. According to Kwiatkowski, no single organization was strong enough for such an action (Kwiatkowski 1966, 296 ff.). Edward Gryń and Zofia Murawska write: "In cooperation with the resistance movement in the camp, a plan for self-liberation was drawn up with the help of the partisans fighting in the Lublin area. This plan could not be implemented, for as the eastern front came closer, Lublin became an increasingly great German military center. Because there was no direct connection with the forests, the camp administration could not be taken by surprise and the inmates could not be evacuated" (Gryń/Murawska n.d., 64). Nevertheless, an attempt was made, and on January 1, 1944, a barracks was set on fire. In Mauthausen, the initiative for developing a militarily oriented organization was taken by the Spaniards, who were most qualified for this by virtue of their battle experience. They started in 1943 and extended their efforts to other national groups.[43] In Auschwitz, Witold Pilecki toyed with the idea of a military uprising as early as 1941, but at that time these plans turned out to be unrealistic (Gárliński 1973, 34 ff.). In the spring and summer of 1944, Combat Group Auschwitz regarded the situation as ripe for military planning. The Russians, who maintained contact with this group, urged this course of action, and the news about the end of Majdanek spurred them on.[44]

In the very last phase, the resistance organizations made efforts to be prepared for the end, and they did so with varying forces and under various conditions. Where the SS dealt severe blows to the organization in the final phase—for example, in Sachsenhausen, Dora, and Auschwitz—the opportunities were limited. Besides, in the camps that were evacuated before the complete collapse of the Third Reich, the situation was different from that in those camps where the SS was no longer able to effect a complete evacuation.

The Actors

8

THE GERMANS IN THE
RESISTANCE

As already mentioned, the National Socialist "racial" thinking created far more favorable conditions for German prisoners than for their non-German fellow sufferers, and they were able to utilize this to resist the SS terror and attempts to corrupt the inmates. This special situation, also, brought German prisoners a favorable position for resistance activity.

Foreigners frequently viewed all Germans, even opponents of National Socialism, as mere members of the nation that was bringing so much misfortune upon their country and themselves. The Germans' privileged position in the camps could be misleading and was probably intended to be. The relatively peaceful life of these German armband wearers "created bad blood," as Harry Naujoks, the respected senior camp inmate of Sachsenhausen, freely admits.[1] Since Germans had more chances than others to establish contact with the camp management, they were tempted to make their fellow inmates quite aware of their nationality. The Pole Wincenty Hein observed this in prominent Germans, and not just among the criminals.[2] Krokowski, who gathered his experiences in Dora, as Hein did, states flatly that all Germans regarded themselves as members of a master race. The dubious nature of any such generalization is indicated by his opinion of two senior camp inmates, Jupp Gamisch and Christl Beham, whose performance of this difficult job he came to appreciate.[3] A number of descriptions of conditions in Dora emphasize that all Germans there were functionaries, but the mortality rate tells a different story. Almost 13 percent of those who died in the first (and worst) six months of the camp were Germans. Unfortunately the percentage of Germans in this camp is known only for a later period; on November 1, 1944, it was 8.6 percent (Bornemann/Broszat 1970, 168, 181). In the same period the number of deaths was smaller than the number of those who were shipped off to extermination camps as unfit to work, and as a rule the SS did not include Germans in such transports. Nonetheless, the large number of German deaths permits one to conclude that not all Germans could have been in privileged positions. The survivors probably remembered the visible functionaries while others remained unobserved. During that period, hardly more than forty politically aware Germans are said to have been in Dora, but hundreds of criminals were (Kiessling 1964, 210). In any case, this too argues against making sweeping statements and confirms that non-Germans frequently had an emotional aversion to Germans.

Alfred Hübsch states that the Dutchmen had a great hatred for all Germans,[4] and Krokowski observed that Poles, Russians, and Frenchmen were against all Germans and wanted to take revenge on them.[5] Helene Potetz remembers that Ukrainian women viewed every German woman as an enemy.[6] The Communist Rudi Goguel gained the impression that "a profound distrust of everything German . . . has taken root among our foreign comrades as well" (Goguel 1947, 174). Since Potetz speaks about Ravensbrück, Krokowski about Dora, Hübsch about Dachau, and Goguel about Neuengamme, and similar statements have been made about other camps as well, this emotional attitude may be regarded as having general validity.

Hans Sündermann, an Austrian, emphasizes the importance of the Germans in the Buchenwald resistance movement and points to a factor that might have contributed to the unpopularity of the Germans: "To be sure, the role of our German friends was often misunderstood. Their treatment of other prisoners was often so rude that they came in for harsh criticism. Despite this, however, I must say today [in 1958] that the accomplishments of the German comrades were enormous."[7] This rudeness may have been the consequence of years of imprisonment that many Germans had behind them when foreigners arrived in the camp—years of far more direct terror in camps that were much smaller in those days.

Erich Rossmann, a former officer of the SPD (*Sozialistische Partei Deutschlands*, German Socialist Party), points to an additional difference between Germans and members of other nations: "This system certainly created an enormous spiritual conflict for the Germans, whose ardent patriotism no one was permitted to doubt. They now had to prefer the defeat of their fatherland, as represented by the National Socialists, to the continuation of the prevailing tyranny" (Rossmann 1947, 144). Rossmann's fellow German, Hans Christian Meier, has given a similar account. Of course a German prisoner wished for the defeat of Hitler's system, but was he to feel the same joy as a foreigner? In Meier's account, which takes the form of a novel, a German Communist said to a friend when news about the landing of the Allies in Italy had reached the camp: "If you were a German, you wouldn't jump for joy either because a German army is being destroyed in Italy. Cousins or friends of mine might be among the fallen soldiers" (Meier 1949, 269). On the basis of his experiences in Dachau the Frenchman Edmond Michelet reports that among his German fellow prisoners there apparently existed, despite everything, "a certain solidarity—resigned but indisputable—with their fellow Germans, who were responsible for the situation." He claims to have discerned an "instinctive patriotism" among some Germans, especially when the Ardennes offensive met with initial success at Christmastime 1944—and he emphasizes that this was very different from the reaction of the Austrians (Michelet 1955, 170).

The Luxembourger Eugene Ost, who was also imprisoned in Dachau, speaks of an embarrassing situation that was created by bombardments: The non-Germans rejoiced, while the Germans feared for their families.[8] This is contradicted by the Bavarian Gustl Gattinger, who was interned in Dachau for years and had a chance to observe the nocturnal bombardments of nearby Munich: "I was happy about every bombing even though I had relatives living there."[9] The Swabian Hans Gasparitsch also resolutely rejects remarks like those of Michelet,[10] and the Austrian Franz Freihaut believes that Michelet's observation may have been true only of those who were bound to have a bad conscience because of their conduct in the camp and thus feared the end.[11] Jacobus Overduin, a Dutchman, has attempted to make an objective judgment: "Those who did not have a good word to say about the Germans could not understand that even an anti-Nazi German did not greet news of Allied victories with the same unalloyed enthusiasm as we did" (Overduin 1947, 315). The historian of the camps, Eugen Kogon, confirms that despite many contrary instances Germans were not popular, yet "most of what has appeared about them in accounts of the concentration camps written by non-Germans is full of one-sided statements, simplifications, and misjudgments" (Kogon 1949, 378ff.)[12] One such simplification is probably the statement of the Luxembourger Leo Bartimes that no German in a concentration camp was free from blame.[13] Such a blanket judgment is inappropriate even if "German" is replaced by "bigwig," certainly not always the same thing.

The Austrian Otto Horn has given a graphic description of the way the German resisters handled the danger posed by the camp administration's preferential treatment of the Germans. As early as 1939, the underground strove for contacts with foreign inmates and tried to get them placed in better details, which was not a simple matter in those days. "At the same time, they began a campaign against the beating methods of the SS, which were, shamefully enough, adopted by some German capos and foremen. The underground German leadership issued this slogan: Every blow against a foreigner is a blow against the German people." "Some day this score will have to be settled," wrote Horn immediately after the liberation, and added: "It must be remembered that this struggle began at a time when German armies were still at the Volga, the English Channel, in Norway, and in Tobruk."[14]

The German Communist Walter Sonntag was the senior inmate of a Buchenwald block in which recently arrested Frenchmen were placed. Realizing "that they regarded as enemies not only the SS but us as well," he immediately told them that he had the same enemy as they and that they should therefore regard them as a friend (*Buchenwald* 1960, 331).[15] It was not only in Buchenwald that German political prisoners tried to gain the confidence of their foreign companions. Foreigners have praised the conduct of Germans in many camps who did not need to be urged not to abuse their privileges. The Pole Mieczysław Mołdawa has named Germans who helped Poles in Gross–Rosen; one of these joined Polish prisoners in listening to Allied broadcasts on an SS radio (Mołdawa 1967, 142, 166). Drahmoír Barta, a Czech active in the resistance organization at Ebensee, confirms that Konrad Wegner, a German political prisoner, also aided this organization in listening to Allied radio stations. "Beginning in April 1945, we joined Konrad Wegner every evening to listen to foreign radio broadcasts." As head of the camp post office, Wegner had his own quarters in the camp storeroom.[16]

Otto Küsel, the German head of the prisoner Work Assignments at Auschwitz, escaped together with Polish members of his detail. This was accomplished on December 29, 1942, when an Allied victory was still years away, and as a V.I.P. Küsel had had all the privileges granted to the first thirty Germans in the transport from Sachsenhausen. When he was asked many years later why he had made such a risky decision, he replied: "The Poles in my detail wanted to escape. Mietek was an officer and could expect to be shot sooner or later. . . . The only choice I had was to denounce them or flee with them. If they had escaped without me, no one would have believed me if I had said that I had not been aware of their preparations for this escape. And then I would have been next. But I did not want to denounce them" (Langbein 1972, 181).

The German capo Georg Arold escaped from a subsidiary camp of Majdanek, also with a group of Poles.[17]Both men joined their Polish friends in their struggle against the Nazis—Arold as a member of a group of partisans, Küsel in the Warsaw underground. In Natzweiler the German capo Hans Gasch helped with the preparations for a sensational escape that five prisoners effected on August 4, 1942 (Eschenbrenner n.d., 35).

Since a large number of Reds were interned in Ravensbrück, the help given by politically aware Germans to their companions in misfortune was able to take more organized forms. Maria Kurcyuszowa confirms that, thanks to German prisoner functionaries, the first Polish women in Ravensbrück occupied positions in the camp administration and thus had a chance to help their compatriots. At first the Polish women were strictly isolated and subjected to particularly harsh treatment.[18] A few months after the liberation of Neuengamme, the Pole Ewald Gondzik wrote: "Luckily for many thousands of foreigners there were among the German prisoners (in addition to Greens and Reds, who had maltreated their fellow inmates) politically sound elements who joined battle with the hangmen and henchmen." In his German-language account he goes on to say: "The foreigners distrusted the Germans, and this need not be explained further. On the other hand, the Germans who were favorably disposed toward them were not identifiable as such. . . . It was necessary to watch out for German informers, but among the foreigners too there were plenty of Fascist elements who performed this kind of service to secure personal benefits in the camp."[19]

Many instances of this kind could be cited, yet what Hans Maršálek has written applies not only to Mauthausen: Many a German, and not just criminals, "expressed Slavophobia and anti-Semitism in word and deed as well as displaying national arrogance." This led many non-German prisoners to dislike Germans, and according to Maršálek, "this feeling was summed up as 'Once a German, always a German' " (Maršálek 1974, 254). The Luxembourger Pierre Grégoire illustrates such feelings when he describes the activity of the German underground organization in Sachsenhausen: "I don't know where the men of understanding are, I don't know them and can't find them anywhere, but I do sense that work is going on in accordance with their principles and that they don't view their neighbor as an adversary in the daily struggle for life but as a human being and a brother sharing the same misfortune." Elsewhere, however, Grégoire generalizes about "the impertinent arrogance of the leadership of German prisoners" and of the German psyche, whose color he describes as "the most depraved grey of hatefulness and bloodthirstiness" (Stein 1946, 157, 178). When the German Communist Rudi Goguel arrived in Sachsenhausen in September 1944, he encountered, in addition to brutal German criminals, political prisoners serving as senior block inmates and capos (one of whom liked to describe himself as an "old Bolshevik") who beat fellow prisoners of other nationalities with whips and clubs. When Goguel protested against this, these prisoner functionaries deprived him of the privileges that Germans enjoyed at that time. Their motto was "We Germans have to stick together in the camp" (Goguel 1947, 151 ff.). In 1944, the Frenchman Jacques Lusseyran met a German in Buchenwald "who was responsible for our quarantine barracks. . . . There was a rumor that he had once been a hero. Now he was killing two or three of us with his own hands every day. . . . To him that was a pleasure he could no longer do without." Lusseyran has attempted to explain how men could sink so low in a concentration camp: "The harm that had been done to them had been so damaging that it had entered their bodies and their souls. Now it had taken possession of them. They were no longer victims but were doing harm themselves" (Lusseyran 1963, 195).

Unlike what happened in Sachsenhausen or Buchenwald, the SS in Dachau broke the solid phalanx of the German political prisoners shortly before the end of that camp by transferring them to other camps. The camp management placed vicious elements among the Germans in the vacant top positions. Thus anti-German sentiments erupted most clearly when liberation seemed near. Heinrich Eduard vom Holt reports how he tried to hide from an evacuation transport on April 26, 1945. He managed to escape to the prison hospital. "A Czech clerk yelled at me, 'Beat it, you German!' " A Dutchman wanted to help him—but " 'Get out of here, you German, and join the murderers and thieves!' " Vom Holt describes the general reaction this way: "A wave of hatred enveloped me." Finally he was able to evade the murderous evacuation transport. When the camp was liberated three days later, a Pole warned him: " 'Speak Polish, English, or French, but don't speak German anymore' " (Holt 1942, 266, 274). Karl Ludwig Schecher reports that in those days the representatives of other nations visibly distanced themselves from the Germans. All national groups staged celebrations after the liberation. Schecher recalls that the celebration of the Germans "was in view of the entire situation a painful, pitiful affair." At that time sixty Germans were arrested. Some of these may have been denounced because of personal resentment or trivial actions, but others really had blood on their hands, and these included people who had worn a red triangle in the camp.[20] In his description of the days following the liberation of Dachau, the German K. A. Gross passes a harsh judgment on his fellow countrymen: "We must, *entre nous*, be glad that they [the foreigners—H.L.] did not bash our heads in, for haven't the various kinds of pashas, moguls, pharaohs, capos, and barracks orderlies done everything to create the misconception that there is no difference between a German who was an SS leader and a German who was a prisoner?" In describing the celebrations on May 1, he goes on to say this about his fellow countrymen: "Too bad that some aren't able to muster a joyful victory mood. . . . We're no longer playing first fiddle in the camp, but what of it? I have reason to fear that the depression of some mopes is due to the fact that they will henceforth be barred from playing this pleasant instrument. Thus every national group carried its banner forward; even the Austrians have a flag of their own, but only the small group of surviving Germans remained without a symbol to rally around. A harsh, harsh fate, but it is not undeserved" (Gross, n.d., 219). In a few camps, the SS was able to risk using armed German prisoners as auxiliary guards on evacuation marches.[21]

Writing about the last days of Dachau, Walter Leitner states that what German anti-Fascists had accomplished at the risk of their lives "opened the hearts of their foreign comrades and gained them their confidence."[22] A few months after the liberation, the Belgian Arthur Haulot confirmed that the foreigners who survived the camps owed this "in large measure to those righteous German comrades" without whom "many more of us would not have lived to be free." Haulot knows whereof he speaks, for he played a decisive role in the international resistance organization of Dachau in its final phase.[23] The truth of these words cannot be doubted any more than the truth of the preceding statements. In the final years, and particularly in the chaotic final days, each camp constituted a confusing complex, and thus each informant was able to report only from his own vantage point.

The anti-German atmosphere that has been described in some accounts should not make us forget what Dutchmen of different political persuasions have reported about the anti-Fascist collaboration immediately after the liberation of Buchenwald: "It would not have been possible without the pioneering work, which cannot be praised enough, and the dynamic fortitude of the German anti-Fascist comrades, which proved its worth to the very last moment."[24] It was this fortitude that was at work in other camps as well.

9

THE ROLE OF THE COMMUNISTS

Walter Bartel estimates that 30 to 35 percent of the 2,000 German political prisoners interned at Buchenwald in 1944 were members of the KPD (German Communist Party)—a high percentage if one considers that numerous more or less apolitical prisoners wore a red triangle in the concentration camps, as did Nazis who had committed some crime (*Buchenwald* 1960, 374). For the above-mentioned reasons, Communists as well as Austrian political prisoners were in a far less favorable position for engaging in any underground activity than others. In addition to Socialists, numerous functionaries of the Schuschnigg regime were taken to concentration camps, since this regime had at various times taken action against National Socialists. However, the activity of the Austrian Communists was more noticeable than would have been in keeping with their percentage among the Austrian political prisoners, a percentage smaller than that of the Germans. They too displayed the special aptitude for conspiracy of men trained in a Communist Party, an activity in which discussions had to be kept to a minimum and absolute discipline was often demanded.

Apart from the Spaniards concentrated in Mauthausen and from the Russians, the percentage of Communists among members of other nations was substantially smaller, though it varied. Among Czechs and French, it was higher than among Poles. Among those imprisoned for "racial" reasons, Jews who had belonged to a Communist Party were in a slightly better position than fellow Jews. Their ideology and education guarded them against the profound demoralization faced by those who always had a worst-case scenario in view. In addition, they found it much easier than politically indifferent Jews to establish friendly contact with like-minded "Aryan" comrades and enjoy their protection.

As a rule, foreign Communists quickly established contact with Germans who shared their ideology. Many knew one another from international meetings. Thus the Czech Communist functionary Artur London, on his arrival in Mauthausen, met the Austrian Leo Gabler, whom he had gotten to know at a conference of the International Association of Young Communists in Moscow (Razola/Constante, 1969, 118).[1] When Franz Freihaut came to Dachau with one of the first Austrian transports in the spring of 1938, he was immediately recognized by a German comrade with whom he had taken a course in Moscow and pulled out of the group of new arrivals, who were always subject to the worst treatment.[2] On November 20, 1939, Antonin Zápotocký, a well-known Czech Communist functionary, arrived at the Sachsenhausen concentration camp, and just a few hours after his arrival, he had contact with his German comrades (Kiessling 1960, 211). Other German Communists met comrades with whom they had had contact during their emigration. The shared ideology bound together even those who were not personally acquainted with one another. Since Communists played a major role in the underground organizations of almost all camps and German or Austrian members of the party led those organizations, it seems appropriate to follow our analysis of the role of the Germans with an investigation of the special problems faced by these groups.

In many instances resistance organizations, particularly in the three old camps, have been equated with an underground Communist Party organization, and not merely by outside observers.

The German Communist Harry Kuhn has described the formation of a party organization in Buchenwald: "On the very day of my arrival I established contact with the party in the camp. It was accomplished through comrade Albert Kuntz, who knew me well from our years of work in the party and its youth organization. . . . In the nature of things, the process of forming the party was still in its early stages. . . . The arrival of the roundup prisoners in September 1939 [at the beginning of the war, a large number of politically unreliable people were sent to the camps—H.L.] changed the situation radically. Around 700 Communists arrived within a few days. . . . This marked the beginning of a tightly organized branch of the German Communist Party" (Kuhn/Weber n.d., 53).

The equation of resistance organizations with the KPD was made most unequivocally in the German publications about Buchenwald. Thus Walter Bartel, a leader of the German Communists in that camp, writes: "The initiators and organizers of the solidarity actions, the political information, and the creation of national committees were German Communists. . . . With their solid, disciplined core and their years of experience with the underground struggle in the camp, the German Communists helped their international friends with words and deeds to organize their underground national committees. Upon their initiative, an underground international camp committee was formed in the summer of 1943 under cover of the infirmary" (*Buchenwald* 1960, 395 ff.). Elsewhere Bartel characterizes the international camp committee as a fighting organization which "initiated and led by German Communists and in close cooperation with underground Communist groups of other countries . . . aimed [to be active] in accordance with the decisions and concrete instructions of the party" (Bartel 1976, 309).

Janez Ranzinger, who until July 1944 represented the Yugoslav group in the international committee, confirms that this was clearly a Communist group.[3] However, a report about the "Polish secret organization in the Buchenwald concentration camp" that was written soon after the liberation states that a group of Polish Communists formed around Henryk Mikolajczak, who as a nurse in the hospital was in a favorable position for illegal activities; it was in contact with the German group, he wrote, but "it was too small to elicit a major response from the Poles as a whole" and thus encountered difficulties. Later "the committee began to function" (evidently by adding others), but a Polish Communist organization continued to be active alongside it.[4] Problems of this kind evidently prompted an anonymous contributor to the *Buchenwald* collection to state that underground national organizations of non-Germans were created "with and without the support of the German Communists" (*Buchenwald* 1960, 323).

Bartel has described how the German Communists dominated Buchenwald to the end. Six days before the liberation, the camp administration issued an order requiring the forty-six prisoners named in it—all of them men who played an important part in the life of the camp—to report (evidently to isolate them, or perhaps even to liquidate them), and this order was immediately delivered to the "leadership of the German Communist Party." These leaders decided that the forty-six men were to hide and then transmitted the order to the international camp committee together with its decision (Kuhn 1975, 303). The anonymous "Preliminary Report about the Military Organization in the Buchenwald Concentration Camp," which was evidently written immediately after the liberation, concludes with this sentence: "At 5 P.M. on April 13, 1945 [two days after the liberation—H.L.], the military leadership ordered the demobilization of the military organizations of the Communist sections in the concentration camp Buchenwald."[5]

In the pertinent works published in East Germany, the Buchenwald resistance organization is virtually equated with the activity of the Communist Party. The chronology of the above-mentioned collection about Buchenwald has this entry under July 1942: "The underground leadership of the KPD is starting to organize military groups" (*Buchenwald* 1960, 585). Harry Kuhn, a member of the executive committee, calls the international camp committee that was formed in the summer of 1943 a committee of Communist parties which, according to him, eventually included representatives of eleven organizations of the Communist Party. "The leadership of the international military organization was comprised entirely of German comrades," he writes. It became "the recognized international military leadership, which meant that its instructions had the force of orders." Kuhn reiterates that "all the military work in the camp was under the direction of the KPD and the international leadership of the Communist parties" (Kuhn/Weber n.d., 54). Two East German officers go so far as to write that "the conception of the Communists . . . was not the result of subjective ideas and wishes. . . . It was based on the decisions and directives of the central committee of the individual Communist parties and of the executive committee of the Communist international" (Kuhn/Weber n.d., 437).

This equation of the resistance movement with the Communist Party cannot merely be traced to the need of East German Communist functionaries to give their party revisionist credit for all the accomplishments of the resistance. Here I shall quote only two competent witnesses who are not members of any Communist Party. The Frenchman David Rousset speaks of an "absolute control by the German Communists" of the secret organization,[6] and the German Max Mayr says that it is to the "undisputed credit of the Communists that they created an underground camp organization and military organization." The fact that both men have criticized various activities of the Communists gives these appreciative statements added significance.[7]

The general resistance and the activity of Communist groups are most clearly exemplified by the case of Buchenwald, but we have similar reports about Sachsenhausen as well. In another collection published in East Germany, it is emphasized that in addition to the camp committee there was a leadership of the Communist Party. The committee is described as follows: "The international camp committee constituted a body that was supported by the party leadership from all countries and had unconditional authority" (Damals in Sachsenhausen 1967, 92, 97). Wolfgang Kiessling bases himself on this version when he writes that, in the last years of the war, the leadership of the international resistance was "primarily in the hands of proven Communists." In this connection he names three German Communist functionaries and adds "and others" (Kiessling 1960, 218). Harry Naujoks states that the leaders of the national groups all belonged to one party, meaning the Communist.[8] To be sure, it must be considered that Naujoks was in Sachsenhausen only until fall 1942. The sectarian nature of such a view is manifested most blatantly in an article by the Czech Communist Bohdan Rossa, who states that the German Communists tried "to counteract the destructive work of the Fascists in concert with the Communist and other prisoners of other nations" (Rossa 1959, 56 ff.).

There are similar reports about the composition of the resistance movement in Mauthausen as well. The Spaniard Mariano Constante writes that
the military organization created there in the fall of 1943 initially consisted of a handful of Communists (evidently Spaniards): "The majority had
been officers of our army in Spain" (Constante 1971, 210). Valentín
Sakharov reprints an address of the Russian major Kondrakov before the
secret Russian committee in spring 1944 in which the following task is
set: "We must create a military fighting organization composed of Communists from all nations" (Sakharov 1961, 10 ff.). However, in Mauthausen
the organization seems to have attached the greatest importance to the
collaboration of everyone from the very beginning. Constante emphasizes
this goal, at least for the Spanish Communists, and he mentions in particular Socialists and anarchists (Constante 1971, 203, 210).

Thanks to continuous contacts, the leading role of the Communists in
Buchenwald was transferred to Dora as well. This is confirmed by the Pole
Wincenty Hein,[9] and Wanda Kiedrzyńska, also a Pole, describes the role of
the Communist Party in Ravensbrück as follows: "Communist women of
all nationalities had close contact with one another. Through them it was
possible to reach the prisoner functionaries on all levels, most of them
German Communists. . . ." (Kiedrzyńska 1960, 96).

In the extermination camps in the East, the small number of Communists interned there, as well as the nature of these camps and the height-
ened brutality of the political department, prevented Communists from
occupying the same kind of exclusive privileged position that they enjoyed
in Buchenwald. In the face of the constant threat posed by the gas chambers, political differences lost their significance. Exceptions arose only
where in the course of the transfer of all Jews to Auschwitz, in October
1942, closed groups of Communists came to an Auschwitz subsidiary
camp, where they could stay together again. Thus a group of German and
Austrian Communist Jews, who had been through the "Buchenwald
school," established a resistance organization in Monowitz, which also
regarded itself as a party organization. This group offered the nineteen-
year-old Fritz Kleinmann, who had been transferred together with it,
membership in the party because he had not informed on anyone under
torture.[10]

Similar tendencies were displayed by a Communist-led organization in
the subsidiary camp Jawisczowicz.[11] In the base camp, the few Communists active in the resistance, some of whom had experience with similar
activity in Dachau, did not regard themselves as a party organization. This
made it possible for the Combat Group Auschwitz to gain an international
character that transcended political boundaries.

In Sachsenhausen, and perhaps even more in Dachau, the Communists active in the resistance did not emphasize their leading role as much as they did in Buchenwald. The German Communist Walter Vielhauer, who experienced both Dachau and Buchenwald, has indicated a reason for this difference: Buchenwald housed a much greater number of German Communists, who had filled important offices in their party, whereas there were hardly any leading German members of the Communist Party in Dachau. Vielhauer writes: "Among the Austrian Communists, there were some prominent ones, and they gave us support. However, because they always stressed the fact that they were Austrians, they were not able to reveal themselves as Communists to the extent that we did."[12] Together with Austrian Communists, the Nazis had packed Social Democrats and members of the Dollfuss–Schuschnigg Fatherland Front off to Dachau. The Austrians' explicit accentuation of their nationality that Vielhauer observed produced a solidarity similar to the one that bound French or Polish Communists to their fellow countrymen.

The discipline to which every member of a Communist Party was accustomed was very useful in the concentration camps. It was frequently difficult to induce a responsible person who was qualified for a position to accept it, for an armband involved not only privileges and opportunities for action but also risks and moral dilemmas. It was easier to induce Communists to disregard their scruples than others. For example, when the position of senior camp inmate had to be filled in Sachsenhausen in the spring of 1939, because the incumbent, the KPD functionary Oskar Müller, had been released, the party leadership decided to utilize its chance to fill this key position and to recommend the appointment of Harry Naujoks to the camp administration. "I had to go along with this, though reluctantly," writes Naujoks.[13] There was a similar reaction from Albert Buchmann when the same party organization asked him to take a leading position in the Labor Service: "That's the decision. Agreed" (Ahrens 1968, 93). In addition to issuing instructions, a Communist organization gave moral support to those whom it had helped to obtain positions. Naujoks emphasizes that its constant control provided an effective aid against the temptations attendant upon the virtually unlimited power of every wearer of an armband.[14]

However, it would be erroneous to assume that the strict discipline of the Communists eliminated all the problems that arose under the conditions of a Nazi concentration camp. The national conflicts that the SS fomented as a matter of course affected the Communists as well. Such conflicts erupted even between Austrian and German members of this party, though the SS put the members of these two nations on an equal footing instead of playing one against the other. As already mentioned, these conflicts prompted Austrian Communists, even under the special conditions of Auschwitz, to write the only theoretical work that was produced in a concentration camp and has been preserved—Alfred Klahr's study of the national problems of the Germans. With reference to Ravensbrück, Toni Lehr makes this guarded statement: "There was no cordial contact between German and Austrian Communist women." This is also reflected in subsequent descriptions of the underground struggle in that camp. Thus Toni Lehr believes that the role of the German Communists there has been "exaggerated and euphemized." Lehr and others have identified the Austrian Communist Mela Ernst as the moving force in the international resistance organization, but it took pressure from the Austrian survivors of Ravensbrück to get her mentioned in the second edition of a book about this camp that was published in East Germany.[15] In late 1944, the German Isa Vermehren, who did not come from the workers' movement, gained the impression that the majority of the women Reds identified as Germans and wearing red triangles were "of Austrian nationality or Austrian Communists." She goes on to say that she "did not encounter any German political intellectuals" and that she found the most intelligent Germans among those who had been sent to the camp on account of *"Rassenschande"* (sexual relations between an "Aryan" and a "non-Aryan") (Vermehren 1947, 95). Margarete Buber-Neumann has this to say about the relationship between the German members of the KPD and their foreign comrades: "The position of the German Communists in Ravensbrück was a peculiar one. The great majority of the unpolitical prisoners of all nationalities equated everything German in the camp with the SS. They hated the SS and the German inmates equally. The majority of Communist women from various nations also rejected their German 'comrades' . . ." (Buber-Neumann 1958, 366). Elsewhere Buber-Neumann uses the German Communist Wiedmeier to explain this rejection. That woman did such good work as the supervisor in the dressmaker's workshop that the SS man in charge said the whole outfit would not function without her. "When we took her to task for this, she gave an astonishing answer: 'What do you want from me? I simply have a sense of duty and have to work. . . .'" Like any sweeping judgment, Buber-Neumann's conclusion that "Communist prisoners are especially suitable for slave labor" must be accepted critically, but her observations cannot be dismissed out of hand (Buber-Neumann 1963, 238 ff.).

Buber-Neumann also gives a reason for the rejection she observed of the German Communists by the foreign women Communists. Because the KPD had not succeeded in preventing Hitler's assumption of power, this party could not have equal rights. The majority of Communists from various nations "enthusiastically adopted the slogan about the guilt of the entire German people, and the German Communists did not dare defend themselves." The Marxist-trained author adds that "no one pointed out that suddenly Marxists were speaking about peoples rather than about classes" (Buber-Neumann 1958, 366).

In an American report written about the situation in liberated Buchenwald and published in October 1946, we read that the underground organization in that camp "was composed of German Communists." This clearly anti-Communist account describes the role of Communists of other nationalities as follows: In Buchenwald there were thousands of non-German Communists, particularly Frenchmen, Dutchmen, and Spaniards. To a certain degree these were absorbed by the German organization and received their orders from Germans. An extensive underground system of councils and meetings had been established in order to make these Communists a solid component of the organization. However, many of them did not love their German overlords. Numerous Russians and foreign Communists spoke of giving the German Communists a beating on the day of liberation" (Robinson 1946).[16] That this statement probably is not a pure invention is documented by Jean Michel, according to whom Friedrich Pröll, who worked as a hospital capo in Dora, told Frenchmen that the German Communists were counting on them and distrusted the Russians, who had only revenge on their minds (Michel 1975, 224).

On the basis of his own ample experience, Hans Maršàlek has attempted an analysis of the conflicts that were apparent in Mauthausen as well: "Among some Austrian, German, French, and Czech Communist inmates of the main camp, there were in 1943 and 1944 disagreements about the forms of organization and the extent of the resistance. Some expressed the opinion that a tight international organization would run counter to the rules of conspiracy, that the SS was bound to uncover it, and that there would be brutal reprisals. Others wanted to create illegal resistance groups only on an international basis. There were also different opinions about the leadership of the resistance in Mauthausen, and some Communists did not want to take 'decisive action' until after the fight. These disputes concerned national differences, the so-called protection of cadres, and the lack of personal courage" (Maršàlek 1974, 258). The Frenchman Michel de Bouard states specifically that German Communists—including Franz Dahlem, who had great authority—opposed the development of an international organization as planned by French and Spanish comrades. To be sure, not all German Communists shared this view; some Czech Communists did, but not a majority of them.[17] More than twenty years later, Dahlem himself discussed these problems with restraint: "There were comrades who wanted to know who the leaders were, who regarded their lack of knowledge as indicative of a lack of confidence in them, and who spoke of 'democracy within the party.' " Finally, however, it was possible to convince even these comrades "of the necessity of a stringent conspiracy" (*Document Notes* 1979, 110).

Differences between national groups of Communists arose not only in Mauthausen. An unsigned report that appears to have been written in Dutch immediately after the liberation of Buchenwald and betrays knowledge of internal affairs in the Communist organization of this camp describes disagreements that repeatedly became apparent between the Russian group of Communists—"for the most part young fellows without experience with conditions in western Europe"—and groups from other Communist parties. Such disputes were resolved in the international camp committee, and in this connection the role of the Austrian Wegerer is given pride of place. The report also states that the Communist Party was the only one that continued its organization in the camp, and "with tremendous energy."[18] Another Dutch report, one signed by representatives of four political parties, describes it as a task of the Dutch group in Buchenwald to oppose the "chauvinistic elements among the prisoners who . . . tried to minimize the accomplishments of the German Communists." This report goes on to say that "one of our most difficult tasks was to change the understandable anti-German attitude of a large number of Dutchmen into an anti-Fascist stance."[19] N. Wijnen recalls the great efforts he had to make to overcome his fellow Dutchmen's antipathy to German Communists. He also mentions personal differences among Dutchmen, who constituted the leadership of that nation's Communist group in Buchenwald. These disagreements stemmed from the fact that initially various Dutch Communists had established contact with German comrades who held different views and thus transmitted these to the Dutch Communist group.[20]

There were disagreements among the tightly organized German Communists as well. These were most apparent in Sachsenhausen, where, according to Heinz Junge, the party was disorganized for a time after the release of leading functionaries in April 1939.[21] Fritz Selbmann, who arrived in Sachsenhausen around that time, writes that there was no organization for a whole year. In August 1939, Hitler and Stalin signed a nonaggression pact. "That was like a blow on the head. The Nazis are grinning, the Greens are laughing at us, and the political prisoners have lost confidence in us"—this is how Selbmann has a German Communist describe the situation to a new arrival (that is, himself). The Communists were divided. "Arguing is no longer the word for it. Many of them have really become enemies" (Selbmann 1961, 72, 88). Selbmann played a leading part in one of the wrangling groups of German Communists, and therefore others have rejected the account of the conflict given in his book *Die lange Nacht*, The Long Night as too subjective.[22] Nevertheless, Heinz

Schmidt confirms that there were heated discussions among German Communists, who had split into three antagonistic groups, and that the situation became confused after the reverses of the Red Army.[23]

Other reports about these differences are not free of a subjective coloration either, for their authors, like Selbmann, belonged to one of the three groups that fought one another from time to time. According to Heinz Junge, the differences of opinion were due to the rejection, by those who had been imprisoned since 1933, of the political line declared official by the Communist International after its seventh world congress. (At that congress, held in the summer of 1935, Georgi Dimitroff had proposed and got adopted the tactic of a popular front against Fascism.) By contrast, the Communists who were still at liberty in 1935 had adopted this new line. Junge himself, who experienced this period in exile, had memorized basic articles of the KPD, and, basing himself on these dogmas, he strove to consolidate conditions among the German Communists.[24]

Hans Pointner, an Austrian Communist who, like Junge, had been able to participate in these discussions as a free man, has given the most detailed account of this factional dispute. This was in a report about the internal situation of the Communists in Sachsenhausen which he wrote immediately after the liberation in July 1945. In the camp, he too belonged to one of the three groups, and he writes that their conflicts came to a dangerous head in late 1940. "Until spring 1941, the discussions in the first and second groups [Pointner himself belonged to the third group—H.L.] were concerned less with political opinions than with the struggle for positions and functions in the camp." According to Pointner, political discussions were carried on in the spring of 1941 about the significance of the Hitler–Stalin pact and the problems raised at the seventh world congress of the Communist International. Among the participants were the Czech Jaromir Dolanský and the German Max Reimann, who had attended that congress in Moscow before their arrest. Pointner writes that, as late as spring 1941, a group including Heinz Junge was of the opinion that nothing should be done to weaken Hitler in his struggle against the western powers, which were considered the main danger to the Soviet Union. Another group condemned the popular-front policy decided upon at the seventh world congress as "rightist opportunism" and expressed the opinion that since Hitler's assumption of power there had been "no substantial change" in the German working class. Pointner names Ernst Schneller and Max Opitz as the spokesmen of this group. According to Pointner, the discussions had the following result: "In the course of ideological clarification we were able to expand our influence considerably. . . . The struggle for political unity which we carried on with all the resources at our disposal placed us in a good position for further political work." This work included the formation of a politically clear executive committee of five, the organization of the leadership of national groups, and the establishment of footholds in all labor details. This did not completely eliminate the disagreements, however.[25] In an article that appeared in East Germany decades later, Max Opitz mentions these conflicts only in passing when he speaks of "heated discussions . . . that are of little significance today" and of "animosities between one person and another" (Opitz 1969, 164, 172). These differences are confirmed by Karl Raddatz, the author of a report written a few weeks after the liberation about an SS roundup in the summer of 1944 that brought the shooting of twenty-seven prisoners and the punitive transfer of 102 others, predominantly German functionaries, to Mauthausen. During an interrogation, Friedrich Bücker mentioned the differences of opinion in the Communist group and gave names. The SS managed to destroy the organizational network of these groups to a large extent, evidently by skillfully exploiting these disagreements and torturing people brutally.[26]

Disputes about the new Communist popular-front line took place in other camps as well. Rudolf Gottschalk, who was in Buchenwald, remembers great political differences between those Communists who had been interned since 1933 and those who had engaged in illegal activity while still in freedom. He also points to disagreements among the German Communists in their evaluation of the Hitler–Stalin pact shortly before the outbreak of the war.[27] Eugen Ochs reports that Hans Ruess, the political leader of a group of Swabian Communists in Buchenwald, was attacked because he had too much contact with members of an opposing KPD group (to which Ochs belonged). These attacks did not cease until a member of the central leadership of the party confirmed the principles of the popular-front policy espoused by Ruess.[28] David Rousset observed that the arrival of French Communists in Buchenwald triggered discussions about the new political line with the German Communists who had been imprisoned there since 1933. At first these men refused to accept their French comrades because of their views, and it took long debates for the French to prevail and contacts with non-Communists to be established in accordance with the new tactics.[29] Klaus Drobisch, who attempts to glorify the role of the German Communists, provides indirect confirmation of this when he cites Walter Bartel, who has described "reporting about the seventh world congress of the Communist International" as his first assignment from the party in the winter of 1939–40. Drobisch writes that Bartel "attached great importance to the creation of a new relationship with the Social Democrats." It evidently was not possible to win over the Communist cadres completely at that time, for, as Drobisch mentions elsewhere, Ulrich Osche, who arrived in Buchenwald in 1943, explained these decisions again. The German Communist Reinhold Lochmann recalls that "in connection with the founding of the national committee Free Germany (among German prisoners of war in the Soviet Union) there were many differences of opinion within the underground organization, especially in the beginning." Lochmann speaks of "sectarian views" (Drobisch 1968, 38, 118). Franz Freihaut reports that in Dachau officials of the Austrian Communist Party who arrived there in spring 1938 changed the political thinking of their German comrades. As a member of the Austrian delegation at the seventh world congress, Freihaut was in a position to transmit the decisions made there authentically. He recollects that at first the German comrades did not understand the idea of a popular front,[30] probably as a result of their years of imprisonment in the camps. Sectarian thinking seems to have been most prevalent among the German Communists interned in Buchenwald, but the Luxembourger George Hess reports that the French Communists in Glau, a satellite camp of Sachsenhausen, were different from the others.[31]

Karl Ludwig Schecher has given a graphic description of the effect of national differences on Communist inmates despite all the discipline and international principles. On the day after the liberation of Dachau, the former prisoners, men who had worked together harmoniously in the camp, split into national groups. Schecher likens this effect of the liberation to a "chemist who is able to separate the components from a mixture in which various substances have been completely dissolved. . . . The morning of April 30 [the day after the liberation—H.L.] already witnessed the radical dissolution of the camp into its national components. Up to then the camp had, so to speak, constituted an integration of the various nationalities. Now the reintegration took place at one stroke. . . . The international cohesiveness of the Communists was no longer in evidence."[32]

An important element of the new line developed at the seventh world congress was the relationship with the Social Democrats. In 1938, it was evidently still bad. With reference to Buchenwald, Walter Poller writes that officials of the SPD (Socialist) were vilified by the "political clique," as he calls the Communists who controlled the internal administration of the camp, as "Hitler boosters and Social Fascists." When a transport to Mauthausen had to be put together, this "clique" placed the name of Steinbrecher, the secretary of the SPD, on the list, though it was common knowledge that a transfer to Mauthausen, which the inmates of Buchenwald called "Mordhausen," was tantamount to a death sentence. However, Poller has this to say about Walter Stoecker, a former Communist Reichstag delegate: "Discussions with him were a pleasure. . . . [He was] well-read, calm, practical, and without any of the disagreeable, presumptuous, subjective fanaticism which, I am sorry to say, I frequently encountered in agitators of his political persuasion" (Poller 1960, 207 ff.). Another report contains similar statements. The Buchenwald camp administration, which was "in the hands of the very well-organized German Communists," initially treated "all Socialists as 'Social Fascists' " and made no attempts to help them. However, "by means of tireless discussions," Roman Felleis, an Austrian functionary of the "Revolutionary Socialists," managed "to make relations with the KPD people" somewhat more productive," and in this endeavor he was supported by some Austrian Communists (Stadler 1966, 190). In a report about Dachau we read that after the signing of the pact between Germany and Russia, Austrian Social Democrats gained the impression that "at least some of the German Communists initially thought of a blending of red and brown—a view not held by the Austrian Communists. The relationship between Socialists and Communists "could not have been worse at that time" (Stadler 1966, 190). These discussions do not seem to have had a sweeping effect, for this attitude is still reflected in an account by the Russian Baky Nazirov, who arrived in Buchenwald years later. He describes how he was able to attend very interesting discussions between German Communists and Social Democrats in which Communists called the opponents conscientious servants of the bourgeoisie who had betrayed Socialism and paved the way to power for Hitler (Nazirov 1959 47). On April 22, 1945, eleven days after the liberation of Buchenwald, Ernst Thape, an official of the SPD, wrote in his diary that the Communists "always treated us Social Democrats, who were never here in large numbers, as enemies, or at least not as friends. This changed a bit during the past year. . . ."[33] At that time a German popular-front committee was created at the initiative of Hermann Brill, a German SPD official, but strangely enough, instead of concerning itself with the problems of the camp, this committee discussed ways of building a different, democratic Germany after the crushing of National Socialism. Klaus Drobisch has stated that when Buchenwald was liberated, 796 members of the KPD and thirty-one of the SPD were in that camp.

This is how the relationship between members of the Communist and the Socialist parties looked in Sachsenhausen from a Communist viewpoint after the new line had been accepted: "The Communists had long since established a relationship of close cohesion and joint struggle with most Social Democratic inmates. Often it was not even clear who had once been a Communist and who a Social Democrat." Fritz Selbmann, the author of this account, has described a Bielefeld member of the Socialists who worked harmoniously with Communists in the underground camp administration (Selbmann 1961, 153 ff.). Heinz Junge reports that in the early years the Communists demanded a single party because, in their opinion, the SPD no longer had a raison d'être. After the quick defeat of France, the Social Democrats' expectation of a victory by the western democracies over Hitler's Germany was not fulfilled, and so the Communists had to "put them back on their feet," as Junge put it. Some of the Social Democrats participated in the discussions among the Communists, but others declined to do so.[34] Stephan Hermlin, a writer living in East Germany, evidently had the period around 1941 in mind when he described the relationship between Communists and Social Democrats in Sachsenhausen: "In the peculiar atmosphere of the camp, the differences between Social Democratic and Communist workers, disagreements that had brought the German working class defeat and streams of blood, were still alive here and there; sectarianism and narrow-mindedness still existed and people stubbornly clung to old errors" (Hermlin 1975, 164 ff.). Provost Heinrich Grüber, who observed the relationship between Communists and Social Democrats as a political outsider, speaks of a strong rivalry between Communists, who were largely in charge of the prisoner self-operation, and Social Democrats, who constituted a minority (Gruber 1968, 161).

I have already explained why the relationship between Communists and Social Democrats in Auschwitz differed so markedly from that in other camps. The initiative for an amalgamation to form an international resistance organization came from the Pole Józef Cyrankiewicz, who had been arrested as an officer of the Polish Socialist Party and established contact with Austrians whom he knew to have a Communist orientation. This is how I have described (from memory) the first conversation in which this idea was expressed; Cyrankiewicz: "If an underground organization here in Auschwitz is to prepare for fighting the Germans, it is quite clear that this can only be an international one." Langbein: "Certainly. And if our two groups [the Polish one with Cyrankiewicz and the one that had formed around the Austrian Ernst Burger and included Czechs, Frenchmen, and "Jewish comrades"—H.L.] work together and later combine, then we'll have such an international organization. All we'll need then are the Russians and the Germans." This conversation took place on May 1, 1943. We made good use of this National Socialist holiday, on which there was no work and a large number of SS men were off, which means that the labor details that were accompanied by guards did not move out. In a subsequent conversation, one in which Burger also participated, it was "decided to prepare a collaboration of the two organizations with a view to turning them into a united organization. Our plan is not to operate on the basis of national groups any more, but to organize our comrades in the form of details" (Langbein 1949, 112 ff.).

Even though the use of the word "comrade" in the above report indicates that it was intended primarily to designate persons who in freedom had been active in the workers' movement, it was not narrowly conceived in terms of a party. In point of fact, in the fifteen months of the Combat Group's activity no disagreements ever arose in its leadership because of different views of political problems on the part of Social Democrats and Communists.

In several camps the Communists continued their tradition of holding indoctrination sessions, despite all the risks this involved. Thus we read in a book about Ravensbrück: "The Communists regularly gave political instruction to small and very small groups. . . . Everyone rejoiced when it became known one day that some printed chapters from a history of the Soviet Communist party had arrived in the camp" (*Die Frauen von Ravensbrück* 1961, 125 ff.). From 1938 on, this book—which bore the official title History of the Communist Party in the Soviet Union (Bolsheviks). A Brief Course—was the basic text for Communist indoctrination.

In other camps, too, Communists developed a systematic instructional activity for which books could be utilized. Fritz Selbmann reports that an inmate of Sachsenhausen found among the scrap material that arrived in the camp by the wagonload for processing "a rather tattered Polish book" that turned out to be Stalin's *Problems of Leninism*, "a find of inestimable value, the first Marxist manual in a Fascist concentration camp. The book was cut into many pieces, and Polish and Czech students began to translate it into German, with German Communists acting as helpers and interpreters" (Selbmann 1961, 188). Harry Naujoks remembers that books by Lenin and Kautsky were also smuggled into the camp and served as the basis for Marxist training classes. Those books were never discovered by the SS. To be sure, some of them were destroyed during a big wave of arrests in Sachsenhausen that spelled the end for numerous German Communists.[35] There was other political literature in the camp as well. A young Polish inmate of the youth block was given a "book about the Reichstag fire" by the German Communist Karl Uhlich and later reported: "Karl had told me that the Communists were organized in the camp and doing political work" (*Damals in Sachsenhausen* 1967, 110). In a collection published in East Germany, the Czech Bohdan Rossa describes the instructional activity in Sachsenhausen in these words: "The direct influence of the German political prisoners on the Czech students increased steadily as the latter learned more German. Then German Communist leaders took the initiative in forming study groups or did so in cooperation with Czech Communist students" (Rossa 1959, 57).

The German Communist prisoners in the subsidiary camp at Berlin-Lichterfelde also managed to make contact with Communists who were working illegally in Berlin. In this way "important material came into the camp—leaflets, writings of the national committee Freies Deutschland, the program of the Saefkow Group." This quotation is from a publication that was evidently edited by East German authorities, and there we also read, "It was possible to transmit the program of the party leadership to the responsible comrade in the camp with instructions to study it and then return it with any emendations." This report concludes that "through its collective of leading comrades, the camp takes an active part in the final version of the document" (Sachsenhausen 113). That is as concrete as the official presentation of the party gets, for, as Heinz Junge has reported, the Saefkow Group's document entitled "We Communists and the National Committee Free Germany" on which the German Communist organization took a stand in February and March 1944,[36] apparently did not fully correspond to the party line.[37] In a communication sent by the Saefkow Group to the Communist Party organization in Sachsenhausen in mid-April 1944, we read: "We send you greetings via our connection. Join us in seeing to it that this contact is not temporary but becomes firm and permanent. . . . Your work inspires, stimulates, enriches, and helps us. . . . We are convinced that the party as a whole will benefit from this collaboration" (Nitzsche 1957, 60).[38]

As Rudi Jahn reports, prisoners in the Buchenwald outside detail at the Erla airplane factory in Leipzig maintained "close contact with the underground national committee Free Germany in Leipzig. Members of this committee discussed our view of the situation and our plans with us and brought to the camp leaflets that were printed illegally in Leipzig" (Das war Buchenwald n.d., 101 ff).

Inmates of other camps were more cautious with written material, but it has been reported that in Dachau it was possible to establish contact between the camp and Communist underground organizations in Munich; this was accomplished via prisoners and civilian workers employed in a porcelain factory. Walter Vielhauer, who established this connection, writes that "information and political analyses, even sketches for leaflets, went back and forth."[39]

In Mauthausen in early 1944, Leo Gabler, an officer of the Austrian Communist Party, organized regular indoctrination sessions with five to eight persons, mostly Austrians but including two Germans and one Czech. In addition to discussing the political situation and problems of the camp, Gabler presented a history of the Bolshevik party. Hans Maršàlek reports that "at one of these sessions a participant made written notes and used these for review. [At the beginning of each session, a participant reviewed what had been covered in the previous one—H.L.] This was called unacceptable. At the time we regarded this as Communist political indoctrination, and I do so today."[40] In Herzogenbusch, Marxist training sessions were organized with young inmates, and there were discussions of current problems and of the way the world should look after the war.[41] The Russian Nikolai Kyung reports that in Buchenwald he was instructed to write a history of the November 1918 revolution in Germany. He was given light block duty so he could devote himself to this work with relative ease—"As I found out later," writes Kyung, "this article was translated and secretly read by German anti-Fascists" (Kyung 1959, 68 ff.). In Buchenwald, Janez Ranzinger was instructed by the international committee to prepare lectures about the history of Yugoslavia and its Communist Party. Evidently the greatest interest was attached to the question of how the population of a [relatively] small country could have resisted the big German Reich.[42] Paul Schnabel remembers political instruction that was imparted in individual conversations in one of the Jewish blocks of Buchenwald and reports that the Czech and Polish groups held some indoctrination sessions.[43] Tadeusz Patzer, a very young Pole on barracks duty, was tapped for a course on Marxism.[44] An instructional leaflet issued by the Communist organization in September 1944 deals with the tasks of the national committee Free Germany; only parts of it have been reproduced (Drobisch 1968, 119). In Gerdauen, a satellite camp of Stutthof, which housed female prisoners, discussions about Lenin and the October revolution were organized (Dunin-Wąsowicz 1970, 18).

The activities of the Communists did not remain hidden, and the decisive influence they were able to exert on the prisoners' self-government in many camps made them an object of everyone's attention and invited a critical view of these activities. The Communists are frequently reproached with having helped only those who shared their ideology.

Every group helped its own members first, and the Communists were no exception. In Fritz Selbmann's formulation, "the foremost task of the prisoner self-operation is the protection of the camp against the harassment and terrorism of the SS as well as the protection of the party and the Communists in the camp" (Selbmann 1961, 43). Heinz Junge writes: "I was under the protection of the party as soon as I arrived in Sachsenhausen and was accredited by the comrades who were active there." This is confirmed by Max Opitz, who had arrived at that camp in September 1941 (Opitz 1969, 149).

In Ravensbrück, the SS once again made a list of prisoners who were unfit for work and were scheduled to be murdered. To a Russian woman who had been selected, another Russian whispered, "Marinochka, we've managed to change the list and cross out your number as well as the numbers of a few Czech Communists" (*Frauen-KZ Ravensbrück* 1973, 179). Those women were not called up to be taken away.

Outsiders noticed this. When Margarete Buber-Neumann was asked what Communist activities she had been able to observe in Ravensbrück, she replied that Communist women procured better details for their comrades, prevented Communists from being placed on transport lists, and cared for sick comrades.[45] Buber-Neumann has given a more incisive formulation in one of her books. In the hospital "no one asked you whether you were in pain or running a temperature but whether or not you were in the party" (Buber-Neumann 1963, 266). On the basis of his experiences in Buchenwald, the Dutchman Wijnen speaks of a "buddy policy" on the part of the German Communists and says that this policy was adopted by their Dutch comrades.[46] Carl Laszlo writes that groups of Russians, Poles, and Communists established a certain internal order in the camps, but "this order benefited primarily the members of these groups" (Laszlo 1956, 12). Albert Guérisse observed in Dachau that the Communist organization endeavored to help its comrades,[47] and Vratislav Bušek, a Czech physician, reports this about his experiences in the Mauthausen hospital: "I would not say that the Communist comrades were prejudiced against the non-Communists, but they preferred helping the Communists. What they 'organized' was for the benefit of the Communists, and what the non-Communists 'organized' was also supposed to benefit the Communists."[48] The Frenchman Jean Michel observed that the Buchenwald Communists kept their comrades from being transported to dreaded Dora (Michel 1975, 88 ff.). When the Pole Wincenty Hein was transferred from Auschwitz to Buchenwald together with some of his compatriots, "only the Communists remained in Buchenwald; the others [including Hein himself—H.L.] were sent to Dora."[49] This is confirmed by Herbert Weidlich, who was in charge of Labor Records and in 1943 was ordered by the SS to compile a list of 2,000 inmates for an earthwork detail. At the same time the senior camp inmate instructed him to "keep as many comrades as possible from being transported." Whenever Weidlich identified a comrade, as the prisoners filed past the camp doctor, he told the doctor the man was a skilled worker. "By way of camouflage" Weidlich asked that "Jehovah's Witnesses and a few Greens" be exempted as well (Drobisch 1968, 99). The Dutchman Antonius van Velsen reports that the Communists in Birkenau saved their German comrade Horst Jonas after he was marked for death in the gas chambers by substituting someone else for him.[50] This was a terrible decision, although, in terms of the situation in Auschwitz, this was sometimes the only way to save a person who was important for personal or political reasons.

The Communists have sometimes been reproached with concentrating on saving those who shared their ideology and using their influence against their political adversaries. This charge has been made most pointedly by survivors of Buchenwald, for there the dominance of the Communists was most in evidence.

Thus the Luxembourger Leo Bartimes recollects that, despite several protests, a Dutchman was placed on a transport list because he had once said something against the Communist Party. Bartimes sums up his Buchenwald experiences in these words: "Those who said they were Communists had a good relationship with the Germans who had something to say in the camp. Others wound up in bad details."[51] When the Englishman Thomas arrived in the camp, a colleague warned him not to say that he was an officer or that he had held an important position in peacetime, for "the internal administration of the camp is in the hands of Communists, and they love neither officers nor capitalists" (Marshall n.d., 181). Pierre d'Harcourt, a Frenchman, confirms that the Communist leadership had little use for Catholics and upper-class people. In fact, he heard a rumor that Communists had killed a religious man in the hospital who had made no secret of his rejection of Communism (Harcourt n.d., 115).[52]

At this point, it is difficult to determine to what extent this attitude was intended as protection against traitors or as punishment for presumed political opponents. The Pole Tadeusz Patzer was transferred to dreaded Dora after he had refused to tell the Communists about acquaintances of Wolff, the recently deposed senior camp inmate, who had chosen Patzer for barracks duty because of his knowledge of languages.[53] Wolff, a former German nationalist who "increasingly worked with the SS against his comrades" (Gryń/Murawska n.d., 267), appears to have been a bad sort. The fact that Patzer later played a positive role in the resistance in Dora would seem to indicate that he was not Wolff's puppet in Buchenwald. It must be pointed out, however, that conditions in the camps made it difficult to establish such things in a quick survey.

Anyone acquainted with the fanatical hatred with which Communist parties pursued the Trotskyites, or those who were regarded as such, will not be surprised to learn that the KPD members in power in Buchenwald immediately shipped the French Trotskyites off to Dora.[54] Actually this did not always happen. Walter Vielhauer, who belonged to the Communist "party" in camp says that a Czech Trotskyite played a positive role in Buchenwald.[55] On the other hand, Karl Fischer, an Austrian Trotskyite, remembers that German and Austrian Communists refused to help Trotskyites—evidently because they were afraid of "being suspected of sympathizing with these pariahs."[56] Margarete Buber-Neumann has given a graphic account of her reception by Communist functionaries in Ravensbrück. Together with many other prominent Communist women who had fallen out of favor, she had been released from Russian prisons in the summer of 1940 and turned over to the Germans, who sent these women to concentration camps. In Ravensbrück some Communists with access to admission papers found out where Buber-Neumann had come from, and thus three inmates with armbands immediately summoned her and began to interrogate: " 'You were arrested in Moscow?' 'Yes.' 'Why?' These questions were asked so presumptuously that I immediately understood I was being interrogated by Communists, and therefore every reply I gave was such that it was bound to cut a Stalinist heart to the quick. Only Minna Rupp, a stolid Swabian, was able to make a response: 'Da bischte äbä a Trotzkischt!' ['Gad, so you're a Trotzkyite, ain't ya?']" From then on Buber-Neumann was ostracized in the camp; in fact, a young Czech Communist who had befriended her anyway was expelled from the Czech Party (Buber-Neumann 1968, 218, 358). Nevertheless, Buber-Neumann was able to become a senior block inmate.

Such behavior frequently gave rise to a negative judgment about Communist armband wearers. An "old camp fox" once explained the internal situation in Dachau to the Luxembourg clergyman Jean Bernard in these words: "Almost all the 'seniors' are Communists. This is because they were the first victims of mass arrests by the Nazis. Some of them have been in the camp for five years or longer and can hardly be considered normal people anymore. For this very reason, and also because the camp discipline has become second nature to them, the SS leadership regards them as the proper instruments." This statement is followed by a description of the method used by the SS to keep the functionaries appointed by it under constant pressure. If a block or a barracks attracted the attention of the SS, the senior inmate received twenty-five strokes with a bullwhip (Bernard 1962, 42 ff.). N. Padt, a Dutch clergyman, confirms that the inmates of the clergy block had good relations with some Communists, but in general there was a lot of distrust. "When the chips were down, they were real Germans," writes Padt.[57] The Austrian Walter Adam, who was sent to Dachau as a leading official of Schuschnigg's Fatherland Front, made a clear distinction between two groups of German Communists. "Most of them were class-conscious, partisan, and often intelligent working men. . . . They stuck together well, openly acknowledged their political persuasion, and had a secret leadership in the camp. There was another group in the camp that also called itself Communist but actually constituted a lumpenproletariat that was rejected by class-conscious Communists. This was the group from which the SS liked to draw its most dangerous collaborators" (Adam 1947, 22 ff.). Kogon believes that the principal charge to be made against the Communist secret organization is that it did not always make such a differentiation consistently and was "reluctant to purge its own ranks, while it was always quick to 'eliminate' those with a different ideology" (Kogon 1946, 311).

The German Communist Rudi Goguel was not blind to the weaknesses of some of his comrades and admits that "in the course of the years some comrades did not stand up to the constant demoralizing pressure, especially if they accepted leadership positions—initially with the best of intentions." As it was explained to him by a Communist in Neuengamme with a great deal of camp experience, the will to live "produced a human type that stayed alive by adapting to camp conditions, while the others perished." With his characteristic openness Goguel sums up: "Even righteous and decent comrades fell prey to demoralization in the course of the years. Anyone who tried to suppress that fact would be telling a tale from the Arabian Nights." This unvarnished admission only gives added weight to his statement that most Communists transcended themselves by "being spurred on to ever new resistance by this moral swamp" (Goguel 1947, 160 ff.).

Non-Communists frequently praise individual prisoner functionaries who were known as members of the KPD. Thus the Austrian Ernst Toch singles out the German Communist Ernst Schneller, who was "uncommonly tolerant and accessible to everyone."[58] Schneller was shot in October 1944 in the course of an action against the underground Communist organization in Sachsenhausen. His comrade Max Opitz reports that Schneller occupied "the key position" on the German Communist team (Opitz 1969, 171). Wolfgang Kiessling writes that this former Reichstag deputy and sometime member of the Politburo was "in the last years of the war, and until his violent death, a member of the KPD executive committee in Sachsenhausen" (Kiessling 1960, 201). The Dutchman Jan van Dijk has described Heinz Bartsch, who was killed together with Schneller, as "a very good and courageous senior camp inmate."[59] The Luxembourger René Kerschen, for his part, praises Rudi Wunderlich of Sachsenhausen, who "helped everyone, not just his group, which made him very popular even with the foreigners."[60] The Pole Patzer describes the infirmary camp of Dora, a young Augsburg Communist named Fritz Pröll, as "a wonderful fellow who tried to help everyone." In November 1944, when Pröll was swept up in a big wave of arrests caused by an informer in Dora, he sent the following message from the bunker to Patzer, who was privy to many underground actions and plans: "Don't worry, tomorrow I'll be dead, and dead men don't talk"—whereupon he committed suicide.[61] Patzer's good opinion of Pröll, whom he knew well from his close collaboration with him, is not shared by J. B. Krokowski, who is very critical of Communist prisoner functionaries in general. This gives all the more weight to his judgment about Armand Bertele, a Frenchman of Austrian descent and a Communist veteran of the Spanish Civil War, whom Krokowski calls outstanding.[62] Many similar statements could be cited. Thus Eugen Kogon feels duty-bound to emphasize the contributions of the two Communist capos Baptist Feilen (from Aachen) and Robert Siewert (from Chemnitz). Feilen was "equally popular with the German and the foreign prisoners because of his fairness, serenity, and objectivity," and Siewert "had the courage to stand up even to SS commanders, putting his life on the line every time" (Kogon 1946, 67 ff.). I, for my part, feel obliged to recall the Viennese Ernst Burger, an official of the Communist youth association, who was highly respected among his fellow prisoners of all nationalities in the Auschwitz base camp because, in addition to his other contributions, he did not use the corrupting privileges that he could have claimed as a "German" and a block clerk for his own advantage (Langbein 1972, 286 ff.).

Several clergymen are among those who have given a positive account of Communists. Thus Père Riquet testifies that the Communists in Mauthausen "furnished fine examples of energy and solidarity" (Riquet 1972, 194) and that the Communist-dominated international leadership helped everyone.[63] With reference to Melk, one of the biggest subsidiary camps of Mauthausen where numerous Frenchmen were interned, Raymond Hallery reports that such a good relationship developed between a Communist and a Catholic resistance group that the Communists stood watch while a French priest secretly celebrated Mass and that it was the clergymen's turn to stand guard while the Communists held a meeting (Bernadac 1975, 324). Louis Maury reports that, in Neuengamme, Germans both Red and Green not only participated in secret religious functions of French Protestants but also pointed out the most favorable hiding places to them (Maury 1955, 53).

With reference to Sachsenhausen, the Dutchman Telling writes that the attitude of the German Communists saved the lives of many thousands of foreigners, since the party members not only protected their own people but also improved the general living conditions.[64] Despite all the critical reservations cited here, such statements may be accorded general validity.

Some critics comment on incautious acts of Communists that sometimes endangered not only the existence of their own cadres but the entire camp. But it should be remembered that the Communists undoubtedly were the most active group, and thus their failures had the greatest consequences.

The above-mentioned Report about the Sachsenhausen Concentration Camp contains an account of the unusual funeral of the former Communist Reichstag delegate Lambert Horn, who died on June 2, 1939: "His comrades laid him out in the mortuary and adorned his coffin with flowers. One by one the Communists in the camp went there and bid their dead comrade farewell." Such a demonstration could not remain hidden from the camp administration. The SS "immediately had all political prisoners who worked in the hospital as orderlies sent to the cellhouse." There they were tortured and put in the penal company. There was another sanction that proved detrimental to the whole camp: "For a time political prisoners were barred from working in the hospital."[65]

Another memorial service had far worse consequences. When Buchenwald was bombed by the Allies on August 24, 1944, the SS murdered the KPD leader Ernst Thälmann, who had been held in solitary confinement, and concealed this crime by putting out the story that Thälmann had been killed during the bombardment. The Communist leaders of the camp organization held a memorial service in the basement of the disinfection station. This had been suggested by Willi Bleicher, the capo of the storage room for personal property.[66] Because the rapid advance of the Allies on all fronts had given the inmates the unfounded feeling of optimism—"that anything could be done now,"—the rules of conspiracy were evidently not observed strictly enough, and so an informer was able to denounce a number of the participants to the SS.[67] Among those arrested were Robert Siewert, who had delivered a memorial address, Willi Bleicher, who had organized the meeting, and other German, Austrian, and Russian Communists in leading positions. "There was great tension in the whole camp at that time," but since even torture did not make those arrested talk and some of them were dragged through various police prisons, the camp administration did not succeed in smashing the entire Communist leadership. "This was the only major reverse suffered by the party in its years of underground activity, and it put some of its members in a state of crisis"— this is how the situation following this wave of arrests has been characterized (Buchenwald 1960, 234, 368 ff.). Eugen Kogon has described the consequences more graphically: "During the months of this affair, a stifling cloud lay over the entire camp, and in the first weeks political activity was almost impossible. The leading forces withdrew into newly organized snail trails" (Kogon 1946, 324). Willi Bleicher put it quite succinctly: "At that time the hard core lost its nerve."[68]

In the 1944 investigation of Sachsenhausen by the special SS commission, which was expanded to cover a secret organization of the German Communist prisoners, the Gestapo was aided by the carelessness of some Communists. Immediately after the liberation Karl Raddatz described how some of his comrades who were doing "political work" in the Heinkel Works detail were arrested and shot. They became the "victims of a stool pigeon who had managed to obtain a somewhat deeper insight into our underground activity."[69]

The most momentous conspiracy mistakes were made in Dora, where the production of V-rockets had prompted the SS to employ an especially large number of informers. It made particular use of an enigmatic person who is the subject of conflicting reports. The ambiguity begins with his biographical data. Some seem to remember that he was an Italian named Grozzo, others believe he was a Frenchman named André Grotzo, and still others call him Grozdof. I shall adopt Tadeusz Patzer's version of his name, Grozdoff,[70] for as a clerk Patzer had a chance to examine personal documents in the administrative office. Grozdoff was of Russian descent and wore a red triangle in the camp. After this arrival the "underground camp leadership," whose confidence he managed to gain in a very short time, quickly made him a senior inmate in a Russian block. He never spoke Russian with the Soviet prisoners: "We all believed he could not speak Russian" (Češpiva/Giessner/Pelný, 54). Grozdoff acted as an agitator, encouraged his fellow prisoners to resist, organized meetings in his block, and thus got to know those who were ready to collaborate with him. One day he betrayed himself by suddenly starting to swear in Russian in his block, which made the Russians realize that he had understood their conversations, whereupon he escaped the revenge of the other inmates of his block by running to the SS. Since he had now been unmasked as a stool pigeon, on November 2, 1944, the SS started a round of extensive arrests and tortures, evidently on the basis of information supplied by Grozdoff and other informers. In this way it broke up the resistance organization, and a long series of executions followed. The only ones spared were the Frenchmen who had been arrested, which led them to spread the rumor that Grozdoff was a double agent and had made contact with western Allies with the knowledge of the SS leadership (Michel 1975, 347). Grozdoff himself had been among those arrested, but later he was observed leaving the camp in civilian clothes, and he spread the rumor among the French that in March 1945 he had carried on discussions in Berlin with Kaltenbrunner, who had been trying to establish contact with the western Allies.

It is obvious that the activity of the German Communists in the camp gave rise to legends that have been perpetuated in the literature. What the Pole Wincenty Hein writes with reference to books about Dora published in East Germany and Poland applies also to a number of other works issued by Communist publishing houses. As Hein has pointed out, a number of these accounts present everything in accordance with present-day political and ideological desires, and some books could be cited as typical instances of adapting what really happened to present needs.[71]

The formation of legends can be most clearly demonstrated in the case of Dora. The Grozdoff betrayal described above caused many German Communists in the resistance organization to be murdered by the SS. Some of them have been unanimously praised for their exemplary conduct by non-Communist fellow inmates. The propaganda emanating from East

Germany, however, concentrates on the glorification of Albert Kuntz. One publication states that "the underground resistance organization of Buchenwald gave him the responsibility for organizing the resistance in Dora" and calls him the foremost "Führer" of those active in the resistance. He evidently headed the German Communist Party organization "which demanded and obtained iron discipline from its comrades in the underground activity of the concentration camp" (Dieckmann/Hochmuth n.d., 36 ff.).[72] Another publication quotes from a letter written by an unnamed Dutch survivor, which says that Kuntz "gave us the strength to go on fighting for life and a lasting peace" (Češpiva/Giessner/Pelný 1964, 31). Such effusive, panegyrical, cliché-ridden propaganda was bound to evoke dissent. The harshest judgment has been rendered by J. B. Krokowski, a Pole deported from France, who writes that Kuntz "played God," totally rejected his pleas for help, and even gave him a beating.[73] Tadeusz Patzer, whose above-mentioned assessment of Pröll proves that he was not a unilateral opponent of all Communists, writes that Kuntz "was tough (he did not even spare himself!), and it is entirely possible that he occasionally beat inmates," but he concedes that Kuntz may well have had reasons for such beatings.[74] While the Pole Wincenty Hein confirms that Kuntz's role in the resistance was "definitely a big one," he also says that he "certainly did not behave well toward the great mass of the prisoners," something that was, in Hein's experience, "common among a majority of the bigwigs."[75] Many of these were "typical old Communists" who regarded only Communists as worth anything.[76] Willi Bleicher, who met Kuntz in Buchenwald, categorically denies that he was a violent type and has a very positive opinion of the man.[77] Since Bleicher is not guided by the official view of the KPD, his judgment carries weight.

In his book *Naked Among Wolves*, Bruno Apitz gives a fictional description of an episode in the Buchenwald resistance and hence claims poetic license. This account revives the emotions with which the work of the party organization in the camp have been adorned in postwar narratives: "The party to which they were bound was in the camp with them— invisible, impalpable, omnipresent." When he has an officer of the KPD converse with the senior camp inmate, also a German Communist, Apitz writes: "The party was facing him in its camp illegality" (Apitz 1958, 39, 41).

Jaroslav Marik, the first Czech to be sent to Sachsenhausen in 1939, has described the organization of the German Communists in that camp as "fabulous and fantastic." His remark that the German Communists in protective custody had more power than the SS men must be treated with caution,[78] for the brutal actions of the SS, which claimed the lives of numerous German Communists, tell a different story. The Frenchwoman

Charlotte Delbo resists the legend about the strength of the French-led Communist organization in the Birkenau women's camp by cautioning that "the Communist women sanitized the situation after the fact."[79]

With reference to a number of passages in publications about the activity of the Communists in Mauthausen, the Spaniard Juan de Diego speaks of a "Communist mythology,"[80] and the Czech physician Vratislav Bušek regards Communist accounts of a resistance organization as exaggerated and calls passages in Bruno Baum's book *Die letzten Tage von Mauthausen*, The Last Days of Mauthausen "ludicrous braggadocio."[81] In the literature Bušek's brave activity in the hospital is repeatedly emphasized, and thus he may be considered as a connoisseur of the situation. Through the exemplary objectivity of his presentation Hans Maršàlek clearly destroys the legends that have grown up around the activity of the Communists in Mauthausen (Maršàlek 1974, 244). Since he occupied a leading position in the Communist-led organization in the camp, his words carry particular weight. Maršàlek candidly describes glorifications in the literature—including *Mauthausen mahnt*, a booklet he himself edited—as "poetic license."[82]

Apart from the legends and despite all reservations, the activity of the Communists in the concentration camps is a subject deserving of respect.

10

SOCIAL DEMOCRATS IN THE RESISTANCE

On the basis of his experiences, the Austrian Social Democrat Benedikt Kautsky wrote that the Social Democrats "were far fewer in number than the Communists; the average ratio was probably ten to one rather than five to one. . . . To be sure, it should be remembered that, in an effort to save themselves unpleasant altercations with the dominant Communists, some Democrats did not stress their political affiliation—unless they preferred to join the Communists." Kautsky evidently has in mind those camps in which Communists were clearly dominant, but he must also have been thinking of Germans: "Most of the Social Democrats were much older, because young members of the German working class only seldom embraced Social Democracy, which is one reason why they were less active." They also found it harder to adapt to life in the camps. However, when Kautsky makes the general statement that they were "not 'hard' enough and not sufficiently 'up to scratch' to be considered for positions in the camp," he ignores the situation in Dachau (Kautsky 1961, 134 ff.).

There were far fewer Social Democrats than Communists, and they did not have the background that facilitated the Communists' underground activity. But these are not the only reasons why their role in the resistance movement has come in for less attention and received less critical treatment than the others. There is no counterpart to those works that glorify the importance of the Communists, like the East German publications cited above. The available documents indicate that the role of the Social Democrats was quite variable. In Buchenwald, for example, they concentrated on discussing the tasks that the Germans were bound to face after the Nazi regime was crushed, while the Social Democrats in Dachau tried to take an active interest in camp affairs, which frequently enough embroiled them in bitter fights with the Communists. The Polish Social Democrats, who played an important part in the Auschwitz resistance movement, also concentrated fully on camp tasks. However, they managed to reduce the conflicts between the most purposeful inmates of different nationalities and political affiliations, which had impeded concerted action.

We have named three camps, but this does not mean that Social Democrats did not play a role in others. When survivors of Ravensbrück have been asked who fought for an improvement of conditions in that camp, they have repeatedly named Austrian Social Democratic women, such as Rosa Jochmann and especially Helene Potetz, who enjoyed "the best reputation"[1] and, according to Margarete Buber-Neumann, was imperturbable and invulnerable.[2] Such praise from an author known for her critical judgment carries great weight.

From Sachsenhausen, we have only scant information about the participation of Social Democrats in the resistance movement. However, in a document dated May 14, 1945, and titled *The Organizational and Administrative Structure of the Sachsenhausen Concentration Camp*—of unknown authorship, although the content indicates that it was probably written by Communists—the sentence "It was primarily the political prisoners who gave pride of place to their communal attitude" is followed by the words "Communists, also some Social Democrats" in parentheses.[3] Harry Naujoks, a member of the KPD and senior camp inmate of Sachsenhausen, has named one of them, the Altona teacher Franz Bobzien, who was in the underground leadership and held the positions of second deputy senior camp inmate and senior block inmate in charge of a block housing young Poles. Naujoks emphasizes that Bobzien had good relationships with these people. A Pole who was a member of this block has confirmed this, describing Bobzien as a "brave young Socialist" and one of the "true Germans" whom Poles encountered for the first time (*Damals in Sachsenhausen* 1967, 110). Bobzien's contributions can only be fully appreciated if one knows how difficult it was in many camps to overcome the Poles' distrust of all Germans. For a time the German Social Democrat Herbert Bender, who later died as a prisoner of war in Russia, also was a member of the three-man executive committee.[4] In another study Fritz Henssler is called "the one constant factor" among a group of Social Democratic functionaries over a period of eight long years; the other members changed, but Bobzien and Bender are not mentioned. Despite comradely contacts with German Communist functionaries, "they clearly kept their distance from them with regard to indoctrination sessions run by KPD members." Political arguments were "carried on very passionately," and after Hitler's defeats on the eastern front, there were discussions about future developments in Germany in which both Communists and representatives of the Catholic Action participated (Pawlak 1978).

The role played by Social Democrats in Dachau has attracted far more attention and frequently the rather critical kind. After Karl Zimmermann became hospital capo in 1941, they established their most influential position there. Like his fellow Bavarian Karl Kapp, who wore the armband of senior camp inmate at that time, Zimmermann was a member of the SPD. Kapp maintained a close connection with the German and Austrian Social Democrats in the hospital, and Kurt Schumacher also had constant contact with it. Some observers had the impression that Kapp received instructions and suggestions from there. This group did all it could to help its comrades. Schorsch Scherer, a German Communist who arrived in Dachau in 1935 and was the first to function as senior camp inmate—and to everyone's satisfaction—remembers that Kapp, then a capo, denounced him and even murdered people in satellite camps at the behest of the officer-in-charge.[5] The Pole Jan Domagala, who was not involved in the conflicts among German Reds, names Kapp among the prisoner functionaries who "had many people on their conscience."[6]

According to two outsiders, "a covert power struggle raged between Communists and Social Democrats, a struggle that the SS administration shrewdly exploited from time to time" (Joos 1946, 82 ff.). A book issued by the International Dachau Committee describes the good cohesion among the political prisoners, though it points out that, in the nature of things, conflicts could not be avoided and heated disagreements between the representatives of the two German workers' parties about the course to be pursued were everyday affairs (Berben 1968, 159). Eugen Ochs, who was interned in Dachau for six months in 1939, speaks of friction between Communists and Social Democrats, particularly between the Communist capo Karl Wagner and the senior camp inmate Kapp, who was "too ready to do the bidding of the SS."[7]

Witnesses who belonged neither to a Communist nor to a Social Democratic party report that this fight reached its climax in the infirmary. Karl Schecher, whose balanced judgment is bound to impress those acquainted with the situation, writes that the early period, when those transferred to Flossenbürg and Mauthausen had returned and Dachau was again in operation in the spring of 1940, brought "the promising makings of a sensible personnel policy." However, "when the camp was filled up again, the old fight between parties and nationalities was resumed and common sense was again replaced by the pursuit of special interests."[8] It is this "old fight between parties" that Eugen Ochs refers to when he writes that "despite the fact that the camp was internally dominated by the political prisoners, great conflicts between the SPD and the KPD erupted to the detriment of the prisoners." Ochs adds that "by contract, there was good collaboration among political prisoners in Buchenwald," where Ochs was transferred at the beginning of the war.[9] The Austrian Walter Neff had been interned because he had informed Austrian authorities of a coup planned by the National Socialists, whose party was illegal at the time. Thanks to his important position as head nurse in a hospital block where SS men were carrying on experiments, a post that made him largely independent of the hospital capo, Neff was able to observe what went on behind the scenes. He believes that Karl Kapp, the senior camp inmate, tried to consolidate his influence among his SPD people in the hospital, where there was "a bitter fight between two groups—Communists on the one side, Social Democrats on the other." Walter Neff characterizes these groups as follows: "The Communists are in the minority, but their people are incomparably better than the Social Democrats—which is not to say that the party ideology is to blame for the inferiority of its representatives." Neff describes the hospital capo Karl Zimmermann as a brute and a bully. In this connection Neff mentions the German Social Democrat Heini St(öhr), an unsurpassably self-sacrificing man, who, however, fell out with his own people because he stood up to their mean tricks. By way of summing up, Neff writes: "What harm this fight did! The very best men were transferred to other camps as nurses because they were an irritant and simply opened their mouths at the right time."[10] Schecher, too, refers to this episode when he writes: "As a result of this conflict, many good nurses were transferred to the hospitals of the dreaded eastern camps in order to make room in Dachau for protégés of the party."[11]

In those days the usual method of getting rid of a *persona non grata* was this: The hospital capo was asked to supply nurses to augment the personnel in Auschwitz, where the SS was trying to control a typhus epidemic that had spread to the military and civilians, and it was up to the infirmary capo and his friends to assemble such a transport. Most of those sent to Auschwitz in 1942 were Communists, whom these men now regarded as troublemakers. This selection was not based on professional considerations—seventeen of them were clerks.[12] I was one of them. Shortly before that, I had had an altercation with the head nurse of the block in which I served as clerk, a young Sudeten German Social Democrat, and with Zimmermann, because I had taken it upon myself to give discharged convalescents slips saying "light block duty," which exempted them from hard work for a few days. No SS man noticed that, but the head nurse, who had refused to issue such slips, regarded my action as undermining his authority and thought that I deserved to be punished.[13]

This was not the only episode of this kind. The Swabian Communist Hans Gasparitsch reports that, in spring 1944, people who had been sent to the camp because of their membership in the SPD provided the SS with material incriminating Swabian Communists; whereupon these men were charged with engaging in underground Communist activities and sabotaging orders of the SS, locked up in the bunker, and later transferred to other camps. When Gasparitsch was asked about his observations of conflicts between Communists and Social Democrats, he replied that Schumacher, Franz Olah, and Knapp were opponents of the Communists.[14] The Communist Julius Schätzle reproaches Schumacher with failing to make Kapp listen to reason; according to him, that man was the only prisoner functionary who supplied the SS with a great deal of information.[15] The Austrian Communist Franz Freihaut believes that the fights between members of Social Democratic and Communist parties were limited to the Dachau infirmary, whereas in the camp there was good comradely collaboration with Alexander Eifler, the former chief of the Social Democratic *Schutzbund* (Defense League, a paramilitary organization) in Austria.[16] After the transfer of prominent Communists to other camps in 1944, Social Democrats filled top positions; the Frenchman Joseph Rovan remembers that there were Austrians among them.[17] The German Provost Heinrich Grüber gained the impression that the camp administration was largely in the hands of Social Democrats, particularly Austrians, and he also stresses the influence of Schumacher (Gruber 1968, 173).

The case of Buchenwald clearly demonstrates how greatly descriptions of the importance of the German Social Democrats can differ—depending on the political orientation of the authors. The following brief account is given in the *Buchenwald* collection published in East Germany: "In the camp there were around fifty or sixty prisoners who belonged to the SPD, and they themselves stated that they were not organized and engaged in little political activity." This report goes on to say that there was "no visible political activity on the part of former members of the SPD" (*Buchenwald* 1960, 323). The German Social Democrat Ernst Thape has described his first experiences upon his arrival in Buchenwald at the beginning of the war: "A short man in prison clothes greeted me [in the office—H.L.] and informed me that he was a Social Democrat from Dortmund and had learned from the admissions list who I was. He said that I should not lose heart, there were more Social Democrats in the camp." About this man, whose name was Heinz Baumeister, Thape writes: "I have many people to thank, but no one helped me more than he" (Thape 1969, 157 ff.). Since Baumeister put Thape in touch with other Social Democrats, there seems to have been some cohesion after all. Eugen Kogon has also repeatedly mentioned Baumeister as an "old concentration-camp hand," who took part in relief actions and calls that man, who was politically from the Christian side, his friend. Kogon also mentions the "Socialist poet Ferdinand Römhild, chief clerk in the prisoner hospital." Kogon consulted these and other men when he encountered problems in his bold and risky work with SS physicians (Kogon 1946, 245 ff., 319).

Only a small number of Social Democrats were included in the underground organization, which was always dominated by Communists. These have mentioned only Armin Walther, who helped make illegal radio sets (Hartung 1974, 207), and Willy Jentzsch in connection with acts of sabotage (Drobisch 1968, 129).

Things took an interesting turn in December 1943, when the SPD official Hermann Brill arrived in Buchenwald. Although the Socialist leadership operating outside Germany rejected the German Communists' efforts to achieve a popular front after their seventh world congress, a Social Democratic group operating illegally in Berlin adopted the collaboration strategy. This group was smashed by the Gestapo, and many of its members were arrested. Hermann Brill, one of its leading members, was sent to Buchenwald after serving a prison sentence and immediately took the initiative there in the same spirit: "After a few days I noticed that Buchenwald was dominated by the KPD. I got in touch with some of its leading members and as early as February 1944 formed a popular-front committee." In addition to Brill, who was elected chairman at its first meeting on July 5, 1944, this committee included Thape (also a Social Democratic officer), a German Communist, and a Christian Democrat (Brill 1946, 88).[18]

Brill emphasizes that the activities of this committee also had the approval of representatives of the French Socialists (Eugène Thomas) and Communists (Marcel Paul) in Buchenwald. Its program consisted entirely of problems concerning the future of Germany after the defeat of the National Socialist regime, and all decisions were unanimous. This activity, with meetings and written manifestoes, was quite unusual in a concentration camp and almost cost the members of the committee their lives. In the course of arrests in the late summer of 1944, the SS found manuscripts written by Brill, and thus the work of the popular-front committee was "considerably curtailed." However, the general process of dissolution paralyzed the activities of the camp administration in the final phase, and so there were no serious consequences (Brill 1946, 88).

This striking dual track—a very efficient underground leadership headed by German Communists on the one hand and a popular-front committee led by German Social Democrats that did not concern itself with camp problems and had a Communist as a collaborator on the other—appears to have been part of the Communists' tactics. According to the *Buchenwald* collection, "the committee limited itself to discussions within its own circle," and its formation facilitated the work of the Communists "without a visible political activity on the part of all former members of the Social Democrats." This may be read in an unsigned report written in 1945 and revised in 1960 (*Buchenwald* 1960, 323 ff.).

The Communists' tactics became apparent at the time of Buchenwald's liberation. As Ernst Thape wrote in his diary eleven days later, "When the camp government was formed on April 11, we Social Democrats were completely ignored."[19] Brill's illusions about comradely collaboration were shattered at that time, too: "As early as the second day after the liberation, we were forced to recognize that the KPD had not changed. They only wanted to use the popular front as a bridge to non-Communist circles." For this reason Brill took the initiative. A committee consisting of five German and two Austrian Social Democrats composed a manifesto that was signed by Social Democrats from other nations as well (Brill 1946, 96 ff., 101 ff.).[20]

As Thape noted in his diary, this had an astonishing effect on the Communists, who were surprised "that we knew so quickly and so exactly what we wanted. Among them there is a great uncertainty about all sorts of questions because they cannot find out what Moscow wants and do not have the courage to stand on their own feet."[21] This, however, is outside the scope of this study.

The Buchenwald resistance organization saw to it that cadres were transferred to Dora. Six German Communists and one Social Democrat "took over the most important functions in the camp: key positions for illegal activity." Four Communists and two Social Democrats were added at a later date (Dieckmann/Hochmuth n.d., 64).[22] No reports of The Social Democrats' activity in the Dora resistance organization are known.

It has already been pointed out that the unusual conditions in the Auschwitz extermination camp precluded theoretical discussions about future developments and made factional fights between party groups even more dangerous than elsewhere. Also, for several reasons, Poles performed a key function in this resistance organization.

As early as October 1940, a group of Polish Socialists who had been arrested in Warsaw banded together and worked independently of the secret organization set up along military lines (Gárliński 1975, 38 ff.). By the spring of 1941, they were able to establish contact with the outside via Polish civilians who had been assigned to work in the camp area (Gárliński 1975, 46 ff.). Because of carelessness, the political department found out that Stanisław Dubois (who used the name Dębski and organized the group of Polish Socialists) was maintaining contact with the outside, and in August 1942 he was shot (Gárliński 1975, 23, 113, 84).[23] A few days later Józef Cyrankiewicz (from Crakow) arrived in the camp, and soon he replaced Dubois as the leader of the Polish Socialist Party group. Since he had held an important position in that party in Crakow, he was able to consolidate the Crakow connection of the Polish secret organization.

Józef Gárliński has given a detailed account of the resistance activity of the Poles in Auschwitz. However, for this period, his work must be used with caution, for he clearly tries to minimize Cyrankiewicz's role in Auschwitz—evidently because he condemns his conduct as the prime minister of Poland after 1945. For this reason he repeatedly seeks to belittle the effectiveness of the Combat Group Auschwitz, in the leadership of which Cyrankiewicz played an important role. Gárliński ignores the fact that my own accomplishments were possible only because I was a representative of this group and acted with its support. He acknowledges them only as my personal successes (Gárliński 1975, 196).[24]

In point of fact, the Polish Social Democrats steadfastly championed international cooperation in the resistance organization and thus opposed the extreme Polish nationalism that on the one hand rejected all Germans, including the German political prisoners and all Russians, and on the other hand led to active anti-Semitism (Langbein 1949, 114 ff.).[25] Thanks to this stance and to the perceptible achievements of the Combat Group Auschwitz, which was active from the spring of 1943, Social Democrats' authority with the underground Polish military organization increased to such an extent that close organizational cooperation could begin in early 1944 (Gárliński 1975, 227). Mass arrests and executions in the fall of 1943 had greatly weakened the Polish military organization (Gárliński 1975, 213/84), and this made the conspirational Combat Group even more important. Its significance was definitively underlined by the Polish underground organization's recognition of Cyrankiewicz as the military leader of the resistance movement in the camp (Langbein 1949, 158).[26]

That cooperation in the Combat Group Auschwitz was achieved and that both national disagreements and party differences were put aside is equally to the credit of the Communists and the Socialists who were active in that organization. The Polish Social Democrats were the ones who were able to overcome the greatest difficulties in that regard.

11

THE SPECIAL ROLE OF THE AUSTRIANS

As has repeatedly been pointed out, the Austrians active in the resistance played a special role in the camps, one that differed markedly from the role of the Germans even though the camp administration treated Austrians as Germans. The Austrians, however, regarded themselves as members of a suppressed nation and not as "Germans integrated into the old Reich."

This awareness activated the same energy in them that members of other nations suppressed by National Socialism displayed in their struggle against the Nazis even behind the electrically charged wire of the concentration camps. This did not go unnoticed. The Frenchman Edmond Michelet observed in Dachau that the Austrians refused to be identified with the regime in Germany "under any circumstances," and in this Michelet saw "the most noticeable difference" between Austrians and Germans (Michelet 1955, 170). The specific mentality that is characteristic of many Austrians was also recognized. Thus Hermann Riemer, who was transferred from Natzweiler to Dachau in the fall of 1944, has described the difference in atmosphere between the two camps as follows: "The block personnel did not administer any beatings. I never even heard a bad word." Trying to explain the difference, he writes: "Was it due to the fact that the Austrian senior block and barracks inmates treated things with that Viennese nonchalance?" (Riemer 1947, 150).

In various camps Austrian Communists strove to distance themselves from Germans. When they found it possible to organize some indoctrination sessions, the national question regularly appeared on the program. In a *Report by Austrians to the Psychological Warfare Division of the American Army*, a document produced immediately after the liberation of Buchenwald, we read that "information sessions about the national question and a thorough discussion of the Austrian problems under Fascism and after the attainment of Austrian independence" were organized and "complete agreement about an Austrian program of reconstruction after the expulsion of the Nazis" had been achieved.[1] In Mauthausen, Leo Gabler, an officer of the Austrian Communist Party, also discussed the Austrian national question in indoctrination sessions and cited "the ideological struggle against the idea of a Greater Germany" (Maršàlek n.d., 57).

Hermine Jursa has named four subjects covered by an Austrian group in Ravensbrück, and one of these was "What is a nation?"[2] Bertl Lauscher confirms that the instruction sessions there gave pride of place to the Austrian national question.[3] It is no accident that the only theoretical work produced in a concentration camp is the work of an Austrian and treats national problems of the Germans from the viewpoint of a Communist.[4] The impetus for this work was given by the complaint of Ernst Burger, a young Austrian Communist, about difficulties in cooperating with German Communists in the Auschwitz base camp. "They always want to dictate to others and refuse to see that Poles, Frenchmen, or Jews cannot be ordered around. In almost every one of them there is a little bit of a German chauvinist" (Langbein 1949, 169 ff.). The situation in Buchenwald was similar. An Austrian report, written immediately after the liberation, enumerated various difficulties, then went on: "An added difficulty for us Austrians arose from the fact that in political discussions about Austrian independence it was less necessary to prevail [over] . . . those who often did not understand this problem or made the misjudgment of espousing German ideas."

This is followed by the statement that the correctness of the Austrian standpoint was confirmed at a meeting of Allied foreign ministers in the fall of 1943. This would seem to indicate that the above disputes had taken place earlier and that the Austrian Communists had evidently been able to convince their German comrades by referring to the authority of the Soviet Union, which at the conference had proclaimed the restoration of an independent Austria as a war aim.[5] Otto Horn, responsible for the Austrian group in the international resistance, wrote this immediately after the liberation of Buchenwald—with reference to the time when Austrians were the first foreigners to be sent to the camp: "The Austrian comrades were not integrated with the German ones but created their own organization, which was independent of the Germans." Another remark by Horn indicates that this process involved some friction; he writes about "the struggle for equality among all nations in the camp and for a proper understanding of the mentality and life-style of the individual nations." This statement refers to relations with other national groups, among whom there undoubtedly were greater problems, but to a certain degree it probably refers to the relationship between Germans and Austrians as well.[6]

Developments in Dachau were similar, but there appears to have been less friction, for the German Communists did not have the same cadre of former high officials as in Buchenwald, and the Austrians were more numerous and include many experienced politicians. In addition, the arrival of several hundred Austrian veterans of the Spanish Civil War on May 1, 1941, markedly augmented the Austrian group (Langbein 1949, 39 ff.). "Among us Austrians in Dachau there was complete agreement about the national question," writes Franz Freihaut, "but among our German comrades there were initial difficulties."[7]

In Auschwitz and Mauthausen Austrians played a leading role in the resistance movement from the beginning—in Mauthausen because numerous Austrians were interned there and could more readily establish contact with their compatriots outside the camp.[8] In Auschwitz the outstanding personality of the Viennese Ernst Burger probably was a decisive factor. The two camps housed only a small number of German political prisoners (Langbein 1949, 115 ff.).

Some Austrian political prisoners regarded differentiation from the Germans as superfluous. That this view was most prevalent in Buchenwald may be due to the appeal of the experienced, tight organization of the German Communists. In connection with disputes among the Austrian Communists, two men are named who regarded a separate organization of Austrians as pointless and argued that the Germans were giving a great deal of help.[9] There probably were other reasons why Austrian Social Democrats in Buchenwald did not deem it necessary to document their national identity. A seven-member committee that included, in addition to five German Social Democrats, the Austrian Socialist functionaries Benedikt Kautsky and Karl Mantler composed a manifesto two days after the liberation of Buchenwald. It begins by stating that a declaration has been issued by representatives of democratic Socialism (from various German *Länder* [states or provinces] and from Austria on an equal basis) in the presence of representatives of other Socialist parties (here five provinces [*Länder*] are named, but Austria is not). This declaration presents the Social Democrats' idea of a free, peaceful, Socialist Germany (Kautsky 1961, 287 ff.).[10] Before Hitler's assumption of power in Germany, Austrian Social Democrats had generally espoused the idea of union with a democratic Germany. Evidently neither Kautsky and Mantler nor the other five Austrian Social Democrats who had signed the manifesto revised this position in the face of developments after 1933.[11]

Certainly there were several reasons why the international character of the resistance organizations was more clearly evident in those camps where Austrians had the same leading role that Germans played in the old camps. In Mauthausen and to an even greater extent in Auschwitz, German Reds formed a smaller percentage of the political prisoners, who by virtue of their privileged position had greater opportunities to engage in underground activity. Unlike most Germans, the Austrians had not had years of camp experience behind them before members of other nations arrived—that is, they did not have the strong organizational cohesion or the sense of superiority displayed by "old inmates" to new arrivals. Last but not least, the Austrians have a tradition of establishing contact with members of other nations more easily than the Germans, many of whom were slow in that regard.

Thus Toni Lehr reports that the Austrian Communists in Ravensbrück had very good contact with Czechs and close connections with French-women but no cordial contact with German Communists.[12] The Russian W. Biktashov describes how the Austrian Communist functionary Josef Lauscher established contact with him and other Russian officers interned in Dachau and helped them build up an organization.[13] The German Karl Ludwig Schecher has described the effect of the Austrians' arrival in Dachau in these words: "They changed the structure of the camp in several respects . . . and, so to speak, reduced the feverish quality of camp life."[14] Edwin Tangl, a Tyrolean, believes that conditions in Dachau became more humane when Austrians began to fill positions.[15]

In Buchenwald, when it was a matter of systematically developing contacts among members of different nationalities, the Austrians played a special role, for their relations "with the other nations were very good, particularly their cooperation with the nations of the Danube area."[16] The Austrian Communist Hans Sündermann emphasizes that, immediately after their arrival, the Austrians had not only "the best and friendliest relations with their German comrades [but] even before the formation of the international camp committee" good relations with comrades of other nationalities.[17] Poles single out the Viennese Gustav Wegerer, "who over a long period demonstrated his liking for Poles."[18] Austrian Communists were not the only ones whose good reputation helped dispel distrust and bridge national differences in Buchenwald, and the Frenchman Pierre d'Harcourt is not the only one who singles out Eugen Kogon, who came from the camp of the Austrian Catholics. Kogon had tremendous influence and was respected by men from all parties. According to Harcourt, whom Kogon successfully championed, this enabled him to influence the camp hierarchy very effectively (Harcourt n.d. 122).

In Mauthausen Austrian Communists took the initiative in organizing solidarity actions, which finally led to the formation of a certain international organization. The Spaniard Juan de Diego, not a Communist, emphasizes that they did not act in sectarian fashion. In reports from a period when any resistance was extremely difficult because the camp was still entirely in the hands of Greens, one repeatedly encounters the names of two Austrians: Josef Kohl—called Pepi or "father," one of the first Austrian political prisoners in that camp—and Hans Maršàlek, who came to Mauthausen with a group of Viennese Czechs and therefore found it easier than others to gain the confidence of Czechs and other speakers of a Slavic language.[19] Diego is not the only author who emphasizes Maršàlek's great courage in the face of the SS,[20] and he was in the best position to observe this because he was his coworker in the camp office. The Italian Pappalettera mentions Maršàlek's name together with the names of two Czechs when he speaks of fifty prisoners who were saved from the gas chambers (which continued to be in operation until the end). It was possible to give these men forged papers identifying them as Frenchmen, and then the International Red Cross took them to Switzerland in April 1945 (Pappalettera 1972).[21] Thanks to his authority and initiative, Leo Gabler became active in the resistance immediately after his arrival in Mauthausen in October 1943. However, on April 13 of the following year he was taken to Vienna and executed.

In Mauthausen too, Austrian Communists had to come to terms with the national problem. Maršàlek, who participated in these discussions, writes that, like the countries of exile, this camp housed "Austrian Social Democratic functionaries and a leading German Communist who did not regard the annexation of Austria as a step backward, at least not from the viewpoint of social policy." This view was vigorously opposed by Kohl and later by Gabler. Thanks to them, these theories remained isolated among the German-speaking prisoners in Mauthausen.[22]

To the last, Austrians were in very responsible positions in the prisoners' struggle against the SS. When an international Mauthausen committee was formed in late March 1945, it was headed by Heinrich Dürmayer, an Austrian who had been evacuated from Auschwitz two months earlier.[23]

The Pole Tadeusz Hołuj has described the development of an international resistance movement in Auschwitz as follows: In the middle of 1943 individual groups were formed in the base camp as well as in Birkenau and in satellite camps "They were in contact with one another and through the initiative of the Austrian group formed, around New Year's 1942–43, a joint international group in which Communists, Socialists, officers of the international brigade, the [Austrian] Defense League, partisans of the western European resistance movement, and Soviet officers held leading positions. Through Józef Cyrankiewicz this group started negotiations with the Poles in May 1943 and formed in the camp a general international anti-Fascist organization under the leadership of Józef Cyrankiewicz, Hermann Langbein, Ernst Burger, and Tadeusz Hołuj. This organization called itself Combat Group Auschwitz" (Smoleń 1960–67, 34 ff.).

Many authors have emphasized the special role of the Austrians, and particularly of Ernst Burger, independently of one another. The Slovene Janez Ranzinger met Burger as early as December 1941 on the transport to Auschwitz and remained in touch with him in the camp. "Ernst and Rudi Friemel [a Viennese member of the Defense League and veteran of Spain whom he had met through Ernst—H.L.] gave me radio news and instructions every day," writes Ranziger.[24] A Yugoslav who evidently belonged to the group around Ranzinger established contact with the Russian major Aleksander Lebedev. Through him the Russian met Burger, who helped him and his group of Russians and remained in contact with them (Lebedjev 1960, 34 ff.). Rudolf Vrba, a Jew who had been deported from Slovakia, describes how he gradually realized that Ernst Burger, "the polite, gracious clerk" of Block 4, was the leader of the underground organization that had helped him without his having known about it at first (Vrba/Bestic 1978, 194). Isaac Liver, another inmate of Block 4, also remembers Burger, who "before the end of 1942" had formed an underground group to which Liver belonged.[25] Roger Abada describes how the Frenchmen deported to Auschwitz attempted to organize secretly and to establish contact with others: "There already was an organization—one of Austrian prisoners that also extended to some Germans and Poles." In December 1942 Abada met Rudi Friemel, who spoke French and strove to make contact with Frenchmen. "We quickly came to an agreement," writes Abada, who brought the French group in contact with the leadership, "in which Germans, Czechs, Russians, Poles, and our Austrian friends" were represented (Abada 1946, 170 ff.). Eugène Garnier, who was active in this group, describes Burger as "our Viennese leader" (Garnier 1946, 183).[26] All these remarks refer to a period before the Combat Group was formed in the spring of 1943.

In the trial of the commandant of Auschwitz in spring 1947, the witness Józef Cyrankiewicz was asked about the resistance movement in the camp. "We [the Poles—H.L.] had friends primarily among the Austrian anti-Fascists and Communists, and it is hard not to speak of them in terms of the deepest friendship and respect," said Cyrankiewicz as he named Burger as "one of our best comrades" (Cyrankiewicz 1964, 17 ff.). In September 1943, the Polish-Jewish physician Alina Brewda was transferred from Majdanek to Auschwitz, where she was put to work in the experimental Block 10 of the main camp and was soon able to make contact with the underground organization. "One of its most important leaders was a young Austrian named Hermann Langbein, who had served in the international brigades in the Spanish Civil War. This man of keen intelligence was of enormous value to the resistance movement [as clerk of the SS doctor—H.L.], Langbein's very close associate in the underground was Ernst Burger, also an Austrian" (Minney 1966, 148 ff.). Bruno Baum also reports that many prisoners owed their lives to Langbein.[27] In a report that Cyrankiewicz was able to smuggle out of the camp he describes Langbein as "an intelligent and good person with whom we are in the closest touch."[28] The Pole Thomasz Sobański emphasizes that Heribert Kreuzmann, the Austrian senior camp inmate in the hospital of the Auschwitz subsidiary camp Jaschowitz, was "imbued with great benevolence" (Sobański 1974, 137). Until the end the leadership of the Combat Group Auschwitz was composed of Poles and Austrians (Langbein 149, 185).[29]

The contributions of Austrians to the resistance movement were acknowledged after liberation. Among those who received letters of appreciation was the Tyrolean Edwin Tangl. Frenchmen who were members of the Dachau labor detail at Landsberg on the Lech river, where Tangl was able to use his position as a camp clerk to make their lives easier, have testified to his irreproachable attitude toward his French comrades.[30]

One reason why survivors of the concentration camps occupied important positions in Austria after the liberation is that many internees had been politicians from different parties. It is largely due to the "spirit of the camp area," which was often cited after 1945, that these men ended the murderous fight that had raged before the occupation of Austria in 1938 between the clerico-Fascist regime headed by Dollfuss and Schuschnigg on the one side and the workers and their organizations on the other. This spirit did not prevent heated disputes from arising, but it did produce a unifying national consciousness—the lack of which was one reason Hitler could occupy that country without a struggle.

12

THE POLES

Apart from the Germans, there is no national group about which there are as many (frequently contradictory) reports and judgments as there are about the Poles, and there are several reasons for this.

For one thing, Poles followed Austrians and Czechs into the concentration camps right after the beginning of the war, and in far greater numbers than these other groups. Big transports of Poles arrived in Buchenwald in mid-October 1939.[1] Between March and September 1940 masses of Poles were sent to Sachsenhausen, and the majority of them were then transferred to other camps.[2] Around that time the arrival of big transports of Poles was registered in Neuengamme and Gross–Rosen.[3] As has already been mentioned, Auschwitz was originally founded as a concentration camp for Poles, and apart from a small number of German prisoner functionaries, Poles were the only inmates of the camp for a considerable period of time after June 1940.[4] For the duration of the war so many Poles kept arriving at the camps that they probably constituted the strongest national group despite the especially murderous treatment they received.

Another reason for the special role played by Poles in camp life and in the resistance is that as Slavs, they were under particular pressure from the SS (Kogon 1946, 232 ff.). This pressure forced the Poles to struggle for their lives.

In addition, the Poles differed from the other national groups in their composition. In their quest for *Lebensraum* (living space) in the East, the National Socialists persecuted Polish intellectuals with particular harshness, in order to deprive this nation of its power of resistance. No other nationality had as many clergymen interned as the Poles, and like most clerics these were, in the course of time, concentrated in Dachau. Polish academicians and students could be found in all the camps; thanks to their youth, the latter found it easier to accommodate to camp conditions physically and mentally.

Finally, Poles held different ranks in the hierarchy of the camps. In Auschwitz, they used their camp experience and their pronounced ethnic cohesion to form the most influential group after the small number of German prisoner functionaries. By virtue of their marked solidarity the Poles were able to occupy practically all important positions in Birkenau, where the SS kept German criminals at the top of the camp hierarchy until the very end. This has been reported by Wiesław Kielar, who is well acquainted with conditions in the Auschwitz complex and adds that Poles managed to tie the hands of the Greens to a large extent (Kielar 1979, 279, 329). However, according to the commandant of Auschwitz, this national cohesiveness should not be overrated, for he claims that "among the Polish prisoners there were three big political groups whose adherents bitterly feuded with one another. The strongest of these was the nationalistic-chauvinistic group. The doctors frequently told me that there always were bitter fights for predominance in the hospital as well as in the Work Assignments. The hospital and the Work Assignments were probably the most powerful positions in prison life" (Höss 1958, 101). The Poles were not able to capture similar positions in other camps, where they were usually among the Slavic groups that were kept out of key positions, and consequently the roles played by Poles in the resistance movement varied greatly in importance from camp to camp. The evaluation of the Poles in the concentration camp is influenced by several factors: their pronounced national feelings, a legacy of their harsh history; the traditional aversion of many Poles to Russians, particularly Ukrainians, an antipathy that had received fresh sustenance from the partition of Poland by Hitler and Stalin in September 1939; and an anti-Semitism that was more pronounced among Poles than in other national groups and could be utilized by the SS to terrorize Jewish prisoners severely.

David Rousset emphasizes both the strong solidarity of the Poles, which he experienced in the camps, and their crassly anti-Semitic and anti-Russian attitude.[5] Another chronicler of the camps, Benedikt Kautsky, writes that virtually all Poles were nationalistic, but he adds that this is not surprising in people who have been persecuted because of their nationality. "The question of anti-Semitism, even among most of the leftist Poles, was more of a problem." Kautsky differentiates between two groups of Polish prisoners. The first consisted of people who had been expelled from their homes in western Poland to make room for German settlers and were able to differentiate Nazis from other Germans, and the second group was composed of "Fascists, mostly from the intelligentsia, and members of the underworld." Kautsky, who gathered his experiences not only in Buchenwald but primarily in Auschwitz, in the satellite camp Monowitz, comes to this general conclusion: "Here the hatred of Germans and Jews amalgamated with contempt for all other nations and produced an unsurpassable incarnation of chauvinism" (Kautsky 1961, 146 ff.).[6]

The experiences gained by the Austrian Heribert Kreuzmann as senior block inmate in the hospital of the Auschwitz base camp give a graphic picture of the difficulties stemming from such an attitude as well as the possibilities of overcoming it. Nationalistic Poles who occupied a jealously defended position in the hospital pitted themselves against him, a Communist and veteran of the Spanish Civil War. When he tried to put "Aryans" and Jews in the same rooms, they enlisted the help of the SS camp doctor to frustrate this plan. However, Kreuzmann was supported by the Polish Socialist Zenon Rozański, one of the nurses in his block. Kreuzmann remembers that "I put Rozański in charge of everything that concerned Polish nationalists, and this changed the Poles' attitude toward me."[7]

Hermann Joseph, a German, was told by a Communist compatriot with camp experience that those camps in which German political prisoners set the tone did not have the anti-Semitic attitude that he observed among the Poles in Auschwitz.[8] After the defeat of the Spanish republic, the Polish Jew David Szmulevski, who had served in that war, had been active in a Communist-led resistance organization in France before he was deported to Birkenau. He reports that an "Aryan" Pole named Edek, with whom he had become friendly, once told him that no Jew should return to Poland after the war, for there would be no room for them there. To be sure, Szmulewski admits that Communists did not differentiate between Jews and non-Jews in their comradely relationships.[9] Filip Müller, a Slovak Jew, characterizes Mietek Morawa, a young Polish capo in a special detail, as a "dreaded murderer" and states that "extreme nationalism and an inexplicable hatred of Jews" had turned him into one (Müller 1979, 66).

Ianko Vexler, a Jew deported to Auschwitz from France and assigned to the Gypsy camp as a doctor, testifies that Polish nurses employed there beat their Jewish colleagues in front of the Gypsies—presumably to demonstrate their power to the latter. Vexler adds, however, that he greatly admired the courage and quiet heroism of some Polish nurses, physicians, and clerks who risked their lives in resisting this, for they were incurring the hatred of their compatriots (Bernadoc 1979, 206). Jósef Cyrankiewicz too, did not hesitate to excoriate the worst excesses of anti-Semitism, which the SS sought to spread so intensively even among its victims. In a report to the Polish underground organization, he wrote that when an SS man was selecting infirm people for killing, their hatred of Jews impelled some Polish physicians in the prison hospital to lead him to the hiding places of such inmates.[10]

Here, too, blanket judgments are off the mark. Igor Bistric had been deported to Auschwitz from Slovakia. As one of the first Jews on the staff of the hospital, he met there both Polish anti-Semites and Polish intellectuals, who always treated him and other Jewish nurses and clerks in a

comradely fashion (Langbein 1972, 97).[11] However, it is also a fact that
Józef Gárliński, a chronicler of the Polish resistance in Auschwitz, endeavors to deny the anti-Semitism of some Poles, which had a deleterious
influence by virtue of the prominent positions held by these men. In fact,
though Gárliński knows about the reproaches of anti-Semitism leveled
against them, he unreservedly glorifies them as resistance fighters.[12]

There are reports from all camps that Poles took an active part in the
resistance. In addition to the participation of Polish groups in resistance
organizations, many Poles are fondly remembered for their personal courage and actions. Thus the Polish physician Władysław Czapliński managed to induce Bachmayer, the officer-in-charge at Mauthausen, to stop the
gassing of patients shortly before the liberation of that camp. He was able
to influence him because he had treated Bachmayer's family (Bernadac
1974, 242). At that time Marian Molenda's refusal to participate in gassings at Gusen cost him his life (Pappalettera 1972). During a daring action
to rescue Allied officers scheduled to be killed in Buchenwald, Eugen
Kogon had the support of the Pole Arthur Gadziński (Salomon 1960, 185).
In Auschwitz, Marian Batko, a secondary-school teacher, and Mak-
symilian Kolbe, a clergyman, volunteered to replace another man in a
group sentenced to starve in a bunker as a reprisal for the escape of a Pole
(Langbein 1972, 277 ff.).

In Dora, the Polish capo Krassowski saved a Pole by substituting a dead
person's number for his.[13] In Buchenwald Gwidon Damazyn, a Polish
engineer, built radio sets and a shortwave station over which he and the
Russian Konstantin Leonov broadcast SOS calls to the American army
three days before the liberation (*Buchenwald* 1960, 517 ff., 543 ff., Czarnecki 1973, 55 ff.). These particularly striking instances are not the only
ones.

Authors have repeatedly mentioned that it was more difficult to integrate Poles into international cooperative ventures than other national
groups. In addition to the above-mentioned factors, the anti-Communist
attitude of many Poles—probably a consequence of their bad experiences
with the Soviet Union—played a part, particularly in those camps in
which Communists set the tone in the resistance movement. Thus Walter
Vielhauer has described how difficult it was to establish contact with Poles
in Dachau, because most of them were Communists. At first this was
attempted via Russian comrades, but the anti-Russian orientation of the
Poles thwarted this.[14] With reference to his experience in Buchenwald,
Otto Horn writes: "The collaboration between the Polish and German
comrades turned into a prolonged process. Again and again misunder-
standings and confusion had to be cleared up before they could reach that
measure of trust on both sides that is a prerequisite for a common strug-

gle." In this connection Horn also mentions "very great difficulties" among the Poles, because they differed in their ideas about the future structure of Poland[15]—evidently meaning that many Poles rejected Communism. It goes without saying that under these conditions the small number of Polish Communists had a special role to play. Henryk Sokolak has described his efforts to convince German Communists in Buchenwald "that Polish Fascists were not the only ones sent to the camps," whereupon Poles were given influential positions as well. "This considerably enhanced the position of the Polish leftists," for "the German comrades helped and supported all anti-Fascists in the camp, first and foremost the Communists." Sokolak also mentions "discussions about Marxism and materialism" and indicates that there were difficulties in this area. "The only short-term goal reached by the organization was the renewed politicization of the Polish prisoners." Together with two of his fellow countrymen he testified that in April 1943 the Polish Communists formed "a united organization" in Buchenwald and added that "in October 1943 the representatives of our party were admitted to the international camp committee" (Kuhn/Weber 1976, 58). Elsewhere Sokolak writes that in January 1944 this group was admitted to the committee as the sixth national Communist Party (*Buchenwald* 1960, 407 ff.). No contact of this kind appears to have been achieved in Sachsenhausen, for Hans Pointner wrote immediately after the liberation: "The Poles were a chapter by themselves. Apart from the fact that they were all nationalists, they were also chauvinistic, Fascist, anti-German, and particular opponents of the Communists and the Soviet Union. Their chief enemy was not the SS or Hitler but the Germans and the Soviet Union."[16] At a later date Heinz Junge remembered that for several years big landowners set the tone among the Poles.[17] As Communists, both Pointner and Junge were active in the resistance movement of Sachsenhausen. According to both of them, the conflicts were so great that Poles furnished the largest percentage of stool pigeons in that camp. However, Communists are not the only ones who have rendered a harsh judgment about the behavior of Poles in Sachsenhausen. On February 2, 1945, the Norwegian Odd Nansen wrote in his diary that among the Poles there were "next to the Germans the worst foremen, the most brutal men, the wildest braggarts, and the meanest 'comrades.'" Elsewhere he mentions the Poles' burning hatred of the Germans (Nansen 1949, 264, 159). Michel de Bouard, a Frenchman who always strives for a balanced judgment, describes the Poles he met in Mauthausen as men held together by a sort of sacred egotism, by means of which they isolated themselves from others. Officers primarily set the tone in this group, and "many vied with the SS in their anti-Semitism." Bouard mentions the clerk of Block 19, a druggist from Posen (Poznan) whom he describes as the leader of the Polish collective. That man gave a beating to a French engineer because he suspected him of being a Jew (Bouard 1954, 57 ff.). Both the German Jew Bruno Baum and the Russian Valentin Sakharov have pointed to similar problems in Mauthausen. The latter mentions that in the final phase the Poles still had no representative on the international camp committee, though he states that this situation was remedied (Sakharov 1961, 204). Elsewhere Sakharov describes bitter conflicts with Poles, who clearly hated the Germans. The German Communist functionary Franz Dahlem told him that these people carried on "an embittered, mendacious propaganda" against the Soviet Union, and Sakharov adds that "there also were such nationalists among the Yugoslavs, the Germans, and even among the Czechs" (Sakharov 1961, 61 ff.). In his description of the same period Baum states: "However, the situation of the Poles was complicated, because there were many bourgeois forces among them. In the final analysis, this affected the unity of the resistance." In this context Baum emphasizes the fate of Józef Cyrankiewicz, who had already successfully striven in Auschwitz to reduce political conflicts within the Polish group and who used the authority he had gained there to the same end when he and many of his compatriots were evacuated to Mauthausen in January 1945 (Baum 1965, 204). Hans Maršàlek was able to register the results of these efforts, and he also paid careful attention to the special situation of the Polish prisoners whose ranks had been decimated by mass executions in the early period. "The constant danger of liquidation, the confrontation with people with an entirely different political and religious orientation, and a skeptical attitude toward any interpretation of Marxism and atheism and toward the Soviet Union [Maršàlek characterizes the Poles as "nationally conscious, very religious, and anti-Soviet"—H.L.] led to an endeavor to help their fellow countrymen." The resultant "partial isolation of the Polish prisoner collective" did not change until "additional Poles arrived from Auschwitz in January 1945," including Cyrankiewicz himself (Maršàlek n.d., 248).

Cyrankiewicz explained to his friends of other nationalities, who frequently criticized the Poles' lack of international solidarity, that among the deportees were not only anti-Nazis, as with other national groups, but men from reactionary circles as well. Their compatriots had to impart political understanding to these men in the camp (Ainsztein 1974, 787).

Cyrankiewicz and his friends do not seem to have exerted any influence beyond the confines of the Mauthausen base camp. The judgment of the Luxembourger Eugène Thomé was that the Poles living in Gusen "remained nationalistic." This had a negative effect, for during the last two years they were able to occupy many positions in that camp (Letzeburger zu Mauthausen 1970, 341). As a consequence of the above-mentioned differences, however, many Poles have given a negative judgment of the attitude of the Communists in the camps.

The Pole Krzystof Dunin-Wąsowicz, a historian who wrote about the Nazi concentration camps on the basis of his own experience, concludes that the Polish resistance groups were formed on a military basis and upon the initiative of leftists. He particularly mentions Socialists in Auschwitz and Mauthausen as well as Communists in Stutthof (where he was interned), Auschwitz, and Buchenwald (Dunin-Wąsowicz 1972, 5).

In addition to the Polish resistance organization in Auschwitz—which, as Józef Gárliński reports, was organized by Witold Pilecki along military lines—Krokowski mentions a group of officers as having been active in Dora from September 1944 and late February 1945.[18] Bogdan Suchowiak testifies that a Polish resistance organization was formed in Neuengamme as early as 1942. He writes that "it was organized and led by former Polish active and reserve officers, and at first it had no political orientation"[19]— by which he evidently means that in its ranks there were no disputes arising from party politics. Jerzy Kwiatkowski reports that in Majdanek there were both a Polish military organization and a group led by Polish Communists (Kwiatkowski 1966, 248), but the effectiveness of these groups was diminished by the fragmentation of the Polish underground groups on the outside with which contact was maintained.[20]

In addition to this militarily oriented core there are reports of another center that strove to organize resistance. Thus officials of the Polish Boy Scouts in February 1941 began a systematic activity which, in contrast to the groups led by officers, aimed at giving young people moral and, if possible, material aid. No anti-Semitic or blatantly nationalistic tendencies were observed in their ranks. Many of these officials were educators who, according to Józef Kret, "in accordance with the principles of all boy scouts gladly came to the aid of their fellow men . . . and gave educational care to youthful prisoners and all those who had fallen prey to resignation and were on the verge of a nervous breakdown" (Kret 1971). In the women's camp Ravensbrück, Girl Scouts formed a group that called itself Mury and had as its "main task training for altruism."[21] Urszula Winska writes that Mury came into being as early as 1941 and acted in accordance with its motto "The Girl Scouts will survive and help others to survive."[22]

In Ravensbrück Polish women organized a type of educational activity that was observed in no other concentration camp. When numerous children were sent to that camp in 1943 and especially in 1944 (after the crushing of the Warsaw uprising), it was possible to give real instruction in clandestine classes. Józefa Kontor, the scoutmistress of Mury, had prepared this by giving teacher training, particularly to girl scouts. Members of this Polish group of girl scouts also established contacts with girl scouts of other nationalities in Ravensbrück.[23] Isa Vermehren, a German, emphasizes "the high intellectual and cultural level" of the "intellectual elite" of the Polish women and believes that this level was not reached by any other national group. Even in the final phase, which Vermehren experienced in Ravensbrück, these Poles occupied "almost all leading positions" (Vermehren 1947, 93). Nothing comparable to the activity of the boy scout and girl scout groups or to that of the officers' organizations is to be found among other national groups.

Some survivors report efforts to eliminate conflicts between Poles and members of other nations that prevented a united, international resistance movement. The German Communist Hans Gasparitsch sums up his experiences in Dachau by saying that the German Communists found it easier to work together with other nationalities, because these had a more political orientation rather than a purely nationalistic one, whereas the Poles were "absolutely chauvinistic" and had hardly any Communists in their ranks (with whom German Communists could, of course, have established contact most easily). Yet Gasparitsch states that it was possible to "slowly persuade" the Poles.[24]

Heinrich Christian Meier writes that the Poles in Neuengamme regarded themselves as being "on a higher rung of the ladder" than the Frenchmen, who had followed them to the camp in large numbers. No sooner had Frenchmen been placed in a better detail than "Poles in favorable positions immediately pulled strings to send the Frenchmen out to do earthwork the next day" (Meier 1949, 405 ff.). Hans Schwarz, who was not transferred to Neuengamme until fall 1944 but then became well acquainted with the secret organization, writes: "Because of the special nationalistic atmosphere, it was not possible to establish contact with our Polish comrades (who had arrived in mass transport in the spring of 1940). The criminal prisoners, who largely dominated the hierarchy at that time, managed to misuse many of these Polish comrades' for their activities. Collaboration with the Polish comrades did not come about until the small active group of political prisoners succeeded in making contact with a like-minded Polish group and creating an atmosphere of trust."[25] Ewald Gondzik's judgment is particularly important because he is himself a Pole and had contact with the resistance movement in Neuengamme for four years. Writing in Hamburg a few months after the liberation, he described the cooperation among the ethnic groups, saying of his compatriots "there unfortunately were many fanatical nationalists whose viewpoint was the same as that of the Fascists. They caused us [the politically aware prisoners, evidently leftists—H.L.] a great deal of trouble. In the latter part of

1944 we took action to reduce the differences between the [presumably Polish—H.L.] nationalists and members of other nationalities, and we succeeded in part. Many people saw the light, but others became our enemies, and we had to guard against denunciations."[26] Elsewhere Gondzik mentions the efforts of the camp administration to play Czechs and Germans out against Poles and Russians,[27] and he denies Józef Gárliński's statement that there were two Polish resistance groups in Neuengamme, which fought each other.[28] "In the camp there certainly were other Polish groups of former landowners, but these could not be regarded as resistance groups; at best they were discussion groups."[29] The German Communist Albin Lüdke also regards Gárliński's statement as off the mark; as far as he knows, the Pole Wojnarski was "the leading intellect of the Socialist, or Communist, group of the Polish resistance movement."[30] Rudi Goguel, a German Communist, gained the impression that the "overwhelming majority" of the Poles were chauvinists of the London orientation (meaning the Polish government-in-exile there) and anti-Russian. He, too, mentions Wojnarski as "one of the few Polish comrades" (Goguel 1947, 172).

Cecile Goldet reports that most nurses in the Ravensbrück hospital were Poles and tried to eliminate members of other national groups from the staff. However, as indicated elsewhere in her account, it should be borne in mind that the Frenchwomen evidently felt slighted by many ethnic groups. For example, she complains that neither Belgian nor Dutch nor Danish women shared the contents of their packages with Frenchwomen (Saint-Clair 1966, 218). Generally speaking, prisoners with an influential position in the hospital building or another key detail endeavored to get their compatriots there. This practice was apt to lead to nationalistic one-sidedness, and only the establishment of a firm cohesion on an international basis managed to end it. Thus an Austrian-led international organization in Auschwitz managed even before its merger with a Polish group to have not only Frenchmen and Czechs but also Jewish doctors placed on the staff of the hospital, which until March 1943 was composed almost entirely of Poles (Langbein 1949, 100 ff.).

A document entitled *The Polish Secret Organization in the Buchenwald Concentration Camp*, evidently written immediately after the liberation and signed by three Poles, gives a graphic picture of the development of the Polish resistance organization in that camp. On October 3, 1943, "a few political prisoners of Polish nationality decided to found a Polish secret committee, a group in preparation since June." This committee established contact with the German Communist group "to enlist its aid in actions in behalf of Polish comrades." In this effort it was assisted by Gustav Wegerer, the Austrian foreman in the pathology section. One of the first tasks of this committee was "to settle disputes between Poles and other national groups." In January 1944 the leadership of the Polish group was augmented, and the three new members represented the teachers, the military men, and the journalists. Their representative on the international committee was the Communist Henryk Mikolajczak, evidently because he had the best qualifications for working with a committee dominated by German Communists. After the liberation of Buchenwald, the Polish committee was "reorganized and expanded."[31] An article by Wacław Czarnecki published in 1968 shows how skeptical one must sometimes be about those named as having been active in a resistance movement, especially if the source is a party official writing years later. Czarnecki names three men as leaders of the Polish group in Buchenwald, though their names do not appear in *The Polish Secret Organization* (Czarnecki 1968). In that report Czarnecki is mentioned as a "representative of the Polish journalists" who was coopted into the leadership of the Polish group, together with two others, in January. Like most accounts written immediately after the liberation, this report seems to be more convincing, if only because of the fact that Czarnecki claims that the Polish-Jewish Communist Leon Stasiak (a man who was transferred from Buchenwald to Auschwitz in October 1942) was a member of the executive committee (founded a year later).

When the Slovenian Communist Janez Ranzinger was transferred from Auschwitz to Buchenwald in March 1943, information he was given by the Auschwitz resistance enabled him to establish immediate contact with Austrian and German Communists in Buchenwald and he was instructed to contact Polish anti-Fascists. Since he spoke Polish and had come to Auschwitz together with Poles, the Buchenwald organization regarded him as especially qualified for this task, and he soon found Polish Communists who helped him.[32] Ranzinger, who maintained contact with the Poles for about six months, remembers that "it was very difficult to work among the Poles because there were many factions, more nationalistic-chauvinistic than leftist ones."[33]

The judgment of non-Communist inmates about their Polish fellow prisoners is frequently negative also, and there are similar reports from various camps. The Luxembourger Pierre Grégoire makes the blanket judgment that in Sachsenhausen Poles were very instrumental in effecting denunciations. In his book, which was published under the name Gregor Stein soon after the liberation, he writes that Frenchmen too "compromised both their human and their national dignity" (Stein 1946, 178). The Frenchman Frère Birin describes how he was beaten by the senior block inmates and those on barracks duty, most of them Poles, when he arrived in Dora in January 1944 (Birin 1947, 38). His compatriot Andrès Pontoizeau, who arrived in Dora around the same time, characterizes the Polish capos as even more terrible than the German criminals and murderers who held that powerful position there: "For the sake of keeping their position or getting a smile from their masters, they were prepared to do anything, even to kill." He goes on to say that they hated France and the French (Pontoizeau 1947, 84, 101); as many Frenchmen appear to have had a strong antipathy to Poles. Léon Halkin, a Belgian who was transferred to Dora a year later, mentions that Polish as well as Serbian and Dutch capos "were already thinking like Germans, and we had nothing to expect from them except beatings" (Halkin 1965, 153). In Gross–Rosen, his former camp, Halkin had already experienced the capos' reign of terror—"almost all of them German criminals or Poles" (Halkin 1965, 102).

The Poles in Mauthausen have been characterized in similar terms. The Spaniard Mariano Constante compares the behavior of Polish capos with that of German Greens,[34] and his compatriot Manuel Razola, who arrived in Mauthausen in April 1941, writes that at first the camp was completely in the hands of the criminals. Only a few Poles were able to occupy responsible positions, "but they were reactionaries and evinced a marked political hostility toward the Spaniards" (Razola 1969, 57). There are similar reports about Poles in Gusen, the largest satellite camp of Mauthausen. Three Spaniards who were transferred to that camp in early 1941 remember that, apart from the senior block inmates who were German criminals, almost all positions were in the hands of the Poles: "They were the cruelest enemies of the fighters for a Spanish republic." The political differences are highlighted by the statement "that the Poles were rich men who regarded it as natural to beat or kill poor men" (Razola 1969, 180). The Frenchman Louis Deblé believes that the Poles were characterized by an "immense presumptuousness" and a "narrow-minded chauvinism," qualities that made them despise their fellow prisoners. Most of them (and Deblé evidently refers to those who were able to hold positions) belonged to the landed nobility or were intellectuals: "For all of them Poland was the hub of the universe." Deblé also points to the reasons for the particular enmity between Poles and Spaniards: "The Poles were Catholics and great admirers of Salazar and Franco, but in the civil war the Spaniards fought for the republic" (Bernadac 1975, 21 ff.). In his diary, the Pole Stanisław Nogaj gives the names of German Greens and Reds, including Communists, in Gusen who were "bloodthirsty murderers," but he also names five Poles who were murderers. However, the SS system was arranged in such a way that inmates "tortured and killed" one another, and thus Russians, Frenchmen, Latvians, and others were murderers, too.[35] Paul Tillard, a French Communist, describes how at the liberation of Ebensee, another big subsidiary camp of Mauthausen, the "German and Polish criminals felt forsaken by their masters and protectors . . . and were afraid." Many in fact, were killed (Tillard 1945, 73 ff.). Evidently the camp administration there managed to exploit political differences as skillfully as national ones. However, the strength of the spirit of resistance with which members of all imprisoned nationalities were imbued proves that national differences could be reconciled repeatedly. Stanisław Nogaj reports that Poles in Gusen strove to proceed against willing tools of the camp administration. Together with other Poles, Nogaj was transferred to Gusen in May 1940 from Dachau, where he, as well as some of his compatriots whom he names, had been taught by German Communists how to organize resistance. In Gusen, Rudi Meixner, an Austrian Green, used his position as camp clerk to get Poles placed in important posts (Nogaj 1967, 158 ff.). Krokowski, a Pole deported from France, emphasizes the aid given by Poles to their fellow sufferers in Dora. In addition to Tadeusz Patzer, who used his clerkship to save lives, he names Józef Radzymiński, whom he characterizes as "one of the finest figures" in Dora. This judgment carries weight because Radzymiński was a Communist and veteran of the Spanish Civil War and Krokowski generally judges Communists harshly.[36] Ernst Israel Bornstein emphasizes that not all Poles in Fünfteichen (a satellite camp of Gross–Rosen in which the top positions were entrusted to Greens, as in Gusen) became henchmen of the SS and that this applies to the Poles in the underground movement. Bornstein's words carry weight because he was sent to the camp as a Jew, and Poles are often accused of anti-Semitism (Bornstein 1967, 139). Harry Naujoks, the German senior camp inmate in Sachsenhausen, remembers that he never had any difficulties with Poles,[37] and the Austrian Helene Potetz remembers with pleasure the cohesiveness and will to resist among the Polish women in Ravensbrück.[38] Other Austrian women recall with gratitude the help given them by Poles when it was a matter of saving three Austrian Jews, who had been transferred to Ravensbrück from Auschwitz after the Poles had learned that these women were scheduled for execution. Danuta, a Polish senior block inmate, was asked to protect them in her block, and when Mitzi Berner tried to inform Danuta, a confirmed Polish nationalist, about the political persuasion of the three, "Danuta immediately interrupted me by saying, 'You are talking about my sister inmates, and everything else is of secondary importance.' " Other Polish women also participated in this rescue action. The Polish physician Grabska removed the tattooed number of a former inmate of Auschwitz, and thus that prisoner could be kept on the rolls under the name of a deceased woman.[39] The German Isa Vermehren has characterized Danuta as indispensable as head of the secret organization of prisoners, a person who managed to gain the respect of the SS (Vermehren 1947, 126).

If further proof is needed that Poles were active in the resistance, it may suffice to state that among those sentenced to death by the SS for resistance activity, sabotage, and other crimes were numerous Poles. The great majority of those shot at the Black Wall in Auschwitz were Poles. Most of the 118 inmates of Dora who were hanged because of sabotage between March 12 and 21 were Russians (ninety-nine, but sixteen were Poles).[40] Wanda Kiedrzyńska reports dozens of death sentences for sabotage in Ravensbrück involving "Russian prisoners of war and also a few Poles" (Kiedrzyńska 1960, 97). It is probably true that the SS was especially quick to sentence both Poles and Russians to death. For example, we read with reference to Sachsenhausen that "the smallest infraction caused especially Soviet and Polish prisoners to be hanged publicly" (*Damals in Sachsenhausen* 1967, 95). However, without the brave actions of numerous Poles, whether they carried on their struggle against the SS regime individually or in groups, there would be no explanation for the number of victims, a percentage that was clearly higher than that of other nationalities, with the exception of the Russians.

13

THE RUSSIANS

"Since there were no Jews in the camp, the Russians occupied the lowest rung. They were not permitted to be in a good detail."[1] This statement by Julius Schätzle refers to the period in Dachau in which all Jewish inmates had already been shifted to camps in the East, but it applies as well to all other camps inside the Reich. The SS forced the Russians to the bottom-most rung of the hierarchy it had created—not counting the Jews.

The first Russian prisoners of war sent to the concentration camps were systematically murdered. Around 300 of them arrived in Auschwitz as early as July 1941, and a few days later not one of them was alive. It is estimated that in September of that year 1,500 were gassed immediately after their arrival, about 600 during the first test of Zyklon B (Brandhuber 1961, 15 ff., 45). Of approximately 10,000 Russian prisoners of war sent to Auschwitz that fall and winter only 186 were still alive on May 1, 1942. In November 1941 alone, 3,726 Russian dead were registered (Brandhuber 1961, 29, 33). Of 1,000 Russians who arrived in Majdanek in August 1941, only 130 were still among the living in May 1942 (*Die Todesfabrik Majdanek* 1946, 20; Simonov 1945, 10).[2]

The first transports of Russians arrived in Sachsenhausen in September of that year, and in November only 2,500 out of around 20,500 were still alive (*Damals in Sachsenhausen* 1967, 144). In the Buchenwald camp area 8,483 Russian prisoners of war were murdered before the first Russians were assigned to the camp as prisoners on October 18, 1941, in accordance with a Himmler order of a week earlier that "in addition to the Soviet prisoners of war slated to be executed, Soviet Russians are to be placed in concentration camps for purposes of labor" (Drobisch 1968, 36 ff.).

On October 20, 1941, the first Soviet prisoners of war arrived in Mauthausen, and further transports followed shortly. Of the 5,333 prisoners of war deported there by the end of 1942, 4,866 did not live to see New Year's Day of 1943 (Maršàlek, 95, 252). I made the following note about Dachau: "In late 1941 the first Soviet prisoners of war arrived at the camp—that is, for a long time only their uniforms arrived. The prisoners were killed somewhere outside the camps, and their uniforms were sent to the disinfection station, where inmates were employed."[3]

Mass murders on this scale were not undertaken later, but the behavior of the Russian prisoners cannot be understood without considering the fate of these first transports of Russians. Also, it appears to be no accident that two of the most infamous concentration camps, Majdanek[4] and Gross–Rosen,[5] were originally intended as camps for Russian prisoners of war.

Apart from the Jews, the Russians found it hardest to gain access to positions in the camp. Fritz Selbmann writes that it caused quite a stir when a Soviet prisoner of war, and a first lieutenant to boot, was given an armband in Flossenbürg. "Never before has a prisoner of war been the foreman of even the smallest detail. Now a former high officer even becomes the chief capo of a detail with many thousands of prisoners. Is the new chief capo a traitor?" On the basis of his camp experience Selbmann gives this answer: "It can't be otherwise" (Selbmann 1961, 305).[6] Ernst Israel Bornstein reports that in the final phase of Flossenbürg the dominant German Greens frequently had the support of prisoners "who performed many of the subordinate functions in the camp" and were registered as Russians. These were Ukrainians. "Some of these fellows had mile-long whips with which they beat us," writes Bornstein (Bornstein 1967, 196). The first lieutenant mentioned by Selbmann was a Ukrainian as well.

Many negative judgments about Russian prisoners concern Ukrainians, who also had to wear an R in their triangles. The Austrian Socialist Helene Potetz met Ukrainian women in Ravensbrück and remembers that "they regarded every German as an enemy."[7] The Pole Maria Kurcyuszowa confirms that these women, like the male Ukrainians, were pushed to the lowest rung of the camp hierarchy: "They had no chance to occupy positions in the camp." According to her, only Belgian women, who did not know German, shared this lot.[8] Those best able to adapt to the camp administration had the best chance of performing functions. Thus Aimé Spitz states bluntly that in Natzweiler Ukrainian nurses murdered inmates—and Poles are the only others about whom he makes such a statement (Spitz 1970, 30).

Those who understood Russian and therefore had contact with Russians were able to make distinctions. The Pole Krokowski has said that the majority of those marked with an R in Dora were anti-Stalinist Ukrainians.[9] Leo Bartimes, a Luxembourger, remembers tensions between Russian prisoners of war and Ukrainians, many of whom had been sent to Germany as foreign workers and had been packed off to concentration camps because of some transgression, and he describes the Russians as "swell fellows."[10] Like Bartimes, the Austrian Communist Otto Horn observed the situation in Buchenwald, and he wrote immediately after the liberation: "The first Russians who came to the camp, so-called Ukrainians, were given a very friendly reception ... but their uncomradely conduct soon caused them to be rejected. This situation changed when the first transports of Soviet prisoners of war arrived in November 1941." The relationship between the Communist-led secret organization, in which Horn was active, and the Russian group seems to have been somewhat problematic, for Horn is careful to say that "eventually a basis for a systematic and thorough collaboration was created after "the Russian comrades had repeatedly taken the initiative in changing their leadership."[11]

Another Austrian Communist, Hans Pointner, who was interned in Sachsenhausen, also wrote down his impressions a few weeks after his liberation. "Among the Russians, we gradually found good comrades, especially among the many young ones. On the other hand, there were many among them who openly expressed their opposition to Stalin." Pointner emphasizes that "there were very strong anti-Semitic currents among the Ukrainians" and states that many of them had gone to Germany voluntarily.[12] With reference to Sachsenhausen the Dutchman Jan van Dijk speaks in general terms of great differences among the Russian prisoners of war.[13] Georg Buch, a German Social Democrat who also experienced that camp, writes that "the Russians were unpredictable, and many of them lumped all Germans together."[14] While admitting that in Flossenbürg there were conflicts between Russian prisoners of war and foreign workers who had gone to Germany voluntarily, Naujoks says that there was no hostility.[15] The Frenchman Michel de Bouard emphasizes the crass difference he noticed in the Russians interned in Mauthausen. Most of them— "pariahs of the camp"—were young lads who had come to Germany as foreign workers and had been sent to the concentration camp for some reason. Groups of them committed organized theft and bullied other prisoners. The small number of prisoners of war stood out from these young men, who had been demoralized by life in the camp (Bovard 1954, 58). The Norwegian Odd Nansen wrote his observations down in a diary he kept in the camp. There he also describes the Ukrainians as "pariahs" and strives to fathom the reasons for their general rejection. "What everyone shares is hatred of the Ukrainians, or contempt for them. Anti-Semitism is latent in everyone, and so is the Germans' aversion to the Ukrainians ... because they are starved, badly dressed, and on a far lower educational level than the average Norwegian" (Nansen 1945, 61, 119 ff.). Nansen tried to give them the same help that he gave to his Jewish companions in misfortune. Both the Frenchman Louis Maury and the German Communist Rudi

Goguel got to know Russians in the last phase of Neuengamme. Maury estimates that around New Year's 1944–45 about 30 percent of the prisoners there wore an R, which means that they were either Russians or Ukrainians, and he emphasizes their cohesion. They cooperated in digging up additional food and cigarettes, doing so much more skillfully than most of the others. Maury writes that "despite the checkered population and the variety of their languages, these peoples seem to have been formed in the same melting pot," but he warns against the generalization that could easily have arisen from difficulties in communication and total mutual misjudgment (Maury 1955, 55). "The Russian problem is giving us a great deal of trouble," he writes. The prisoners of war were in the minority; the majority were criminal elements who "made no distinction between a German comrade and a German fascist." He noted that the Russian block "teems with stool pigeons and agents provocateurs" and describes it as "the bottommost rung of hell." This is his explanation for his observation that "even good Russian comrades turned into out-and-out nationalists" (Goguel 1947, 168). Eugen Kogon has summarized the situation as follows, presumably on the basis of his experiences in Buchenwald: "The Russians were divided into two entirely disparate groups; one consisted of prisoners of war and Russian civilians, the other of Ukrainians, who constituted the great majority. Whereas the prisoners of war were a well-disciplined group, the mass of the Ukrainians was a motley crew." Kogon confirms that at first the Ukrainians received preferential treatment from their German fellow Communists; however, "the insolence, indolence, and uncomradely conduct of many of them rapidly brought about a complete change, and they no longer had a chance to occupy leading positions" (Kogon 1946, 378).

All this also posed problems for international cooperation in resistance. Where there was such cooperation, Russians urged military actions. On behalf of the Combat Group Auschwitz, Ernst Burger strove to establish firm connections. "We have been looking for a connection for a long time, but so far we have not succeeded. They are especially cautious"—this is how Burger describes the first organizational contact in the Auschwitz base camp, probably in early 1944. Burger reported to the leadership that the Russians were exerting pressure and asking what preparations the Combat Group had made for an armed uprising and the organization of mass escapes. In those days their initiative gave a new impetus to the leadership of the Combat Group. "The Russians are soldiers, and they see everything in military terms"—this was the assessment of the leadership, which certainly did not disparage such a viewpoint (Langbein 1949, 157). A report by the Russian M. S. Sobochenii has been shown to have been adapted to the Communist Party line after the fact, but it confirms that an international cooperation was achieved with the help of Austrians and that the Russians pressed for placement on details where they would have access to weapons (Sobochenii 1965). The Dutchman Antonius van Velsen has described how contacts with Russians were made in Birkenau. He too differentiates between nonpolitical men, who had run away from their place of work in Germany and had been sent to the camp for that reason, and political prisoners. The latter were quite ready to help plan an uprising, but they wanted to decide the timing. Van Velsen believes that they wanted to wait until Russian armies were approaching.[16]

A certain confirmation of what has been said about the Russian problem in this camp is provided by a report by the Russians Stepan Baklanov and Nikolai Kyung about underground activities in Buchenwald. Initial "isolated actions" of various Russian groups "caused disagreements in the general resistance." On March 25, 1943, however, the Russians active in the resistance managed to unite (*Buchenwald* 1960, 415 ff.).

The organizational development of the Russian resistance is best documented in Buchenwald, and they appear to have been most effective there. This impression may be caused by lack of such detailed reports about Russians from other camps as are available in the collection *War Behind Barbed Wire* (though this volume, like Russian publications on this subject generally, could not be published until long after Stalin's death).[17] In February 1944, a Russian military organization was formed under the leadership of officers, and Ivan Smirnov has described it as the spearhead of the international resistance movement (Nazirov 1959, 50; Kyung 1959, 72). According to him, it included 2,000 of the 5,000 Russian prisoners of war who were interned in Buchenwald in its final phase (Smirnov 1959, 86; Dronov 1959, 138). Eugen Kogon has confirmed that these activities had a positive result: "During the past year the Russian prisoners of war have begun, in concert with a few outstanding Komsomols [members of the Soviet youth organization—ed.] from the ranks of the Ukrainians, to train at least the usable members of this group, which had absolutely no inhibitions [Kogon means the Ukrainians—H.L.], and to integrate them into the whole. In this difficult task they even succeeded, partially and in some instances" (Kogon 1946, 378).

Since some confusion had been caused by parallel organizations—one political (Simakov 1959, 118) and one military—it was decided to merge these in the summer of 1944 (Smirnov 1959, 88). Their leader Nikolai Simakov, the former head of the Russian political organization, writes that the Russians in Buchenwald also pressed for preparations for an uprising. In early 1944, his group instructed him to urge this upon the international center, for it regarded what had already been done to this end as insufficient. According to Simakov, this prompted other national groups to begin military activities (Simakov 1959, 120).

There are no equally concrete descriptions about Russians in the resistance at Sachsenhausen, but the few available reports do indicate a certain parallel. Major General Sotov, evidently the head of the Russian group there, discussed with the German Communist Ernst Schneller "the organization of an armed uprising based primarily on the French and Soviet prisoners, the greatest military potential" (*Damals in Sachsenhausen* 1967, 97, 113). There are only scant reports about a Russian military organization in the Stutthof concentration camp. Kryzysztof Dunin-Wąsowicz gives as one reason the strict secrecy of this group and as another the fact that there were only few survivors. He points out that the first Russian prisoners of war did not arrive in that camp until 1943, and he stresses their high morality (Dunin-Wąsowicz 1970, 194).

The Russian secret organization in Mauthausen has been described by its head, Valentin Sakharov, who repeatedly describes it as Communist. It is obvious that he constantly gives Communists pride of place in his accounts of other groups as well. After uncertain beginnings—which, as Sakharov emphasizes, were encouraged and guided by Franz Dahlem, a German Communist official and veteran of the Spanish Civil War—organized military work was started in spring 1944 under the leadership of officers (Sakharov 1961, 79 ff.). Dahlem gave this instruction to Sakharov, evidently in the name of an international committee: "A group of higher (Russian) officers must form a staff which will develop plans (for an armed uprising)" (Sakharov 1961, 111). According to a very concrete description by the Spaniards Manuel Razola and Mariano Constante, a Russian and a Spaniard shared the leadership of the international military organization in 1944—for conspiracy as well as linguistic reasons. The Russian had charge of the Czechs and Yugoslavs and the Spaniard of the Frenchmen, the Belgians, and the Poles—the last-named evidently because of the Poles' antipathy toward the Russians (Razola 1969, 151). At the time of the liberation the Russian major Andrei Pirogov was in charge of the prisoner units (Razola 1969, 147). Sakharov indicates in passing that "the group of Soviet citizens imprisoned in Mauthausen was very diverse in its composition." Most of them were prisoners of war, but there also were "traitors in the service of the Fascists and a few criminals who had committed some transgressions against the Germans" (Sakharov 1961, 122 ff.).

As early as the summer of 1942, when the Russians in Dachau were still strictly isolated, Soviet officers conducted initial discussions about the organization of resistance, and, according to Biktashov, they were aided by Austrian and German Communists.[18] When, immediately before the liberation, a Communist-led organization was joined by an international committee that was already preparing to assume the leadership of the camp after liberation, the Russian general Nikolai Mikhailov participated in the first nocturnal discussion, which had attracted sixteen representatives of various national groups. He is said to have requested the chairmanship on the grounds that the Russians were numerically the strongest ethnic group in the camp at the time.[19] However, since Poles and Frenchmen also claimed the leadership, it was finally agreed to elect Pat O'Leary, the representative of the smallest national group, as leader. This prisoner had been transferred to Dachau from Natzweiler in late September 1944 and was the only person registered in the camp as a Canadian. Actually, he was a Belgian, real name Albert Guérisse. Mikhailov did not participate in future meetings; he and the Belgian Arthur Haulot had been elected deputy chairmen, and O'Leary maintained contact with him (Brome 1957, 230 ff.). Guérisse believes that "he probably was the only Communist on our committee." The committee remained in contact with the group led by German Communists.[20]

In a later chapter about open rebellions there will be repeated mention of Russians. Russians refused to work for the German arms industry, including fifty-four female Russian prisoners of war in Ravensbrück, even after they had received harsh punishment. Their resistance was broken only after the SS picked out a few and threatened to shoot them, whereupon the women decided to commit systematic sabotage (*Die Frauen von Ravensbrück* 1961, 199 ff.). The Dutchman Wijnen remembers the refusal of Russian prisoners of war to work in the Gustloff Works at Buchenwald. They too did not give in until the SS threatened to shoot them. Wijnen observed that "the great strength of the Russians consisted in their doing everything in groups."[21] In an account of escapes and attempted escapes from the camps, we shall also name Russians more frequently than members of other nations.

In addition to the special situation that led them to incur more risks than others, other elements seem to have played a role. Thus René Gille reports from Melk, a satellite camp of Mauthausen, that more than anyone else, Russians attempted to escape whenever any opportunity presented itself— "seldom with any preparation and without any precaution." They seemed to be possessed of a fixed idea and persisted in the face of reprisals from the camp administration. The Frenchman Gille spent thirteen months in that camp and remembers only one successful escape, which took place a few days before the approach of Russian troops (Bernadoc 1975, 305). On the basis of his observations in the Flossenbürg subsidiary camp Leitmeritz (now Letoměřice) the Czech Franz Heřmánek believes that "frequent and repeated attempts to escape were typical" of the Russians, who were distinguished by "an urge for freedom coupled with courage to the point of risking their lives in foolhardy fashion" (Krivsky/Krizkova 1967). In connection with mass escapes from Birkenau, the Dutchman Antonius van Velsen writes that Russian soldiers had obligated themselves to make every attempt to flee if they became prisoners of war.[22] Wiesław Kielar, a Pole, speaks—evidently in the same connection—of the "iron discipline" of the small number of Russian prisoners of war who had stayed alive after the "liquidation" of most of them in Birkenau (Kielar 1979, 317 ff.).

We know of no parallel in any other camp to one special activity of the Russian group in Buchenwald: Episodes from the history of the Soviet Union—called "reports"—were written down. Baklanov and Kyung have reported that "the main aim of this work was to show the Soviet reality to our foreign comrades and to unmask the Fascist propaganda" (Buchenwald 1960, 418). According to Nikolai Kyung, "members of the Russian underground" went even further and in the spring of 1943 decided to issue a newspaper; twenty-six issues appeared, each in two handwritten copies of four to six pages. It was written at night in a storage room for the clothes of patients. Eugen Jalzew, whom Kyung identifies as the editorial "secretary," writes: "Our first issue of the fighting journal called upon the prisoners of war to organize and practice self-discipline and friendship" (Buchenwald 1960, 419 ff.).

A number of observers have spoken of an anti-Russian atmosphere. Jean Michel writes that Russians, whom "no one helps," behaved like animals, and he stresses their patriotism (Michel 1975, 114). The Frenchman David Rousset reports that the Russians displayed great solidarity and were regarded as wretches by the others—in fact, a real scandal arose when he shared the contents of his first package with Russians, who were not allowed to receive any packages.[23] This happened in Helmstedt, a satellite camp of Neuengamme, and Michel's observation refers to Dora.

The Luxembourger Pierre Petit has given an impressive description of his experiences with Russians in the last months before the liberation of Bergen–Belsen. There he had become friendly with a young Russian named Piotr, and through him "I met a number of his compatriots and for the first time had contact with a small opposition group composed entirely of Russian Komsomols. They were brave lads, former partisans with a devil-may-care attitude who had not abandoned their anti-Fascist struggle even in the camp. . . . They laughingly risked their health and their lives. . . . They were fanatics, a kind of inverted SS." Petit says that they sometimes went too far and destroyed even camp institutions that were useful to the inmates, but they were "good and dependable comrades, camp comrades with whom one could go through thick and thin" (Petit 1965–68).

Surely similar observations could have been made in other camps as well if the observers had gained the trust of their Russian fellow prisoners.

14

OTHER ETHNIC GROUPS

In addition to Germans and Austrians, Poles and Russians, the numerically strongest groups, members of other nations also played an important part in the resistance. In this connection, Frenchmen and Czechs are given pride of place.

Considerable numbers of Czechs began to arrive at the camps as early as 1939[1] and Frenchmen in 1943.[2] Reports about the latter have come primarily from Buchenwald, Dora, and Dachau, and about Czechs chiefly from Mauthausen and Sachsenhausen, but members of these two national groups were active in the resistance movement of other camps as well. Opportunities for such activity varied, for the experience of long-time prisoners gave them an advantage, and "old" prisoners had a greater chance of being awarded armbands by the camp administration. But more than their longer imprisonment—many of the Czechs spoke German, whereas knowledge of this language, essential for attaining an endurable position, was far less common among the French. One of them, Michel de Bouard, also emphasizes the unity and dignity of the Czech group in Mauthausen (Bouard 1954, 57); its members received numerous packages from relatives (Bouard 1962, 61), and this was a considerable advantage. Nevertheless, in many respects the composition of the two groups was similar. Compared to others, the number of intellectuals among them was above average. In one month, February 1942, seventy-five professors and lecturers at the University of Brünn (now Brno) arrived in Mauthausen (Maršàlek 1974, 251). Also, both the Czech and the French groups included numerous Communists, among them internationally known officials, and these could easily establish contact with German Communists, who had captured key positions, especially in Buchenwald and Sachsenhausen.

In their relationship with other nationalities, the French differed greatly from the Czechs. According to the Austrian Helene Potetz, the Frenchwomen in Ravensbrück were a "closed society," and there were no conver-

166

sations with them.[3] The German Willi Bleicher observed that French intellectuals were helpless, depressed, and more apt to break down than others.[4] No such statements are found about the Czechs, though both Potetz and Bleicher emphasize that there was a good relationship between Germans and Frenchmen—or, as Potetz put it, "between French intellectuals and German intellectual Communist women." David Rousset, the French chronicler of *univers concentrationnaire*, believes that the French had the greatest difficulties in adapting to life in the concentration camps,[5] and Eugen Kogon confirms this when he writes that "their pronounced individuality and generally high intellectual level caused them many difficulties" (Kogon 1946, 376). Isa Vermehren, a German, remembers that the well-developed national pride of the Frenchwomen gave them important moral support (Vermehren 1947, 93).

Frenchmen were frequently the objects of the contempt that other nationals had for the French government, especially, Spaniards, Czechs, and Poles. The Frenchman Jean Michel avers that, even toward the end of the war, the Czechs still distrusted Frenchmen because of the French capitulation to Hitler in Munich (Michel 1975, 226). J. B. Krokowski has stated that the French were despised by others,[6] and there are similar reports from Mauthausen. The Frenchman Fernand Alby believes that some people blamed the French for their quick defeat in 1940 as well as the ensuing collaboration with the Nazi government and that the Spaniards resented them for their unfriendly reception in France after the defeat of the Spanish republic. "To be sure, only a minority were involved," he writes and adds that the majority were able to distinguish between the responsibility of the government and that of the people (Bernadac 1974, 369). Louis Deblé concludes that "the Spaniards' only experience of France was its internment camps" and that this was the reason for the bad reception they gave the Frenchmen arriving in Mauthausen (Bernadac 1975, 22). Georges Parouty sums up the situation by saying that the Spaniards blamed the French for their nonintervention in the Spanish Civil War, the Czechs held them responsible for Munich, and the Poles resented the fact that the French army did little to help them when their country was attacked by the Nazis (Bernadac 1975, 17). Manuel Razola and Mariano Constante confirm that this was the atmosphere that greeted the French when large numbers of them were deported to Mauthausen in the spring of 1943, but they also point out that the Spaniards patiently fought this prejudice, which was detrimental to the consolidation of international solidarity, and that most Frenchmen had been sent to the camp because of their active resistance against the Nazis. "Some [Spanish] Socialists, republicans, and anarchists helped us bring about this change of opinion," write Razola and Constante (Razola/Constante 1969, 104 ff.). However, the German Karl Ludwig

Schecher writes, with reference to Dachau, that this development was not completely successful everywhere: "Anyone who might have believed that the resistance here would constitute a model for a united Europe would have been greatly disappointed. Among the foreigners in the camp, whose national life had been so severely affected by Hitler's brutal interventions and whose national pride had been hurt, an ever more clearly discernible nationalism developed."[7] Where there were only few politically aware prisoners who were able to counteract such an atmosphere, the weaker national groups suffered the most. "We were only a handful of Belgians and Frenchmen in the midst of a hostile group"—this is how the Belgian Léon Halkin has described the situation at the evacuation of Gross–Rosen on February 8, 1945 (Halkin 1965, 45). This was the camp in which the development of an international resistance had encountered the greatest difficulties.

Among both the French and the Czechs, there were more doctors than among other groups (with the exception of the Jews, only a small number of whom were employed in the camp hospitals—for example, in Auschwitz after the spring of 1943[8]—and were thus able to practice their profession.) There are reports about the successful activity of the French and Czech doctors in the hospitals of many camps.

In appreciative reports about prisoner doctors, one often encounters the name of Josef Podlaha, a professor at the University of Brno. SS men used him to treat members of their families.[9] When one of them, Willy Eckert, asked Podlaha at the end of a treatment what he wanted, evidently expecting a request for food or cigarettes, the doctor replied, "I want you to be less cruel when you beat prisoners" (Pappalettera 1972). In May 1942 he became physician-in-chief at the camp hospital (Maršàlek 1974, 142) and used this position for the benefit of many of his fellow prisoners.[10] The Russian Communist Valentin Sakharov writes that "under the direction of the outstanding Czech professor Podlaha, prisoner physicians saved many lives every day" (Sakharov 1961, 97). In fact, he finally "used the authority he enjoyed with the camp commandant to induce him to reduce the number of patients who were to be burned (immediately before the liberation of the camp)" (Sakharov 1961, 196). In this rescue action, Podlaha's colleague and compatriot, Vratislav Bušek, also distinguished himself; the Spaniard Juan de Diego has described him as a man of "particular bravery" who acted without contact with the secret organization in the camp.[11] The Frenchman Paul Tillard writes: "Among the prisoner doctors in the infirmary the French were the most numerous and the most experienced. Their medical knowledge gained them the respect of the SS doctors, who frequently consulted them. A case in point was Dr. Quenouille, born in 1884, who used this respect to procure many benefits for the patients." Hundreds owe their lives to this man (Tillard 1945, 58 ff.). Reports about positive activities of prisoner physicians in the Dachau infirmary usually include the name of the Czech doctor Frantisek Bláha; the Austrian Father Lenz describes him as the only physician who could be asked for advice (Lenz 1956, 258). Albert Guérisse (O'Leary), who headed the Dachau resistance movement in its final phase, states that Bláha helped endangered men by giving them the prison numbers of dead men.[12] In reports about the terrible last months of Bergen–Belsen, one encounters the name of G. L. Fréjafon, a French medical man. "We 'westerners' in particular were pleased finally to have a doctor from our midst in the infirmary who broke the 'eastern monopoly.' " This statement by the Luxembourger Pierre Petit, who describes Fréjafon as "helpful and full of human understanding," also indicates national conflicts among the hospital personnel at Bergen–Belsen (Petit 1965–68).

The list of doctors who are fondly remembered by many could be greatly extended and, of course, supplemented with names of members of other nationalities: Polish doctors in Auschwitz, particularly Władysław Fejkiel, the last senior camp inmate in the hospital building (Langbein 1972, 247 ff.); the Yugoslav doctor Nadja Persic in Ravensbrück, who saved patients from selections by making false diagnoses (Saint-Clair 1960, 221); the Polish doctor Maria Grabska, who joined Persic in removing the prison numbers tattooed in Auschwitz so the camp could not locate Austrian women slated to die;[13] and her Russian colleague Lyuba Semiovna Konnikova, who in defiance of all reprisals and torture refused to work in an arms factory (Bernadac 1972, 197 ff.; *Die Frauen von Ravensbrück* 1961, 148). Twelve prisoners in Sachsenhausen of ten different nationalities wrote immediately after their liberation: "Through the activity of some internationally known (prisoner) doctors, the patients received considerable help. Thanks to their initiative, the International Red Cross made valuable medicines available to the camp."[14]

Although the list of doctors who refused to carry out the orders of the SS and did their sworn duty even in Nazi concentration camps is bound to remain incomplete, it must include the name of the French physician Adelaide Hautval, who openly refused to participate in the pseudomedical experiments of the SS in Auschwitz (Langbein 1972, 264 ff.). After she had testified about them in a London court, the judge called her "perhaps one of the most impressive and most courageous women who have ever testified in a British court of law" (Hill/Williams 1965, 255).

Officers of the Czech Communist Party established contact with comrades very quickly. Thus the Austrian official Hans Pointner writes about Sachsenhausen: "We were able to connect with our Czech comrades very rapidly, because we had some well-known comrades here."[15] This also applies to Buchenwald, and Pointner's compatriot Otto Horn writes: "It was relatively simple to make contact with our Czech comrades. There were a number of personal connections from the time when German anti-Fascists lived in Czechoslovakia as emigrants."[16] In Mauthausen, Artur London, a Czech who had fought in the Spanish Civil War, had no trouble gaining the confidence of the Spaniards active in the resistance. Hans Maršàlek reports from his own experience that "between February and March 1944 an underground executive group was formed in the main camp with the help of French Communists and the Czech Communist Artur London, who had come from France"—in spite of German Communist functionaries, who had earlier been of the opinion that camp conditions did not permit an international form of organization. Maršàlek was himself a member of this group (Maršàlek 1974, 258 ff.). The French Communist Michel de Bouard remembers that after the arrival of London, who spoke all the languages important in the camp, a Czech group was formed that had contact with other national groups (Bernadac 1974, 269). Artur London himself describes how, thanks to the young Spaniard Constante, he had immediate contact with other veterans of the Spanish Civil War as well as comrades of various nationalities (Razola/Constante 1969, 119). To be sure, London's name is no longer found in a number of publications issued after the notorious trials in Czechoslovakia in the early 1950s, for that is when London was sentenced and regarded as an "unperson" by Communists who followed the party line. Thus the Russian Communist Valentin Sakharov, who gives numerous names, only mentions the "connection with the underground Czechs" (Sakharov 1961, 80), and Franz Dahlem, a top official of the German Communist Party, who knew London well from the international brigades in Spain and worked with him again in Mauthausen, also suppresses his name (Document Notes 1979, 110). The Frenchman Jean Lafitte mentions Drahomír Bárta, a young Czech Communist student who worked in the office at Ebensee and, aided by his extensive knowledge of languages, promoted an international organization in that large satellite camp of Mauthausen (Lafitte 1970, 254 ff.). From Ravensbrück there is a report that German Communist women promptly helped Czech comrades obtain positions, thus giving them an opportunity for effective activity.[17]

Evidently prominent French Communists could not be smoothly integrated into the organizations led by their German comrades—probably as a result of the popular-front policy, which in France was seen as resulting in the victory of Fascism in Germany. The French Communists felt more independent and flexible than the monolithic German Communists had been in the pre-Hitler period.

We have detailed reports about conflicts in Buchenwald. When large numbers of Frenchmen arrived there in the summer of 1943 and big transports further augmented this ethnic group in January 1944 and thereafter,[18] "only the minority group of French Communists established close contact with the internal camp leadership." The others were, according to Eugen Kogon's observations, "incredibly splintered" (Kogon 1946, 376).

Frédéric Manhès, who later headed the French group, confirms that Communists were the first to make contact with other national groups. The others, who have been designated as "Gaullists" (according to Manhès, often not justifiably so), found this much more difficult, for there was a tendency to form a unified anti-Communist group. In early February 1944, however, a four-man executive committee was created—"luckily for us and for these inept people," as Manhès puts it. This committee provided the leaders of other nationalities (and here Manhès evidently has German Communists in mind) with the assurance that those Frenchmen who did not belong to the Communist Party were "loyal to republican ideas." In June of that year this group merged with the Communists to form a united French organization (Manhès n.d., 18 ff.). It was probably this merger that led members of those national groups still in contact with the French, if only for reasons of language, to believe that the Frenchmen, including the Communists, were "in a certain conflict with the Germans"[19] and that there had in fact been power struggles.[20] These differences were caused by the more flexible attitude of French Communists, who recognized the need to respect different ideologies of fellow sufferers. Hence Günther Kühn and Wolfgang Weber, who emphasize the Communist character of the secret military organization, also feel impelled to speak of a "specifically French organization of military mass resistance after the pattern of the Résistance in France" (Kuhn/Weber 1976, 429). Frédéric Manhès, whose presentation may be regarded as a sort of accounting, writes that although the German Communists, who dominated the internal administration of Buchenwald at a time when large numbers of Frenchmen arrived, invited other national organizations to form military groups, they regarded themselves as in charge—responsible for the entire international military organization and for the planning of actions. However, as Manhès reports with some pride, in June 1944 the French managed to get this scheme revised: The defensive plan devised by the Germans was to give way to more offensive actions, and the cadres were to be expanded. Though Manhès does not directly mention it, this seems to have involved greater use of non-Communist experts, particularly officers (Manhès n.d., 44 ff.). Evidently the French Communists and their leader, Marcel Paul, played an important part in the adoption of this new perspective. Shortly before the liberation of Buchenwald, Paul started a discussion among the leaders of the international organization to ascertain whether the time was ripe for an attack on the camp administration. The Germans thought it was certain that the camp would be neither destroyed nor evacuated and that they should therefore postpone such an action, "but events proved the French right" (Manhès n.d., 47 ff.). Thousands, including numerous Frenchmen, were evacuated from Buchenwald at the last moment, and for many this meant death. According to Manhès, the French pressed their point to the very end (Manhès n.d., 50 ff.). The leadership of the French organization that was installed in June 1944 was composed of representatives of thirty-four regional and political groups (Manhès n.d., 57 ff.)—proof of the great diversity in this organization and also of the special opportunities in Buchenwald, a camp internally dominated by Reds. In most other camps the need for secrecy would have precluded such an extensive organization. Finally, Manhès can report that, six days after the liberation, the activity of the French leadership was unanimously approved by the remaining Frenchmen in Buchenwald (Manhès n.d. 60 ff.).

The Pole Wincenty Hein observed that in Dora, whose resistance movement was influenced by Buchenwald's, the French national committee went "its own way," for it had been organized by adherents of Charles de Gaulle.[21] The numerically strong French group in Dora included only a small number of Communists; according to the Poles Wacław Czarnecki and Zygmunt Zonik, most of them were Gaullists, and these had no contact with the "German anti-Fascists"—presumably meaning the group led by German Communists (Zarnecki 1973 220, 224). In Buchenwald, French Communists were protected by the German resistance movement, but it did nothing to keep large numbers of other Frenchmen from being transferred to dreaded Dora. As has already been pointed out, no organization of prisoners was able to save everyone from being transferred to a bad detail and therefore always had to choose those whom it wanted to give special protection.[22]

Michel de Bouard remembers that in early summer of 1944 the Communist resistance in Mauthausen attempted to organize non-Communists too in the various national groups. "I believe that the French were the first who responded to this appeal," writes de Bouard and names four Frenchmen, including himself, who formed an expanded leadership and maintained contact with the Communist-led organization (Bouard 1954, 71). In Gusen, where the opportunities for the development of an organization were still much more favorable than in the Mauthausen base camp, the French cleric Père Jacques helped many through his personal efforts—materially to the extent of his very limited opportunities, but especially morally. He also established a good connection with the Poles, who occupied more influential positions than the French (Bouard 1962, 62 ff.).

As far as is known, in Sachsenhausen the collaboration of the German Communists with the Czechs and the French was probably limited to the Communist functionaries. Heinz Schumann reports that internationally known officers of the Czech Communist Party quickly made contact with their German comrades. "Just one day after the arrival of the first group of Czech comrades (on November 20, 1939) we met for a discussion in barracks No. 65. Antonin Zápotocky, Jaromir Dolanský, and Ernst Schneller [a leading German Communist in the resistance movement—H.L.] already knew one another from their earlier activity in the international workers' movement and from congresses."

Together these men indoctrinated a group of Czech students, "sons of the bourgeoisie who regarded living together with Communist workingmen as undesirable" (Damals in Sachsenhausen 1967, 86 ff.). They seem to have succeeded in this endeavor, for when these students were released before Christmas 1941—"An unexpected event.... Never before have such a large number of prisoners been released," writes Fritz Selbmann, who also mentions spirited discussions, in the pathology section, "between Czech bourgeois students and German Communists" (Selbmann 1961, 190)—German and Czech Communists arranged a political farewell party that was characterized as an "assembly" and evidently showed the fruits of this political indoctrination. Selbmann merely describes how the students acknowledged the speech of a German Communist with applause and shouts (Selbmann 1961, 195), but a propagandistic publication states that after the German's address, a Czech philosophy student promised in the name of all the students in attendance "that they would all work toward the victory of progressive forces in Czechoslovakia" (Rossa 1959, 59).

The first major transports of Frenchmen arrived in Sachsenhausen in the summer of 1943.[23] On October 11, 1944, the SS staged a mass execution in an attempt to smash all resistance activities of the prisoners, and three "French comrades" were shot, together with twenty-four Germans (Damals in Sachsenhausen 1967, 99). The designation "comrades" seems to indicate that the French were Communists, whose collaboration with the Germans was sealed by their common death.

Resistance activity on the part of the Frenchmen deported to Dachau began under different conditions. When large numbers of French Reds began arriving there in June 1944, around 100 leading Communists had been transferred to other concentration camps, having been betrayed to the camp administration by informers (Schätzle 1946, 34 ff.). At that time Edmond Michelet had already been in Dachau for a year. Since he had been part of the Catholic movement in France, he soon established contact with German and Austrian Catholics in Dachau. By obtaining for him a position in the disinfection detail, they enabled him to help his compatriots who arrived later, and his effective aid gave him great authority among these.[24] According to Michelet, the Communists "shrewdly" attempted to choose as the French representative in the international organization (dominated by them) a French fellow traveler, but the Frenchmen never bowed to their authority. General Delestraint became their representative, and after he had been shot by the SS, his place was taken by Michelet (Michelet 1955, 214). Joseph Rovan has made an interesting statement in this connection: The activities of the French Communists obliged those Frenchmen who refused to subordinate themselves to them to form an organization of their own.[25] Albert Guérisse remembers that finally, in late 1944, an international organization was established that had contact with the Communist-led one (which had existed for a long time). According to Guérisse, "the Communists later put out the story that they had created this organization, which was recognized by the Americans after the liberation."[26] Mentioning all Frenchmen or Czechs who played a role in the camps would be beyond the confines of this study, but I shall name the French Communist Marthe Desrumeaux, whose attitude and activity in Ravensbrück has been emphasized not only by those sharing her ideology.[27] Margarete Buber-Neumann, who was ostracized and even persecuted by the Communist organization in that camp, has called her a "fabulous exception" who was "charming" to her, though Desrumeaux must have known that Buber-Neumann had been arrested under Stalin and deported to Hitler's Germany.[28]

In Mauthausen the international resistance movement managed to remove a criminal from the post of chief clerk and obtain this key position for the Czech Kuneš Pany. Pany did "outstanding work for the movement" and was even able to smuggle weapons into the camp (Maršàlek n.d., 20, 39). Michel de Bouard speaks of the "immeasurable services" rendered to the organization by Pany (Bovard, 1954, 270). Even people who did not share his ideology have praised his conduct, and his compatriot Vratislav Bušek, who is generally critical of the activity of Communists in Mauthausen, has said that "his behavior was above reproach."[29]

When a new satellite camp was established at Melk in April 1944, the resistance movement saw to it that a group of Frenchmen was transferred there and reliable comrades occupied the most important positions. André Ulmann, who adopted the name Antonin Pichon and thus managed to conceal his Jewishness from the SS, served as camp clerk and was able to maintain contact with the secret organization in the Mauthausen base camp. Several French Communists have reported that in Melk they managed to form a unified organization nationally as well as internationally, including both Catholics and Gaullist officers. Ulmann is said to have played a decisive role in this (Bernadac 197, 320, 327 ff., 330; Bovard 1954, 267). When Russian troops approached, the inmates of this subsidiary camp were evacuated to Ebensee, and the French group brought the resistance organization there valuable reinforcement. At the initiative of

Communists a "national front" had been formed in Ebensee in the spring of 1944, which collaborated with other national groups. It was led by a Frenchman, a Czech, and a Yugoslav (Bernadac 1976, 248 ff.). Frenchmen pursued the same course in the satellite camp Loiblpass: "We have formed a group without regard for the political orientation of the members. It is normal that Communists should take the initiative"—if only because they established contacts with Russian and Polish Communists, who in turn were in touch with Slovenian partisans operating in the nearby mountains. "We call our organization National Front, and its members are not only Communists but also Gaullists, Socialists, and those who belong to no group. The only criterion is patriotism" (Lacaze 1978, 256 ff.). Similar reports have been made by Frenchmen who were interned in the satellite camp Linz (Bernadac 1976, 156 ff.).

If the participation of other nationals is not given equally detailed treatment here, this is not intended to indicate that their contributions were insignificant. In another connection we shall give the names of courageous, resolute, and resourceful individuals who took an important part in frustrating plans of the SS and improving the situation of their companions in misfortune, or at least keeping the situation from getting worse. Let us briefly indicate a few problems of these ethnic groups here.

We have already mentioned that Spaniards were deported primarily to Mauthausen, where they played an outstanding role in forming action groups against the camp administration. In the early period their ranks were horribly decimated; of around 7,500 who arrived there between 1940 and 1942, 4,200 were killed by the end of 1942. Groups of prisoners that arrived later had to suffer the fate of those whom the SS forced onto the lowest rung of the ladder. Hans Maršàlek, the chronicler of Mauthausen, does point to different political ideologies as well as to separatist endeavors among the Spaniards; in addition to anarchists, Socialists, and Communists, there were middle-class democrats and syndicalists as well as Catalan and Basque separatists in the camp. However, all this was transcended by "a shared boundless love of their homeland and hatred of Franco's and Hitler's system." Their military discipline enabled them to adapt to the conditions of camp life more easily than others, and their solidarity gained them great respect (Maršàlek 1974, 294 ff.). Drahomír Bárta, a Czech who was one of the leaders of the resistance in Ebensee, emphasizes both the camp experience and the special skills and firm cohesiveness of the Spanish group, qualities that enabled it to do valuable work.[30] Other concentration camps housed only a small number of Spaniards, but this is true of these as well. Thus David Rousset states that the Spaniards he encountered in satellite camps of Neuengamme were distinguished by very good cohesiveness.[31] However, as Jorge Semprun reports, the Spaniards who headed the national party organization in Buchenwald were nevertheless subjected to Russian-style proceedings and sentenced after the liberation (Semprun 1978, 129).

Only a small number of Norwegians were sent to National Socialist concentration camps, and since the SS regarded them as "Nordic people" they were given preferential treatment there. In January 1944, 349 students at the University of Oslo were deported to Buchenwald and housed separately from the other prisoners. "They kept their civilian clothes, were given the same food as the SS men, and for several months received instruction and political indoctrination by the SS. Not a single one of them volunteered for duty with the SS." After the failure of this attempt at indoctrination, which was unique in the annals of the concentration camps, they were assigned to heavy labor building entrenchments.[32] Many informants have stressed their solidarity with their comrades living under far harsher conditions. Thus Otto Horn writes that "a good relationship" developed between the Norwegians "and many other nations, though for linguistic and social reasons these students were strangers to the great majority of camp inmates."[33] When children were sent to Buchenwald, these students gave "many of the things they received from the International Red Cross to the little ones, who were always hungry and mortally malnourished" (Konzentrationslager Buchenwald 1945, 24). Leo Eitinger reports that these students also smuggled weapons into the camps when they had to carry wounded men there after bombardments.[34]

The effect of the students' extraordinary behavior has been described most incisively by Leo Eitinger, a Jew who emigrated from Czechoslovakia to Norway, was deported to Auschwitz, and after the evacuation of that camp was transferred to Buchenwald: "They were all kindly and friendly. It is a strange experience to be treated as a human being again. They consider it their duty to help whenever possible."[35] Similar acts of solidarity by Norwegians have been reported from Sachsenhausen, e.g., by Pierre Grégoire: "The Norwegians, who seem to be drowning in Red Cross donations, have agreed to share some of their surplus with the sick and infirm" (Stein 1946, 177). Karl Raddatz reports that "with the approval of the camp administration, the Norwegians have regularly placed their surplus Red Cross packages at the disposal of the Russian prisoners of war."[36] Following the Russian victory at Stalingrad, "Norwegian inmates made part of their food available" for a celebration (Damals in Sachsenhausen 1967, 95 ff.). In Dachau too, Norwegian students made a positive impression. Karl

Ludwig Schecher, a German, is among those who have called them "exemplary in their general attitude."[37]

It was similar with the Yugoslavs. Most of them had participated in partisan struggles before their arrest, and thus they were physically tough and continued to regard themselves as fighters. There were few of them, but as the Pole Mieczysław Mołdawa has written about the Gross–Rosen camp, they were the most popular (Mołdawa 1967, 155). There is a report that the inmates of Buchenwald viewed this group, which became numerically somewhat stronger after fall 1943, with favor (Buchenwald 1960, 432). To be sure, it has been stated that the Yugoslav group was more differentiated than others "linguistically, religiously, and as far as their original environment was concerned" (Buchenwald 1960, 428). On the basis of his observations in Mauthausen, Hans Maršàlek formulates this even more clearly: "Among the Yugoslavs there were two groups. The majority of these prisoners were adherents of Tito; there also were adherents of the Chetnik general Mihajlović; and differences existed between Croats and Serbs as well" (Maršàlek 1974, 256).

All other national groups had problems of their own. The only reason why these are not detailed here is that they played no great part in international resistance activities.

We have repeatedly referred to one difficulty that runs through the entire history of the international secret organizations of all camps: the aversion to all Germans that many people felt on the basis of their experiences with National Socialism. An effort to combat these feelings of resentment is clearly evidenced by a camp newspaper published by the Czech group eight days after the liberation of Buchenwald. The headline "Our Relationship with Our German Comrades" is followed by this admonition: "Let us not forget that the majority of our German comrades who occupied leading positions in the camp had been there for years because of their anti-Fascist attitude and their struggle against Nazis." After emphasizing their contributions, the article concludes as follows: "It is necessary to view our German comrades in this light. For this reason we would like our relationship with our German comrades to remain a good one to the end" (Das war Buchenwald n.d., 124).

15

GROUPS IN A SPECIAL POSITION

Other groups were distinguished not by their nationality but by the reasons for their internment, and hence they occupied a specific position in resistance against the SS.

Beginning in 1937, German Jehovah's Witnesses were sent to concentration camps, evidently in the course of general preparations for war, for they were conscientious objectors to any military service, and the National Socialists feared that they might influence others in that direction. Those who signed a pledge to obey all orders of the authorities, including military service, were released "after a considerable period of time, and later immediately" (Höss 1958, 74 ff.; Kogon 1946, 264). At the beginning of the war they were expressly called upon to perform military service. "For each person that refused, ten were shot [in Sachsenhausen—H.L.] After forty victims, the SS gave up" (Kogon 1946, 265). Twelve inmates who remained in the camp at the evacuation in 1945 could still remember the public execution of August Dickmann, a German Jehovah's Witness, who refused to serve when war broke out.[1] Rudolf Höss, at that time adjutant of the commandant of Sachsenhausen, has described the "delight and rapture" with which two Jehovah's Witnesses went to be executed. "This is how I imagined the early Christian martyrs," writes Höss about the conduct of these men (Höss 1958, 73). The Jehovah's Witnesses were threatened with shooting in Buchenwald as well, but when all of them refused to sign the declaration, they were only forced to do punitive labor and barred from treatment in the prison hospital (Kogon 1946, 265).

A few typical examples may illustrate the steadfastness of this group of inmates. In 1942 the German farmer Ernst Raddatz, an inmate of Neuengamme, refused to sign a military service agreement, though he was assured that his signature would cause him to be released and enable him to resume his farming without being called up (Poel 1948, 105 ff.). In Ravensbrück, where many hundreds of Dutch Jehovah's Witnesses had been sent, Heinrich Himmler noticed a beautiful young Dutchwoman

178

and, evidently because of her "Germanic" appearance, personally invited her to renounce her faith, but she was brave enough to refuse the Reichsführer-SS.[2] Hans Maršàlek reports that on September 29, 1939, a few weeks after the outbreak of the war, "the first and largest group of German and Austrian Jehovah's Witnesses, 144 persons" arrived in Mauthausen. At first these people were subject to "systematic liquidation," and this did not cease until March 1940, when large numbers of Poles were brought to the camp and now engaged the attention of the SS. In late December 1944, there were eighty-five Jehovah's Witnesses in Mauthausen—forty-six Germans or Austrians, thirty-six Poles, and three Czechs. Over the years only six German or Austrian Jehovah's Witnesses were released. From this it may be concluded that only such a small number were willing to join the Wehrmacht; the SS was not so interested in having non-Germans sign a pledge to this effect. Other inmates did not have a "particular relationship of trust" to the Jehovah's Witnesses, but Maršàlek describes them as generally "helpful." They "were a community of quiet, modest, disciplined, tolerant, industrious people who were devoted to their faith" (Maršàlek 1974, 219 ff.). The Pole Stanisław Nogaj emphasizes the outstanding solidarity and camaraderie of the Jehovah's Witnesses, which he learned to appreciate in Gusen.[3]

Despite their small numbers, the Jehovah's Witnesses as a rule made a positive impression in other camps as well. In Auschwitz there were hardly more than two dozen men and a somewhat larger number of women; in August 1944, 122 of the latter were counted. Those whom I met personally there or about whom I heard were invariably "proper, helpful, and friendly; they unmistakably rejected National Socialism and did not let their privileged position corrupt them" (Langhein 1972, 280).

This privileged position was the result of their principle not to escape. According to the commandant of Auschwitz, "they needed no supervisors or guards. They did their work industriously and willingly, for this was Jehovah's commandment." For this reason they were given service positions "in the homes of SS families with many children, in the building of the Waffen-SS [military arm of the SS], and even in the commandant's home. Höss voices one regret: "Unfortunately there weren't enough of them"—older German women and younger Dutchwomen. There were "strange creatures" among them, as Höss put it: "One served an SS leader and anticipated his every wish, but as a matter of principle she refused to clean uniforms, caps, boots, and anything connected with the military; in fact, she never even touched such things" (Höss 1958, 113).

Understandably, opinions about Jehovah's Witnesses vary in accordance with the personal experiences of the observer. Whereas Provost Heinrich Grüber describes their conduct in Sachsenhausen as exemplary (Grüber

1968, 153 ff.), and Julius Freund writes that the Jehovah's Witnesses in Buchenwald constituted a real combat group against the Nazis (Freund 1945, 129), the Dutchman Wijnen believes that in the struggle between the Reds and the Greens, they were on the side of the political prisoners, though as a kind of "negative appendage."[4]

Margarete Buber-Neumann probably got to know the Jehovah's Witnesses best, for she was their senior block inmate in Ravensbrück for almost two years. She has given an account of around 600 of them, "Germans, except for a few Dutchwomen." They were the only "unified ideological community" that Buber-Neumann encountered in Ravensbrück. "The camp management could not imagine more ideal slaves as regards their devotion to duty, industriousness, absolute honesty, and strictest obedience to all SS commands." (Buber-Neumann 1958, 244 ff.). However, their religious persuasion forbade them to do any work in the service of war, though the interpretation and scope of this commandment were not certain. Following a heated discussion between fanatics and moderates, some ninety Jehovah's Witnesses refused to continue working in the Angora-breeding and gardening details, because the wool was being used for military purposes and the vegetables were being sent to an SS field hospital. This refusal, which had hitherto been inconceivable in a concentration camp, caused them to be locked up in a bare rooms without jackets and blankets, to be whipped, and to be fed only every fourth day (except for bread), but they stuck with their refusal. "They were walking skeletons covered with welts. Undernourishment had given them dysentery, and they looked like mental patients," writes Buber-Neumann (Buber-Neumann 1958, 278 ff.). They were finally transferred to Auschwitz,[5] and it is easy to guess what fate they suffered there.

We know about other refusals to work, too. Thus Jehovah's Witnesses in Ravensbrück "categorically refused to produce sewing kits for the Wehrmacht or to unload straw for army horses" (Die Frauen von Ravensbrück 1961, 147). Hermine Jursa, an Austrian, has reported that because of a woman's refusal to appear for roll call, Jehovah's Witnesses were doused with cold water and locked up in a bunker.[6] Buber-Neumann recalls a Second Adventist who was shot for refusing to work on Sundays,[7] and Jean Michel tells about a Russian Jehovah's Witness in Dora who refused to participate in the manufacture of arms (Michel 1975, 218 ff.). Other than that, only isolated instances of pointblank refusal to work—on the part of Russians—have become known. Only one of these, occurring shortly before the collapse of the Third Reich, was not followed by reprisals. After Amstetten, a satellite camp of Mauthausen, had been bombed by the Allies on March 20, 1945, a female labor detail refused to return to that camp, and the camp commandant was apprised of this by "a delegation consisting of several Frenchwomen and an Englishwoman." Hans Mar-šàlek goes on to say that "this was the first open and successful refusal to work that had no deleterious consequences. Some time earlier, such an action would inevitably have meant the killing of the entire delegation" (Maršàlek 1974, 264 ff.). Eugen Kogon writes that, on New Year's Day 1942, the Jehovah's Witnesses in Buchenwald were punished by being deprived of their undergarments and leather shoes and assigned particularly hard labor because they had unanimously declined to make a contribution toward woolen clothes for the German troops on the eastern front, something that all inmates had been urged to do (Kogon 1946, 265). Otto Horn believes that this incident occurred in 1943.[8]

The German Johann Wrobel, who worked as a foreman on the garage-building detail in Sachsenhausen, has testified that two Jehovah's Witnesses refused an SS man's order to "baptize" an old Jew on that detail, as the SS man put it, whereupon the latter drowned his victim himself by holding the Jew's head under water until he was dead.[9]

There are repeated mentions of female Jehovah's Witnesses whose friendly and humane conduct was morally uplifting to others. Erich Kret-schmer, himself a Jehovah's Witness, did more than that; together with the German Communist Robert Siewert, he helped children in Buchenwald, who were imprisoned in a separate block (Korschak 1968).

There is less information about the behavior of the Gypsies in the concentration camps, for they were more isolated than others. In accordance with a directive from the Central Security Office, dated January 29, 1943, a section of Auschwitz–Birkenau was established as a Gypsy camp, and whole families were interned there—a process hitherto unknown (Czech 1959–64). Apart from Ravensbrück, where large numbers of Gypsy women had been interned as early as 1939[10] and where those inmates of Birkenau were finally transferred who were to be exempted from the general liquidation in early August 1944, there were no appreciable number of Gypsies in the camps. It would be wrong to regard the internment of entire families as an indication that the situation of the Gypsies was easier than that of other inmates. In the first winter of the war, the Gypsies from the Austrian province Burgenland furnished "a particularly high proportion" of the large number of casualties in Buchenwald.[11] Even by Birkenau standards, the conditions in the family camp were catastrophic.

On one occasion the SS sentenced Georgette Ducasse, a Frenchwoman imprisoned in Buchenwald, to twenty-five blows. Gypsy women who were supposed to administer this punishment "categorically refused and declared that they were prisoners, just as I was" (Bernadac 1972, 268).

Another Frenchwoman, Simone Saint-Clair, wrote in her secret diary in Ravensbrück on November 23, 1944, that "there was a revolt in the camp." Gypsy women did not observe the discipline of the roll call because their children had been taken away from them, and they were put on a transport (Saint-Clair 1966, 132).

The SS called it "liquidation of the Gypsy camp in Birkenau," and when the Gypsies were loaded on trucks that were to carry them to the gas chambers, there evidently were desperate attempts at resistance. None of the victims were around to report about it later, but other inmates who had contact with the Gypsy camp heard cries like "Criminals!" and "Murderers!" and they remember that shots rang out and that they saw blood in the empty section the next morning (Langbein 1965, 523, 527, 109). How many heroic attempts to resist this murderous action of the SS have remained obscure?

There were other inmates that should be considered separately as a group, though they belonged to various nations—those volunteers for the international brigades who fought Fascism in Spain and after the defeat of the Spanish democracy were forced into Nazi concentration camps because the way to their homelands was cut off.

On May 1, 1941, a group of Austrian veterans of the Spanish Civil War arrived in Dachau. Edgar Kupfer-Koberwitz, who was politically unaffiliated and thus may be trusted to make objective judgments, emphasizes that these men were well liked and therefore drew good details, something that I can confirm from my own experience. "Their camaraderie was still regarded as exemplary, and so was their solidarity" (Fréjafon 1954, 59; Langbein 1949, 43). Pierre Grégoire, a Luxembourger imprisoned in Sachsenhausen, put it in similar terms: "The Red Spain fighters [the SS term—H.L.] are already the darlings of the leading *dii minores* [lesser gods, the political prisoners, who were occupying key positions—H.L.]. Vacant prominent positions were theirs. Together with their spiritual brothers, the Communist functionaries, they enjoy some privileges" (Stein 1946, 157 ff.). When the SS roll-call officer, referring to twelve newly arrived veterans of the Spanish Civil War, threatened that "in six weeks all of them will be gone," the men were saved by first being hidden and then put on a transport to Neuengamme (Ahrens 1968, 96). The Pole Wacław Czarnecki writes that, in Buchenwald and other camps, veterans of the Spanish Civil War were instrumental in facilitating contacts with newly arrived international groups (Czarnecki 1968, 53). Jean Pierre Schmit, a Luxembourger, observed that the Spanish veterans formed a separate group that was not always in accord with "the others" (evidently meaning the dominant

German Communists). According to Schmit, this group included not only Germans and Austrians but also a large number of Czechs. Both Schmit and his compatriot, Leo Bartimes, especially mention a man named Seidel, who gave them his support.[12] A statement by Alfred Hammerl, an Austrian veteran of the Spanish Civil War, indicates that in Dachau, where many Austrian members of the international brigades were interned, these also formed a separate closed group. Hammerl learned about the successful escape of his friend Sepp Plieseis, a Spanish veteran from Ischl, from an outside detail near Hallein, and the news of this escape acted "like a spark." He and his friend Leo Jansa secured, "from the party," permission to flee. Jansa remembers that he probably "discussed it with Peter Loisl"— also an Austrian member of the international brigades. Hammerl and Jansa then talked over their plan "only with our Austrian Spanish veterans," and they organized their escape from the same outside detail to which they had managed to be transferred. This escape was successful as well.[13] Heribert Kreuzmann, another Austrian veteran of the Spanish Civil War, also speaks of a "party section of Austrian Spaniaken," as these veterans were frequently called.[14] In a report of the Austrian committee, written immediately after the liberation of Buchenwald, we read that experienced soldiers or veterans of the Spanish Civil War were particularly prized in the creation of a secret military organization, for these "constituted the foundation of a military group."[15]

We have already referred to the special significance of these veterans in the Mauthausen resistance movement, which had been started by Spaniards. This is also emphasized by Vicenzo Pappalettera, an Italian who arrived in Gusen with a group of his compatriots in February 1944. The solidarity of Italian veterans of the Spanish Civil War helped them overcome the initial difficulties (Pappalettera 1972, 211). Hans Maršàlek, who does not shirk touchy questions, stresses that "the small group of veterans of the international brigades, who had close contact with the Spaniards and acted as liaisons to their national communities . . . constituted a solid supranational block of staunch anti-Fascists." Maršàlek points out, however, that within this group of "predominantly Communist activists" there were "heated arguments." These arguments concerned such matters as their volunteering to return to Germany from French camps (in accordance with a directive of the Communist Party, issued after Hitler's occupation of France and before his attack on the Soviet Union) as well as measures taken by their military leadership, shortly before the members of the international brigades crossed into France in February 1939 (Maršàlek 1974, 250).

The group of Spanish Civil War veterans also included Jews. The SS lumped these together with others who were persecuted for "racial" reasons, but the non-Jewish (and thus far better off) former members of the international brigades helped them in comradely fashion and hence often constituted a link between "Aryans" and Jews who had decided to resist. This became most evident in Auschwitz, where the greatest numbers of Jews were transferred from other camps after fall 1942. It is not possible to determine their total number in the camp, for the SS did not list the "Aryan" veterans of the international brigades separately either; rather, like other political prisoners, they had to wear a red triangle. Also, some Spanish veterans died in Auschwitz before their comrades learned of their arrival and had a chance to help them. Only in isolated instances did this become known at a later date, and a list of twenty-two Polish veterans of the Spanish Civil War was compiled from memory. Most of these had lived in France before the outbreak of that war, and were sent from France to Auschwitz on Jewish transports. Austrian veterans of the Spanish Civil War remember thirteen comrades, six of whom had to wear the Star of David and four of whom did not survive Auschwitz. Rudi Friemel, who was in the camp as an "Aryan," was hanged because of his resistance activity.[16] The leadership of the Combat Group Auschwitz included a Spanish veteran,[17] and among its activists greatest credit is given to such veterans—frequently Jews, who were at far greater risk and yet fully participated in resistance activities.[18] Alter Feinsylberg, a Polish veteran of Spain, has stated that the need for a resistance organization in Birkenau was first articulated by Spanish veterans (presumably Jews) who knew one another from an earlier period.[19]

Istvan Balogh, a Hungarian veteran of the Spanish Civil War, reports that a small group of fellow veterans—Romanian Jews—was systematically murdered by the SS in Mauthausen. When these men could no longer have any doubt about the fate decreed for them, they decided to die with dignity. Intoning the Internationale, six survivors marched toward a watchtower on October 11, 1940, and when they disregarded the guards' cries of "Halt!" they were killed by machine-gun fire (Strzelecka 1973, 71 ff.). Balogh mentions that he was a member of the Spanish Communist Party in Mauthausen—further proof of the political closeness of Civil War veterans to the Spaniards interned there (Bernadac 1974, 99 ff.).

It was the Jews in the extermination camps who finally dared to engage in armed struggle with the powerful murderers. The uprisings in Treblinka, the special detail at Auschwitz,[20] and the best-organized rebellion in Sobibor will be discussed at a later point. Suffice it to say here that veterans of the Spanish Civil War were involved in planning both the uprising in Auschwitz and the heroic revolt in Sobibor (Ainsztein 1974, 752).

Acts of resistance in the camps repeatedly include veterans of the Spanish Civil War. Though few in number even in relation to those imprisoned for political reasons, they played a role whose significance cannot be disregarded. One reason is that, on their own, they had taken up the task of fighting Fascism. By volunteering for the international brigades, they made plain the international character of the Spanish struggle. Their appreciation of international collaboration was an immense help in thwarting the camp administrations' deliberate practice of setting one nationality against another.

The SS also endeavored to infect the inmates with its murderous anti-Semitism and frowned upon comradely contacts between "Aryans" and Jews, even punished them. The German Communist Willi Marker was on barracks duty in a Jewish block at Sachsenhausen whose inmates were, upon orders from the camp administration, subjected to indescribable tortures. "Since he, despite warnings, did everything in his power to ease the sufferings of the doomed men, he was replaced with a professional criminal, transferred to a punitive outfit, and hanged in the washroom a few nights later. On April 22, 1940, his wife received this announcement: 'Spouse committed suicide' " (Simon, 1974, 9). When, in the fall of 1943, I was denounced and locked in a bunker, one of the charges made against me was that I had had friendly relations with Jews and attempted to help them (Langbein 1949, 136). In a "Report of the Communist Party Group of the Jawiszowice Concentration Camp," which was issued shortly after the liberation of Buchenwald on May 16, 1945, we read: "Germans from the Reich were at first prohibited from having comradely relations with Jews."[21] This was a great additional impediment to the resistance activities of Jews. Furthermore, it should be noted that, with a few exceptions, Reds were persecuted because of their fight against German National Socialism, or at least because of their negative attitude toward it, whereas all Jews, regardless of their political orientation or activity, were classified as "racially inferior" by the Nuremberg Laws and were arrested, deported, and destined for extermination for that reason. It is to the Jews' everlasting credit that, despite this, many of them, surely far more than can be documented after the fact, participated in resistance activities.

After the organized pogrom of *Kristallnacht*, November 9–10, 1938, numerous Viennese Jews were sent to Dachau and tortured there. This gave rise to acts of solidarity, described by Ludwig Göring, a German political prisoner who was serving as the senior inmate of a Jewish block: "Among the arrivals there were rich Jews but also very poor ones. (In those days the Jews were not yet stripped of everything, and they were able to make purchases in the prisoner canteen.) Therefore the Jews, with the connivance of the block personnel, started communal kitties with payments from the moneyed Jews." When the camp administration got wind of this, it immediately acted "by confiscating the kitties, and the entire block personnel was punished."[22]

At a later date, when the systematic extermination of the Jews began, those allowed to live for as long as they were able to work were also harassed. They were immediately stripped of their entire property, and with rare exceptions they were not permitted to receive any parcels or remittances of cash. Since these Jews were concentrated in Auschwitz, most accounts of their conduct are from there, though they greatly vary in nature.

Erich Hoffmann, an inmate of the satellite camp Jawiszowice from August 1942 on, writes that of the 1,500 Jews interned there only a small number could be induced to join the resistance group, formed by about thirty Jewish Communists. Later around eighty joined and finally 140 young men in whose block Hoffmann had become the senior inmate (Schmidt 1958, 240 ff.). In the above Jawiszowice report Hoffmann refers to "a number of difficulties" which the party group had with the Jews, "most of whom were indifferent," for they had lost all hope, become resigned, and thought that waiting was the only thing they could do.[23] Heribert Kreuzmann, a cosigner of the report, emphasizes the particularly difficult situation of the Jews, whom he characterizes as weak-willed. According to him, "something could be done" only with those who had once had some contact with the workers' movement.[24] Hermann Joseph, a German, observed on the quarantine block in the Auschwitz main camp that the Polish Jews, who constituted the great majority there, "hated everybody" and "resisted being bossed around by western Jews. They were frightened people driven into a permanent panic by cruel experiences and suffering."[25] Sim Kessel, who had been deported from France, reached the conclusion in the base camp and in Jaworzno that the international Jewish solidarity, which Nazi propaganda depicted as dangerous under the catchword "world Jewry," was nothing but a myth. Whenever he was able to observe Jews banding together, these groups were formed according to nationality and together with non-Jews (Kessel 1970, 51). Eugène Garnier reports that a group of French Communists who established contact with the Combat Group Auschwitz consisted of "Aryans" and Jews (Garnier 1946, 178), and Jews from other countries were also active in this group. Here, too, veterans of the Spanish Civil War frequently acted as liaisons, and they were quickest to inspire the requisite relationship of trust (Langbein 1949, 68).

Harry Naujoks, the politically active senior camp inmate of Sachsenhausen, made observations that were similar to those made in Jawiszowice by Hoffmann. Young Jews gathered around a group of Jewish Communists.[26] Many of them were transferred to Auschwitz in October 1942, and there they sought contact with like-minded people who were active in the resistance.

Beginning in the spring of 1944, able-bodied Jews were transferred from Auschwitz to camps in Germany, where they were needed for the arms industry. After the evacuation of Auschwitz in January 1945, the number of Jews in German camps increased markedly. The Communist Emil Carlebach, one of the approximately 200 Jews who were requisitioned as skilled workers at Buchenwald in 1942 and thus escaped transfer to Auschwitz, writes that these Jews in the big transports "constituted a heterogeneous group and consequently had no leaders" (Buchenwald 1960, 130) and that "a considerable number of them had no experience with political resistance" (Carlebach 1969, 11). Carlebach does mention one exception: "The evacuation transport from Auschwitz–Monowitz had a pure, clear-sighted anti-Fascist leadership—our Buchenwald comrades who had been sent there two-and-a-half years earlier" (Buchenwald 1960, 130). The Jews deported from Buchenwald at that time formed the focal point of a resistance organization in Monowitz, a satellite camp of Auschwitz.[27] Curt Posener believes that while in Monowitz there was "no international camp committee on the Buchenwald pattern," there was a "group of politically reliable men" which was led "primarily by German and Polish Jews."[28] Gerhard Harig and Max Mayr, the statisticians of Buchenwald, counted 11,860 Jews who arrived in the overcrowded camp between May 24, 1944, and January 20, 1945,[29] the majority of them deported from Hungary or Siebenbürgen, which was part of Hungary at that time. In his description of the terrible conditions under which these new arrivals had to exist, Ernst Thape characterizes them as "very difficult people" and explains that once a person gets in a state of panic, he is helpless. On April 9, 1945, he made this diary entry about these unfortunates, who had been waiting for days to be transported to another camp: "The unbridled people pounce upon the food pail and the bread carts, and they pour the hot food, which they can't even swallow, all over one another, but there's no keeping them in check."[30] Here as everywhere, any generalization would be misleading, and this is proved by a statement by André Ulmann. A group of Hungarian Jews, large numbers of whom had been sent to Mauthausen and its subsidiary camp Melk, smuggled several loaded revolvers to Melk, and according to Ulmann, they were Communists. When Melk was evacuated, it was possible to take these weapons along to Ebensee (Bernadoc 1975, 333).

According to men active in Dora, Jews were admitted to a secret organization ("Dora" 1967, 18 ff.). A number of Russian officers were sent to Dachau because they had formed a secret organization in prisoner-of-war camps, and ninety-two of them were shot on September 4, 1944. The leaders among them were Jews (Guri 1965).[31] Israel Gutman has named Polish Jews who took a leading part in the Auschwitz resistance organization despite the virulent anti-Semitism of many Polish inmates. Gutman mentions one success of the common activity: Three Jewish activists were able to become block clerks, which gave them far greater opportunities for action (Gutman 1958, 158). In Herzogenbusch Jews were able to replace German criminals in leading positions, because the latter had completely discredited themselves even in the eyes of the camp administration. According to Presser, these Jews headed resistance activities, and in addition to Dutch Jews, he particularly praises the German jurist Dr. Lehmann (Presser 1968, 468, 477).

There was collaboration between "Aryan" and Jewish Poles in Buchenwald as well, as is evidenced by the fact that after the liberation three representatives of the Jewish group were included in the reconstituted Polish committee, which had been formed as part of the resistance.[32]

Just as a Communist orientation united many people, Zionism offered cohesion and moral support. Curt Posener mentions camouflaged afternoon and evening sessions of young Zionists in Monowitz, at which Jewish adults tried to give support to young people.[33] A Zionist youth organization was especially effective in the section of Birkenau that served as a family camp for deportees from Theresienstadt, where this organization had already established a solid structure and created a training program. These people were fated to be murdered in the gas chambers, but during the six months in which the inmates were allowed to live in this section under much easier conditions than the other inmates of Birkenau, this Zionist group endeavored to continue its activities. Fredy Hirsch, whose "Zionist idealism" had made him "an inspiring model, particularly for the smaller children" in Theresienstadt, did pioneer work in this regard (Adler 1960, 548 ff.). Since his reasonably well-groomed appearance and his Prussian discipline "had always satisfied and even impressed the Germans," he became the camp capo and was eventually allowed to get the children together and establish a school of sorts for them. German was taught for the sake of the SS, which often inspected the children's block and showed it off to visitors, but the general emphasis was on Jewish history.[34] It was also to Fredy Hirsch's credit that, after the grace period of six months, a small group of young people were able to escape the general carnage. A few SS men who had gotten to know the children on their frequent visits had championed them (Langbein 1972, 283). To be sure, the planned rebellion on the day of the liquidation, which had become known to some prisoners, failed. The plan was to set fire to the barracks and thereby give a signal to the inmates of the other sections of Birkenau.[35] The resistance organization had been able to smuggle gasoline into the family camp, and Fredy

Hirsch, who undeniably enjoyed the greatest authority in that section, was slated to lead the uprising. However, on March 8, 1944, the eve of the rebellion, he killed himself by taking poison (Czech 1959–64). This disrupted the plans prepared by the special detail in the crematories (Kulka 1965, 199) and other sections of Birkenau.[36] When the six months' grace period for the second transport from Theresienstadt was over, the inmates of the family camp refused to be loaded unresistingly on trucks and driven to the gas chambers. This time an action was planned by Růžena Lauscher and Hugo Lengsfeld, but it could not be carried out either. On July 11, 1944, the SS was able to commit this mass murder too undisturbed (Czech 1959–64).

It is not clear what conditions led to the so-called Budy revolt in the fall of 1942. The satellite camp Budy was the location of the penal company of the women's camp, which housed 300 to 400 women, primarily Jews but also Ukrainians and Poles, many of them deported from France. German criminals and prostitutes had been selected to wear armbands, and under the benevolent supervision of the SS, these women appear to have exercised a reign of terror. It can probably never be established whether French Jews attempted an uprising or whether the prostitutes merely feared that their intimate relations with SS guards might be revealed by Jewish women. Around ninety predominantly French Jewesses were murdered by the criminals; the commandant of Auschwitz remembered that they were "torn to pieces, killed with axes, choked to death" (Höss 1958, 112 ff.; Czech 1959–64). Elfriede Schmidt, the "axe queen," and five other German inmates were killed as accomplices by injections of poison (Czech 1959–64, 133; Langbein 1972, 137 ff.), which indicates that an investigation of the facts would have implicated members of the SS as well.

On July 29, 1942, thirteen Jews attempted what appears to have been an organized mass escape from Birkenau; twelve of these had arrived only five days earlier on a transport from Drancy near Paris, and all of them were shot (Roux 1968, 38 ff.; Czech 1959–64),[37] many just outside the camp. Marian Zelman has testified that a group of about ten Jews, who had already formed a secret organization in the Lódź ghetto, continued their activity in Gleiwitz IV, a satellite camp of Auschwitz. "They helped one another, but also gave aid to nonorganized comrades" (Strzelecki 1974, 166).

Jewish inmates who were forced to work in gas chambers and crematories on special detail repeatedly rebelled against this horrible activity, but very little has become known about this.

Weiss, a foreman of the night shift who had been deported from Slovakia, planned a breakout together with others and was able to establish contact with civilians. However, the day-shift foreman betrayed this plan because he was not able to go along and evidently feared punitive sanctions by the SS. Consequently 300 members of the special details were gassed on December 3, 1942, but not before they had killed the traitor (Langbein 1972, 230; Czech 1959–64). Filip Müller, a member of the special detail at that time, remembers that slips of paper found at the burning of the dead bodies indicated that men on barracks duty had revealed an escape plan (Müller 1979, 80). On July 22, 1944, 400 Jews, who had been brought to Birkenau from Corfu more than three weeks earlier and had presumably learned what was happening in the crematories, refused to work on the special details. They too had to die in the gas chamber (Langbein 1972, 226 ff.; Czech 1959–64). As a rule, such work was given to Jews who had recently arrived in Auschwitz and therefore could not know what they were in for. The long-prepared uprising of the special detail will be discussed elsewhere, together with rebellions in the extermination camps. These actions constitute the most unambiguous documentation of the Jews' will to resist.

On orders from Himmler, all Jews from the concentration camps in the Reich were transferred to Auschwitz. In October 1942, when the Jewish inmates of Sachsenhausen were being prepared for a transport, they took defensive action, one that was later surrounded by legends. But what was written about it immediately after liberation? A report signed by twelve prisoners of various nationalities and political persuasions, liberated in Sachsenhausen, says the following: "In late October 1942, the remaining 500 or 600 Jews were transported to Auschwitz. The fact that all personal items were taken away from them led the Jewish inmates to the logical conclusion that they were on their way to the crematorium. The bravest among them broke through the cordon of block leaders, knocked them down, and stormed through the camp crying 'We won't let ourselves be slaughtered! We want to die fighting!' This happened during roll call in the presence of all inmates of the camp. Sauer, the officer-in-charge, recognized the danger of the situation and calmed the Jewish prisoners down."[38]

Reports differ about the number of the Jews involved. In an article evidently written by Horst Jonas, we read that 700 were transported, forty-one of whom were able to survive Auschwitz (*Damals in Sachsenhausen* 1967, 109 ff.). According to a chronicle compiled by the Auschwitz museum on the basis of preserved documents, 454 Jewish prisoners from Sachsenhausen were registered as new arrivals in Auschwitz on October 25, 1942. This entry does not say that these new arrivals were subjected to a selection (Czech 1959–64).

Heinrich Lienau states that on October 22, 1942, the inmates gathered for the evening roll call heard "shots, cries of help, and the curses of the block leader. Suddenly fleeing Jews emerged between the barracks and were driven to the road by the block leaders. We heard them cry out in fear and desperation: 'Go ahead and shoot us!' Some of the would-be escapees flung themselves down on the camp road and waited for the relief of a pistol shot. . . . In the roll-call area the officer-in-charge managed to calm down the excited and frightened Jews" (Lienau 1949, 156 ff.).

In the collection of essays about Sachsenhausen that was published in East Germany, we read how young Jewish Communists prepared to resist the transport, for the measures taken by the camp administration gave them reason to believe that it was going to the gas chambers. Finally "a window was smashed, the SS guards were overwhelmed," and the young people rushed down the camp road. "Any SS man who resisted, such as the deputy officer-in-charge, was knocked to the ground." In the end "eighteen young comrades were beaten up and lay by the gate." All the chroniclers mention the fact that the camp administration calmed the inmates down and did not order the reprisals that everyone expected (*Damals in Sachsenhausen* 1967, 106 ff.). Johann Hüttner (then known as Nathan Hirschtritt), who was on that transport, speaks of hand-to-hand fighting in which numerous SS men were seriously wounded,[39] but Ernst Toch, who was also on it, states that this affair was later embellished by myths.[40]

One statement in the above-mentioned report points to a problem that repeatedly arose in various camps. After the young Jewish Communists had made a plan for open resistance—after all, their lives were at stake— they informed "the responsible comrades" (evidently Communist comrades in the leadership of the resistance) of their plan. "Few are enthusiastic about the decision of our Jewish friends. Many react reservedly, and some express their misgivings. A number of people are afraid there will be consequences for the whole camp" (*Damals in Sachsenhausen* 1967, 106). Frequently those with responsibilities for everyone were bound to think differently from members of a group that was subject to extreme personal terror.

Individuals achieved the greatest fame, or notoriety, when their position lifted them out of the anonymous mass. Only a small number of Jews stood out, by virtue of their activity, from the faceless army of their fellow sufferers—in Louis Maury's phrase, "dead men before their deaths" (Maury 1955, 57). For this reason there are fewer reports about the helpful activity of individual Jews than there are, say, about German armband wearers. Yet such reports do exist.

For example, Mala Zimetbaum became generally known in the Birkenau women's camp, and not only because of her sensational escape with a Polish man and her death. After she had been captured, brought back to the camp, and placed under the gallows, she cut her veins with a razor blade she had been able to obtain and, in the presence of all her fellow inmates, hit an SS man in the face with her bleeding hand (Czech 1959–64). She had been known and highly esteemed before these events. At the age of twenty-four, she was deported to Auschwitz from Antwerp, where her family had emigrated from Poland, in September 1942. Thanks to her knowledge of languages, her self-assurance, and her intelligence she became a camp messenger and interpreter. She managed to gain both the confidence of Margot Drechsler, the dreaded chief supervisor, and the affection of her comrades, whom she helped (though this help was often not readily apparent).[41] Because she did not use her special position for her personal advantage, she succeeded in "doing those she was able to help much good. She had particular affection for Belgian and French women" (Birnbaum 1946, 129 ff.). Zimetbaum also strove to influence capos by reminding them that they all faced the same fate. According to her relative Giza Weisblum, "she had infinite patience, and someone was always asking her for help. She was a *Mensch* [a humane person] in the truest meaning of the word, and to remain human in Auschwitz was not easy." Apparently the education received in a Zionist youth organization in Antwerp to which Mala had belonged bore fruit (Weisblum 1968, 199).

Rudolf Vrba is one of the informants drawing attention to David Szmulewski, a Polish Jewish veteran of the Spanish Civil War who was a "leader in the underground movement" in the Birkenau men's camp (Vrba/Bestic 1964, 207). Jósef Cyrankiewicz states that Szmulewski was a liaison between the Combat Group that was formed in the main camp in spring 1943 and the special unit (*Sonderkommando*).[42]

Róza Robota, who was also educated in a Zionist youth organization, was even younger than Zimetbaum. She was taken to Auschwitz from nearby Upper Silesia and helped the resistance movement in its search for a way to smuggle explosives out of a munitions factory. Róza was able to interest young Jewish girls who were working in the factory in this smuggling operation and organized it. With these explosives the special unit blew up a crematorium (reported in detail elsewhere), but with the aid of an informant the SS was able to find out how the explosives had been brought in. Róza and three girls from the explosives factory—two Poles and one Belgian—were arrested and tortured. One night a male friend from the youth organization was able to visit Róza, and he had trouble recognizing her, for the political department had really battered her about. Róza assured her friend that the other participants in the smuggling had nothing to fear. When she was interrogated, she blamed everything on a man she knew to be dead, and on a slip of paper she wrote words of farewell to her comrades along with the greeting of her organization: "*Chazak v'emats*" [Be brave and strong.] On January 6, 1945, the four girls were hanged in the women's camp—the last execution before the evacuation of Auschwitz (Suhl 1968, 237 ff.; Gutman 1958, 273 ff.).

How was it possible for a friend to visit Róza Robota in her cell in the strictly isolated bunker? When Jakob Kozelczuk arrived in Auschwitz with a transport of Jews from East Poland in late January 1943, he attracted the attention of the SS with his athletic build and height. His uncommon physical assets gained him the position of bunker attendant, in charge of keeping the cells in the cellar in order and also of leading the victims of the regular firing-squad executions to the black wall. In addition, he had to assist at executions in the roll-call area, but in return the SS gave the bunker attendant certain privileges: He received adequate food and drink as well as his own room in the bunker block. Jakob corrupted the SS men on duty so skillfully that he was eventually able to obtain great freedom of movement.

The SS having appointed him a hangman (which is what he was generally called in the camp), Jakob did his best to help many people, and not only his coreligionists. Jakob's conduct came in for a great deal of discussion in the camp. Among inmates who had not met him in the bunker, he had a bad reputation. The Pole Wiesław Kielar, an old camp hand, mentions this but adds that Jakub (his phonetic spelling) took care of Mala Zimetbaum and Edek Galiński, who had been put in the bunker after their escape, and even enabled them to converse there (Kielar 1979, 403). I myself was able to observe him in the bunker, and I am not the only one who can testify that he courageously helped many. Jakob also helped Alina Brewda when she was locked up in the bunker.[43] And he took the risk of secretly admitting Róza Robota's friend at night.

The argument that many have used to excuse themselves for participating in crimes—If I had refused to take part in heinous deeds as I was ordered to do, I would have lost my life, but the crimes would have been committed anyway, and probably more cruelly—is generally unacceptable. Every opportunist could justify himself in this fashion. But I am convinced that Jakob did more than that; he put up with the role of a hangman in order to be able to help. This is why many people came forward to testify in his behalf when proceedings were started against him in Israel after the war.

On April 5, 1945, when the SS attempted to evacuate Buchenwald, starting with the Jews, Kurt Baum resisted and was shot. Reports differ about this episode. Eleven days after it happened, Carolus wrote: "A few Jewish inmates had hidden in the cellar of Block 49. Two block leaders immediately began to beat them; a Jewish prisoner fought back, stole an SS man's pistol, and tried to shoot, but the gun wouldn't work. Another SS man came in and shot the inmate in the head."[44] Ernst Thape wrote in his diary that this Jew had been shot because, in his panic, he had flailed about.[45] Alfred Bunzol, who, like Carolus, wrote his report in the newly liberated camp, describes this incident as follows: "While the SS was hunting for inmates on April 5, the Jewish comrade Kurt Baum, from the Ruhr region, was shot by SS Squad Leader Müller at 9 A.M. Having hidden in the cellar of Block 49, he was cornered by the SS, and when he refused to be evacuated, he was mowed down" (Bunzol 1946, 39). Decades later Emil Carlebach embellished this episode: When Kurt Baum "saw that he had been discovered, he picked up a spade and rushed at his mortal enemies in an effort to sell his life as dearly as possible. Before he was able to strike, he was hit by a bullet," whereupon "all SS men precipitously left the inmates' area. . . . A paltry little spade in the hand of a half-starved Jewish prisoner had sufficed to cause thousands of heavily armed SS men to retreat" (Carlebach 1969, 11). Walter Bartel has adopted this version: "Kurt Baum resisted with a spade. A shot in the head was lethal" (Bartel 1976, 303).

Eugen Kogon has described an incident in Buchenwald in 1941: "In the troops-garage detail Squad Leader Abraham had thrown the Viennese film producer Hamber into a water hole and trampled on his victim until he died a miserable death. Hambler's surviving brother went to the officer in charge of the 'protective custody' section and reported the murder. . . . The brother said: 'I know that I shall die because I made this report. But perhaps these criminals will restrain themselves a bit in future if they know that they might be reported. In that case I shall not have died in vain." Four days later the brother's corpse was taken from the camp prison. The Hamber brothers had been arrested for "racial reasons," and with the exception of one man, who received a lucky break, the other Jews in the detail were exterminated (Kogon 1946, 114).

These examples, which were known only to few, prove that Jews ready to fight existed not only in the extermination camps.

Jews displayed courage in another form of resistance as well. At one of the artistic evening programs in Sachsenhausen, which the SS men not only tolerated but also attended, Fritz Hirsch, a Viennese Jew, presented some of his own songs. Heinz Schmidt still remembers one line—"*Und schlägst du's Zebra lahm, das Zebra wird nicht zahm*" [You can make a zebra lame, but the zebra won't get tame]—and recalls that the SS applauded it.[46] Zebra is what the inmates' striped attire was called.

We have had to refer repeatedly to anti-Semitic tendencies among the prisoners that impeded joint action against the guards. It is not surprising that these tendencies fomented hatred. Fania Fénelon, who was deported to Auschwitz from Drancy, writes that the Jewish political prisoners considered killing all "Aryan" Poles some day (Fénelon 1976, 310). She observed that the same chauvinism prevailed everywhere: "The Zionists despised all those who were not Zionists, and the Germans treated Polish women as subhuman. The Aryan women never missed an opportunity to use us [Jewish women] as scapegoats for every misfortune" (Fénelon 1976, 316).

It would be wrong to ignore the atmosphere described by Fénelon, who gathered her impressions in the orchestra of the women's camp, a group in which there were probably more impassioned power struggles than in other details, but it would be equally wrong to make generalizations. "Aryan" inmates helped their Jewish companions in misfortune on a number of occasions and in a number of camps.

Albin Lüdke writes that in 1938 the Jews were strictly separated from the rest of the inmates in Sachsenhausen and were not admitted to the infirmary. Medicines were smuggled into their separate quarters.[47] In Buchenwald Robert Siewert managed to organize a masonry course (*Buchenwald* 1960, 376 ff.), and this detail was staffed particularly with Jews and Poles who had hitherto not been admitted to specialized work, which carried a number of privileges. According to Kurt Hirsch[48] and Erich Fein, this masonry course saved the lives of many Jews, because it was possible to exempt Jewish skilled workers from the transport to Auschwitz in October 1942 (*Buchenwald*, 378 ff.). Fritz Kleinmann remembers that, on the basis of a decision of the underground organization, forty young men from Jewish transports from Austria became apprentice masons at that time.[49] This masonry school had another favorable effect: The SS leadership liked the idea of training masons in the camp, and therefore similar training details were established in other camps as well, to the benefit of young men there. Thus masonry schools were established in Birkenau in June 1942, in the Auschwitz main camp in the winter of 1942–43, and finally in Monowitz (Langbein 1972, 104 ff.). Albin Lüdke remembers that when fourteen-year-old Russians were transferred from Dachau to Neuengamme, details with skilled workers were assigned young men as apprentices.[50] Other ways of helping were found as well. Herbert Weidlich reports that inmates employed in Labor Statistics at Buchenwald managed to obtain for "Jewish comrades"—presumably Communists—easier work details, though this had been prohibited by the SS (*Buchenwald* 1960, 339). When late in the war, mass arrivals, plus the destruction of the political sections, documents in an American air raid, caused the camp administration to lose precise control, the men working in the office used this opportunity to "Aryanize" Jews (*Buchenwald* 1967, 341).

There are reports about comradely help for Jewish fellow sufferers even in camps where conditions did not permit any organized resistance movement. Julien Unger, a French Jew interned in Stutthof, gratefully recalls such help, but the chronicler of this camp, Krysztof Dunin-Wąsowicz, adds that an atmosphere of solidarity could be created only after the brutal terror of the SS had abated in 1943 (Dunin-Wąsowicz 1970, 192). In Gross–Rosen it was possible to shield a Jewish professor at the University of Berlin for three years in the "construction office" detail; this man was the only survivor of a Jewish transport from Dachau. In that camp too, the atmosphere improved as the front moved closer.

Of all the groups that were forced to live in Nazi concentration camps, the Jews were undoubtedly the worst off. The fact that many Jews nevertheless mustered the moral strength to resist demoralization, think of resisting, and engage in resistance under the most unfavorable conditions is the most convincing refutation of the notion that Jews generally went to their deaths unresistingly and apathetically.

The Actions

16

THE SAVING OF LIVES

In 1970 the district court of Essen had to concern itself with the resistance organization in Dora, camp Gestapo officials having been accused of numerous crimes in their endeavor to uncover such an organization in that camp. Inmates there had been assigned to work on V-rockets, and any sabotage activity was supposed to be prevented. After hearing the testimony of more than twenty witnesses about the existence and activities of such an organization, the court concluded that one of its aims had been "mutual aid in an effort to survive despite the prevailing living and working conditions."[1]

This judgment has general validity. The safeguarding of lives and the saving of lives from destruction—that was a goal of those inmates of Nazi concentration camps who wished to continue their struggle against the murderous intentions of their overlords. As Walter Poller, who served as a medical clerk in Buchenwald, put it, no one who could muster the requisite courage and strength was able to escape that terrible dilemma, "the horrendous compulsion to choose one inmate out of a thousand" whose life one could save—at considerable risk and usually only on an ad hoc basis. As a rule, Poller adds, a person had to watch helplessly "how thousands of inmates mercilessly wasted away, died, or were killed" (Poller 1960, 92 ff.). The Frenchman David Rousset also speaks of a principle that prevailed in the camps: Since it was impossible to save everyone, it was necessary to choose those whom one could attempt to rescue.[2] In the course of the years those active in the resistance were frequently able to increase their opportunities. Immediately after the liberation of Buchenwald, a group of Austrians who had been active in the resistance wrote that "in 1940 it was possible to save comrades from being liquidated by the SS only in isolated instances," but in 1944 and 1945 a number of Austrians could be saved, and names and methods have been given.[3] Nevertheless, Ernst Martin believes that large-scale help was not possible,[4] and as a former medical clerk he has a right to make such a judgment. According to

Heinrich Christian Meier, who gathered his experiences in Neuengamme, solidarity behind the barbed wire also meant "determining the fate of others in merciless fashion." Meier points to those responsible for this: Only the SS was to blame "if, by saving human beings, we had to send other poor human beings to their deaths" (Meier 1948, 113 ff.). It is obvious that such decisions were a burden on a person's conscience, but that burden would have been far greater if that person had not mustered the courage for such a decision and had remained passive. It is equally understandable that those who were under a compulsion to play God were later subjected to attacks. "We felt that it was our responsibility to save as much of the core as possible," writes the German Communist Walter Vielhauer, "and now we are being blamed for this."[5]

To be sure, Martin, Meier and others cited above were not aware of procedures intended to bring about general improvements; the knowledge of such activities had to be strictly limited to a small circle. Only a very few people knew, or even suspected, the reason why, in the spring of 1943, the main camp of Auschwitz abandoned the everyday method of killing patients unfit for work: by injecting poison into their hearts. No one can estimate how many lives were saved thereby, whether permanently or not. According to documents that were smuggled out of the camp in November 1942 and reached the Polish underground organization in Kraków, thirty to forty people were "spritzed" every day. In late April 1943, ten a day were recorded, and a document from the first part of May says: "General relaxation. The patients will remain in the hospital until they are completely cured and regain their strength" (Langbein 1972, 48 ff.). We know that the number of deaths in Auschwitz in May 1943 amounted to 5.2 percent of the camp population; in May of the preceding year this percentage had been 14.8 percent (Langbein 1965, 100).

Very effective help could be given in the winter of 1939–40 to those German political prisoners in Flossenbürg who had been transferred from Dachau, when that camp was temporarily evacuated. These men had to endure both the SS and the revenge of criminal capos whom they had ousted from their privileged positions in Dachau. In the first half of December, the incidence of dysentery increased sharply, and soon the number of cases reached the point where the helpless SS camp doctor could no longer ignore the epidemic. He then took the unusual step of calling in Dr. Anton Hittmayr, a prisoner who had been physician-in-chief at the hospital in Wels. Hittmayr managed to "make the SS men understand that they too were in danger of being infected and that this necessitated the complete isolation of the inmates from the SS." A strict quarantine was imposed, "and for weeks we did not see any SS men" (Adam 1947, 77 ff.). In Dora, too, inmates succeeded in getting a quarantine because of suspected typhus, which meant that the murderous labor ceased for days (Kiessling 1960, 221). J. B. Krokowski, who is generally quite skeptical about Kuntz, confirms that Kuntz managed to get that quarantine imposed by making false reports about cases of typhus.[6] We have already mentioned the courageous and effective help given by doctors imprisoned in Mauthausen shortly before the liberation of that camp. Hans Maršàlek, who estimates the number of men saved at that time at more than 600 (since Mauthausen was free a few weeks later, the majority probably was not in mortal danger anymore), reports that during that period of about fifty days the SS received false reports about the number of inmates (Maršàlek 1974, 239 ff.). This entailed a great risk for those people, including Maršàlek himself, who had to prepare the daily roll-call lists, and presumably only the disintegration of the final weeks made it possible.

Edgar Kupfer-Koberwitz has given an account of an action by the inmates of Block 9 in Dachau. In spring 1941 the camp administration ordered that the food rations for the inmates of that block, in which patients suffering from scabies were quarantined, be reduced to bread. This prompted the block personnel to ask the officer-in-charge to be "relieved of their duties because they could not bear to watch any more deaths. There was a great row, but the men remained firm and said they would rather be locked up in the bunker than continue to look on. This caused the food rations to be restored." Kupfer-Koberwitz also gives the name of the brave senior block inmate: Hugo Guttmann (Kupfer-Koberwitz 1960, 32).

Actions of this kind were possible only in exceptional instances. The handiest and relatively least dangerous way to help was to get additional food for others, though this was based on the premise that the helper himself was not starving and was able to procure such food. Ways of doing this were constantly sought and such sources as storage rooms, kitchens, and food businesses where inmates worked were found. When the receipt of food parcels was permitted—though never to everyone, Jews and Russians always excluded—an additional source opened up. Many survivors from all camps have reported how they were helped in this way and how they were able to help others. In addition to the aid given to individual friends, political comrades, or compatriots, there were general relief actions.

Heinrich Christian Meier has described such an action in Neuengamme that was organized at the initiative of André Mandryckx, a young Belgian who figures in numerous accounts of acts of resistance. "The German foremen and capos give their evening bread ration away [armband wearers had many opportunities to procure additional food and thus were not wholly dependent on such rations—H.L.]—regularly and for weeks. . . . A large number of weakened men from all ethnic groups feed on this soldarity fund," and this practice acts as "a shot in the arm" (Meier 1949, 408 ff.).[7] The effect of such actions on the prisoners' morale, was no less significant than the concrete nutritional help. Similar actions were organized in Mauthausen as well. During a few weeks in the winter of 1943–44, Pepi Kohl, a Viennese, started Project Slice of Bread, and this was expanded later, when it was possible to make a political prisoner the bread capo. Hans Maršàlek, the chronicler of Mauthausen, who avoids any revisionist idealization, cautions that "there were many problems with this bread" (Maršàlek n.d., 16).

A similar relief scheme in Sachsenhausen shows how dangerous such actions were. The German Communists in the resistance called it *"Rote Kuhle,"* *Kuhle* being a term for the daily bread ration. They had been ingenious enough to secure the consent of the camp administration, but informers told a special commission of the Gestapo, which was hunting for a Communist conspiracy among the inmates, that this relief work was being run by a secret organization of this type. The deputy assistant senior camp inmate, a German "Baltic fighter and bandit . . . used this *Rote Kuhle* action to charge that it was a *Rote Hilfe* [Red Relief] for political prisoners." The political prisoners used the armbands they had won after struggling against the Greens to start another relief movement: "In the spirit of communality, recipients of packages who had leftover food had to give up their bread rations from time to time in favor of weakened prisoners."[8] In another account, which was also written immediately after the liberation, we read: "With the approval of the camp administration, the Norwegian inmates regularly placed their surplus Red Cross packages at the disposal of the Russian prisoners of war. After consulting Bartsch [the senior camp inmate, a German Communist—H.L.], the camp administration approved a scheme by which each recipient of a parcel gave his bread ration of that day to another inmate." The special commission regarded this as a "Communist relief action," whereupon Heinz Bartsch and others were arrested and shot.[9] This solidarity action has been mentioned by numerous survivors of Sachsenhausen. The German Communist Rudolf Wunderlich calls it "an especially glorious chapter in the history of our legal and illegal work in the camp," though understandably it had to be preceded by "a certain amount of convincing."[10] The many people who were executed by the Gestapo because of this action and subsequent activities are remembered with reverence.

In the face of all danger, inmates of many camps who worked in the hospital or the office, or occupied other key positions, found ways of keeping especially imperiled prisoners out of the clutches of the SS by replacing their numbers and records with those of dead prisoners. The prisoner at risk was then reported as dead and took over the number and name of the one who was actually deceased. After a swap of this kind, most of those men were assigned as quickly as possible to be transported to another camp in order to minimize the danger of discovery.

In Auschwitz, the SS stopped this method of saving lives in early 1943 by ordering every inmate to have his number tattooed on his left underarm, but it did not take this measure in other concentration camps, evidently because these were not extermination camps like Auschwitz.

We know about life-saving number-exchange schemes in Stutthof (Dunin-Wąsowicz 1970, 8), Dora,[11] and Sachsenhausen (Lienau 1949, 84). Wim Zwart, a Dutchman, reports that fifteen inmates of Sachsenhausen whom the SS had evidently destined for death were transferred to Bergen–Belsen on a transport on February 8, 1945. As a rule transfers made under such circumstances were soon followed by orders to liquidate. A British major in that group was shot by the SS shortly before the liberation of that camp, but a Russian doctor interned in Bergen–Belsen was able to save three Dutchmen by reporting them as dead and giving them numbers of deceased prisoners. Zwart never learned about the fate of the others.[12] In Leitmeritz (Litoměříce), a subsidiary camp of Flossenbürg, where two recaptured escapees from Brieg, a satellite camp of Gross–Rosen, were interned, experienced inmates exchanged the numbers of the pair just before the SS started looking for them. All too often attempted escapes were punished by death, but by the time the SS got around to carrying out this death sentence, the two inmates were already registered as deceased.[13] Several reports confirm that, in the prison hospital at Ravensbrück, inmates working in Work Assignments and in the clothes depot collaborated in exchanging numbers of endangered inmates for those of dead prisoners.[14] According to reports by Polish women, young compatriots of theirs—who had been chosen as "guinea pigs" and whose legs had been mutilated by operations—were saved during the confusion of the final phase. Wanda Kiedrzyńska has described this as follows: "When the victims of experimental operations were ordered, on February 4, 1945, to leave the block, everyone realized that the SS was preparing to execute this living evidence of the Nazi doctors' crimes. . . . In those days, there was indescribable chaos as well as great overcrowding, and thus we were able to hide them among the mass of prisoners. The women in the Work Assignments were able to give a few of them the numbers of dead prisoners and place them on a transport leaving for a factory" (Kiedrzyńska 1960). According to another Pole, Maria Kurcyuszowa, information about those mutilating experiments had previously been sent to a Polish resistance organization that was active outside the camp, and these people passed it on to the Allies. At the decisive moment the "guinea pigs" informed the camp commandant that their fate was known and being followed in other countries. This was done in February 1945 and caused the commandant to delay his execution order, which left time for victims to be smuggled out as described above.[15]

In Mauthausen, as the war was winding down, prisoner functionaries organized in the resistance were able to utilize the chaos caused by overcrowding and the progressive demoralization of the SS. Hans Maršálek writes: "By the winter of 1944–45 the underground solidarity in the main camp had developed to the point where office armband wearers were able to collaborate with inmates working in the hospital and save some particularly endangered prisoners by switching numbers and making false reports." Maršálek has described one specific case: There were certain signs that Leopold Kuhn, an Austrian Communist sent to Mauthausen in early March 1945, was in danger of being executed. He was quickly admitted to the hospital, and the inmates waited for a patient ("preferably of the same nationality and similar in age and appearance") to die. On March 31, 1945, Robert Litterer, a man who had been transferred from Gross–Rosen just a few weeks earlier and therefore was not known in the camp, died of typhus. Kuhn was reported as dead in place of Litterer, discharged from the hospital with Litterer's number, and transferred to a satellite camp (Maršálek 1974, 261). Kuhn has confirmed this account and mentioned that, after his liberation, he had a great deal of trouble proving his identity because his discharge papers bore the name Litterer (Kuhn 1975, 40). In April 1945, when most other camps had already been liberated and the Allies were in the vicinity of Mauthausen, the camp administration permitted the International Red Cross to take French, Belgian, and Dutch prisoners to the safe haven of Switzerland (Maršálek 1974, 240). At that time Hans Maršálek, the deputy clerk, and two Czechs managed to pass off around fifty inmates of other nationalities, including numerous Italians, as Frenchmen and have them placed on that transport (Pappalittera 1972).[16] Another rescue attempt made in those last, hectic days was less successful. When an order was issued, on April 27, 1945, to execute a group of Austrians who had been arrested for underground activities in the fall of 1944, the devil-may-care inmates working in the office exploited known disagreements in the ranks of the SS and managed to delay the lineup of the victims by one day. That done, they urged the latter to flee during the night and provided them with secretly obtained weapons—three pistols and a few hand grenades. At that time the chances for escaping were improved by the fact that the electric current in the camp fence had been turned off and the camp was no longer being guarded by the SS but by older soldiers from units of the Luftwaffe. However, "the condemned men refused to believe that they were to die on the eve of the liberation. . . . Their starvation existence and the arduous camp conditions had broken their will to resist. They did not have the strength to incur the risk of an escape." After the morning roll call the courageous camp clerks made one final attempt and tried to take the endangered men to the hospital, where in the general confusion of those days at least a few people would have had a chance to hide. However, only one man made use of it, and the SS escorted the other thirty-three men from Upper Austria to the gas chamber and killed them (Maršàlek 1974, 240 ff.).

"From the political departments [where inmates were employed—H.L.] we learned about imminent executions, and so we managed on a few occasions to save the lives of some comrades whose records were exchanged for those of dead people." The Pole Ewald Gondzik, who wrote this after the liberation of Neuengamme in the best German he could muster,[17] knows whereof he speaks, for he was part of the resistance movement in that camp. Hans Schwarz heard about another case there: "When the two British flyers who had been shot down near Hamburg in March 1943 arrived at the hospital seriously wounded, it was soon learned that the SS was planning to liquidate them. Inmates saw to it that they 'died' during the same night and were switched with two dead men lying in the mortuary. This action was successful despite the screaming of the SS, and the two 'casualties' disappeared in an outside detail" (Schwarz 1960–67, 80). Gregor, a commissar of the Red Army who was being sought by the SS, could also be saved in this fashion. "Gregor lived under the name of a deceased Soviet inmate, and we had put him in a place where he was hardly noticed and was never detected," writes Fritz Simon, another active member of the resistance organization in Neuengamme. "In that way we managed to save many . . . especially comrades at particular risk" (Emmerich n.d., 386). The same practice was followed in Dachau. Albert Guérisse, whose camp name was O'Leary, learned from a friend that the SS was planning to kill a Russian who was a patient in the infirmary. Guérisse, who was on the staff there, substituted the number of a Pole who had just died for that of the Russian. When this trick worked, nurses wanted to save other lives in that fashion (Brome 1957, 231 ff.). The camp clerk alerted anyone who was in danger. Upon questioning, Guérisse admitted that such life-saving number swaps could not be effected frequently.[18] The Frenchman Joseph Rovan, who was a clerk in Dachau, has described the case of "a Dutch captain of Jewish origin who was to receive 'special treatment' (*Sonderbehandlung*), which meant execution. An SS man came with a letter and asked whether the man was there. . . . I looked over his shoulder and saw what was involved. The man hadn't arrived yet. I took note of his name, and a few weeks later that man was actually delivered by the Gestapo. At that point I hid his file card. From time to time the SS squad leader came looking for the man, but he still hadn't arrived, and so it was reported that the man couldn't be found. All this while the man had been sitting peacefully in his barracks." Rovan concludes his account by saying that this Dutchman later died of typhus (Kuby n.d., 120).

This type of life-saving activity has been documented most fully for Buchenwald, too. Actions of this type (Leibbrand n.d., 48) reached the point where it was decided—in August 1944—to start a *"Totenreserve"* [corpse bank] so as to save time when an exchange had to be made in a hurry.[19] Specific cases have also been recorded. Thus Willi Grünert has described how the life of Erich Hoffmann, a veteran of the Spanish Civil War from Hamburg, was saved by an exchange of numbers (Schmidt 1958, 264 ff.). Baky Nazirov, a Russian prisoner of war, reports how the Belgian Robert Villus was saved in the same way, though "this risky method permitted only the saving of a small number of lives" (Nazirov 1959, 54 ff.). Nazirov's compatriot Nikolai Kyung describes the risks such actions involved, but he does conclude that "dozens of comrades could be saved from being executed in this way" (Kyung 1959, 77).

In another account, three Russians state that between September 1, 1944, and the liberation of Buchenwald, the lives of twenty-six Russian inmates were saved, and they name several of these. Even though this report does not state unequivocally that all twenty-six were saved by a swap of numbers with dead prisoners, this may be assumed from the mention of this method immediately preceding that statement (*Buchenwald* 1960, 353). The Polish Communist Henryk Sokolak remembers that this technique began to be applied as early as 1943, "but always in individual cases only, and even then with extreme caution." He adds that "after the swapping of names the inmates involved were immediately placed on a transport so they would not be recognized by any fellow prisoner." Sokolak estimates that about 130 changes of identity were accomplished (*Buchenwald* 1960, 353). A man who has been approvingly mentioned by many, Ernst Busse, the German capo of the infirmary in which many of these life-saving actions took place, wrote in 1945 that the lives of three Belgians whose names could be ascertained, twenty-six Soviet prisoners of war, a German Jew, and a Jewish foreigner could be saved by "having the men at risk die on paper and go on living under another name." Busse also describes how it was possible to help inmates in the Buchenwald hospital by declaring them as "unfit for transport;" this saved them from being transferred to a worse camp or delivered up to the Gestapo, which wanted them. Here, too, Busse documents his statement with names (*Buchenwald* 1960, 350 ff.). Walter Wolf, a German, has described another opportunity for saving lives that arose after the American air raid on Buchenwald on August 24, 1944. Since documents of the political department were destroyed, it was possible to list "a considerable number of endangered inmates under assumed names" and to "Aryanize" Jews (*Buchenwald* 1960, 341).

In Buchenwald organized life-saving through the switching of numbers differed from the above-mentioned schemes in several respects. It involved agents of the Allied secret services who had been captured in France, and the action was not led by the resistance organization headed by German Communists. On August 17, 1944, the Paris office of the Gestapo delivered to Buchenwald thirty-seven French, Belgian, and Canadian officers and agents under circumstances that immediately made experienced inmates recognize them as uncommon prisoners. The French inmate Alfred Balachowski quickly established contact with the new arrivals, and after a few days the threat to this group became clear: On September 9, sixteen of them were lined up and killed.[20] It was easy to guess that the same fate awaited the others. French friends approached the "secret German Communist organization," but it declined to intervene on the grounds that they themselves were being investigated by the SS, for having smuggled arms into the camp after the bombing of the Gustloff Works a few days earlier. In its search, the SS used some informers, and under these circumstances the resistance organization regarded the proposed action as too risky.[21] Thus a rescue action was started by the Austrian Eugen Kogon, a Catholic, who was serving as a clerk to the SS doctor and displayed "remarkable diplomatic abilities" (Hessel 1954, 358), and the German Socialist Heinz Baumeister. Under adventurous circumstances and with the aid of a number of friends—including, in addition to the Frenchmen, the Pole Arthur Gadcziński and the Dutchman Jan Schalker (Salomon 1966, 183 ff.)[22]—they were able to place three members of the imperiled group in the infirmary. With the help of Dr. Erwin Ding-Schuler, the SS doctor, who by this time was anxious to make points with the inmates,[23] Hessel was put in the strictly isolated typhus section, which was avoided by the SS (Kogon 1946, 246). "Of course, only a very limited number of those at risk could be considered [for this action—H.L.] It was a tragic moment when its leader, Dodkin of the Royal Air Force, made the selection and because of his importance was urged by his comrades to put himself at the head of the list. . . . It was possible to save only three men" (Kogon 1946, 246).[24] Owing to linguistic difficulties, these three could only take the place of dead Frenchmen. Dodkin and Peuleve, the two Englishmen, spoke fluent French; because the third man, the Frenchman Stéphane Hessel, was hidden in the section for infectious diseases, he had to be exchanged for a man who had died of typhus. "On October 5 another twenty-one members of the group, including Peuleve, were called up. . . . By means of a milk injection Peuleve was given a high temperature; he was put on the sick list, and the SS physician was able to convince the commandant that it would be easiest to kill this moribund inmate by giving him an injection of poison. Dietzsch, the senior inmate of the section for infectious diseases— a fascinating person who had been induced to cooperate—served Wilhelm, an SS chief squad leader who had been ordered to do the killing, "a splendid supper with schnapps. . . . When the SS man was tipsy enough, Dietzsch showed him a dying patient, said that this was the man he was looking for and that, since he could expire at any moment, he was not worth wasting an injection on. Wilhelm actually left and told the camp doctor that Peuleve had been executed" (Kogon 1946, 247). On that very day, "like a gift from heaven," a transport from Cologne arrived in Buchenwald with dozens of Frenchmen suffering from typhus, and one of them died almost immediately (Kogon 1946, 258). This offered a chance to exchange numbers, and by the end of October it was possible to change the identity of the two others. They were quickly assigned to a transport to a satellite camp, which enabled them to survive (Kogon 1946, 252; Salomon 196, 190 ff.)

There was a similarly adventurous rescue of three Austrian Jewish women who had been arrested by the Gestapo because they had returned to their homeland in the guise of foreign workers and were active in underground organizations there. These women were deported to Auschwitz on December 1, 1944, and as in similar cases, it was likely that this would be followed by a death sentence. After the evacuation of Auschwitz, the Austrian resistance group managed to send news of these especially endangered women to Ravensbrück where they were shipped. Toni Lehr, one of the three, reports that the "Austrian group immediately took charge" of her and her comrades and pulled them out of the transport while the other inmates were being detained in the roll-call area of the camp.[25] The SS did not call those three out until March. Having received a timely warning from prisoner armband wearers, the three did not obey this call but were hidden by their comrades, and thanks to their help were not found, despite a feverish search by the SS. To keep them alive, it was necessary to remove the tattooed Auschwitz numbers, for these could have identified them even if they had been given the numbers of dead inmates. Nadja Persic, a Yugoslav doctor, agreed to perform this operation at night.[26] The three prisoners received the numbers of deceased Frenchwomen and could be placed on a transport of Scandinavian, French, and Belgian women, which the International Red Cross sent to Sweden on April 22, 1945, at the time of the general breakup.[27]

Mitzi Berner recalls that this rescue action, too, was possible only "because by that time the SS had grown increasingly nervous, gave orders, and later revoked them."[28] Most of these rescue actions would have been inconceivable before the chaotic final phase of the concentration camps. Nevertheless, this period also brought the greatest number of casualties.

By various routes the Combat Group Auschwitz had sent out maps of the railway lines and the crematoria with built-in gas chambers, urging that the machinery of extermination be bombed and trying to dispel scruples that such attacks might kill inmates too (Langbein 1972, 293 ff.).[29] This was yet another attempt to save lives. At the time this information was sent out, the greatest campaign of destruction—of the Hungarian Jews between mid-May and early July 1944—was in progress, and by then the Allies had advanced to the point where a bombardment of the area would have been possible both from Italian and Russian bases. This information did reach the Allies, which is proved by a secret report of the German Foreign Ministry dated July 5, 1944. A telegram from the British Embassy in Bern to the Foreign Office in London had come to the attention of the Germans. In it the destruction of the Hungarian Jews in Auschwitz is described and the following actions are proposed: "Reprisals against Germans in the hands of the Allies; bombing of the railway lines from Hungary to Birkenau; precision bombing of the machinery of the death camp."[30] It has never been established why this rescue attempt was not carried out. The I. G. Farben factory was bombed on September 13, but the gas chambers and the crematories, the railway lines, and the Auschwitz station remained unscathed (Czech 1959–64).

In summary, the following is from a report written by Austrians after the liberation of Buchenwald: "The fact that, despite the bloody terrorism of the SS, consistent anti-Fascist activities could be carried on in the camp was psychologically significant. Thanks to this, thousands—and particularly the anti-Fascist forces—could be kept alive. Even though it was never possible to discuss these things openly and many of the measures taken could not be explained, this aspect of work in the camp was decisive. It must be emphasized that all this was accomplished under the greatest difficulties imaginable, under constant SS terrorism and in the face of incomprehension on the part of many inmates."[31] Hans Sündermann, an Austrian active in the resistance at Buchenwald, has described easements that the secret organization had been able to secure; these "benefited all inmates, but even more important was the support of individual prisoners, whose camp life was improved by obtaining better labor details and other privileges for them."[32]

Sometimes it appeared that Communist-led organizations were primarily interested in helping their comrades,[33] which is humanly understandable but under the inhumane conditions of a Nazi concentration camp led to harsh decisions. Thus the German Communist Hans Gasparitsch remembers that in Work Assignments at Dachau transport lists were falsified by removing the names of comrades and entering those of other inmates.[34]

Frédéric Manhès, a Frenchman who in the final year represented the French resistance group on the executive committee of the international organization in Buchenwald, justifies his activity to his French comrades. At a time when Frenchmen still had no contact with the international organization, most of the French prisoners sent to Buchenwald were transferred to Dora. "This was the period when Frenchmen had a bad reputation, were not organized, and thus could be used as substitutes for those inmates of other nationalities whose names their organizations removed from the lists [for transfer to dreaded Dora—H.L.]." In an effort to make himself better understood, Manhès adds that Frenchmen never amounted to more than 13 percent of the inmates and "all important positions were in the hands of members of other nations, most of them enemies or declared adversaries of the French." This situation changed when, in May 1944, French Communists too were deported to Buchenwald. Now they were able to create an organization and establish contact with the international leadership, which gave them a chance to support their compatriots. By giving numerous names, Manhès attempts to prove that the French group by no means limited its support to Communists. He describes the difficulties that arose when a certain number of inmates had to be selected for transport, and each national group favored its own. There was always a struggle to remove compatriots from the list. Manhès attempts to silence his critics by inviting them to "imagine the difficult and ticklish situation" of an inmate who had to plead the case of fellow nationals before the committee (Manhès n.d., 18 ff.).

The French historian Olga Wormser raises the question whether the resistance in Buchenwald, "particularly that of the Communists, was good for the inmates in general or not."[35] Those who have experienced Buchenwald give an unambiguous response to this question. As Benedikt Kautsky puts it, "it was the international solidarity that overcame National Socialism" (Kautsky 1961, 179), and Eugen Kogon writes: "Would we have been more successful in our struggle against the SS if the Communists had been consistently democratic from the beginning? In the face of the abnormal and exceedingly difficult conditions in the concentration camps, I cannot venture to answer this question. The only certain thing is that many positive things were accomplished with great sacrifices and that some things could probably have been achieved at lower cost and, above all, more fairly" (Kogon 1946, 314 ff.).

Neither Kogon nor Kautsky was a Communist.

17

AGAINST THE INHUMANITY
OF THE SYSTEM

Prior to 1939, the SS gathered experience in building an all-powerful machinery of terror that was capable of keeping every prisoner under constant pressure and making him feel his impotence drastically. After the outbreak of the war, when the camps were increasingly flooded with prisoners from occupied countries, the SS men reinforced this apparatus by utilizing inmates to whom they had given armbands. These inmates were supposed to act as an extension of the SS, and to this end it attempted to corrupt them and to compromise them in the eyes of their fellow inmates. But prisoner functionaries, prepared for the struggle and morally unbroken, strove to provide visible proof that they had not become an arm of the camp administration.

It is reported, from the earliest phase of the concentration camps, that Fritz Männchen, a German political prisoner, refused to participate in the public execution of the criminal inmate Bargatzki. (Bargatzki had killed an SS man while attempting to escape from Buchenwald and had been captured and returned.) Männchen was the deputy senior camp inmate at the time, and on June 4, 1938, a criminal prisoner took over his hangman's job. (*Buchenwald* 1960, 583). At Whitsuntide 1941, Harry Naujoks, the Communist senior camp inmate of Sachsenhausen, was ordered to hang another escaped criminal who had been recaptured. After he had said that he could not do this, another inmate carried out the public execution.[1]

In February 1944, the SS was preparing the public execution of two recaptured escapees from Dora, and it ordered Georg Thomas, the senior camp inmate, to perform the hanging. All the inmates assembled in the roll-call area heard Thomas say, "I refuse to carry out this order!" The order was then given to Ludwig Szymczak, the deputy senior camp inmate, but he gave the same answer. After both men, German Communists active in the resistance, had been arrested, a German criminal finally obeyed the

211

execution order. Thomas and Szymczak were soon discharged from the bunker and resumed their camp jobs, but their position was taken by the Green who had done the hanging. Naujoks, however, continued as senior camp inmate in Sachsenhausen, but as Götz Dieckmann and Peter Hochmuth report, this change took place in Dora: "The criminal prisoners gained the upper hand" (Dieckmann/Hochmuth n.d., 73). Their description of this heroic episode has been confirmed by several writers.[2] There is a laconic report that in Majdanek a prisoner was hanged because he had refused to put the noose around the neck of another inmate, whom the SS suspected of planning to escape, though the details are not known.[3] Those who refused to become executioners had no way of knowing what the reaction of the SS might be in any given case.

One day an SS medical officer named Bahr ordered Fritz Bringmann, a nurse in a subsidiary camp of Neuengamme, to participate in killing infirm Russian prisoners of war with injections of carbolic acid. Bringmann refused, and so did other nurses; Bahr gave them a beating but did not otherwise discipline them.[4]

Even in the final phase, the SS attempted to turn inmates into accomplices of their crimes. In early April 1945, during the evacuation of the Hinterbrühl satellite camp of Mauthausen, a German prisoner (whose name has not been recorded, though it is known that he was from the Lake Constance area) was ordered to shoot the 150 patients in that camp. (In those days, some camp administrations were using German inmates as auxiliary guards.) According to the Luxembourger Jean Brausch, that man "refused and was shot at the barbed wire. But there were other Germans" who were willing to do this work (Brousch 1970). When the Mödling subsidiary camp of Mauthausen was to be evacuated on March 31, the prisoner physicians were ordered to kill the patients who were not capable of marching by injecting them with poison. Despite all threats, they refused to do so, and nothing happened to them. A Viennese criminal who was a nurse in the camp carried out this order and killed fifty sick prisoners (Bernadoc 1976, 146 ff.).

Around the same time the Austrian capo in the disinfection section of Gusen received the order to prepare the gassing of 600 fellow inmates. When he resisted, the SS threatened to kill him, whereupon he passed the order down to his subordinates. One of them, the Pole Marian Molenda, responded that, although he knew that he could not do anything to save those 600, he would not participate in the mass murder: "Let the SS men do it if they want to, but I won't. I'd rather be killed myself." And the expected beating did kill him (Pappalettera 1972).

A vaguely phrased remark by Walther Piller, the deputy officer-in-charge at the extermination camp Chelmno, allows us to infer that Jews who were forced to work with the machinery there frequently refused to participate. After his arrest Piller testified that sometimes "new inmates started out by inciting the old ones to refuse to do this work." Since this had led "to a certain unrest," those in charge refrained from replacing the "workers."[5] Piller does not say what the SS did with those who had caused such an "unrest," but in an extermination camp, only those were allowed to live who did the SS's bidding—and only for as long as their work was needed.

The SS liked to use prisoner functionaries not only as hangmen; but also to administer public beatings. Sometimes they refused to execute such orders also. Thus the Pole Tadeusz Patzer, a capo in Dora, refused to give fifteen blows to a Russian who had fallen asleep at work. Patzer's friend Krakowski has explained how he was able to do so without perceptible consequences: "Patzer was an exceptional person: blond, blue-eyed, very young (qualities that the SS particularly appreciated), with excellent manners and a knowledge of many languages."[6] In Herzogenbusch a Dutch senior block inmate, the prizefighter Benni Brill, refused, in front of his lined-up fellow inmates, to give another prisoner a whipping. Lehmann, a German Jew, writes that "this was the first time in my two-and-a-half years in concentration camps that I witnessed or heard about such a refusal" (Presser 1968, 470).

Even individuals who had not been sent to a camp for political reasons did not let the SS use them as henchmen. Heinrich Christian Meier tells about a "Bavarian pimp" in Neuengamme, a man notorious as a brutal bully, who refused to obey when he, along with other capos, was ordered to administer whippings in the roll-call area. "He said he hadn't beaten anyone on orders in his life and would never do so" (Meier 1949, 197 ff.). He was given a beating and taken to the bunker, but Meier is silent about his further fate. Margarete Buber-Neumann has told about the German prostitute Else Krug, an inmate of the penal block in Ravensbrück, who was ordered to whip a woman slated for punishment but refused—and this despite assurances that she would be released from the penal block and receive additional food rations (Buber-Neumann 1958, 230). Shortly after her refusal to obey this order, Krug was assigned to a transport that was destined for gassing. In both cases others quickly came forward who were willing to do the bidding of their masters.

In 1942, the central office ordered that henceforth beatings were no longer to be administered by SS men but by inmates, but in Dachau, according to Walter Vielhauer, the Dachau resistance organization was able to delay the execution of this order for a long time.[7] Conditions were very bad in the subsidiary camp Allach, partly because of the conduct of unprincipled armband wearers, including some Reds. Karl Wagner, a German Communist who had been imprisoned since 1934 and at the initiative of the resistance group was transferred to Allach as senior camp inmate, was the first prisoner who openly refused to administer punitive whippings to Russian, Polish, and Yugoslavian fellow inmates. "I don't give beatings!" he said. Wagner believes that this happened in the spring of 1943,[8] and he states that "among the leading comrades in Dachau the question of whether or not to refuse to give beatings was seriously discussed. . . . Whether an inmate could refuse such an order depended on the closeness of his political ties to his comrades and on the influence exerted by the SS." He points out that "in some camps German criminals obeyed orders to administer beatings in return for additional bread rations . . . and there the political prisoners were spared such orders."[9] After the incident described by Wagner, other German political prisoners refused to give beatings; among these were Hans Biederer, Karl Frey, and Kaspar Bachl.[10] Wagner was taken to the bunker in Dachau, given twenty-five blows, discharged, and reinstated in his position as capo (Pingel 1978, 192). Biederer's refusal netted him three teeth knocked out on the spot, whereupon he received a whipping and was locked up in the bunker; later he was transferred to the penal block and finally to another concentration camp. Bachl suffered a similar fate.[11] In compliance with a decision by the party, Hans Vetrofsky, an Austrian Communist serving as senior block inmate in Dachau, refused to obey orders to give a beating. He was himself whipped but retained his armband.[12] The effect of such staunch actions has been described by Leopold Arthofer, who writes in connection with Frey's refusal to administer beatings: "His glory lives on in the hearts of a thousand grateful former camp inmates" (Arthofer 1947, 102).

Even in an extermination camp, a Jew was brave enough not to obey the order to beat a comrade. Shaul Fleischhacker from Kalisz preferred suffering a beating himself to being the one to punish the "twenty-five" in Sobibor (Novitch 1978, 65).

From the beginning it was part of the SS system of total terror to use a network of informers in the camps. The more overcrowded and intricate the camps became, the more importance the SS attached to stool pigeons. Thus we read in a letter sent on March 31, 1944, by the SS Economic Office to the commandants of all concentration camps: "It has proved to be absolutely necessary . . . to have the camp inmates kept under surveillance by suitable fellow inmates [informers]."[13] There are reports about the deleterious activities of such informers from all camps. In Gross–Rosen, the roll-call officer Helmut Eschner developed an entire system of informers; Andrzej Kaminski has described him as a "talented organizer" in this area.[14] Kornelis Hofman reports that agents provocateurs were infiltrated into Herzogenbusch in order to pump the inmates.[15]

The chief informer in Majdanek is said to have spoken seven languages.[16]

The political department in Auschwitz used the bunker there as a regular "stoolie factory." Since it was especially afraid of underground activity of Polish prisoners and their contacts with the Polish population of the area, it concentrated on those who spoke Polish and gave them a choice between providing it with information and being put up against the Black Wall and shot (Langbein 1972, 207 ff.). There were also people who volunteered their services in hopes of an easier life.

In Sachsenhausen too, the camp administration made vigorous attempts "to build up an effective snitcher service," for it had noticed that an anonymous authority "was at work [in the camp] every day" (*Damals in Sachsenhausen* 1967, 92). The number of informers is estimated at around 200, and they were under thirty or forty inspectors, whose duty it was to verify the information supplied by them. The informers were paid off with cigarettes (Dam/Giordano, 302). Max Opitz speaks of a "system of spying and snitching" (Opitz 1969, 170). However, things got even worse. In the clothes depot of the SS military arm, inmates were put to work checking the shoes and other leather goods of murdered men for hidden valuables. When these items were cut open, gold, diamonds, watches, and foreign money were sometimes found, so the SS men used criminal prisoners to get their hands on as much of this property as possible. These shady activities became known, and on November 1, 1943, a special commission was charged with an investigation. It immediately clashed with the camp administration, which was interested in covering up the transgressions of SS men.

By virtue of its special powers, the commission used a number of German prisoner functionaries who "over the years had tried to break the influence of the political prisoners by means of intriguing and informing against them."[17] Among these were many Reds and "broken-down German Nazis," as Rudolf Wunderlich has characterized them.[18] On March 27, 1944, the SS accidentally discovered a radio and typewritten leaflets in a camp workshop, and the commission took charge of the investigation— presumably at the instigation of its agents; these men hoped to win their fight against those German Communists who had long been trying to limit the authority of the informers. The special commission was enlarged and its authority expanded. In the course of its investigation, it arrested German Communist armband wearers. These were not merely tortured in Gestapo fashion; their interrogators also skillfully exploited "disagreements among the Communists on such matters as the dictatorship of the proletariat and popular rule" by carrying on political discussions with individuals, whose self-importance they promoted.[19] Eventually a number of informers were sent to Berlin for further training.[20] Pierre Grégoire, a Luxembourger who was himself a victim of this action and was assigned to a punitive transport to Mauthausen, has described the atmosphere in the camp in these words: "From all lairs of meanness and insidiousness the depraved vermin comes crawling and cozies up to him [the head of the special commission—H.L.], blissfully betraying their acquaintances and friends, opponents and human dignity itself. . . . The golden age of all unprincipled persons has dawned" (Stein 1946, 176 ff.).

The prisoner functionaries who had not been arrested found themselves in the "unprecedented, tragicomic situation" of having to side with the camp administration against the special commission. Intrigues and counterintrigues were plotted, provocations were unmasked, and informers' reports were secretly read (the senior camp inmate was given fresh carbon paper to make his report legible), whereupon these were skillfully refuted and counterreports written.[21] Despite all the inmates' defensive maneuvers the results of this most extensive SS effort to uncover a Communist secret organization in a camp with the aid of informers were bad. In a report written shortly after the liberation, Karl Raddatz stated that "this big network of informers failed to gain a deeper insight into our illegal activities and did not get beyond the periphery,"[22] but the observations in an anonymous report, also written by Communists, seem more realistic: "By means of the unscrupulous revelations of the criminals, they managed to gain an ever deeper insight into our ranks."[23] And Max Opitz has written: "The rampage of the special commission created a very critical situation for the inmates who were still politically active. Some lost the courage to participate in the resistance struggle under the more severe conditions" (Opitz 1979, 178). It is true that, on orders of the camp administration, the commission had to release thirty inmates from the penal block because the incriminating material "stank [all too obviously] of the informers' intentions."[24] However, twenty-seven prisoner functionaries, Germans and three Frenchmen, were shot on October 11, 1944, and 103 put on a transport to Mauthausen on October 20 (*Damals in Sachsenhausen* 1967, 149).

Here, too, the resistance organization was able to exploit disagreements among the SS. The senior camp inmate Kuhnke, "the greatest murderer of the special-commission period, was brought down by the camp administration with our assistance. Beaten and reviled, he had to march at the head of the 103 . . . a heartless murderer who was now trembling and crying for his life."[25] In a diary entry of October 20, 1944, the Norwegian Odd Nansen characterizes this whipped senior camp inmate as follows: "He was the devil behind everything. His power was very great. He had the lives of many of his fellow inmates on his conscience" (Nansen 1949, 212). Thus ended the terrible period of the special commission in Sachsenhausen.

Among the other informers who were transferred was Kokoschinski, "originally a Pole" (he had evidently signed an ethnic list and was hence-forth registered as a German), who had endeavored to find among the Poles helpers "for the common fight against Communists."[26] After having been transferred to Ravensbrück, he later returned to Sachsenhausen and was "assigned to a foreman with instructions to liquidate him by appropriate treatment." In connection with a mass shooting in February 1945, the camp administration "brought down [among others—H.L.] almost all in-formers involved in that matter. . . .[27] They had served one SS faction, and the other one undertook to reward them for their slimy services." Earlier, the senior camp inmate Herbert Volck had been dropped by the Gestapo, and he was "sent to a penal camp where he was pursued by the vengeful camp administration and met his deserved fate."[28]

In all camps, the inmates who wanted to resist the methods of the SS had to silence those fellow prisoners who were acting as its henchmen. "The struggle against the henchmen of the Gestapo and the SS in the camp . . . had to be carried on with extreme ruthlessness and severity. . . . Those who could be recognized as stool pigeons at their arrival were less dangerous than those who became informers in the camp. The latter sometimes already had a more or less profound insight into existing forms of organiza-tion, knew the moving and leading forces in the anti-Fascist struggle, and hence were particularly dangerous."[29] This is how Austrians summed up their experiences in this field immediately after the liberation of Buchen-wald. Otto Horn, one of the authors of that report, also states: "The moral pressure was so strong that only few people dared to curry favor with the administration by informing. And it was at this point, where morality no longer availed anything, that organized opposition to betrayal and talebear-ing set in. Within a matter of days,—or, in especially severe cases, of weeks—the day of reckoning came, and it always ended with the death of the traitor." Horn also describes a method that could be followed: Almost all officers-in-charge and roll-call officers were systematically corrupted and used "for killing their procurers themselves."[30] The Dutchman Wijnen has described how a man who had already informed on others in Amster-dam was lured into the hospital at Buchenwald and killed there.[31] Several reports by Russians record that they were obliged to do likewise to traitors within their ranks (Gurin 1949, 149). One night an informer tried to get to the SS unobserved, but he was accused of stealing bread, an action punish-able by death according to an unwritten law of the camp (Kyunz 1959, 75). On another occasion, Russians found in the clothes of a fellow prisoner a piece of paper with a list of names. Before he had a chance to take it to the commandant's office, "the traitor was executed in the washroom" (Sap-unov 1959, 18). If an informer was a German, the Russians enlisted the aid of their German comrades. The German senior inmate of Block 13 secretly kept a list of those whose anti-Fascist orientation he had noticed. The Russians informed the German Communists of this, and when the spy was called to the commandant's office over the loudspeaker, the authorities were informed "that the head of Block 13 was dead, which was true" (Simakov 1959, 123).

The Dutchman Eugene Heimler heard that when capos transferred to Buchenwald from other camps were denounced by fellow transferees as murderers, they were sentenced to death and executed by a secret court (Heimler 1961, 155). The Pole Tadeusz Patzer remembers a decision to kill the camp interpreter of Dora, a man who had caused the death of numerous fellow inmates, and this was accomplished in the hospital building.[32] Another Pole, Stanisław Nogaj, tells about a five-man court that sentenced informers to death in Gusen (Nogaj 1967, 159). In Bergen–Belsen, one night in early September 1944, a court composed of capos, doctors, and nurses pronounced the German criminal Karl Rothe, who was present, guilty of having committed mass murder and other crimes. As head nurse this man had killed innumerable fellow prisoners by injections of poison. Those judges could venture to pronounce this death sentence because Rothe's protector in the SS happened to be on leave. "Not a muscle in Rothe's broad, puffy face moved when he begged to be allowed to execute himself. Without a word someone handed him the rope that had been in plain sight on the table the whole time, and Rothe disappeared with it in the washroom." He tried to escape from there, but he was caught, and now "justice turned into vengeance." Rothe was lynched and his corpse was strung up to make his death appear as a suicide. "The SS did not conduct an investigation; after all, Rothe had not always murdered on his own initiative but frequently at the behest of SS men, and once such accomplices had served their function, they were glad to get rid of them" (Petit 1965–68, 95, 189; Fréjafon 1954, 388).

In Auschwitz the resistance movement found another way of getting rid of the numerous informers. When a new commandant arrived in November 1943, the movement explained to him that the stoolie system of the political department was causing considerable unrest among the inmates. On the basis of this intervention, the commandant ordered the transfer of the informers to another camp. The list was compiled by the Combat Group Auschwitz. "They are trying very hard to get out of the transport, but all their ruses are in vain. . . . Everyone says 'express orders from the camp commandant.' " On February 9, 1944, 112 inmates were sent to Flossenbürg; most of these were known to the resistance movement as informers of the political department (Langbein 1949, 148 ff.; 1972, 61 ff.; Czech 1959–64). Before that time, however, inmates had been obliged to use the severest tactics to immobilize stool pigeons. For example, the two most dangerous Polish informers of the political department were killed by their compatriots, against whom they had been working (Langbein 1972, 208 ff.; Brol/Wloch/Pilecki 1959, 35). When the Russians interned in Birkenau learned that the political department was employing an informer to stop the numerous escapes in 1944, "he met with an industrial accident. . . . The Russkies liquidated him," as the Pole Wieslaw Kielar put it (Kielar 1979, 399).

Those condemned to work in extermination camps could protect themselves against traitors only by killing them. In Sobibor, a Jew nicknamed Berliner who had revealed an attempt at escape was given this punishment.[33] In Treblinka a blanket was put over an informer's head at night, and he was hanged. Since suicides were not a rarity, this did not attract the attention of the camp administration (Willenberg 1961–63).

Where it was not possible to immobilize informers, there were acts of revenge after the evacuation or liberation. A case in point is Gross–Rosen, where informers for the SS got their "just deserts" on the day of the liberation, "predominantly from the inmates themselves." These included five Polish capos who had distinguished themselves in a most wicked way (Mołdawa 1967, 64). The senior camp inmate, a German Red who had gone on terrible rampages, was lynched at the time of the evacuation.[34] Lynch law was also applied at the liberation of Gusen, where, as in Gross–Rosen, henchmen of the SS had terrorized the camp until the very end. Thus men who had been tormented took revenge on two Berliners, the deputy senior camp inmate Hermann Amelung and the camp clerk Anton Jahnke, who has been characterized as a "Pole-baiter."[35] The Luxembourger Eugène Thomé has given a graphic description of the day of liberation in Gusen: "The severely oppressed human dignity brought about an explosive reckoning with the capos, senior block inmates, and criminals. Some had cleared out, but others were pulled out of their hiding places and mercilessly abandoned to an inglorious death" (Thomé 1970, 361). In Ebensee too, "a squaring of accounts with the capo henchmen" took place on May 5, 1945; they were "hunted down like game, stoned, beaten to death: their deserved punishment!" (*Letzeburger zu Mauthausen* 1970, 212).

In the final phase of Dachau, the camp administration had given top positions to two men who had repeatedly served them well— Thessaloniki-born Johann Meanssarian[36] was appointed senior camp inmate, and the German Wernicke, a former member of the Horst Wessel brigade in Berlin, was made capo of the camp police. Wernicke, whom the two Luxembourgers Jupp Feltes and Paul Langers have characterized as a son of a bitch, informed the camp administration that a prisoners' organization was planning an uprising and had hidden weapons, whereupon the camp was searched on April 14 (Fénelon 1976, 62). Shortly before the liberation, politically canny prisoners managed to get the two informers removed because of their shady dealings,[37] but on April 24 the camp authorities "found out that there was an organization in the camp. To meet this danger they pulled their old collaborators Meanssarian and Wernicke . . . out of the bunker. . . . They know the camp, and they also know which people are capable and courageous enough to start a fighting organization under the eyes of the SS."[38] But the two never got a chance to do what they were supposed to do. When Dachau was liberated five days later, Point 12 of the first report of the international camp committee stated that "the former inmates Meanssarian and Wernicke were arrested and summarily shot on orders from the American commandant."[39] Karl Ludwig Schecher comments on their end by saying that "both men deserved to die more than a hundred times over."[40]

There was another way of weakening the SS's all-powerful machinery of terror. We have already referred to prisoners' chances to corrupt their guards and to the susceptibility of many SS men. Individual prisoners were not the only ones who were interested in buying the good will of a guard, whether by illicitly working for him in a workshop or by "organizing" things he wanted. In probably all camps, systematic attempts were made to loosen the firm front of the guards through corruption, and men with a lot of camp experience have had a great deal to say about this.

Albin Lüdke reports how the SS leaders in Neuengamme were systematically bribed by catering to their personal needs in the camp workshops. They could then be enlisted to help curb the activities and influence of dangerous criminals. A Green senior camp inmate and a capo in the Work Assignments were put on transports by corrupted SS men. Thereafter the Work Assignments became a solid and important bastion of the resistance movement. Lüdke points out, however, that to the end the Greens could not be entirely immobilized.[41] With reference to Sachsenhausen, Heinz Junge remarks that "we were not able to stop the SS men from giving beatings, but they were careful not to beat anyone who was part of our clique," for they were afraid that the sources from which they drew might dry up.[42] There are reports from Buchenwald that "the corrupted SS men" looked the other way when inmates in key positions wished "to carry out policies of their own" (Czarnecki 1968, 53). Even before the outbreak of the war, political prisoners "in power" managed "to bribe many SS men, up to the rank of company commander (*Sturmführer*)." After *Kristallnacht*, large numbers of German Jews were sent to Buchenwald. With the aid of corrupt SS men, moneyed Jews were able to instruct their relatives on the outside to pay ransom for them, and this actually effected their release (and evidently their subsequent emigration).[43] It was the same in Dachau. As Oskar Müller puts it, "despite strict instructions from the commandant's office that a block leader could not have inmates make anything for him, when a bastard could be controlled by making something for him in the tailor's or carpenter's workshop,"[44] we [prisoners and the illegal prisoner committee—H.L.] gave permission. The Austrian Franz Freihaut believes that all SS men were corrupted in this fashion.[45]

The central administration tried to keep the inmates from influencing the SS in this way. Something that has been written with reference to Buchenwald probably applies to other camps as well: "The work of undermining was pushed as a mass effort. There were no major successes. The constantly changing SS staff made it impossible to maintain a proper connection."[46]

In the extermination camps, the terrorism was even more brutal than in the "ordinary" concentration camps, but there were far greater chances of corrupting and demoralizing the guards because the property of the murdered men was sorted and searched for valuables by details of inmates. Even threats of severe punishment could not keep prisoners from taking things that were of use to them. The SS men who managed to gain access to these details stole like magpies, and since they could not do so without the help of the prisoners working there, they could of course not deprive those of the chance to "organize" things for themselves, too. Thus members of the SS and inmates were dependent on one another. "The 'organizing' inmates had to bribe the SS men to escape their control, and the SS men who wanted to appropriate something needed the connivance of the prisoners" (Langbein 1972, 161). The description of Rudolf Höss, the commandant of Auschwitz, applies to the other extermination camps as well: "The valuables of Jews caused the camp enormous and uncontrollable difficulties.... Unsuspected possibilities opened up for the inmates.... Money, watches, rings etc. could be traded for anything with SS men and civilian workers" (Höss, 164 ff.). It must be added, however, that only a very small percentage of prisoners had such opportunities, and they sometimes found themselves in grotesque situations.

For example, the Jews in a special Auschwitz detail, working on the clothes left in the antechambers of the crematories by those destined to be gassed, were brought alcohol and (unwittingly) even weapons in the containers by an SS man named Stefan Baretzki—in return for a great deal of money.[47] On one occasion Viktor Capesius, the chief pharmacist and as a major one of the highest-ranking SS officers in Auschwitz, wanted a diamond brooch and promised the inmate who was supposed to "organize" one for him twelve bottles of schnapps in return. The Polish prisoner obtained the desired brooch for him, for his assignment in the SS pharmacy was to search for valuables among the medicines, toiletries, and the like from the luggage of people who had been taken to the gas chambers. In the interest of getting the schnapps into the camp safely, he induced Capesius to take the twelve bottles there himself, for it goes without saying that an SS major was not subjected to the same inspection at the gate as the prisoners (Langbein 1972, 395).

Such opportunities multiplied over the years—for one thing, because the unfavorable news from the front increasingly demoralized the SS, which caused many of them to look for a prisoner who could later give him a good testimony, and for another, because an increasing number of ethnic Germans were brought in as guards. If, for example, a man in an SS uniform spoke Polish better than German, not an infrequent occurrence in Auschwitz, his German "comrades" let him feel their contempt. It was frequently easier for Polish prisoners to establish human contacts with such a man. Sometimes it was not even necessary to pay for services. Heribert Kreuzmann, the Austrian senior camp inmate in the hospital of Jawiszowice, a satellite camp of Auschwitz, remembers a Croatian SA man who was employed as a chauffeur in 1944 and regularly brought (clandestine) letters to Jawiszowice from the main camp. In this way Kreuzmann maintained constant contact with the Combat Group Auschwitz.[48]

The administration of the extermination camps was in the hands of a small number of German SS men, and Ukrainian volunteers were employed as guards. With reference to Treblinka, Yankel Wiernik reports that "gold was tremendously attractive" to them, and thus they "constantly made deals with the Jews and always gave a bottle of schnapps for twenty dollars' worth of gold" (Wiernik n.d., 45).[49] Another statement by Wiernik graphically illustrates how the German camp administration treated its "volunteers." If a Ukrainian SS man was caught giving inmates some food, he was brutally beaten by the German SS (Wiernik n.d., 36). It is self-evident that such methods were not designed to make the Ukrainians feel they were full-fledged members of the SS. It should not be supposed that the "business connections" between the prisoners and the Ukrainian guards were a simple matter. According to Shmuel Willenberg, guards did take money but more often than not brought nothing in return (Willenberg 1961–63). Nevertheless, the Jewish doctor Julian Chorążycki, who was planning an uprising, was able to buy small arms from a Ukrainian guard. (He was caught making preparations and committed suicide to escape being tortured before his execution.) "Many transactions worked out well," writes Shalom Kohn, a survivor of Treblinka who remembers that this arms purchase was accomplished on a purely materialistic basis (Kohn 1945).[50]

Similar cases of corruption have been reported from Sobibor. Stanislaw Szmajzner has made this report: "I gave the Ukrainian a great deal of money; he got me schnapps and food and sometimes also brought me letters from (the strictly isolated) camp III."[51] In one place or another, there were also other reasons for the modification of the hostile attitude of the guards toward the inmates. A Ukrainian SS man gave a Russian Jew the news about an uprising in Treblinka that was of decisive importance for the organization of the prisoners' rebellion in Sobibor. According to a report by Szmajzner, "the two men already knew each other from previous military service." The Ukrainian guard also alerted his acquaintance— Sascha Pečerskii, one of the organizers of the uprising—to the impending liquidation of the inmates of Sobibor.[52] Hermann Posner, who also understood Ukrainian, has confirmed that for various reasons Ukrainians were good to the inmates: "Some of them wanted to get money from us in that way. . . . But there also were Ukrainians who sympathized with us on idealistic grounds. The Ukrainians also told us about what was going on outside the camp."[53] Ilona Safran remembers that "Ukrainians gave some of us weapons from the ordinance depot."[54] Koszewadski, a Ukrainian guard from Kiev who was in charge of the kitchens, confided in the inmate Herszel Zukerman that he had friends among the Russian partisans who were working on a scheme for liberating the camp. However, on orders from the central administration, the inmates were removed from the SS kitchen. They were still able to smuggle some money to Koszewadski, but that plan evidently was not feasible, and Koszewadski escaped and joined the partisans. Szmajzner believes that Koszewadski was the one who warned Pečerski (Novitch 1978, 127; Ainsztein 1974, 751 ff.).[55]

Abraham Margulies confirms that the inmates of Sobibor received information about events at the front and the partisans' spheres of action, but he warns against generalizations: "There were some Ukrainians who sought amicable relations with us, but we knew that the Germans had put them up to it."[56]

In Stutthof a group of Russian prisoners was able to establish contact with several Ukrainian guards, who were presumably anxious to use them as "insurance" (Dunin-Wąsowicz 1970, 195; Dunin-Wąsowicz/Matusiak 1969, 38). Albert Jouannic has described what is probably a unique case. Among the guards of Loiblpass, a Mauthausen satellite camp at the Carinthian-Slovenian border, was an Austrian policeman whose son was, in the fall of 1944, fighting with the partisans in the nearby mountains. According to Jouannic, he was perhaps the only man in the camp who was never observed committing a brutal act (Bernadoc 1975, 134). The partisans told the resistance organization of this satellite camp that an Austrian named Zimmermann—"perhaps more a Slovenian than a German"—was a person to be trusted, and he gave daily reports about what was going on among the guards (Langbein 1949, 417). Several inmates of Dachau have described another case that is probably unprecedented. Having been released from that camp, Walter Neff, an Austrian political prisoner, was hired as a country policeman in late 1942, for his work in the medical experimental station in Dachau had been appreciated by the SS. (Neff had also tried to save the lives of many of his fellow inmates) (Langbein 1949, 53 ff.).[57] According to Gustl Gattinger (and others), "he helped us in the uniform of a country policeman."[58]

In the last year of the war, the central administration of the camps found itself obliged to use Wehrmacht soldiers as guards, for the steadily increasing number of subsidiary camps required an augmentation of the guards, and all those fit for service had to be sent to the front. (However, as a rule, all the SS men who were recognized as specialists after long service in the concentration camps were allowed to stay in their posts).

Dora and its numerous satellite camps were staffed with soldiers from the Luftwaffe, presumably because the air force was involved in the construction of V-rockets there. Karl Feuerer has reported that "contact was made with antiaircraft outfits that were defending the installations around the mountain.[59] Inmates of a satellite camp were able to make contacts with the outside because their guard, a Wehrmacht soldier, drew the attention of German civilians to messages that they dropped while marching to work (Dora 1967, 32). The satellite camp Harzungen also was administered by members of the Luftwaffe, and their commander, Capt. Wilhelm Frohne (who later held the same rank in the SS), could be induced "to collaborate with the inmates within the bounds of possibility."[60] For example, Willi Gardini, a German who served as chief capo in the arms factory detail in Majdanek, has stated that, although a certain soldier in the military administration was sympathetic toward him, he was afraid to help Gardini escape.[61] The Frenchman André Ulmann, a key figure in the secret organization of the Mauthausen satellite camp Melk, writes that although the SS was in command of the guard detail, the troop itself was composed of airmen, many of whom were Austrians. "We tried to influence them in various ways," writes René Gille and Robert Monin. Gille remembers a Czech guard who regularly gave him food as well as an Alsatian who carried on private conversations with him, and Monin recalls a conductor of the Vienna State Opera who was doing guard duty and sided with them against their capo (Bernadoc 1975, 174, 277).

It stands to reason that the most effective, and also the most difficult, method was to mitigate the SS's organized reign of terror by influencing top SS leaders. According to Eugen Kogon, who gathered a great deal of experience in this area in Buchenwald, such an attempt was "most likely to be successful with a certain type of SS doctor" (Kogon 1946, 318).

Dr. Benno Adolph was one such doctor in an SS uniform. The infirmary capo of Neuengamme, the German political prisoner Mathias Mai, has described Adolph, in contrast to other SS doctors, as "a decent fellow." After the end of the war, Adolph was released from a Russian prison because former inmates had testified in his favor, and when the Americans interned him again, Poles and Russians again exonerated him.[62] The Luxembourger Pierre Schneider, who worked in the hospital as a nurse, remembers that upon his arrival in Neuengamme Adolph asked, "Where can I help?" "That was unprecedented," writes Schneider; "he did not treat us as prisoners at all." Adolph requested that imprisoned medical men be assigned to the hospital.[63]

In Dora too, an SS doctor could be induced to help. After the liberation, the Pole Wincenty Hein testified as follows: "It must be considered that Dr. Kurzke's activities were selfless and deliberate, and since they were in conflict with instructions from the camp authorities, they involved great personal risk."[64] Jan Češpiva, a Czech physician imprisoned in Dora, states that Dr. Kurzke got him released from the bunker by requesting his services for an important operation (Češpiva/Giessner/Pelný 1964, 55). Kurzke's testimony in a trial at Essen a year later proves that he had contact with prisoners active in the resistance. He was able to demonstrate that a secret radio transmitter built by the Czech inmate Jan Chaloupka had been housed in the diet kitchen and for a time in the therapy room of the hospital. At the time he did not use this information against the prisoners.[65] The regular SS doctor in Dora, an Austrian named Dr. Karl Kahr, has also been described as "humane."[66] According to Hein, he also knew about the inmates' organization and did not betray it—"there was no figuring him out."[67]

Benedikt Kautsky has made the following statement about Dr. Waldemar Hoven, the camp doctor of Buchenwald: "In every respect Dr. Hoven did not fit the usual SS pattern. . . . On the one hand, he readily participated in all lethal injections, experiments with typhus, and the like that claimed thousands of victims. On the other hand, he quite openly allied himself with the political prisoners who dominated the infirmary, fought for medical and hygienic improvements in the camp, looked after maltreated inmates, and played a decisive role in internal camp politics. In the battle between the Greens and the Reds, he was clearly on the side of the political prisoners and helped them against the criminals wherever he could. He went to the point of acting as an executor of secret judgments against criminals" (Kautsky 1961, 122). Eugen Kogon, the greatest expert on conditions in the Buchenwald prison hospital, confirms that Dr. Hoven was capable of killing dozens of inmates by means of lethal injections in one week, but "at the same time did a great deal for the camp as a whole and for individual prisoners." Kogon mentions one case in which Hoven, "who had been well-lobbied and was on the side of the leading prisoner functionaries," helped to eliminate one of the most dangerous informers (Kogon 1946, 147, 309).

According to Rudi Gottschalk, Hoven had already been corrupted with the money brought into the camp by the Jews who arrived in the camp in large numbers after *Kristallnacht*. He wound up "selling us even his pistol."[68] The Austrian Communist Gustav Wegerer wrote Hoven's doctoral dissertation together with the Czech physicist Kurt Sitte (Kogon 1946, 302) and managed to use his attendant influence on Hoven systematically for the benefit of the camp.[69] An American military court in Nuremberg sentenced Hoven to death for numerous murders, but on the basis of the evidence, it concluded that Hoven had served both the SS and the political prisoners in the camp and had saved numerous inmates from being executed (Mischerlich/Mielke 1949, 206).

Two physicians could be induced to help the inmates to an extent that was of decisive importance for the general development of the camps. These two men—Dr. Eduard Wirths, the regular SS doctor in Auschwitz, and Dr. Erwin Ding-Schuler, the camp doctor of Buchenwald—were quite dissimilar, but there were many parallels between the methods by which they were won over and the results of this exertion of influence.

Eugen Kogon, who served as Dr. Ding-Schuler's clerk, got to know him as well as I got to know Wirths, for whom I performed the same function. Kogon exerted a "direct political influence" on him, and as a result of hour-long private conversations, Ding-Schuler "did a great many positive things for us, or at least permitted them to be done" (Kogon 1946, 318 ff.). Sixty-five inmates were employed in Block 50 of the Buchenwald prison hospital, which housed Ding-Schuler's department for typhus and viral research, "a true island in the camp." The detail was comprised exclusively of political prisoners. Inmates slated for execution and even seven Jewish inmates "found a shelter there with Dr. Ding-Schuler's knowledge and approval . . . protection from direct actions and death transports. *'Ultimum refugium judaeorum'* [the last refuge of the Jews]—that is what Dr. Ding-Schuler once called Block 50—jocularly but aptly" (Kogon 1946, 176 ff.). In the last days before the liberation of Buchenwald, Dr. Ding-Schuler provided the inmates with important information and also arranged for Kogon to be taken, on April 8, 1945, to Ding-Schuler's Weimar apartment in a box containing medical material so that he could transmit a warning to the camp commandant [not to commit atrocities—ed.] (Kogon 1946, 338 ff.). Alongside such activities, and especially in earlier periods, Ding-Schuler acted as a murderer. This has been testified to by Walter Poller, who was the doctor's clerk in 1939–40 (Poller 1960, 97 ff.).

Dr. Wirths also took a leading part in mass murders in Auschwitz.

Beyond this, he conducted experiments on inmates that caused at least two casualties (Langbein 1949, 164 ff.). Nonetheless, his conduct cannot be compared to Ding-Schuler's. He was capable of being influenced—not because he was corruptible, but because he was inwardly opposed to the murderous enterprise. Since his attitude differed basically from that of other SS leaders, including most of the SS doctors under him, I could dare to inform him about the murderous goings-on in the hospital buildings that his subordinates were covering up. I have already mentioned that as a result, and with Wirths' help, the daily killing of weakened patients in the hospital was stopped. He could also be induced to requisition imprisoned doctors to serve in the hospital buildings; in March 1943, I had no trouble getting "Aryan" doctors so assigned. When this encouraged me to suggest that Jewish physicians be pulled out of the transports and added to the hospital staff, Wirths replied: "But then the hospital rooms would have to be assigned in such a way that the Jewish doctors don't treat any Aryans, because that's impossible." Under this condition, Wirths ordered the integration of Jewish physicians into the hospital (Langbein 1949, 100 ff.). There was no parallel to this in any other camp; on the contrary, the general tendency was to keep doctors away from the hospitals. In late 1943, Wirths served as a liaison for contact with the new commandant, Arthur Liebehenschel, who had replaced Höss, and, as already mentioned, this had a positive effect on the camp in several respects. In the spring of 1944, the military situation had reached a point where Combat Group Auschwitz issued threats against those SS men who bore the chief responsibility for the mass murders in the camp. These threats were broadcast by the BBC and had a noticeable effect. After a year-and-a-half of personal contact with Wirths, my relationship with him had developed in such a way that I could risk telling him that I was speaking with him on behalf of a secret organization (Langbein 1949, 156 ff.). Wirths helped us get ahead, and Rudolf Höss, the former commandant of Auschwitz, later characterized the chief camp physician in these words: "Wirths frequently complained to me that he could not reconcile the killings demanded of him with his medical conscience and that this caused him suffering. . . . He often told me in confidence that he had scruples about the whole extermination of the Jews." Regarding Wirths's relationship with the inmates serving under him, Höss has this to say: "He particularly favored the imprisoned medical men; in fact, I often gained the impression that he treated them as colleagues" (Langbein 1972, 413 ff.). Testifying before a Frankfurt court, the Polish physician Władysław Fejkiel described Wirths as "an intelligent doctor and not a bad person" (Langbein 1972, 417). Upon my suggestion, Wirths had in early 1944 appointed Fejkiel as senior inmate of the hospital in the main camp, and Fejkiel did an excellent job in that sensitive position.

Despite all this, systematic attempts to influence an SS leader were always fraught with perils, not the least of which was the risk of becoming an unwitting tool of the SS. To guard against this, Eugen Kogon and I used the same method: We discussed every step with reliable friends (Kogon 1946, 319; Langbein 1949, 85). Another parallel may be noted between the two cases: Both Wirths and Ding-Schuler committed suicide, and both in September 1945 (Kogon 1946, 319; Langbein 1972, 432).

We also know about the help given by two Austrian doctors who were not members of the SS. The Frenchman André Ulmann mentions the air-force doctor Josef Sora, who interceded with the officer-in-charge in Melk—a satellite camp of Mauthausen—on behalf of the inmates, regularly gave them information, and finally even placed a small radio at their disposal (Bernadac 1975, 333). Edwin Tangl, an Austrian, recalls an old Viennese staff doctor who "had no use for the Nazis" and consequently gave effective aid in concert with some of Tangl's fellow Tyroleans, who were guards at Landsberg am Lech, a subsidiary camp of Dachau. On one occasion, this doctor, at Tangl's request, certified a particularly brutal SS chief squad leader as fit for service at the front and ordered that he be assigned to a combat outfit.[70]

However, with reference to doctors in SS uniforms, one must warn against generalizations. On the basis of his experiences, Benedikt Kautsky writes: "Almost all SS doctors were rabid representatives of racist thought and therefore far more dangerous than ordinary SS men" (Kautsky 1961, 121). Numerous SS doctors were fanatics and thus impossible to influence.[71] The following cases should be regarded as exceptions—well remembered because of their unusualness.

The Pole Ewald Gondzik, on the basis of his experiences in the resistance at Neuengamme, remarked that it was impossible to posit any harm. There were SS people and Greens with whom it was possible to work, just as there were so-called political prisoners who were totally unreliable.[72] The Luxembourger Joseph Dichter, described "an SS man with human impulses" who enabled him, while working in a detail outside Natzweiler, to speak with his brother, who was at liberty.[73] On December 26, 1943, the Norwegian Odd Nansen wrote in his diary at Sachsenhausen that SS Squad Leader Hellwig, in command of his detail, had seen his entry and returned his diary to him without saying a word. "I believe I can trust him," wrote Nansen. When a Dutchman's diary was discovered at a later date, Nansen entered in his: "A thing like that can lead to a catastrophe" (Nansen 1949, 130 ff., 146). Ernst Martin, a Tyrolean whose service as the clerk of the SS doctor in Mauthausen brought him in contact with medical officers, has characterized Walter Metzler, an SS staff sergeant, as "one hundred percent positive."[74] This has been confirmed by the Viennese Alois Stockinger, who knew Metzler from his work in the SS pharmacy.[75]

Eugen Kogon memorialized August Feld, a medical officer, in his standard work *The Theory and Practice of Hell*. Feld was "naive and ignorant" when he was assigned to the hygienics institute at Buchenwald as a courier in the spring of 1944. "Without any ulterior motive, out of pure humanitarianism" he was prepared to take all risks that active support of the inmates involved. Thus he escorted the Dutch prisoner Jan Robert to Jena so that he might examine specialized works about typhus in the university; the SS doctor Ding-Schuler approved this unusual trip under this pretext. Feld left Robert unsupervised in Jena, and this enabled him to carry out all the assignments he had been given. Feld also visited Kogon's family in Vienna, and helped to smuggle Kogon out of the camp shortly before the liberation. According to Kogon, no one else obliged the prisoners in Buchenwald as much (Kogon 1946, 130, 327, 340 ff.).[76] Walter Poller, who met the SS men working in the Buchenwald infirmary years earlier, calls the Berlin medical officer Rose the only man "whom I cannot condemn." Even though he was able to "give only a limited amount of help, he did help to the best of his ability." Rose, an elderly man and "not the Buchenwald type," had been transferred there at the outbreak of the war, when the concentration camps were expanded (Poller 1960, 275 ff.).

The inmates' organization in Buchenwald systematically tried to uncover weaknesses among the guards. This assignment was given to the Dutchman Wijnen, who became the barber of the SS toward the end of 1943.[77]

Old Dachau hands remember Brückelmann, the head of the SS canteen, who may have been "a bit too self-confident." He even shook hands with Jewish inmates, which was inconceivable, and did not last long at Dachau.[78] The Jews interned in the satellite camp Allach told American officers that the SS man Gerhard Schmidt had helped the Jews there.[79]

Even in extermination camps, some SS men could be induced to break the solid chain of isolation and terror that surrounded the inmates. Here we shall mention only an SS man from Berlin named Steinberg, a guard in the special detail at Auschwitz, of whom one can only speak "in the highest terms." It seems that the reason for this unusual conduct was Steinberg's Jewish brother-in-law, an inmate of Auschwitz.[80] Inmates of Birkenau who were active in the resistance received information about the imminent liquidation of the family camp in Theresienstadt through Hans Schwarzhuber, the officer-in-charge; he was having an affair with a female prisoner and let out the secret to her.[81] The German court that investigated the crimes committed in the extermination camp Sobibor came to the conclusion that the SS supervisor Klier had indicated to the inmates "that he was on their side and did not approve of what he was forced to do." This man was rebuked by his superiors for being "much too soft on the inmates." He is said to have warned the inmates in the late summer of 1943 that the camp did not have much time left and they should somehow get out.[82] Chaim Engel sums up his judgment of this man in these words: "Klier was kind, but not kind enough to allow us to run away."[83]

As the defeat of National Socialism became more and more imminent, acts of kindness toward the inmates multiplied—obvious attempts on the part of the SS to make points with the prisoners. This is why most of these reports have come from the camps that were liberated last.

At Dachau, the Belgian Albert Guérisse, who as head of the international resistance movement surveyed the situation in the final phase, says that in those days there were young SS men "who were entirely on our side, particularly ethnic Germans."[84] Karl Ludwig Schecher, a German, made this comment about the last days: "The inmates' crossconnections were now expanded by a number of SS men who were 'hedging their bets.' Hardly a telex arrived at the commandant's office that did not become known to the inmates within a few hours."[85] According to Schecher's compatriot Walter Leitner, at that time SS men were "available for the subversive work of German anti-Fascists."[86] Toward the end, Dachau, or its satellite camps, housed female prisoners as well, and these were guarded by women wearing SS uniforms. In the very last days of the camp, female SS supervisors gave guns to inmates who assured them that, in return, the prisoners would help them as soon as the situation changed. In this way a total of four revolvers came into the possession of the resistance organization (Brome 1957, 232 ff.). On April 26, three days before the liberation, a prisoner detail was able to leave the camp, together with two SS men, to make contact with the Americans. These two men, with whom those active in the resistance had already had contact, were prepared to throw their lot in with German inmates.[87] In the Dachau satellite camp Landsberg, an SS guard simply opened the gate for four inmates who were anxious to escape in late April 1945, and he received a can of meat in return.[88]

There are several documents about similar developments in Mauthausen, the last camp to be liberated. The Russian Valentin Sakharov writes that toward the end of 1944 some SS men already approached prisoners and offered them their help; "German and Austrian comrades told us this" (Sakharov 1961, 177). The Spaniards Manuel Razola and Mariano Constante gained the impression that in the final period the demoralization of the SS was far advanced. Evidently impressed with the solidarity and high morale of the Spaniards, some SS leaders sought conversations with them, assured them that they would henceforth treat them fairly, and expressed the hope that if the war turned out badly, the Spaniards would not harm them. Even earlier the Spaniards had managed to infiltrate the inmate personnel of the SS junior officers' home, where their man was able to make contact with one of the officers, who helped him and gave him information about the morale of the troop (Razola/Constante 1969, 134). Hans Maršàlek, speaks of a "general picture of demoralization" of the SS in the final phase. "Many SS men procured civilian clothes and ID cards with false names, and some of them conspired with certain prisoner functionaries" (Maršàlek 1974, 239). Utilizing such conditions, the lives of several inmates could be saved by bribing SS men (Maršàlek n.d., 26, 39). However, to the very last days, numberless inmates were murdered on orders from the SS leadership.

Obeying an order from the central administration to the very last, the SS leaders tried to herd the inmates of Gusen into a tunnel in which they had been forced to work. The SS men were going to pretend that there was an air raid and then stage an explosion to block the entrance to the tunnel. The inmates learned about this from SS men who no longer wanted to participate in such actions. The Pole Stanisław Nogaj states that this scheme could be aborted by SS men and inmates who jointly cut the electric cable to the tunnel, thus rendering a blast impossible. It has been reported that SS men, primarily Ukrainians, suggested that the inmates join them in fighting those who had remained under the Nazi spell even after Hitler's suicide.[89]

The administration of Ebensee also wanted to drive the inmates of that satellite camp of Mauthausen into a tunnel whose opening had already been prepared for blasting. The guards were under the command of the Austrian captain Alfred Payrleitner, who was not a Nazi, had previously established contact with inmates via Josef Poltrum, an Austrian noncommissioned officer, and had supplied them with weapons. On May 3, Poltrum informed other inmates about the plan of the officer-in-charge and advised them to refuse to obey his order to go into the tunnel, which would be on the pretext of sheltering from an American air raid. On May 3, the officer-in-charge *asked* the inmates to seek protection in the tunnel; five days after Hitler's suicide, he no longer had enough authority to issue an order. The inmates said "No" in one voice. The weapons had so enhanced their self-confidence that they were able to muster the strength for one final act of life-saving resistance. The officer-in-charge left the camp, together with his block leaders, his world turned upside down. (*Letzeburger zu Mauthausen*, 1970, 245 ff.).[90]

The officer-in-charge of Leitmeritz (Litoměřice), a satellite camp of Flossenbürg, where prisoners had to work for the arms industry in subterranean tunnels, also received orders from the central administration to drive the inmates into the tunnel upon the approach of the enemy and then to blow it up. Willi Gardini, the German capo of the disinfection station, wanted to flee, together with Russian friends, in a last-minute attempt to escape destruction. There followed a grotesque episode. A Gestapo man tried to make points by offering Gardini food and also promising to shelter him in his apartment in Leitmeritz if he decided to escape. He even gave Gardini directions. After Gardini had taken this daring step, he was received in the apartment "with open arms, for I had been expected"—by the Gestapo man, who had learned of the escape. Gardini was given food and a pistol, which tided him over the short period till the end of the war.[91] We also have earlier reports about connections between prisoners and those who guarded them. "Corruption was an important indication" of such contacts (Trhlínová 1974).

The prisoners strove to open all imaginable routes for breaking out of their isolation. When very few inmates were assigned to work in arms factories, contacts with the civilian population were only accidental, and the experiences gained then were not encouraging.

When Eugen Ochs was escorted to Buchenwald after the outbreak of the war, he had to pass a row of civilians on his way to the camp. "They were all hostile, except for one young man who whispered to us, 'Chin up!' "[92] In 1939, Eugen Kogon was taken from Vienna to Buchenwald and had this encounter: "In Leipzig we—sixty men chained together—were led through the railway station, and all the people, every one of them, looked the other way" (Langbein 1976). Others also experienced German civilians' reactions to concentration-camp inmates for the first time at railroad stations. When I passed the main station in Munich in my striped prisoners' garb on my way from Dachau to Auschwitz in August 1942, I did not see a trace of compassion on the faces of those who were staring at us. The Luxembourger Pierre Petit, who was marched through the same station almost two years later, was reviled and physically attacked there (Langbein 1972, 504 ff.). On his way to Mauthausen in September 1944, Joseph Drexel noted at the railway station of St. Valentin (Upper Austria) how a transport of inmates "in deplorable condition" was watched by people "on the crowded track": "Not one face had an expression of horror, or at least of shame and sadness" (Drexel 1978, 66 ff.). Walter Vielhauer and Karl Wagner made different observations on their way from Dachau to Buchenwald in July 1944. In Munich there was a "wave of unspoken sympathy"; people slipped them food-ration coupons, money, and cigarettes. The citizens of Weimar, however, gave them a wide berth, and some even spat contemptuously. That may have been a reaction to the news of that day; it was July 20, the day of the attempt on Hitler's life.[93] The Pole Mieczysław Mołdawa remembers mocking remarks by Germans at the Gross–Rosen station (Mołdawa 1967, 170) and comes to the general conclusion that "the Gross–Rosen camp had no hinterland in which clothes or food could be obtained" (Mołdawa 1967, 140). In late 1944, when an evacuation transport from Auschwitz arrived at a siding of the Regensburg station after a long odyssey and in indescribable condition, civilians threatened the utterly exhausted inmates and reviled them. "It was enough to make one puke," writes Hermann Joseph.[94] In March 1945, inmates of the Mauthausen satellite camp in Linz were assigned to clearing operations at the railway station, and on the way there they were able to observe the population. Gaston Vezes remembers that "no one gave our sad group a compassionate look. . . . I saw women laughing at our appearance and children throwing stones or spitting at us" (Bernadoc 1975, 195 ff.). Inhabitants of Gleiwitz put pieces of broken glass on the streets on which barefoot inmates of the Auschwitz satellite camp had to walk every day on their way to work (Piper 1978, 76). The Dutchman Siegfried van den Bergh remembers that Germans shouted to SS men, who were guarding inmates unloading wagons, that they did not understand why they did not beat those dirty Jews to death (Langbein 1972, 505). An experience reported by Eugen Kogon may be the worst of all those bad experiences: "In Weimar, nurses denied even a drink of water to inmates of Buchenwald who were digging out buried people and cleaning up after an air raid in February 1945. The municipal hospital refused to give first aid to seriously wounded men from the local Gustloff Works."[95] Inmates of Sachsenhausen, who were marched through Mecklenburg after the evacuation of the camp in late April 1945, remember that "even when the rumble of the American artillery had already become audible, people had neither a kind word nor a glass of water for us" (*Damals in Sachsenhausen* 1967, 126).

These examples indicate the attitude of the German population with which concentration-camp inmates had to reckon. Incidents reflecting the opposite are all too rarely encountered. The Frenchman René Gille reports about compassion and clandestine signs of sympathy from the population that he and his fellow sufferers noticed both in Melk and in Amstetten, and he concludes that "with rare exceptions, the Austrians were not hostile to us" (Bernadoc 1975, 301, 370).

In evaluating reports that civilians helped inmates in Ebensee and Ischl, it must be borne in mind that these descriptions were written in the final period and not by prisoners. The Austrian physician Dr. Rudolf Pekar, a member of the Wehrmacht who was assigned to Ebensee as a doctor for the troops and the inmates three months before the camp's liberation, believes that most of the population of Ebensee had a neutral attitude toward the inmates. "A minority of the inhabitants wanted to help them. In those final months I did not notice a hostile attitude." Like other observers, Pekar points out that it was very hard to help; for example, if someone tried to throw the inmates some food, their guards beat them if they tried to pick it up.[96] Josef Steinkogler, a civilian who in the fall of 1944 worked in the tunnel to which inmates of Ebensee had been assigned,[97] remembers trains that were carrying inmates to Ebensee after the evacuation of other satellite camps of Mauthausen. When corpses pulled from the railroad cars were dragged through the town, female inhabitants "rebelled" and the SS had to cancel this transport. The reactions of populations that had themselves been oppressed by National Socialism were different. When Eugen Kogon was on his way from Vienna to Buchenwald, and before the above-mentioned experience with the inhabitants of Leipzig, this transport of inmates passed through Prague. "There people slipped us cigarettes and other things—as much as they possibly could" (Langbein 1976).

French prisoners who were assigned to the Loiblpass detail have unanimously confirmed that the surrounding Slovenian population displayed active sympathy, which quickly created "a climate of hope such as was known to only a small number of details." The Luxembourger Edy Kapgen writes: "The Yugoslavian population was wonderful; it helped wherever it could. . . . Thus we found bread and cigarettes in the pits that had been dug" (Letzeburger zu Mauthausen 1970, 173, 163). In fact, a civil engineer took the initiative in making contact with French inmates—and this happened in September 1943 and not shortly before the end of the war (Bernadoc 1975, 91, 100, 103f.). Those who had been transferred from Buchenwald to an outside detail on the west coast of France had similar experiences. The Pole Tomasz Kiryłłow remembers that "after the French had learned that we were political prisoners, we received food every day."[98] The people of Cernay (Alsace) also did their utmost to ease the lot of the inmates who were sent there from Natzweiler to work. "We became friends," avers a Luxembourger, who also reports that civilian workers who came in contact with them created an organization in their town, with the assistance of the mayor and other important persons, that set itself the task of supporting the inmates with food, even though they had hardly enough to feed themselves.[99]

There is no doubt that the most effective help was given by the Polish population to inmates of Auschwitz. Despite extremely stringent measures taken by the SS—such as resettlements, arrests, and tortures—this help remained continuous. In Gliwice, where Germans maliciously endeavored to exacerbate the sorry situation of the inmates, this help caused Poles to be sent to concentration camps (Piper 1978, 76). The Viennese Karl Dubsky has testified that the chained prisoners who were escorted from the Auschwitz satellite camp Jaworzno to work in a coal mine every day found little food parcels on the road, gifts from the Polish population. On their prison uniforms, most of the prisoners wore evidence that they were Jews. Charles Goldstein, who had been sent from Auschwitz to Warsaw for cleaning work together with Jewish fellow sufferers, reports that strangers tried to cheer them up and greeted them with something akin to reverence (Langbein 1972, 505 ff.).

In this atmosphere, well-organized acts of support and the regular contact of the Combat Group Auschwitz with the Polish resistance on the outside were able to thrive, whereas similar contacts from camps in Germany were possible only in exceptional cases—for example, in Dachau, where clergymen were concentrated and received support from the clergy in Munich (Berben 1968, 170). In the final phase German Communists interned in Dachau were able to receive help from their former comrade Georg Scherer, who had been a generally respected senior camp inmate there; he had been discharged in 1941, and was now living in the town of Dachau.[100] Thanks to a secret organization that had been formed in camps housing Russian prisoners of war, the Anti-Fascist German Popular Front Munich established contact with political prisoners in Dachau and sent them an encouraging letter. It had even considered liberating the camp. But its unconspiratorial conduct—it issued membership cards and vouchers—made it easy for the Gestapo to smash this organization.[101] From outside details of the Sachsenhausen camp that had been assigned to work in nearby Berlin, German Communists were able to establish contact with groups of the German Communist Party that were operating illegally in the capital.[102] The Buchenwald resistance had contact with Belgians doing forced labor in the arms factories of Sömmerda and included these in their plans for an uprising (*Buchenwald* 1960, 498).[103] Otto Horn reports that there were 30,000 civilian workers in Sömmerda.[104]

When the course of the war required ever-increasing numbers of inmates for the arms industry, the prisoners' opportunities to get together with civilians, skilled workers, and specialists employed in such plants—that is, with Germans who had not been drilled in the spirit of the SS— multiplied. The SS did everything it could think of to prevent human contacts; it incited the civilians against "the scum of the earth" and wherever it had any doubts about lasting success, it tried to intimidate those who were bound to come in contact with inmates at their place of work. Private conversations were strictly prohibited, but the SS had no way of making sure that this ban was observed everywhere. The inmates, for their part, were seeking people who had not been shaped by the inhuman system of the SS state.

The pressure on the civilians employed in Dora was especially strong, for the inmates assigned to the production of secret weapons were to be isolated even more strictly than elsewhere. The result has been summarized as follows: "Most of the civilian workers ... acted as agents of the Fascists. Only a small number of them were able to withstand this pressure, and thus there were only few opportunities to establish contact with civilian workers and inhabitants of surrounding towns" (Dieckmann/ Hockmuth, 67). The Pole Tadeusz Patzer, whose function enabled him to survey the situation well, believes that "many civilians behaved worse than the SS," but he also states that many others helped.[105] The Frenchman Andrès Pontoizeau did not observe a trace of compassion in the civilians and even says that many administered beatings like those of the SS and the capos, but he does mention two Germans who aided the inmates and adds that in general German civilians became gentler as their hope of a victory faded (Pontoizeau 1947, 86). On the basis of his studies about the Dora concentration camp, Götz Dieckmann also comes to the conclusion that civilian workers generally treated inmates badly and even beat them. However, he also mentions cases that reflect the opposite—for example, a civilian chef and a woman in Harzungen who were sent to concentration camps because they helped prisoners.[106]

The Frenchman David Rousset had contact with German master craftsmen in Helmstedt, a subcamp of Neuengamme. Some of them identified themselves as Social Democrats. However, after the start of the Ardennes offensive in December 1944, "a bad period began for us," for in those days they evidently believed in Hitler's victory again.[107] In September 1944, I endeavored to establish a personal connection with a master craftsman in the Borgward Works at Bremen. Since I was working in the Work Assignments in the satellite camp, I was able to have regular dialogues with him in his workroom. When he learned that I had been sent to the concentration camp as a veteran of the Spanish Civil War, he identified himself as a former member of the KPD. I had found a way of carrying on a correspondence: Outwitting the equally ignorant and lethargic guard that escorted me from the camp to the plant, I simply dropped my letters and those of my friends into the mailbox that we passed. When I ran out of stamps, I asked the master craftsman to give me some, and when he hesitated, I suggested that he leave them lying around. If they were found in my possession, he could say that I had stolen them from his work station. However, he was not prepared to help me in this way" (Langbein 1949, 198).

Although "almost all the German civilian foremen, master craftsmen, engineers, etc. . . . who supervised inmates [working on arms production] were staunch Nazis," which has been reported about Buchenwald,[108] the contact with civilian workers did make it possible "to isolate the real Nazis or Gestapo agents, or to make them known to the inmates, and also to give the civilian workers a more or less positive attitude and the strength to help us."[109] The Communist Gerhard Zipperer, an engineer employed in the Erla Works at Leipzig–Thekla, facilitated contact with the underground leadership of the KPD that was active in Germany (Drobisch 1968, 123), and useful contacts were made also with Soviet civilian prisoners ("splendid fellows") who had been assigned to the Gustloff Works (Hartung 1974, 81). The Pole Matilda Brożek reports open conversations between her and several German masters at the subcamp Leipzig–Schönfeld in 1944; a few Communists among them even joined female inmates in damaging machines.[110]

There are similar reports from Ravensbrück. "The men serving as masters in the arms factories were mostly Fascists. . . . Even if they were not Nazis, they lived in constant fear of unpleasant consequences . . . [for] masters or workers with whom the management was dissatisfied were simply packed off to the front" (Frauen-KZ Ravensbrück 1973, 201 ff.). However, there are positive examples from this camp as well. "A number of things could be fixed" with a civilian worker at the Siemens plant.[111] When it became known that a civilian worker employed in breeding Angora rabbits was helping inmates, he, his wife, and his daughter were sent to concentration camps (Buber-Neumann 1976, 150).

Zacheusz Pawlak has given a graphic account of the situation in Wesserling (Alsace), a satellite camp of Natzweiler. "The German civilians working at the machines generally consisted of fanatical Nazis, and if there was a German who held a different political opinion, he was so surrounded by Hitlerites that he was afraid to exchange a few words with the Poles" (Pawlak 1978, 212). There are reports about several subcamps of Natzweiler located in Württemberg where the surrounding population gave food to inmates on their way to work. However, it should be noted that only two such cases have been reported by former prisoners (Schabet-Berger 1978, 82; Keverleber-Siegle 1978, 140); the other information was given by civilians (Risel 1978, 116; Walter-Becker 1978, 163; Bockle 1978, 198; Holoch 1978, 258). Also, all these incidents are said to have occurred in the last months of the war. The behavior of German foremen and masters in the subcamp Echterdingen has been reported as "not bad." In another subcamp, Rappenau, a civilian worker is reported to have cooked peas and lentils for the prisoners (Keverleber-Siegle 1978, 141) and a "good-natured old man" to have invited the Pole Zacheusz Pawlak to visit him in his workshop every day and fed him there (Pawlak 1979, 230). By contrast, the master in charge of an excavation crew of inmates of the subcamp Hailfingen has been characterized as "one of the most cruel torturers" who is said to have killed several Jewish prisoners (Walter-Becker 1978, 157). In 1944, the Dutchman Floris B. Bakels had similar experiences at the subcamp Dautmergen: "The higher-ranking OT men [the letters stand for the

Organization Todt, which supervised the work—H.L.] acted like the SS, the lower-ranking ones were on our side and sometimes slipped us bread crusts." Bakels calls special attention to the collaboration of an Austrian worker named Glauninger (Bakels 1979, 267).

There is more positive information about Sachsenhausen. In the Klinker Works "Master Gamm, before 1933 a member of the Social Democrats, supported the political prisoners whenever he could" (*Damals in Sachsenhausen* 1967, 69). The political prisoners assigned to the Heinkel Works were able to establish "contact with around 100 civilian workers," who, according to report issued in East Germany, "were given regular political instruction" (*Damals in Sachsenhausen* 1967, 89). A letter from the SS dated July 3, 1944, indicates that at least one of these had to pay dearly for helping inmates. "The civilian Walter Gau ... an employee of the firm of Heinkel in Oranienburg, was arrested today because on several occasions he smuggled letters and packages out of the plant for the Dutch inmate van Kampen and transmitted them. Gau is to be admitted to the concentration camp Sachsenhausen as an inmate and to be kept in isolation forthwith."[112] Here, too, the more favorable incidents have been reported from subsidiary camps, where it was not possible to exercise the strict supervision of a main camp. The Luxembourger George Hess has testified that the German civilian supervisors of a construction site in the satellite camp Glau "behaved well," and this was also true of SS men assigned there as technicians.[113] The situation was particularly favorable for German political prisoners assigned to one of the small crews that worked in SS offices in Berlin. Rudolf Wunderlich, whom his connections with Berlin Communists enabled to escape at a later date, has singled out the Berliner Annie Noack, a cleaning woman in the adjutant's office of the Main Security Office: "She was a plucky, courageous woman with no interest in politics who helped inmates whenever she could"—and she found many opportunities. For example, she walked off with the official stamp of this office, which enabled prisoners to prepare false papers. There were also a boiler-room attendant who, "in return for a few appropriate 'presents,' did everything he was asked to do" and another cleaning woman who helped bravely.[114] Wunderlich comes to this conclusion: "The best contacts were ... the plainest people in such offices, like boiler-room attendants, craftsmen, and cleaning crews" (*Damals in Sachsenhausen* 1967, 91).

Subsidiary camps of Dachau were located near Hallein. Sepp Plieseis has testified that he was helped by Sepp Hofer, a site foreman there.[115] Plieseis was able to make contact with comrades, and they helped him escape on August 20, 1943. His friend Leo Jansa, like Plieseis an Austrian veteran of the Spanish Civil War, was also anxious to escape and at a later date managed to get transferred to the same subcamp. In November 1944, the

German manager of the Adnet quarry enabled him to carry on a conversation with his brother, who had come to Hallein from Vienna, and in this way Jansa was able to prepare his escape.[116]

Karl Wagner feels obligated to publicize the conduct of the inhabitants of Neustift in the Stubai valley. When an additional subcamp of Dachau was established there, the inmates were able to make contact with several inhabitants, and this developed to the point where there was "a permanent illegal food-collection center for us inmates, organized and directed by Luise Kempf. Week after week our comrades went to the sacristy to pick up the additional food that we so badly needed for the preservation of our lives." Beyond this, the sacristan Alois Kuprian and his wife Anna provided two prisoners who planned to escape in March 1945 with food and clothes (Wagner 1979, 3, 17).

The Frenchman Robert Monin did forced labor in a quarry near Melk, a satellite camp of Mauthausen. Both its manager, an old Austrian monarchist, and the SS guard, "an Austrian anti-Nazi who had been conscripted into the SS," made the inmates' lives as easy as possible. The manager of the quarry and his wife were imprisoned because they had given the inmates food and so severely tortured that one foot of the old lady had to be amputated (*Aktenvermerk*, File Notes 1979, 120 ff.). In the camp at Wiener Neustadt, another subsidiary of Mauthausen, a master whose first name was Günter not only brought the inmates food but also treated the wounds inflicted on them by beatings (*Aktenvermerk* 1979, 120 ff.). The Luxembourger Eugène Thomé was employed in the Steyr Works together with other inmates of Gusen. There he met a master craftsman named Kettner, a South Tyrolean who had been conscripted. "He eventually did whatever I told him," reports Thomé; a genuine friendship had developed between the two men (Thomé 1970, 274 ff.).[117] However, in the same factory Thomé also encountered cruel and unscrupulous masters (Thomé 1970, 284, 305). In the satellite camp Ebensee a site foreman named Achleitner, who was from that town, even killed some inmates.[118]

There are positive reports about Alsatians who came in contact with inmates in Natzweiler. Edouard Barbel, a Luxembourger, feels that all Alsatian foremen of details working on the dismantling of aircraft engines were on the side of the prisoners.[119] Inmates of Stutthof also managed to establish contacts with the civilian population, and from subcamps with French and Italian prisoners of war as well (Dunin-Wąsowicz 1970, 99/ 15, 18). Czechs encountered by inmates of Leitmeritz, a subsidiary camp of Flossenbürg, rendered them substantial assistance, which made it possible to smuggle so many medicaments into the camp in the final months that inmates were able to nurse the patients (Trhlínová 1974, 198). Poles living in Lublin found ways of giving secret aid to inmates of nearby Majdanek;

civilians working for construction firms in the camp area had the greatest chance to do so. Also, in late February 1943, Polish charitable organizations managed to obtain permission from the camp commandant to send food and medicines to the camp (Gryń/Murawska n.d., 60). During that period the central administration of all concentration camps permitted food parcels to be sent to inmates, and this probably promoted the Polish relief action. Polish civilians who had to work in the vicinity of the camp "formed a secret bridge between the prisoners and the charitable organizations as well as their families on the outside," writes Zacheusz Pawlak, who also remembers with pleasure that the civilian populations slipped the prisoners little food packages whenever it was possible (Pawlak 1979, 69, 165). Thus, in Auschwitz there were far greater opportunities than elsewhere of making contact with persons living on the outside, who were themselves being oppressed by the Germans. Via Polish civilians working in the camp area, there was regular contact between the Combat Group Auschwitz and the Polish underground organization in Cracow, though the political department did its utmost to prevent such contacts.[120] In addition to the continuous contact between Polish prisoners in the main camp and compatriots who had been conscripted to work there, connections were made from Birkenau—for instance, by the Polish foreman of the leveling detail, which also worked outside the immediate camp area (Sobański 1974, 200). Here, too, it was easiest to make contacts from a satellite camp. On the extensive premises of I. G. Farben's Buna Works, civilians of different nationalities and British prisoners of war worked side by side with inmates. Leon Stasiak, a Polish Jew who was active in the resistance organization in Monowitz, has testified that prisoners made contact with Polish civilian workers, members of various nationalities doing forced labor, and British prisoners of war at the IG construction site.[121]

Another report sounds similarly optimistic: "My work brought me in contact with civilians of all nationalities—Frenchmen and Belgians, but also German anti-Nazis, Communists, and prisoners of war. All these people helped us a great deal."[122] Fritz Kleinmann, a Jew from Vienna, remembers two Germans with a positive attitude toward the prisoners: Jakob Preuss from Mainz and Sgt. Alfred Wocher, a Bavarian who lived in Vienna and spoke to Kleinmann when he noticed the latter's Viennese pronunciation. As a disabled veteran, Wocher had been assigned to the Buna Works, and with reference to what was going on in Auschwitz [the mass gassings], which could not remain concealed from anyone, he said to Kleinmann: "This isn't what I was fighting for." Kleinmann closes his report by saying that both men gave effective aid; "both were genuine anti-Nazis, but they didn't do anything free of charge."[123]

Leon Stasiak continues his report as follows: "We appealed to the civilian workers of IG Auschwitz [I. G. Farben's Buna Works at Monowitz—
H.L.] to slow down their work and not return from leave. We issued several
appeals to the French workers in particular."[124] To prevent a one-sided
picture from emerging from these optimistic-sounding reports, we must
point out that there is also testimony about German superiors in IG plants
who acted toward prisoners in accordance with National Socialist ideology
(Levi 1979, 110 ff.).

There are a number of reports about contacts with civilians working in a
coal mine to which prisoners of the satellite camp Jaworzno had also been
assigned (Kessel 1970, 159). Karel Bulaty reports that inmates working in
this mine were able to obtain money and civilian clothes; evidently these
were Poles.[125] A different picture has been painted of German pit foremen
and masters: "The majority of them belonged to the SA, and they received
appropriate instructions at the party meetings that took place on Tuesdays
and Fridays." As a result they were "greatly prejudiced against the inmates"
and even murdered some of them in the mine. This went so far that the
officer-in-charge had to remind them that mine workers were forbidden to
maltreat prisoners. On the other hand, "many workers selflessly helped the
inmates" (Piper 1970, 91 ff.). There are similar descriptions about other
satellite camps. Inmates assigned to work on freight cars in Gleiwitz I
report that while "many workers were indifferent or hostile toward the
prisoners," others sought and found opportunities to smuggle food, cigarettes, and newspapers to them despite the strict supervision. Polish forced
laborers, male and female, were particularly helpful (Strzelecka, 104). Reports from the neighboring satellite camp Gleiwitz II are almost identical.
There were German masters who beat inmates, whereas others treated
them fairly. Polish prisoners were able to establish useful connections with
sympathetic Polish workers, masters, and technicians as well as inhabitants of the city of Gleiwitz (Strzelecki 1973, 148, 141). The situation in
other subsidiary camps did not differ significantly from what has been
described above. A report of the Communist organization of prisoners
employed in the mine at Jawiszowice, which was written by three Germans and an Austrian in May 1945, describes the "appalling incidence of
anti-Semitism among the Polish mine workers" as a serious impediment
for the inmates, the overwhelming majority of whom were Jews, and states
that the miners were incited by German pit foremen. The maltreatment of
inmates by these foremen was "not infrequently" applauded by the mine
workers.[126] In the Fürstengrube, where inmates of another satellite camp
of Auschwitz had to work, civilians kicked and slapped inmates they did
not like and made deals with others like the best of friends.[127] Some of the
men working at the mine face and their foremen, among the latter a man

named Goletz, maltreated inmates so often that the officer-in-charge issued a warning. According to Rudolf Ehrlich's testimony, "anyone who fainted and was unable to go on working was regarded as a malingerer" and given a beating (Iwaszko 1978, 56 ff.). In a report dated September 1944, the management of the refinery in Trzebinia, where inmates of Auschwitz worked, stated that productivity could be increased only if block leaders, guards, and capos kept the prisoners under relentless pressure (Piper 1978, 116).

Survivors of Auschwitz have gratefully acknowledged the beneficial activity of a German and an Austrian who came in contact with inmates at their workplace in the main camp. Curt Reinicke came to Auschwitz in 1941 as head of the soil service, and the inmates assigned to work on surveying and soil improvement were under his direction. According to the Pole Józef Kret, "he treated them very benevolently and tried to ameliorate their harsh lot." Reinicke also organized advanced chess courses—"a boon" for the participating prisoners. His humane conduct was an irritant to the camp administration, and in the summer 1943 it managed to get him transferred.[128]

The Carinthian nurse Maria Stromberger requested transfer to Auschwitz when she learned that terrible things were happening there and that nurses were needed to care for sick SS men. "Perhaps I can do some good," she wrote her sister, who had been trying to dissuade her from taking this step. On October 1, 1942, Stromberger was transferred to the SS infirmary in Auschwitz, and there she became acquainted with the machinery of extermination as well as with inmates working in the SS hospital. "It was hard to gain the confidence of those young, bitter men," she said later, but she did gain that confidence to a greater extent than any other civilian in that extermination camp. By virtue of a character that was strengthened by honest faith, her palpable revulsion at the murders and the murderers, and her daily help for those whom she could reach, her relationship with the prisoners developed in such a way that she was finally able to smuggle personal letters and even secret documents out of the camp. In the final phase, she even brought the inmates some weapons. In my memoir of this unusual woman, I wrote: "None of us would have thought of offering her some 'payment' for her help, which was customary when one asked an SS man for a favor." After the end of the war Stromberger wrote as follows to Edek Pyś, a young Pole who had worked under her direction in the diet kitchen of the SS hospital: "I am still choked by the fear that I felt every morning until I saw you before me safe and sound. . . . It seems that I expended my wealth of love in Auschwitz. I have fulfilled my function. What more should I do?" (Langbein 1972, 517 ff.).

It is worthy of note that both Curt Reinicke and Maria Stromberger grew

up in a period when National Socialist though was as yet not being disseminated. He was born in 1894 and she in 1898.

No one should be deceived by the cases mentioned above. Many tens of
thousands came in contact with inmates of concentration camps, whether
in SS uniforms or in civilian clothes. Very few of these placed the elementary commandments of humanity above the inhumane prohibitions of the
SS leadership.

18

BREAKING OUT OF THE
ISOLATION

Isolation from the outside world was part of the psychic pressure that was exerted upon the inmates. Letters that the prisoners (though not all of them) were allowed to write every two weeks were subjected to censorship, and in the early years it was very strict. Practically speaking, a prisoner could write only stereotypical phrases, and even those only to a specific family member, who in turn could give the prisoner only family news—unless both letter writers had prior skill in the use of a "slave language" that could outwit a censor. In several concentration camps, inmates were forbidden to get newspapers; in others subscriptions to National Socialist journals were permitted. The reasons for these divergent practices are not known.

The prisoners' efforts to resist the psychic terrorism included attempts to break out of this isolation. For the morale of the inmates this was of great significance, and its importance increased from year to year as the military situation developed. Where inmates were officially barred from receiving newspapers, they tried to obtain them clandestinely. This has been reported, among others, by the Pole Stanisław Nogaj from Gusen[1] and Shmuel Willenberg from the extermination camp Treblinka (Willenberg 1961–63). The transmittal of news was relatively simple in camps where newspaper subscriptions were permitted in one part and prohibited in another—for example, in the Auschwitz main camp, where "Aryans" (with the exception of Russians) were able to order newspapers, provided that family members had deposited funds for them in a bank account, whereas this was impossible in Birkenau and some satellite camps. The transmission of news by the privileged "Aryans" to their fellow sufferers in the same camp posed even less of a problem, though it did involve some risks. After all, a prisoner had to make sure that the fellow prisoner with whom the contents of a newspaper, especially the daily report of the Wehrmacht, were shared did not blab, for this would have enabled informers to tell the SS about such a contact and put both persons at risk.

There are reports from virtually all camps that individual prisoners found ways of secretly listening to the radio. Those inmates who worked in SS offices with radios had the most favorable opportunities for doing so. Karl Röder writes that it was possible to listen to the radio in the SS quarters of Dachau, "occasionally to foreign stations, too."[2] Sepp Eberl listened to the news in the SS canteen of that camp and transmitted it.[3] On June 6, 1944, inmates working in the officers' home in Dachau were able to disseminate the news about the Allied landing in Normandy throughout the camp as early as 9 A.M.; they had heard it while secretly listening to the radio, and one of them hurried to the camp under the pretext of taking care of the laundry.[4] In Sachsenhausen, prisoners were able to listen to foreign stations when they had been assigned, as specialists, to overhaul a communications truck of the Wehrmacht (Lienau 1949, 151). Radio London was listened to in the motor pool of Majdanek (Mołdawa 1967, 142), in the commandant's and construction offices in Neuengamme,[5] and in the garage of Natzweiler.[6] Before the start of work we listened to Radio London and other foreign stations in the office of the chief SS doctor. Our detail moved out early because the SS hospital had to be cleaned before the SS started work there. This was by no means the only opportunity of listening to Allied stations in Auschwitz.

That such listening was not as easy as this enumeration may indicate is shown by an account written by Fritz Selbmann. A nocturnal attempt to listen to the radio of an SS man in Sachsenhausen "was not repeated because of the danger it involved (Selbmann 1961, 165). Mieczysław Mołdawa remembers that on one occasion such a listening action was "busted" in the weather-station detail at Gross–Rosen. The Russian who was caught was sent away that same evening, never to be heard of again (Mołdawa 1967, 147). Specialists frequently collected radios belonging to the SS for repair and kept them for as long as possible, and if conditions permitted, this enabled them to do some secret listening.[7] However, a report by Schorsch Scherer, the first senior camp inmate of Dachau, indicates that such opportunities did not always exist. He occupied this position in 1939–40 prior to his release and does not remember hearing about such broadcasts, but since he was in close contact with German and Austrian Communists, who were eager to get news from abroad, he would surely have known about such an activity.[8]

Despite all dangers, prisoners in many concentration camps endeavored to become independent of these unsafe and irregular news sources by putting together their own sets or stealing radios. Thus the Luxembourger Arthur Hansen reports that the German Communist Valentin Gabel, an electrician, "organized" a radio in Flossenbürg and listened to it in the camp.[9] In Leitmeritz, a satellite camp of Flossenbürg, inmates were able to listen to news secretly after the fall of 1944; that radio appears to have been sent to the camp for repair and kept there (Krivsky/Krizkova 1967, 38). According to Krysztof Dunin-Wąsowicz, a Russian and a Polish group each had a hidden radio in Stutthof (Dunin-Wąsowicz 1970). Russian prisoners who worked on the dismantling of airplanes smuggled a radio receiver into Auschwitz–Birkenau (Kraus/Kulka 1957, 220). In the shoe factory of Sachsenhausen the German Communist Rittwagen, who was employed as an attendant of the SS, built a set into the wall of a storeroom on which it was possible to listen to Moscow and London regularly for a long time (Opitz 1969, 159 ff.). Even in the extermination camp Sobibor, a Czech Jew named Schwarz, who was an electrician by profession, managed to build a receiver from components that had been smuggled into the camp. The news about developments at the fronts did a great deal to keep the morale of the totally isolated prisoners from deteriorating and give them strength for a successful uprising (Ainsztein 1974, 748).

There are several reports from Mauthausen. With the help of a Spanish group, Istvan Balogh, a Hungarian veteran of the Spanish Civil War, built a radio set in September 1941 with parts he had "organized" at his place of work. To keep the risk of betrayal at a minimum he shared the news he heard only with comrades he knew and trusted (Razola/Constante 1969, 92, 137; Bernadoc 1974, 99 ff.) Vratislav Bušek, a Czech doctor, writes that at times he had a crystal set in the hospital building, and apparently there was another radio in the crematorium.[10] The French radio technician Serge Choumoff has been described as the "radio chronicler" of Gusen (Pappalettera 1972, 212). Harry Naujoks, the German senior camp inmate of Sachsenhausen, recalls a radio set hidden in the drawer of a table in the Russian block on which the Russians listened to Radio Moscow.[11] The Luxembourger Emil Peters tells about a radio put together in Neuengamme by a German engineer, a political prisoner whose first name was Walter.[12] The "ingenious" Pole Jerzy Luda smuggled a crystal set into the concentration camp Gross–Rosen (Moldawa 1967, 151). We have already described the deleterious consequences of the discovery of a radio set in the camp for the leading Communist inmates of Sachsenhausen. It was only natural for the prisoners to try to listen to Allied stations. BBC London and, in the final phase, Radio Luxembourg, were the stations most likely to be received. We have detailed reports from Dachau, Buchenwald, and Dora about the procurement of radios and the dissemination of the news heard on them.

In Dachau the prisoners obtained several sets. The Austrian Communist Franz Freihaut reports that in the detail Cleaning of SS Quarters a radio was hidden in a watering can on which it was possible to listen to a speech by Stalin in 1941.[13] The German Willi Eifler writes about a set concealed in Block 20,[14] and his compatriot Karl Röder tells about another built in the workshop in which he was employed and on which they listened to foreign broadcasts as early as spring 1939.[15] There is a detailed account of inmates regularly listening to Allied broadcasts in the camp laundry.

Gustl Gattinger, a man from Munich who was working as a specialist in the electricians' detail of the security workshop, used replacement parts obtained by inmates from the cable-dismantling detail (where radio sets of shot-down Allied airplanes were stripped) to put a supposedly unrepairable set in working order and took it to Fritz Burkhardt, the German capo of the camp laundry. As far as Gattinger remembers, this was in late 1943 or early 1944. Because of Allied bombings, the SS had ordered Gattinger and others to sleep in the rooms of that detail as the so-called firewatch. The Luxembourger Albert Theis, a friend of Burkhardt's, has described the hiding place of the radio set as follows: "Since the laundry was connected to the central heating system of the camp, the required pipes were located in a walled-in corridor that was concealed by a steel plate in the laundry. We used this corridor as a hiding place. . . . After hours, when the SS had left the camp, we locked and bolted all outside doors . . . turned out all the lights, and with the aid of a shaded flashlight brought the radio into a wonderfully suitable room, which was centrally located in the laundry and surrounded by other rooms. . . . Neither a beam of light nor a sound could penetrate to the outside. In this way we received the latest news every day." Theis adds that, in addition to Burkhardt and him, the listeners were a Pole, a Czech, "and sometimes others as well"—convincing evidence that there were trustful international contacts in that detail. The news was cautiously shared with dependable colleagues. Gustl Gattinger, who also slept in his detail (Security Workshop) on firewatch, also obtained a radio. An SS chief squad leader had brought his set to the workshop for repair and had been sent to the front shortly thereafter, so the radio stayed in Gattinger's possession, and he listened to Russian, Swiss, and British stations night after night.[16]

There are varied reports about Dora. The generally well-informed Pole Tadeusz Patzer believes there was no need to incur the risk of building a set, because every evening inmates listened to news in the infirmary on a radio provided, in return for gold teeth, by an SS junior squad leader on duty there.[17] However, the Czech Jan Češpiva writes that his compatriot Jan Chaloupka, a radio mechanic, constructed a receiver (Dieckmann/Hochmuth 70). The Pole Krokowski remembers a receiver put together by his compatriot Marek Kolczyński, which was hidden in the crematorium and destroyed when the SS started an investigation in November 1944 on the basis of information supplied by informers. The SS found remnants of this set, and as a result there were numerous arrests, tortures, and executions as well as searches in other camps.[18] Chaloupka also attempted to build a transmitter, but it could not be established whether it ever was operational before its components, like those of the receiver in the crematorium, had to be destroyed.[19] The German court in Essen that interrogated the witnesses available to it came to the conclusion that "the existence and activity of a transmitter could not be definitively established."[20]

On this subject, too, we have the most numerous reports from Buchenwald. The Austrian Communist Otto Horn wrote shortly after the liberation: "Listening to foreign stations since around 1939; still unorganized, however, and on a very small scale, impeded by SS control and the paucity of sets. . . . When Berlin ordered, in September 1943, that all receivers be removed from the camp and that repairs be made only outside the camp, opportunities for clandestine listening were immediately created, or existing plans were put into practice. In an effort to utilize the nights, chances to sleep outside the blocks were created (on the pattern of Dachau). Prisoners began to build small receivers in neutral containers that could easily be disassembled, and camouflaged antennas also."[21] Armin Walther, an inmate who was employed as a master electrician, writes: "We regularly received news from around the world with well-camouflaged short-wave receivers" (Kautsky 1961, 309). Others have reported that Walther constructed and built receivers, and he had to keep repeating this work, for "every time the SS conducted a raid in the camp the little receiver had to be destroyed. . . . New sets were built two or three times" (Hartung 1974, 177). National groups created their own opportunities; for example, a group from Pilsen built a receiver and hid it in a gasoline drum (Buchenwald 1960, 404), and Russians concealed their radio under a false bottom in a bucket containing shoe polish. Ivan Smirnov writes that news could be received on that set after mid-1944 (Smirnov 1959, 91 ff.), but Julius Mader, who was not in the camp, believes that this receiver was in use a year earlier (Mader 1973). An unsigned report dated 1945 points to problems faced by Communist-led organizations in listening to news: In addition to places they evidently created and controlled, there were also "so-called 'wild' listeners." Although it was important to the organization "to derive a clear political line from the political news," the 'wild' listeners transmitted this news "indiscriminately, from objective as well as personal points of view" (Buchenwald 1960, 363).

In discussions of the building of radio sets in Buchenwald, the name of the Polish radio engineer Gwidon Damazyn is repeatedly mentioned. It was due to his expert help that Russians were able to construct their set. Damazyn built a total of "seven radio receivers in three-and-a-half years. . . . He built most of them at night in the film projection booth with parts that had been smuggled there from the detail Garrison Administration [Where Damazyn was employed as a specialist—H.L.] or stolen from SS radios under repair." His compatriot Teofil Witek, the author of this account, characterizes Damazyn as a "righteous, sober-minded, and keen-witted man" (*Buchenwald* 1960, 517 ff.). Together with the uncommonly accomplished German radio technician Helmuth Wagner, who was not affiliated with any political party, Damazyn also initiated the construction of a short-wave transmitter. According to a study published in East Germany, "this was not done on instructions from the underground resistance organization; rather, the group of electricians acted on their own initiative." East German publications usually give credit to the Communists (Hartung 1974, 115 ff, 72). In the collection *Buchenwald*, Damazyn, Wagner, the German Social Democrat Armin Walther, and several German Communists are named as collaborators on this transmitter (*Buchenwald* 1960, 519). According to an anonymous report written immediately after the liberation, "We had these sources of communication: 1 mains receiver, 1 battery receiver, 1 super mains receiver for the party headquarters, 1 mains receiver (prisoners of war), 1 transmitter, 12 walkie-talkies with 3,000 meters field cables and equipment. The transmitter was started by Russian prisoners of war and completed and put into operation by Polish friends."[22] Armin Walther's testimony before the American authorities that had liberated Buchenwald indicates how risky the procurement of all this equipment was. After experimental transmissions of recorded music and announcements that worked very well, a "comparable receiving and transmitting station was betrayed and detected [in Dora]. Twenty-nine inmates were arrested, eight were shot, and two took their own lives. An order was issued to search all camps for transmitters. . . . With a heavy heart we had to destroy ours." However, it was possible to rebuild one transmitter, and on April 8, 1945, it broadcast an SOS that was answered by American outfits approaching Buchenwald (Kautsky 1961, 309 ff.).

A statement by Joseph Joos, who was interned in Dachau, proves that the dissemination of clandestinely heard news was also capable of causing bad blood. "The savvy people in the camp had other reports, but you couldn't mention or even whisper them. Only certain people listened regularly, and they transmitted what they had heard only to certain other people" (Joos 1946, 193). The mass executions in Mauthausen have already been mentioned, and the history of that camp also shows that strict secrecy was absolutely necessary. On November 4, 1944, two electricians, the capo Franz Steininger and Anton Güttlein, were tortured and shot because the Mauthausen administration had heard that they had been listening to a radio in their barracks (Maršàlek 1974, 181; (*Aktenvermerk* 1979, 141 ff.). In Gusen, two young Poles, Władysław Wozniak and Piotr Grzelak, were killed on April 21, 1945, shortly before the liberation, after an SS man had reported that they had listened to a radio in the construction office at the quarry and had marked the positions at the front on a map.[23]

After it had been revealed that inmates had been listening to broadcasts on a radio smuggled into Sachsenhausen, the SS also searched for a secret transmitter in the hospital building, but because the informers' reports were groundless, nothing was found.[24] There are divergent reports about a transmitter in the Auschwitz main camp. The Pole Eugeniusz Niedojadło has testified that he took the components for such a transmitter from the SS hospital, where he worked, to the camp wrapped in blankets. To prevent an inspection at the gate, he wrote "Infectious! Handle With Care!" on the package and took it to Block 20, the infection station, which was shunned by the SS. As far as he can remember, this was in late spring or early summer of 1942, and he believes that the transmitter was in operation for only three months, broadcasting to Cracow and from there to London.[25] The Pole Józef Gárliński has confirmed this and stated that, for reasons of conspiracy, the transmitter had to be dismantled in the fall of 1942, for too many inmates already knew of its existence and the SS was looking for it. However, he believes that the secret organization of Polish officers had already been able to use it for seven months (Gárliński 1975A, 100; 1975B, 67). Since he was not in Auschwitz at that time, he must have heard about it at a later date. It must also be remembered that Garliński is bent on emphasizing the accomplishments of the officers' organization headed by Witold Pilecki. Józef Cyrankiewicz, who began to participate in the Polish resistance organization shortly after his arrival in Auschwitz in early September 1942 and later was the liaison with the Polish underground movement in Cracow on instructions from the Combat Group Auschwitz, states that there was no transmitter in Auschwitz during that period,[26] and thanks to the well-functioning constant correspondence connection, it would have been irresponsible to incur the risk of operating a transmitter.

To seek contact with the world outside by means of a transmitter certainly constituted the most spectacular attempt to break out of total isolation, but it was not the most effective one, for it was too risky. Hence transmissions were the exception rather than the rule. The most frequent method, one probably employed in all camps, was to use contacts with guards or civilians to smuggle out mail. This was the simplest way of transmitting information to outsiders (and, if the intermediaries were willing, of receiving mail). Of course, "simple" must be understood in relative terms.

Most of the news sent out of the camps in this fashion was probably personal in nature. Obviously, resistance organizations also looked for intermediaries who could establish contact with like-minded people living in freedom. We have already mentioned the intensive written contact between the Combat Group Auschwitz and Cracow as well as some results of this connection—such as the replacement of both the commandant and the head of the political department in the fall of 1943 (Brückner/Horn 1975). In various ways, the International Red Cross received information that made relief actions possible. As early as 1941, it received from a Swiss man living in Linz who evidently had contact with Mauthausen "an accurate report and even a site plan."[27] Lists of inmates secretly smuggled to Geneva enabled the Red Cross to secure permission to send packages to concentration camps. When these were not distributed to the inmates whose names they bore, the Red Cross was informed (and the camp administration was bypassed) (Red Cross 1947, 18 ff.). Lists with inmates' numbers and blocks were smuggled out of Auschwitz and reached Geneva via Cracow. In a covering letter dated June 20, 1943, we read: "It is necessary for people living abroad to receive our addresses en masse, for it is important to prove to the Germans that the whole world knows about Auschwitz. . . . It would be helpful also to give addresses of Germans in the camps, of Czechs, and others, e.g., Soviet Communists." This action actually brought Red Cross packages to Auschwitz, and even though the SS confiscated many of them, they had an effect (Jarosz 1978, 157 ff.). When the catastrophic military situation eventually obliged the German government to give up its rigidly negative attitude toward interventions by the Red Cross, information that was secretly sent out also facilitated the relief actions, which were now permitted. Thus the Norwegian Silvia Salvesen secretly sent out "a detailed report about the catastrophic conditions" in Ravensbrück, which enabled the Red Cross to evacuate several groups of inmates, principally French and Scandinavian women, to Sweden during the last weeks before the final collapse of the Third Reich (Buber-Neumann 1958, 368 ff.; Die Frauen von Ravensbrück 1961, 150; Arndt 1970, 128 ff.).

Contacts that could be established by clergymen, who were concentrated in Dachau, effected improvements as well. The Austrian Father Johann Lenz reports that a German parson assigned to a block of invalids managed to smuggle out news of the fate of those incarcerated there, who were destined for starvation or gassing at one of the institutions in the "euthanasia project." "Berlin finally acted to prevent such facts from becoming known abroad," but evidently this news had already been transmitted to other countries. This probably happened in the latter part of 1942, and from then on clergymen could no longer be used for experiments and had "a right to normal treatment in the infirmary" (Lenz 1956, 170). There were other contacts between Catholic clergymen and clergy living outside.[28] For example, through an underground correspondence with Cardinal Faulhaber in Munich and the bishop of Münster, all documents and religious paraphernalia required for the consecration of a mortally ill deacon in Dachau could be obtained in December 1944 (Goldschmidt 1954, 266 ff.) Thanks to his privileged position in Gusen, the clergyman Johannes Gruber was able to make contact with his sister in nearby Linz–Urfahr and through her with places in France, Czechoslovakia, and Poland. Gruber, the capo of a detail charged with the conservation of prehistoric artifacts found during excavations, gathered information about events in the camp and transmitted it, but the success of this written contact (and soon also exchange of packages) evidently made him careless. The Vienna Gestapo got wind of it, and a search turned up notes and documents relating to this correspondence in Gruber's possession. He was beaten and shot on April 7, 1944; his contacts outside the barbed wire—an SS man from Romania and a building contractor—as well as many others were arrested and tortured. When the central administration of the camps was informed about this incident, it immediately prohibited the use of clergymen for any secretarial duties.[29] The Frenchman Louis Deblé has described how Gruber helped young French Catholics materially and morally and characterized him as "goodness incarnate" (Bouard 1942, 62).

An unusual relief action was initiated for Polish prisoners who had been transferred from Auschwitz to Gross–Rosen, where they were deprived of the normally permitted correspondence with their relatives and had to live under oppressive conditions. In the summer of 1944 Władysław Plaskura, an "old" inmate of Auschwitz employed as a specialist in the construction office, was ordered to travel to Gross–Rosen. He was escorted by the SS lieutenant colonel who headed the water-supply and drainage department of the SS construction inspectorate for Silesia and a guard, because overcrowding created by numerous transfers had caused difficulties with the water supply. Plaskura knew that inmates of Auschwitz had recently been transferred to Gross–Rosen. When he wanted to establish contact with the Poles employed in the construction office, he was at first rebuffed because they could not trust someone who had arrived together with an SS officer. To dispel this distrust, Plaskura invited his colleagues to check with former inmates of Auschwitz, among whom were friends who had worked with him in the construction office there. This created an atmosphere of trust, and the Poles agreed to compile a list of those who had no contact with their families. After telling his superior that he had to complete his assignment in Auschwitz because he did not have the necessary tables and books in Gross–Rosen, Plaskura concealed the list—about 200 names—in a secret compartment built into a tube containing drawings which the SS officer himself carried to Auschwitz. There Plaskura gave the list to the resistance organization, which saw to it that those on it received packages through the good offices of the Polish secret organization in Cracow.[30]

Special efforts were made to disseminate information about the production of V-rockets, to which the inmates of Dora and its satellite camps had been assigned. Bretons interned there included in their letters, which had to be written in German, some Breton words. The SS censor did not understand these, of course, and might have taken them for proper names, but they did give the recipients some idea of what was going on in Dora.[31] Romuald Sztaba, a Polish physician interned in Majdanek, learned from transferred prisoners that V-rockets were being manufactured in Dora, Ellrich, and Nordhausen. Having found a way of sending letters, he wrote to an acquaintance, an inmate who had been discharged, about this arms production in invisible ink (Kwiatkowski 1966, 304 ff.; Pawlak 1975, 174 ff.).

The boldest way of transmitting information about Dora was found by Eugen Kogon. He used the telephone of the SS camp doctor in Buchenwald, whom he was serving as a clerk, told the operator that he was the doctor, and called a police station in Unna, where a friend of his comrade Heinz Baumeister, like the latter a Social Democrat, was an officer of the civil defense. Using a prearranged pseudonym, he told Baumeister that blueprints of the subterranean buildings of Dora, to which both men had access because they were stored in the hygienics institute of Buchenwald, would be worked into a book jacket and sent to him.[32] From Auschwitz plans of the crematories with built-in gas chambers were sent out. Věra Foltýnová, a Czech who worked in the construction office and copied plans there, commented: "Perhaps they are not all accurate; many of them were drawn in the dark, and often our eyes were more on the door than on the paper" (Kraus/Kulka 1957, 20 ff.). Such copies were sent to Poland as well as Czechoslovakia.[33] The Pole Stanislaw Klodzinski, who worked as a nurse in the Auschwitz hospital, sent out a preparation that the SS tested on sick inmates with the request that it be analyzed. The doctors among the inmates did their best to sabotage such experiments (Klodzinski 1969, 81).

The inmates were very anxious to learn what was going on in the world, particularly how the military situation was developing, but it was also very important to them that the world found out what was happening in the concentration camps, and especially the extermination camps. In several camps they concealed documents so that the realities could be proved after the liberation of the concentration camps, even if there might be no witnesses alive to testify.

Thus Mieczysław Mołdawa reports that inmates utilized the chaotic conditions in Gross–Rosen caused by overcrowding in the latter part of 1944 to "save notes and documents about past crimes in order to make them accessible to an international public." A Pole who worked in the SS photo laboratory was able to hide photos of great documentary value in the camp, and these were found after the liberation (Mołdawa 1967, 155). Francisco Boix, a Spaniard who worked in the SS police-records department in Mauthausen, secretly made copies of important photos, both of prominent visitors to the camp and of inmates who had been killed, and these were concealed by the Spanish secret organization for two years, until the liberation.[34] In December 1944, a twenty-man detail was transferred from Mauthausen to Hartheim Castle with orders to remove all evidence that for years human beings had been killed by poison gas in that "euthanasia institution," and these inmates had reason to assume that they too would be killed once this work was done, in order to eliminate all living witnesses. Thus a Spaniard placed a slip of paper in a bottle and immured it in the wall that served to lock the door to the gas chamber. This slip was later found.[35] Czech inmates working in the office at Mauthausen saved the death records, which contained information about those who died in that camp between January 7, 1939, and April 29, 1945, and the Spaniard Sibile José Bailina safeguarded registers of Work Assignments (Bouard 1954, 39). The Pole Krystyna Zywulska worked in the property room of the Birkenau women's camp. There she had contact with women who were being discharged from the camp, particularly so-called reformatory prisoners, who had been sent to the camp for a certain term because of some misdemeanor at their places of work. She came to trust one of these, sewed a description of the extermination process in Auschwitz into her garter, and asked her to transmit this information to her relatives in Warsaw. In a covering letter she requested that the next package sent to her include three hard-boiled eggs as a sign that the information had been received. Soon after this woman was released, Zywulska received this proof (Zywulska 1979, 212, 323). The Austrian Jew Otto Wolken, a doctor in the quarantine section of Birkenau, was able to keep statistics about arrivals, gassings, and murders. When he was ordered, before the evacuation, to turn all documents over for burning, he managed to bury them, because the SS no longer took the time to check the papers that had been turned in. At a later date, his notes were retrieved.[36]

In Majdanek too, inmates endeavored to preserve documents about Nazi crimes. The Pole Zacheusz Pawlak writes: "[I made] a list of the patients who had been gassed after the first selection, which I myself survived. I copied their personal data from the patients' register of Block 4, wrapped the list in wax paper and parchment, and then cemented it into the washroom floor of Barracks 3, where a sewerage system was being installed. . . . A few days later I prepared a second list, which contained a description of the selection and additional information about those who had been gassed. . . . That was in May 1943." When inmates were ordered, on May 1 (which the National Socialists observed as a holiday), to put up a monument, they immured in its base ashes of murdered prisoners as well as a list of murdered members of the Polish underground movement (Pawlak 1975, 82 ff., 124).

The documents that were buried by members of the Auschwitz special detail at the crematories are an even more moving source—and historically more important. These men knew that they were privy to secrets and would therefore be killed. After the uprising of the special detail on October 7, 1944, had been put down, Salmen Lewental added the following sentence to his notes about what was happening in and around the gas chambers: "From now on we shall hide everything in the ground" (Lewental 1972, 188). Salmen Gradowski started his account with these words: "I buried it under the ashes, for I had reason to assume that this is where they would dig in order to find the traces of millions of murdered people" (Gradowski 1972, 79). At a later date several documents were dug up and deciphered, and they helped to break through the wall of secrecy that the National Socialists had put up to hide their mass murders from the world.[37]

The Combat Group Auschwitz tried to immobilize the SS Senior Squad Leader Wilhelm Boger, one of the most dangerous and most corrupt men in the political department. Shortly after the liberation, I described this attempt as follows: "We sent an anonymous letter [via our intermediaries on the outside—H.L.] to the commandant in which we enumerated all objects in Boger's apartment that had been 'organized' [that is, stolen—H.L.] and also stated where and under what circumstances they had been obtained. All statements could have been verified, but nothing happened to Boger."[38]

In the last year of the war, the resistance group in Monowitz sent, in the same way, "a letter to the officer-in-charge Schöttl and director [of the IG Buna Works—H.L.] Walter Dürrfeld in which we called on both men, in view of the impending events, to treat the inmates decently."[39] The effect of this letter was harder to determine.

Another method of getting out information developed in places from which escapes could be organized. On August 4, 1942, there was a spectacular escape of five inmates from Natzweiler, which was organized by the Czech captain Josef Mautner (born in 1899) and the Austrian Karl Haas (born in 1910). The inmates fled in an SS automobile procured by Haas, who was working in the SS garage as a mechanic. Two of them had put on SS uniforms obtained by a stateless criminal, who as foreman in the SS laundry had access to such uniforms. For this reason he had been included in the group, but he was the only one who lost his head after the successful escape; he separated from the others, was captured, returned to the camp, and hanged. Mautner writes that he had a long struggle with himself before deciding to go along, for he had reason to fear reprisals against his family: "On the other hand, I felt an urge . . . to reach freedom and be one of the few witnesses to German brutality and the terrible sadism in the concentration camps." Thanks to careful planning and the support of Frenchmen they encountered, he did gain this goal. On November, he and Haas reached England with the help of the French resistance, and there he was able to give detailed reports. Haas, a pilot, volunteered for the Royal Air Force, and on a flight undertaken on July 19, 1944, he took an aerial photo of Natzweiler.[40]

Understandably, the desire to get news out was strongest in those who had to witness the daily mass murder in extermination camps. Both escapees and those who helped them escape attached immense importance to the transmission of authentic information. "After the Pole Kazimierz Hałoń had fled from Auschwitz on February 20, 1943, at the behest of the Polish resistance, he was hidden in a Cracow apartment and instructed not to leave it and to write as detailed a report as possible about the camp and to draw a map of it. The latter was to "include the main camp, Birkenau, Rajsko, and Budy [two satellite camps in the immediate vicinity—H.L.] This documentation was to be given to the Allies in order to inform the world about the atrocities" (Sobanski 1974, 55 ff.; Iwaszko, 32).

Several Czech and Slovak Jews escaped from Auschwitz in the spring of 1944, which revealed to the world a great deal about the extermination machinery in that camp. On April 5, the Czech officer Vítěszlav Lederer managed an adventurous escape from Birkenau. In late 1939, a secret Czech military group to which Lederer belonged had been betrayed to the Gestapo. After his arrest he had been dragged from one prison to another while the Gestapo tried to extort further details from him. He finally landed in Theresienstadt, and from there he was transferred to Auschwitz on December 19, 1943, where he was given the position of a senior block inmate in the family camp, to which the Theresienstadters were assigned. The political department repeatedly summoned Lederer for interrogations, and these involved torture. The SS man who had been ordered to produce Lederer was Viktor Pestek, an ethnic German from Bucovina (Romania), and he had a chance to examine Lederer's file, which indicated that Lederer would sooner or later be executed; if the Gestapo charged a Jew with political crimes, it usually followed this with a death sentence. On the other hand, Lederer's file also indicated that he had good connections with his homeland. This induced Pestek, who was disgusted with his activity in Auschwitz, to suggest to Lederer that they flee together; he would help Lederer get out of the camp, and in return Lederer would help him drop out of sight in Czechoslovakia. Having nothing to lose, Lederer agreed, and the preparations were quickly made; Pestek obtained an SS uniform and papers for Lederer. The escape was successful; Lederer was able to get to Prague and used his freedom to warn the Jews interned in Theresienstadt. He sneaked into the town several times, in order to describe to his acquaintances the fate of those who had been deported to Auschwitz, but his warnings remained futile. At precisely that time the administration of Theresienstadt was preparing a great comedy.

The Red Cross had been permitted to make an inspection, and so improvements were effected and amenities installed. In fact, a film about the "social life" in Theresienstadt was made, and the inmates allowed themselves to be impressed, thinking that the Nazis needed them as an alibi and would therefore let them live. Lederer also attempted to make contact with the Red Cross in Switzerland and was able to travel to Konstanz, but these efforts are not known to have produced any concrete results.[41]

A successful escape from Birkenau about the same time had a greater effect. Two young Jews, Alfred Wetzler (born in 1918) and Walter Rosenberg (born in 1924, later assuming the name Rudolf Vrba) had been deported from Slovakia in the spring of 1942. Since they had had uncommon freedom of movement in various functions, eventually as block clerks, they became intimately acquainted with Auschwitz and the functioning of the extermination machinery. They were also in touch with the underground organization and could thus count on help with their escape. The motives for their attempt may be learned from their own accounts.[42] Wetzler, whose story is told in the third person, writes: "How gladly he would assure them [those active in the resistance—H.L.]: Believe me, dear friends, we don't forget anything, we shall do our best to tell the world what monstrous crimes against humanity the Nazis are committing behind this barbed wire" (Lanik 1964, 138). Vrba writes: "For almost two years I had thought of escaping—at first only for egotistical reasons, because I wanted to have freedom, but later with a more general aim: I wanted to tell the world what was going on in Auschwitz" (Vrba/Bestic, 226). With the aid of their friends, the two men gathered documents; their compatriot Filip Müller, who was working in the special detail, was able to remove the label from an empty container of the poison gas Zyklon B and give it to them (Müller 1979, 194 ff.). We are not dealing here with a legend written after the war. The two men wrote a report for the Jewish council in Žilna after their successful escape, and this historic document has been preserved.[43] This is what Wetzler has to say: "In the course of three days we composed a report of about fifty typed pages. We described everything we had seen in the camp and also gave statistics about murdered people. These were not compiled from memory but were based on notes we had brought along from the camp" (Iwaszko 1964, 39). In his book Wetzler gives a more detailed report. Several little rolls of paper contained data given them by inmates working in the main office and the political department: "On these dirty scraps of paper they recorded the dates of the construction and expansion of the various camps as well as the numbers of victims who had been dragged there first from Poland, then from Germany and France, and finally from all occupied European countries and 'nonoccupied' Slovakia" (Lanik 1964, 264). Their report gives the number of Jews gassed before April 7, 1944, the date of their escape, as 1,715,000 ("a careful estimate").[44] These statistics are arranged by country of origin, but they evidently do not include those Jews who were added to the camp as inmates and then died.

On May 27, two other Jewish inmates, Arnošt Rosin and Czesław Mordowicz, managed to escape from Birkenau. They too were able to make their way to Slovakia, where they met with the Jewish council and their comrades Wetzler and Vrba (Drexel 1978) and provided concrete information about the destruction of Hungarian Jews, a murderous roundup that had been started eleven days before their flight from Auschwitz. "Their declarations supplemented the first report, particularly with reference to the arrival of Hungarian Jews in Birkenau."[45] The fugitives also had an opportunity to hand their completed documents and maps to the papal nuncio in Slovakia.[46] Together with the report of a Polish major who had also been able to escape from Auschwitz, this detailed documentation of the organized mass extermination in that camp was turned over to the pope and the governments of the United States and Great Britain as well as the press. This happened in early July of 1944, and the public was alarmed. Interventions by churchmen and several governments with Regent Míklos Horthy induced him to have the deportation of Hungarian Jews to Auschwitz stopped.[47]

Individual inmates who had successfully escaped from one of the extermination camps in eastern Poland also endeavored to make known what they had had to experience there and to issue warnings. Thus Haim Lejst reports that in spring 1942 an escapee from the special detail at Belzec told him about the organized mass murder there, "but no one would believe him" (Novitch 1978, 137). Samuel Rajzman remembers that Jews interned in the Warsaw ghetto were told by a young man who had managed to escape from Treblinka what was going on in that camp: "But we didn't believe it."[48] In her graphic description of the lives of Jews in Berlin, Inge Deutschkron writes: "Listening to the BBC in November 1942, we heard for the first time about gassings and shootings, but we couldn't and wouldn't believe it" (Deutschkron 1978, 107). A young Jew from Warsaw who had escaped from Sobibor wanted to disseminate the truth about the extermination of Jews and took his reports from ghetto to ghetto. It seems that he too failed, for normal human minds boggled at the idea of death factories. That man was finally captured, returned to Treblinka, and killed (Ainsztein 1974, 748).

The first eyewitness account of an extermination camp was published in Warsaw in early 1944, when the city was still under German occupation. Yankel Wiernik, a Warsaw Jew, had been deported to Treblinka. During the uprising organized by Jewish inmates on August 2, 1943, he managed to escape and made his way to Warsaw, where his Polish friends protected him by providing him with "Aryan" papers, and he wrote down his experiences in the extermination camp. Two thousand copies of this report, entitled *Ein Jahr* in *Treblinka*, were produced and distributed by a secret printshop, and copies were sent to London and the United States.[49]

19

ESCAPES AS LIFESAVERS

One driving force for organizing an escape was the need to tell the world about the murderous character of the camps. But other inmates attempted flight purely in order to save their lives. In this context we shall discuss primarily escapes that were prepared in advance rather than spontaneous ones, for prepared escapes were part of resistance in a narrower sense.

If the escapee was to have a chance, he needed two things: an opportunity to get out of the camp and someone ready to help him once he was free. The camps were closely guarded; the central administration had to be notified of every escape, and nothing irritated Himmler more than such reports. This caused the commandants to make frequent checks of the arrangements and use every attempt as an occasion to block the loopholes that had been utilized. Thus the officer-in-charge at Sachsenhausen made the Polish student Tadeusz Owczarek, who had been recaptured after his getaway, "reenact his escape with a ladder that he had used. This convinced the officer-in-charge that the electrical power barrier was not deep enough, and he promptly remedied the situation by having several kilometers of wire newly installed and insulated."[1] A letter sent by Glücks, the inspector of the concentration camps, to the commandants on July 16, 1941, contains this warning with reference to successful escapes of Poles and a "Red Spain fighter": "Every member of the SS who is responsible for the successful escape of an inmate can expect very severe punishment."[2]

The retaliatory measures ordered by the commandants ranged from making the prisoners stand in the roll-call area until the fugitive had been found to incarcerating the comrades of the escapee and leaving them to starve in their cells—a method used by the commandant of Auschwitz, Rudolf Höss.[3] Such reprisals frequently worked, and they made resistance organizations abandon any thought of escapes; a case in point is the Polish officers' organization in Auschwitz (Gárliński 1975A, 66). According to Emil Carlebach, the expectation of reprisals against the entire camp caused the camp committee of Auschwitz to organize no escapes, at least until fall

1944.[4] At a time when concentration camps existed only in Germany and Austria, one great deterrent was the extreme difficulty of escaping detection by the police after a successful flight. Escapees had to expect that the population would report suspicious individuals to the authorities—not only because many convinced National Socialists regarded this as their duty, but also because those who knew of an escape and failed to report it were threatened with dire consequences. Hias Neumeier, a Bavarian, was able to escape from Dachau with the help of a friend, but he was tracked down and taken back to the camp together with his helper.[5] Walter Adam reports that almost all of the small number of fugitives were brought back to the camp after a few days; he remembers only two successful escapes. Adam arrived in Dachau in the spring of 1938 with the first transport of political opponents from Austria and was detained there until July 1943 (Adam 1947, 67). Edgar Kupfer-Koberwitz confirms that escapes from Dachau were impossible before 1943 (Kupfer-Koberwitz 1960, 158). As a rule, recaptured fugitives, especially non-Germans, were hanged in front of the inmates assembled in the roll-call area as a deterrent, and frequently this execution was preceded by torture. The Pole Stanisław Nogaj, who, like Kupfer-Koberwitz, managed to keep a secret diary in the camp, wrote after his successful escape from Gusen that only one in a hundred attempts succeeded and that all other fugitives were captured and murdered. He tells about a Pole who got as far as 40 kilometers from Gusen but was captured when he begged for food in a village.[6] Even in the last months of the war, the inhabitants of the Württemberg town of Schörzingen and its vicinity informed the SS about escapees from the local satellite camp of Natzweiler, and, according to the camp commandant, in many instances the fugitives could not have been recaptured without this information (Holoch 1978, 258). Hans Maršàlek, the chronicler of Mauthausen, has summed up the situation as follows: "The close-meshed security network inside and outside the camps as well as a populace that was, until fall 1944, intimidated, fearful, and often antagonistic toward the inmates greatly diminished the chances for a successful escape. Only in rare instances were inmates helped by the population, and without such support as civilian clothes, food, temporary shelter, and the like no escapee could get far" (Maršàlek 1974, 193).

We have statistics about escapes from Mauthausen (Maršàlek 1974, 200) and Sachsenhausen.[7] The parallels are clear: In its first year, 1938, Mauthausen reported no escape; in 1939 there were four escapees, two of whom were recaptured; in 1940 all seven escapees, in 1941 six out of eight, and the following year eight out of eleven were returned to the camp. Sachsenhausen reported its first three fugitives in 1942. In both camps the number of escapees later grew by leaps and bounds. As early as 1943 there were forty-four in Mauthausen, and the Gestapo was able to seize only nineteen of these; in 1944 there were 126, ninety-eight of whom were taken back to the camp; but in the frequently chaotic conditions of early 1945, only twenty-nine of the 339 escapees became prisoners of the SS again. In Sachsenhausen there was no successful escape in 1943, but ninety-six were reported the following year and 288 fugitives in the first three-and-a-half months of 1945. Dachau reported 338 escapes between March 11, 1943, and January 18, 1945, but before that there had been only isolated cases (Berben 1968, 165).

This rapid rise in the number of escapes, including successful ones, was due not only to military developments (which encouraged the prisoners and probably many of those living in the vicinity of the camps as well). The great increase in the number of satellite camps also favored escapes, for satellites could not be guarded as closely as the main camps, and there were incomparably greater chances of establishing contact with civilians, including foreign workers and prisoners of war, who frequently worked in the same plants as the prisoners. Of the 509 escapees from Mauthausen who were reported between early 1943 and May 1945, only twenty had been able to flee from the main camp, and eighteen of these not until 1945.

The (incomplete) record of escapes from Auschwitz differs from the above-mentioned ones. To be sure, the number of fugitives in 1940 and 1941 is also small (two in 1940, one of whom was recaptured, and six in the following year, all of whom were returned to the camp), but in 1942, 120 escapees were reported, and only sixty-five of these fell into the clutches of the Gestapo again. In 1943, there was a further rise in the number of escapees (to 310) and also in the percentage of successful escapes (only 156 were captured). The incomplete record for the last year lists 209 escapees, forty-two of whom were recaptured.

Only in 42 percent of these cases do the extant documents indicate what camp the inmates escaped from. Unlike what happened in Mauthausen, one-fourth fled from the most closely guarded Auschwitz main camp and more than 37 percent from Birkenau. These documents, as well as the 144 names of escapees (1942–early 1944) mentioned in letters from the Combat Group Auschwitz, indicate that a majority of the escapes were organized with the knowledge and support of that resistance group. Without the help of an organization, it was extremely difficult to escape from a well-guarded base camp.

A letter from the central administration to all concentration-camp commandants dated June 20, 1943, indicates the consequences of this development. It says that the steadily increasing numbers of escapees has "made a very unfavorable impression on the Reichsführer-SS" (Himmler). It also confirms indirectly that many escapes were accomplished with the help of fellow inmates; this probably refers primarily to Auschwitz. As investigations showed, in almost all cases the inmates first concealed themselves and did not escape until the guards had withdrawn from the camp area.[8] It was the Combat Group Auschwitz that had created such hiding places within the great chain of checkpoints (Langbein 1949, 160, 180 ff.; Iwaszko 1964, 30 ff.).

Despite the most severe punishments meted out to inmates suspected of planning to escape and to the surrounding Polish population (those living in the immediate vicinity of the Auschwitz camp were resettled), the SS could not keep an ever-increasing number of prisoners from escaping (Iwaszko 1964, 4). Almost half of these were Poles, for they were the most likely to receive support from the surrounding population. Evidently these civilians could not be intimidated, for they continued to help their compatriots. Hans Maršálek has pointed out that the inmates of Loiblpass, a subsidiary camp of Mauthausen, had a greater chance of "finding among the local Slovenian population someone who was willing to incur the risk that supporting an escapee involved" (Maršálek 1974, 193).

Many fugitives received support from the Polish resistance organization, which had established bases in the vicinity of the camp where fugitives were given what they needed and then sent on. Having been provided by the Combat Group Auschwitz with maps, foods, and medicines, such escapees were also helped by Polish partisan groups that operated in the nearby Beskids Mountains and later even in the vicinity of the camp. These groups consisted to a considerable extent of escapees from Auschwitz (Smoleń 1960–67, 40). The organization of Polish officers that had been active before the formation of the international Combat Group also organized successful escapes of its members. Thus Wincenty Gawron and Stefan Bielicki escaped on May 16, 1942, on instructions from this organization, which was headed by Witold Pilecki (Jarosz 1978, 146). Even those Poles who dared to flee even without contact with the Combat Group had better chances than inmates of other concentration camps. Józef Gárliński has described how clergymen helped a Polish fugitive (Gárliński 1975A, 171).

With reference to the first escape from Auschwitz on July 22, 1940, a high SS and police official wrote that any inmate "who manages to escape can expect any kind of help as soon as he reaches the nearest Polish farm" and summarily characterized the population as "fanatically Polish and ... ready for any action against the hated guards" (Oswiecim 1977, appendix). This may be an exaggeration, but the above figures do show that this assessment is not a pure invention.

One incident reported by Rolf Weinstock may serve to illustrate the

Poles' willingness to make sacrifices. A Polish family was hanged because it had hidden an escapee from the satellite camp Jawiszowice for two days (Weinstock 1948, 106). However, not all escapees could count on such supprt. Thus Ota Kraus and Erich Kulka report that people living in the vicinity of Birkenau "were not always friendly" toward Russian escapees from there (Kraus/Kulka 1957, 52).

The conduct of the Polish population was at its most problematical when Jewish fugitives came looking for help. Shalom Kohn writes that very few of the Jews who had managed to escape from the extermination camp Treblinka were saved. "Most of these fugitives were betrayed by the Polish population and the Polish police and turned over to the Gestapo."[9] Ada Lichtmann, who managed to break out of another extermination camp, Sobibor, together with others, remembered that peasants used a pretext to search the forest in which the escapees had taken refuge and then told the Germans where they could be found (Lichtmann 1961–63). The worst behavior was that of some Polish partisan groups toward Jews who had broken out of extermination camps in eastern Poland, for these groups could not have been motivated by fear of reprisals. After escaping from Sobibor together with some comrades, Stanisław Szmajzner encountered partisans who identified themselves as members of the Native Army, a Polish resistance movement. First they took the Jews' only gun and their money, then they chased them away and shot at them. Szmajzner concludes his report by saying that only three of the fifteen-man group remained alive.[10] Kurt Thomas remembers a Dutch Jewish woman who was shot by partisans.[11] The record of the jury trial in Hagen, which concerned itself, among other things, with the uprising in Sobibor, contains this conclusion reached on the basis of the testimony: "Many of the escapees faced new dangers outside the camp area—from collaborating Polish peasants who betrayed them to the Germans or from anti-Semitic Polish partisan groups."[12] George Pfeffer, a successful escapee from Lublin–Majdanek, was anxious to join the active Polish underground movement and fight with it for the liberation of his homeland, but he was turned down because he was a Jew.[13]

Here, too, a generalization would lead to false conclusions, for there is much evidence that Poles aided Jewish fugitives without consideration of the risk this entailed. Mayer Ziss, who regained his freedom during the uprising in Sobibor, was able to join a partisan group. Several comrades were hidden by Polish peasants,[14] and Mordechaj Goldfarb hid out on such a farm for several months.[15] Ilona Safran reports that she was helped by Poles, and she also recalls a young German-Jewish woman who had been shot in the stomach during the uprising and was cared for by Polish peasants.[16] Numerous participants in the uprising at Treblinka are grateful to Poles who concealed them from German search parties. Platkiewicz[17] and Berek Rojzmann[18] were hidden by peasants until the final liberation, and the wounded Mayer Ziegelmann was taken in by a peasant.[19] Leo Lewi also found shelter with a Polish peasant and then went to Warsaw, where he was hidden by an "Aryan."[20] Sol Weisberg[21] and Heinrich Poswolski[22] found hiding places in Warsaw, and Jozef Siedlecki was provided with "Aryan" papers by a pharmacist in that city.[23] Rudolf Reder, who managed to escape from Belzec, was hidden in L'vov for twenty months by a woman he knew.[24] When Auschwitz was evacuated in January 1945, Alter Feinsylberg was able to save his life by running away from the evacuation transport. A Polish woman took in him and a friend, even though he identified himself as a Jewish refugee from the camp, and she concealed him for five weeks. In Auschwitz, Feinsylberg had been in the special detail, and when this transport arrived in Mauthausen, the members of this detail, as was to be expected, were killed as persons privy to secrets.[25]

Sometimes, to be sure, it was not advisable to identify oneself to helpers. For example, Martin Gray reports that after his escape from Treblinka, a Polish peasant sheltered him for several weeks. One day, however, the peasant got drunk and told him, "If you're a Jew, I'll kill you" (Gray 1971, 188 ff.).

Josef Meisel, an Austrian Jew, escaped from Auschwitz together with his Polish comrade, Szymon Zajdow. The Combat Group had organized this escape of their particularly endangered members. Meisel reports that, although he was aided by the Polish resistance in Cracow, Zajdow was dropped by it. These Poles knew that Zajdow was a Jew, but evidently they did not know that Meisel was also Jewish.[26] By way of a precaution, after his escape from Lublin–Majdanek the German Willi Gardini told the Polish woman whom he was asking for help that he was Dutch; evidently he was not sure that he would have received support as a German.[27] Opportunities to escape were diminished not only by anti-Semitism and a widespread aversion to all Germans. After a successful escape from the Auschwitz satellite camp, Gleiwitz I, a Russian managed to hide in a nearby camp for Ukrainian forced laborers, but a Ukrainian betrayed him—evidently because he hated Russians (Strzelecka 1973, 98).

After their successful escapes, members of various ethnic groups had to contend with prejudices on the part of the surrounding population, but if that population was not German, escapees had at least a chance of not being betrayed right away. This is true of inmates who worked in Hesdin (western France), a satellite camp of Buchenwald. The prisoners were

already fully acquainted with the attitude of the inhabitants of the surrounding area, for the latter slipped food to inmates whenever they could.
According to Tomasz Kiryłłow, who was able to escape from the camp on
May 12, 1944,[28] a French partisan group facilitated escapes of Poles and
Russians. Frenchmen interned in the Mauthausen satellite camp Loiblpass
were in turn aided by the surrounding Slovenian population, which even
enabled them to venture spontaneous attempts. When Jean-Baptiste Che-
valier and Gaston Charlet escaped from that subsidiary camp on October
7, 1944, they were helped by every civilian they encountered and established a connection with Slovenian partisans for the French (Bernadac
1975, 127 ff.). Frenchmen who had managed to escape from Loiblpass
earlier, on September 17, 1944, were passed on to a partisan group by local
people. However, a Pole who after his escape encountered Austrians rather
than Slovenians was turned over to the SS by them (Bernadac 1975, 117 ff.).
As already mentioned, after their flight from the Sachsenhausen satellite
camp Fichtengrund, the Luxembourger Paul Müller and the Frenchman
Alex Louns were concealed by French officers in a Berlin prisoner-of-war
camp for six weeks and provided with civilian clothes. In that way they
were able to travel all across Germany and get to Luxembourg in March
1944 (Bezant 1978, 11 ff.).

   According to Andrzej Kamiński, the fact that the environs of the concentration camp Gross–Rosen were inhabited by Germans constituted, in
practical terms, an impediment to escapes. He documents this by reporting that, after an escape by Poles from the satellite camp Brieg, the police
were supported in their hunt for the fugitives by the populace, the Hitler
Youth, and similar organizations.[29] This observation is valid for all other
camps situated in Germany or Austria. Suffice it to adduce one example.
On April 5, 1942, three Spaniards managed to escape from Vöcklabruck, a
subsidiary camp of Mauthausen—thanks to a maid who had obtained a
wire cutter they had requested—and were able to make their way into the
mountains. When they encountered a forest ranger, he shot at them without warning and wounded one of them (Santos 1967). The small number of
known exceptions that follow cannot refute Kamiński's general observation. Georg Rajgrodzki, who was able to make his way to Warsaw after the
uprising in Treblinka, was taken in by a German woman who was married
to a Czech, and a forged identity card enabled him to survive.[30] The
German Fritz Mühlhoff protected two fugitives from Treblinka in Rad-
kow, and he also helped other Jews escape the Gestapo.[31] Hermann Wiener
and Jakob Estreicher used the freedom of movement their positions gave
them (Wiener was roll-call clerk and Estreicher chief capo) to flee from
Fünfteichen, a satellite camp of Gross–Rosen. A German master craftsman provided them with bicycles and workers' identifications, and a Ger-

man farmer gave them shelter until they were liberated by the Red Army (Bernstein 1967, 143 ff.).

Some German and Austrian Communists managed to make contact with comrades on the outside and use this connection for the organization of escapes. This worked for the Berliner Josef (Jupp) Pietzschmann and Franz Primus, a veteran of the Spanish Civil War, both of whom escaped in early April 1944; Herbert Tschäpe, a German veteran of that war, who successfully escaped together with Fritz Reuter (Perk 1979, 82) on April 22 of that year; and Rudi Wunderlich, who regained his freedom on June 10. The Communist Party group in Sachsenhausen expressly instructed Tschäpe to strengthen the party group operating in Berlin. Before organizing his escape, Wunderlich too secured the permission of the party leadership. All the above-named were able to escape from Sachsenhausen's outside details that worked in Berlin, and they utilized contacts with Berlin women whom they encountered there.[32] Austrian veterans of the Spanish Civil War managed to make contact from a Dachau satellite camp near Hallein with comrades living there and through them with relatives. In this way, their escape and subsequent protection from search parties could be ensured.[33] Sepp Plieseis served as an example by forming a partisan group in the Salzkammergut [district in western Austria—ed.] on August 20, 1943 (Plieseis 1946, 235 ff., 313 ff.). From Klagenfurt, where he was employed in a subsidiary camp of Mauthausen, the German Kaspar Bachl was able to maintain contact with his wife, and she helped him with his successful escape on November 15, 1944, after which he was able to stay with anti-Nazis in Fuschl until the end of the war.[34]

In the final phase of the war, escapees found it easier to secure the support of Germans and Austrians as well. This was the experience of the Austrian Communist Josef Lauscher, when he escaped from a Vienna outside detail of Mauthausen on February 1, 1945. A building superintendent admitted him to her apartment, which enabled him to shake off his pursuers and later go to an address that had been given him in Mauthausen.[35] All that Hans Maršàlek writes about this escape is that the endangered Lauscher was able to escape "under particularly adventurous circumstances" (Maršàlek 1974, 198). Lauscher himself describes how Maršàlek used his key position in the office of the main camp to get him suitable clothes, money, a razor blade, and addresses of "safe houses" in Vienna. In addition, Maršàlek arranged Lauscher's transfer to the satellite camp in Vienna and in the file changed Lauscher's place of residence from Wien to Wiener Neustadt, because no one could be transferred to an outside detail located in his own city.[36] Since Lauscher had been punitively transferred to Mauthausen because of his resistance activity in Dachau, his escape was prepared by the Mauthausen resistance organization. In April 1945, the Viennese Franz Freihaut escaped from the evacuation transport out of Flossenbürg, and he was hidden by German women until the Americans reached the area.[37]

Some escapes were accomplished under quite adventurous circumstances. On June 4, 1944, four inmates of the Buchenwald outside detail in Arolsen escaped without contact with any organization or knowledge of any bases in the area. They were Pierre Schaul and Nicolas Wolff, both from Luxembourg, the Belgian Fernand Labalue; and the Pole Adolf Korzyński. The Pole was over thirty, the others not much more than twenty. In the camp, they had managed to occupy positions that offered good chances to escape: Korzyński and Wolff in the automobile repair shop, Labalue in the SS clothing depot, and Schaul as an SS barber. Schaul obtained keys from SS offices and had copies made; Labalue took SS uniforms, and in the SS garage Korzyński and Wolff put a broken-down car that had been discarded into running order. One Sunday morning they started their daring enterprise. Korzyński put on the uniform of an SS general (since Arolsen was the site of an SS officer-training school, there were such uniforms in the clothing depot), and the younger ones also slipped on SS uniforms. Marching orders for a courier trip to Saarbrücken as well as road maps and a compass had been prepared. The three men got into the car, the guard at the gate gave them a military salute, and they drove west, stopping only when they ran out of gasoline. They concealed the car off the road, continued their flight on foot, and then were bold enough to board a train bound for Trier. When they found the controls at that station too risky, they split up and made their way to nearby Luxembourg, where they exchanged the SS uniforms for civilian clothes at the homes of friends and were able to drop out of sight. All four men lived to see the liberation.[38]

We have already reported about a similar flight from Natzweiler, although in that case the escapees did not have to traverse half of Germany. There was a successful escape of this type from Auschwitz as well. On June 20, 1942, four Poles employed in the troop-management section—Lieut. Stanisław Jaster, Józef Lempart, Eugeniusz Bendera, and Kazimierz Piechowski—drove out of the camp area in a Steyr 200 automobile. Three of them had been able to obtain SS uniforms, and they "escorted" the fourth man, who was tied up. When they reached the barrier, the highest-ranking officer, recognizable as such by his uniform, ordered the guard with a vigorous movement of his hand to raise it. They drove for another 80 kilometers and then abandoned the car, which they had rendered unusable, in a ditch (Iwaszko 1974, 12; Jarosz 1946, 146). Another daring escape was effected from Auschwitz. It involved three Poles and Otto Küsel, a German inmate who wore the number 2 and whose unusually comradely conduct has been described in another context. Küsel headed the Work Assignments, where two of the Poles were employed, and he managed to gain the confidence of SS men. The prisoners stole an SS uniform, and Küsel requisitioned from the farming section a horse-drawn wagon for purposes of transportation, which he drove to the camp. (In view of his top position, this was not unusual.) They loaded the carriage with chests in which the Poles hid, and Küsel, who was well known to the guards, was able to drive the wagon out of the camp uninspected. Before the next guard's station, one of the Poles put on an SS uniform, sat down in front next to Küsel, and at the next checkpoint displayed the forged permit that entitled one to escort an inmate (Küsel) out of the camp area. The men had chosen to escape on December 29, 1942, because they knew that numerous SS men were on leave between Christmas and New Year's. By the time the SS noticed their escape, the four men had been able to reach Warsaw with the help of Poles with whom they had secretly made contact at an earlier date. Many months later, the Gestapo arrested Küsel there, took him to Auschwitz, and tortured him. However, because there was a new commandant and a new head of the political department, recaptured escapees were no longer being executed, and so Küsel was transferred to Flossenbürg (Iwaszko 1974, 27).

The consequences of another escape from Auschwitz made it more memorable than many others. On May 20, 1943, three Poles escaped from the surveying service detail. Since the members of this detail were surveying a large area outside the camp, they had especially good opportunities of making contact with the surrounding population. As "old" prisoners, they had been able to establish good relations with their guards, and this further enhanced their mobility. One day a Polish woman from the surrounding area, who had maintained contact with Polish prisoners on behalf of the resistance movement, was arrested. Since the Poles in the surveying crew now had reason to fear that in its search for the connections, the political department would arrest and torture them, they decided to flee. As they had done on previous occasions, they gave the sentry a drink, but this time the drink contained a sleeping potion. It worked, and they were able to escape. They were known in the surroundings of the camp, and there were compatriots ready to help. Thus far it was one escape among many; however, it was the reprisals that set it apart from the numerous others. The political department had appointed one of its most reliable informers as capo of that detail. On the basis of information supplied by him, thirteen members of the detail were shot in the bunker and twelve others, also Poles, were hanged on July 19, 1943, in the roll-call area in the presence of all inmates (Sobański 1974, 154).

In view of the extraordinary attention that this escape evoked, it is appropriate to refer once more to the escape of Edward Galiński and Mala Zimetbaum. On June 24, 1944, this Pole from the first transport and this Jewish woman, who was well-known and well-liked in the women's camp as a messenger, fled together from Birkenau. Wearing an SS uniform, he pretended to be escorting his girlfriend. Mala had been able to procure from the office of the women's camp a permit that enabled Galiński to get an inmate past the big series of checkpoints, just as a Pole in an SS uniform had been able to get Küsel out of the camp. Once free of that area, they were helped by Poles with whom Galiński had established contact. The apprehension of his friend that they might not be able to count on aid if people recognized "her Semitic features" proved groundless. However, as they approached the Slovakian border, they fell into the hands of a patrol, were returned to the camp, tortured, and hanged (Kielar 1979, 401 ff.).

At least one of the escapes from Majdanek should be mentioned here. Georg Arold, a German capo, escaped together with nine Poles shortly before the evacuation of the camp in the summer of 1944. Other Poles who managed to escape at that time met up with Arold, who has been called a Communist by some and a Catholic journalist by others, and his Polish comrades in a partisans' unit.[39] Shortly before the evacuation of Gross–Rosen there was a mass escape from Brieg, a satellite camp. Polish inmates, probably thirty or forty, who were working in a storeroom outside the camp, overpowered their guards on their way back to the camp. Some of the prisoners put on SS uniforms and used the truck that was supposed to take them back to the camp to drive east. They happened to meet a police car, and thinking they were being pursued, jumped off the truck and ran into a nearby forest. They were hunted for a few days, and several of them were shot, the others captured.[40]

It is evident that the spectacular escapes mentioned here were organized by inmates whose position lifted them out of the herd. Only they were able to gain the required perspective and utilize opportunities that were bound to remain unavailable to prisoners who held no favorable positions.

From virtually all camps, we have reports about numerous and often quite daring escapes of Russians. At Christmastime 1941, Russians attempted to break out of the Flossenbürg concentration camp; a few were shot, and eight were hanged on Christmas eve (Heger 1972, 119). The SS also got wind of plans for a mass escape of Russians from Natzweiler, and five officers were hanged as ringleaders (Spitz 1970, 32). Russians broke out from Wöbbelin, a subsidiary camp of Neuengamme,[41] but their number is not known nor has it been established whether they regained their freedom permanently. Two Russian officers managed to escape from Buchenwald. Comrades had given them a pistol that had been bought from Hoven, a corrupt SS doctor, and these officers were not brought back to the camp.[42]

The murderous treatment that Russian prisoners of war had to endure in the early period was probably one reason for the numerous escapes and attempted escapes. It is obvious that camps located in the East offered Russians an additional inducement, both because of the surrounding Slavic population and (particularly in the final phase) the proximity of the Russian front.

There is documentation of Russian escapes from the Stutthof concentration camp, and it has been possible to reconstruct details about escapes of Russians from Majdanek. In March 1942, several dozen prisoners of war escaped from that camp, and only one of these was recaptured (Gryń/ Murawska n.d., 66 ff.). Another successful mass outbreak followed in the summer of that year. Petrick, an SS man, believes that eighty to a hundred men were able to escape from a field at night.[43] Konstantin Simonov has given a description of the outbreak of these prisoners of war, who were evidently destined for destruction: "The prisoners of war gathered the available blankets together, arranged them in piles of five, put these over the barbed wire, and fled. Since it was a dark night, only four of the fugitives were shot, and the others escaped." The Russians who had not participated in this outbreak were shot in the camp. This is said to have happened in late June 1942.

The Russian prisoners of war who had been deported to Auschwitz were used to build Birkenau in the winter of 1941–42. As commandant Höss put it; "They died like flies of physical exhaustion. . . . The dampness and the impossibility of drying out, especially in the half-finished, primitive, hastily slapped-together brick barracks in the early days of Birkenau, did the rest to produce a steady increase in the number of deaths." This desperate situation prompted the Russians to incur any risk to save their lives. Höss remembers a mass outbreak: "A large number of them were shot, but many did manage to escape" (Höss 1958, 102 ff.). Jerzy Brandhuber, who has tried to reconstruct the fate of the Russian prisoners of war in Auschwitz, believes that this mass flight took place in March 1942. A hundred and twenty prisoners of war are said to have participated in the mass breakout, and 103 deaths were recorded (Brandhuber 1961, 17). Witnesses remember a breakout of Russians from Birkenau in the fall of 1942. Russians are supposed to have simulated an escape by hiding the body of a fellow prisoner. Thus the evening roll call was off, and, in accordance with regular practice, a search for the missing man began. The Russians volunteered for this task. According to Höss, the few Russians who were left "did excellent work and were put on floating details wherever some project had to be completed quickly" (Höss 1958, 104). Favored by the darkness and a thick fog, the Russian volunteers toppled a watchtower and broke out of the camp area they were supposed to search.[44] We have the names of four survivors of this breakout. Kazimierz Smoleń tells about "more than ten" who successfully escaped and then joined a partisan group operating in the vicinity (Smoleń 1960–67, 40). It cannot be clearly established whether this refers to the same breakout, for which the wrong time has been given, or to two successive ones.

Numerous Russians escaped from Birkenau at later dates as well. "When the siren sounded [the alarm for escapes—H.L.]," writes the Dutchman Antonius van Velsen, "we asked ourselves how many were involved this time." One time eleven Russians managed to flee together. Van Velsen adds that the Russians had outside contacts that they utilized in their escapes, but that they refused to tell others about them.[45] Tadeusz Iwaszko, who analyzed the escapes from Auschwitz, writes that "of eighty fugitives from Birkenau in 1944, thirty were Russians." With almost 20 percent of all escapees from Auschwitz, the Russians were in second place after the Poles, who comprised more than 48 percent, though this is based on incomplete data (Iwaszko 1964, 52 ff.). There is almost complete documentation about the nationality of escapees from Mauthausen, including those who were caught attempting to escape. Where the surrounding population did not favor any nationality, the ratio was almost exactly reversed: More than 50 percent were Russians, followed by not quite 19 percent Poles (Maršàlek 1974, 199 ff.) We know the nationality of twenty-seven escapees from Dora or its satellite camps; nineteen of these were Russians (Dieckmann/Hochmuth n.d., 74). Even in the last days, and at extreme danger to life, it was Russians who mustered the courage for a daredevil flight. When, after the evacuation of Neuengamme, thousands were put on ships in Lübeck Bay, seven Russian prisoners of war placed themselves at the disposal of an action committee composed of three German Communists that attempted to make contact with the Allies from one of the boats. Wearing life jackets, they secretly left the *Cape Arcona* in the night April 29–30, 1945. One of them was unconscious when he was fished out of the water, and three were dead when they washed ashore. "The other three comrades were never seen or heard from again. Probably they too had to pay for their sacrificial act with their lives (Schätzle 1946, 44).

Others who found themselves in a similarly hopeless situation as the Russians in the early months attempted to escape their fate with the courage born of desperation. Those who were subjected to daily torture in the penal company at Birkenau dared to break out on June 20, 1942, virtually a suicidal act. Around fifty men made this daredevil attempt; thirteen of these were shot, nine managed to escape, the rest were captured and killed together with over 300 other members of the penal company who had not participated in this venture. Their names indicate that all of them were Poles.[46] An escape attempted by Jews in Birkenau probably represented a similar act of desperation. Little is known about it. All fourteen were shot; twelve of them had been deported to Auschwitz from France only five days earlier (Rutkowski 1970, 38 ff.).

Similar desperate attempts have been reported from Sobibor. Thus a fairly large group of Dutch Jews once planned an attempt that is said to have been organized by a high-ranking Dutch officer. The attempt was betrayed, and seventy-one Dutchmen were killed.[47]

On numerous occasions inmates planned to escape from satellite camps by digging tunnels. Invariably large groups had to band together to manage the digging and, what was perhaps even more difficult, the removal of the earth. Hence it was inevitable that the preparations were noticed by many.

There are reports about attempts to reach freedom in this way from several subsidiary camps of Auschwitz. In Jaworzno inmates dug a pit about 1 meter deep in their barracks and made a tunnel that led to a forest approximately 50 meters from the camp enclosure. The initiators of this bold attempt were a Pole and a Czech Jew. One of them "was an experienced mason and had evidently devised the plan of the tunnel. Two to four men from this group always did the laborious work of digging and shoveling at night. . . . The loosely dredged-up sand was leveled underneath the block [which stood on wooden pilings in the sand—H.L.]. . . . The group had been provided with money and civilian clothes, the latter traded for in the tunnel." This is from a report by the Czech senior block inmate Karel Bulaty, who had been informed.[48] However, the plan was betrayed, and the Pole Wladyslaw Smigielski has identified a German capo with a black triangle as the traitor.[49] According to Bulaty, it was the Czech Hnátek who told the SS about the attempted escape, and he was lynched by the inmates with whom he had later been transferred to Buchenwald. Mass arrests followed, and after the usual interrogations and tortures twenty-six inmates—"around half of them Poles and the other half Czechs, most of the latter Jews"[50]—were hanged in the roll-call area of the camp;[51] others were assigned to the penal company. There are reports about similar attempts that were made in Jawiszowice and Fürstengrube and were also betrayed (Strzelecki 1975, 244; Iwaszko 1978, 72 ff.). On August 16, 1944, however, I succeeded in passing a group of eleven Russians under the enclosure at subcamp Gleiwitz I, through a tunnel that was dug under the floor of their barrack and ended in a meadow outside the camp. In this case, the retaliatory measures of the SS already differed markedly from the norm; the camp administration contented itself with making the inmates stand in the roll-call area for one day and transferring all Russians and Poles to another concentration camp (Strzelecka 1973, 98 ff.). Seven prisoners, evidently Russians as well, effected an escape through a tunnel from the Buchenwald subcamp in Schwerte (Gurin 1959, 149). Desperate attempts to escape a murderous fate by digging tunnels have also been reported from extermination camps. Two prisoners in Sobibor successfully escaped in this fashion in 1942. For many weeks in the summer of 1943, other inmates dug a tunnel, but after that successful attempt the SS had laid mines in the environment of the camp. As they dug an exit from the tunnel outside the camp, the inmates set off a mine, which alerted the SS and caused all 150 men of this detail to be shot (Ainsztein 1974, 748). In Treblinka, inmates attempted this mode of escape as well. The passage through a tunnel was successful, but unfortunately that night brought the first snowfall, which enabled the SS to track the escapees, though apparently not everyone was captured. A survivor of Treblinka reports that the escapees fought with their pursuers on the outside. Lindwasser remembers that in spite of terrible reprisals—recaptured men were subjected to inhuman tortures before they were finally killed—there were a great many attempts to escape.[52]

Some escapes stand out from all the rest by not having been organized solely to save lives. For example, in early 1945 the French resistance movement in Auschwitz facilitated the escape of Jules Frank so that he might, in view of the impending liberation of the camp, establish a connection between the Frenchmen in the camp and a resistance group composed of French prisoners of war and civilians doing forced labor who were housed in the vicinity. It was possible to get him assigned to an outside detail working in Weimar, and with the help of French prisoners of war he was able to escape and make the desired contact (Wormser 1954, 251 ff.).

In individual cases, the resistance organization in Auschwitz, which facilitated numerous escapes, was also guided by motives other than a desire to save the lives of comrades at especial risk. A case in point is the escape of Witold Pilecki (whose camp name was Tomasz Serafiński), the leader of the Polish officers' organization. One motive was the fact that a Pole who had escaped together with Otto Küsel at Christmastime 1942 had fallen into the hands of the Gestapo and under torture might reveal what he knew about this organization. Another was the lack of response to his repeated messages to the Polish resistance organization on the outside that the camp was ready to fight and that he was waiting for joint action. "Warsaw remained silent and sent neither orders to plan a struggle nor information about preparations for help from the outside." Pilecki grew impatient and decided to flee in order to convince the underground organization in person. The escape was planned from the camp bakery, which was located outside the camp and where inmates worked at night. The night of April 26–27 was chosen as the most propitious time; this was shortly after Easter, when many SS men were on holiday leave. Pilecki effected a successful escape together with two companions (Czech 1959–64; Gárliński 1975A, 165).

Pilecki's plan to organize an uprising in early 1943 was unrealistic and was evidently so regarded by the Polish underground organization, but the same idea seemed feasible in the summer of 1944, for Majdanek had been evacuated, offensives of the Red Army had brought Russian troops to Polish territory, and it could be expected that the next push would bring them as far as Auschwitz. There was reason to fear that the SS would leave no eyewitnesses to the mass exterminations, so the leadership of the Combat Group Auschwitz decided to send out the two Austria heads of this organization, together with two Poles, so that they might unite with the Polish partisan groups in the vicinity and do their utmost to prevent a liquidation of the camp. By that time organized flights had almost become routine for the Combat Group. Those designated for escape concealed themselves inside the great chain of guard stations. They remained in place for three nights, in case any inmates were noted as missing at the evening roll-call. After this period, the hidden prisoners sneaked out of their hiding places and to a prearranged spot where members of the Polish underground were waiting for them and helped them along. In this way the escape of the Austrian Alfred Klahr and the Pole Stefan Bratkowski was accomplished on June 15. They got to Warsaw, but there Klahr fell into the hands of the Gestapo and was killed. On June 27 the two Poles Konstanty Jagiełło and Tomasz Sobariski escaped and joined a partisan group; on July 19 their compatriot Lucjan Motyka followed them; Roman Cieliczko escaped a few days earlier, and so three days later did the Austrian Josef Meisel together with the Pole Szymon Zajdow, two Jewish veterans of the Spanish Civil War (Langbein 1949, 177, 180 ff.; Iwaszko 1964, 30 ff.; Jarosz 1978, 162).

The escape of the Combat Group's executive committee, however, was to be organized differently, for it could be assumed that, since the fugitives were known to it, the SS would not content itself with the search methods that had become routine. For this reason an SS uniform and a pass were "organized." Under the pretext that I had to mark on a map all swamps and stagnant bodies of water so that these breeders of malaria could be effectively treated, I scouted the route, map in hand and escorted by guards, to the meeting place, where the partisans were to await us with clothes and weapons. A day in August 1944 had been selected for the escape, but a day earlier the Combat Group was notified that the partisans had run into difficulties, which meant a postponement (Langbein 1949, 172 ff.). A second attempt was made on October 27, and this time the help of two SS men from the motor pool could be enlisted. They were to drive five members of the Combat Group out of the camp in a box of dirty laundry bound for Bielitz and take them to a spot agreed upon with the partisans. Among the five was the Viennese Ernst Burger, a member of the executive committee of our underground organization; the others were Poles. Since the preparations for my own escape had attracted attention, causing it to be postponed, I had by that time been transferred to a subcamp of Neuengamme. One of the two SS men was a traitor, however. Those hidden in the box were not driven out of the camp but to the bunker, and the partisan group was waylaid at the meeting place. Among the casualties was Jagiełło, who had escaped in June. When the five noticed that they had been betrayed, they took the poison that they carried with them by way of precaution. Two Poles died, and the others had their stomachs pumped, for the SS was anxious to interrogate them and break up their organization, but the arrested men remained firm. Together with two other Austrians, who were known to the traitor because they had recruited the SS men for this escape in the motor-pool detail, they were hanged on December 30, 1944, in front of the inmates lined up in the roll-call area (Czech 1959–64).

In some instances prisoners escaped after killing their guards. On May 8, 1938, two Germans—Bargatzki, who had been interned because of his criminal past, and Forster, a former member of the Foreign Legion—who were working outside Buchenwald struck down the SS guard, who died soon thereafter, and fled. The consequences, as described by Bruno Apitz, were terrible: "There were some corpses in the roll-call area. The dead men had had nothing to do with the escape of those two. They had gotten under the rifle butts of the SS and been beaten haphazardly into bloody bundles" (Buchenwald 1960, 181 ff.). Reprisals for the entire camp were ordered. Bargatzki was captured a few weeks later and Forster, who had managed to get to Czechoslovakia, after the occupation of that country. Both men were taken back to the camp and hanged in the roll-call area.[53]

A similar episode is mentioned in an article published in the SS's military newspaper Für die Waffen-SS. On November 24, 1939, the German prisoners Franz Brönner and Anton Kropf, who had been sent to Mauthausen at the beginning of the war as "soldiers difficult to train," escaped from the camp after striking down an SS guard "according to a preconceived plan." Both men were captured shortly thereafter and hanged on December 9 (Waffen-SS 1978, 36 ff.). In this case the SS guard did not die of his injuries.[54]

In the early period, these two escapes involving force were undertaken by Germans; at that time few members of other nations were in the camps. Later non-Germans tried to gain their freedom in this fashion.

Several escapes involving acts of violence were accomplished by inmates of the Mauthausen satellite camp Loiblpass. As already mentioned, the proximity of Yugoslav partisans constituted an inducement. On April 19, 1944, a Pole on an outside detail beat his guard to death and fled into the mountains, but he was recaptured six days later, subjected to terrible torture, and finally murdered (Bernadac 1975, 106). On November 23, 1944, four Frenchmen who were laying telephone lines outside the camp area disarmed their two guards, knocking down the younger one, who put up a fight, and escaped to the mountains, where they joined the partisans (Bernadac 1975, 144 ff.). In late April 1944, three Russian officers accomplished an adventurous escape. They were able to knock down three guards and disarm, undress, and tie them up before fleeing to the partisans. Wearing SS uniforms, they encountered no obstacle in driving through the tunnel to the other side of the pass. The SS search was futile, but as a reprisal all Russian members of this detail were transferred to the Mauthausen main camp and evidently murdered there (Bernadac 1975, 106 ff.; *Letzeburger zu Mauthausen* 1970, 166; Lacaze 1978, 279 ff.). André Lacaze has given a graphic report about the preparation and implementation of the escape of three French members of the same detail. With the support of a Croatian civilian worker, they rode out of the tunnel, in which men were working on the night shift, in a false bottom built into a dump truck used to remove earth from that tunnel. These escapees also joined the partisans (Lacaze 1978, 460 ff.).

Russians dared to attempt forcible breakouts in other camps as well. In May 1942, seventeen Russian prisoners of war, under orders to bury men who had been shot in a nearby forest, slew seven SS guards with their spades and fled. Only two of them were recaptured (Simonov n.d., 10). As a consequence the Russians remaining in the camp were isolated, and since they had reason to fear that they would be liquidated, they decided to break out. (An account by the SS man Petrick has been given earlier.) In August 1943, thirteen Russian prisoners of war on reaping duty killed four guards with their scythes and fled. Six were captured, but seven managed to escape. In December of the same year, two inmates of Majdanek doing outside work choked their guard to death. One put on the SS man's uniform and with the aid of his gun escorted his friend out of the camp area. Both men were from L'vov and thus probably Ukrainians (Gryn/ Murawska n.d., 66).

In the Bullerhuserdamm School in Hamburg, where an outside detail of Neuengamme had been installed, as late as April 21, 1945, SS men murdered prisoners who were not to be liberated by the Allies at any cost. Twenty Soviet prisoners of war were also taken there at that time. After a few of them had already been hanged, those who realized that the same fate was in store for them attacked their guards, threw salt in their eyes, and attempted to flee. Five or six of them managed to escape (Bringmann 1978, 19).

In the extermination camp Sobibor, Shlomo Podchlebnik and Józef Kopf, who had been assigned to a forest detail, beat a Ukrainian guard to death on their way to get water, took his gun, and cleared out. The SS was alerted, and whereas the Dutch Jews on the same detail let themselves be escorted back to the camp, twenty Polish Jews, who knew they were about to be killed, attempted to flee. As Thomas Blatt reports, "at that point a number of men hurled themselves at the Germans."[55] Eight presumably managed to escape, and the inmates who had been returned to the camp were shot. The surrounding population helped the ten escapees and saved them from being recaptured.[56]

When Russian troops were approaching and the extermination camp Chelmno had to be liquidated, the Jews of the labor detail were shot, five at a time, during the night of January 17–18, 1945. According to a report written by Walther Piller, the deputy officer-in-charge, a few months afterward, "when the third group was brought out [of the prison that served as a shelter—H.L.], the Jewish cook [Max Zurawski] fled." After more executions "the upper cell with the twenty . . . craftsmen was left. Lenz [a police officer who, along with Piller, was among those who had shot the prisoners—H.L.] went to the upper cell, as he had previously gone to the lower cell, to get five Jews to be shot. As soon as he had unlocked the door, four Jews rushed up to Lenz and pulled him into the cell, where they snatched his pistol and opened fire." The prison was set on fire, and the inmates perished together with Lenz.[57]

20

RESISTANCE AND REBELLION

Not every attempt to fight back by inmates destined for death has become known. There was no room for pathos-filled gestures in the concentration camps, with some exceptions, and as a rule there were no witnesses to report how condemned prisoners went to their deaths. Nevertheless, some acts of resistance have been documented.

The night of February 1, 1945, was to bring yet another shooting—that of prisoners in Sachsenhausen, who had been isolated in the penal company. Nineteen Luxembourg policemen had refused to join the SS, and they were to die, together with Russian officers and British prisoners of war. The doomed men were tied up and led out of the camp. When they could no longer have any doubt about the fate that awaited them, they broke loose, and the Luxembourger Viktor Reuland was able to wrest a pistol away from a guard and shoot him, whereupon he and all the others were felled by SS bullets.[1] On February 3, 1945, the Norwegian Odd Nansen made this entry in his diary: "When a group of men who had been taken out of the blocks in the dead of night was marching through the gate and turning right, the men understood where they were going, broke ranks, and ran into the small park between the outside walls, The guards opened fire, and they were mowed down right then and there." This shows that the events of that night were discussed in the camp. Nansen adds his own observation: "It was the rattling of the guards' machine guns that pierced the stillness of the night." Nansen lost his British friends, and Russian officers "and many others" were also liquidated that night, as were "all lackeys of the special detail . . . that had done the Gestapo's bidding" (Nansen 1945, 266 ff.).

On October 28, 1942, the camp administration of Auschwitz carried out another retaliatory action, this time in response to acts of resistance by Poles in the Lublin area. Almost 300 Polish prisoners from that region were called out and taken to Bunker Block 11, the place of execution. When a few men tried to break out of that isolated block, the SS called for reinforcements, and all the men were shot (Czech 1959–64; Gárliński 1975A, 144).

Near the gas chambers there were repeated incidents that could not
be documented afterward. The officer-in-charge, Franz Hofmann, who
often acted as a supervisor there, years later told an examining magistrate:
"There were, of course, disturbances among the inmates who had been
selected to die. Then I had to act to restore law and order" (Langbein 1972,
144).

The Combat Group Auschwitz informed Cracow that on May 25 and 28
a considerable number of men deported from Hungary had tried to flee
when they were herded from the railway platform to the gas chambers.
They wanted to hide in a copse that was surrounded with electrically
charged barbed wire. The SS scoured the area with searchlights and shot
all the prisoners (Czech 1959–64).

Another act of resistance became better known because of its consequences. On October 23, 1943, 1,700 Jews were once again escorted to the
gas chambers. They had been deported from Warsaw to the Bergen–Belsen
concentration camp, where they were told that they would be taken to
Switzerland. Instead they were sent to Auschwitz to be exterminated, and
on the basis of their experience, they were not ignorant of their fate. When
about two thirds of them, predominantly men, had already entered the gas
chambers, "a rebellion broke out among the last third in the undressing
room," as Commandant Höss put it. "Three or four armed SS noncommissioned officers (*Unterführer*) entered the room to speed up the undressing.
The electric wires were cut, the SS men were attacked and deprived of their
weapons, and one of them was stabbed to death. Since the room was now
completely dark, there was a wild shootout between the guards at the
entrance and the prisoners inside. When I arrived, I ordered the doors shut
and the gassing process of the first two thirds stopped. Then the guards and
I entered the room with hand-held searchlights, and we herded the inmates
into a corner, from where they were led out individually and upon my
orders shot with small-bore rifles in a room next to the crematorium."[2]
The infamous SS roll-call officer Schillinger died of his wounds and SS
Squad Leader Emmerich was seriously injured. This episode showed the
inmates that SS men "were also mortal," as Wieslaw Kieler put it, and it
gave rise to legends. Schillinger is said to have torn a woman's bra off in the
undressing room, and the woman, who was reputed to have been a dancer,
fought back and was able to take his pistol away from him. Kielar also
remembers that, on the afternoon of the same day, some men fought back
in front of Crematorium IV. When he heard shooting, he tried to see what
was happening: "The grove [next to the crematorium—H.L.] was strewn
with corpses. They were mostly men and still had their clothes on" (Kielar
1979, 250).

On October 17, 1944, Hanna Lévy-Hass wrote in the diary she was able to keep in Bergen–Belsen: "Something has happened in the adjoining camp, which houses Polish women, though it isn't quite clear whether these are political prisoners or Jewesses. It appears that they revolted today. Rumors of this have reached us. Suddenly everyone was ordered to return to barracks. The laborers came home early, and in the kitchens the fires had to be extinguished and the personnel dismissed. The big gates that separate our blocks from the rest of the camp were closed. Everywhere panic and absolute quiet. We shall never find out exactly what the result of the women's rebellion was. Meanwhile it is clear that the Germans have 'restored order' after their fashion and committed new crimes. The crematorium is operating nonstop in front of everyone's eyes" (Levy-Hass 1979, 26).

No other source gives more information about this event. How many similar revolts were there that are not even hinted at in any diary?

Let us refer again to another rebellion about which little is known, the uprising of the Russian prisoners of war in the Flossenbürg satellite camp Mülsen–St. Micheln during the night of May 1–2, 1944.[3] It seems to have been triggered by cuts in the food rations "for disciplinary reasons" as well as the terrorism perpetrated by Georg Weilbach, the German senior camp inmate, on orders from the SS. However, the Russian inmates appear to have acted in concert with comrades doing forced labor in Leipzig, who had formed a resistance group there, rather than spontaneously. They set fire to their pallets, "largely burning down" the plant in which they were working, and caused a bloodbath among the (apparently Polish) prisoner functionaries.[4] Toni Siegert, who attempted to reconstruct what happened from the records of the American Flossenbürg trial that took place in Dachau in 1946–47, writes: "The men who had been working there [in Mülsen–St. Micheln—H.L.] were primarily Russian prisoners of war, former inmates of Buchenwald. Georg Weilbach was brought in from Flossenbürg as senior camp inmate [or foreman] of this detail. After the SS leader Burke had cut the food rations several times and conspiratory messages had been exchanged, via the transport of materials, between the arms factory in Leipzig and the Mülsen detail, a revolt broke out in the night of May 1–2. Russians had previously removed the electric fuses of the building and then set fire to some mattresses in the sleeping quarters. Others pulled out homemade knives and in the darkness started a terrible bloodbath among the Polish prisoner functionaries." Basing himself on the trial record, Siegert describes the end of this rebellion as follows: "The guards used force of arms to break this rebellion. There was not a single successful breakout." A hundred and ninety-five inmates died of stab wounds and burns. "On May 13, the presumed ringleaders were transferred from Mülsen to Flossenbürg, and at least forty of them were executed between June and September" (Siegert 1979, 460). Senior camp inmate Weilbach also returned to Flossenbürg, where he is said to have bragged that he had joined SS men in shooting at the prisoners in his charge.[5]

Russian prisoners of war also attempted to break out of Mauthausen in what appeared to be a completely hopeless situation. Most of them had been strictly separated from the rest of the camp as "incorrigible" because they had attempted to escape from prisoner-of-war camps, caught committing sabotage, or the like. There were many rather high-ranking officers among them. Later SS Senior Squad Leader Josef Niedermayer, who was responsible for the isolated Block 20 where they were interned, testified that "in accordance with orders they were so badly fed . . . that they were bound to starve." The following figures forcefully illustrate the effects of this "treatment." It is likely that around 4,700 persons had been assigned to this block since March 1944. In early February 1945 only 570 of these were still alive—in addition to Russian officers, five or six Poles who had been captured during the Warsaw uprising, and a few Yugoslavs (Maršàlek 1974, 203 ff.).

Higher officers who had been incarcerated in this death block since January 1945 decided to attempt a breakout, no matter what the cost. The organizers whose names are known were Lieut. Col. Nikolai Vlasov, Cols. Aleksander Isupov and Kiril Chubchenko as well as Captain Mardovzov. These officers had been able to make contact with the underground prisoners' organization in the camp by means of slips of paper tossed over the wall that separated the isolation block from the rest of the camp. Since their total isolation prevented them from knowing even what was in the immediate vicinity of their block, they requested a map of the camp. When the air force officer Ivan Bityukov was sent to Block 20 at the beginning of the year, he informed his comrades that the Czech camp barber, an inmate who had been able to speak freely with him for a moment while cutting his hair, had suggested that they attempt their escape soon, for they were all marked for extermination in the near future. The camp barber added that the desired map would be sent to Block 20 affixed to the bottom of the food pail.

The senior block inmate who dished out the food, a German criminal who subjected the inmates under his command to murderous treatment in order to prove himself to his masters, had to be kept ignorant of the connection with the prisoners in the camp. So Capt. Genadi Mardovzov employed a ruse. He was "always the first to rush up to the bucket when the senior block inmate gave out second helpings, and this started a scuffle. He tried to get hit so he could fall down, and then he had a chance to search the bottom of the pail quickly and unobtrusively. This maneuver failed twice, but on the third attempt he felt a pellet that was pasted onto the bottom of the pail. He quickly scraped it off and managed to put it in his mouth unobserved. However, his habitual scuffling for second helpings had attracted the attention of the senior block inmate, who took down his number." This meant that Mardovzov did not have much longer to live, and the senior block inmate actually murdered him that evening, but not before Mardovzov had given the pellet to his friends. It contained, on cigarette paper, a map of the camp and its vicinity.[6]

The breakout was to be accomplished during the night of January 28–29, but a few days before that, the SS took twenty-five inmates who were still in fairly good physical condition out of the block and shot them. Among them were Vlasov, Isupov, and Chubchenko. The traitor was never identified. Nevertheless, the plan was not abandoned, though the date had to be changed to the night of February 1–2.

First the senior block inmate had to be killed. This task was undertaken by his barracks orderlies, two Poles and a Russian, who had been under his protection but knew that they would not be allowed to stay alive either. After a higher officer had delivered an address at night, the inmates armed themselves with stones, pieces of coal, ersatz soap (which the senior block inmate had not distributed), and two fire extinguishers. Boards torn from the barracks floor were used as projectiles and striking weapons. Ignoring the shots fired at them, the men stormed the watchtowers at 1 A.M. The jets from the fire extinguishers and the hail of projectiles prevented the guards from shooting accurately. Blankets that the senior block inmate had stockpiled for himself instead of distributing them were thrown over the electrically charged barbed wire or torn up and used as foot cloths. Approximately seventy-five inmates from that block were too weak to participate in the breakout, so they gave their clothes to their comrades. Some men caused a short circuit with their bodies, and others climbed over these to scale the fence.

An Austrian inmate has described the appearance of the site the next morning. "The electric wires at the top of the wall were torn down and blankets hung over them. Corpses of inmates were lying under the wall, and the dead could be seen in the fields as far as the forest below. The dead were just skin and bones, completely starved, badly dressed, without shoes. Some had rags wrapped around their feet. I heard that the watchtower on the front side of Block 20 was stormed, hit with wooden shoes and other objects, and sprayed with fire extinguishers."[7]

According to a report by the gendarmerie station of Schwertberg, a nearby village, the escapees carried the tables of their barracks to the wire fence, "put their almost empty pellets and other rags" over it, climbed over this electrically charged barrier, and attacked the guards with fire extinguishers and wooden shoes. "Because the guards were older reservists from the Viennese police and fire department as well as the Wehrmacht, they were easier to overpower."[8]

Of the almost 500 prisoners who took part in that breakout, 419 managed to scale the fence and get out of the camp area—despite the fire from the guards, their reduced strength, and their unfamiliarity with the immediate vicinity. The SS alerted its units, the Wehrmacht, and all military and paramilitary outfits down to the Hitler Youth. There began what appears in the history of Mauthausen as the Mühlviertel Hare-Hunt. A police report written shortly after the liberation gives some idea of what it was like. In the snow, guards found "bloody footprints of barefoot people. From some of these, one could recognize that rags had been wrapped around their feet with string." The following order was issued: " 'No one is to be captured; everyone is to be killed immediately.' A killing spree began, a real bloodbath. The slush in the street turned red from the blood of the men who had been shot. There were cruelties that one would never have believed the Mühlviertel people capable of."

On the first day, over 300 were captured, and more on the succeeding days. The dead bodies were taken to the camp and counted. In the end, the SS listed only seventeen as missing. Those who remained in Block 20 had been murdered the night of the breakout.

Only very few farmers in the vicinity dared to give the fugitives food and not betray them to the searching parties. Only the Langthaler family from Winden was brave enough to shelter and feed two Russians till the liberation three months later. And, despite all threats, the Mascherbauer and Wittberger families also helped. A remark in a diary kept by a clergyman vividly illustrates the prevailing attitude of the population: "People are afraid and don't give [food]. . . . They are so cowardly that they have no compassion, and some of our people already act like SS men, who mercilessly mow down everyone they can get their hands on."[9]

The well-organized Spanish inmates in the main camp knew about the breakout, and others may have known as well. On the evening of February 1, one of the Spanish leaders told his friends it would be a good idea not to undress that night (Razola/Constante 1969, 142 ff.).

This event, which is unique in the history of the concentration camps, could not be reconstructed until much later and thus only incompletely, for, as Smirnov cautiously puts it, "for a long time [in the Soviet Union] there was a certain prejudice against people who had returned from Fascist imprisonment."[10] Not until years after Stalin's death did a radio talk by a French survivor of Mauthausen prompt a search in Moscow for survivors of this breakout. It was possible to locate seven of them, and they were, quite belatedly, officially honored.[11]

Those prisoners who were made to do forced labor in the crematories and gas chambers of Auschwitz were much better nourished than other Jewish inmates, but they knew from experience that eventually the SS would kill them as being "privy to secrets." Salmen Lewental, who buried a description of life in that special detail next to one of the crematoria, describes in this moving document—later retrieved and deciphered in part—that the idea of a breakout was always alive in the prisoners. However, "we could not bring ourselves to act, because there was always someone who felt tied to the camp, whether through the good food or through a girl with whom he was in love." In short, even in such a hopeless situation the camp administration was able to corrupt people and sap their fighting spirit. When, however, "preparations were made to burn the Hungarian Jews" in early May 1944, "this led every member of the detail, no matter from what class or walk of life, and even the worst people, to urge that this game be stopped at last" (Lewental 1972, 163 ff.). Such extensive preparations foretold that this was the beginning of a most overwhelming extermination. Lewental stresses that it was Jósel Warszawski (real name Dorębus, born in 1900) and Jankiel Handelsman (born in 1908) who took the initiative in this matter. Both men had emigrated from Poland to France in 1931 and, having been arrested by the Gestapo because of their activity in the French Resistance, had been transported to Auschwitz in March 1943 (Lewental 1972, 157 ff.).

These men maintained contact with the resistance movement in the camp and with partisan groups that operated in the vicinity. Both outfits warned them that the time was not ripe for a general uprising. The partisans feared that they would not be able to take in and protect a large number of people after a successful outbreak, and the Combat Group Auschwitz did not think the chances for a general struggle were good. However, once alerted, the SS was more likely to quell an uprising at a later, more opportune date.[12] Lewental wrote that the inmates active in the resistance wanted to wait until the front came even closer. "From their standpoint they were right, especially because they did not feel *they* were in immediate danger of being exterminated." The members of the special detail, however, "concluded that if we wanted to accomplish anything in life, we would have to act sooner." They urged such action, "but unfortunately they [the resistance organization] kept putting us off" (Lewental 1972, 164 ff.). On May 16, 1944, the special detail was expanded to its maximum size before the greatest extermination project began, involving the Jews deported from Hungary. A report from that time lists members of the detail as 952 inmates, and Filip Müller recalls that these comprised around 450 Jews from Hungary, 200 from Poland, 180 from Greece and smaller groups from other countries, nineteen Russian prisoners of war, five Poles, and one German capo (Müller 1979, 211). After completion of the extermination the detail was reduced. The camp administration announced that more than 200 men would be transferred to the subcamp in Gleiwitz; these were loaded on wagons and given food for the journey—and then they were driven to a disinfection station near the main camp and gassed.[13]

The inmates on the special detail found out about this action. The dead bodies were taken to the crematoria and SS men, "for the first time in the history of Auschwitz," burned the corpses themselves at night—and the next morning tried to make members of the special detail believe they were those of civilians killed in an air raid. But workers were able to identify the incompletely burned bodies of their slain comrades (Müller 1979, 246 ff.).

In the meantime nineteen Russians and a German capo had been transferred to the special detail of Auschwitz from Majdanek, a camp that was being evacuated at the approach of the Red Army. These Russians managed to make contact with Russian prisoners of war who were dismantling destroyed airplanes in Birkenau. Lewental emphasizes that these Russians "were able to help us a great deal in our activities, especially with their spirits and their strength," although he also states that they did not have the conspiratorial attitude and clear understanding necessary for such a complicated project (Lewental 1972, 167 ff.).

At that time the resistance movement in the camp procured explosives from the Union factory. Jewish women who worked there smuggled small quantities into the camp, helped by a group of Jews active in the resistance. Róza Robota, a young Polish Jew, passed the powder on to Borodin, a Russian technician, who placed it in empty tin cans together with other chemicals. Thus the special detail received "material," as Lewental put it (Lewental 1972, 166; Gutman 1962, 273 ff.; Kagan 1946, 283). On October 7 the special detail was informed by the resistance organization that another "transport to Gleiwitz"—meaning another death roundup—was being planned. "This created utter chaos in the detail," writes Lewental.

Finally there was an incident. A Russian member of the detail got drunk and made a row, whereupon an SS man beat him. "When the Russian tried to run away, the SS man fired a shot and wounded him. The SS man tried to take the Russian away, but the latter jumped from the wagon and attacked the German, snatching his whip away and giving him a blow on the head. The German shot him on the spot" (Lewental 1972, 177).

This appears to have impeded the execution of the plan. What happened next can be reconstructed only in part because all eyewitnesses lost their lives. Mikos Nyiszli, a physician who had to autopsy the bodies of experimental subjects of the SS doctor Mengele in one of the crematoria, writes that activists on the special detail had notified him a day in advance that the uprising was planned for the evening of October 17. Thus he was surprised to hear an explosion and shots at noon on that day (Jarosz 1978, 157). Lewental, who had been assigned to the special detail of another crematorium, remembers that the SS came "at 1:25 P.M." to collect 300 members of the special detail for the transport—that is, for destruction. These people "raised a loud outcry, rushed at the guards with hammers and axes, wounded some of them, beat the others with whatever was handy, and simply threw stones at them" (Lewental 1972, 178). Filip Müller's description of these events is similar; the 300 men, mostly Hungarian and Greek Jews, did not obey the order to line up. Suddenly "a hail of stones" came down on the SS men; "some of them were wounded and overpowered, others managed to run away. . . . In the meantime, the crematorium had been set on fire" (Müller 1979, 248 ff.). Müller confirms that "the timing of the uprising was [on account of the selection—H.L.] spontaneous and not organized. Nor did it take place as planned" (Langbein 1965, 132). Sigismund Bendel, a physician on the special detail, became convinced that the revolt was badly organized, even though members of the detail had been making preparations for it since early 1944. However, the crematorium in which it broke out was on fire.[14] According to other reports, a German criminal assigned to a crematorium as a capo overheard a conversation about the planned rebellion and threatened to betray it, whereupon the inmates killed him—Lewental reports that they threw him into the oven[15]—which forced them to start the action sooner than planned. Then they attacked the SS men, blew up the crematorium with the explosive smuggled into the camp, and cut the fence, which enabled some members of the detail to break out. Thereupon the inmates of another crematorium disarmed their SS guards and killed them, but the inmates on the details that worked in the two other crematoriums were unable to join in the uprising (Czech 1959–64). Filip Müller heard that Russians simply threw "the hated chief capo Karl Konvoent" into the fire and greeted the SS men with one of the three hand grenades they had in readiness. The inmates utilized the ensuing chaos to cut the barbed wire with pliers with insulated handles and ran out into the open (Müller 1979, 256 ff.). All reports agree that large and heavily armed SS forces were immediately deployed to quell the uprising and pursue the fugitives. "Armed SS men roared down the main road alongside the railway platform on motorcycles and bicycles," writes Wieslaw Kielar, an observer in Birkenau who had to watch out for stray bullets (Kielar 1979, 355).

Thus the uprising and attempted escape were limited to the units housed in those two crematories. Neither the special details employed in the two other crematories nor those housed in the Birkenau sections of the camp were able to join in, though rebels had cut the barbed wire that separated the women's camp from the crematories, and it had been arranged to drench the barracks with gasoline (which was in readiness) and set them on fire. In accordance with the plan, this was to be done during evening roll-call and the SS men in the camp for that purpose were to be attacked. However, the premature outbreak of the rebellion prevented the implementation of this plan. After the initial panic, the heavily armed SS rushed to the crematoriums whose details were rebelling. Besides, as Feinsylberg has pointed out, the homemade hand grenades were inferior.[16]

The SS was able to overpower all inmates at the burning crematorium; they were shot and those who had broken out were pursued. The latter barricaded themselves in a barn at Rajsko in the vicinity of Birkenau. The SS set the barn on fire and massacred these men, too. This has been confirmed by inmates who, as members of the camp's fire brigade, had to work first on the burning crematorium and then on the blazing barn.[17] Before the outbreak there had been 663 members of the special detail, but two days later 212 were listed. There are no reports of a successful escape, but the rebels were able to kill three SS junior squad leaders and wound twelve SS men. The blown-up crematorium could not be used anymore.

There ensued arrests and tortures, and the political department sought to retrace the route taken by the explosive from the Union factory to the special detail. Finally, on January 6, 1945, four young Jewish women were hanged in front of the assembled inmates—the last public execution before the evacuation of Auschwitz (Kagan 1946, 282 ff.).

Despite its bloody suppression, the rebellion of the Auschwitz special detail demonstrated that Jews were capable of fighting and defending their lives. As Israel Gutman wrote, Jews were the ones who killed the first Nazis in Auschwitz.[18] In addition to those already mentioned (Handelsman and Warszawski/Dorębus), other Polish Jews as well as Greek officers and French and Hungarian Jews have been named as organizers of this action.[19]

The only details about attempted uprisings in extermination camps have been furnished by survivors. Since none of those who did forced labor in Belzec have survived, we have only vague information about isolated acts of resistance there. On one occasion a group of arriving Polish Jews refused to leave the wagon. Another time a woman tried to fight back with a razor blade, but each time those who rebelled were shot. When the members of the special detail of Belzec were taken to Sobibor after the liquidation of the camp and noticed that their new camp had the same extermination machinery as their old one, they attempted to resist, but the SS had expected that and stifled the attempt with machine-gun fire.[20]

Several inmates who had been forced to be cogs in the machinery of destruction in Treblinka managed to escape and survive, and thus we have more concrete reports about people who attempted to fight back there.

When Jews were once again transported from Grodno to Treblinka, probably in late 1942, they resisted the order to undress and enter the gas chamber that was camouflaged as a shower. All that Eliahu Rosenberg remembers—according to his testimony about this incident in a Düsseldorf court in 1970—is that these Jews (90 percent men, he estimates) refused to enter the gas chamber, broke ranks, and were shot.[21] Kalman Teigmann, who had been questioned about this same incident nine years earlier, reported that people shouted to one another not to obey the command to undress. They were beaten, but continued to refuse. "Then there was an explosion; apparently someone had thrown a grenade or something like that. A badly injured Ukrainian [Ukrainian volunteers were used as guards—H.L.] was taken away."[22] In 1948 Shmuel Willenberg testified that Jews from Grodno rushed at the SS men and that a fight ensued. They fought so effectively with knives and bottles that three SS men had to be taken to the hospital. However, all of them (a total of 2,000, according to Willenberg) were shot (Willenberg 1961–63). Here is an excerpt from the testimony of Kurt Franz, a former SS first lieutenant and one of the defendants in the Düsseldorf Treblinka trial: "On one occasion I was attacked by a Jew and suffered a stab wound. One of the Jews had thrown a hand grenade. . . . It was a Jew who was about to be taken to the gas chamber." This probably refers to the same incident; Franz stated that the Jew was shot and his wound was treated for four or five weeks.[23] It may be assumed that the testimony of Franz's fellow defendant Arthur Matthes ("Several rushed at me, and I was also wounded with a knife and bled pretty badly") is also connected with this incident.[24]

When a Ukrainian auxiliary policeman did not permit a young Jew to say farewell to his mother on August 26, 1942, the Jew is said to have wounded the Ukrainian with his knife, whereupon he and everyone else on the transport from Kielce were shot (Ainsztein 1974, 726).

Another desperate act of rebellion came up at the Treblinka trial in Düsseldorf. A young Jew named Meir Berliner, who had been selected for labor from a Warsaw transport on September 11, 1942, hurled himself at SS Junior Squad Leader Max Biala with the words "I can't take it anymore," and he inflicted such serious knife wounds that Biala died soon thereafter. As Biala's SS colleague August Miete testified, "we pulled the knife out of Biala's back."[25] Berliner had just had to watch his wife and child being taken to the gas chamber. By way of reprisal Berliner and more than 100 Jews of his labor detail were cruelly killed (Kohn 1945; Ruckerl 1977, 231). "There was a massacre," testified Georg Rajgrodski.[26]

The thought of rebellion and breakout long occupied those who had to operate the machinery of extermination. Their number fluctuated between 500 and 1,200.[27] Prisoners who took sick or were otherwise rendered unfit for work were killed and replaced with new arrivals. Anyone who made a bad impression on an SS man suffered the same fate. However, in an effort to obtain greater productivity from their slaves, the camp administration put a stop to too frequent replacements. This did provide experienced workers, but it also gave the inmates greater opportunities to organize (Glazar 1973).

The prisoners were housed in two camps that were strictly separated from each other. In the bigger one the "four initiators of the uprising" met at night "after the daily hellish experiences" in their barracks in order to devise a plan. Stanislaw Kohn has named especially the aged Warsaw physician Julian Chorążycki, the Slovakian officer Želo Bloch, the capo Zew Kurland, who had also been deported from Warsaw, and Lubling, who was from Silesia.[28] Chorążycki organized the purchase of weapons from corrupt Ukrainian auxiliary guards, which has been mentioned in another context.

However, Chorążycki did not live to see the beginning of the uprising. The SS Lieutenant Kurt Franz described to a Düsseldorf court Chorążycki's end. When Franz went to the hospital on April 19, 1943, he noticed a bundle of banknotes in Chorążycki's pocket; Shmuel Willenberg had just brought him 750,000 zlotys for an arms purchase (Willenberg 1961–63; Ainsztein 1974, 731). Franz asked him what he was going to do with the money, and Chorążycki, who did not want to implicate his comrades, replied that he was preparing his escape. Knowing that his situation was now hopeless, he rushed at Franz with a dissecting knife. "I quickly picked up a chair, the knife bounced off, and I fell backward. Dr. Chorążycki took poison."[29] Eugen Turowski observed the following scene in front of the hospital barracks: "We heard screaming. Dr. Chorążycki came jumping out of the window, and behind him came Franz. . . . He beat the doctor with his whip. . . . When Dr. Chorążycki came out later, we could no longer recognize his face. It was like black pulp.[30] Arie Kudlik also remembers this scene: "I was standing outside when they carried the doctor out. They tried very hard to revive him. . . . The doctor no longer looked like a living human being. Rogossa [one of the guards—H.L.] poured water in the doctor's mouth. Lalka [a nickname of Franz—H.L.] stood on the doctor's belly, and he tried to make the water go into his body by jumping up and down on it. Before this the doctor had been beaten."[31] However, Chorążycki died of the poison and the beatings before the SS was able to whip more out of him.

Even though this was a grave loss for the organization, it could not keep it from pursuing its plan further. Others took Chorążycki's place. In addition to Jews from Poland—such as Alfred Galewski from Lódź, reputedly a baptized Jew whom the SS had appointed senior camp inmate (Ainsztein 1974, 728), there were Rudolf Mašárek from Prague, who had been deported as a person of mixed blood (*Mischling*) because he had refused to leave his Jewish wife, and the mechanic Stanislaw Lichtblau from Morawska–Ostrawa [city in the Czech Republic—ed.]. Shortly before Chorążycki's death, the punitive transfer of Želo Bloch to the second camp also caused a change of plans and consequent delay. Kohn has characterized Bloch as a "military expert" and "the soul of the rebellion." In those days, the inmates of Treblinka learned of the uprising in the Warsaw ghetto because the last transports of Jews went to Treblinka. According to Kohn, these were "no longer the usual transports of apathetic, broken men, women, and children," and Glazar remembers that, along with the news of the Warsaw uprising, they brought the message "Now it is up to you!"[32]

The organization continued to look for ways of procuring weapons, and one was found in this fashion: One day the lock on the door of the armory got broken. The Jewish camp locksmith was ordered to repair it, and he used the opportunity to make an impression and then a copy of the key, which was "guarded like a relic" (Kohn 1945, 4; Rajzman 1968, 146). Richard Glazar remembers that the fourteen-year-old Edek, who had greater freedom of movement because he was almost a child, had put a sliver of metal into the lock so that it would have to be repaired (Glazar 1973).

The number of those who were privy to the plan for a rebellion and participated in preparations was large. Shmuel Willenberg believes that about ten groups were formed, each with five or ten members (Willenberg 1961–63). This is in approximate agreement with an account written by Stanisław Kohn shortly after the end of the war: "Only sixty persons are familiar with the precise plan of the rebellion, and these form the core of the combat organization. They are divided into three groups" (Kohn 1945, 8). Yankel Wiernik, who worked in the strictly separated upper camp, found a way of maintaining a connection with the main camp. In that camp groups of five were formed, and each was assigned a special task. Despite numerous SS informers, this Treblinka organization was never exposed.

Several dates, including June 15, were considered, but there were constant postponements. Wiernik had a hard time persuading young fellow conspirators to be patient (Wiernik n.d., 35). There were probably around 700 inmates in the two camps at that time.[33]

Stanisław Kohn has given the following account of the plan that was devised: "First catch and finish off the chief slavedrivers; disarm the guards, cut the telephone connections; burn and destroy all the equipment of the death factories so they cannot be made operational anymore; liberate the penal camp for Poles in Treblinka 2 kilometers away, join forces with them and make our way into the forests to form a strong partisan group there" (Kohn 1945, 8).

The exterminating activity of the SS seemed to be coming to an end. No more transports arrived. The pits into which bodies had been thrown before they were burned on a large grill were soon empty, and the bodies dug up with an excavator were also burned. Realizing that they would be killed as witnesses as soon as this work was finished, the inmates urged the implementation of their plan, and finally it was set for August 2, 1943, at 5 P.M. (Kohn 1945, 8).[34] "Commandant Galewski is finally giving the signal for an uprising," writes Kohn. Wiernik managed to notify the conspirators in the upper camp of the time (Wiernik n.d., 44).

That morning "there was a tremendous tension in the camp." All those in the know endeavored to stick to the routine of an ordinary day. "The distribution of guns did not begin until 2 P.M. Little Salzberg and a few other lads who performed personal services for SS men and thus had access to their lodgings started rummaging in their masters' barracks in the morning, looking for more weapons, and they managed to steal guns, grenades, and munition. They took everything to the garage. . . . On that day there was a trash collection not far from the arsenal, and that was a great help to us. However, our work was disturbed by the SS man Hiller, the business manager of the camp, who had arrived a short time earlier and wanted to sleep. The agronomist Sudowicz, who was in charge of gardening, called Hiller out under the pretext of having to inspect some plants. Meanwhile Markus and Salzberg were taking carpets to the corridor opposite the arsenal for cleaning, which caused the guards to turn away for a moment. At that, the door to the arsenal was opened with the copied key, and Jacek, the nimble fourteen-year-old Hungarian, slipped in. He tiptoed to the window on the other side of the arsenal, cut a piece out with a glass cutter, and handed grenades and munition to people outside. Together with the garbage, they were loaded on a vehicle and taken to the garage. . . . By now it was impossible to guard the secret, and therefore the leaders decided to start the rebellion in an hour. At 4 P.M. sharp, messengers were dispatched to all groups with instructions to go to the garage immediately and get weapons. . . . Everyone had to give the password 'death,' and the response was 'life.' There were spirited shouts of 'death,' 'life,' 'death,' 'life,' and hands reached for the longed-for weapons" (Kohn 1945, 9). Others believe that the beginning of the uprising had to be advanced because there was reason to fear treason, and that is why not all the weapons could be distributed.[35] Richard Glazar remembers that an informer, who was a senior barracks inmate, had been responsible for the premature outbreak of the rebellion, which was not entirely successful for that reason.[36]

At the same time, the disinfector was splashing liquid on the barracks; however, this time he had not filled his canister with the usual disinfectant but with gasoline from the garage. An unsuspecting SS junior squad leader watched him. At 3:45 P.M. a shot was fired as the agreed-upon signal (Rajzman 1968, 147).

It was understood in the upper camp. A Ukrainian was doing guard duty on the watchtower, and since Ukrainians frequently made deals with inmates, a Jewish inmate showed him a gold piece. He came down in hopes of bartering something. Instead, he was knocked down and relieved of his revolver (Wiernik n.d., 45).

According to Richard Glazar, after the shot and explosion of hand grenades, the SS Junior Squad Leader Suchomel came running out of the SS barracks "in his shirtsleeves, evidently having had his afternoon coffee. He stopped in astonishment and, at the burst of the next grenade, immediately disappeared."[37] Years later Suchomel was interrogated about the events of August 2 by a German court. "When the uprising broke out," he testified, "I was in my room working at the cutting board. I had noticed all day that the Jew workers were restless. Suddenly I heard two bangs; it was pineapple hand grenades. I looked out the window. Küttner [an SS man] was kneeling with his pistol in firing position. Next to him lay a dead Jew worker whom the others had killed as a stoolie. . . . Molotov cocktails were flying around, setting fire to barracks all over the place. I heard shots. . . . Some Jews were lying up there on the rampart [between the upper and the lower camp—H.L.] and shooting into the camp with rifles."[38] During another hearing Suchomel said: "The fence [to Camp II—H.L.] was torn down and wooden boards were used to get past the tank trap. Two guards were disarmed. The shootout lasted for a quarter of an hour. The whole thing had been prepared very, very well." The overwhelming majority took part in the uprising, but "the Jews who wanted to stay in the camp put their hands up."[39]

There was such a rush of events that postwar statements differ. Kohn reports that Želo Bloch "rushed at two SS men with an axe, made his way to us [from the upper camp], and assumed the command" (Kohn 1945, 10). Glazar also draws attention to the other leaders of the conspiracy, who joined battle with the SS to enable their comrades to escape and fell in the process.[40] It was possible to arm 200 prisoners with the weapons taken from the guards (Kohn 1945, 10). Willenberg believes that only the premature outbreak of the rebellion, necessitated by an informer, prevented the prisoners from distributing all weapons and leaving the camp in an eastward direction in the two armored cars of the SS (Willenberg 1961–63). Nevertheless, there were fires all around, a large reservoir of gasoline exploded, and the way to freedom had been opened by force. When Teig-mann was asked at a later date how he had gotten over the fence, he replied: "There were beds, there was wood, and I simply got over the fence."

To the extent that a balance sheet of this uprising can be drawn up, it looks something like this: Since the rebels did not manage to destroy the telephone wires, presumably another consequence of the premature break-out, the SS could quickly alert units in the vicinity. Teigman recalls that "we were pursued with horses and trucks,"[41] and that is why the escapees were not able to reach the Polish penal camp. Nor did they manage to render the entire extermination machinery inoperable. The SS continued to use it for a while after August 2, 1943, though to a greatly reduced extent. This is how the Düsseldorf judges summed up their findings: "After the uprising, the camp was not rebuilt in its original form. In the gas chambers that had remained intact, a few smaller transports from Bialy-stok were exterminated. The buildings that were left, including the gas house, were torn down (Rückerl 1977, 240). In late November 1943, the last Jews who had been doing forced labor in Treblinka were murdered, and those parts of the camp that had not been destroyed in the uprising were demolished as well.

There are different estimates of the number of successful escapees. They range from 150 to 600, and the great discrepancy may be explained by the fact that the estimates by SS men (500 to 600) refer to all those who got beyond the camp fence, whereas the rebels include only those who were able to reach the protective forests.[42] As we have already reported, many of the latter either fell as partisans or were killed by anti-Semitic Poles.

The greatest discrepancy, and the one for which it is hardest to find a satisfactory explanation, concerns the number of guards killed during the rebellion. Kohn, who speaks of "a regular battle" that lasted six hours, assures us that they succeeded in killing "200 German and Ukrainian Fascists." When he was confronted with the testimony of SS Lieutenant Kurt Franz that "to my knowledge, no one from the German camp person-nel was killed; one of the Ukrainians was sent to the hospital with a bullet in his lungs, and another Ukrainian was wounded by hand grenades,"[43] Kohn averred that he saw many dead SS men and Ukrainians, some of whom he knew by name, lying on the ground.[44] Other survivors of the rebellion have also given eyewitness reports about the killing of guards. On the other hand, the former SS men Willi Mentz and August Miete join Franz in claiming that the masters of the camp suffered no losses in the uprising.[45] They had no apparent reason to withhold such information from the court, for exaggerating losses would have emphasized the danger posed by the inmates, whose brutal suppression they were charged with.

The German prosecutors who had prepared the Treblinka trial in Düsseldorf were able to determine that fifty-two inmates, including two women, lived to see the definitive liberation after the end of the war.[46] Richard Glazar concludes his report about this revolt as follows: "On that blazing afternoon in August, the flames from elsewhere were even higher than the usual ones from the enormous burning grill near the gas chambers. The fiery glow that poured forth over Treblinka that night had a different color, a different origin, and a different interpretation than the one of all previous nights" (Glazar 1973).

The former SS man Erich Bauer has testified that the Jews deported to Sobibor did not have a clue and did not begin to suspect anything until they already were in the gas chambers. "However, by that time there was no turning back," said the well-informed Bauer. "Resistance was offered very rarely" (Rückerl 1977, 181). Nevertheless, reports by survivors do mention some attempts at resistance. For example, on April 30, 1943, prisoners deported from Wlodawa rebelled at the railroad platform and managed to injure some SS men and Ukrainian henchmen before they were killed. When deportees from Minsk were getting off the train in September of that year, they pelted guards with stones, pots, bottles, and whatever else was handy (Ainsztein 1974, 746 ff.).

As in Treblinka, and presumably also in the other extermination camps about which no one could report afterward, those doing forced labor in Sobibor considered a breakout over a long period of time. Simcha Białowicz remembers two plans. One involved putting poison into the guards' food (some inmates were working in their kitchen) and the other called for setting the barracks on fire and using the ensuing tumult to break out. Neither plan could be put into practice.[47]

Dov Freiberg has stated that the Jewish chief capo Moshe planned an uprising together with two other capos but was betrayed by a Jew nicknamed Berliner. The three capos and others were shot, and as his reward, Berliner received Moshe's position, but his fellow prisoners lynched him.[48] On the basis of extensive evidence, the Hagen court that dealt with the Sobibor complex reached the following conclusion: "Although acts of violence applied a constant paralyzing pressure on the majority of the inmates, plans for an uprising . . . were made repeatedly and never abandoned."[49]

A group that concerned itself with such ideas, which considered various plans, formed around Leon Feldhendler, a Polish Jew.[50] These men were spurred on by the fate of the Jewish slave laborers who were brought to Sobibor around the end of May and the beginning of June 1943 and murdered there. What happened to them was a graphic illustration of what was in store for the inmates of Sobibor. They established contact with some Ukrainian guards from the Soviet Union, whose aversion to the German SS they had noticed (while no such attitude was discernible in Ukrainians from Poland), and they hoped that these guards would act as a liaison with partisan groups with whom they could collaborate on liberating the camp. The Ukrainians did try, but in the end the inmates escaped alone.

On September 23, a transport from Minsk arrived in Sobibor. Among those selected for work were Russian Jews who had served in the Red Army as officers and thus had military experience, including partisan fighting. Their arrival evoked curiosity and hope in the camp. "They listened to what we said," wrote Aleksander Pecherskii (on September 27, 1943) in the diary which he had kept since his arrival (Pecherskii 1968, 26).[51] Pecherskii had immediately attracted attention by the uncommon pride with which he turned down a reward offered him by an SS guard for his fast work (cigarettes, later bread and margarine) (Pecherskii 1968, 23 ff.). As a result of the hopes stirred by the arrival of the Russian officers and the prisoners' respect for Pecherskii's conduct, a fellow inmate called on Pecherskii to flee—this on September 29, a scant week after his arrival. His response was that escapes of individuals would cause bloody reprisals against those left behind; instead ways would have to be found to give the largest possible number of inmates a chance to escape. This answer was as impressive as another of his, this one to the question why the Russian partisans were not liberating the camp: "Our work won't be done for us by others." This, within an astonishingly short period of time, caused the members of the resistance group to offer Pecherskii the leadership.[52] "We owed our ability to accomplish the uprising" to the Russian prisoners of war, wrote Stanislaw Szmajzner. "The idea of organizing a rebellion came from Russian inmates who as former soldiers were better informed."[53] Moshe Bachir believes that Moshe Feldhendler prepared the uprising moralewise and Pecherskii on the technical level.[54] Feldhendler was born in 1910 and Pecherskii the following year. The former was murdered in a pogrom in Poland after the war, but Pecherskii has stated that Feldhendler invited him to participate in the planning and was in daily contact with him until the uprising (Pecherskii 1968, 30 ff.).[55]

Observing strict conspiratorial rules, an executive committee (of seven, according to Pecherskii)[56] communicated about necessary preparations. Tuvia Blatt believes that the "staff" consisted of ten members, that fifteen people had been entrusted with special tasks, and that thirty, including himself, knew about the plan (Blatt 1961, 26). According to another source, a group of twenty Czech, German, French, and Polish Jews had been formed prior to the arrival of the transport from Minsk. Its leadership was comprised of five Polish Jews, for the Poles were in the majority.[57]

As already mentioned in another context, the conspirators received warnings. A Ukrainian guard who knew Pecherskii from the Red Army informed him that an uprising had taken place in Treblinka and that the liquidation of Sobibor was imminent. Samuel Lerer remembers that few transports were arriving in Sobibor by that time and "the camp was coming to an end."[58] Ilona Safran also heard the rumor that the camp was in its last days and the inmates could therefore not wait for help from the outside any longer. In those days people whispered to one another that they should put on warm clothes every day in order to be prepared for a possible breakout.[59] Stanislaw Szmajzner offers this recollection: "In the fall of 1943, we heard the rumor that our camp was being broken up. This would have meant that in the end even the working Jews would be gassed, and that is why we organized the uprising."[60]

The court in Hagen endeavored to reconstruct the course of events immediately preceding the breakout: "Since there was little work, the camp administration permitted all inmates of Camp I to pray together in a barracks on Yom Kippur, the evening of October 9 or 10. This gave the uprising committee a pretext for a general discussion among all inmates. The women were asked to pray as loudly as they could while the Feldhendler group was briefing the men about the plan and assigning specific tasks to subgroups" (Rückerl 1977, 195). Jakob Boskovitch has given the following account of this discussion: "All 600 of us gathered in the barracks and we prayed. . . . In a corner we saw a group whispering."[61] Ilona Safran recalls that she learned about the escape plan on that occasion.[62]

Pecherskii, who had in the meantime briefed Jewish capos and included them in the planning, has reported about a final leadership discussion in the carpenter's shop on October 12, in which nine persons, eventually including the capo Bjetzki, participated. The exact time and the assignments of each group were decided upon. "I submitted the plan of the uprising and the escape to the underground committee, and it was adopted together with some additional proposals," writes Pecherskii[63] and adds that it was decided on the evening of the 13th to stage the uprising on the 14th (Pecherskii 1968, 41 ff.). According to some reports, the uprising was originally scheduled on the 13th but had to be postponed by a day.[64]

Pecherskii begins his account of the great event by saying that "October 14 was a fine, sunny day. . . . During the night we distributed the knives that we had obtained and almost a dozen small axes that had been made for us by blacksmiths and were easy to hide. Anyone who needed warm clothing was given some. Only the leaders knew exactly when and how we were going to break out" (Pecherskii 1968, 43). Everything had been carefully and prudently organized. Years later the judges in Hagen formulated the result of their hearings objectively and concisely: "Since commandant

Reichleitner and the dreaded top sergeant Gustav Wagner were on leave on October 14, the committee called on the prisoners to revolt on that day. . . . At midday the first weapons were stolen" (Ruckerl 1977, 195). Because youths had greater freedom of movement, as they did in Treblinka, they had been entrusted with the procurement of weapons. One of them, Jakob Boskovich, later testified as follows: "We had no weapons, except for a few hand grenades, rifles, and pistols as well as a submachine gun. These had been stolen and brought into the camp a few days earlier by children and girls, who were employed in shining SS men's shoes and cleaning floors."[65] Stanislaw Szmajzner, who was sixteen and a half years old at the time, has reported how he carried out the orders he had been given: "Since I was a plumber and had access to the Ukrainian barracks, where I had installed iron stoves, I was ordered to steal rifles from there and take them to Camp I at 3:50 P.M. I was able to steal three rifles, put them in iron stovepipes, wrapped blankets around them, and took them to the camp at 3:50 sharp. I gave two to Russian inmates and kept one for myself."[66]

The plan was predicated on the fact that SS men had prisoners do work for them in the workshops, and it also took into account the punctuality of the Germans. Individual SS men were invited to come to various work-shops for fittings at specific times, and there they were killed. This started in the tailor's shop with the deputy commandant, Josef Niemann, who was killed when he had put his gun down and was trying something on.[67] There followed blow upon blow. "We killed six SS men in the tailor's and shoemaker's shops, where we had asked them to come, at fifteen-minute intervals after 4 P.M., to try on or pick up some article of clothing or shoes. After 3:30, four SS men were killed in Sector II, where we had lured them into the storeroom one by one, to pick up a leather coat that we had found among the effects of dead inmates. This proved to be an excellent decoy. One Fascist was killed in the garage. In this way, eleven of the fourteen SS men, who were then presiding over the extermination of human beings, were killed; two were absent from the camp." Pecherskii, the organizer, has given an objective account of the action.[68] If an SS man could not be lured into a workshop, the inmates tried a different tactic. After SS Junior Squad Leader Wolf had been slain in the clothing depot, his colleague Falaste "rode by in a truck, and we told him, 'Herr Squad Leader, Squad Leader Wolf is looking for you.' Falaste came in and was given the same treat-ment." When the first stab did not kill the SS man Beckmann, and he screamed, "someone rang a bell to drown out the screams. . . . A little boy ran from Camp I to Camp II and kept tabs on the number of dead."[69] According to Simcha Bialowicz, "two Ukrainians came on bikes, and we mowed them down, too."[70] A German Jew named Schwarz, who was working as an electrician, disconnected the light and the telephone.[71]

Thus far the precisely prepared plan had worked. Then the SS man Bauer "unexpectedly returned to the camp in a truck . . . and called some inmates, who had just killed Squad Leader Floss, out to unload the vehicle. When Bauer saw the dead man, he shot at the inmates" (Rückerl 1977, 196). Pecherskii reports that the camp administrator Frenzel did not keep his appointment at the workshop, and because the inmates could not wait any longer, he instructed the capo Byetzki to give the signal with his whistle. "People came flocking from all directions. Seventy inmates, mostly Russian prisoners, formed the vanguard. . . . The rest were a mass of uniformed prisoners who could only guess that something had been prepared." The ensuing tumult made it impossible to march in the customed formation and thereby continue to deceive the SS guards. "Thus I called out 'Comrades, forward!' " Thunderous calls echoed throughout the camp and "immediately brought together Jews from Russia, Poland, Holland, France, Czechoslovakia, and Germany. With a loud 'Hurrah' 600 undernourished and exhausted people started a charge for their lives and their freedom. The attack on the arsenal failed; heavy machine-gun fire stopped us on our way there" (Pecherskii 1968, 49 ff.). The plan also called for a Russian to speak with the Ukrainian guards, "for some of them would have liked to come along. This did not work out because one of the Ukrainians started shooting, which forced us to run toward the gate and the fence rather than the arsenal."[72]

As Stanisław Szmajzner put it, "at first we met with no resistance from the SS. My explanation is that the SS men who were still alive and even the guards on the towers [surrounding the camp] were so surprised by the events that they could not think straight."[73]

Karl Frenzel testified that he and Bauer sounded an alarm. "When I reached Camp I, Jews came running toward me and past me. . . . The guards shot at the fleeing Jews. . . . The guards in Camp I, some of the Ukrainians, and German camp personnel were killed."[74] Frenzel's subordinate Franz Wolf, a brother of the man killed in the clothes depot, gave this report: "On the day of the uprising, I heard shots from the arsenal. I ran to the office to make a call. Beckmann's body lay on the desk and next to him was a dead Ukrainian. The telephone wires were down. Frenzel told me to guard the gate with a machine gun."[75] Simcha Bialowicz confirmed that the inmates could not pass the gate "because someone was standing there and shooting. . . . There was shooting from the tower as well. . . . Many people were killed by shots from the tower."[76]

Pecherskii has described various escape routes. "The field around the camp was mined 15 meters deep. When Frenzel opened fire from his machine gun, some of the inmates ran to the fence, tore the barbed wire, and fled across the minefield. Many were killed, and this opened the way for others."[77] Smajzner, who was among them, writes: "Many Jews died when they were caught in the wire entanglement, but even more were killed in the minefields. . . . I was able to save my life by climbing to freedom over the dead bodies lying on the mines."[78] Pecherskii and his group ran toward the SS lodgings next to the minefield. "We thought the Fascists would be afraid of laying mines next to their habitations because fragments might come in through the windows. Those who had been assigned that task by the underground committee made openings in the wire with scissors, and many got through." The assumption was correct, and that area was not mined. Despite this, three friends were felled, for they ran into a cross fire on this escape route. "Many people were killed by bullets in the open area [after they had already managed to escape from the camp—H.L.] between the camp and the forest."[79]

The Lublin police drew up the following balance sheet: "On Oct. 14, 1943, ca. 5 P.M., rebellion of the Jews in the SS camp Sobibor, 40 km north of Chelm. They overpowered the guards, took possession of the arsenal, and after a gun battle with the other camp personnel they fled in an unknown direction. . . . 9 SS men killed, 1 SS man missing . . . 1 SS man wounded . . . two foreign guards shot. Around 300 Jews escaped, the others were shot or are in the camp. Troops, police, and Wehrmacht were immediately notified and secured the camp around 1 A.M. The area south and southwest of Sobibor is being combed by the SS and the Wehrmacht" (Sauer 1974). The SS man Erich Bauer gave the following testimony before the Hagen court: "I took seven coffins to Chelm; the other coffins were transported there in a wagon, and I took them from the railway station to the town hall. In all twenty-one or twenty-three persons were killed, among them a Ukrainian." Bauer also mentioned the names of wounded SS men.[80]

Karl Frenzel, who had initiated the pursuit of the escapees, took stock before the same tribunal in these words: "Approximately eighty Jews were shot while trying to escape. Some of the Jews, about thirty or forty, were caught and taken back to the camp. The Jews who were still in the camp after the uprising [the court estimated that these amounted to about half of those interned there—H.L.] were shot in Camp III on orders from Sporrenberg (Rückerl 1977, 196).[81]

The Hagen trial began on September 6, 1965, and the prosecutors who had prepared it were able to get the addresses of thirty-two survivors of that extermination camp and establish that at least three others, including Feldhendler, had died after the liberation in 1945. They estimated that of the 500 to 600 inmates of the camp at the time of the uprising, fifty to sixty had been able to survive.[82]

Understandably, the known rebellions of inmates that have been discussed in this chapter were ventured by those who were in the most

hopeless situation. During the period of the concentration camps' existence, Jews killed SS men in Treblinka, Sobibor, and later in Auschwitz as
well. The great symbolic significance of this has been emphasized in a
report written on November 15, 1943, by an underground Jewish national
committee in Poland and published in England shortly thereafter.[83]

21

SABOTAGE

Presumably, any prisoner who is forced to work prefers to perform as little as possible, unless the fruit of his labor benefits him and his comrades. This applies to an even greater extent to the inmates of concentration camps, who were deprived of their liberty without any awareness of their own guilt.

A prisoner who was assigned to the hospital building, the inmate kitchen, or similar work projects—unless he was completely demoralized—was spurred on by the realization that his labor could benefit fellow victims. If one had no such assignment, however, work was intended primarily as punishment and organized accordingly, with guards and frequently capos or foremen enforcing a killing pace. Those who tried to shirk could easily be kept in line by beatings.

This situation changed when it became apparent that the war would last a long time and the SS was obliged to make prisoners available for the arms industry. This period began in the spring of 1942. Eventually, the majority of prisoners were assigned to arms factories, for their managements requested them. In fact, some war plants were purposely built around concentration camps, so they could utilize the prisoners' labor. And if an inmate was working at a machine, a cudgel was hardly the appropriate instrument for getting the most out of him [so there was an automatic improvement in inmates' positions—ed.].

But a prisoner who knew that his labor was intended to help assure the victory of the Nazi armies—or, at a later date, at least to prolong the war— was unwilling to contribute to delaying the final defeat of National Socialism. With few exceptions, he could not hope to regain his freedom before such a defeat. Thus it was natural for inmates to think of sabotaging this work even before there was organized resistance activity.

Realizing that the customary methods of terror no longer brought results, Oswald Pohl, head of the Economic Office, ordered on May 15, 1943, that inmates doing satisfactory work be granted certain privileges (Georg

1963, 116). He did so after Himmler had called upon him to "concern himself intensively with the question of a system of piecework among our prisoners" (Heiber 1968, 194 ff.). In accordance with this order, vouchers were issued as premiums, though these had little practical value, for they could rarely be used to obtain something useful. There were attempts to refuse them. There is a report from Ravensbrück that the underground organization of Polish women tried to sabotage the assigned work systematically and managed to get "the overwhelming majority of Polish inmates to refuse premiums. Not all ethnic groups regarded this gesture as the right way to go about it." Maria Kurcyuszowa, the author of this report, also states that as a rule Polish women received packages from home,[1] something that might have promoted this attitude. In Dora, too, there reportedly was a conscious sabotage of the premium system "to prevent a stimulating effect on productivity."[2]

Two statements may illustrate the problems involved in carrying on sabotage. The Austrian Communist Otto Horn has described a certain type, the skilled worker who had been sent to a concentration camp because of his political or union activity. "After years of grueling imprisonment, it was often a great boon for these workers to stand at an anvil, a vise, or a lathe again. . . . In the early period, only jobs were done for the camp in which all inmates had an interest. If the doors worked well or iron toilet grates were available, if there were solid banisters at the staircases or the water pipes and drainage worked well, then this benefited all inmates and no one came in conflict with his own political past if he practiced his craft." However, after Stalingrad—the point in time chosen by Horn— when the plants concentrated on war production, "a politically responsible inmate did not always find it easy to locate the exact boundary between being killed as a saboteur if he refused to work and keeping his professional pride in check."[3] Maria Kurcyuszowa, the chronicler of Polish women in Ravensbrück, sees the significance of sabotage in arms factories "not so much in material losses—after all, the work of unskilled laborers was not very successful in any case—but in moral resistance against the criminal compulsion. . . . This is illustrated by a phrase frequently used by Polish women: 'Sabotage is like wine.' "[4] Horn, who gathered his experience in Buchenwald, has primarily German and Austrian political prisoners in mind, and Kurcyuszowa mainly non-Germans—but not trained specialists, for presumably there were hardly any among the female inmates.

Horn also points out that it was hard to distinguish which plants (to which inmates were assigned) were armament factories and which not, for increasingly all work was intended to benefit the war effort, directly or indirectly. Is it sabotage of the German armament industry if, as Frenchman Roger Abada recalls, mechanics in the Auschwitz motor-pool systematically disabled those vehicles (Abada 1946)? Or if the Luxembourger George Hess, together with a Frenchman and a Belgian, cemented thirty or forty automobile batteries into the ground while building a barracks in the Sachsenhausen subsidiary camp Glau?[5]

One much-discussed act of sabotage has nothing to do with arms and war but is important nonetheless. When the old crematorium in Dachau could no longer handle the increased demand, the camp management on May 9, 1942, ordered the construction of a new and larger crematorium with several ovens and a gas chamber, to be called Barracks X. This work was assigned to a detail of inmates headed by Karl Wagner, a German Communist and a mason by trade. Wagner did his best to delay the building, and Sepp Plieseis, who was assigned to that detail for a time, has described his instructions as follows: "Comrades, the gas chamber through which all of us may be intended to march must never be finished! Work slowly? No, sabotage wherever you can!" And "the cement did not bond properly, the foundation turned out to be too weak, and the mortar in the brickwork crumbled so that whole units had to be torn down and put up again" (Plieseis 1946, 208). This action later became legendary.[6] The stout-hearted Wagner, who was highly respected by all, has described his activity modestly by saying that since the construction could not be sabotaged completely, the best he could do was delay work on the gas chamber until the crematorium was finished and the SS had lost interest in the completion of the gas chamber.[7] By that time, inmates who were to be killed could be assigned to "invalids transports" bound for the "euthanasia project" in Hartheim Castle near Linz, where inmates were dispatched with poison gas, or for an extermination camp. This happened in March 1943, when the incineration room and the morgue, but not the gas chamber, were put into operation.[8]

There are reports from practically all camps about acts of sabotage by inmates forced to work on the production of weapons, and it is certain that many similar acts went unrecorded.

In Sachsenhausen inmates buried steel plates intended for tanks under rubble.[9] In Rajsko, a satellite camp of Auschwitz, where researchers sought a way of making rubber out of the coxagis plant, women sabotaged these experiments by using their expertise to avoid reaching the desired results (Smoleń 1960–67, 38). Heribert Kreuzmann, an Austrian veteran of the Spanish Civil War who was in charge of giving out material in the Präzifix detail of Dachau, used his position to misplace screws and other parts important for production. He did this at his own initiative, and when he was "busted," friends assigned him to a transport of nurses to Auschwitz, and so he escaped punishment.[10] In the subsidiary camp Leipzig–Hasag, the Pole Matilda Brózek damaged machines in the cartridge factory in which she was working with other women. She did so with the approval of German foremen, and when she was betrayed, she was able to escape punishment—in the case of sabotage, public execution—because the functionaries shielded her, and the chief supervisor came to her aid, Brózek having bribed her with packages received from her family. To eliminate any danger, Brózek was placed on a transport as well.[11] Polish prisoners working in the construction office at Gross–Rosen did not meet deadlines for the production of basic materials, thus upsetting the work schedule of other details. Workers in the garage put a flamethrower out of commission (Mołdawa 1967, 142, 145). Poles employed as stonemasons in Gusen damaged both their tools and bricks ready to be used for large buildings (Nogaj 1967, 169). A group of prisoners (Luxembourgers, Dutchmen, and Norwegians in particular) who were dismantling damaged airplane motors in Natzweiler, destroyed some parts that had remained complete and intact; since the foremen, Alsatian civilians doing forced labor, were on the side of the prisoners, this action went unnoticed.[12] Similar actions have been reported from Flossenbürg.[13] French engineers and technicians assigned to an aircraft plant in the satellite camp Flöha produced parts in such a way that heavy use was bound to bring out defects, though they easily passed inspection. They also devised a special system of riveting airplane parts defectively (Siegert 1979, 460). These acts of sabotage stand for many similar ones.

Wherever resistance groups had formed, they included the organization of sabotage among their tasks. This began with Work Assignments.

In Dachau inmates on this detail did not place skilled workers on those outside units that had to work for arms factories;[14] instead they assigned inmates without special skills to such plants as "experts."[15] Since the inmates in Work Assignments kept a card index listing special skills, they were able to manipulate such assignments as long as they were safe from traitors within their ranks. Sabotage in Dora followed the same pattern. Although electrical engineers were much in demand there, Krokowski, who had such training, was not tapped as an expert by the inmate-run labor-statistics detail.[16] On the other hand, efforts were made to steer experts to workplaces where their knowledge enabled them to commit effective acts of sabotage. Jan Češpiva, a Czech doctor assigned to the hospital, called himself a "sabotage dispatcher" and said that he had "the task and the opportunities . . . to assign skilled workers to the appropriate places [via the hospital—H.L.]. Electrical engineers, experts on low-tension current, and other specialists were immediately identified by the underground leadership and assigned to the installation of the steering device at the tail end of the missile and to other important work. They were instructed to change the voltage in the relays of the receivers after the

Palný 1964, 36). In Mauthausen, inmates in Work Assignments even managed to keep a considerable number of prisoners from being assigned any
work by giving false reports about the number of inmates (Maršàlek n.d.,
23). In Ravensbrück Margarete Buber-Neumann acted in similar fashion
on her own. As senior block inmate, she took it upon herself to assign
women of her block to inside duty, thus keeping them from having to go
out with a labor detail.[17]

The German Communist Oskar Müller has described acts of sabotage
that were organized in various workshops at Dachau.[18] His comrade Albin
Lüdke has reported such acts in a factory producing automatic rifles in
which inmates of Neuengamme worked. "It was the task of the resistance
movement to impede production by lying down on the job and committing
acts of sabotage, and in this endeavor it succeeded." He also reports about
the Belgian Communist Pierre Tollenaire, a welder who effectively sabotaged welding operations on ships in the Jastram engine factory at
Hamburg–Bergedorf.[19] This caused both Tollenaire and a Czech officer,
whose sabotage activity in the Dachau workshops had come to the attention of the SS, to be hanged.

The Combat Group Auschwitz also tried, "when sabotage in the arms
industry became relevant, to infiltrate cadres in those details that offered
an opportunity to do so." A number of successful actions have been
reported. "Roger Abada has testified that at the German Armaments
Works production declined by 50 percent within a few months after systematic sabotage had been organized. According to Thérèse Chassaing, the
success of the activity of the women's detail assigned to the Union Works, a
munitions factory, could be gauged by the daily complaints that grenades
manufactured there had failed to explode. Frequently machines broke
down because of defects. Inmates working in the engineering office of the
Rheinmetall Company, Düsseldorf, which had a branch at Laurahütte,
found a way of damaging the mechanism of guns manufactured there after
they had already passed inspection" (Langbein 1972, 303 ff; 1949, 159;
Smoleń 1960–67, 37). We also have concrete statements about the results
of sabotage in the Jawiszowice coal mine. The leadership of a resistance
group, German and Austrian Communists, has enumerated the following
actions: "Hollow spaces were left when wagons were loaded; when coal
and wood were being bunkered, rocks were included; hard-to-obtain steel
parts disappeared.[20] In addition, conveyor belts and haulageways were put
out of commission—there is a letter extant in which the mine administration complains about inmates damaging conveyor belts—fuel for locomo-
tives was poured into crevices of rocks, and mine timber was thrown in to
inaccessible places (Strzelecki 1975, 240).

Russians who were in contact with the Buchenwald underground have described systematic sabotage activity. After Yuri Sapunov's arrival there, he was checked and observed by comrades and then instructed to organize work on the shaft detail in such a way that as little as possible was done without incurring punishment. A Polish foreman who was known as a slavedriver and might have stood in the way was pressured into giving Sapunov no more trouble (Sapunov 1959, 23). Alexej Gurin, a Russian physician, was instructed by compatriots in the Buchenwald resistance to organize sabotage in the subcamp Schwerte, where inmates had to work in a locomotive repair shop. In cooperation with other Russian officers, much could be achieved—for example, the destruction of a valuable lathe. When this detail was disbanded, the inmates were transferred to Bad Salzungen, where they continued their organized sabotage in an aircraft factory, which had been installed in the tunnel of a salt mine (Gurin 1959, 148 ff.).

Another Russian, Valentin Sakharov, has given a graphic description of an action in Mauthausen that had the same aim: "The underground organization continually concerns itself with the problem of organizing the forced labor of the inmates in such a way that it does the Fascists the smallest amount of good." In the fall of 1944, when the Messerschmitt Works installed a plant in the camp area to produce parts for airplane wings, "our comrades devised a method of mass-producing unusable parts." The Russian Georgi Arapov, who was responsible for the production of rivets, utilized an arrangement of the SS to save workers' time—a latrine between the workshops. As he passed these pits every day, Arapov threw in the proper rivets and then gave the workers rivets that were too small, which rendered the riveted parts unfit for use. The SS whipped the culprits within an inch of their lives but did not kill them—evidently because the technical personnel of the plant had had a hard time "teaching the simplest things" to the inmates, who pretended to be slow on the uptake. The factory management had had to train unskilled workers because the camp clerks had put the requested skilled workers on a transport to a subcamp as quickly as they could (Rutkowski 1970, 162 ff.). The Spaniard José Sanz reports that a civilian worker in that plant stood up for him when he was suspected of sabotage, and thus he escaped punishment. He managed to get himself transferred to another detail (Razola/Constante 1969, 189).

According to a report out of East Germany, the following "directive" was issued by the international camp committee of Sachsenhausen: "Work slowly, produce substandard articles, waste materials, cause machines to break down" (Damals in Sachsenhausen 1967, 89). The administration of that camp was able to strike the most momentous blow against organized sabotage. On March 27, 1944, SS leaders found typewritten leaflets that called upon civilian workers to offer passive resistance and commit acts of sabotage. We have reported about the deleterious consequences in another context.

The Dutchman Telling remembers that Russians in Sachsenhausen sabotaged the completion of a munitions factory so successfully that newly erected sections of a wall collapsed, and as a result, that plant never became operational.[21] An international group in the Mauthausen satellite camp Melk, which included specialists, managed to delay the construction and installation of a factory in a mine tunnel for several weeks, and with the approach of the Russian army, the camp had to be evacuated before work in the plant could start (Bernadac 1972, 334).

Several camps were dominated by a large armaments plant, and thus sabotage activity concentrated on them. The Heinkel aircraft factory played such a role in Sachsenhausen, and according to the East German report, activities were "particularly successful" there (Damals in Sachsenhausen 1967, 89 ff.). The 5,000 inmates of different nationalities who worked at Heinkel "helped silently and steadily when it was a matter of damaging all equipment and machinery needed for military purposes in such a way that they were unfit for use." Young Russians specialized in removing small valves from airplanes, and it took a long time to obtain replacements. An "extraordinary amount" of Plexiglas was used, for the inmates made cigarette holders from it, a commodity much coveted by the civilian workers in the plant. Heinrich Lienau sums up these activities by saying that "it was an unwritten law to do anything that might shorten the war" (Lienau 1949, 157 ff.).

The most important arms factory in which Mauthausen inmates were forced to work was the Steyr Works—both the plants in the town of Steyr itself and the factory built near Gusen. There are various reports about acts of sabotage in the production of armaments. The Frenchman Hippolyte Samson writes that everyone sabotaged in his own way there (Bernadac 1975, 58 ff.), but the Italian Antonio Galiano reports about an Italian-organized sabotage in the production of machine guns that was carried on till the liberation, despite all threats and reprisals, and caused many unusable guns to be delivered (Pappalettera 1972). Patricio Cruz has described the systematic sabotage carried out by a solid Spanish group that managed to shut the factory down on several occasions, once for as long as four days (Bernadac 1976, 209). The Pole Emil Samek has given a detailed report about efforts to slow down production in the Steyr plant at Gusen: "I worked there from spring 1943 to the liberation on May 5, 1945, mostly as a setter. . . . This gave me many opportunities for sabotage by setting the devices incorrectly, and other setters did the same thing. However, we soon stopped doing it, for it would have been easy to trace such acts. . . . Only during the final inspection in a separate shop were there greater oppor-

during the final inspection in a separate shop were there greater opportunities for passing larger numbers of improperly dimensioned parts for the final montage, which was done outside the plant, or for putting the right parts on a junk pile to be scrapped. I only worked on the final inspection for a few months, but I know that organized sabotage took place there. . . . However, a 100 percent sabotage was not possible until after the installation of a tempering facility in our plant." In this endeavor young Poles acted so conspiratorially that Samek did not learn until after the war "what excellent work was done" there. The improper hardening of some parts of a gun sufficed to make the gun fail after a short period of use.[22] Samek's compatriot Stanisław Nogaj has mentioned Józef Ladowski as the organizer of this very effective sabotage in the heat-treating shop, and he has also reported about Poles who gave out damaged implements in the toolhouse. During the nightshift, other Poles substituted defective parts for good ones and sent them to the main plant in Steyr. The good parts were taken back to the plant and added to the production lists for a second time. According to Nogaj, others carried out individual acts of sabotage and were helped by some civilian masters (Nogaj 1967, 167 ff.). The Luxembourger Eugène Thomé remembers how one of these, the south Tyrolean Kettner, saved him from being punished (*Letzeburger zu Mauthausen* 1970, 287 ff.). Kettner, for his part, recalls that on one occasion, when 1,200 pieces of scrap were reported, he covered up for the inmates when this excessive figure led to an investigation.[23] In this connection, both Kettner and Samek name Petrak, an Austrian civilian who took part in this sabotage.[24]

The most detailed reports about sabotage actions in Buchenwald concern the Gustloff Works, where up to 6,000 prisoners were employed in twelve large shops. "In cooperation with the comrades on the labor-statistics detail, we excluded skilled workers who were known as lackeys of the Nazis or whose orientation was dubious; instead, we filled the most important specialized positions with dependable anti-Fascists of every nationality, men who were ready to take personal risks. . . . As a matter of principle, plans were made to order more machines, tools, and materials than were required for a given production job. . . . In one instance, orders for a long-abandoned production project were 'inadvertently' placed over a period of months and burdened several suppliers with tens of thousands of wasted man-hours. . . . By fostering jurisdictional disputes among sections of the bloated bureaucracy of the plant management, it was often possible to produce delays lasting for months. The numerous regulations of the Wehrmacht, which governed such matters as inspection and purchases down to the smallest details, were carried *ad absurdum* so that arms that had been delivered had to be subjected to a time-consuming overhauling because of small, unimportant flaws or imperfections, while major defects

that were difficult to detect went unnoticed." On one occasion the
Wehrmacht had to send back the entire nine months' production of automatic carbines as unserviceable, even though a testing committee had
been unable to find the source of the defects (Leibbrand 1945, 38). The
Russian Leonid Iosem gives the credit for this very effective action to a
specialist, his compatriot, Anatoly Skobtsov, and identifies himself as the
leader of the sabotage activity in the Gustloff Works (though it is not clear
whether he led the Russians working there or an international group). He
concludes his report by saying that "for security reasons even I was not
informed of many methods of sabotage" (Iosem 1959, 109 ff.). Iosem's
compatriot Nikolai Simakov writes that at the behest of the Russians all
ethnic groups sent their best people to the Gustloff Works. When, in 1944,
an especially urgent order came in, doctors among the inmates told the
commandant that they had diagnosed typhus in workers at the plant,
whereupon the commandant, who feared that an epidemic might spread to
civilian workers, ordered that all inmates working in the plant be quarantined for two weeks. This delayed the filling of that urgent order (Simakov
1959, 121).

The sabotage started during the construction of the Gustloff Works.
"Thousands of bags of cement were wasted when the foundations were
laid. . . . The shafts for hydraulic elevators and lifts, the big montage shaft
for the rocket missiles, and the test range behind the plant were never
made watertight. . . . When connections to the power lines were made, a
great number of interference elements were built in. This sabotage caused
production in the Gustloff Works to start with a few months' delay"
(Siewert 1960–67, 49).

The Frenchman Frédéric Manhès has pointed out that the delaying and
sabotage activities were greatly intensified in May 1944, when numerous
metal workers from France arrived in Buchenwald and were assigned to the
Gustloff Works (Manhès n.d., 28).

Many figures have been given to illustrate the dimensions of the sabotage, but one example must suffice here. "The production of carbine bar-
rels . . . had been set at 10,000 per month; the machines that had been
ordered and delivered were adequate for a production of 15,000. After a
year and a half the maximal production amounted to 8,000 pieces, but four
to ten times as many expensive special tools were used up as had been
stipulated by offices of the Wehrmacht." In this summary Eugen Kogon
also points out that "direct sabotage, such as the damaging of machines or
weapons, was possible only in isolated instances. In general, methods had
to be employed that were hard to detect." These methods could be found
because the technical and organizational know-how of the German civilian foremen, masters, and engineers was so scanty that "they were often

dependent on the specialists among the inmates" (Kogon 1946, 328; Bunzol 1946, 38; *Buchenwald* 1960, 357 ff.; Manhès n.d. 29 ff.; Iosem 1959, 110; Kyung 1959, 64 ff.).

The proliferation of acts of sabotage caused an investigating committee to be sent to Buchenwald. "When it was about to start its work, Allied air raids (on August 24, 1944) almost completely destroyed the Gustloff Works, the German Armaments Works, and all military installations in Buchenwald, preventing an effective investigation (Siewert 1960–67, 49). As the German capo of the Gustloff Works, Heinz Gross, has pointed out, this almost completely stopped the production of arms (*Buchenwald* 1960, 357 ff.). The inmates utilized this bombardment as well: "The toolhouse had fared best; a considerable number of high-class machines remained undamaged there. During the clearance work the prisoners helped things along a bit by putting most of these machines out of commission" (Leibbrand 1945, 41). After the Hermann Göring Works in Linz had been bombed on July 25, 1944, the members of a Mauthausen outside detail who worked there did likewise. Gaston Vezes writes: "I am convinced that during the month in which we had to clear up in the factory we destroyed as much as the bombing itself, if not more" (Bernadac 1976, 178).

However, even in the final phase, the chief engineer of the Gustloff Works still tried to combat the sabotage, which had its center in the toolhouse. At his behest, the capo of this detail, the Pole Bruno Falkenberg, was locked up in the bunker as a saboteur on April 1, 1945, but by then it was too late for an investigation. Ten days later Buchenwald was liberated, and so was Falkenberg.[25]

When, in late August 1943, inmates of Buchenwald were transferred to a newly established subsidiary camp with the mysterious cover name Dora, it leaked out that new "miracle weapons" were to be produced there, by means of which the tides of war were to take a favorable turn. The Buchenwald resistance organization sprang into action and was able to assign "dependable comrades experienced in underground resistance" to the very first transports. In this connection, six German Communists and one German Social Democrat have been named, and later they were followed by other Germans—four members of the German Communist party and two of the German Socialist party (Dieckmann/Hochmuth n.d., 64). Members of other nations also reacted to the special nature of work in Dora. Having been assigned to a transport to Dora, the Frenchman Claude Lauth volunteered for a dreaded detail that was directly involved in the production of V-rockets. This, even though he had previously been able to work in the open air, whereas the "miracle weapons" were produced in a tunnel dug into the mountain which the inmates were initially not permitted to leave

No other work made the prisoners feel that so much depended on their activity—and thus also on their sabotage—as the production of the new weapons did. This is why we have reports of numerous individual acts of sabotage in Dora, and many of these agree that Russians urinated on transformers and other sensitive parts of rockets or that cables were cut.[26] Together with a Frenchman, the Pole Stanisław Kamiński put a powder into the oil used for the missiles, hoping to damage them thereby.[27] His compatriot Józef Gabis has also given accounts of individual acts of sabotage.[28] Another Pole, Zygmunt Karwat, believes that none of those who committed such sabotage was following orders,[29] and Krokowski agrees that it was a matter of personal initiative that cannot be credited to an organized action after the fact.[30] The judges in Essen, who had to concern themselves with acts of sabotage in Dora because SS men had been charged with tortures and mass executions of prisoners for alleged or actual sabotage, reached the following conclusion: "It cannot be ruled out . . . that it was one of the goals of the resistance organization in Dora to carry out sabotage, that this was done, and that some of these acts were not arranged for by the resistance organization but were based on the decision of individual inmates, though it has not been possible to determine the extent of organized and unorganized sabotage."[31] As the Pole Wincenty Hein told this court as an expert witness, "everything hinged on the sacred word 'sabotage.' It could happen that a person was hanged for a trifling transgression, for in concrete instances no one knew what sabotage was."

There are numerous reports about an organized sabotage of the V-rockets. In the same expert opinion, Hein characterized sabotage as "part of the struggle of the resistance organizations, a part that presupposed a high measure of awareness and organization."[32] The Frenchman Jean Michel has identified French, Czech, Russian, and Yugoslav groups that engaged in sabotage activities but had difficulties with joint action (Michel 1975, 133, 204 ff. 220, 237). His statements have been disputed by others,[33] and, in general, accounts of sabotage activities in Dora diverge greatly. Wincenty Hein, a former inmate of Dora whose balanced judgment, influenced by no party or group, was so highly valued by the Essen court that he was called as an expert witness, states that German Communists undoubtedly formed an organized group. However, it was composed of old Communists who collaborated only with other Communists; Poles, for example, had reason to be afraid of them. Russians engaged both in individual and in organized sabotage in the plant, particularly after the arrival of Russian officers in Dora in 1944. Hein is not certain whether there were organized groups of Frenchmen and Czechs; he believes that the French went their own way.[34]

In their endeavors to reconstruct the resistance struggle of the inmates of Dora, Götz Dieckmann and Peter Hochmuth came to the following conclusion: "Sabotage was carried out by virtually every prisoner who had an opportunity. Frequently this was done out of altogether selfish motives. Someone would remove the rheostat from the switch of a grinding machine in order to have coils for an electric stove. Electric wires would be torn or cut, and this immediately disrupted the power supply.... Many saboteurs carried on their sabotage to take revenge on their masters or engineers, and they did not think of larger contexts. Despite this, their actions had more far-reaching consequences than they suspected. Organized and wild sabotage existed side by side, and they ultimately combined with the chaos of production to stop the production of V-rockets. The organized resistance fighters supported this spontaneous resistance" (Dieckmann/Hochmuth n.d., 75 ff.).

Dieckmann and Hochmuth wrote their account on the basis of documents available in East Germany, and if the research on the same subject carried on by Manfred Bornemann and Martin Broszat in the Institut für Zeitgeschichte (Institute of Modern History) in Munich has led them to somewhat different conclusions, this may be due in part to their divergent political points of view. Warning against an overestimation of the network of illegal organizations that Communists have described as a "widely ramified organization," Bornemann and Broszat write: "On the whole, the unorganized, spontaneous activity of individuals who operated skillfully and did not attract attention, particularly in carrying out sabotage in the tunnels, probably was no less significant than prepared and organized acts of sabotage. Also, not all of those who pioneered here were Communists by any means. In view of the importance of the production of V-rockets, which the inmates were aware of, decisions to engage in sabotage were frequently made independently. Not least among these were the non-German prisoners, who as former soldiers and officers of their countries felt in particular measure that they were at war with Germany.... Soviet and French inmates working as technicians appear to have been most active in sabotaging the production of rockets by intentionally damaging or improperly mounting special parts" (Bornemann/Broszat 1970, 189).

There is documentation about the public refusal of a group of Italian prisoners of war to work on rocket production, and these men based themselves on the Hague Land Warfare Convention (of 1899). This caused seven officers to be shot on December 15, 1943 (Dieckmann/Hochmuth n.d., 75; Bornemann/Broszat 1970, 189).[35]

Understandably, the special importance of the V-rockets in the final phase of the war caused the sabotage activity of the resistance to be occasionally dramatized after the fact. On February 2, 1944, the Czech physician Jan Češpiva, a member of the Communist Party, was transferred from Buchenwald to Dora "with instructions from the resistance center" and was able to occupy a key position in the hospital there. The German Communist Albert Kuntz has been described as the "leader of the international resistance organization" and Češpiva as the head of a Czechoslovakian resistance group (Češpiva/Giessner/Pelný 1964, 17; Dieckmann/ Hochmuth n.d., 63 ff.). However, Wicenty Hein, who has been listed as one of the leaders of the Polish group, has denied it, and this indicates the problematic nature of such descriptions (Češpiva/Giessner/Pelný 1964, 34). Nevertheless, the Czech publisher of Češpiva's book still listed the author as having performed that function in a later edition.[36]

Concerning the waste of weapons, different figures have been given. The first V-1 rocket was fired at England in the night of June 15–16, 1944. Of a total of 11,300 rockets, about one-fifth are said to have failed at the start (Mader 1963, 262). The first V-2 rocket was fired on September 7 of that year. "Only one-half of the 10,800 V-2 rockets fired until the end of March 1945 could be directed into the intended target area; over 5,000 fell apart in the start area, exploded in the air, or fell into the North Sea" (Kiessling 1964, 219 ff.). Bornemann and Broszat, however, feel constrained to warn against drawing far-reaching conclusions from these figures: "The rockets produced in the first half of 1944 had a particularly high failure rate (up to 80 percent), which delayed the employment of V-2 until September 1944, but this rate was appreciably lower in the second half of the year. Although the underground organization was undoubtedly tighter in that period than before, nevertheless figures would seem to indicate that most of the failures were due not to sabotage but primarily to technical flaws in the mass production that initially went unrecognized and were later remedied" (Bornemann/Broszat 1970, 190).

Whatever the reason may have been, it is certain that the production managers had to come to terms with the problem of sabotage by prisoners. Former members of the Wehrmacht, who had worked in the office that examined weapons before taking delivery—men who would "logically have been most likely to know about acts of sabotage"—testified before the court at Essen that they had not seen or heard about sabotage and that "because of the technical complexity and imperfections of V-2, it was practically impossible to determine whether a possible defect had been deliberately caused or was due to something else." On the other hand, the verdict of the same court cites twenty-six witnesses who gave testimony about acts of sabotage.[37] The most convincing evidence of the effects of sabotage may be found in documents of the management. In a special directive dated January 8, 1944, we read: "We must point out that on a number of occasions our installations have been deliberately and maliciously damaged by disruption, destruction, and theft" [the last four words are underlined in the original—H.L.] (Dieckmann/Hochmuth n.d., 51). A letter of December 8, 1944, states that, out of 150 items, twenty-two did not pass inspection and were returned to the manufacturer. The list of defects noticed in these rockets includes some that former inmates of Dachau described to the court as a result of their acts of sabotage. Because of this sabotage, the letter closes with a request that the cause of these defects be most painstakingly investigated (Dieckmann/Hochmuth n.d., 77). Another letter, one dated February 8, 1945, contains this statement from a technical liaison officer: "The statistics [of January 1945—H.L.] show an alarming increase in the number of misses. The activity of the investigating commissions has not produced any improvement. The technical liaison staff has determined that the troops are not at fault!" (Bartel 1970, 20).

There is no doubt that the inmates' sabotage caused "a network of agents" to be developed in the plant;[38] in fact, the security service transformed the camp into "a jungle of stool pigeons and agents provocateurs" (Dieckmann/Hochmuth n.d., 78). We have already described the devastating consequences of the activity of André Grozdoff, one of the latter, and the carelessness of those active in the resistance. On November 2, the SS began a series of arrests, and these became so extensive that it finally managed to "smash the core of the resistance" (Dieckmann/Hochmuth n.d., 63). A total of 300 or 400 inmates were arrested; men who had been fingered by informers were tortured and executed. These mass executions had the intended deterrent effect. Between March 10 and 21, 1945, 118 inmates were publicly hanged (ninety-nine Russians, sixteen Poles, two Czechs, and one Lithuanian). This orgy of murder concluded, shortly before the evacuation of the camp, with the shooting of seven German Communists, who had performed key functions in the camp and in the resistance movement, though executions no longer took place during a roll call.[39] It is interesting to note that the Gestapo dealt much more severely with Russians and Poles than with Frenchmen and Belgians, who had also been betrayed and arrested.[40] The fact that the Czech Jan Češpiva was discharged, while the German Albert Kuntz was among the last victims of the Gestapo, gave rise to rumors.[41]

Some statements about sabotage in Dora could not be substantiated when their authors appeared as witnesses in Essen.[42] The Pole Tadeusz Patzer, who has clearly tried to reconstruct the truth, has pointed out that after the war many people liked to be characterized as "heroes."[43] Even if one makes allowance for this as well as for the momentous conspiratorial mistakes of the resistance organization in Dora, one must nevertheless conclude that, in the final phase of the war, inmates—regardless of the most severe terror—took any risk to prevent the National Socialist regime from delaying its defeat by means of the new miracle weapons.

Originally the escape of an inmate was regarded as the biggest crime, and every conceivable measure was taken to deter attempts. However, in January 1943, when prison labor in the arms industry was given top priority, Hitler himself ordered that preventive terrorist measures, such as the shooting of every tenth inmate, be taken if production defects in that industry gave rise to the suspicion that inmates working there might be engaged in sabotage (Maršàlek 1974, 11).

This order was carried out most radically in Dora, but in the last two years of the war numerous prisoners were executed as a deterrent in other camps as well. However, neither premium vouchers nor the gallows could effectively keep prisoners from sabotaging the production of arms for their enemies.[44]

This is evidenced by a letter to the commandants of the concentration camps dated April 11, 1944: "In an increasing number of cases commandants have recommended the death penalty for inmates who have engaged in sabotage in arms factories. I now ask you to request henceforth death by hanging in demonstrated cases of sabotage. The execution is to be carried out in the presence of all inmates of the labor detail that is involved, and the reason for the execution is to be announced as a deterrent" (Frauen-KZ Ravensbrück 1973, 205).

22

RESISTING DEMORALIZATION

Wherever the system of the camp administrations had succeeded in breaking the prisoners' self-confidence, morale, and human dignity, the speedy death of the victims could be predicted. As a rule, a person who had lost his inner fortitude was no match for the harsh living conditions of a camp. Therefore any effort to counteract total demoralization was helpful. It is impossible, of course, to measure the success of such endeavors, but all camps report that they were made, often systematically organized and carried out persistently.

In no other area of resistance, broadly defined, were there so many efforts by small groups and circles, and few descriptions of life in a concentration camp fail to include accounts of such efforts and their results. But it is impossible to give a comprehensive description of such activities, for they were too variegated and too dependent on individual free will. For this reason we can make only brief comments and illustrate these with specific examples.

Many commentators on camp life have described the incomparable effect of music. The camp administrations attached great importance to having good orchestras. These had to play march music as the prisoners walked to and from work to help the columns keep in step and make the prisoners easier to count. In addition, they had to give concerts for the SS bigwigs, and for this they had to be given an opportunity to rehearse. Auschwitz was one of the camps where the administration had many first-class musicians at its disposal. They rehearsed in their free time in a room in Block 24, and anyone who could squeeze in was allowed to sit on the floor or lean against a wall and listen. I remember such hours: "On more than one occasion I stood in that rehearsal room and felt more strongly than ever before or afterward the power of music, which said that outside Auschwitz there was a human world, one that was capable of giving individual features to the faces of the listeners and dissolving the dull, gray mass that constantly surrounded us, that helped preserve us from

317

drowning in the humdrum of the extermination camp" (Langbein 1972, 151). The Pole Jerzy Brandhuber has summed up his reaction to listening to such rehearsals: "That was the only moment that made me forget the camp around me" (Brandhuber 1962, 92). Such an effect has been described from all camps: "The feeling of not having been expelled completely from humanity." Even in Gross–Rosen, where (barring the extermination camps) the most unfavorable conditions prevailed, Poles were able to put on "Sunday evenings of Polish songs and Polish music" (Mołdawa 1967, 151).

Here and there courageous, humane prisoner functionaries found additional ways of giving their fellow inmates hours of contemplativeness, forgetfulness, and a gathering of their moral reserves.

The German Communist Rudi Arndt, who became senior block inmate in Buchenwald despite his Star of David, "made the greatest efforts to pit against the Nazis' degradation of everything human all true manifestations of this humanity. He consequently encouraged gifted comrades to write poems and songs and finally managed to form a string quartet that . . . played Mozart, Haydn, and Beethoven" (Hermlin 1975, 41 ff.).

Olga Benario, an officer of the German Communist Party and senior block inmate in Ravensbrück, set a similar task for herself and organized in her block "lectures, courses and literary evenings at which Goethe, Schiller, and Mörike were recited" (Hermlin 1975, 62). "Sometimes women softly recited poems in their free hours on the camp road. They discussed books they had read and plays they had seen. They practiced 'mental acrobatics,' as some of them jocularly called it, for they wanted to use their mental powers instead of becoming dull and apathetic." It has been reported that the Russian Kudryavzeva and the Austrian Jew Käthe Leichter, a Socialist official, recited poetry they had written in Ravensbrück for their comrades (*Frauen-KZ Ravensbrück* 1973, 195 ff.). Dutchwomen even wrote a three-page leaflet reflecting the lighter side of everyday life in the camp and intended to cheer their compatriots up; its motto was "May this sheet bring some cheer/into lives that are painful and drear"[1] (*Für die Kranken in Not und Pein/ soll dieses Blättchen eine kleine Ablenkung sein"*). Eugen Kogon has mentioned the enduring effect, in Buchenwald, of a reading of scenes from Georg Büchner's play *Danton's Death* and revolutionary-satirical poems by Heinrich Heine (Kogon 1946, 326).

In Dachau inmates managed to secure permission to organize theatrical performances. I remember a performance of one-act plays by Johann Nepomuk Nestroy at Christmastime 1941, which was attended by SS men, who sat in the first row. The Austrian journalist Rudolf Kalmar has given a graphic description of the "premiere" of his farce *Die Blutnacht auf dem Schreckenstein, oder Die wahre Liebe ist das nicht,* The Bloody Night on the Schreckenstein, or That Is Not True Love, which was permitted to take place in the summer of 1943. The main figure had unmistakable elements of Hitler, and the inmates in attendance greeted political allusions with laughter and applause. "The parody was obvious. The majority of the SS [men who occupied places of honor in this auditorium as well—H.L.] were so dim-witted that they would not have caught on even if the farce had been broader still. The more intelligent among them did smell a rat, but they regarded what they were hearing as too improbable to merit further thought, and the few men who knew what was going on ignored it." Gustl Eberle, a Viennese veteran of the Spanish Civil War, portrayed the Critical Thinker, and his Nestroyan wit and overtones of Viennese lyricism produced both laughter and emotional silence (Kalmar 1946, 183 ff.).

In Sachsenhausen the senior camp inmate Bender endeavored to raise morale by means of "songs and literary evenings." "Some theatrical performances, e.g., scenes from *Faust*, met with an enthusiastic response in the camp."[2]

At Christmastime 1943, Dutchmen sang a song that was integrated into the history of their country's libertarian struggles and ended with the lines "Pierce the dike, open the locks, drown the foreign tyrants."[3] Other poems were written in that camp as well; many years after the liberation a notebook with forty Russian poems was found in the foundation of a building (*Damals in Sachsenhausen* 1967, 115). Hans Maršàlek has given the names of seven Poles who wrote poetry or musical compositions in Gusen. The titles of some poems show that they could hardly have been recited with the approval of the camp administration: "Hunger," "Golgatha," "Living Stones," "The Fallen Man." Maršàlek comes to this conclusion: "In Gusen it was the Poles and in Mauthausen the Czechs and Spaniards who, beginning in the summer of 1943, were able to develop a relatively open and also an underground cultural life within the framework of their ethnic groups.... On various special occasions, Poles and Czechs recited, individually or in groups, poetry from the rich treasure of their ethnic literature, which dealt with the rebirth of their people" (Maršàlek 1974, 263). Heinz Junge has described how cultural evenings, which were at first put on underground in Sachsenhausen, were later given semilegal status and finally even required tickets of admission.[4] To be sure, as Georg Buch points out, most inmates had no opportunity to attend them.[5]

In Majdanek the Polish pediatrician Miecysław Michałowicz gave medical lectures (Gryń/Murawska n.d., 63); in Gusen the Polish professor Ormicki gave geography lessons and with the aid of secretly obtained newspapers presented in his block nocturnal commentaries on the world situation.[6] There also were organized Sunday lectures in Ravensbrück blocks that housed Polish women.[7] However, the imparting of knowledge was not the most important thing about such activities; they were motivated primarily by a desire to resist the demoralizing feeling of having been permanently expelled from mankind and having no future behind the electrically charged barbed wire. Presumably this was the motivation for the discussions about the future of their country held by groups of Dutchmen interned in Herzogenbusch.[8] When groups composed of Germans in Buchenwald drew up a constitution for a Germany liberated from National Socialism, this "political quixotism" was intended to help counteract the effects of the stultifying humdrum of camp life.[9]

Stanisław Wolny, a Polish official of the Boy Scouts, has furnished a convincing explanation of the value of the evening lectures that he was able to organize alternately with other Boy Scout leaders: "Picture 400 tormented, often despairing colleagues who, having been subjected during the day to hard labor and abusive treatment by the Green scoundrels, forget the daily nightmare every evening before they fall asleep, who breathe a normal, human air, escape the hell of the camp for a few moments, and thanks to our narratives are transported to a free world" (Kret 1973, 34).

Along with helping them resist total demoralization and neglect, the instruction given to young people was intended to plug to some extent the gaping hole that had been produced when children had been pushed into the world of the concentration camps instead of being allowed to develop in a school. In Buchenwald Jewish children, a considerable number of whom were interned there by late 1944, were given instruction in Yiddish, reading, writing, and history (Korschak 1968). For Russian children between seven and twelve, a secret school was organized (*Buchenwald* 1960, 379 ff.), and the same was done in the women's camp in Auschwitz (Sobochenii 1965). In the men's camp, a group of Polish boy scouts tried to give systematic instruction to youthful compatriots (Kret 1971). Seven hundred children were inmates of the Theresienstadt family camp that had been established in Birkenau, and there it was even possible to start a school legally (Langbein 1972, 281 ff.). In Ravensbrück, Polish women organized a school in which 200 children were eventually taught by forty teachers in various grades.[10]

In the diary that she kept in Bergen–Belsen, Hanna Lévy-Hass wrote on August 28, 1944: "I have undertaken the task of caring for the children. In our barracks there are 110 children of different ages, from three-year-olds to boys and girls of fourteen and fifteen." She describes the difficulties of teaching in a concentration camp, only one of which was the lack of even the most primitive instructional material: "The children are wild, uninhibited, starved. They feel that their lives have taken an extraordinary turn, and their reaction to this is instinctive and brutal. . . . A small minority of them show a certain interest in learning; the others remain indifferent." Lévy-Hass also comments on the demands by adults, made irritable by the strain of camp life, that children who had insulted them crudely be punished: "As though children here could be persuaded to be nice and polite, in this monstrously inhuman milieu where nerves are overstrained, grown-ups whip one another, offend one another, steal from one another, abuse one another shamelessly and crudely, where everything is soiled and corrupted" (Lévy-Hass 1979, 11 ff.). Such words in a diary kept in a concentration camp describe more incisively than any postwar reflections both the problems and the value of educational work in a Nazi camp.

Inmates made great efforts to celebrate festivals in such a way that they were lifted out of the grayness of everyday life in the camp, and this too was intended to prevent apathy and resignation. There is a report about a Christmas celebration at Sachsenhausen in 1939 that already had an international flavor and with its "fighting songs and recitations" was intended to instill fresh courage in the prisoners (*Damals in Sachsenhausen* 1967, 142). Christmas celebrations were organized in Majdanek as well (Gryń/Murawska n.d., 63), and such a celebration in Neuengamme in 1943 was intended to help produce as frictionless a collaboration among the nations as possible.[11] In Ravensbrück women went to a great deal of trouble to make Christmas Day 1944 festive for the children interned there, and they managed to persuade the camp administration to permit a celebration.[12]

Other celebrations had a more marked political character. On August 31, 1944, Dutch Jews in Bergen–Belsen celebrated the birthday of their queen, and Hanna Lévy-Hass wrote in her diary that "even a theatrical performance took place—for the children" (Lévy-Hass 1979, 18). In 1944, Frenchwomen celebrated the 14th of July in the washroom (Bernadac 1972, 188), and women in the Buchenwald subcamp Bad Salzungen tried to celebrate the international Women's Day in March 1945 (Gurin 1959, 151). Such celebrations were intended to enhance patriotic feelings and raise the fighting spirit.

The meaning of secret rallies on traditional fighting days of the workers' movement is even more unmistakable. There are reports about May Day observances in Stutthof (Dunin-Wąsowicz 1970, 191) and Buchenwald (Schmidt 1958, 260 ff.; *Buchenwald* 1960, 405), and surely there were similar commemorations in other camps as well. This opportunity arose from the fact that the National Socialists had also proclaimed May 1 as a holiday, which meant that the SS guards wanted to celebrate and only a limited amount of work was done in the camps on that day. The Austrian Communist Otto Horn has described how November 7, 1943 (the anniversary of the Russian Revolution), and May 1, 1944, were celebrated in Buchenwald: "In accordance with a uniform plan five representatives from each of several nations assembled . . . at a prearranged place and discussed the meaning of the day and the task of the comrades in the camp."[13] The Pole Urszula Wińska reports about a November 1942 celebration in Ravensbrück with a program that consisted of "a talk about the uprising, songs, and recitations."[14] The German Communist Karl Raddatz remembers that his comrade Josef Schupp was brutally tortured in Sachsenhausen because an informer had reported to the SS that, at a celebration of the revolution on November 7, he had distributed bread and cigarettes to the many Russians in his block.[15]

An action by the Spaniards in Mauthausen was demonstratively combative in nature. After the death of the first Spaniard to have been deported there, they observed a moment of silence in his memory, and then one of them made a brief speech.[16] Such a demonstration could take place only immediately after arrival in the camp, for later the large number of murdered people made this sort of thing impossible. A report written by Austrians, after the liberation of Buchenwald, mentions a rally put on jointly by Austrian Social Democrats and Communists on February 12, 1944, the tenth anniversary of the fights between Austrian workers and the Dollfuss regime. Such evenings, which included celebrations of May 1, July 14, and November 7, were given an "anti-Fascist character."[17] Fellow inmates remember a "big speech" given on February 12, 1944, by the well-known Socialist official Roman Felleis.[18] The deleterious consequences of two funeral ceremonies in Buchenwald have already been described in another context.

Countless discussions, lectures, and reports (and it is hard to differentiate among these terms as used by writers) were devoted to political orientation and thus constituted a counterpoise to the Nazi propaganda that had made its way into the camps. When the German armies were still marching from victory to victory, Hitler's speeches were broadcast over loudspeakers in some camps. The effect of this constant drumming, particularly on German prisoners, was to be neutralized. The German Communist Hans Gasparitsch, who was interned in Dachau at a very young age, tells of receiving political instruction from an experienced Austrian colleague while the two men were walking up and down the camp road in their free time.[19] This is just one random case among many, as is a report by Bruno Matthies about indoctrination sessions of the German Communist Ernst Schneller in Sachsenhausen, in which four German and two Czech comrades participated (Kiessling 1960, 209). For such instruction, it was necessary to find a room where people could talk without attracting attention in the chronically overcrowded camp or being eavesdropped on. The pathology room in Buchenwald offered protection against these dangers, and therefore the Austrian Communist Gustav Wegerer gave real training courses there.[20] We have already discussed such political indoctrination in connection with the role of the Communists in the concentration camps (we have scarcely any reports about sessions conducted by others), and there are various views about their value. The Austrian Socialist functionary Rosa Jochmann, who was acquainted with the indoctrination sessions led by Communist women in Ravensbrück, believes that the camp itself offered sufficient practical instruction, and therefore, in view of the great risks involved, attempts at indoctrination constituted sheer madness.[21]

Despite all these dangers, politically motivated inmates in several camps even produced written documents in order to give heart to their comrades. There are reports about leaflets issued by Russians interned in Dachau[22] and weekly written material of the Yugoslav Communist group in Buchenwald.[23] Materials produced in Auschwitz were intended for a general political orientation and indoctrination as well as concrete goals. In an effort to promote collaboration among resistance groups, the Combat Group Auschwitz listed the goals of resistance activity in twelve points.[24]

The French Communist Roger Abada has mentioned an article written by his group with the aid of "Polish intellectuals," in order to counteract the anti-Russian sentiments that were very much in evidence, particularly among Polish fellow prisoners. Several copies of this article were distributed without incident. In 1943, they circulated a four-page manifesto, translated into several languages, that called upon the inmates to prepare for the liberation of the camp (Abada 1946, 174). Urszula Wińska reports about a systematically organized activity of the Polish women in Ravensbrück that was also intended to improve international contacts and combat demoralization. "In the outside detail Neubrandenburg, which was attached to a plant making airplane parts, the fear of bombardments and the low spirits caused by work in an arms factory was combated with acts of sabotage and discussions of political questions in international groups."[25]

Other activities of this kind could be enumerated, but these should not convey a false picture, for under the conditions of a Nazi concentration camp they could reach only a very small percentage of the internees. The complaint of the German intellectual Johannes Maas, who arrived in Dachau in the summer of 1944, that he was not able to find any political discussions[26] surely expresses the feeling of many who were outside the circle, of those who helped one another on this road, a group necessarily kept small. It meant that such outsiders had no one to help them overcome their despondency.

The French clergyman Père Riquet is undoubtedly correct when he characterizes religious activities in the concentration camps as another form of resistance, the combating of total demoralization. He was able to observe such activity in Dachau.[27] In that camp, where clergymen of different denominations and nationalities were concentrated in special blocks, the celebration of Masses was permitted during some periods and prohibited at other times. Sometimes a permission applied only to German clergymen. Since there already are detailed accounts of life in the "clergymen's blocks" at Dachau, and thus also of the effects of religious activity, we shall here refer only to such sources.[28]

Like most orders from the central administration of the SS, the one calling for all imprisoned clergymen to be transferred to Dachau was not completely obeyed, and thus there are reports from several camps about the activities of the clergymen, who kept prisoners from turning into animals.

Mieczyław Mołdawa has described how the Polish pastor Szymański brought relief to the sick and the dying in Gross–Rosen (Mołdawa 1967, 153). The Dutchman Kornelis Hofman has emphasized how important it was for the Catholics interned in Herzogenbusch to be able to hear Mass and go to confession there: "It made them forget for a while that they were in a camp."[29] According to the Dutchman Floris B. Bakels, religious services that could be held on Sundays in Natzweiler made people feel a "surge of strength." Bakels reports that although Franz Gutmann, the senior block inmate, thought they were foolish, he made no trouble. "We met between the plank beds in the sleeping quarters—ten, twenty, sometimes sixty or eighty shadowy figures who sat on the bottommost beds. A man stood watch at the entrance to the bedroom and another at the barracks entrance. The service could begin." Bakels had borrowed a Bible from a Norwegian fellow prisoner and asked another Norwegian to translate suitable Bible passages for him. "The Bible text was read and then interpreted. The text had been chosen for its relevance to our miserable situation. There followed a prayer.... These services were attended by particularly unrefined inmates, too, even by malevolent ones. Unbelievers did not stay away either, and there were some Communists among us" (Bakels 1979, 218 ff.). The French clergyman Frère Birin had been cautioned by a camp-wise coreligionist in Buchenwald not to come forward when clergymen were asked to identify themselves, and therefore he was transferred to Dora rather than Dachau. Although religious practices were strictly forbidden in Dora, he managed, together with others, to hold services "as in the catacombs in days of yore," and they even managed to make Eucharist wafers (Birin 1947, 192). Thanks to his moral strength, the Frenchman Frère Jacques was so highly regarded in Gusen that, after the liberation, he was unanimously elected the leader of the French group—a clear recognition of the succor that his religious activities had given his comrades. "He organized solidarity," writes Père Riquet

(Riquet 1972, 198). A Polish parson who had secretly celebrated Masses and heard confessions was betrayed, and as punishment he and some of his coreligionists had to kneel for hours (Nogoj 1967, 156). Many writers have emphasized the great effect of the sermons that the German Protestant pastor Paul Schneider shouted through the bars of the bunker window across the roll-call area. "He was never able to speak more than a few sentences before the slaps of the bunker guards rained down on him," writes Leonhard Steinwender, who has described the effect of this absolutely fearless man in these words: "The long ranks of prisoners stood there stirred to the depths of their souls by the strength and willpower of this brave man. It was as if an admonishing voice had called out to them from another world." After no torture had been able to stop Schneider from giving his sermons, he was murdered by the SS on July 18, 1939 (*Buchenwald* 1960, 393 ff.; Simon 1974, 13).

Eugen Kogon has summed up the experiences that he gained in this field in Buchenwald in these words: "There is no doubt that if even a modicum of pastoral care had been possible, it would, especially among Poles, have prevented a great deal of neglect, meanness, and sadness; it would have uplifted thousands, heartened hundreds in their last moments, given countless sick people new inner strength, and promoted their physical recovery as well"—but the SS permitted no such spiritual care ("naturally," adds Kogon). He also describes the dangerous conditions under which Masses were secretly celebrated. "Only among the Dutch and the French was . . . underground pastoral care possible in the very last period— for example, in Buchenwald" (Kogon 1946, 326 ff.).

Jehovah's Witnesses also sought comfort in their religion. Harald Abt, whom his faith caused to be interned in Sachsenhausen, has reported that in 1942 seven copies of their periodical *The Watchtower* and some Bibles could be smuggled into the camp by "brethren who had not been arrested yet." "On Sunday afternoon we would all crowd together in a wing of a barracks for Bible study. There were around 200 of us. A few people had to stand watch outside and give us a signal when an SS man approached." When some Bibles were discovered, "about eighty brethren were transferred from Sachsenhausen in a labor detail. The remaining Witnesses were distributed among the various barracks in the camp. Even though this prevented us from having our big meetings, we now had more frequent opportunities of preaching to fellow prisoners" (Abt 1980, 10).

Jews were in an incomparably worse position in the concentration camps, and religious comfort probably played an even more important role for the devout among them. Rivka Kuper has described her first impressions after being sent to Auschwitz from Cracow. "On Friday evening ten or twelve comrades gathered on the uppermost bed in complete darkness. . . . and quite softly sang Sabbath songs. After a short pause, we suddenly heard stifled sobbing from all the plank beds around us" (Hausner 1967, 253). We have this report from Gleiwitz I, a satellite camp of Auschwitz: "There was, of course, no chance that we would be permitted to hold religious services or pray together in the camp. Nevertheless, one Saturday evening I decided to gather ten comrades in a corner so I could pray with them and say kaddish for my father. . . . Although we prayed and said kaddish as softly as possible, this made such a great impression on the inhabitants of the barracks that the entire block of a few hundred people started to cry."[30] In Monowitz too, well-disguised services were held on the major Jewish holidays.[31] Elie Wiesel, who had lost his faith after his arrival in Auschwitz, has described a cantor's chanting of prayers on Yom Kippur in the fall of 1944. "Thousands of lips repeated the blessing." Wiesel mentions heated discussions of the question whether inmates should fast on the Day of Atonement, and he states that before an imminent selection "a number of them prayed" (Wiesel n.d., 95 ff.). Thomas Blatt, who was in Sobibor, writes that "many Jews said evening prayers, which was punishable by death." To keep the praying Jews from being noticed, other inmates made music.[32]

The religious activities of Jews could surely be described in far greater detail if more eyewitnesses had survived.

The End

23

THE END IS IN SIGHT

In June 1942, a step was taken in Buchenwald that had more far-reaching consequences than could be surmised at the time. The leadership of the inmates induced the camp administration to form the Camp Defense, a security force, from among the inmates. (Karl Keim calls this leadership the inmate camp administration (*Häftlingslagerleitung*); Wolfgang Kiessling's term is party leadership (*Parteileitung*), meaning the leadership of the KPD, the German Communist Party). "After much back and forth, this was finally approved, and the original complement of twenty men was soon raised to thirty" (*Buchenwald* 1960, 499 ff.; Kiessling 1964, 198). Eugen Kogon believes that this security force, which was supposed to "constitute an extension of the SS in the camp, in reality served the well-understood aims of the prisoners. At that time [June 1942—H.L.] there was no longer great danger that the SS would effectively use this organization against the inmates." Kogon confirms that the SS was "literally tricked into giving its approval" (Kogon 1946, 69).

The point of this initiative was twofold: to keep the SS away from the camp at night (the Camp Defense undertook to guard the food supply and other objects), and also to have the inmates take charge of the reception of new arrivals, in order to spare them the usual harassment by the SS. Keim, the capo of the Camp Defense, admits that "there were incidents here and there, which was inevitable in a camp of 40,000 to 50,000 inmates of different types," but he also states that "we were able to maintain order and discipline without the methods of the SS (beatings, etc.)." The Austrian Communist Otto Horn, who was not a member of this force, wrote shortly after the liberation of Buchenwald: "The Camp Defense was not always regarded as an organization in the best interest of the entire camp, but this deficiency was more than compensated for by the positive results."[1]

The administration of Buchenwald had previously attempted to use inmates for that kind of work. Walter Poller has mentioned HansSchulenburg, who enjoyed great popularity as a camp constable in the winter of

1938–39 (Poller 1960, 74, 184), but there is no mention of a camp police in reports about the succeeding period. This institution was revived only by the above-mentioned initiative of the secret organization, and thanks to the efforts of the inmates and as a consequence of the enormous expansion of the camp it was then extended. As early as 1943 the Camp Defense prevented the clandestine celebration of the first of May from being discovered by the SS (Schmidt 1958, 260 ff.).

The resistance organization systematically worked toward an expansion of the Camp Defense. In August 1944, following a number of unsuccessful attempts, it was able to convince the camp administration that linguistic difficulties made it imperative that all nations be represented in the Camp Defense, which had hitherto been composed exclusively of Germans. "Frenchmen, Germans, Belgians, Luxembourgers, Russians, Poles, Czechs, Yugoslavs, and Italians were now added to the force, and its size was increased to around 100 men."[2] The Luxembourger Leo Bartimes, who became a member around that time, believes the Luxembourgers were the first foreigners and non-Communists in that detail,[3] and the Russian Nikolai Kyung states that although Russians had long been barred, five or six of them now became members. "It was not easy work, because most prisoners regarded the Camp Defense with undisguised mistrust," adds Kyung (Kyung 1959, 74 ff.). The Frenchman Frédéric Manhès refers to this attitude, which was widespread among his compatriots also, when he writes that the critics finally realized that the addition of Frenchmen to the force was useful (Manhès n.d., 50).

Opinions about the activity of the Camp Defense in Buchenwald diverge, but the German Eugen Ochs has given a positive evaluation of it, for he is convinced that it was beneficial when inmates kept order in place of the SS.[4] The Czech Paul Schnabel, on the other hand, believes that the role played by the Camp Defense was not an entirely good one. There were "some gangsters with a political orientation,"[5] but on balance it appears to have been a positive institution that was able to play an important part in the final phase.

The scene in other camps was different. There the SS adopted this institution because it felt that it had been successful in Buchenwald and was in line with Himmler's intention to save guards by playing one group of inmates off against another and turn some of them, particularly Germans, into auxiliaries of the camp administration. Wherever the idea to form a security force originated with the administration, the resistance groups could not always manage to exert influence on this detail.

The Camp Defense of Dora had a bad reputation. That camp had originally been a subsidiary of Buchenwald, and it never lost its connection with that camp, which is why such a force was formed there at an early

date. Krokowski reports that this Camp Defense administered beatings and
that "its capo Runki used his stick more than his mind." New arrivals were
also beaten with clubs. "When the SS got tired, the Camp Defense administered the corporal punishment," writes Krokowski,[6] and Bykadorov recalls
that the entire Camp Defense joined the SS in a hunt for *Muselmänner*
[prisoners who had lost the will to live and were vegetating] who were to be
transferred to an extermination camp (Besymenski 1968, 214).

The Luxembourger Jean Majerus has painted an even crasser picture of
the Camp Defense in Mauthausen. According to him, the arrogant attitude of these camp policemen proved that, despite their status as inmates,
they were infected by the notion of *"Herrenmenschentum"* [belief that
they were members of a master race]. Majerus writes that, both in the
main camp and in the Ebensee subcamp, the Camp Defense was composed
of Germans and that in the latter "they did not shrink back from killing
people" (*Letzeburger zu Mauthausen* 1970, 207).

In early 1944, the commandant of Auschwitz requested twenty German
prisoners from Flossenbürg to serve as camp policemen, evidently because
the SS was afraid that Germans who had been in Auschwitz for some time
had too many connections with others to be used as docile henchmen.
Almost all of those transferred were Greens. The Combat Group saw to it
that the only political prisoner in this group was soon removed to keep him
from compromising himself. For the rest, the Combat Group could only
try to restrict the functions of this camp police as much as possible.[7]

The authority of the camp police in Sachsenhausen was about as broad
as it was in Buchenwald, but this outfit appears to have fully carried out
the wishes of the camp administration. It was composed entirely of Germans, former members of the Wehrmacht who had been sent to the camp
because of some offense. Their capo was a Green. They gave beatings and
were feared.[8]

There are somewhat divergent reports about the camp police in Ravensbrück. Margarete Buber-Neumann writes that it constituted "a staff of
professional informers" and describes a camp policewoman, a German
Communist, who "flogged, bellowed, threatened to report people" and
thus "was tailor-made for this responsible position" (Buber-Neumann
1958, 279). The Frenchwoman Irene Bloncourt-Ottelard mentions the
camp police and the SS in one breath (Bernadoc 1972, 235), and the German
Isa Vermehren reports that the beatings of the chief of the camp police, an
Austrian woman named Thury, were dreaded (Vermehren 1947, 114 ff.).
Bertl Lauscher, also an Austrian, confirms that Thury, who wore a red
triangle, was hated and occasionally beat inmates, but she also states that
"she always informed us and helped us whenever she could"; by "us"
Lauscher means the members of an Austrian resistance group.[9] Mitzi

Grassinger, whom that group had placed in the camp police to work for the benefit of her fellow prisoners, remembers that Thury tried to help when the camp police were ordered to search for three Austrian Jewish women who were to be killed. It was possible to warn these in time and have the resistance movement hide them in the camp.[10] According to a report published in East Germany, the Camp Defense (which was evidently the official name of the camp police), was composed mostly of anti-Fascists after 1943 (Frauen-KZ Ravensbrück, 174).

The camp police in Dachau was under the command of a former storm trooper named Wernicke, who caused "the death of hundreds." Nevertheless, the resistance organization was able to smuggle "representatives" into that detail.[11] In the final phase, it managed to get inmates of all nationalities added to it. The camp administration agreed to that expansion under the condition that Russians be excluded, but despite this Russian inmates eventually became members of the camp police.[12]

Thus the step taken by the Buchenwald resistance movement in the interest of its camp had various consequences. The inmates of Buchenwald could not have foreseen that the other camps would follow suit and obtain different results.

In Buchenwald the resistance movement moved with the times. The increasingly frequent bombings by Allied planes caused the SS to institute camp fire brigades and to use inmates for this service. Representatives of various nations were infiltrated into these brigades, and this meant the open creation of a quasi-military outfit. To be sure, a number of things had to be done to make it appear that this detail was on the side of the camp administration. Heinz Mühler, one of the leaders of this fire brigade, writes that "sometimes our comrades may have got annoyed at our rough manner" (Buchenwald 1960, 503 ff.). In a memoir written in the camp, Karl Barthel describes how in March 1944 one of three Russians who had been sent to Buchenwald to be executed broke loose in the crematorium and concealed himself in the small camp. The camp's fire brigade had to participate in the search; an inmate on this detail found the Russian in an unused part of the heating system and turned him over to the camp administration, which killed him (Barthel 1946, 71 ff.). This case illustrates the problems of using official means in resistance activities. Eventually the resistance organization obtained the formation of a strong rescue team and medical corps, which meant that eventually about 1,500 inmates of Buchenwald were members of these outfits (Biermann 1945, 31).

Fire brigades played a role in other camps as well. On January 17, 1945, the Norwegian Odd Nansen wrote in his diary that the German Manske, a former official of the German Socialist Party, had "reached the peak of his desires" as an "antiaircraft general" in Sachsenhausen and was behaving like a madman, even escorting fellow inmates to their execution (Nansen 1949, 252). The development in Neuengamme, however, appears to have been similar to the Buchenwald system; disguised military cadres are reported to have become members of the fire brigade and camp police.[13]

The SS even recruited German inmates for special units of the SS when more soldiers were needed for the war effort, thus making them its helpers and setting them against their fellow prisoners. When both criminals and political prisoners were invited to join the special Oskar Dirlewanger Unit, the resistance groups had to take a stand. This became urgent when a letter from Himmler dated October 15, 1944, approved Dirlewanger's suggestion that commandants of concentration camps select "former political opponents of the National Socialist movement" who desired to demonstrate their inner transformation by participating in the struggle of the Greater German Reich. Himmler's letter states that fitness for military service should be determined "generously" and that men up to forty-five years of age, and "in exceptional cases up to fifty," should be accepted. The "voluntary" nature of such recruitment is exposed by the fact that this letter contains the numbers of political prisoners who were to be conscripted: 375 in Sachsenhausen, 248 in Dachau, 117 in Neuengamme, 108 in Auschwitz, 69 in Buchenwald, and fewer than 25 in the other camps (Buchenwald 1960, 371 ff.).

In October 1944, the commandant of Buchenwald informed the assembled Reds that Himmler was now offering them an opportunity to fight for National Socialism. Since he evidently had no interest in losing German inmates (whose role in the prisoners' hierarchy was useful to him), he did not exert any particular pressure on them. As Otto Horn put it, this matter "was not pursued aggressively."[14] The Dutchman Wijnen has testified that some of the German Red Front fighters seriously considered volunteering for this unit so they could desert at the front. "Other Germans and all Dutchmen [who, as "Teutons," had evidently been offered the same choice—H.L.] agreed that the possibility of a collective desertion was an illusion. They felt that they should not volunteer."[15] Walter Bartel, a leader of the resistance, reports that nine Germans came forward, "members of the Wehrmacht who had been sent to the camp because they had committed a crime." He too mentions discussions: "Thoroughly honest political comrades argued that the main thing was to get out of the camp and obtain weapons; everything else would then fall into place. The counter to this was that there was no guarantee that the former political inmates would get arms; rather, there was reason to believe that they would be completely dispersed, in order to nip any joint action in the bud." Bartel sums up as follows: "Our intensive action that night [after the meeting of the Germans—H.L.] prevented" volunteering by those who were under the influence of the resistance organization (*Buchenwald* 1960, 374). The German Communist Hans Gasparitsch believes that the only people who volunteered for the Dirlewanger Unit were those not under the discipline of the Communist Party.[16] The Russian Nikolai Kyung, who could have known about this episode only from hearsay, has given a more dramatic account of it, writing that at the meeting "two hostile classes" confronted each other and that there was not a single volunteer (Kyung 1959, 82).

In contrast to the commandant of Buchenwald, the head of Dachau was seriously interested in having many volunteers for the Dirlewanger Unit, for he told the assembled Germans (and he included Austrians and Sudeten Germans) that anyone under age forty could volunteer for military service. According to Karl Ludwig Schecher, who was sixty-one at the time, and thus did not have to make a personal decision and could be a disinterested observer, "the announcement was so ambiguous that people could assume it was a matter of joining the Wehrmacht. As always, there were pros and cons. It was feared above all that if the appeal was unsuccessful, all inmates would be subjected to far worse treatment. However, the SS had speculated correctly: The urge to regain freedom, even the questionable freedom of war, and the hope of joining the Wehrmacht and thus finally escaping the clutches of the SS prompted many to come forward."[17] Karl Röder was among these, and he reports that about 500 out of 600 volunteered, 192 of whom were chosen—according to Schecher, on the basis of a physical and an examination of personal files by the political department. Röder has described his reasoning and that of his comrades at the time: "They did not face a very difficult decision; the choice was between unresisting extermination in the camp and a tiny chance to perish in an action against the Nazis. They chose the latter, because that gave their death a meaning." Röder writes that he actually allowed himself to be deceived, for he did not notice that he had not been placed in a Wehrmacht unit until, upon his departure from the camp on November 10, 1944, he received an SS paybook.[18] Gustl Gattinger was another man who had let himself be deceived in that fashion. According to him, some had argued that those who did not volunteer would be transported to another camp and perish there, while others had pointed out that volunteers would receive weapons and be able to do something. He himself was among the last men to come forward reluctantly.[19] At that time clergymen were confronted with this decision as well. At first "only a few [volunteered] for medical duty," for they suspected an SS trap. As Father Lenz, an Austrian, relates, "under the leadership of a dean and with reference to canon law, we all decided that we would not volunteer, or, if force was used, only for medical duty, unarmed service." Lenz reports that almost all nonpriests came forward, "first and foremost camp bigwigs, and this freed and delivered us from them" (Lenz 1956, 208). The Dutchman Padt has also criticized this mass volunteering: "They remained genuine Germans when they were called upon to be."[20]

In Sachsenhausen this "recruitment" took place a few weeks after the special commission of the SS had finished its reign of terror, involving mass executions and deportations. According to a diary entry by Odd Nansen, "on October 23, 1944, all Germans who had been sentenced for high treason were given an opportunity to volunteer for front-line duty within twenty-four hours. On November 1, they were all conscripted, whether they were willing or not," and on November 10 the first batch of "volunteers" departed (Nansen 1969, 214 ff., 221). In reports written shortly after the liberation this episode is described as follows: "These recent events [executions and transfers—H.L.] caused many of the inmates involved to misinterpret the situation, and that is why 300 men came forward."[21] According to the Austrian Communist Hans Pointner, who was acquainted with the discussions of the Communist group, "having been traumatized [by the shooting of twenty-seven of the best comrades and the punitive deportation of 102 others—H.L.] comrades like Max Opitz and others expressed the following view: 'The liquidation has begun. For us there is only one chance: volunteering for Dirlewanger.' This view was corroborated by the officer-in-charge, who told those who had committed high treason: 'This is your last chance.' " Pointner emphasizes that "we all knew what cruel acts the Dirlewanger Unit was used for." He also recalls Opitz's argument: "Revolutionary action means a decision in favor of Dirlewanger. Let us take up the weapons that are being forced upon us and act accordingly." This prompted many comrades to come forward.[22] The Dutchman Nicolaas Wassenaar has mentioned an additional argument that probably convinced many: In those days the camp police had been "busted" for making deals, and evidently the members of that detail volunteered to escape punishment.[23] An additional factor was the procedure followed by Kolb, the officer-in-charge: He asked the assembled inmates "who among them was not ready to fight for their threatened fatherland. . . . Everyone knew that nonvolunteering was tantamount to admitting opposition and was aware of the consequences of such an admission."

In the satellite camp Lichtenfeld the recruitment appears to have taken place in September 1944, and 350 men volunteered for the Dirlewanger Unit there (Auerbach 1980, 71). In Neuengamme the commandant's office seems to have wasted no time; on November 5, 1944, seventy-two political inmates, most of them with years of camp experience, were conscripted into the SS without being consulted.[24] According to another source, the inmates earmarked for the Dirlewanger Unit were individually called in by

the officer-in-charge, who informed them that they had now been assigned
to a probationary unit of the SS. It seemed pointless to refuse (Auerbach
1980, 72). In Auschwitz, the camp administration acted like the one in
Dachau. Following an initial announcement by the SS that Germans (and
Austrians) imprisoned for political reasons could now volunteer for service, those who had no contact with the Combat Group agreed that no one
should volunteer for the SS but that service in the Wehrmacht could not be
refused. To be sure, the camp administration formally stuck to the principle of voluntarism, but "in practice the list of volunteers soon included
men who had not come forward." The author of this statement, the Austrian Franz Danimann, found a way of evading this "transfer to the troops,"
to use the official phrase: "The day after receiving a summons, I was a
patient in the section for infectious diseases, running a high fever and
suspected of having typhus." A friendly Polish nurse had produced this
fever by means of an injection. However, forty-five inmates with red triangles were conscripted on November 7, 1944, and assigned to the Dirlewanger Unit of the SS.[25]

There were increasing signs that the war would end with the defeat of
Germany, and so as not to be completely at the mercy of the camp administration when the critical moment came, the resistance groups made preparations. In camps that were closest to the front, this problem arose earlier
than in those located in the heartland of Germany.

Auschwitz had a battle-ready international resistance organization that
was in constant contact with the Polish underground operating in the
vicinity, and thus it had more opportunities than other camps.

In an executive discussion of the Combat Group Auschwitz, held in a
basement room in Block 4 where he was the clerk, the Viennese Ernst
Burger reported that it had finally been possible to establish contact with a
Russian resistance group, and they urged the Combat Group to prepare for
an armed rebellion in cooperation with the partisans. "The perspective of
our work is clear to all of us. Our combat group must join the fighting
when the Allied armies approach Auschwitz. . . . Our organization in the
camp must be reorganized in such a way that it can deliver a military
punch. Until now we have endeavored to place comrades from our Combat
Group in various details so we could have our eyes and ears everywhere,
and our people could have the greatest possible number of contacts." Now
they were to be concentrated in the motor pool, the SS clothing depot, the
cleaning detail in the troops' quarters (where there were weapons), and in
details working outside the great chain of checkpoints. "Ernst proposes
that our organization be given a military leadership that would concern
itself exclusively with preparing for action" (Langbein 1949, 157). Such a
leadership was created, and the Polish officer Bernard Świerczyna was able

to establish contact with Polish resistance groups in the camp that were not under the authority of the Combat Group (Friedmann/Hołuj 1946, 93). It is no longer possible to determine exactly when this reorganization was accomplished, but a detailed letter dated August 22, 1944, and addressed to the headquarters of the Polish resistance organization in Cracow proves that it had been completed by August.[26] From the outset, this plan was based on collaboration between the two groups. "Our preparations were for an uprising in cooperation with Upper Silesia. In this case the prisoners constituted an auxiliary army for the rebellion," writes Józef Cyrankiewicz, whom the Polish resistance had accredited as the military leader of the camp (Langbein 1949, 158).[27] One of the principles of the military council was that "the planned military action can be carried out only in concert with the actions on the outside." A detailed plan was devised, and the following were determined: the strength of the SS and the military and police forces in the camp area, their weaponry and equipment, the location of the arms depots, the alarm system of the SS, and the number and operational capability of the inmates—135,000 in Auschwitz and its subcamps, including the foreign workers in the vicinity, especially in the Buna Works of I. G. Farben (Czech 1959–64). Various possibilities were considered, including the evacuation or mass liquidation of the inmates, Allied air attacks, and even an Allied parachute landing. In a document that was sent out of the camp and has been preserved, we read: "The military command of the Combat Group believes that an action to liberate all or part of the camp is of enormous moral importance in view of the international significance of Auschwitz as one of the dismal symbols of Nazi Germany. The military command of the Combat Group declines to view the liberation of Auschwitz exclusively as a relief action for the inmates. [Instead, it] regards the Auschwitz camps as a huge reservoir of people who are ready to fight" (Smoleń 1978, 96 ff.; 1977).

The Polish underground organization made a thorough study of all options. The organization active in Cracow, partisan groups operating in the vicinity (which included Polish escapees from Auschwitz who were best acquainted with camp conditions), and representatives of the Polish underground army held a number of discussions. The Polish government-in-exile in London sent Stefan Jasieński, an officer who parachuted into Poland and established contact under the code name "Urban." The partisans familiar with the camp were the most skeptical, for in the immediate vicinity of Auschwitz there were no extensive woods in which large groups of people might hide. Where should the people liberated from the camp be taken, how could civilian clothes and food for so many be procured, and how could they be housed? Finally Tomasz Sobański, who had joined the partisans after escaping from Birkenau on June 27, 1944, and met with "Urban" in August, noticed that his contact had little experience with conspiratorial activity. One night the latter fell into the hands of the Germans near Auschwitz, and since he was carrying plans for actions to liberate the camp, he was sent there (Sobański 1974, 97; Gárliński 1975A, 253 ff.). On September 29, 1944, the Combat Group Auschwitz notified both the partisans and the Cracow organization about this mishap (Czech 1959–64).

The SS had feared an uprising of the prisoners in Auschwitz even before it had a chance to examine these documents, but despite all its informers and tortures it had not been able to get a line on the Combat Group. Thus it transferred large numbers of Polish and Russian prisoners to other camps in the latter part of 1944. After Urban's arrest, the Combat Group Auschwitz decided to organize escapes of its executive members in order to be ready for the critical phase that was bound to come when the Russian army approached Auschwitz. This plan had been made earlier, but its execution had had to be postponed. However, the attempt to escape failed, and on October 27, 1944, Ernst Burger, Bernard Świerczyna, and other Poles were sent to the bunker. The plans for the liberation of the camp had to be shelved, for neither the resistance in the camp nor the resistance on the outside was strong enough to venture such an action, and the camp administration was forewarned. Even though the latter was subsequently unable to seize all other members of the Combat Group leadership, it transferred more Poles and Russians—people it regarded as potentially most dangerous—to other camps. Parallel efforts to prepare the liberation of some subsidiary camps with the support of Polish partisans had to be stopped as well.[28]

At the approach of the Red Army, the underground groups in Stutthof faced the same situation as the resistance movement in Auschwitz. A Polish group led by officers and a Russian group jointly discussed the possibility of an uprising at the critical moment. The Russians had established contact with Ukrainian guards. However, plans for an uprising and a mass escape were finally abandoned because no one could assume the responsibility for its consequences. True, the two groups might have broken out and reached a nearby forest, "but what would happen to the other inmates, particularly those of different nationalities who understood neither German nor Polish? Surely the National Socialists would take terrible revenge against them" (Dunin-Wąsowicz 1969, 37 ff.; 1970, 13 ff.; n.d.).

After the Allies had succeeded in landing in Normandy, June 1944, and opened a second front, a French resistance group in Natzweiler devised a plan for an uprising in an effort to forestall a liquidation or evacuation. However, the camp was evacuated in early September before the plan could be implemented.[29]

At various times the resistance groups began to prepare for the end of their camp—however it should come about.

As with other matters, we have the greatest amount of information from Buchenwald. In the frequently cited report by Otto Horn, which was written shortly after liberation, we read: "The organization of the military-political cadres began in the summer of 1942. At first these comprised only Germans."[30]

This has been confirmed by Robert Siewert: "The possibility of an armed contest with the SS was already under consideration in the early years of World War II. After the first great defeats of Hitler's Wehrmacht before Moscow in the winter of 1941–42, the anti-Fascists proceeded from theory to practice and created a military organization. The military-political leadership was assumed by German comrades" (Siewart 1960–67, 52). Another Buchenwald report, also apparently written shortly after liberation, agrees: "The organization of the military-political cadres began in the summer of 1942, initially only in the German section."[31] Harry Kuhn, who was placed in charge of this project, had this to say about it in a conversation held in the early 1970s: "As early as the middle of 1942, our party [the KPD—H.L.] had started vigorously organizing military groups. The internationalization began early the following year. At that time, the KPD already had a solid military basis, and . . . [we debated] ideas about the options and variants of an armed uprising, though the planning of combat was still rudimentary" (Kühn/Weber 1976, 54 ff.). The Russian Nikolai Simakov probably refers to this qualification when he writes that in early 1944 the Russian secret organization had instructed him to urge the international center to prepare for an armed uprising, "since we believed that they had not done enough about this." This effort was successful (Simakov 1959, 120), but Kühn emphasizes that "the leadership of the international military organization consisted entirely of German comrades." In this connection he names Studer, Roth, and himself (Kühn/Weber 1976, 54 ff.).

In the other camps in Germany and Austria, similar preparations did not start until the military situation suggested them. Wolfgang Kiessling believes that in Sachsenhausen preparations for armed actions already assumed concrete form in late 1943 or early 1944 (Kiessling 1960, 218), but there appear to have been more conversations than concrete organizational measures (Damals in Sachsenhausen 1967, 113); we have reports about talks between the German Communist Ernst Schneller and the Russian Major General Aleksander Sotov. Apparently, the snooping of the special commission—mentioned several times already—prevented the inmates from maturing their plans.

We have already mentioned that the Spanish resistance group in Mauthausen was working on the creation of a military structure as early as the spring of 1944. According to the Russian Valentin Sakharov, it was the French Communist official Frédéric Ricol who suggested that the Russian group devise a plan for an uprising, and his suggestion was accepted.[32] The Frenchman Michel de Bouard speaks of long-range plans for a military action and names the year 1944 (Bouard 1954, 75), and the Spaniard Miguel Serra-Grabulosa confirms that precise preparations were made by an international military leadership comprised of highly qualified officers.[33] In an East German publication, we read: "In late 1944 and early 1945 the military resistance organization already comprised ten ethnic combat groups—three Soviet, two German, one Austrian, one Czech, one Spanish, one Yugoslav, and one Franco-Belgian. In addition, there later was a Polish combat group" (Aktenvermerk 1979, 145). The chronicler of Mauthausen, Hans Maršàlek, writes: "The first plans in the main camp for establishing military units of Spanish, Czech, German, and Soviet inmates were discussed and devised in the winter of 1944–45 by veterans of the international brigade in the framework of the leadership of their national groups, and they were implemented in the spring of 1945." He also reports that the first deliberations were made by ethnic groups: "There were several plans for an uprising by inmates in case of an impending mass liquidation, and these were independently worked out by Spaniards as well as Czech and German veterans of the international brigade" (Maršàlek 1974, 261).

The inmates of Dora planned an uprising at Christmastime 1944, but were betrayed by an informer infiltrated by the SS, and the ensuing mass arrests prevented the implementation of this plan. It called for fires as a signal for an uprising, together with the Dora and Buchenwald subsidiary camps in the Harz Mountains.[34] A document indicates that in Neuengamme there was a "military command" that set itself the tasks of reconnoitering the strength of the SS in the camp and outside the camp area and of establishing contact with groups of prisoners of war and interned civilians.[35] In early 1945, the inmates of Ravensbrück began to prepare for the liquidation of the camp. "They considered the possibility that the SS guards might leave the camp as the Soviet army approached, and they tried to prepare to be on top of the situation at the decisive moment. International communication was achieved" (Kiedrzyńska 1960, 97). There is evidence that in those days Polish women "organized squads of five on instructions from the [Polish—H.L.] national army."[36] In Dachau the need to prepare for an evacuation or liquidation of the camp in some form prompted the inmates in late 1944 to create a broad-based international organization.[37] When Johann Steinbock, a Catholic clergyman interned in Dachau, writes that "a direct uprising was out of the question, for it would have involved the irresponsible murder of many thousands" (Steinbock 1946, 21), he repeats the arguments of the resistance groups in Stut-thof, where conditions were less unfavorable, because the environs of the camp were not populated solely by Germans.

In the reports from Buchenwald, we encounter not only expressions that were not common among other resistance groups, such as "military cadres"; we also read about block men and flank men, instructors and chief instructors, and discipline exercises at which written orders of the day were issued[38]—in short, about concepts that were taboo in other camps for reasons of secrecy. The SS was nevertheless unable to track down this organization, no matter how ramified and active for so long, and this was probably the result of efforts by the Buchenwald resistance to develop self-administration in the camp and to take it away from the camp administration. A report written after the liberation states that around 850 prisoners had been members of the military organization one month earlier. Most of these were Russians, and they were followed by Germans, Austrians and Dutchmen (who are lumped together), Frenchmen, Czechs, Yugoslavs, and smaller national groups.[39] The military organization had originally drawn up two plans, one offensive and one defensive. According to a publication of the East German military publishing house, "by agreement with the international camp committee, the leadership of the international military organization stopped working on the offensive plan in the summer of 1943." It was foreseeable by then that even further advances of the Allied armies would create "no favorable external conditions for an uprising by inmates" (Kühn/Weber 1976, 432). It was this realization that probably kept the resistance organizations of the other concentration camps from even beginning to devise offensive plans.

Anyone who thought of military actions also had to consider how to obtain weapons. Both resistance groups and individual inmates had tried here and there to procure some. For example, there were a few revolvers in Herzogenbusch, but Kornelis Hofman's caveat that reports about it indicate an "abundant imagination" applies not only to this concentration camp.[40] We have already detailed how prisoners in Auschwitz obtained weapons by trading with corrupt SS men. In Monowitz Fritz Kleinmann "purchased" two pistols and two submachine guns from Sgt. Alfred Wocher and a junior officer of the Luftwaffe; he remembers prices of thirty and one hundred dollars.[41] The Dutchman Antonius van Velsen writes that in Birkenau a pistol with fifteen bullets cost thirty $20 gold coins.[42] Prisoners who were assigned to work in the airplane-dismantling plants near Birkenau were able to smuggle into the camps weapons that had remained undamaged or needed repair (SS on Trial 1957, 42). This was probably how the special detail—those condemned to work in the crematoria—obtained weapons (Müller 1979, 204). The most effective booty were the explosives obtained from the Union Works, which were used during the rebellion of the special detail to blow up one of the four crematories (Suhl 1968, 239). The Combat Group Auschwitz, however, was guided by a principle that was later formulated by Józef Cyrankiewicz as follows: The procurement of arms seemed unncessary and much too dangerous to possess. Instead, we reconnoitered where the weapons of the SS were stored and how we could quickly obtain them in an emergency.[43]

The attitude of the resistance movement in Buchenwald in the matter of obtaining arms was in keeping with the unique conditions in that camp. It had a chance to make a long-range effort to obtain weapons, most likely from the nearby Gustloff Works, where inmates were working on arms production. The German Kurt Köhler believes that, as early as October 1942, he received a carbine for safekeeping, put it in a hollow tree trunk, and later hid it in the false ceiling of the toilet in the dental station, where he was employed (Kühn/Weber 1976, 59). According to reports written shortly after the liberation, the camp military command in August 1943 was able to "put aside" ten guns from the Gustloff Works and conceal them in various hiding places in the camp, including the coke depot of the corpse incineration chamber, Block 7, Block 9, the medicine cellar of the inmate hospital, and the bath.[44] Kurt Leeser, who worked as a pharmacist in the SS hospital, has indicated another source of arms procurement. In 1943, SS men were sent to Buchenwald from the SS penal camp Matzlau near Danzig, and Leeser was able to become friends with one of them, a man assigned to the armory. Together with the canteen capo, Heinz Schäfer, he "purchased" pistols from the rather starved SS man for margarine. It was possible to hide these weapons in Leeser's workplace, but not to bring them into the camp (Kautsky 1961, 307). We owe the most concrete report to Franz Bera, an Austrian Communist. Since he had been assigned to work as a foreman in the SS armory, he was put in charge of the procurement and care of arms, and he soon managed to "put aside" two pistols as well as hand grenades. In a report dated June 5, 1945, Bera writes: "To 'put aside' ammunition was not particularly difficult, because the SS was unable to exercise exact control." Bera also reports about instruction sessions held evenings in the pathology section through the good offices of the Austrian Gustav Wegerer, who was the capo there.[45]

When a bombardment largely destroyed the Gustloff Works on August 24, 1944, it was relatively easy to overcome what had hitherto severely impeded the smuggling of weapons into the camp—the close supervision in the plant and the checkpoint the labor detail had to pass as it marched back to the camp. The plant was in chaos, and since numerous prisoners had been killed or injured, the inmates' medical corps was activated. Erich Dlabaja writes: "In addition to its duty to bandage the wounded and recover the dead, the medical corps also salvaged military material for the camp" (*Buchenwald* 1960, 508; Manhès n.d., 46). Leo Eitinger recalls that Norwegian students, special prisoners who had also been assigned to the transport of wounded men, joined the corps in bringing weapons into the camp.[46] According to Erich Fein, the medical corps was instructed to take the pistols and bayonets of SS men killed in the bombardment to the camp, together with the dead bodies of inmates. The military organization took charge of these weapons and hid them.[47] Thus the decision of the resistance organization to develop such medical details and place reliable comrades on them had paid off.

Reports written after the liberation agree that there was military training. "Some 7.65–08 and Mauser pistols were used to train men on German small arms, and a carbine with a sawed-off barrel and butt served for instruction in the handling of a gun. Particular importance was attached to training in marksmanship. Concerning training in the use of a bazooka, the military command issued a special instruction to the staffs.[48] The Russian Yuri Sapunov has described how his group was instructed on a "German automatic" in the washroom (Sapunov 1959, 27 ff.). Robert Leibbrand remembers that "Soviet Russian prisoners of war, fighters from the French Maquis, Red Spaniards, Yugoslav partisans, German and Austrian veterans of the Spanish Civil War, and former Czech and Polish soldiers and officers gave practical instruction in the handling of weapons as well as theoretical instruction in topography and tactics" (Leibbrand n.d., 46 ff.). Eventually the weapons in the camp included ninety-one carbines with about 2,500 bullets and a light machine gun with 2,000 bullets. This is how the latter was brought into the camp in February 1945: The Austrian Franz Meixner, a member of the medical corps who had been assigned to unload a transport of prisoners from Auschwitz, noticed that a machine gun with ammunition had been left in the rear escort vehicle, covered with the bodies of prisoners who had died during the transport. This gun was taken to the camp and hidden in the hospital building. The inmates who ventured to do this speculated correctly that the SS man who had forgotten the machine gun would not report it for fear of being punished (*Buchenwald* 1960, 512). According to the report, the arsenal also included twenty small firearms, 200 Molotov cocktails, makeshift hand grenades, and homemade cutting and stabbing weapons.[49] Russians busied themselves with the construction of these hand grenades, and they were helped by inmates who were chemists (Iosem 1959, 108; *Buchenwald* 1960, 513). Chemicals for the Molotov cocktails were smuggled into the camp by inmates employed in the German Armaments Works and the SS pharmacy. After the bombardment that burned down the SS arsenal, Franz Bera was able to put aside and repair five slightly damaged pistols, and he even managed to test these pistols on the SS rifle range in the basement of the arsenal.[50] These impressive figures, however, should not blind us to the crass inequality in the strength of the two sides, even if one allows for the demoralization of the SS in the days before the liberation. Because they had been stored away for a long time, many weapons were not immediately functional. Thus Rudi Jahn writes in a pamphlet issued by the Communist Party of Leipzig that on April 10, the day of liberation, thousands yearningly looked up at the cloudless sky, "for this was where they expected first aid from. All options were considered and the appropriate preparations were made. Only a small number of weapons were on hand; what else was needed was expected from the sky" (Das war Buchenwald n.d., 110).

Those interned in Mauthausen and its satellite camps also attempted to secure weapons over a long period of time. Inmates of Gusen were assigned to the Steyr Works where, as in the Gustloff Works near Buchenwald, arms were manufactured. In 1944 the Pole Ladowski put aside and concealed ten submachine guns there; missing parts that were not produced in the Steyr Works were secretly made after sketches by other Poles (Nogoj 1967, 169). In the Mauthausen base camp it was primarily Spaniards working in the SS arsenal who were able to smuggle pistols and hand grenades into the camp and "even start smaller arms depots" (Maršàlek n.d., 23, 39; Sakharov 1961, 161) under the wooden floor of their barracks.[51] In the final phase it even was possible to smuggle a submachine gun into the camp, and the Spaniard Juan Pagès hid it under the floor of the Block 3 room for which he was responsible as the camp barber.[52] In the last weeks before the liberation, the systematic pressure on SS men, who evidently could no longer believe in a German victory, bore fruit. The Czech Kuneš Pany, who as chief camp clerk was in the best position to maintain such contacts, received several pistols with ammunition from the SS Senior Squad Leader Josef Kirsch, and in March 1945, the SS roll-call officer Heinz Bollhorst gave the two camp clerks two 7.65 Walther pistols with ammunition for "self-protection." Thus it was possible to start an additional arsenal under the wooden floor of the office. That spring, sixteen bottles filled with petroleum and gasoline were hidden in a barracks wall of a block whose prisoner personnel had been specially selected by the resistance organization (Maršàlek 1974, 260 ff.). The senior camp inmate in the hospital building, the Austrian Alfred Siebitz, was able to "purchase" a pistol from an SS man shortly before the liberation (Baum 1965, 89 ff.). Eventually the international resistance organization had at its disposal about twenty pistols, thirty-four hand grenades, and forty-seven Molotov cocktails. This has been reported by the Spaniards Manuel Razola and Mariano Constante, and they include even fire extinguishers in this arsenal, "valuable weapons for immobilizing tower guards" (Razola/Constante 1969, 155).

It was possible to smuggle arms into some subsidiary camps of Mauthausen as well. Thus the Frenchman André Ulmann believes that a group of Hungarian Jewish Communists were able to bring seven revolvers with bullets into the Melk camp, and when this camp was evacuated to Ebensee, it was possible to take these weapons along (Bernadoc 1975, 333 ff.).

The situation in the subcamp Ebensee, whose prisoner personnel had increased to more than 18,000 in the final phase (Maršàlek 1974, 58), was different from that in other camps, because in August 1944, after the SS guards had been relieved by members of the Wehrmacht, the Austrian Capt. Alfred Payrleitner assumed command of the guards. Like one of his subordinates—Josef Poltrum, a native of Ebensee and a junior officer of the Luftwaffe—Payrleitner was an anti-Nazi, and both men established contact with prisoners who appeared trustworthy to them. When Payrleitner learned from the SS officer-in-charge, in early 1945, that there was a plan to liquidate the inmates upon the approach of Allied troops, he arranged with Poltrum, who could more easily maintain contact with prisoners without being detected, to warn them and give them arms. To this end, Payrleitner requisitioned pistols for his guards under the pretext that a man carrying a rifle could easily slip on the icy roads. Poltrum gave the pistols and bullets to Camille Scholtes, an inmate from Luxembourg.[53] This immeasurably increased the self-confidence of the inmates of Ebensee shortly before their liberation, though Drahomír Bárta, a Czech active in the leadership of the resistance organization, carefully avoiding any exaggeration, speaks of "meager weapons" (Barta 1944).

The German resistance group in Sachsenhausen used various methods of obtaining arms. Rudi Wunderlich and others working in SS offices in nearby Berlin utilized unguarded moments to appropriate pistols and ammunition. Thus the underground leadership "possessed six pistols in early 1943," according to Wunderlich, and this smuggling continued.[54] Max Opitz, a member of a detail working in a shoe factory, made a skeleton key that enabled him to gain access to SS weapons in a time of need without having to take the risks involved in the concealment of weapons in the camp (Opitz 1969, 161).

In Dora, too, prisoners were able to procure hand grenades, explosives, poisons, and similar weapons, though it is not known how they did this.[55] Internees of Stutthof were also able to "organize" weapons from arms factories (Dunin-Wąsowicz 1970, 10 ff.; n.d., 38). The same was done in Neuengamme[56] and undoubtedly in other camps as well, even though no detailed reports about this have been preserved.

The approaching end of the war and the news of liquidations of inmates before the Allies could reach their camps—as well as of murderous death marches at the evacuation—prompted those inmates of concentration camps located in Germany and Austria who were still physically and morally strong enough to think of resistance to prepare themselves for the critical moment to the best of their ability.

24

THE LIBERATION OF THE CONCENTRATION CAMPS

A considerable period of time elapsed between the evacuation of those concentration camps which armies approached from the East or West and the liberation of the camps situated in central Germany or Austria by Allied armies. Gross–Rosen was the last eastern concentration camp to be liberated—in February 1945—and Dora was the first in the heart of Germany—reached by the Allies on April 9, 1945. In the scant four weeks between that day and the fifth of May, when the last concentration camp, Mauthausen, was finally liberated, the collapse of the National Socialist regime became more obvious each day. Thus those who were bent on opposing the last murderous attempts of the SS camp administrations faced different conditions; especially after Hitler's suicide on April 30. It therefore seems appropriate to give a chronological description of the actions taken by prisoners before the liberation, beginning with Dora.

Like similar organizations in other camps, the resistance movement in Dora had originally set itself the task of "taking precautions to escape possible destruction at the collapse of National Socialist rule."[1] By means of arrests and executions as a consequence of the repeatedly mentioned betrayals by infiltrated informers the camp administration had managed "to smash the core of the resistance" (Dieckmann/Hochmuth n.d., 233), which meant that in the last critical days, the resistance organization was deprived of its leadership ("Dora" 1967, 37). When the evacuation of Dora and its numerous subcamps began on April 4, the SS formed a "Commando 110" from about sixty German Greens and assigned it the task of "keeping the other inmates in check in case of parachute landings by the Allies." In the very last days, this commando was armed with pistols and rifles, and chaos reigned in the camp ("Dora" 1967, 27; Češpina/Giessner/Pelný 1964, 46; Pontoizeau 1947, 132). The evacuation transports were no less chaotic—not only because of the general conditions in those days but also because ethnic conflicts erupted among the evacuees; we have striking descriptions of such conflicts between Russians and Frenchmen as well as Frenchmen and Belgians (Gauesen 1966, 217 ff.). Where inmates were left behind at the evacuation, as in Nordhausen, the situation was as follows: Although the SS and the capos were no longer around, there were also no hospitals, no medicine, and no food. German troops were just as likely to come at any time as American bombers. Those who had been left behind in Nordhausen had to endure such an interregnum for a week before they were finally liberated on April 11 (Halkin 1965, 175). These were consequences of the complete smashing of the resistance organization in Dora.

The corresponding organization in Buchenwald, which was not far away, had made thorough preparations for the moment when Allied armies would approach the camp area, and it remained intact. In mid-February it began working on a plan that provided for three stages of alert and also divided the camp area into combat zones, which were in turn subdivided into sectors. "Our groups were trained according to these plans," wrote the Austrian Communist Otto Horn shortly after the liberation. The organization even distributed maps to the staffs "for actions in the camp area on a scale of 1 to 25,000."[2] According to Frédéric Manhès, "beginning in early 1945, the leaders of the French Communist section urged the international political and military organizations to take offensive action as soon as conditions permitted" (Manhès n.d., 47). We also have reports that the Russians made long-range preparations for an armed rebellion (Smirnov 1959, 84 ff.; Kyung 70). According to Nikolai Simakov, as early as December 1944 he urged the international leadership, at the request of his comrades, to fix a definite date for an armed uprising. At that time he only had the support of the French and Czech representatives on the committee, while the others agreed with the German comrades that the time was not ripe and they could not risk the lives of 80,000 fellow prisoners (Simakov 1959, 123 ff.). This figure probably includes the satellite camps as well.

As in Dora, the administration of Buchenwald began to evacuate the camp in early April 1945. On the third of the month a first transport of 1,500 inmates left for Theresienstadt (Die Wahrheit n.d.).[3] Being acquainted with the fate of those evacuated from Auschwitz to Buchenwald, the inmates knew that an evacuation would have been tantamount to a liquidation of most of them. "Fewer than half . . . actually reached Buchenwald. The others, weakened from long marches, were simply finished off by being shot in the neck by the roadside. Hundreds of others died of thirst, hunger, or asphyxiation while traveling in sealed cattle cars for weeks and arrived in Buchenwald as corpses" (Das war Buchenwald n.d., 103). For this reason it was decided "to use any imaginable means to delay the evacuation, for every hour gained saved many lives" (Drobisch 1968, 148). However, "we still could not risk open rebellion and mutiny. . . . The American troops were not close enough to the camp yet" (*Das war Buchenwald* n.d., 104).

The atmosphere of those days is described in a report written in Buchenwald three days after the liberation. On April 3 Commandant Pister declared before the 800 inmates of the rescue team—"mostly German political prisoners who had been in the camp for years and had been chosen by the inmates themselves [that is, their resistance organization—H.L.]" that the camp would be turned over to the Allied troops in orderly fashion. This speech "affected the thousands of inmates just as the Fascists had intended. They became less nervous, and most of them believed that the camp would not be evacuated." At the same time, the commandant attempted to play the German prisoners off against the foreigners by telling the chief senior camp inmate that he had heard the foreigners were planning to bump the Germans off the next night. In the camp, it was rumored that leaflets warning against acts of violence against inmates had been dropped over Weimar nearby. "If anything like that came to the attention of the Allies, the entire province of Thūringia would be punished by punitive attacks in the style of the bombardment of Dresden."[4]

Nevertheless, on the evening of April 4, all Jews were ordered to come forward, and this led to open resistance. "We [the senior block inmates— H.L.] realized that they wanted to evacuate our Jewish comrades to parts unknown, and our sabotage of the evacuation measures of the SS began. The Jews did not appear in the roll-call area, except for a few who came forward voluntarily" (Bunzol 1946, 39). Two "air-raid alarms may have been the reason why the SS did not take the Jews from their barracks by force. The senior block inmates were ordered to identify the Jews in the various barracks and report them." By that time numerous Jews had already removed the telltale Star of David from their prison garb. At the roll-call the next morning, the senior block inmates said that they had been unable to carry that order out, "whereupon the camp administration sent twenty heavily armed SS men to the roll-call area, who examined each prisoner's racial status, block by block, and immediately pulled out those they identified as Jews. Afterward they searched all buildings and institutions in the camp for Jews. . . . The Jews they had selected, about 1,500 men, were isolated under heavy guard."[5] The index file of Jews had previously been destroyed (Bunzol 1946, 39). "With our help a large number of the Jews slipped into the other ranks of inmates." The author of this report, the German Communist Rudi Jahn, emphasizes that both the inmates' Camp Defense and the inmates' fire brigade had been ordered to surround the selected Jews, but they evidently sympathized with them and thus enabled them to break through the chain of guards (*Das war Buchenwald* n.d., 105). Rolf Weinstock confirms that the Camp Defense carried out "all orders as slowly as possible"; he himself was aided by an acquaintance on that force (Weinstock 1948, 163 ff.). The Belgian Omer Habaru reports that not everyone received the same impression, for he remembers that capos and members of the Camp Defense "from all nationalities" administered beatings and prevented people from escaping (Habaru 1946, 248). A statement by Benedikt Kautsky seems to explain how such divergent judgments could arise: "At that time the Jews were divided into two groups—a small one of perhaps 600 or 800 who were housed in the big camp, almost exclusively old prisoners, and a big one of that many thousands in the small camp [where Habaru was—H.L.], composed of those who had come from Auschwitz, Stutthof, and the subsidiary camps in western Germany." The smarter Jews from the big camp found ways of hiding, and the Camp Defense "readily let them pass the chains." Presumably those herded together for the evacuation transport were primarily from the small camp. Kautsky remembers that they were "mostly emaciated, non-ambulatory types who broke down after a few hundred meters. In the camp we could hear the shots with which those fallen by the wayside were finished off" (Kautsky 1961, 279 ff.). This report indicates that even a well-organized resistance movement had limited opportunities to help even at a time unusually propitious for action. Otto Horn admits that the tactics of delay and sabotage which were employed in those days "could not be 100 percent successful,"[6] and by way of summing up, Eugen Kogon writes that "1,500 of the approximately 6,000 Jews in the camp were gathered, and their number was augmented on the following day by the Hungarian Jews arriving from Ohrdruf" (Kogon 1946, 337). Still, Rudi Jahn was able to report that "on the evening of April 5, the Jewish roundup was finally completed. After two days the camp administration had collected some of the Jews for a transport. Thanks to our tactics of obstruction and sabotage, a process that would normally have been finished in two hours took two full days" (*Das war Buchenwald* n.d., 106).

The commandant was clearly alarmed at the refractoriness of the prisoner functionaries, and on the evening of April 5, he gave the clerks a list containing the names of forty-six inmates who were ordered to line up by the gate the next morning. Otto Horn assumes that this list was compiled on the basis of an informer's report,[7] and it included the names of inmates in key positions, especially Germans imprisoned for political reasons, also five Dutchmen, four Czechs, three Austrians, two Poles, and one Frenchman—which indicates that the camp administration suspected members of various nations of being the ringleaders of activities directed against it. Interestingly enough, this list also included three Jews (an Austrian and two German senior block inmates).

Hours earlier, the SS doctor, Erwin Ding-Schuler, had told Kogon, in confidence, that such a list had been compiled, adding that those on it were scheduled to be executed before the evacuation of the camp—evidently to prevent renewed resistance to an evacuation order. "This warning was of inestimable value, for it gave us almost eight hours' head start," writes Kogon and adds that the entire machinery of the internal camp leadership was alerted in a trice (Kogon 1946, 338). Other reports do not mention this valuable early warning.[8] At night there was a meeting of the underground camp committee. The proposal to stage an armed rebellion was renewed but rejected again,[9] for "the military situation has not improved in the camp's favor." However, it was decided that the forty-six inmates would not obey the order to line up but would instead be hidden in the camp. "If the SS tries to drag one of the forty-six inmates to the gate by force, force will be used against it." During the same night this decision was made known in all blocks. The announcement included the first mention of an "international camp committee" that would not tolerate "the murder of our best people" (Bartel 1970, 304). No one spoke in his own block, and thus the spokesmen of the resistance organization operated under the cover of darkness. Hiding places were prepared. On the next morning the French manufacturer Bloch was the only person who showed up at the gate. "No one knew how he had got on the list. After some time Bloch was dismissed, evidently for tactical reasons, to lull his fellow victims into a false sense of security."[10] The Camp Defense was ordered to search for the forty-six. "In spite of the threat of the officer-in-charge that some members of the Camp Defense would lose their lives if the prisoners were not found, this search was fruitless" (*Buchenwald* 1960, 541 ff.).

At that time there were also other ways of preventing a liquidation of the inmates of Buchenwald. On April 3 "four important foreigners in the camp—the Belgian minister Soudain, the French undersecretary of state Marie, Captain Burney, and the Dutch naval officer Cool—were induced to send a letter to the commandant in which they cleverly assured him of their loyalty and probity. The signers of the letter also expressed the hope that, after returning to their homelands, they would have an opportunity to bring this to the attention of the general public in their countries. The commandant's barber delivered this letter, and it had the desired effect. Pister regarded it as a document that would bring security to him and his family. "He thought that, if need be, there could be a respite between an order and its execution. . . . He hesitated, and that was the main thing."[11] This act was evidently not organized by the international camp committee, for there is no mention of it in the reports written or inspired by its members.

Another and even more important step was taken at that time. In accordance with a decision by "the responsible people in the camp," Eugen Kogon, one of the forty-six who were in hiding after the night of April 5, had himself smuggled out of the camp in order to reach the Allied lines from Weimar. From there he planned to send a letter to the commandant of Buchenwald that gave the appearance of being from an officer of British parachutists and contained a warning against further lethal evacuation transports. This letter had been suggested by British officers whom Kogon and his friends had helped save from being shot, and they had also drafted it.[12] Kogon emerged from his hiding place, "presented [himself] to Ding-Schuler [the SS doctor whose clerk he was and whom he had long influenced—H.L.], who had been notified by Junior Squad Leader Feld [about whose cooperation with infirmary inmates known to him we have already reported—H.L.], and arranged the daring undertaking with him. On April 8, a police truck was to be sent to Weimar to pick up valuable instruments and vaccines. I was to sit in one of those boxes and be taken to Ding-Schuler's house in Weimar." An air raid delayed the departure, but around 12:45 the loading of the boxes proceeded smoothly under Feld's direction. "Four hours later the letter to the commandant was mailed in Weimar. It too was effective. Pister vacillated even more" (Kogon 1946, 339 ff.). Pierre d'Harcourt appreciated this episode so much that he made the following entry in his diary on April 13: "All of us owe our lives to him [Kogon—H.L.]" (Harcourt n.d., 178). Walter Bartel, the head of the resistance organization, ignores it (Bartel 1976), and although other Communists, who wrote their reports shortly after the liberation, mention it, they suppress Kogon's name.[13]

At the same time the international camp committee endeavored to make direct contact with the American troops. Now it was possible to risk using the transmitter that had been constructed some time ago. This was on April 8 toward noon, in the movie room. The Pole Teofil Witek has given a graphic description of the Morse code transmission, in Russian and English as well as in German, of the following SOS: "To the Allies. To the army of General Patton. This is the Buchenwald concentration camp. SOS. We request help. They want to evacuate us. The SS wants to destroy us." This text had been formulated by the leadership of the resistance organization.[14] Witek goes on to say: "While the text was being transmitted in German, the electric current was turned off in the camp. Within three minutes our own generator was operational. The English and German texts were transmitted by Damazyn [a Polish engineer—H.L.], the Russian text by a Soviet prisoner of war [Konstantin Ivanovich Leonov—H.L., Bartel 1976, 307]. After another transmission, the transmitter was switched to reception. Gloomy silence. No reception. The transmission was repeated. [According to another report, the transmission was "repeated about twelve times"—H.L.][15] After listening hard for three minutes, Damazyn received the following Morse message in English: 'KZ Bu. [Buchenwald concentration camp]. Hold out. Rushing to your aid. Staff of Third Army.' This message caused Damazyn to faint from nervous tension, exhaustion, and excitement" (*Buchenwald* 1960, 543 ff.).

On April 10, one last attempt was made to influence the commandant. With reference to the Geneva Convention, the Czech surgeon Horn suggested that Pister leave an SS doctor and a small protective force with the patients who were to be spared evacuation measures. Upon the Allies' arrival in Buchenwald, it would be testified that these SS men had acted honorably. There were no visible results of this plea, and evidently the attempt had not been cleared with the underground camp leadership, for it is not mentioned in its reports. In fact, the Luxembourger Bourg-Bourger writes that he regarded this attempt as hopeless and undignified and therefore refused to be among the signers of the letter (Biermann 1945, 42).[16]

Evidently Horn was motivated by his not unfounded worry about the sick, for the evacuations proceeded. On April 7, the assembled senior block inmates were ordered to make preparations for the evacuation of the entire camp. After a brief deliberation, the senior block inmates agreed to ignore this order. After the command "Line up for roll call," the roll-call area remained empty. When the senior block inmates were called out and asked to explain, they said that the inmates had refused to line up because they were afraid of low-flying planes. Everything imaginable was done to gain time. "Thanks to our sabotage, only 6,000 inmates could be evacuated on April 7, not the entire camp, as planned by the SS. . . . On April 8, no one was evacuated, for the SS seemed to be battle-weary. Air-raid warnings sounded almost all day. . . . On April 9, 9,600 men had to line up and were evacuated. There was no way out. . . . On April 10, the members of the commandant's staff packed their things. In the crematorium all papers were burned under the supervision of the SS, and the SS evacuated 9,280 more inmates." This report was written shortly after the liberation of the camp by Alfred Bunzol, who was wearing the armband of a senior block inmate (Bunzol 1946, 41 ff.). Leo Eitinger, a Jewish inmate, wrote right after the liberation: "A number of our comrades constantly took the hard walk to the gate and toward an uncertain fate, while we knew that every day and every hour was bringing our liberation closer. When the order 'Line up for roll call' was no longer obeyed, some 500 heavily armed men marched into the camp. When they came to a block, they cried 'Everyone out!', but only very few obeyed voluntarily. Most men remained passively seated and had to be chased out by force; a very few offered direct resistance. Most had to be driven out with kicks. It was a horrible spectacle, and it was an eternity before a block was cleared."[17] On April 9, Ernst Thape made this entry in his diary: "A handful of SS men can force the inmates to do whatever is deemed necessary. I hope that this lays many romantic illusions to rest once and for all."[18] Those evacuated on the last day included primarily Poles, Czechs, and Soviet prisoners of war. The underground camp committee had decided "to yield to superior force."[19] Years later, the German head of this committee wrote about it: "We were not able to keep the Soviet prisoners of war from marching off, but we managed to make sure that they did not begin their death journey unarmed. They were handed revolvers, hand grenades, cutting and stabbing weapons. . . . Our friends marched out of the camp in military discipline (Bartel 1976, 307). On the basis of his fresh memory, Otto Horn recorded this event as follows: "On April 10, 1945, 2 P.M., a large number of Poles were evacuated and almost the entire military organization of the Polish section went with them. At 4 P.M. those [Soviet] prisoners of war departed who had agreed to be evacuated."[20] In another, anonymous report we read: "On April 10, we had to give up parts of the real anti-Fascist core. Among the evacuees were the Soviet prisoners of war and a considerable number of Polish anti-Fascists" (*Buchenwald* 1960, 533 ff.). The camp administration managed to evacuate 28,285 inmates,[21] but the projected total evacuation could be prevented. On the morning of April 11, there were still around 21,000 prisoners in Buchenwald.[22]

To the extent that it is possible to reconstruct the fate of the evacuees, it was no different from the fate of those who had been forced to go on death marches from other camps. However, the 21,000 inmates who had remained in the camp—thanks to efforts to influence the powers that be, systematic obstructionism, and frequent air-raid alarms—lived to see their liberation on April 11, 1945. Since descriptions of the dramatic events of this last day of the Buchenwald concentration camp diverge and legends were created after the fact, it is advisable to reconstruct these events from notes made at the time.

While still in the camp, Alfred Bunzol wrote: "April 11 began with intensive air activity. American fighter planes and bombers circled over the camp. At 7 A.M., the air-raid warning sounded, and it never stopped. The SS no longer carried out the planned evacuation. . . . At 11 A.M., a siren announced that the enemy was approaching. Over the public-address system all SS men were ordered to leave the camp immediately. The rumbling of artillery got closer and closer to the camp. Rifle and machine-gun fire was clearly audible. We noticed the SS fleeing along the fence to the woods east of the camp" (Bunzol 1946). Other reports agree in substance, though the times given are somewhat different.[23]

Leo Eitinger has given a graphic account of his observations at that time.

"I was standing on a slope in the camp, and so I could see with my own eyes that the SS was leaving Buchenwald. It was the SS men who were evacuating it, and they ran down to the highway with all the rucksacks and hand luggage they could carry. Down there we were able to watch the German retreat almost as in a movie. Horses running without riders, fleeing soldiers. . . . Cars driving heedlessly, and in the midst of all this 'our' SS men."[24] Before all this, Commandant Pister had called in Hans Eiden, the senior camp inmate, and Edelmann, a German prisoner functionary, and turned the command over to them (Kogon 1946, 342; Burney 1946, 135).[25] The resistance organization ascertained that the entire camp administration had cleared out of the camp. "At 1:30 P.M. we called all offices, such as those of the officer-in-charge and the commandant, on the telephone. No answer anywhere" (Kautsky 1961, 309). Fritz Freudenberg recalls that when the members of the inmates' detail working in the SS kitchen marched back to the camp, they had to open the gate themselves, for there no longer was any guard there.[26]

For a time the watchtowers surrounding the camp were still manned.[27] Ernst Thape wrote in his diary: "In fact, there is no SS in the big camp any longer, but the towers are still manned and the barbed wire is still electrically charged."[28] As Eitinger noted in those days, "a few guards are still around the camp and shooting wildly into it—for the last time, in order to show who is boss. But that lasts only a few minutes."[29] Carolus has given a graphic description of what happened next: "Suddenly, at 5 minutes before 3 P.M., someone cried, 'Guards immediately down from the towers!' They hesitantly withdrew, and the intermediate guards cleared out, too. Two Russian SS men [evidently Russian volunteers—H.L.] cautiously sneaked up the mountain slope to get out of the line of fire. A Russian inmate asked them to throw their weapons away, and they readily obeyed."[30]

The German Fritz Freudenberg, one of the first to take advantage of this situation, has given an exact description of his venture: "On the watchtower over the camp gate an LMG [light machine-gun—H.L.] was on a stand as always, but there was no SS. I told my comrade that I was going to get it down. After a moment of hesitation, I picked up a handy ladder and raced to the gate. I lay down and waited, but nothing happened. Then I jumped up, put the ladder in place, rushed up to the roof, lay down flat again, and looked over the ridge into the area of the commandant's office. Nothing was to be seen. Everything seemed deserted. My next move was to the railing of the watchtower, and again I lay on the ground and waited, but nothing happened. . . . It was equally quiet inside the camp, which I was able to see well from the tower. I saw only parts of a few heads peering out of some barracks. Now I took the machine gun off its stand and put it on the ground; there was no ammunition. . . . To avoid exposing myself to the side where the commandant's office was located, I climbed through an open window facing the camp into the topmost room. Then I tiptoed down the spiral staircase, carrying a sharpened triangular file as a weapon. In that room there were three long boxes containing bazookas. I had never had such things in my hand, and so I had to stop and think about how to use them. Suddenly I heard footsteps and saw two legs descending the winding staircase: it was August Bräucker, the smith on our detail. This had really frightened me. In a whisper he explained the function of a bazooka to me. Then I went down the nearest staircase with one of those things under my arm. I came to the room of the head of Work Assignments and to the exit door. The room . . . was empty. . . . When I ventured out, I suddenly saw a man in uniform below the detention cells. I cried 'Hands up!' He was unarmed and obeyed. When I asked him where he was coming from and going, he said he was a member of the Wehrmacht, that his group had dispersed and everyone was shifting for himself. From him we learned that for the past hour the first American tanks had been moving over the Ettersberg [hills north of the city—ed.] in the direction of Weimar."[31]

Another report, one written shortly afterward, gives a more concise account: "Around 3 P.M. the first American tanks entered the camp area. The German defense was very weak, for the SS guards had already marched off, and the commandant and his staff had fled. . . . When they saw those first tanks, our young comrades armed themselves and stormed the wire entanglement. No shot was fired—the SS had fled" (The Truth n.d., 25). The German Communist Karl Barthel has given the following description of what must have been the most impressive hour in his long incarceration: "Masses of tanks and armored reconnaissance cars rolled over the Buchenwald mountain. The hitherto restrained enthusiasm of the inmates assumed the proportions of an avalanche. Human streams surged toward the liberators from the inmates' barracks. Those patients who were at all ambulatory got out of bed, for they too wanted to be there. . . . The hitherto dreaded barbed-wire fence—death-dealing and electrically charged—was knocked and torn down with big poles, and the SS guards still on their towers were disarmed and arrested. . . . At 4 P.M. the first American liberators shook hands with those they had liberated" (Barthel 1946, 159). Alfred Bunzol has described how, at that time, the weapons hidden in the camp were taken out and distributed, and he has also given an account of the storming of the camp fence: "At the same time [he believes it was at 3:40 P.M.—H.L.] the white flag was raised on Tower 1. Over the public-address system Hans Eiden, the chief senior camp inmate, spoke the following words: 'Comrades, we are free! The SS bandits have run away from our liberators, the American army" (Bunzol 1946, 44 ff.). However, in Otto Horn's version of this first address of a prisoner over the camp's public-address system, there is no reference to the American liberators.[32] Eitinger has described the events of this historic hour in these words: "Then we saw two American tanks rolling up to the camp, on the same road the SS men had just used for their flight. We ran toward them waving and screaming. They were not excited: 'Hallo boys, you are prisoners?'—'Yes. That's Buchenwald.'—'Oh, yes. Is everything all right now?'—'Yes.'—'All right, we are in a hurry, we must [go on] to Berlin. Bye, bye.' And then they went back to the main road. It was unreal. We were free."[33] The German Eugen Ochs, who worked in the inmates' kitchen, remembers that when he walked through the camp around 2 P.M., after serving a meal, he saw an SS man on a watchtower who had taken off his shirt and hung it out for everyone to see. "He evidently wanted to hoist the white flag in time." Around 4 P.M., the first American tanks reached the camp, "while most of them continued on the main road in the direction of Weimar. I remember one tank very well; it was on one of the camp roads, and numerous French inmates had gathered around it. There was a lot of cheering. Those were French soldiers who had fought alongside the Americans."[34]

Alfred Bunzol writes: "In order to be prepared for anything if the SS fired on the camp, the weapons that had been hidden in the camp were taken out around 3 P.M. amidst great cheering from all the inmates, who were already standing outside the block. Certain groups were armed" (Burney 1946, 44 ff.). The Austrian Communist Franz Bera, a member of the "military high command and a specialist in arms and ammunition," was in charge of distributing the weapons and the ammunition, and he has described this activity as follows: "The distribution of arms to various national groups took place in accordance with precise instructions from the military leadership. The main gate and the watchtowers were occupied by the cadres, exactly following Plan A (offensive plan). The SS retreated in the direction of Weimar."[35] Ernst Thape made the following entry in his diary: "3:45 P.M. It's all over. Now begins the chaos. A babble of voices. The rescue team has a hard time keeping the inmates in the block ... 4 o'clock. Suddenly inmates are walking through the camp streets with ready-to-fire carbines. All those who were roaming around the camp have been gathered together. In three minutes the situation was clear. ... The members of the Camp Defense are on the march with carbines, hand grenades in their belts, and pistols."[36] According to Rudi Jahn, "the international committee sprang into action immediately after the first tanks appeared" (Das war Buchenwald n.d., 115). Carolus remembers that "our resistance groups went on the attack the moment the first tanks arrived."[37] Another report reads as follows: "At 3:15, a white flag was fluttering on Tower 1. The camp is in an uproar. All want weapons and surge toward the outside. The barracks of the SS and the Wehrmacht are stormed. Everywhere weapons are taken and brought into the camp; new groups are armed with them. The first prisoners are brought in."[38] Bunzol adds to this: "By 10 P.M., our armed groups had arrested more than one hundred SS men" (Bunzol 1946, 45). In these last hours of Buchenwald, two inmates were killed, evidently the victims of wild shooting in the first paroxysm of rapture.[39] Eugen Ochs believes that a man from Leipzig by the name of Paul Geissler (or something like that) suffered a fatal abdominal wound "in that senseless shooting."[40] Carolus's comprehensive judgment is in line with other reports: "As soon as the first American tanks appeared, the international committee started acting with complete legal authority, and it did not lose control for one moment."[41]

The further activities of this committee—thanks to which the chaos with evil consequences, observed in other camps, was avoided in liberated Buchenwald—are outside the scope of this book, for the liberation on April 11, 1945, marked the end of the resistance against the former masters of Buchenwald.

The composition of the liberated inmates indicates which ethnic groups were most numerous after the great evacuations of the final days. The biggest was the Russian group with 4,380 persons, and this was followed by the Poles (3,800), Frenchmen (2,900), and Czechs (2,105). After those came the Germans, who were probably the easiest to keep from being placed on evacuation transports, with 1,800. (The 550 Austrians are already listed separately). There were 1,467 Spaniards and 1,240 Hungarians (probably Hungarian Jews who had been evacuated to Buchenwald in the final phase; unlike the SS practice, we no longer counted Jews as a separate group). Among the smaller ethnic groups, Belgians (622) and Yugoslavs (570) are at the top.[42]

In line with this ethnic composition, the liberated inmates formed an executive committee that consisted of a Russian, a Frenchman, a German, a Czech, and an Italian. Recognition of what the resistance organization had done for the inmates was widespread, as is indicated by the fact that the German representative on the executive committee, Walter Bartel, was also head of the resistance and that the French and Italian members had also had leading parts in it. The conduct of the German senior camp inmate Hans Eiden gained him a particularly impressive vote of confidence: He was made head of the administration, and the Americans accredited him in that position.[43] On the first day of freedom, after Eiden had expressed everyone's thanks "to our liberators, the American army" a mightily cheered American officer responded: "We admire you for having managed to preserve such unity, order, and strength under the Nazi terror.

You are the best of Europe. You have taken 150 SS men prisoner" (Bunzol 1946, 45).

I have described the liberation of Buchenwald in such detail because, in those critical days and hours, a resistance organization acted in a disciplined manner and passed a generally recognized acid test. Another reason is that a "self-liberation" of Buchenwald was constructed after the fact—for transparent political purposes. However, no episode in the highly dramatic story of the resistance movement in the concentration camps ought to be distorted.[44] If a newspaper published in East Germany writes that "bourgeois falsifiers of history would have us believe" that Buchenwald was liberated by the American army (Dittmar/Fricke 1975, 468), we can set the record straight by quoting from a resolution that was signed in Buchenwald on April 19, 1945, by representative of eleven Communist parties: "The military cadres of all nations liberated Buchenwald shoulder to shoulder and in cooperation with the Allied American army" (Drobisch 1968, 159).

Soon thereafter, on April 15, Bergen–Belsen was liberated. After evacuations had been started on April 6, Bergen–Belsen became the only camp turned over to British troops following negotiations. In the early months of 1945, Bergen–Belsen had been flooded with evacuees from other camps, and it was completely unprepared for such overcrowding. Conditions there were so chaotic that "there was no functioning prisoner self-administration or underground resistance organization of the inmates that could automatically have brought order into chaos in the leadership vacuum of those days" (Holt 1947, 169). As a consequence, the "law of the jungle" reigned in the camp, as Louis Martin-Chauffier put it (Kolb 1962, 146). On April 1, Abel Herzberg entered in his diary: "Roll calls are not being held any longer, nor is any work being done. All people do is die" (Kolb 1962, 282).

What the Allies found in the liberated camps Buchenwald and Bergen–Belsen was far more convincing than all the secret reports that had reached them earlier. Photographs of piles of corpses and reports of survivors filled the world press. Heinrich Himmler, who at that time was negotiating with a representative of the World Jewish Congress and with the Swedish Count Bernadotte and therefore had ordered Bergen–Belsen to be turned over to Allied troops, complained bitterly about the "mendacious horror stories" that were not an inducement "to continue to surrender the camps" (Fraenkel/Manvell 1965, 213). Nevertheless, despite the ever-increasing space problem [apparently in those camps still receiving prisoners shipped out of about-to-be-liberated ones—ed.], evacuation trains and marches were assembled once more.

In mid-March 1945, the Danish and Norwegian prisoners of Sachsenhausen were turned over to the Swedish Red Cross (*Damals in Sachsenhausen* 1967, 150). When Russian troops approached, the following situation arose in that camp, whose resistance organization had been greatly weakened by murders and transfers to Mauthausen: "April 15 to 20. Daily inspections and call-ups of inmates for the Dirlewanger Unit. Gypsies are outfitted and quickly shipped out. Among the German political prisoners, in particular, there is growing unrest about possibly being put in uniform. There are rumors that all Germans will be conscripted. In point of fact, most of the Germans are outfitted and go to work in uniforms."[45] At that time, the German Communist Max Opitz, evidently an influential member of the German resistance group, was laid up in the hospital with injuries, having been buried in a bombardment. He asked his contact to find out "the group's opinion" about the impending evacuation. The latter emphasized that "we, the activists in the camp, have no way of stopping the northward march of 40,000 inmates" (Opitz 1969, 181 ff.). Retrospectively the following decision of the "underground camp committee" has been reconstructed: "1. Courageous and disciplined political prisoners will accept the offer of the camp administration and assignment as auxiliary guards of the columns on the evacuation march. They are to keep the SS from killing all inmates. Especially qualified inmates with military experience shall bring up the rear. 2. The 'hose guard,' which had secretly been developed as a military unit and engaged in firefighting exercises by way of camouflage, was to undertake the protection of the camp and the 5,000 patients left behind, in addition to preventing the hospital from being blown up."[46] Heinz Junge has confirmed that the camp committee that drew up the above order was composed entirely of Germans; he speaks of a decision of the German party.[47] Georg Buch, who was sent to Sachsenhausen as an officer of the SPD, writes: "I was a bit cautious in dealing with members of the fire brigade, though I have no evidence against them."[48]

"The evacuation began on the evening of April 20. Dirlewanger people received rifles and submachine guns with ammunition . . . and went along as guards, together with SS men. There were groups of 500 women, and later the same number of men. . . . The evacuation went on all night and until 11 P.M. on the following day, when it was over. Höhne, the officer-in-charge, had the gate shut and told the block leaders to hurry up and leave the camp. No SS men are left in the camp. The towers and everything else are vacant. The radio is still on in the block leader's quarters, and there are about 3,000 inmates in the camp, including women and around 2,000 patients in the infirmary."[49] About 400 healthy inmates, among them 200 women and forty German Reds, stayed behind of their own free will and in defiance of SS orders."[50] These included Georg Buch, who lay low under a pretext. According to him, a large number of prisoners—he believes almost a thousand—concealed themselves as he did, among them about a dozen Germans. The Russians are said to have turned rancorous and threatened to hang the Germans.[51] In front of the gate, five Germans and a young Russian were shot.

These last shootings involved a dramatic episode: "Ernst Mönkemöller and a few other comrades from the 'hose guard' came out of their hiding places and confronted the Beier group [named after the last senior camp inmate, a German criminal who had joined SS men in their search for hidden prisoners—H.L.]. They had revolvers and one carbine. Both sides avoided a shootout—Beier because the SS was already leaving the camp, Mönkemöller because he did not want to have the SS back. The camp gate was secured with chains and locks. The SS left the commandant's area through the outer gate. The 'hose guard' immediately went to work. The lock was forced open, and the towers were occupied. The machine gun of Tower A was dismounted and installed on the camp road. Storage rooms and food supplies were taken over and guarded. Some SS men were driven out or disarmed."[52]

The situation after the departure of the SS has been described as follows: "In the camp 3,000 inmates are waiting for coming events in dramatic tension, but things remain quiet. . . . Thus we wait till about 3 o'clock, but all remains calm, and we finally lie down fully clothed. Sunday morning, the 22nd. For the first time no reveille, no SS in the camp. A prisoner stands guard at the gate. Machine guns with ammunition have been left behind on the towers. Nothing has been destroyed. At 11 o'clock, suddenly shouts in the camp: Russkie, Russkie, the Russians are here! Everyone rushes out to the roll-call area. There, by the door, Red Army men! . . . We immediately embrace them, kiss them, caress them, lift them on our shoulders. . . . The Red Army men don't stay but move on. Some enthusiastic Russian inmates . . . go with them, but they are soon sent back to the camp."[53] This last clause is omitted in a later version published in East Germany—a version that makes more than stylistic corrections (*Damals in Sachsenhausen* 1967, 131 ff.). There is an astonishing parallel with the above-mentioned episodes at the liberation of Buchenwald.

The misery and the mass murder of those who were driven across the country on evacuation marches resemble the conditions on the death marches during the evacuation of other camps. There were isolated rays of hope. Thus Wolfgang Szepansky writes: "The column in which I marched was guarded by some prisoners who had been given SS uniforms in Sachsenhausen. That was good for us, for they were on our side" (*KZ Sachsenhausen* n.d., 38). We have the following description of the rescue of the almost sixty-year-old Fritz Henssler [sent to the concentration camp as a deputy of the SPD—H.L.], who had dropped from exhaustion at the side of the road and had to "expect to be shot in the neck by a rearguard detail of the SS": In accordance with a direction of the resistance organization, prisoners had placed "a secret military group, mostly veterans of the international brigades in Spain, on a baggage cart at the end of the line. When Karl Sauer [a Sudeten German veteran of the Spanish Civil War—H.L.] spotted Fritz Henssler in the ditch, he said to his group: 'All right, here comes the first test of strength. There sits a former member of the Reichstag. We won't let them shoot him; we will take him with us.' There was an argument with an SS officer, but the prisoners insisted that Henssler be put on a wagon. They still weren't able to stage an open rebellion, but suddenly the SS no longer dared to use its arms to enforce its will" (Pawlak 1978, 29).

Internees of the subsidiary camp Falkensee were able to prevent an evacuation. In early April, the guards had been replaced with older men. "The new guards treated the inmates with restraint," writes Max Mikloweit.[54] When, on April 20, the prisoners were ordered to line up for departure, the senior camp inmate, a man wearing a black triangle, intervened with the camp commandant together with a German Red. In view of the inmates' resoluteness the commandant rescinded his order. After some of the SS men had left the camp on April 25, "we [evidently a German resistance group—H.L.] occupied the towers at the four corners of our camp and included inmates who were members of the Soviet army in our actions. Around 11 P.M., the commandant came into the camp and noticed that some changes had taken place there and that the Germans who were supposed to help the SS keep order and had been given light weapons were beginning to strike out on their own together with the foreign inmates." Thus he handed "all keys to the senior camp inmate, who was still officially in charge of the camp" and disappeared. The inmates obtained weapons, and when SS men approached the camp once more, they avoided a fight. The next day the camp was definitively liberated by Russian troops.[55]

When the administration of Flossenbürg started, in February 1945, to use German inmates for guard duty, these formed a "camp police" of about 400 men (Siegert 1979, 481). "We were not able to determine whether or not pressure was really brought on them; in any case, they informed on numerous inmates," writes Ernst Israel Bornstein and points out that this unit consisted primarily of criminals (Bornstein 1967, 212). The evacuation began on April 16. In the final phase, Germans with red markings were added to the camp police. The Austrian Communist Bruno Furch has testified that "after a heated discussion, we political prisoners deliberately joined it in order to keep the camp police from becoming the exclusive domain of the Greens."[56] Furch's comrade and compatriot, Franz Freihaut, believes that this decision was made by the Russian leadership of a resistance group.[57] However, on April 20, which the chronicler of Flossenbürg, Toni Siegert, has called "the day of the great residual evacuation" (Siegert 1979, 483), the German and Austrian Reds, who as camp policemen were armed but escorted their foreign comrades without any ammunition, evidently had few opportunities to avert the worst. As Bruno Furch has testified, "we were unable to prevent a special detail, which marched along at the rear of the individual columns, from shooting those who dropped from exhaustion. But we helped as much as we could—by helping people escape and providing them with food, cigarettes, etc."[58] Members of this camp police tried to escape these marches,[59] evidently because they realized how powerless they were.

There are rumors that the 1,526 people left in the camp—mostly patients, but also some who had hidden or were feigning illness—offered resistance to the SS men. On the morning of April 23, they were liberated by American troops.[60]

When the evacuation of the women's concentration camp Ravensbrück was begun on April 21, 1945, patients and some doctors and nurses were not the only ones who stayed behind. Several women concealed themselves, and in the vacuum created by the departure of the SS, they took care of the sick women. The rush of events prevented the implementation of the plans the prisoners had prepared for that period, but these nevertheless made it easier "to organize life in the days of transition," as Wanda Kiedrzyńska puts it. "On April 30 the outposts of the Russian army appeared on the camp road, and on May 1 regular detachments of Soviet troops moved in" (Kiedrzyńska 1960, 94), which meant that Ravensbrück too was liberated.

As Allied troops approached Dachau in those eventful weeks, the situation there was even more chaotic. "Mass transports of thousands arrived, and not all of them could be taken to the bath and the disinfection station, as smaller transports had been. These people had to set down their things, their clothes, and their underwear in the roll-call area. . . . Then they had to stand there naked for hours and wait until a room was vacated in the blocks. . . . There were reports from the outside that numerous bodies of exhausted and shot people were lying around in the streets. . . . It was also said that a transport which had arrived by train was waiting on the tracks in front of the camp and could not be unloaded for lack of space. Unfortunately this turned out to be true, and later we saw that most of those people had died from hunger, heat, and thirst in the sealed cars. [This was an evacuation transport from Buchenwald—H.L.] We had only one question: If everything is to be funneled into Dachau, where shall we get the space?. . . Or are the masses to be driven somewhere else, and if so, where?" (Steinbock 1946, 20 ff.).

This description by an Austrian clergyman is supplemented by diary entries of the Belgian Arthur Haulot and the Albanian Ali Kuci, both of whom were active in the international combat organization and wrote on April 22, 1945: "Something has to be done. We must at least try to do something. In the present situation we can risk anything." "The atmosphere in the camp changes from hour to hour—from extreme optimism to the blackest pessimism." "On the one side the camp administration, the higher and lower officers, and the SS men—a total of 1,400 men armed to the teeth and in possession of explosives and poison gas, in the grip of both hatred and fear. On the other side 35,000 human beings, among them 10,000 sick people and 5,000 unreliable ones, crowded together, weakened by hunger and fear, deprived of everything, with their numbers as their only means of defense. And between these two groups there are a handful of people, also without any weapon but equipped with experience and courage and imbued with the will even to take on the devil."[61]

Oskar Müller, an officer of the German Communist Party, had been installed as senior camp inmate a short time earlier. Arthur Haulot has testified that Müller's conduct in those days helped to avoid an unimaginable catastrophe,[62] and the Frenchman Edmond Michelet, another active member of the resistance organization, has called him a "decent comrade" (Michelet 1955, 249). Years later Müller wrote that "contact was established with the national committees of the various nations at that time, measures for the internal security of the camp were discussed, and security groups were formed (including the barracks) to keep the camp firmly in our hands and prevent provocations by shady characters." Müller also indicates more far-reaching plans: "If the SS had attempted a massacre now, the camp would have implemented the plan for a breakout, albeit with great sacrifices."[63]

At 1 P.M. on April 23, an order was issued "to immediately evacuate all Jews, without exception. . . . In a short time, 2,400 Jews have been rounded up, all of them weak and emaciated, many lying on the ground without a glimmer of hope. We others are gripped by fear, for everyone knows what a transport of Jews means. Our representatives walk back and forth between the groups" and try to instil courage into them. However, Green camp policemen "watch our people and drive them back. Slowly night falls, and the Jews, a confused, buzzing mass, are still there. . . . In the morning, sixty dead bodies have to be taken away." At 8 A.M. the Jews start marching, and "the camp police, consisting of Greens, escorts the procession."

Haulot/Kuci's diary goes on to say that during the next night "there is no rest for us. We have to use it to centralize our information service. Our measures must be coordinated, the individual tasks must be prepared, and appropriate instructions must be given. We already have a number of responsible people at our disposal. In several sections of the camp, work has ceased, and in others it has been reduced. Our general staff has been installed in the hospital block and in Blocks 9 and 17, where we are best shielded from the curiosity of the camp police. There we are constantly receiving reports from our people: news heard on the radio, movements of the SS."[64] The Alsatian Felix Maurer, who worked in the SS training institute, reported that camp commandant Weiter had suffered a nervous breakdown in the night of April 24.[65]

Haulot/Kuci's diary affords us insight into the dramatic events of the last days and the actions of the international resistance movement. The entry of April 24 reads: "The typhus epidemic is spreading—more than 200 dead each day—and the quarantine blocks resemble scenes from hell. . . . They [the SS men—H.L.] are taking away the valuables of the prisoners recently arrived from Natzweiler. . . . In accordance with our agreed-upon tactics, our people participate in this work; it is the best opportunity to get larger amounts of civilian clothes. If there is an evacuation, it will facilitate the escape of many of us." In the evening the SS put together "an auxiliary police force of about ninety men."

April 25: "An air-raid warning was in effect all night. . . . Another one in the morning; it has lasted practically the whole day, and everyone is glad, because this prevents evacuations. However, the alert does not keep the SS from shooting inmates who have been isolated in the bunker. When will it be our turn to die? Tomorrow or the next day? And yet the Americans are so close! At the moment our life resembles a breathless race with time. . . . The auxiliary police formed from prisoners that is 'to maintain order in case of evacuation' has been augmented by the camp administration to 900 men. We shall infiltrate our people into it—dependable, resolute comrades. The SS continues its feverish destruction of compromising papers. Under the pretext of helping them, we burn all lists and card files. From now on it will be impossible to ascertain who is in the camp and who is not. . . . While our masters are busy in this way [plundering Red Cross packages and other valuables—H.L.] we conceal in safe places, especially in the hospital block, those people whom we don't want to lose under any circumstances but who are directly threatened by the expected evacuation transport: Austrians, German and Italian resistance fighters, Russian officers, veterans of the Spanish Civil War, etc. . . . The famine is increasing."

The diary entries of April 26 begin with the reproduction of documents that "a woman close to the SS whom we had appropriately influenced" had found on the commandant's desk and copied. Himmler wrote as follows to the SS Lieutenant General Pohl (who evidently transmitted his order to the commandant of Dachau): "The surrender of the camp is absolutely out of the question. The camp is to be evacuated immediately. No prisoner must be allowed to fall into the hands of the enemy alive." This is how Himmler motivated his order: "In Buchenwald, the prisoners maltreated the civilian population cruelly."

The prisoners received this telling warning of what evacuation meant: "The Jews loaded on wagons on the 24th have still not been able to leave, 700 of them have died to date." This was the information gathered by those active in the resistance when an order was issued on the 26th of the month that at 12 P.M. everyone had to be in the roll-call area ready to march. "This means the end, but we are firmly resolved not to obey this order. We may have to sacrifice our lives, the lives of the few people who have been directing the underground movement for the past five days. But what does this mean if thousands of lives are saved? We gather in the well-known Block 17 for a council of war and decide to sabotage the distribution of food, to delay the assembly, to remove the letters indicating their nationality from the red triangles of the prisoners, and to use any means to spread chaos and anarchy. . . . The powers that be don't manage to form the first column until around 2 P.M. . . . The Germans are to march off first, followed by the Russians." The inmate population on that day, evidently including the satellite camps, has been given as over 67,000. The Poles were the most numerous group with 15,000, and they were followed by Russians (13,500), Hungarian Jews (12,000), Germans (more than 6,000), and Frenchmen (almost 6,000).[66]

Felix Maurer attempted to change the commandant's mind while serving him coffee in the SS officers' home, and in his presence the commandant ordered the officer-in-charge to dismiss the lined-up inmates again. "However, he had already lost his authority." The commandant left the camp, and the order to evacuate the assembled prisoners stood. Once more the SS "managed to divide the camp. It spread the word that only Germans, Russians, and Jews were going to be evacuated and that the members of nations belonging to the International Red Cross would remain in the camp and be turned over to the Americans." In point of fact, the security police, which was composed of members of those nations, used force to keep prisoners from escaping from the columns that had been herded together for evacuation. "Thus 8,100 inmates . . . had to march off on that Thursday."[67] The diary of Haulot/Kuci gives a different figure: "Seven thousand men, at least 5,000 of whom already resembled skeletons, passed through the camp gate for the last time." The atmosphere in the camp on April 27 is described in these words: "No one is sleeping tonight. Everyone is nervous and irritable. We know that our lives are more directly endangered than ever before. . . . All inmates are providing themselves with civilian clothes and putting on their striped prisoners' uniforms over them. The SS looted the room in which the private effects of the prisoners from Natzweiler were stored, and this was extraordinarily beneficial to us."[68]

The German Karl Ludwig Schecher has described how he prepared for the evacuation march together with a capo. The two men obtained compasses and "were determined to flee west, if possible at the first nocturnal stop, where Allied troops were approaching." However, when he had reason to fear that an SS roll-call officer, who hated him and was making unmistakable threats, would finish him off on the transport, he had the hospital capo admit him as a patient. "He wasn't going to look for me in the infirmary with its 5,000 or more patients, if only out of fear of an infection."[69]

Utilizing conflicts within the SS leadership, German clergymen sent "a sort of delegation" to the commandant in an effort to preserve as many people as possible from the threatening evacuation. "That man gave them a friendly reception [a sign of the times—H.L.] and solemnly assured them that those German clergymen who were not fit for marching would not be transported" (Gross n.d., 189). "The second group was scheduled to march off on April 27, but this never happened."[70] "The remaining Russians and all Italians" were supposed to march off. The distribution of provisions for the march was delayed. "Even the shortest period of time that we gain thereby increases our chances to save our comrades, for the Americans are getting closer and closer." The rumble of artillery could be heard, and "the whole operation was plunged into hopeless confusion." The "long-expected air-raid warning" finally sounded at 10:30 A.M. The sirens kept sounding, and "we rushed into one another's arms, for now we were finally saved. . . . This prolonged alert meant that troops had landed by parachute."[71]

Another rescue attempt was made in those critical days. "The trash-collection detail of Comrade Eichmüller received the order to burn empty Red Cross packages that had been plundered by the SS outside the camp in order to destroy evidence of such vile acts. This detail was taken over by an

SS file leader with whom contact had already been made and who wanted to use this as an opportunity for his own escape. Thus the trash-collection detail [which included eight German Reds—H.L.] passed through the camp gate at 5 P.M. on April 26, 1945."[72]

Karl Riemer, who was to play a decisive part in the succeeding days, gave a graphic account of the daring enterprise—on May 11, 1945, while it was still fresh in his mind. When, on April 26 at twelve o'clock, everyone was ordered to prepare to march off, "I definitely decided to clear out, and, as I noticed, so did many other comrades. In record time we obtained civilian clothes." When capo Eichmüller received the above order, he "immediately gathered seventeen comrades he knew with whom we wanted to venture an escape. . . . Eichmüller told me . . . that an SS file leader named Pfeiffer wanted to join us. Pfeiffer was going to take charge of the detail and then give us free passage." SS patrols outside the camp forced the group to hide and break up. After all kinds of adventure in the succeeding hours, Riemer managed, by the 29th at noon, to make his way to Pfaffenhofen, a town already liberated, and to draw the attention of the American commander to the critical situation of the inmates of Dachau, saying that "not a moment should be lost." The officer dismissed Riemer with "a promise of immediate help."[73]

In addition to this group, other inmates appear to have escaped from the camp. They hid out in the town of Dachau, where they were sheltered in the apartment of Walter Neff, who had been discharged from the camp and had to do forced labor, but had always maintained contact with his comrades. They were given civilian clothes[74] and were also supported by Georg Scherer and his family. (Scherer, formerly senior camp inmate in Dachau, had also been released from the camp).[75] On the morning of April 28, the radio repeatedly broadcast an appeal from a "Bavarian Freedom Action." After a while, the Nazi mayor of Munich went on the air, but the appeal had already triggered a joint action of inhabitants of Dachau and escapees from the concentration camp.[76] They occupied the town hall but were attacked by SS units. Among those who fell in the battle, or were shot after being captured, were three inmates of Dachau—a German and two Austrian veterans of the Spanish Civil War.[77] This blood sacrifice appears to have prompted the SS to leave the camp and led to the installation of men from the Home Guard as camp guards.[78] Haulot and Kuci write: "In any case, their action, in conjunction with our sabotage activity, prevented any further evacuation."[79]

According to Heinrich Eduard vom Holt, "the capos left the camp [together with the SS]. Some of those left behind strove to establish good relations with the prisoners." Since Holt was not part of the prisoner organization, he lacked the requisite perspective and may have generalized too much. However, there are rumors that several capos from Buchenwald, who had evidently come to Dachau with one of the evacuation transports, were lynched by the inmates they had harassed there. The German clergymen Gross, who noted this in his diary, went on to say that "since noon today [April 28—H.L.] the wearers of striped garb have been in control; the leadership has passed to them completely.... The armbands with the imprint HP [*Hilfspolizei*, auxiliary police] are multiplying like rabbits." They appeared to give their wearers "protection . . . from unpleasant surprises" (Gross n.d., 201).

Haulot and Kuci write: "A kind of truce has actually developed between the SS and the prisoners. The latter no longer observe any discipline toward their guards. Our contacts are on the job as never before. What is behind this apparent calm in the commandant's office? ... At 11 P.M. one of our most reliable scouts confirms that the last squads of soldiers have departed.... We issue two instructions: Fill all available receptacles with water. In case of an explosion (there were rumors that preparations were being made to blow up buildings) be sure to keep calm, and no matter what may transpire, maintain iron discipline at all costs. We all have the feeling that the last card will be played soon. At 11 P.M. fifteen men quietly gathered in Block 24." These were members of twelve nations. "Almost all of these performed various functions in the underground actions of recent weeks." Only the representative of the Russians did not participate in this deliberation due to illness. "If the SS really is gone, it is important that life in the camp continue undisturbed at daybreak and that order be maintained until the Allies bring us freedom. Currently there are 32,000 men in the camp, two thirds of them sick and enfeebled, and some of them dying. If we distribute it carefully, we have enough food for twenty-four hours at most . . . and no medicines. . . . Everywhere there are smouldering national hatreds, personal rancor, jealousy, and vengefulness. All this must be kept under control and discipline must be maintained. . . . The important thing now is to snatch those 32,000 human beings from the jaws of death. . . . This is the problem we will try to solve. We are constituting ourselves under the chairmanship of Major O'Leary [the camp name of the Belgian Albert Guérisse, who gave his nationality as Canadian—H.L.] . . . and from this moment on we regard ourselves as the only legitimate authority in the camp." The work indispensable for life in the camp was organized, and passes were issued.

April 29: Müller and Haulot met after sleeping for three or four hours. "In front of us, on the flagpoles, two big white flags are fluttering in the morning breeze. The last SS men have left during the night, and two groups of one hundred under the command of an officer have taken their place. . . . We gain access to the officer's office, and for the first time, two prisoners wearing caps enter the room that, until just a few hours ago, housed the worst torturers. They managed to get permission for the work details that were necessary to keep the camp going to leave the camp, though at first the officer refused to permit even one inmate to do so. The instructions of the camp committee "are conscientiously followed. The representatives of the various nations give a presentation of the situation in all barracks and interpret the measures that have been taken."

The diary of Haulot and Kuci contains a graphic description of what happened during the next hours: "The international camp committee has its regular meeting place in the library. . . . An enormous amount of work must be done: work details, special details to keep order, squads of the camp police charged with identifying all those who must be taken to task, a judicial commission to decide the fate of the murderers who have fallen into our hands, the procurement and distribution of food, and information service—all this has to be considered and regulated."[80]

Oskar Müller has described the definitive liberation as follows: "Toward 4:30 P.M. [on April 29—H.L.], the thunder of cannons came closer, and we heard machine-gun fire from the direction of Dachau. Suddenly grenades from an SS combat group in the southeast roared past the camp. Bursts of machine-gun fire whizzed over the camp, and some of them hit it.

Our next thought was this: Should we now implement our plan and break out of the camp? However, the American combat group that had been assigned to liberate our camp fought its way through, and at 5:15 a storm of joy and vibrancy greeted the great deed of liberation."[81]

Jules Jost, a clergyman from Luxembourg, gives the exact moment of the liberation as ten minutes later. As he remembers it, a jeep drove into the camp at 5:25. It was "driven by a German Jew who had escaped from Dachau earlier," and this released everyone from the "extreme tension" that had reached its climax around 4 P.M. because of the "prolonged full alert with screams of 'Everyone in the barracks!' "[82]

Haulot writes: "Now restraint, silence, stiff muscles, and physical and emotional tension are suddenly gone. Patrick [O'Leary, i.e. Guérisse—H.L.] and I are already outside and running toward the gate."[83] The American major to whom Guérisse and Haulot (two Belgians!) presented themselves gave them complete authority over the camp, while the American troops undertook to protect it from the outside.[84] The last victim was a Polish prisoner, felled by an SS man shooting from Tower B. "The Americans immediately brought down the crew on the tower."[85]

At the last roll call on the morning of April 29, the count was 32,335 inmates, including 385 women or children.[86] An appeal of that date lists a camp committee of fourteen, with Patrick O'Leary as chairman and the Pole Leon Malczewski as secretary.[87] A list made later contains the names of seventeen members. In addition to a Greek and a Norwegian, representing two nations with few inmates in the camp, the German senior camp inmate Müller was now a member, while the original list had contained an Austrian but no German (Berben 1968, 285). The hatred mentioned by Haulot and Kuci was evidently rooted not only in national conflicts, which may have caused the omission of a German representative from the list, even though the committee had always collaborated with Müller. Rabbi Max Eichhorn, who came to Dachau with American troops on April 30, mentions that Poles were hostile toward Jews, even Polish Jews.[88]

There were some similarities between the course of events at Dachau on April 29 and at Buchenwald on April 11. Nevertheless, there was no postwar legend about a "self-liberation of Dachau," and one reason may have been the fact that neither one nationality nor one political ideology dominated the leadership of the resistance organization in Dachau.

Three days before the liberation of Allach, a big satellite camp of Dachau, the SS man Gerhard Schmidt gave Jewish inmates, with whom he had already had a friendly contact, two machine guns with ammunition and told them that if need be he was ready to fight alongside them.[89] Notes made by the German Alfred Hübsch clearly indicate that there, too, national hatred, primarily animosity toward the Germans, erupted when the approach of American troops had diminished the authority of the camp administration. "Soon there was no discipline any longer. Everyone foresaw the breakdown, and no one obeyed the German block personnel anymore. What surprised me was the insolent and unruly behavior of the Polish inmates. . . . As early as April 24, there were severe attacks on the Germans, and some of them were badly manhandled. There were no deaths, but the foreign inmates no longer worried about the SS." Evacuations were still going on there. When the SS moved out during the night of April 27, "an international committee was formed to maintain order in the camp until the arrival of the liberation army. The watchtowers were manned by inmates carrying rifles." However, this committee was unable to keep several German inmates from being severely beaten on April 29, "the one day without non-German supervision. One of them, the senior block inmate Hans Pauli, was beaten to death."[90]

Since the liberation of the subsidiary camp Hallein took place even later, on May 5, a determined group of Hallein Communists, who had been in contact with Austrian inmates for a long time, made use of the favorable situation in the last days of the war. Agnes Primocic has given the following account: "The end of the Hitler period was approaching; the Americans were already supposed to be in Traunstein; and the SS had already moved out of Hallein but had left no food for the inmates. . . . One of them wrote me [via a secret route, of course—H.L.] to come to terms with the officer-in-charge. Wearing my Red Cross uniform, I rode my bicycle to the quarry where the barracks camp was located." In the office she threatened the officer-in-charge that "if anything happened to the political prisoners, he would bear the responsibility; in a few days the Americans would be here and he would be taken to task." The prisoner with whom Primocic was in contact was brought into the discussion, and they "finally persuaded the officer-in-charge to escort the inmates into town, provided that the mayor had no objections. . . ." Primocic prevailed, "and so we went to town, at 11 P.M., with forty-seven prisoners and the guards."[91] This feat saved this small subcamp from unforeseen developments in the very last hours and also from starvation.

In Neuengamme too, the approach of the end alerted those who had set themselves the task of counteracting the SS machinery of extermination. The Austrian Hans Schwarz recalls a sort of dress rehearsal of the international camp committee. On the evening of February 23, 1945, established groups of three and five assembled at prearranged places. "The eyes of the comrades were gleaming," writes Schwarz (Schway 1960—67, 81). The German Albin Lüdke, whose support of his fellow inmates has been generally recognized, puts it more conservatively when he writes: "There were contacts between individual groups, and there were discussions about the end of the camp." However, Neuengamme had information about the smashing of resistance groups in Sachsenhausen and Dachau because of informers and about the cruel consequences (after all, Schwarz was among those transferred to Neuengamme from Dachau), and so the inmates were cautious. "Security in the camp was among our assignments," writes Lüdke.[92] Rudi Goguel, another German Communist, believes that in the final analysis the secret organization would have been too weak and too irresolute to offer resistance (Goguel 1947, 176). True, a five-man military committee headed by the Russian Bukreyev was formed, but it was not possible to make contact with the approaching British troops. The arrival of a representative of the Swedish Red Cross opened up "new, hitherto unknown perspectives" (Goguel 1972, 43 ff.), and evidently these impeded a decision to act.

The actions of the camp administration resembled those of the commandants of other camps. To the last, there were executions and evacuations. Since the commandant of Neuengamme saw no place where he could have the inmates taken—Allied troops were approaching from the West, the South, and the East—he had them escorted to Lübeck, where they were put aboard ships. There "transports of prisoners arrived from Neuengamme every day between April 19 and 26. At the same time miserable processions of emaciated prisoners" from various satellite camps streamed there. A total of "almost eleven thousand persons" were loaded on the ships (Leroy/Vieville/Nevers/Linet n.d., 25).

The Germans retained in the main camp were inducted into the SS Dirlewanger Unit at the last moment, on April 29. The spokesmen for the Communist groups saw fit to have their names put on the list. However, some of them, among them Rudi Goguel, refused and thus even incurred a breach of party discipline (Goguel 1947, 174 ff.). Three hundred and eighty-six men were put into SS uniforms at that time, though they were not given arms. Most of these (or, in Hans Schwarz's more cautious formulation, "the majority") were political prisoners (So ging es zu Ende, How the end came 1960, 42).[93] Albin Lüdke, who, like Schwarz, left the camp in that way does not recall the prisoners being asked whether they wished to volunteer for the Dirlewanger Unit.[94]

These events overwhelmed the secret organization. Shortly before the evacuation, on April 18, there were heated discussions in the executive committee, which reportedly was composed of one Russian, one Pole, one Frenchman, one Belgian, and one Austrian.[95] Evidently representatives of other ethnic groups were included as well, for, as the Czech doctor Bohumil Došlik noted, "the Russians insisted on an armed coup d'état. . . . If we don't revolt as soon as possible and utilize the favorable moment of the camp administration's chaotic perplexity, we shall condemn the camp to death." However, the group had only three pistols and little ammunition. Moreover, the camp was still being guarded by a few companies (So ging es zu Ende 1960, 60; Goguel 1972, 45). Any decision would undoubtedly have been momentous, but none was made. "The very next day disaster struck the prisoners": the evacuation began.

The evacuees who had been placed on boats in Lübeck Bay formed an "actions committee" that strove to make contact with a captain (Goguel 1972, 45 ff.; So ging es zu Ende 1960, 62; Schätzle 1946, 45). Seven Russians were prepared to jump overboard from the largest ship, the Cape Arcona, in an effort to reach the shore and thereby the Allies, but this heroic attempt failed. Only the captain of one steamer refused to obey the orders of the SS and take his vessel out on the open sea, where every ship was being bombarded and sunk by the Allies, but unfortunately that boat was the smallest. The two others, the Cape Arcona and the Thielbek, put out to sea and were sunk on May 3. Only a very small number of prisoners were able to save themselves.

Those inducted into the SS were able to break out "in the general melee" that had confused the "real" SS on May 2 and establish contact with resistance groups in Hamburg. On May 5 British troops reached the empty camp (*So ging es zu Ende* 1960, 43, 67 ff.).

The situation in Mauthausen has been vividly characterized by Hans Maršàlek: "A chaotic confusion; hectic activity on the part of the SS in destroying documents and effacing the traces of their crimes; starvation rations for the inmates; cannibalism; more than a hundred deaths a day in the main camp, the tent camp, and the hospital; the danger of extermination hanging over all inmates: that was the situation in April 1945. . . . Those were days of fear, worry, and wondering whether the SS would carry out its threat to liquidate all prisoners. Hope alternately rose and waned. Many inmates became resigned, but on others the circumstances had a stimulating effect." As in the other camps, the SS did not give up its murderous intentions by any means. "The gas chamber and the contraption for shooting prisoners through the base of the skull were constantly in operation" (Maršàlek 1974, 236).

German prisoners were recruited in Mauthausen as well. "In mid-March more than 200 German and Austrian inmates, including those who had been imprisoned for a long time because of their political convictions, were called to the commandant's office and inducted into the SS. . . . They were isolated from the other inmates and released on April 14, 1945. . . . The members of the committee [of the resistance organization—H.L.] disagreed on how the prisoners forced into SS uniforms ought to behave. A minority demanded that release, uniforms, and weapons be rejected, but the majority believed that this would be tantamount to suicide" (Aktenvermerk 1979, 155 ff.). In an effort to thwart the plans of the SS to use these special units against inmates or as cannon fodder, the international committee instructed the forty-nine members of the Vienna fire brigade, who had been sent to Mauthausen in late March 1944, "the majority of whom were Socialists" (*Die Geschichte des Konzentrationslagers Mauthausen*) and about eighty other members of the resistance movement under the leadership of Pepi Kohl to join these special units. At the decisive moment these men were to aim their guns at their protectors" (Maršàlik n.d., 36). Pepi Kohl told the Austrian Fritz Kleinmann, who after his transfer from Auschwitz had managed to conceal the fact that he had been sent to the concentration camp for "racial" reasons, that he had to volunteer for the SS. "I was put in the training unit; they were looking for young men," writes Kleinmann. However, because he did not feel good about it, he acted in such a way that he was punished for sabotage and returned to the camp as a prisoner.[96]

According to Maršàlek, the men active in the resistance began to advocate joining these SS units around the middle of March. Since early in the month, there had been a number of rallies at which the camp administration urged the assembled Germans (as well as Austrians and Luxembourgers) to volunteer. Maršàlek points out that at first the executive-committee—"at that time consisting, more or less, of Kohl, London, and me; there was no firm organization as yet"—had a negative attitude.[97]

The SS proceeded in similar fashion at subsidiary camps. Ottokar Mĕřinský has described the consequences of this recruitment in the labor camp Linz III: "At first the Austrians and Germans with black and green markings were put in khaki uniforms and sent to the front. Some with red triangles came forward as well, and they too were given uniforms. This enraged the comrades, though no one could be sure that some of these men were not comrades acting under orders."[98]

To everyone's surprise a convoy of white vehicles with the insignia of the Red Cross appeared in Mauthausen one day. On April 22, 756 female prisoners, most of them French and Belgian, and sixty-seven men were called and told that these vehicles would take them to Switzerland.[99] The secret organization was alerted: "Was this part of an extermination plan? Was it a trick?" (Constante 1971, 223). Jean-Maurice Rubli, a Swiss physician who had come to Auschwitz with this convoy, has described the reaction of the prisoners: "That very night the guards herded the prisoners [selected for the transport—H.L.] together in the center of the camp. There was snow on the ground, and it was cold. The people thought they were being transported to the gas chambers. . . . It was deathly quiet. When the trucks arrived, I gave this order in French: 'Chauffeurs, get out!' An unforgettable tumult ensued: Now they believed it!"[100] Subsequently the Red Cross took charge of another 596 male prisoners, predominantly Frenchmen (Maršàlek 1974, 240). The resistance movement managed to smuggle some functionaries of other nationalities into this group—for example, Artur London, a Czech veteran of the Spanish Civil War who had been arrested in France as a member of the Résistance (Constante 1971, 224). After that, the Red Cross had to abandon its efforts, for the last routes to Switzerland were already blocked (Bouard 1954, 74).

Three days after the liberation, the German committee described the effect of this action as follows: "The return of French, Belgian, and Dutch comrades to their homelands rid all of us of a feeling of desolation and affected us like the liberating removal of a leaden weight that had oppressed us" (Gagern 1948, appendix).

The SS, however, saw to it that this euphoria was soon dampened. Aged and infirm prisoners were to be removed from the hospital section to make room for real patients, as the commandant put it. "In point of fact, they were slated to be murdered in the gas chamber." Those experienced in resistance, particularly the inmates who worked in the office, did all they could. "Between April 21 and 25, the SS killed 1,441 prisoners with Zyklon B gas, but 378 could be saved," writes Maršàlek (Maršàlek 1974, II/322). That man became more familiar with this rescue action than anyone else, for as camp clerk he had an important part in it.

Two days later, the SS struck again. Thirty-four Upper Austrian Communists, who had been sent to the camp in the fall of 1944 because of resistance activities, were scheduled to be executed—"to deprive the Allies of constructive forces in the Alpine regions," as Gauleiter [district chief] Eigruber put it in a telex. Making use of conflicts among SS men, some of whom had been conspiring with them for weeks, the inmates employed in the office were able to delay the presentation of the thirty-four men, whereupon Maršàlek notified the members of the international Mauthausen committee (which was already in existence at that time). A momentous decision had to be made—and quickly, for there was little time left: To what extent and in what way could the Upper Austrians be helped? Some members pleaded for an immediate general uprising. The Spaniard Manuel Razola has specified that the Czechs (with a few exceptions), the Russians, the Spaniards, and the Yugoslavs advocated an action by the military forces (Razola, Constante 1969, 135 ff.). The absolute majority, however, rejected this idea because such an uprising required longer preparation as well as the solution of many particular military and organizational problems. For one thing, there was not enough time, and for another, the prisoners as a whole were not ready to participate in a rebellion, because they knew that the liberation would start within a few days, and the SS no longer had the strength to kill all inmates. Finally, in a general uprising many thousands of victims could have been expected, for in the main camp and the hospital section alone there were around 10,000 patients who were incapable of participating in any action. Thus it was decided to enable those destined for death to escape during the night—the night that had been gained by the delaying tactics of the clerks. The Upper Austrians were given the weapons kept concealed in the office—"three pistols with bullets as well as six or eight French 'pineapple' hand grenades." However, "most of the condemned men refused to believe that they were to die such a short time before the liberation. . . . They were not strong enough to incur the risk of an escape." Even the final bit of advice— "to go to the hospital section right after the morning roll call, either individually or with the help of the clerks"—was taken by only one man. "The other thirty-three Upper Austrians were murdered in the gas chamber on April 28 at noon. . . . On the next day the machinery of the gas chamber was dismantled." (Maršàlek 1974, 240 ff.).

The impending end of the war and these dramatic events prompted the camp activists to develop an organization with a military orientation. There are conflicting reports about it. According to Spaniards, who had long taken the initiative in this area, 771 prisoners representing eight nations belonged to such an organization in early April; Russians were the most numerous group by far, and they were followed by Frenchmen and Spaniards. The leaders knew about Himmler's order to kill all inmates if the war was lost, and they were also aware of signs of decay within the SS; in addition to fanatics, there were some who wanted to save their skins. Many members of the guard at that time had been forced into the SS months earlier; in fact, some soldiers declared that they would side with the prisoners if they decided to resist. "Some offered to notify us of any suspicious preparations [on the part of the commandant's office—H.L.]" (Razola/Constante 1969, 148 ff.). This is how Hans Maršálek has described this: "The first plans in the main camp to form military units from Spanish, Czech, German, and Soviet Russian prisoners were discussed, devised, and implemented by veterans of the international brigades within the framework of their ethnic groups." Maršálek is cautious about the time: "Presumably the military unit of the Spaniards was formed in the first months of 1945, that of the Czechs in late April, and the military units of the Soviet Russians on May 5, 1945." Maršálek goes on to say that "the creation of underground military units was presumably discussed in 1945 by Spaniards and perhaps also by Poles in the hospital section and in Gusen I, and such a plan was implemented by Spaniards in late April." He also explains why there are divergent statements about these steps: "There were several completely independent plans for an uprising if a mass liquidation was intended; these plans had been developed by Spanish, Czech, and German veterans of the international brigades" (Maršálek 1974, II, 308 ff.). Elsewhere Maršálek points to additional reasons for a stepped-up activity: "The arrival of around 8,000 prisoners from the evacuated Auschwitz, including the underground leadership, as well as the depression caused among the SS by the defeats of the Wehrmacht gave the underground organization in Mauthausen renewed confidence and marked the beginning of a new stage in the underground struggle." Maršálek too emphasizes that the leadership was "everywhere assumed by the former Spanish freedom fighters" (Maršálek n.d., 28), and he summarizes the situation as follows: "In the last March days of 1945 an international Mauthausen committee was created in the main camp under the direction of Heinrich Dürmayer, an Austrian Communist [and veteran of Spain—H.L.] who had been evacuated from Auschwitz in late January" (Maršálek 1974, 265). Manuel Razola, the Spanish member of the executive committee, explains this choice by saying that the camp was located on Austrian territory and Austrians should therefore be given greater responsibility. In addition to

Heinrich Dürmayer, he mentions Maršàlek and Kohl (Razola/Constante 1969, 134).

Both the above-mentioned events and general developments have repeatedly been discussed. Since Mauthausen was the last camp to be liberated, the collapse of Hitler's armies determined these developments more clearly there than it did in other camps. The Russian Valentin Sakharov sums up his recollections of this final phase in these words: "Every day the international committee concerned itself with the question of when to begin the uprising. . . . The military members of some nations urged an immediate strike, independent of the international committee. With reference to the young inmates, the leader of the Spanish group espoused this view and motivated it by pointing out that, in case of an evacuation, the majority of the inmates would die anyway and that it was preferable to die more honorably in an open battle. A few comrades in the international committee were inclined to support him, but the majority were of the opinion that it was the main task of the illegal organization to keep the many thousands of prisoners alive and to preserve the party cadres. The international committee came to this decision: "We shall not allow ourselves to be evacuated. If the SS tries to start the evacuation or the mass extermination of the prisoners, we shall attack" (Sakharov 1961, 208).

As previously mentioned, there clearly were disagreements among those active in the resistance, and these were probably rooted in the problematical contacts among different ethnic groups. There are frequent reports about differences of opinion with Germans, among whom Franz Dahlem had great authority by virtue of his leadership role in the German Communist Party. The Russian Valentin Sakharov (Sakharov 1961, 122), the Luxembourger Pierre Grégoire, and the Pole Józef Cyrankiewicz (the most experienced organizer of resistance among those transferred from Auschwitz) have given an unreservedly positive picture of Dahlem's role in the underground organization.[101] Grégoire is a non-Communist, has often made critical remarks about Communists, and was surely not motivated by political solidarity, but other observers have made a more reserved judgment. Since Dahlem was exiled in France for a considerable period of time and spoke French, it was primarily French Communists who made contact with him. According to Octave Rabaté, the threat of reprisals caused Dahlem to oppose the formation of an organization (Bernadoc 1974, 263). Another Frenchman, Michel de Bouard, states that despite the urging of several French Communists, for a long time German comrades could not persuaded of the need to form an international organization. De Bouard stresses that Dahlem had previously given many proofs of his courage, and so his repeated rejection of that idea as crazy was surely not due to personal cowardice (Bernadoc 1974, 270). The Austrian Hans Maršàlek also recalls Dahlem's negative attitude and says that Dahlem insisted on German leadership if the various national groups formed an international organization. According to Maršàlek, it took a great deal of urging for Dahlem to agree to work with the international committee in April 1945.[102]

By that time virtually all other concentration camps had been liberated, and numerous satellite camps of Mauthausen, particularly the eastern ones, had been evacuated. The commandant saw no way of evacuating the prisoners, who had been driven out of other camps and were swamping Mauthausen. According to the Italian Vincenzo Pappalettera, the daily more noticeable activities of the prisoners, combined with the declining discipline of his troops, probably induced the commandant to abandon plans for the complete extermination of the inmates (Pappalettera 1972).

Finally, the SS leadership faced a further impediment. As a result of negotiations carried on by the central administration, another convoy of trucks sent by the International Red Cross arrived in Mauthausen on April 28. The leader of this transport, Louis Haefliger, carried a letter from the president of the Red Cross, which cited pledges from the central administraticn and demanded that the delegates of the Red Cross be allowed to "move about the camp freely and make contact with all foreign inmates" (Croix Rouge 1947, 85). While Commandant Franz Ziereis was waiting for a reply to his telegraphic inquiry from his superior Ernst Kaltenbrunner, Haefliger took lodgings in the vicinity of the camp. After waiting for three days, Haefliger managed to be given the room of an SS officer in the camp area. During the next days, he tried to effect an improvement in the catastrophic sanitary conditions and get more food, and he was also able to have a discussion with the commandant and the physician Josef Podlaha, a Czech inmate. Under the pretext of needing to have various things made or repaired, he was able to make contact with other inmates as well (Croix Rouge 1947, 137 ff.).

Hitler's suicide and the news of the rapid advances of Allied armies in the West and the East had an effect on the guards of the last intact Nazi concentration camp. "During the night of May 2, some SS men left the camps Mauthausen and Gusen in civilian clothes; others left on the morning of May 3 in groups and in uniform. . . . Some SS leaders [including Commandant Ziereis—H.L.] hid out in the Alpine area. Together with the military unit the SS had formed from prisoners a few weeks earlier [and given ammunition for the first time on May 3—H.L.], a very small number of troops took a stand against the advancing Russian units east of Mauthausen. They never joined battle" (Maršàlek 1974, 267 ff.). The majority of the SS men surrendered to the Americans advancing from the West.[103] Units of the Vienna fire brigade under the command of Captain

Kern undertook the guarding of Mauthausen and Gusen.[104] On May 3, the Spaniard Ramon Bargueño, who was employed in the Mauthausen jail, was ordered to carry suitcases of SS officers out of the camp. "A Wehrmacht captain remained behind to be in charge of the jail. When we returned, he started crying and said that he was not responsible for what had happened in the jail. We demanded that he give us his pistol and leave. . . . Then we opened all cells and told the inmates that they were free and could return to their blocks in the camp" (Razola/Constante 1969, 145).

The departure of the SS "changed the atmosphere and the situation with the speed of lightning." Heinrich Kodré has furnished a graphic description of the situation on the afternoon of May 3: "No one did any work. The inmates formed groups everywhere, and the camp appeared to be breaking up. The only thing still functioning was the guard, and we also got the same food as before, that lousy grub."

Maršàlek supplements this account when he writes: "For several days some members of the international committee had been meeting in the office. . . . The contact between the camp clerks and the former inmates who now were part of the SS was completely disrupted on May 3, 1945." In a nocturnal shootout, one inmate was injured. This and the general disintegration prompted the international committee to send two representatives, Dürmayer and Maršàlek, to Captain Kern on May 4, and these men "asked him to turn the administration of the camp over to them. On the afternoon of the same day, members of the international committee attempted to take over the internal administration of the camp" (Maršàlek 1974, II/328). At that time Kern agreed that members of the fire brigade would not enter the camp anymore;[105] however, the Vienna fire brigade continued to guard the camp" (Maršàlek 1974, II/328). No detail went out of the camp on that day (Mersch 1970, 176; Frieden 1970–75, 168). The first impressions of a prisoner not tied to the leadership of the resistance movement have been given by the Luxembourger Metty Mirkes: "There was general confusion, and it was even worse in the roll-call area. There the Spanish fighters [evidently meaning the Spaniards who had fought on the side of the republic—H.L.] began to settle accounts with some SS men and senior block inmates who were known to have committed atrocities in the camp. . . . Men were hanged and shot. . . . Our senior block inmate had disappeared" (Mirkes 1970, 181).

According to Maršàlek, "the military units of the prisoners, some of them armed, formed at various places in the camp and remained on the alert. Spaniards put up banners over the main gate of the base camp" that said: "*Los españoles antifascistas saludan a las fuerzas liberadoras*" [The Spanish anti-Fascists greet the armies of the liberators] (Maršàlek 1974,

268). This banner had been prepared three days earlier by the Spanish organization (Constante 1971, 228 ff.).

On the morning of May 5, Louis Haefliger, the delegate of the Red Cross, decided to meet the Americans in Linz together with the SS officer whose room he was sharing in order to guide them to the camp as quickly as possible. This was done and led first to the liberation of Gusen and later of the main camp. "Around noon on that glorious day, we first heard the loud noise of motors from the fog-covered access road and then . . . what then slowly emerged into the sunlight were a white automobile carrying Haefliger and two American armored reconnaissance cars! These vehicles stopped near the hospital section. At the same moment, the gates of the first-aid station were flung open and a stream of inmates—hundreds upon hundreds of men, women, and children—surged toward the vehicles . . . half-starved creatures, living skeletons. It was as if a mass grave had opened." Maršàlek, usually a sober chronicler, remembered that outburst of emotion when he wrote this (Maršàlek 1974, II/330). The American armored cars "remained in the camp area for an hour or two and then rejoined their units. . . . The entire area of the camps Mauthausen and Gusen became a no man's land," and those two were the last concentration camps of the SS state to be liberated.[106]

To Heinrich Kodré we owe a vivid description of this dramatic moment: "Then there were great shouts of joy. . . . The guard at the Jourhaus opened the gate and an American armored scout car drove in. . . . An officer got out and ordered all members of the camp guard to assemble. They came with their weapons from the Jourhaus, the camp, and the watchtowers. While this was happening, I was able to observe some prisoners walk past the Americans and out of the Jourhaus gate and others mounting the watchtowers. I saw one inmate come down with a machine gun. Meanwhile the guards laid down their arms and ammunition. . . . From that moment on the camp was without guards."

Maršàlek goes on: "When the crew of the armored car was about to drive off, Dürmayer talked to one of them in English and asked the Americans to stay in the camp and protect the liberated inmates. However, after one of the soldiers had telephoned his commanding officer, the crew was ordered to continue its interrupted reconnaissance work, and so the American armored vehicles left the Mauthausen main camp after a stay of two or three hours" (Maršàlek 1974, II/331).

"We have weapons from the arsenal, the SS storage rooms, and the Vienna police," wrote the Spaniards Razola and Constante (Razola/Constante 1969, 147). According to Hans Maršàlek, probably the greatest expert on this development, "several nonpartisan national committees were formed in the days of the liberation [May 3 to 7—H.L.], and they sent elected representatives to the international Mauthausen committee, which meant several turnovers in the personnel of this committee." Maršàlek names twelve nations that were represented on that committee "among others." Upon instructions from the international Mauthausen committee, the military units of the prisoners, which occupied strategic points in the vicinity of Mauthausen and Gusen, were under the command of the Austrian officer Heinrich Kodré from May 5 on (Maršàlek 1974, 265 ff.). Kodré has described how this came about: "I believe that Dr. Dürmayer came to see me that evening [May 5—H.L.]. I had never met him before. He asked me to take charge of security in the camp since there was danger that the SS or the Wehrmacht would return and massacre the inmates. He also told me that the bridge in the town of Mauthausen was being guarded by a troop of Spanish comrades who had combat experience from the Spanish Civil War and had been provided with arms" (Maršàlek 1974, II/332).

The Spaniard Mariano Constante has supplemented this report with a description of events in the first hour of freedom: "Total confusion reigned in the camp, and thus it was necessary to restore order immediately. Fortunately we had a well-organized and disciplined military structure. All men were at their posts and expected orders from the staff. As soon as the Americans left, our military leaders met for a discussion; it was the first such meeting. Decisions were made in a few minutes. . . . Where the SS had ruled a few days earlier, our staff was now in charge. In less than two hours we had the situation completely under control" (Constante 1971, 229 ff.). The Spaniard Juan de Diego, who had worked in the office, was the first person to make a telephone call from liberated Mauthausen. He is among those who have emphasized the contributions of the resistance movement after the liberation: "They guarded the storage rooms and took care of the sick."[107]

Others remember chaotic conditions (Croix Rouge 1947, 142; *Aktenvermerk* 1979, 165). In Gusen, where there was no disciplined organization to stop excesses, chaos, lynch law, and pillaging were particularly rampant (Razola/Constante 1969, 165). The Luxembourger Eugène Thomé remembers that "human dignity, which had been so severely suppressed, led to an explosive settlement of accounts with capos, senior block inmates, and criminals" (Thomé 1970, 192). Michel de Bouard has named several capos who were "summarily executed" at that time as well as others who managed to escape (Bouard 1962, 67).

The further activity of the liberated inmates is outside the scope of this study. However, we must briefly discuss military actions of the inmates of Mauthausen because they took place in the vacuum between the liberation on May 5 and the final arrival of American units.

Jean Brausch, a Luxembourger, has provided a description of his experiences. The members of the secret organization "stormed the arsenal, where there also was a repair shop for arms. Most of them were Spaniards, front-line veterans, and they helped themselves to heavy arms. I, a layman, took an Italian carbine. We formed a guard chain around the camp. Down at the railroad station, two truckloads of armed prisoners guarded a carriage containing sugar. The Germans had crossed the Danube to get their hands on that sugar. There was a fight, and the prisoners emerged victorious. Thus the Germans no longer dared to go up the hill [on which the camp was situated—H.L.], and we in the camp were spared a fight. Every ten meters around the camp there was a man with a rifle or a machine gun" (Brausch 1970, 180).

Maršàlek has given an account from the vantage point of those who led the armed units: "It was important to act quickly.... Reconnaissance patrols were dispatched, and at the Danube bridge in Mauthausen prisoner units fought against strong SS formations" (Maršàlek n.d., 44). A Spanish unit that appeared to have been heavily involved in these battles suffered one casualty, a man named Badian, and three wounded men (Razola/Constante 1969, 147). The report written by this group about these events on May 16, a few days after the liberation, is even more vivid than later accounts. After the arsenals, the garages, and the food-storage depots had been occupied, all means of transport were confiscated and units were sent to the town of Mauthausen to set up checkpoints on the roads and occupy the post office, the Danube bridge, and the landing. Unfortunately the telegraph office was not operational. By the end of the day, the camp had been secured. Fifteen heavy machine guns, a few dozen bazookas, eighty submachine guns, pistols, a few thousand hand grenades, and more than 3,000 rifles were available for defense. These weapons were handled by 3,500 disciplined and efficient comrades.... There were also a few small uncontrolled groups that did some pillaging, but they were disarmed during the night and interned in the camp. The Russians shot three of their own who had misbehaved in farmhouses while drunk. The leadership received information all night (Razola/Constante 1969, 163 ff.). These announcements, which were written on forms the SS had used for telex messages, have been preserved.[108] From the same room in which Commandant Ziereis and his staff had until recently devised their extermination plans, Major Pirogov and Colonel Kodré now issued instructions to the combatant units of the inmates" (Maršàlek n.d., 46). At 3:30 P.M. on May 6, Kodré acceded to the request of the Russian major Andrei Pirogov and turned the leadership of the armed prisoners over to him (Maršàlek 1974, II/333).

The situation in neighboring Gusen, with which telephone communication could be established, took a different turn. The lack of a disciplined organization caused the complete disintegration of more than 20,000 people. The food supply had been plundered. According to the above-mentioned report of the Spanish group, Poles, who were in the majority, and some hated capos got hold of the weapons turned in by the guards and terrorized the camp. There were dead and injured people. Miguel, the head of the Spanish group in the main camp, urged the Polish leaders to form an international organization and restore order, pointing out that this was the only way to assure the delivery of food to Gusen. This and threats had the desired effect. In the morning nearly all Russians, Czechs, Spaniards, Frenchmen, and Yugoslavs left Gusen and placed themselves under the protection of the main camp (Razola/Constante 1969, 165 ff.).

In an Order Concerning the Regulation of Military Authority that was issued on May 6 we read: "To maintain order and safety in the camp and to make it tactically secure, the national groups will form appropriate units. . . . The national groups will appoint the leaders of these units. . . . The heads of the national associations will provide each member with a pass entitling him to bear arms."[109]

SS men were captured, German criminals who had blood on their hands from their time as inmates were executed, attacks on the bridge—the nerve center of the camp area's defenses—were repulsed, and the military leadership was reorganized. At 6:30 P.M. on May 6, American units reached the camp and a little later the town of Mauthausen. This marked the end of the vacuum (Razola/Constante 1969, 168 ff.). The various national committees sent greetings and public appeals all over the world.[110]

In the satellite camp Linz III, whose inmates worked in the Hermann Göring Works in Linz, all political activities ceased for a considerable period of time after the factory was bombed on July 25, 1944. This bombardment caused great losses among the prisoners as well, "because the rest of those who had escaped with their lives had been scattered." In the spring of 1945, however, Russians, Czechs, Poles, Frenchmen, Yugoslavs, and Italians managed to band together again, and of course they concerned themselves with the question of "how to behave upon the approach of the liberators." Contact was made with foreign workers in the plant, and it was agreed that they were to aid the prisoners during an evacuation of the camp. There, too, the guards included old soldiers who had been forced to join the SS. "A relationship of mutual trust developed between a majority of the new guards and us." One of the guards assured a Czech inmate: "When the time comes, I shall give you my rifle and pistol. I've had enough of this crap."[111] By late April, work details were no longer leaving the camp (Aktenvermerk 1979, 167).

"The time came during the night of May 4. At 3 A.M., the alarm sounded; the block leaders came into the camp and shouted 'Line up for roll call!' In

accordance with our instructions, we stayed in the block, and those who
wanted to leave it were stopped. . . . The representatives of the various
nations met in Block 3. . . . It was decided not to leave the camp until 7
o'clock"—and even this only on condition that food was given out first.
"Half an hour later everything was granted." The approximately 4,000
inmates were evacuated to a forest on the outskirts of Linz, where an
American vanguard arrived in the afternoon. However, the Americans
disarmed only the SS leaders and not the guards, who took the inmates
back to the Linz camp. "There those comrades who had stayed behind with
the sick people fought against Hitler youths and some SS men. . . . After we
had arrived as reinforcements, it was easy to repulse the bandits who were
shooting into the camp, but our side had three dead and several wounded
men."[112] Thus this satellite camp too was finally liberated.

The Luxembourger Albert Raths has given the following account of the
liberation of the subcamp Loiblpass on the day of the German capitulation: "Hidden Tito troops appeared, and a brief battle ensued. The Polish
and French inmates attacked the SS from the rear. There were dead and
wounded people. The overpowered SS men were mercilessly shot" (Raths
1970, 190).

The liberation of the satellite camp Ebensee was the most dramatic of
all. A fanatic to the end, the officer-in-charge filled most of the positions in
the camp with German inmates who were willing to do his bidding; as the
Luxembourger Jean Majerus put it, the two senior camp inmates were
"known as unscrupulous murderers." The camp police, which was augmented toward the end, was also composed of criminal bullies (*Letzeburger zu Mauthausen* 1970, 207). As usual, the most accurate index of the
situation is the number of casualties in this camp, which even in the final
weeks was overcrowded because of transfers from other subsidiary camps
that had been evacuated. There were thirty deaths in August 1944 (Lafitte
1970, 351), and 4,547 people died in April 1945 (Bárta 1966). There was
unimaginable misery, but those with enough strength to think of organizing resistance had reason for hope. The young Czech Drahomír Bárta, who
was working in the office, the Yugoslav camp interpreter Hrvoje Mac-
anovič, and the Frenchman Jean Laffitte headed such an organization, and
the Russian major Vladimir Sokolov (whose camp name was Kostev) was
responsible for military preparations. This hope was based on the fact that
members of the Wehrmacht,—as in other camps, these men had been
assigned to Ebensee as guards during the final phase—had not only established contact with inmates but had also smuggled weapons into the camp
for their use. There are conflicting reports about the extent of this smuggling, which was accomplished by Josef Poltrum, a noncommissioned officer. Drahomír Bárta believes that "presumably seven revolvers and several

hand grenades" came into the possession of the organizations in this way (Bárta 1966). The Austrian physician Rudolf Pekar—who originally cared for the civilian workers in the plant to which the prisoners had been assigned and later extended his medical care to the inmates of the camp as well—wrote after the liberation of Ebensee that Poltrum and he managed to "regularly get weapons and food into the camp."[113] He remembers that a secret organization developed along clandestine lines comprised members of the Luftwaffe company and of the labor camps as well as inmates of the concentration camp. In addition to Poltrum and Payrleitner, he names eight soldiers who were prepared to help the prisoners.[114] According to Jean Laffitte, "Poltrum had a secret organization of forty soldiers" (Lafitte 1970, 360). Shortly after the liberation, the Pole Wacław Małecki confirmed that Pekar "inconspicuously [brought] bread, weapons, and news into the camp."[115] It goes without saying that this greatly enhanced the self-confidence of those who were bent on resisting.

Bárta has described the dramatic situation as follows: "In the late afternoon of May 4, Poltrum's group warned us that plans were being made to prepare the tunnel in which inmates were working for detonation." During the night of May 4, Anton Ganz, the officer-in-charge, suddenly appeared in the office. Bárta then entered in his diary: "At night Ganz in the office between 2 and 3 o'clock. In the morning roll call; we are supposed to leave for the mine." According to a later supplement, "his behavior was unusual; he was pale and trembling. He spoke in a surprisingly gentle tone of voice that we had never heard from him before." The inmates were supposed to go into the tunnel, for his units would defend themselves to the last man against the approaching American troops. This might place the camp under fire, whereas the tunnels would offer the inmates certain protection.

After officer-in-charge Anton Ganz had left the camp, the leaders of the secret organization met and immediately decided to persuade everyone before the morning roll call not to obey his instructions to go to the tunnels. This decision was made very quickly.

Then came the decisive moment. On May 5, around 10,000 prisoners showed up for the morning roll call; another 6,000 were in the hospital. The officer-in-charge was accompanied by the block leaders, and behind him SS men with submachine guns stood in a semicircle. Ganz ordered the inmates to seek protection in the tunnels, and the camp interpreter repeated this in several languages. In response there were resolute cries of "No, no!" "It was a great moment, such as we had never before experienced in the camp. For the first time masses of inmates refused to obey; it seemed as if the prisoners were no longer prisoners at that moment."

Ganz stood motionless for a long time—pale, perplexed, and silent. He was utterly astonished. After a brief deliberation with his people, he said that the prisoners need not go into the tunnels if they did not want to. Then the SS men walked out of the camp, and in the afternoon they left the camp area. Poltrum's group stayed. The international committee emerged intact from its underground existence. Criminal inmates who held positions were removed, and here, too, there were actions based on lynch law. "It was a horrendous, merciless onslaught that burst forth like flood water and could not be stopped."

On the next day, May 6, American armored vehicles arrived at the camp gate at 2:50 P.M. Bárta wrote in his diary: "A scene full of joy and rapture. The masses are storming the SS barracks. Plundering, shooting, fraternizing with the population. . . ." (Bárta 1966).

The last National Socialist concentration camp was liberated. Since then these camps have been part of history. The resistance of the prisoners, which was accomplished under conditions that do not lend themselves to any comparison, has also become a chapter in modern history, and not the least important one.

25

A PERSONAL WORD IN
CONCLUSION

In describing the resistance of those imprisoned in National Socialist concentration camps I have endeavored to use all accessible sources, and, wherever possible, to consult eyewitnesses concerning conflicting statements in order to make the total picture as objective as possible. I have drawn on my own experiences only if there would have been a gap without them. I wanted to prevent these experiences from adding a subjective note to the total picture, and they have, in any case, been preserved in my firsthand report *Die Stärkeren* [The Stronger].

However, after presenting the resistance in all its problematical aspects, I would like to add some personal conclusions of general significance.

My experiences relate to three concentration camps. In Dachau, where I was from May 1941 to August 1942, I was in contact with an Austrian resistance group. In Neuengamme (October to December 1944), the resistance organization established contact with me, and in the subsidiary camps Borgward Works Bremen (August to October 1944) and Lerbeck (December 1944 to April 1945) I—along with friends—strove to make improvements. I managed to engage in the most effective activity in Auschwitz (August 1942 to August 1944), from May 1943 on as part of the leadership of the international Combat Group.

This list is not given to highlight my contributions. Rather, these data are intended to show that it would be quite wrong to assume that those with resistance activity to their credit were exceptionally courageous and self-sacrificing. My example can show that favorable circumstances enabled some men to engage in activities that were not possible for others less fortunate.

On May 1, 1941, I arrived in Dachau together with many other Austrian veterans of the Spanish Civil War. For over two years, we had been interned in camps in southern France, and only internees who live together day and night can get to know one another as well as we did. We also acquired a certain experience in acting jointly without allowing the camp administration to get a line on such organized activity. In Dachau, some of us encountered acquaintances who had already gained camp experience. For example, right after being admitted to the camp, I was accosted by Hans Schwarz, who had been politically active in the same Vienna district as I (and whom I was to meet again in Neuengamme at the end of my journey through the concentration camps). We had just come out of the bath, where our whole bodies had been shaved, and we had already received our first beatings. Schwarz and others from the clothing-depot detail were distributing underwear and prisoner's garb. He gave me better clothes, and, to keep the SS guard from noticing our conversation, whispered that I should tell him my number (so that he could later more easily find me in the block for new arrivals) and who had come with me. Other prisoners also met people they knew. These brief encounters mitigated the shock of arrival, which the SS wanted to exacerbate by particularly brutal treatment. The general expressions of support from the old political prisoners that greeted us, the first large group of veterans of the Spanish Civil War to arrive in Dachau, did us good morally and in some instances helped us concretely as well.

Kind words and pieces of bread were not all we received. Old camp hands told us that the important thing was to survive the first weeks without being worn down by the constant drills, controls, harassment of every kind, beatings, and humiliations. They told us that they would do their best to keep us from having to stay too long in the arduous labor details to which we, like new inmates generally, were assigned after we were released from the block for new arrivals. I was assigned to a work unit whose members were harnessed like horses to a wagon which, among other things, hauled dead bodies to the crematorium every day. However, I spent only a few weeks in this detail; then my friends saw to it that the prisoner making Work Assignments—a German Communist who had been interned for many years—presented me to his SS boss, who had had a request for a clerk from the prison hospital. My high number gave the SS man pause, for it told him that I was a new arrival. However, the Work Assignments man told him that no other inmates were available who had the proper qualifications—the ability to spell correctly, use a typewriter, and take shorthand. He had prepared me in advance to answer the SS man's questions in such a way that I made a positive impression. With surprising speed, I was placed on a detail with exceptionally good working conditions. Because we also slept in the infirmary, we were not subject to the harassing checks in the blocks. We did not need to show up for the morning and evening roll calls, and we had a roof over our heads as we did our physically undemanding work. To my mind, the greatest advantage offered by our detail was the fact that our work, if done well, benefited the patients. I regarded it as my task to help sick people whenever I could, for the secret organization had helped me so quickly and so effectively. In the infirmary, I also came into contact with old political prisoners who worked there. Thanks to these acquaintances I was able to help some comrades outside the hospital as well. Thus I managed to get Peter Loisl, an Austrian veteran of the Spanish Civil War who was my friend at the time, placed on a good labor detail. He was in bad physical condition from the heavy labor to which he had been assigned. Together with others, the two of us constituted a kind of leadership which, in concert with other Austrians (of whom I still fondly remember Pepi Lauscher), endeavored to take care of the "Spaniaken" (Spainies), as we were called.

If I had arrived in Dachau without company and had not met any acquaintances there, I would today not be able to point to some successes that could be wrung out of the camp administration, though this would not have made me any less courageous.

The fortunate circumstances that were so beneficial to me in Dachau had a favorable effect later on as well. I was a clerk in the department of internal medicine of the Dachau prisoners' hospital, which was housed in Block 3. The head nurse of this department, a young Sudeten German with a red triangle, enjoyed the privileges connected with his position, but he cared very little about the patients in his block. The SS doctors who headed this department changed frequently. Some only made sure that there was no dust anywhere; others saw only patients with illnesses in which they were interested, and they conducted experiments on them; and a third kind rarely set foot in our station.

One day a new SS doctor was assigned to the internal section, and he really made rounds, going from bed to bed—something that I had never experienced before. This gave me an opportunity to put pressure on the lazy head nurse. I conscientiously took down all orders of that SS doctor, whose name was Eduard Wirths, and repeated them the next time he came. For this reason, the head nurse could not risk ignoring any of them. Of course, Wirths could not have known my motivation, but he remembered me as a conscientious clerk. After I had been transferred to Auschwitz (I have already described the circumstances), Wirths, who had been sent to Neuengamme, was transferred there as well. Since the SS clerks were not up to his standards, he requested German inmates as clerks. There was no German clerk in the prisoners' hospital, and so I was sent to him. He immediately recognized me and appointed me as his clerk. Since his basic attitude differed markedly from that of other doctors in SS uniform, the daily contact with him offered me extraordinary opportunities to exert some influence.

Before my transfer to Auschwitz, Pepi Lauscher had told me to contact the Austrian Ernst Burger in that camp. I never found out how Lauscher knew about him, but I did look for Burger and soon located him. He put me in touch with a cell that was trying to counteract the murderous activities of the SS. After combining with a Polish group around Cyrankiewicz, it later constituted the core of the Combat Group Auschwitz. If Wirths had not made me his clerk, or if the physician whose secretary I became had had the SS doctors' usual attitude toward the murderous goings-on in the extermination camp, I would not have met Burger and could not possibly have achieved the useful things that were facilitated by these fortunate circumstances.

Thanks to the routine I had acquired as an experienced inmate, I was able to perform key functions in the small subsidiary camps of Neuengamme in Bremen and Lerbeck—in Bremen as Work Assignments and in Lerbeck as roll-call clerk—and use my position, together with friends, to wring some easements out of the inexperienced camp administration. After our Bremen camp had been destroyed by bombs on October 12, 1944, and we had been transferred to the main camp of Neuengamme, the young Belgian André Mandryckxs, whose very beneficial activities have already been detailed, quickly made contact with me. From the documents he had been able to examine in the office, he had learned that I was in protective custody as a veteran of the Spanish Civil War. This had made him anxious to meet me, and a first brief conversation sufficed, for people in the camp learned to make quick judgments. Mandryckxs got me transferred to the office of the Work Assignments, which the resistance organization of Neuengamme had turned into a solid base.

The comrades wanted to have me there as a reinforcement, but I believed that in the final phase everyone should try anything to escape from the camp, for experience had shown that the SS would attempt to eliminate all eyewitnesses to their crimes before the arrival of the Allied armies. Albin Lüdke, the leading man in both the Work Assignments and the resistance, did not share my view, but he did obtain warmer winter clothes for me when a transport to the small subcamp Lerbeck was put together and I assigned myself to it. There I was able to prepare my escape in such a way that I wore two suits at the evacuation of that camp—my inmates' uniform and under it clothes that were barely recognizable as prisoners' garb. On April 11, I fled from the Salzwedel switchyard together with a Bavarian friend. This, too, worked out only because, unlike our foreign fellow prisoners, as Germans we were not constantly kept in sealed freight carriages. Like most Germans, Lüdke was assigned to a Dirlewanger Unit in the final days of Neuengamme, and together with the majority of the other non-Germans, André Mandryckxs was herded on board the ships that were bombed and sunk in Lübeck Bay on May 3. This was also the fate of the evacuation transport from which I had escaped. I never saw any of these men again.

This brief summary indicates that uncommonly favorable conditions permitted me to do useful work in the Nazi concentration camps and thereby keep from becoming demoralized. Without the above-mentioned chain of lucky accidents, even the best of intentions and the courage to incur any risk would have availed little. And in any case, as a "German," I had access to many things that were unattainable to a non-German. I believe that similar documentation could be added for all others who were able to play an important part in the resistance.

It would therefore be a great injustice if one presumed to divide the inmates into those who accepted their fate without resistance—that is, allowed themselves to be led like sheep to the slaughter—and an elite clearly distinct from the great masses that continued its struggle against National Socialism even in a concentration camp. Whether someone was emotionally broken and physically destroyed by the atmosphere in the camp often depended on what elementary prerequisites for action or rebellion he encountered. Sometimes a virtual accident—meeting like-minded persons, gaining camp experience, surviving the period of permanent hunger that rendered thinking impossible—could transform a spineless and despairing person into a resolute resister.

As chance would have it, my case can also be used to show that successful resistance activities have frequently remained unknown even if those involved have survived. When in November 1943 the new commandant of Auschwitz ordered the cessation of the worst acts of terror as well as of the selections of infirm inmates, the camp breathed a sigh of relief. However, in January of the following year, Jews already in the camp were subjected to such a selection. On behalf of the Combat Group, I urged Wirths to intervene with the commandant in this matter, for we had reason to believe that this selection had been made without his knowledge. In a report I wrote in the winter of 1947–48, when this episode was still fresh in my mind, I included a brief account of the result of the conversation between the doctor and the commandant as given me by the former on the next day: "The commandant knew about the transport [of those selected for the gas chamber]. It was not done behind his back, Langbein, as you believe. The order for this action came directly from Berlin. From the Work Assignments, which had received information that there are too many prisoners in the camp who are not fully fit for work."

Thus our intervention seems to have failed in this case. Many years later, when I was gathering material for this study and discussed this episode with Cyrankiewicz, his recollection of it was the same as mine. He later attempted to procure the letters that he sent to the Polish underground organization from the camp, and a recapitulative report contains this more detailed account of this episode:

"The Jews are to be selected for gassing. More than 800 have been selected in the hospital building, and over 300 in the camp. We agree with Hermann that it is necessary to intervene. Hermann will speak with the SS doctor." The latter refers to "explicit orders from Berlin" and requests arguments he can use with the commandant. "He receives the following: 1. Panic in the camp. The Poles believe that after the Jews it will be their turn. 2. People will avoid the hospital, because there they run the greatest risk of being selected for gassing, and the infections will spread throughout the camp, which will decrease production. In a word, arguments to fit the mentality of the recipients. . . . After some time the SS doctor returns to his office and tells Hermann, "The commandant gives his approval. Selections will be limited to Jews with incurable illnesses.' " Finally all 300 of those selected in the camp were released from the block in which they had been kept in isolation. "In front of the block, a large number of other Jews, many of them sons and brothers of the selectees. They can't believe their eyes. . . . On the next day another examination in the hospital of those destined for gassing. Of the more than 800 selectees [from the hospital] only 300 are certified as being incurably ill."

Thus the Combat Group managed to save the lives of 800 comrades, at least for the time being. Cyrankiewicz and I were involved in this action, but we forgot its result. How many other successful resistance actions must remain unmentioned because the onrush and jumble of the many events in the camp caused those involved to forget the details and because there are no written documents from that period to bear witness?

If a person managed to become involved in a resistance movement, this meant additional risks for him, but such an activity also provided strong moral support by helping the prisoner overcome the paralyzing feeling of being helplessly at the mercy of an all-powerful, abysmally evil force.

This helped me a great deal during my four years in Nazi concentration camps, and most of all where moral support was of the greatest necessity— in the extermination camp Auschwitz. When our Combat Group there, which had many failures, was able to influence the destiny of the camp, we knew that we were no longer mere objects in that "univers concentrationnaire," in the hermetically sealed world created by the SS in which its misanthropic ideology about members of a master race and persons not worthy of living was to achieve an absolute triumph. We knew that we would not allow ourselves to be broken and would knowingly incur additional risks to pass muster before ourselves as active subjects. We knew that we would not let ourselves be deprived of our natural human feelings.

Die Stärkeren [The Stronger] is the title I gave to my autobiographical account that is based on these feelings.

National Socialist theory and practice, which justified and executed the mass murder of entire peoples on the grounds of "race," cannot be compared with the ideologies of other Fascist or totalitarian regimes any more than the concentration camps of the National Socialists can be compared with camps in other countries. Thus a study of the laws governing life in the world of these concentration camps, which was isolated by electrically charged barbed wire, is important for all those who see a need to combat tendencies pointing in a direction that made the creation of extermination camps in twentieth-century central Europe possible.

It is good to know that this closed world ruled by a misanthropic spirit was not dominated exclusively by an absolute contempt for mankind based on the elimination of all natural inhibitions and the arousal of evil instincts. In that world, defenseless human beings who were at the mercy of seemingly insuperable powers mustered the strength to resist them nevertheless.

Our knowledge of death and life in the Nazi concentration camps would be incomplete without this information, but this is not the only reason for providing it. The main reason for having this knowledge is to derive hope from it that even in extreme situations humaneness can be stronger than inhumaneness.

I undertook this work to present this as objectively and irrefutably as possible.

Notes

2. THE CONCENTRATION CAMPS FROM 1938 TO 1945

1. Author's conversation with Harry Naujoks, November 3, 1973.
2. Heinz Junge, "Gab's im KZ Kämpfe zwischen 'Rot' und Grün'? [Was there in the concentration camps a struggle between Red and Green?]" In *Sachsenhausen-Information* No. 73, Dortmund, May 20, 1973.
3. In Lienau, the name is given as Ernst Guggenhahn, but I use the name as it appears on the transport list preserved by the International Search Service at Arolsen. On February 22, 1945, Guckenham was reported as deceased.
4. Alfred Hübsch, "Die Insel des Standrechts: Geheimaufzeichungen des Pförtners von Dachau [The island of martial law: Secret records of the Dachau gatekeeper]," unpublished (Dachau Museum), p. 184.
5. Karl Ludwig Schecher, "Rückblick auf Dachau [Dachau in retrospect]," unpublished (Dachau Museum).
6. Selbmann writes that they owe their survival to "this solidarity of the 'green' camp functionaries" (Selbmann 1969, 367).
7. Order No. 1/41 of the commandant's office of Natzweiler, April 28, 1941 (Red Cross International Search Service, Arolsen).
8. On July 15, 1937, 149 inmates of Sachsenhausen, including fifty-two political prisoners, were transferred to Buchenwald in order to help develop that camp, and after a few days they were followed by criminal and political prisoners from other camps (Drobisch 1968, 12).
9. Author's conversation with Albin Lüdke, November 4, 1973.
10. The information about discharges from Buchenwald was taken from "Zahlenmässige Entwicklung des Konzentrationslagers Buchenwald [numerical development of the concentration camp Buchenwald] 1937–1945" by Gerhard Harig and Max Mayr, unpublished manuscript (in the possession of Mayr). The information about releases from Buchenwald was taken from the chronological table on page 326.
11. Franz Hammer writes that Neubauer and Stoecker, together "with other reliable comrades," formed the political core, and he cites Stefan Heymann, who states that under Neubauer "the system of our party groups was created the way it remained in Buchenwald until the end" (Hammer 1956, 76; *Buchenwald* 1960, 93 ff.).
12. Karl Röder, "Nachtwache [Night Watch], unpublished (Dachau Museum).

13. NS Bu, rep. 128 (Federal Archives, Koblenz); Harig/Mayr, op. cit.

14. Detailed statistics in Harig/Mayr, op. cit. Of the 9,828 Jewish "roundup prisoners" admitted to the camp at that time 9,374 were discharged again, 216 died during the brief period of their internment (Pinzel 1978, 95).

15. Barbara Distel, "Die 'Reichskristallnacht und das KZ Dachau [The Reich Kristallnacht and the concentration camp Dachau]," unpublished manuscript (in the author's possession).

16. Compilation of the archives in the Dachau Museum, February 17, 1976 (in the author's possession).

17. Harry Naujoks, "Wie SS-Lagerführer Rudolf Höss den Jahrestag der Reichsgründung am 18. Januar 1940 beging [How Commandant Rudolf Höss celebrated the anniversary of the founding of the Reich on January 18, 1940]." In *Der Appell—Sachsenhausen-Information*, Düsseldorf, February 1, 1974; also *Damals in Sachsenhausen* [Those Days in Sachsenhausen] 1967.

18. Cf. Maria Kurcyuszowa, "Die Polinnen im Kampf gegen die biologische Vernichtung im Konzentrationslager Ravensbrück [Polish women in the struggle against biological destruction in the concentration camp Ravensbrück]" (unpublished manuscript in the author's possession).

19. From "Die Geschichte des Konzentrationslagers Neuengamme [History of the concentration camp Neuengamme]" (unpublished), The Wiener Library, London.

20. Belzec, Sobibor, and Treblinka are in eastern Poland; Chelmno is in western Poland.

21. In a letter dated October 5, 1942, the Economic Office informed the commandant's office in Auschwitz that around 1,600 Jews were being transferred there, so that the concentration camps in the Reich would finally become *judenfrei* (Jew-free). As early as October, 6,522 Jewish women were transferred to Auschwitz from Ravensbrück, and between the 19th and 25th of the month, there were transfers from other concentration camps; the most numerous ones were from Sachsenhausen (454) and Buchenwald (404). After feeble prisoners had been selected for death in a gas chamber, around 800 prisoners were transferred to the newly established subsidiary camp Buna-Monowitz (Czech 1959–64).

22. Telex from Himmler to the inspector of concentration camps, January 26, 1942 (Federal Archives, Koblenz).

23. In a report to Himmler, dated April 30, 1942, about the integration of the office of the inspector of concentration camps into the SS Economic Office, Pohl writes that he has informed all camp commandants about the "new developments" on April 23 and 24. In this letter Pohl defines the "visible change in the structure of the concentration camps" as follows: "The emphasis has now shifted to the economic side. The mobilization of the prisoners' labor—at present for military purposes (intensification of armaments) and later for peaceful purposes—is increasingly assuming paramount importance." (From the records of the Nuremberg trial).

24. Thierack file (Nuremberg document PS-654).

25. Letters from the inspector of concentration camps to the camp doctors, dated

December 28, 1942, and to the camp commandants, dated January 20, 1943 (Nuremberg document NO-/523).

26. According to a list I was able to make as clerk of the SS doctor of Auschwitz, on the basis of secret reports from his office, and to smuggle out of the camp to Vienna in spring 1944, an average of 20.5 percent of all registered inmates died each month in the third quarter of 1942 and 20.4 percent each month in the last quarter (Langbein 1965, 100).

27. These figures were taken from Pohl's report to Himmler, dated September 30, 1943 (Nuremberg document PS-1469). According to the same report, the population of all concentration camps increased from 143,100 in February 1943 to 203,000 in May of that year.

28. Cf. note 26.

29. The death records do not list prisoners who were not registered in the camp or prisoners of special categories.

30. A detailed description of this development in the nature of the Bergen–Belsen camp may be found in Kolb 1962.

31. A survey of the subsidiary camps may be found in *Vorläufiges Verzeichnis der Konzentrationslager und deren Aussenkommandos sowie anderer Haftstätten unter dem Reichsführer SS in Deutschland und deutsch besetzten Gebieten* [Preliminary catalog of the concentration camps and their outside units as well as other prisons under the Reichsführer-SS in Germany and German-occupied territories] (1933–1945), published by the International Committee of the Red Cross, International Search Service, Arolsen, 1969.

32. Arthur Haulot/Ali Kuci, "Dachau," written in Dachau in May and June 1945, unpublished, (Dachau Museum).

33. Ernst Thape, "Buchenwald-Tagebuch vom 1. April bis 1. Mai 1945 [Buchenwald Diary April 1–May 1, 1945]," unpublished (Dachau Museum).

34. "Angaben des Wilhelm Boger [Statement of Wilhelm Boger]," Ludwigsburg, July 5, 1945. Auschwitz Museum.

35. According to statistics reported by the Economic Office on August 15, 1944, there were 379,167 men and 145,119 women in the concentration camps at that time (Nuremberg document NO-399). A document dated January 15, 1945, lists 511,537 men and 202,674 women. Schumacher Collection 329, Federal Archives, Koblenz.

36. Wanda Kiedrzyńska, "Einleitende Erwägungen [Preliminary Reflections]" unpublished (in the possession of the author). Incompletely preserved transport lists contains the names of 25,038 inmates of Ravensbrück, of whom 19.9 percent were Germans.

37. According to a report to the American Ministry of Defense, of 20,000 living inmates found on April 16, 1945, 1,800 were Germans and 550 Austrians (*Buchenwald* 1960, 554).

38. According to SS statistics dated March 11, 1945, of the 83,595 inmates 5,396 were Germans from the Reich, evidently including every type of prisoner except the "Sicherheitsverwahrte", those imprisoned for reasons of security; the number of these criminals is given separately as 2,881.

39. Götz Dieckmann, *Existenzbedingungen und Widerstand im Konzentra-tionslager Dora–Mittelbau unter dem Aspekt der funktionellen Ein-beziehung der SS in das System der faschistischen Kriegswirtschaft* (Living conditions and Resistance in Concentration Camp Dora–Mittelbau Under the Aspect of Functional Inclusion of the SS in the Fascist System of War Econ-omy). Dissertation, Humboldt University, Berlin, 1968. In Appendix 9, the nationalities of the inmates, including all satellite camps, are given as of April 1, 1945. Of the 40,202 prisoners in the camps on that day, 3,227 were Germans.

40. A "Bericht über das Konzentrationslager Sachsenhausen" [Report on the con-centration camp Sachsenhausen] was written and signed by twelve inmates, representing ten different nations, who stayed behind after the evacuation of that camp. The quotation is from page 36 of that report, unpublished (Royal Institute for War Documentation, Amsterdam), which also states that the majority of the German prisoners consisted of career criminals, antisocial and apathetic people, and former members of the SS and other fascist outfits.

41. Of the 31,432 inmates of Dachau on the day of liberation (April 29, 1945), 1,173 were Germans (including six women), 253 Austrians, two ethnic Germans (*Volksdeutsche*), and three Sudeten Germans.

42. Author's conversation with Andrzej Kamiński, December 14, 1974.

43. "Historische Skizze des Konzentrationslagers Neuengamme bei Hamburg–Bergedorf [Historical sketch of the concentration camp Neuengamme near Hamburg–Bergedorf]," edited by the Arbeitsgemeinschaft [collaborative] Neu-engamme, May 1959, unpublished (in the author's possession), p. 7.

44. A report by the American liberators of Neuengamme, dated May 16, 1945, lists 140 Germans. The total number of inmates was 11,686. However, some Ger-man capos accused of crimes may previously have been arrested. Another element of uncertainty is the fact that the Americans did not list the Jews separately, though there is no reason to believe that a large number of German Jews were interned in Ebensee (Chêne 1971).

45. A letter written by the resistance movement to the Polish resistance organiza-tion in Kraków on May 11, 1943, gives the total number of inmates as 25,912; this figure probably did not include the Birkenau complex. Of these 708 were registered as Germans, but some of the 1,008 inmates who were listed as "others and ethnic Germans" should be added to this number. "Ethnic Ger-mans" evidently referred to Poles from Upper Silesia who had signed the so-called *Volksliste* (Ethnic Register). In another letter, one dated August 22, 1944, the resistance organization reports that among the 15,971 prisoners in the main camp Auschwitz I, there were 950 Germans. At that time, 200 Germans were registered in the Birkenau men's camp, which housed 19,424 prisoners. The percentage of Germans was lowest in the Birkenau women's camp: 300 out of 39,234. The above letter contains this statement about the future development of the camp: "Changes in the ethnic composition of the camp are being planned. The Germans, the Poles, and the Russians are to be transferred, and the camp is to be stocked with Jews." (The letters are in the Auschwitz Museum.)

46. The exact number of all satellite camps and the periods of their existence may be found in a publication of the International Search Service (Red Cross 1969).

47. Author's conversation with Willi Bleicher, November 20, 1976.

48. Letter from Himmler, May 11, 1944. Schumacher Collection 437, Federal Archives, Koblenz.

49. Author's conversation with Andrzej Kamiński, December 14, 1974.

50. Bakels believes that around 7,000 inmates were evacuated at that time (Bakels 1979, 258 ff.).

51. Cf. note 40.

3. THE SELF-GOVERNMENT OF THE INMATES

1. Himmler's Sonthofen address to Wehrmacht generals on June 21, 1944. MA 315 Bl. 3949f. (Institute for Contemporary History, Munich).

2. Arthur Haulot/Ali Kuci, "Dachau," written in Dachau in May and June 1945, unpublished (Dachau Museum).

3. J. B. Krokowski, unpublished manuscript (in the author's possession).

4. Author's conversation with Paul Schnabel, February 13, 1977.

5. In his "Ausführlicher Bericht über das Konzentrationslager Buchenwald [Detailed report on concentration camp Buchenwald]" Otto Horn writes: "He [Hoven—H.L.] took an active part in the fight between the political prisoners and the Greens in 1942. The miserable acts of treachery on the part of the latter caused a big reaction against the political prisoners . . . some of whom were removed from the list for gassing, through Hoven's good offices. It goes without saying that in return for his services, Hoven expected the inmates to further his private interests by obtaining all kinds of things for him. The only reason that the political prisoners were able to exert any influence on him was that he was accessible to certain things." Unpublished (Documentation Archive of the Austrian Resistance, Vienna).

6. In late August 1943, the Polish doctor Władysław Dering became senior camp inmate in the prisoners' hospital in the main camp. After his discharge in January 1944, he was succeeded by the Polish doctor Władysław Fejkiel, who remained senior camp inmate until the evacuation of Auschwitz.

7. The diary entry of February 22, 1944, indicates that August was caught with a Ukrainian lad and transported (Nansen 1949, 128, 143).

8. This unpublished report is dated July 12, 1944 (Archives of the Red Cross International Search Service, Arolsen). However, the SS did find another way. On September 14, Harter was put in the isolation block 58 and from there transferred to Mauthausen, where he arrived on October 25. (Information from the International Search Service, Arolsen).

9. Harry Naujoks, "Wie SS-Lagerführer Rudolf Höss den Jahrestag der Reichsgründung am 18. Januar 1940 beging [How SS Commandant Rudolf Höss celebrated the anniversary of the founding of the Reich on January 18, 1940]." In Der Appell—Sachsenhausen-Information, Düsseldorf, February 1, 1974.

10. According to Stanisław Nogaj ("Gusen-Tagebuch eines Journalisten [Diary of a journalist]," unpublished), Rudolf Meixner was chief clerk in Gusen from May 26, 1940, to February 21, 1942. His successor was Anton Jahnke. In Nogaj's diary, Meixner's conduct is described as follows: "Whenever he could, he tried to ease their [the Poles'—H.L.] lot. . . . He filled the secretarial positions under him with Poles exclusively. . . ." Nogaj also quotes this statement by Meixner: "I protect and support you [Poles—H.L.] not because I like you but because I hate those *Jeckels* and *Marmeladenfresser* [derogatory terms for Germans—H.L.] (From the records of the Mauthausen trial, Central Office in the Province Nordrhein-Westfalen for the compiling of Nazi mass crimes in the Concentration Camps, Cologne.)

11. Hans Maršàlek writes: "Only after Josef Leitzinger, the chief clerk of the main camp, had been removed on March 12, 1944, was it possible to fill certain influential positions in the main camp and the subsidiary camps with political prisoners' (193/40).

12. J. B. Krokowski, op. cit.

13. Unpublished notes by Tadeusz Patzer, in the author's possession.

14. Cf. note 40, Chapter 2.

15. O. Horn, op. cit.

16. Cf. note 10, Chapter 2.

17. Author's conversation with David Rousset, November 16, 1973.

18. Author's conversation with Albin Lüdke, November 4, 1973.

19. Cf. note 10, chapter 2.

20. Kornelis Hofman, "Verklaring [Statement]," January 25, 1951, unpublished (Royal Institute for War Documentation, Amsterdam), p. 57.

21. Cf. note 5, chapter 2.

22. Author's conversation with Heinz Junge, November 6, 1973.

23. Letter from Hans Maršàlek to the author, November 25, 1975.

24. J. B. Krokowski, op. cit.

25. Unpublished (Royal Institute, Amsterdam).

26. Author's conversation with Georg Buch, November 22, 1973.

27. Selbmann also outlines the tasks of the camp clerk: "He keeps the internal camp files, prepares the prisoner counts and roll-call reports, and compiles transport lists." Selbmann describes the office as "the center of the camp's self-operation" and states that the staff included "the three senior camp inmates, the head of the Work Assignments, the camp clerk, and the messengers" (Selbmann 1961, 76 ff.).

28. Herman Joseph, "Der Fall 104338 [Case no. 104338]," unpublished manuscript, p. 203 ff.

29. NS 4, AAu. rep. 5, Federal Archives, Koblenz.

30. Conversation between Emil Carlebach and Falk Pingel, May 2, 1974.

31. In addition to Carlebach, Jewish senior block inmates assigned to "Jewish blocks" included August Cohn and Rudi Arndt. The latter was removed by the officer in charge of the protective-custody section and put in a penal company, where he perished. "They were the political leaders of the Jews" (author's

conversation with Erich Fein, December 28, 1976). That the camp administration regarded them as "politically dangerous" is evidenced by the fact that Carlebach and Cohn were on the list of the forty-six men scheduled to be murdered as the presumed ringleaders shortly before the liberation.

32. J. B. Krokowski, op. cit.

33. "In January 1938 three Polish prisoners, among them Walter Krämer, the former representative of the German Communist Party in the Prussian parliament, started work in the infirmary, which had until then been a domain of the Greens" (Kiessling 1964, 179).

34. Author's conversation with Pierre Schneider, November 19, 1973.

35. Thus Cornelis Fels writes in his "Verklaring [Statement]" of October 21, 1947, that the Dutch doctors in the infirmary were able to work independently. Unpublished manuscript in the possession of Fels's son Hans Fels, Amsterdam, p. 11.

4. THE BATTLE BETWEEN REDS AND GREENS

1. Author's conversation with Heinz Junge, November 6, 1973.

2. Letter from Jerzy Kwiatkowski to the author, March 5, 1974.

3. Further information about Brodniewicz may be found in Langbein 1972, 174.

4. Letter from Tadeusz Patzer to the author, April 15, 1976.

5. Unpublished notes by Tadeusz Patzer, in the author's possession.

6. From Stanisław Nogaj's "Gusen–Tagebuch eines Journalisten [Diary of a government]," unpublished, (Central Office in the Province Nordrhein-Westfalen for the Compiling of Nazi Mass Crimes in the Concentration Camps, Cologne), p. 175. The names of the senior camp inmates and their terms of office are given there.

7. Gostner characterizes Rohrbacher as "an intelligent type of criminal who is not brutal or violent" (Gostner 1945, 156).

8. Penal order of August 4, 1943 (from the record of the Dachau Flossenbürg trial, Washington). Born received ten days in jail.

9. Author's conversation with Gustl Gattinger, March 5, 1976. The capo Christl Knoll and the Austrian infirmary capo Sepp Heiden were especially notorious. After the liberation, Knoll was executed because of his atrocities, and Heiden committed suicide while awaiting trial. Alfred Hübsch has described Max Schnell as a tramp; after the inmates of Dachau had been transferred to Flossenbürg, he was the only man wearing a red triangle who was accepted by the dominant Greens and made a capo. Cf. "Die Insel des Standrechts [The island of martial law]," unpublished (Dachau Museum), p. 183. Many survivors have bad memories of the senior camp inmate Karl Kapp; Walter Neff calls him "a bad sort." "Recht oder Unrecht [Right or Wrong]," unpublished (Dachau Museum), p. 24).

10. O. Horn, op. cit.

11. Benedikt Kautsky, entry in Ernst Thape's diary, written in Buchenwald on May 16, 1945, unpublished (Friedrich Ebert Foundation, Bonn).

12. Unpublished report by E. Büge, Red Cross International Search Service, Arolsen.

13. From "Bericht über Erlebnisse in Berliner Gestapo-Gefängnissen und KZ Buchenwald auf Grund der Mitteilungen des Herrn Ernest Platz [Report on experiences in Berlin Gestapo prisons and concentration camp Buchenwald on the basis of reports from Mr. Ernest Platz]," unpublished, (The Wiener Library, London).

14. Author's conversation with Albert Hommel, November 18, 1973.

15. Juan de Diego, "1943: Cosas Vividas [Things Experienced]." In *Hispania, Boletín de la Federacion Española de Deportades y Internades Políticos*, Paris, September 1967. Also, author's conversation with Diego, July 9, 1974.

16. K. L. Schecher, op. cit.

17. A. Hübsch, op. cit.

18. The first quotation is from Hans Maršàlek's letter to the author dated November 25, 1975, the second one from the author's conversation with Ernst Martin on June 11, 1973.

19. Jan Češpiva writes: "The hospital . . . was in the hands of Polish chauvinists" (Češpiva/Gressner/Pelný 1964, 218), and Ota Kraus and Erich Kulka have this to say: "The leading elements in the camp [Birkenau—H.L.] included, in addition to the German criminals serving as capos, numerous Polish Fascists. Their Nazi-fed anti-Semitism caused them to regard the extermination of the Jews as a postponement or prevention of their own fate. . . . The Nazis encouraged this attitude of the Polish Fascists and directed and rewarded their brutality and ruthlessness, for openly manifested hatred of the Jews was the prime prerequisite for the granting of easements and the assignment of positions to inmates" (Kraus/Kulka 1957, 215). Antonius van Velsen writes: "The Poles were so chauvinistic that they lumped all Germans together and because of their bad experience with criminals established no contact with German political prisoners. They had no liking for the Jews." Unpublished February 5, 1948 (Royal Institute for War Documentation, Amsterdam), pp. 48, 52).

20. In a letter dated October 30, 1942, the commandants of the concentration camps were informed that all "Aryan" prisoners, with the exception of Russian citizens, were permitted to receive parcels. However, it was some time before packages could actually be sent to the camps. (Federal Archives, Koblenz).

21. Author's conversation with Edouard Barbel, November 19, 1973.

22. In May 1943, the first concentration-camp inmates were released to the Dirlewanger Unit, which at first was composed of convicted poachers. According to testimony from Hermann Pister, the commandant of Buchenwald, burglars, sex offenders (with the exception of homosexuals), men convicted of manslaughter and murder as well as loafers and pimps were admitted to this unit. Cf. also Auerbach 1962. The degree of voluntarism may be gauged from the fact that in 1944, when the central office pressed for more volunteers, every

commandant of a concentration camp was given the number of men who had to "volunteer" in his camp.

23. Author's conversation with Arthur Hansen, November 19, 1973.
24. Statement by Bruno Furch from the record of the Dachau Flossenbürg trial, Washington, unpublished.
25. O. Horn, op. cit.
26. Testimony of February 25, 1976.
27. Author's conversation with David Rousset, November 16, 1973.

5. WHAT IS MEANT BY RESISTANCE?

1. Wanda Kiedrzyńska, "Einleitende Erwägungen [Preliminary Reflections]," unpublished (in the possession of the author).
2. K. Röder, op. cit.
3. Letter from Tadeusz Patzer to the author, May 17, 1976.

6. SOURCES AND CRITIQUE OF SOURCES

1. There are conflicting reports about the number of letters smuggled out of the camp. Kazimierz Smoleń's explanation is that the Auschwitz Museum constantly receives letters and slips of paper, many of which are not from an organization in the camp but from individuals who had an opportunity to send such letters out. (Letter form Kazimierz Smoleń to the author, July 31, 1978). Cf. also Smoleń 1960–67, 36; Strgelecka 1974–76, 4; Gárliński 1975A, 46ff.
2. The Czech Véra Foltýnová has described how plans of the crematoria with built-in gas chambers were copied and smuggled out from the camp's construction office," principally to Bohemia" (Kraus/Kulka 1957, 21). Hermann Langbein has described how death statistics were sent to Vienna (Langbein 1965, 100 ff.).
3. Letter of November 24, 1942 (Auschwitz Museum).
4. Declaration of the Combat Group Auschwitz, Summer 1944 (Auschwitz Museum).
5. "Zeichnen als Widerstand [Sketching as resistance]." In *Die Zeit*, September 7, 1979.
6. Józef Cyrankiewicz, "Briefe von ausserhalb der Welt [Letters from outside the world]," March 25, 1944, unpublished (in the author's possession).
7. Untitled article by Alfred Klahr in Weg und Ziel. *Monatsschrift für Fragen der Demokratie und des wissenschaftlichen Sozialismus*, Vienna, January 1957, p. 29 ff. Concerning the origin of this article, cf. Langbein 1949, 169.
8. Author's conversation with Josef Meisel, September 6, 1976.
9. Urszula Wińska's essay about educational work as a special form of the resistance movement of the inmates of Ravensbrück (German version in the author's possession).

10. Maria Kurcyuszowa's essay about the struggle of Polish women against biological destruction in Ravensbrück (German version in the author's possession).

11. Cornelis Fels, "Verklaring [Statement]," October 21, 1947, unpublished (Royal Institute for War Documentation, Amsterdam).

12. Kornelis Hofman, "Verklaring," January 25, 1951, unpublished (Royal Institute, Amsterdam).

13. Stephan Hermlin has supplied information about the escape, on February 2, 1944, of Herbert Tschäpe, a German veteran of the Spanish Civil War, who was given the party's decision that he should flee by an old girlfriend (Schmidt 1958, 321 ff.; *Damals in Sachsenhausen*, 91 ff.).

14. "Konzentrationslager Sachsenhausen: Die Periode der Sonderkommission von Ende 1943 bis 1944 [Concentration camp Sachsenhausen: The period of the special commission from the end of 1943 to 1944]," Oranienburg, May 1945, unpublished, (Royal Institute, Amsterdam), p. 5.

15. Author's conversation with Heinz Schmidt, November 8, 1973.

16. Unpublished Büge manuscript, Red Cross International Search Service, Arolsen, Bl. 204.

17. Letter from the Red Cross International Search Service to the author, May 25, 1976.

18. Büge manuscript, op. cit., Bl. 147f.

19. Testimony by Stanisław Nogaj at the jury trial in Hagen on March 3, 1967. In passing sentence, the court emphasized that Nogaj altered and supplemented his notes after the war. "On the basis of his testimony and the assessment of his notes made on March 18, 1968, by the institute for customs fraud in Cologne and read during the trial the court is satisfied that he actually kept a diary in Gusen."

20. Alfred Hübsch, "Die Insel des Standrechts: Geheimaufzeichnungen des Pförtners von Dachau [The island of martial law: Secret records of the Dachau gatekeeper]," unpublished, (Dachau Museum).

21. Arthur Haulot, "Journal de Camp," unpublished (Dachau Museum).

22. Ernst Thape, "Buchenwald-Tagebuch vom 1. April bis 1. Mai 1945 [Buchenwald diary, April 1–May 1945]," unpublished (Archives of the Friedrich Ebert Foundation, Bonn–Bad Godesberg).

23. Lévy-Hass began to keep a diary in Montenegro, where she had been arrested. In Bergen–Belsen she found it "not so impossible" to continue it, for the SS "was very careful not to get too close to the inmates" (Lévy-Hass 1979, 61).

24. Charles Dubost, "Le Procès de Nuremberg: Accusation Française [Nuremberg trial: French indictment]," Information Service for War Crimes, Paris, p. 141 ff. Also, declaration by Felipe Yebenes-Romo, Paris, December 5, 1978, unpublished (in the author's possession).

25. Cf. "Bericht über das Konzentrationslager Sachsenhausen [Report on concentration camp Sachsenhausen]," signed by twelve liberated inmates of ten different nationalities, unpublished (Royal Institute for War Documentation, Amsterdam); Gerhard Harig/Hans Mayr, "Die zahlenmässige Entwicklung des Konzentrationslagers Buchenwald, 1937 bis 1945 [the numerical development

of concentration camp Buchenwald 1937–45]," unpublished (in the author's possession); "Bericht des Niederländischen Komitees über die illegalen Vorbereitungen zur internationalen, antifaschistischen Zusammenarbeit im Lager Buchenwald [Report of the Netherlands committee on the underground preparations for the international anti-fascist collaboration in camp Buchenwald]," signed by representatives of four Dutch parties, unpublished (Royal Institute); "Die polnische Geheimorganisation im KL Buchenwald [The Polish secret organization in concentration camp Buchenwald]," signed by three Poles on behalf of the Komitet Polski, unpublished (Royal Institute, Amsterdam); Arthur Haulot/Ali Kuci, "Dachau," written in Dachau in May–June 1945, unpublished (Dachau Museum). The initial report that served as the basis of Eugen Kogon's book *Der SS-Staat* (published in English as *The Theory and Practice of Hell*) was completed by the author in the first weeks after the liberation in Weimar (near Buchenwald) "in constant contact with the camp and numerous groups of former prisoners."

26. Fa 506/12, Bl. 271, Institute for Modern History, Munich.

27. Rene Trauffler, "Kurzer Bericht [Short report]," unpublished (in the possession of the author).

28. From the opinion of the Essen district court, May 8, 1970 (Az. 29a Ks 9/66, unpublished).

29. Concerning transfers to Buchenwald, cf. Walter Vielhauer/Karl Wagner, "Solidarität sprengte unsere Ketten [Solidarity burst our chains]," in *Die Glocke von Ettersberg* No. 61, III/75; to Sachsenhausen, cf. the interview with Ludwig Göring of May 8, 1973 (Dachau Museum); to Neuengamme, cf. Julius Schätzle (1946), who was himself transferred there from Dachau in October 1944. In Neuengamme I reencountered Hans Biederer and Hanz Schwarz, whom I knew from Dachau, where I was interned prior to my transfer to Auschwitz. On July 19, 1944, four Germans and four Austrians were transferred to Flossenbürg (cf. testimony of Bruno Forch in the records of the Dachau Flossenbürg trial, Washington, unpublished), among them Fritz Frühwald (cf. Hans Popp's letter to the author, August 2, 1976).

30. Author's conversation with Walter Vielhauer, November 21, 1976. Vielhauer was transferred to Buchenwald in the course of this procedure.

31. Secret letter from Józef Cyrankiewicz to "Adam," later translated into German by Cyrankiewicz, unpublished (in the author's possession).

32. Thereafter Poles and Russians were transferred to other camps in increasing numbers. It cannot be ascertained how many Poles and Russians were on general transfer transports. Between April 26, 1944 (the day on which the first transport, consisting entirely of Poles and Russians, was registered), and the end of the year more than 14,500 members of these two nations were transferred to other concentration camps, mostly Buchenwald, in transports containing only Russians and Poles. Sign. Eich 1063, Institute for Contemporary History, Munich.

33. Stenographic minutes of a meeting of the fighter pilots' staff on May 2, 1944 (Nuremberg doc. NOKWS 389, p. 3017f.).

34. Eugen Kogon was imprisoned in Buchenwald from September 1939 to the liberation. After a brief imprisonment in Dachau, Benedikt Kautsky was transferred to Buchenwald on September 23, 1938; from there he was transferred to Auschwitz on October 19, 1942, and finally to Monowitz. After the evacuation of Auschwitz he was sent back to Buchenwald in January 1945 and remained there until the liberation. David Rousset was quarantined in Buchenwald from late January 1944 to February of that year, whereupon he was transferred to Porta Westfalica, a satellite camp of Neuengamme. About a month later he was transferred to Helmstedt, another subsidiary camp, and finally to Wöbbelin.

35. Albert Beffort, "Buchenwald: Befreiung und Selbstbefreiung [Liberation and self-liberation]," in *Rappel*, Luxembourg, April/May/June 1975, p. 262.

36. Herbert Weidlich's report "Der Beitrag der Arbeitsstatistik zur illegalen Arbeit [The contribution of Labor Records to the work of the underground]" bears this notation on p. 355 ff.: "Report of April 22, 1945 (revised in 1958)"; Heinz Mühler's report "Lagerfeuerwehr ans Tor [Camp fire brigade to the gate!]" has this note: "Report written in 1946 and revised in 1956," p. 503ff.; the unsigned report "Zur Geschichte der Organisation der Kommunistischen Partei Deutschlands im Konzentrationslager Buchenwald [History of the organization of the German Communist Party in Concentration camp Buchenwald]" (p. 315 ff.) bears this notation: "Report written in 1945 (revised 1960)." In the book with the same title and editorship that was issued in the same year by the Kongress Verlag (publishing house) of East Berlin, the last-named report appears with this note: "Report written in 1945, revised 1958." The signature is the same. The above-mentioned differences may be found in this publication.

37. The unpublished original report is in the Royal Institute for War Documentation in Amsterdam. The chapter "Die Befreiung des Lagers [The Liberation of the Camp]" begins on p. 130 of the booklet *Damals in Sachsenhausen* [Those Days in Sachsenhausen]; at the end of this article is this notation: "KLS [concentration camp Sachsenhausen] Archives, report of the political prisoners remaining in the camp, written 1945." Apart from the above-mentioned divergences, which are not identified as revisions, it is identical with the original text.

38. Author's conversation with Juan de Diego, July 9, 1974.

39. Hans Maršàlek, *Mauthausen mahnt* [Mauthausen Admonishes] (Maršàlek n.d.,/35), and a letter from Maršàlek to the author dated October 17, 1975.

40. Maršàlek's letter to the author dated October 17, 1975.

41. Letter from Leopold Mayer to the author dated November 9, 1975, and author's conversation with Mayer on January 3, 1976.

42. In the course of proceedings against persons accused of involvement in mass crimes committed in Auschwitz, public prosecutors in Frankfurt brought action against Stefan Budiaszek, a resident of Hannover under the assumed name Buthner. Numerous physicians who served under Budiaszek in the Monowitz hospital when they were inmates furnished incriminating evidence, but others testified for him, and so the public prosecutors finally decided to drop the proceedings. Cf. also Langbein 1972, 257 ff.

43. Dr. Władysław Dering, a resident of London, brought suit for defamation of character against the American writer Leon Uris, who had written in his book *Exodus* in connection with SS doctors' human experiments in Auschwitz that Dr. Dehring (*sic*) had performed 17,000 such operations without anesthesia. Uris offered to prove his statements, but the trial, which took place in London from April 13 to May 6, 1964, ended with a judgment against Uris because the figure 17,000 undoubtedly represented a gross exaggeration. Dering received compensation in the amount of a halfpenny (Hill/Williams 1965).

44. Some of those named in Gárliński's book have disputed other assertions of his. Thus Stanisław Klodziński has stated that he was not a member of the Polish military organization (p. 136 in Gárliński's book) but only had contact with him (author's conversation with Klodziński on September 6, 1976). Kazimierz Smoleń avers that he had contact only with Klodziński and not with Pilecki's military organization, as Gárliński claims on p. 62 (author's conversation with Smoleń on November 10, 1975). Jerzy Pozimski also denies having had any contact with that organization, as Gárliński states on p. 136 (author's conversation with Pozimski on May 26, 1977). It could be pointed out that the above eyewitnesses are living in Poland today and are denying any contact with an organization whose leader, Witold Pilecki, was executed in Poland in March 1948. However, this hedge does not apply to the statements of the Polish physician Tadeusz Gonta, who lives in Sweden. He has testified that while carrying corpses he saw Alfred Stössel kill inmates in Block 20 by injecting them with carbolic acid. According to Gonta, both Dering and Dr. Rudolf Diem, whom Gárliński has named as an associate of the Polish military organization, told him in Auschwitz that after the selections made by the SS, they substituted Jews for Poles (author's conversation with Tadeusz Gonta on May 31, 1977).

45. Gárliński repeatedly misquotes from my book *Die Stärkeren* (The Stronger) (e.g., on p. 195) and, in contrast to what I wrote, recognizes the results of my underground activity only as a personal success and not as the work of the Combat Group Auschwitz, in which Cyrankiewicz played a leading part.

46. The book appeared in three editions: the first 1949 in the VVN Verlag, Berlin–Potsdam; the second, enlarged edition 1959 in the Kongress Verlag, Berlin; and the third was issued by the same publisher, with a Foreword dated July 31, 1961. Although the descriptions of Langbein's activities are nearly identical in the first and second editions (pp. 8f., 23 and 66 ff., 80 respectively), in the third edition Langbein's name has been replaced with "an Austrian" on p. 66 and omitted on p. 79. In the first two editions Heinz Brandt is named as a member of the resistance group (pp. 23, 79), but his name does not appear in the third edition (p. 78).

47. Albin Lüdke has stated that André Mandryckxs was posthumously put on trial in Belgium (author's conversation with Lüdke, November 4, 1973).

48. Author's conversation with Emil Peters, November 19, 1973.

49. Author's conversation with Pierre Schneider, November 19, 1973.

50. Author's conversation with David Rousset, November 16, 1973.

51. Since the book (Meier 1949) was conceived as a novel and fictitious names are used, the character is named André Marcel, but the context makes it clear that André Mandryckxs's activities are described.

52. "Historische Skizze des Konzentrationslagers Neuengamme bei Hamburg-Bergedorf [Historical Sketch of the Concentration Camp Neuengamme]," edited by the Cooperative Neuengamme in May 1959, unpublished (in the author's possession), p. 5.

53. Author's conversation with Heinz Junge, November 6, 1973.

54. Cf. also Himmler's diary entry with the heading "Wolfsschanze [Wolf's Lair, Hitler's HQ in East Prussia, now Ketezyn], Aug. 14, '44, Führer." Item 12, "Thälmann is to be executed," proves that the inmate Thälmann did not die during a bombardment of the camp but was killed on Hitler's orders.

7. DIFFERENT CONDITIONS AND CHANGED GOALS

1. Author's conversation with Harry Naujoks, November 3, 1973.

2. Author's conversation with Hans Gasparitsch, November 20, 1976.

3. Author's conversation with Walter Vielhauer, November 21, 1976.

4. Author's conversation with Kazimierz Smoleń, November 10, 1975.

5. Mariano Constante, "Les republicains espagnols dans la lutte antinazi [The Spanish republicans in the anti-Fascist struggle]," unpublished manuscript; (Razola/Constante 1969 71 ff.; Constante 1971/203, 210).

6. According to Hans Maršàlek, the first international executive committee, formed February–March 1944, was composed of the Austrians Leo Gabler (who was transferred to Vienna on April 13, 1944, and murdered there), Josef Kohl, and Hans Maršàlek as well as Artur London, a Czech veteran of the Spanish Civil War. Octave Rebate also names Leo Gabler as the leading official of the international organization (Bernadac 1974, 263).

7. M. Constante in Rezola/Constante, op. cit. In a conversation with the author on July 9, 1974, Juan de Diego characterized Kohl as a very intelligent man and a fine human being. On the other hand, the Austrian Ernst Martin believes that he was turned into a hero after the fact. (Conversation with the author on June 11, 1973.) Martin's compatriot Alois Stockinger shares his view; according to him, Kohl helped only those who shared his ideology (i.e., Communists). (Conversation with the author on December 2, 1975.)

8. J. de Diego, op. cit.

9. "Die Geschichte des Konzentrationslagers Neuengamme [History of Concentration Camp Neuengamme]," unpublished manuscript (Wiener Library, London).

10. Author's conversation with Pierre Schneider, November 19, 1973.

11. Letter from Urbonas to the author, February 26, 1975.

12. Author's conversation with Franz Graczoll, October 12, 1975.

13. Author's conversation with Rudolf Gottschalk, February 12, 1977.

14. Mołdawa writes that it was forbidden to form groups and talk in the roll-call area. Cf. also Alfred Konieczny's letter to the author, June 6, 1975.

15. Author's conversation with Andrzej Kamiński, December 14, 1974.

16. Cf. also F. Graczoll, op. cit.

17. Author's conversation with Fritz Kleinmann, December 12, 1976.

18. "Bericht über das Konzentrationslager Sachsenhausen [Report on Concentration Camp Sachsenhausen]," written shortly after the liberation by twelve former inmates, and Karl Raddatz, "Die Sonderaktion vom 2. August 1944 gegen KPD-Funktionäre im KL Sachsenhausen [The special roundup of August 2, 1944 aimed at the KPD Functionaries in Concentration Camp Sachsenhausen]," written on May 20, 1945, both unpublished (Royal Institute for War Documentation, Amsterdam). Cf. also (Stein 1946, 187 ff.).

19. Conversation with F. Graczoll, op. cit.

20. Sworn statements made by Leon Staischak on September 3, 1947 (Nuremberg document NO.NI-10928), and Curt Posener on June 3, 1947 (Nuremberg document NO.NI-9808), both unpublished.

21. Cf. also Karl Feuerer, "Widerstand in Dora [Resistance in Dora]," in *Frankfurter Rundschau*, August 14, 1947.

22. Author's conversation with Toni Lehr on September 19, 1975. She, Gerti Schindel, and Edith Rosenblüth-Wexberg were deported to Auschwitz on December 1, 1944. Since several women's transports had left for Ravensbrück in the last weeks before the final evacuation of Auschwitz (on January 18, 1945), it was possible to transmit news.

23. Walter Vielhauer and Karl Wagner, "Solidarität sprengte unsere Ketten [Solidarity burst our chains]," in *Die Glocke von Ettersberg*, No. 61, III/75, Frankfurt.

24. Antonius van Velsen, "Verslag (Report)," February 5, 1948, unpublished (Royal Institute, Amsterdam), p. 1.

25. Otto Horn, "Ausführlicher Bericht über das Konzentrationslager Buchenwald [Complete Report on Concentration Camp Buchenwald]," unpublished (Documentation Archive of the Austrian Resistance, Vienna) Best., No. 1458.

26. "Vorläufiger Bericht über die militärische Organisation im Konzentrationslager Buchenwald [Preliminary report on the military organization in concentration camp Buchenwald]," unpublished (Royal Institute, Amsterdam), page 1.

27. Author's conversation with Karl Wagner, September 19, 1976.

28. Quoted from "Die letzten Skeptiker müssen überzeugt werden: Der Prozess gegen 31 Angeklagte des Konzentrationslagers Buchenwald hat begonnen [The last skeptics must be convinced; The proceedings against thirty-one defendants of the concentration camp Buchenwald have begun]," in *Oberbayrisches Volksblatt*, April 15, 1947, p. 3.

29. Max Heinl, "Widerstandskampf im Lager Dachau [Resistance struggle in camp Dachau]," November 9, 1948, unpublished (in the author's possession).

30. Author's conversation with Georg Scherer, April 2, 1979. Scherer was appointed senior camp inmate when the first Poles arrived in Dachau in the fall of 1939. He was released at a later date and succeeded by Karl Kapp. Scherer has

NOTES

named the German Communists Hans Meiler and Karl Röder as well as the Austrian Communist Josef Lauscher as men with whom he had regular discussions.

31. "Bericht über Erlebnisse in Berliner Gestapo-Gefängnissen und KZ Buchenwald auf Grund der Mitteilungen des Herrn Ernest Platz, geb. am 25. February 25, 1906 in Brühl/Köln/ (Rheinland) [Report on experiences in Berlin Gestapo prisons and concentration camp Buchenwald on the basis of the reports by Mr. Ernest Platz, born February 25, 1906 in Brühl]," unpublished (in the possession of the author).

32. Gerhard Harig/Max Mayr, "Die zahlenmässige Entwicklung des Konzentrationslagers Buchenwald, 1937 bis 1945, bearbeitet auf Grund vollständiger Unterlagen der zuständigen Dienststellen [The numerical development of the concentration camp Buchenwald, 1937–45, compiled on the basis of complete records of the appropriate departments]," unpublished (in the author's possession).

33. O. Horn, op. cit.

34. "Zeittafel des Konzentrationslagers Sachsenhausen [Chronological table of concentration camp Sachsenhausen]," in *Internationale Hefte der Widerstandsbewegung*, Vienna, 1960–67.

35. "Die ersten Polen in Auschwitz [The first Poles in Auschwitz]," in Bulletin of the Auschwitz International Committee, Warsaw 1974–76.

36. Conversation between Emil Carlebach and Falk Pingel, May 2, 1974.

37. Heinz Gross, the former capo of the Gustloff Works detail (Buchenwald), wrote in 1945: "From the beginning it was . . . the endeavor of the responsible inmates who were employed as capos, foremen, engineers, and specialists not to leave sabotage activity to anyone and everyone, but to direct it systematically. Individual actions that could easily lead to detection were rejected" ("Die Sabotage der Häftlinge in den Buchenwälder Gustloff-Werken [Prisoner sabotage in Buchenwald's Gustloff-Works]," unpublished, [Documentation Archives of the Austrian Resistance, Vienna]). The same principle was applied in Dora: "Acts of sabotage on the V-rockets were under no circumstances left to chance—for two reasons: In the first place, spontaneous sabotage would not have been effective, and in the second place, the SS would have quickly identified the participants in such spontaneous actions and executed them" (Češpiva/Giessner/Pelný 1964, 35).

38. E. Carlebach, op. cit.

39. O. Horn, op. cit.

40. Author's conversation with Jozef Gárliński, November 10, 1973.

41. See note 26.

42. Franz Bera wrote in Vienna on June 5, 1945: "My activity . . . began with my leadership of an Austrian group in the spring of 1942." ("Meine Tätigkeit im internationalen militärischen Kader im KL Buchenwald [My activities in the international military cadre in concentration camp Buchenwald]," unpublished [Dokumentations-Archiv, Vienna], order number 958). However, Baky Nazirov writes that the first meeting of the future Russian military

NOTES 411

center took place on an evening in December 1943, and he names the five Russian participants (Nazirov 1959, 48ff.). With reference to Buchenwald, Wolfgang Kiessling writes: "In late 1942, when the victory of the Soviet army at the Volga marked the turning point of World War II, the party leadership thought the time had come to prepare for military contests with the SS" (Kiessling 1964, 199).

43. M. Constante, op. cit. Elsewhere he writes that the first military organization was founded by Spaniards in the fall of 1943 and that it was expanded into an international organization thanks to the Frenchmen who were arriving in the camp and Artur London, a Czech veteran of the Spanish Civil War, who was deported to Mauthausen along with them (Constante 1971, 210). Manuel Razola and Mariano Constante give spring 1944 as the inception of this military organization (Razola/Constante 1969, 126).

44. Kazimierz Smoleń cites Witold Pilecki's 1941 statement that the important thing was to have control of the camp "for the moment when help will come from the outside, be it in the form of an order or an invasion" (Smoleń 1960–67, 40). Elsewhere he cites a letter from the Combat Group Auschwitz dated September 8, 1944, which gives the relative strength, the lodgings, the armaments, and the alarm system of the SS as well as a defensive plan (Smoleń 1960–67, 41). Hermann Langbein has described the preceding discussion of the Combat Group leadership and mentioned the Russians' urging that preparations for an armed uprising be made (Langbein 1949, 157); this is also described by M. S. Sobochenii (1965). Tomasz Sobański has discussed the formation of a military council in the camp in the spring of 1944, whose leadership comprised three Poles and one Austrian, as well as a conference held in Kraków in July 1944 that concerned itself with the question of how the camp could be given military aid if the SS planned its total destruction. This subject was discussed on a number of subsequent occasions (Sobochenii 1961, 93 ff.).

8. THE GERMANS IN THE RESISTANCE

1. Author's conversation with Harry Naujoks, November 3, 1973.
2. Author's conversation with Wincenty Hein, February 8, 1976.
3. Letter to the author from J. B. Krokowski.
4. Alfred Hübsch, "Die Insel des Standrechts: Geheimaufzeichnungen des Pförtners fron Dachau [The island of martial law: The secret records of the Dachau gatekeeper]," unpublished (Dachau Museum), p. 331.
5. J. B. Krokowski, op. cit.
6. Author's conversation with Helene Potetz, February 12, 1976.
7. Unpublished letter from Hans Sündermann dated March 3, 1958 (Documentation Archives of the Austrian Resistance, Vienna).
8. Author's conversation with Eugene Ost, November 19, 1973.
9. Author's conversation with Gustl Gattinger, March 5, 1976.
10. Author's conversation with Hans Gasparitsch, November 20, 1976.

11. Author's conversation with Franz Freihaut, July 11, 1978.

12. Kogon points out that it seems impossible to him to characterize the Germans in the camp in a few words, which would of necessity make this picture "one-sided and even distorted."

13. Author's conversation with Leo Bartimes, November 18, 1973. Bartimes made this statement in the camp and was urged to revoke it. He did not do so, but consulted Seidel, a German veteran of the Spanish Civil War, who reassured him and said this was not cause for concern.

14. Otto Horn, "Ausführlicher Bericht über das Konzentrationslager Buchenwald [Complete report on the concentration camp Buchenwald]," unpublished (Documentation Archives, Vienna).

15. Sonntag said this in a sort of welcoming speech that he had translated by an interpreter, who feared that the speech could be brought to the attention of the camp administration. Nothing of the sort happened, and the end of the speech was greeted with "rapturous applause."

16. Letter to the author from Drahomír Bárta, March 2, 1980.

17. Letter from Jerzy Kwiatkowski to the author, July 9, 1974.

18. Maria Kurcyuszowa's essay about the struggle of Polish women against biological destruction in Ravensbrück (German version in the author's possession). Kurcyuszowa states that candidates for various positions in the camp hierarchy were selected randomly and that this process was somewhat flawed. Knowledge of the German language was the decisive factor.

19. Ewald Gondzik, "Zusammenarbeit der Nationen in deutschen Konzentrationslagern [Collaboration of the nations in German concentration camps]," unpublished manuscript written on October 29, 1945 (Royal Institute for War Documentation, Amsterdam).

20. Karl Ludwig Schecher, "Rückblick auf Dachau [Dachau in retrospect]," unpublished (Dachau Museum), p. 327.

21. There is a report that in Dora a special detail comprising about sixty criminal inmates was formed and armed in the final period (Češpiva/Giessner/Pelný 1964, 466). In Gross–Rosen, Greens were also armed and on the side of the SS in the last weeks (Kautsky 1961, 277). In the final weeks of Flossenbürg the commandant appealed to German Reds to defend the fatherland. Some came forward and then played a positive role on the evacuation transport (author's conversation with Harry Naujoks, November 3, 1973). On April 30, 1945, German Reds and Greens in Neuengamme were, without being consulted, transferred from the camp to an SS barracks to be used for military operations. In the course of the general disintegration, they left the barracks again two days later. (Author's conversation on November 4, 1973, with Albin Lüdke, who was himself a member of that group, which he estimates as comprising 300 to 350 men). In an unpublished manuscript entitled "Die Geschichte des Konzentrationslagers Neuengamme [History of the concentration camp Neuengamme]," the number of Germans is given as 368 and the day of their military mobilization as April 29, 1945 (Wiener Library, London). Between April 15 and 20, 1945, most of the Germans and Gypsies in Sachsenhausen received uniforms and

weapons, and they had to go along on the evacuation marches as guards, together with SS men. They remained in touch with their comrades, who continued to wear prisoners' garb, and kept them informed (*Damals in Sachsenhausen* 1967, 128, 130). In the final days the commandant of Mauthausen too formed special units consisting of Germans. The international prisoners' committee induced the interned Viennese firemen and about eighty others to join these special units, which were provided with fancy uniforms. During the night of liberation, they were able to join their armed comrades who were wearing inmates' uniforms (Maršàlek n.d., 36, 47; 112). On the last day of Loiblpass, a subcamp of Mauthausen, the senior block inmates exchanged their prison garb for SS uniforms and performed drills (Bernadac 1975, 162).

22. Walter Leitner, "Die letzten Tage im Konzentrationslager Dachau [The last days in concentration camp Dachau]," unpublished (Dachau Museum). Leitner mentions that in the last year "honorable German and Austrian comrades" were betrayed and persecuted and that many "sleazy elements who did not deserve red markings" hobnobbed with the SS.

23. Arthur Haulot, "Kameradschaft im KZ [Comradeship in the concentration camp]," in *Süddeutsche Zeitung*, December 11, 1945.

24. "Bericht des Niederländischen Komitees über die illegalen Vorbereitungen zur internationalen, antifaschistischen Zusammenarbeit im Lager Buchenwald [Report of the Netherlands Committee on the illegal preparations for the international, anti-Fascist collaboration in Camp Buchenwald]," signed by representatives of the antirevolutionary, Liberal Democratic, Social Democratic, and Communist parties of the Netherlands, unpublished (Royal Institute, Amsterdam). There we find the following statement about the Germans: "This upright, combative attitude was the well from which the strength demonstrated here in the camp could be drawn."

9. THE ROLE OF THE COMMUNISTS

1. On March 26, 1944, Artur London arrived in Mauthausen from France, where he had been arrested as a former member of the international brigades and active member of the French Resistance.

2. Author's conversation with Franz Freihaut, July 11, 1978.

3. Author's conversation with Janet Ranzinger, October 30, 1976.

4. This report was signed on behalf of the Komitet Polski by Stefan Szczepaniak, Pawel Kwoczek, and Władek Nowak, unpublished (Royal Institute for War Documentation, Amsterdam).

5. "Vorläufiger Bericht über die militärische Organisation im Konzentrationslager Buchenwald [Preliminary report on the military organization in concentration camp Buchenwald]," unpublished (Royal Institute, Amsterdam).

6. Author's conversation with David Rousset, November 16, 1973.

7. Letter to the author from Max Mayr, May 26, 1976.

8. Author's conversation with Harry Naujoks, November 3, 1973.

9. Letter from Wincenty Hein to the author, July 13, 1974.

10. Author's conversation with Fritz Kleinmann, December 12, 1976. At that time Kleinmann declined to join the Communist Party.

11. "Bericht der kommunistischen Parteigruppe des KL Jawiszowice [Report of the Communist Party group of the concentration camp Jawiszowice]," written by four members of that group on May 16, 1945, unpublished (in the possession of the author); author's conversation with Heribert Kreuzmann on January 27, 1978.

12. Author's conversation with Walter Vielhauer, November 21, 1976. Vielhauer identifies himself as one of the organizers of the German Communists in Dachau.

13. Author's conversation with Harry Naujoks, November 3, 1973.

14. H. Naujoks, op. cit.

15. Author's conversation with Toni Lehr, September 19, 1975. In a conversation with the author on December 3, 1975, the Austrian Communist Bertl Lauscher confirmed that Mela Ernst took the initiative in founding an international organization. In "Bericht über das Konzentrationslager Ravensbrück [Report on the concentration camp Ravensbrück]," unpublished (Documentations Archives of the Austrian Resistance, Vienna), the Austrian Hermine Jursa writes that Mara Gincburg and Mela Ernst, two Austrian women who arrived in Ravensbrück in late 1943 or early 1944, immediately began to develop an international organization. After Gincburg had been shot, Mela Ernst became the focal point of the entire enterprise.

16. There the following analysis of the report by the U.S. Army is cited: "Sustained by the sacred egotism of their mission and the vital idea of forming a Communist Germany, they [the German Communists—H.L.] lost their human idealism. Not for themselves but in the name of a future proletarian Germany, they became hard and justified many remnants of extreme methods."

17. M. de Bouard (1954, 71) names the members of the executive committee of the international organization in its various stages (Bartel 1976, 270 ff.). The leaders of the French resistance group that was formed in mid-June 1944 worked toward an international amalgamation together with Artur London (who appears to have had equally good contacts with the Czech and French groups) and the Spanish group (with which London, a veteran of the Spanish Civil War, also had contact). Bouard emphasizes the special contributions of the Czech resistance group, which had been able to occupy some key positions, to the formation of an international organization. The Austrian Communists agreed to the appointment of an international executive committee, which at first consisted of three Austrians. Dahlem did not join this organization until 1943, but he had been in contact with it before he became a member.

18. According to this unpublished report, 90 percent of the activists were Communists and the other 10 percent Socialists (Royal Institute, Amsterdam).

19. "Bericht des niederländischen Komitees über die illegalen Vorbereitungen zur internationalen, antifaschistischen Zusammenarbeit im Lager Buchenwald [Report of the Netherlands Committee on the illegal preparations to the inter-

national anti-Fascist collaboration in Camp Buchenwald]," signed by representatives of four Dutch parties, unpublished (Royal Institute, Amsterdam). "It was always necessary to point out that the German Communists had already fought Hitler before their years of imprisonment, long before most Dutchmen regarded Hitler and his National Socialism as a menace, and that these Germans must never be placed on the same level as the National Socialists."

20. Unpublished manuscripts written on February 23, March 1, and March 10, 1948 (Royal Institute, Amsterdam).

21. Author's conversation with Heinz Junge, November 6, 1973.

22. Heinz Junge (op. cit.) believes that many statements in Selbmann's book do not stand up, and in a conversation with the author on November 3, 1973, Harry Naujoks said that this novel cannot be taken seriously. In a conversation with the author on November 8, 1973, Heinz Schmidt said that it was a bad book.

23. H. Schmidt, op. cit.

24. H. Junge, op. cit.

25. Hans Pointner, "Zur politischen Lage in Sachsenhausen [The political situation in Sachsenhausen]," Berlin, July 1945 unpublished (Royal Institute, Amsterdam).

26. Karl Raddatz, "Die Sonderaktion vom 2. August 1944 gegen KPD-Funktionäre im KL Sachsenhausen [The special roundup of KPD functionaries, August 2, 1944, in concentration camp Sachsenhausen]," Berlin, May 20, 1945, unpublished (Royal Institute, Amsterdam). Raddatz states that the special commission made use of agents provocateurs and career criminals. He characterizes Bücker's activity as "altogether unconspirative" and Bücker himself as hungry for attention. The Gestapo officials utilized this and described him as the most intelligent inmate and a man with whom they wanted to have political discussions.

27. Author's conversation with Rudolf Gottschalk, February 12, 1977.

28. Author's conversation with Eugen Ochs, February 6, 1977.

29. Author's conversation with David Rousset, November 16, 1973.

30. Author's conversation with Franz Freihaut, July 11, 1978.

31. Author's conversation with George Hess, November 21, 1973.

32. Karl Ludwig Schecher, "Rückblick auf Dachau", 1945, unpublished (Dachau Museum), p. 325.

33. Ernst Thape, "Buchenwald-Tagebuch vom 1. April bis 1. Mai 1945 [Buchenwald diary, April 1–May 1, 1945]," unpublished (in the author's possession), p. 25. Thape goes on to say: "We Social Democrats were also completely ignored when a camp government was formed on April 11" [the day of liberation—H.L.]. The situation did not change until the publication of their manifesto.

34. H. Junge, op. cit.

35. H. Naujoks, op. cit.

36. *Sachsenhausen-Information: Mitteilungsblatt für ehemalige Häftlinge des KZ Sachsenhausen-Oranienburg, deren Angehörige und Hinterbliebene* [Bulletin for former inmates of concentration camp Sachsenhausen-Oranienburg,

their family and survivors, No. 73, May 1973, Dortmund-Hombruch, p. 4 (obituary of Wilhelm Knop).

37. H. Junge, op. cit.

38. On page 81 a female comrade, who had evidently participated in the KPD group, calls the connection a very good one: "It was possible to exchange valuable political analyses."

39. Walter Vielhauer, "Ein Arbeiter aus der Stadt Dachau [a worker from the city of Dachau]," in *Mitteilungsblatt der Lagergemeinschaft Dachau*, Munich, May 1973.

40. Letter to the author from Hans Maršàlek dated November 25, 1975. In that letter Maršàlek corrected an earlier statement that Leo Gabler wrote indoctrination letters that were studied by hundreds (Maršàlek n.d., 16).

41. Cornelis Fels, "Verklaring [Statement]," Amsterdam, October 21, 1947, unpublished (in the possession of the author), p. 13.

42. Janet Ranzinger, "Wie sich die Jugoslawen mit dem Internationalen Komitee im Konzentrationslager Buchenwald verbunden haben [How the Yugoslavians allied themselves with the international committee in concentration camp Buchenwald]," written on February 1, 1964, unpublished (in the author's possession).

43. Author's conversation with Paul Schnabel, February 13, 1977.

44. Note by Tadeusz Patzer, unpublished (in the author's possession).

45. Author's conversation with Margarete Buber-Neumann, June 21, 1973.

46. N. Wijnen, op. cit.

47. Author's conversation with Albert Guérisse, March 2, 1976.

48. Letter to the author from Vratislav Bušek, October 11, 1973.

49. Author's conversation with Wincenty Hein, March 18, 1978.

50. Antonius Franciscus van Velsen, "Verslag [Report]," Den Helder, North Holland, February 5, 1948, unpublished, (Royal Institute, Amsterdam), p. 21.

51. Author's conversation with Leo Bartimes, November 18, 1973.

52. Pierre d'Harcourt also describes a constant covert struggle between Communists and members of other political parties. According to him, the Communists wanted to retain power in the camp so they could use it to fight capitalism after the war (pp. 116, 157).

53. Letter to the author from Tadeusz Patzer, May 17, 1976.

54. Author's conversation with David Rousset, November 16, 1973.

55. Author's conversation with Walter Vielhauer, November 21, 1976.

56. Fritz Keller, "Aus der Biographie des österreichischen Revolutionärs Karl Fischer [From the biography of the Austrian revolutionary Karl Fischer]," in *Rotfront*, No. 7–8, Vienna, July–August 1979.

57. Letter from N. Pandt to L. E. Winkel, Oostzaan, North Holland, January 10, 1951, unpublished (Royal Institute, Amsterdam).

58. Author's conversation with Ernst Toch, September 3, 1976.

59. Author's conversation with Jan van Dijk, November 8, 1973.

60. Author's conversation with René Kerschen, November 20, 1973.

61. Letter to the author from Tadeusz Patzer, April 15, 1976.

62. Unpublished manuscript by J. B. Krokowski (in the author's possession).

63. Author's conversation with Père Riquet, November 15, 1973.

64. Author's conversation with Joop Telling, November 8, 1973.

65. "Bericht über das Konzentratoinslager Sachsenhausen [Report on the concentration camp Sachsenhausen]." Cf. note 40, Chapter 2.

66. Author's conversation with Willi Bleicher, November 20, 1976. Like Robert Siewert, who gave the memorial address, Bleicher had been a member of an opposition group within the KPD that was led by Brandler, which means that he had a critical attitude toward Thälmann.

67. Author's conversation with Eugen Ochs, February 6, 1977. Ochs, who attended this memorial, admits that its organizers were careless. He believes that the informer was a Belgian.

68. W. Bleicher, op. cit.

69. K. Raddatz, op. cit.

70. Letter from Tadeusz Patzer to the author, April 15, 1976.

71. Letter to the author from Wincenty Hein, February 8, 1976.

72. There we read: "Shortly after his arrival in Mittelbau-Dora, Albert Kuntz organized the first underground meeting of the German anti-Fascists. . . . Under their influence national resistance groups formed one by one."

73. J. B. Krokowski, op. cit., and conversation with the author on November 2, 1974.

74. Letter to the author from Tadeusz Patzer, April 15, 1976.

75. Letters to the author from Wincenty Hein dated June 10, 1974, and February 8, 1976.

76. Author's conversation with Wincenty Hein, March 18, 1978.

77. Author's conversation with Willi Bleicher, November 20, 1976.

78. Undated letter to the author from Jaroslav Marik (presumably written in September 1975).

79. Author's conversation with Charlotte Delbo on November 16, 1973.

80. Author's conversation with Juan de Diego on July 9, 1974.

81. Letters from Vratislav Bušek to the author dated August 7, 1973, and May 17, 1974.

82. Letter to the author from Hans Maršàlek, October 17, 1975.

10. SOCIAL DEMOCRATS IN THE RESISTANCE

1. Author's conversation with Toni Lehr on September 19, 1975.

2. Author's conversation with Margarete Buber-Neumann, June 21, 1973.

3. Unpublished (Royal Institute for War Documentation, Amsterdam).

4. Author's conversation with Harry Naujoks, November 3, 1973.

5. Author's conversation with Georg Scherer, April 2, 1979.

6. Unpublished notes by Jan Domagala (Dachau Museum).

7. Author's conversation with Eugen Ochs, February 6, 1977.

8. Karl Ludwig Schecher, "Rückblick auf Dachau," unpublished (Dachau Museum).

9. Letter to the author from Eugen Ochs, December 15, 1976.

10. Walter Neff, "Recht oder Unrecht [Right or wrong]," unpublished (Dachau Museum).

11. K. L. Schecher, op. cit.

12. The Germans Fleischner and Zeibig, the Sudeten German Karl Lill, and the Austrian Hermann Langbein. There were some others who were not particularly qualified to fight typhus—e.g., the heads of the diet kitchen or the X-ray station.

13. "Hermann Langbein, a veteran of the Spanish Civil War, obtained for him a fourteen days' rest period in the convalescents' block. Despite the fact that this was strictly prohibited, he had repeatedly looked after the inmates, and he had actually saved the lives of some of them. He was found out . . . which meant transport to Auschwitz . . . intended to send that inmate to his death" (Plieseis 1946, 201).

14. Author's conversation with Hans Gasparitsch, November 20, 1976.

15. Author's conversation with Julius Schätzle, February 5, 1977. However, Schätzle emphasizes that in the Work Assignment, he and Kuno Rieke, an official of the SPD, worked together harmoniously.

16. Author's conversation with Franz Freihaut, July 11, 1978.

17. Author's conversation with Joseph Rovan, March 2, 1976. According to Rovan, Austrians from the Catholic camp also filled such positions at that time.

18. Thape became a member of the popular-front committee in March 1944; the Communist Walter Wolf joined it in May, and Werner Hilpert of the Center Party in June of that year. Klaus Drobisch, who endeavors to give Communists credit for all achievements of the resistance organization, has stated that the German Communists Harry Kuhn and Walter Wolf took the initiative (Drobisch 1968, 83 ff.).

19. Ernst Thape, "Buchenwald-Tagebuch vom 1. April bis 1. Mai 1945 [Buchenwald diary April 1–May 1, 1945]," unpublished (in the author's possession), entry of April 22, 1945.

20. The members of this committee were Heinz Baumeister, Gottlieb Branz, Hermann Brill, Erich Schilling, and Ernst Thape from the SPD and Benedikt Kautsky (who was put in charge of reports) and Karl Mantler from the SPÖ (Austrian Socialist Party). The manifesto was also signed by twenty-six German Socialists, five Austrian, two Czech, one Belgian, and one Dutch.

21. E. Thape, op. cit., entry of April 22, 1945.

22. The following have been named as members of the original group: The Communists Georg Thomas and Ludwig Szimczak (both senior camp inmates), Karl Schweizer and Fritz Pröll (capo and clerk in the infirmary), Otto Runki (capo of camp security), Albert Kuntz (camp technician), and the Social Democrat August Kroneberg (capo of the carpentry detail). In the course of 1944, the Communists Christian Beham, Josef Gamisch, Heinz Schneider, and Paul Luzius as well as the Social Democrats Fritz Lehmann and Johann Ackermann were added.

23. Debski-Dubois has been described as "one of the leaders of the underground

resistance movement in the camp." One day someone sent Dubois a parcel. Since the receipt of parcels was not yet permitted at that time, the political department guessed that Dubois was maintaining secret contacts with Poles outside the camp.

24. Referring to a conversation with me, Gárliński has stated that Ernst Burger's position in the resistance movement was weak. However, in every conversation with Gárliński, I stressed the great authority that Burger's conduct in the camp gave him as well as the effects of his actions. On p. 211 Gárliński writes the opposite of what I told him without citing a source that might refute my statements. In the conversations to which he refers, I made it plain that while I condemn many actions of the Polish prime minister Cyrankiewicz, I am not willing to disparage his activity in Auschwitz.

25. The nationalistic attitude is expressed by Gárliński (1975A, 198 ff.). Concerning the active anti-Semitism of leading members of the Polish resistance movement, cf. Gárliński (1975A, 210 ff.); regarding Rudolf Diem, cf. (Langbein 1972, 260 ff.; about Wladyslaw Dering, cf. Gárliński 1975A, 220, and Langbein 1972, 255 ff.

26. Józef Gárliński (1975A, 236) believes that Cyrankiewicz was so recognized in August 1944, but as I recall it, this happened much earlier.

11. THE SPECIAL ROLE OF THE AUSTRIANS

1. Unpublished (Documentation Archives of the Austrian Resistance, Vienna). Excerpts from this report are contained in the collection *Buchenwald* (1960, 399 ff.) under the title "Bericht des österreichischen Komitees über das KZ Buchenwald [Report of the Austrian Committee on concentration camp Buchenwald]." There Otto Horn and Kurt Gardner are listed as the authors.

2. "Bericht über das KZ Ravensbrück [Report on concentration camp Ravensbrück]," unpublished (Documentations Archive, Vienna).

3. Author's conversation with Bertl Lauscher, December 3, 1975.

4. Cf. note 7, Chapter 6.

5. "Bericht der Österreicher an die Abteilung für psychologische Kriegsführung in der amerikanischen Armee [Report of the Austrians to the unit for psychological warfare in the American army]," op. cit. In the collection *Buchenwald* (op. cit.) this passage is printed with minor changes that are not identified as such. Thus *deutsche Gedanken* [German ideas] "*was changed to grossdeutsche Gedanken* [Greater German ideas]." (*Buchenwald* 1960, 401).

6. Otto Horn, "Ausführlicher Bericht über das Konzentrationslager Buchenwald [Complete report on concentration camp Buchenwald]," unpublished (Documentations Archives, Vienna).

7. Author's conversation with Franz Freihaut, July 11, 1978.

8. According to Michel de Bouard, the first executive committee of the international organization (which was evidently created by Communists) consisted of the Austrians Kohl, Maršàlek, and Gabler (whom he calls Mayer) (Bernadac

1974, 271). Guatav Rabaté writes that he and his French comrades wanted an Austrian to head the international committee—"because Mauthausen is located in Austria." At Kohl's suggestion Gabler was given this position (Bernadoc 1974, 263).

9. Author's conversations with Fritz Kleinmann (December 12, 1976) and Erich Fein (December 28, 1976). In this connection Kleinmann mentions the Austrians Paul Springer, Fein, and Kurt Mellach.

10. Here is an excerpt from the passage in question: "Representatives of Democratic Socialism from Berlin, Brandenburg, Central Germany, Saxony, Thuringia, Anhalt, Hannover, Brunswick, Westphalia, Rhineland, Saarland, Bavaria, and Austria . . . in the presence of . . . representatives . . . of the French, Belgian, Dutch, Czech, and Polish Socialists. . . ."

11. These five were August Bergmann, Leopold Brünler, Josef Cmejrek, Ed. Goldmann, and Fritz Pollak (all from Vienna) (Kautsky 1961, 292).

12. Author's conversation with Toni Lehr, September 19, 1975.

13. W. Biktashov, "Wir haben unseren Tod überlebt [We have survived our death]," Moscow, 1975, unpublished (partial German translation).

14. Karl Ludwig Schecher, op. cit.

15. Author's conversation with Edwin Tangl, February 16, 1977. According to Tangl, there was a harmonious relationship between the leading officials of the SPD and the SPO (he mentions Schumacher and Olah), but the other members of these two brother parties were by no means in agreement. For example, Tangl himself, an Austrian Social Democrat, was bitterly opposed by members of the SPD.

16. "Bericht der Österreicher an die Abteilung für psychologische Kriegsführung [Report of the Austrians to the unit for psychological warfare]," op. cit.

17. Unpublished letter from Hans Sündermann to Walter, March 3, 1958 (Documentations Archives, Vienna). He mentions connections with "the Czech, Yugoslav, Polish, French, and Dutch comrades."

18. "Die polnische Geheimorganisation im KL Buchenwald [The Polish secret organization in concentration camp Buchenwald]," written on behalf of the Komitet Polski by Stefan Szczepaniak, Pawel Kwoczek, and Władek Nowak, unpublished (Royal Institute for War Documentation, Amsterdam). Wegerer, through whom the first "official contact" of the Polish group was made, is described as a leading German Communist, but he is also identified as a Viennese chemist. As a matter of fact, he took a leading part in the Austrian group.

19. Author's conversation with Juan de Diego, July 9, 1974.

20. Mariano Constante, "Les republicains espagnols dans la lutte antinazi [The Spanish republicans in the anti-Nazi struggle]," unpublished (in the possession of the author). Constante emphasizes that Kohl felt duty-bound to make contact with the Spaniards immediately after their arrival, and through his good offices they were able to establish the first international connections. The German Hans Seigewasser has described Pepi Kohl as the initiator of brotherly solidarity (Sakharov 1961, 237), and Bruno Baum has characterized him as the good spirit of the inmates (Baum 1965, 32).

21. In addition to Maršalek, the two Czechs Marecek and Hrbek have been named. At that time the International Red Cross took 596 male prisoners to Switzerland. These included 531 Frenchmen, forty Belgians, and twenty-one Dutchmen—13 percent of the members of these nationalities who were interned in Mauthausen (Maršàlek 1974, 240).

22. Letter from Hans Maršàlek to the author, November 25, 1975.

23. "Blut und Granit [Blood and granite]," interview with Hans Maršàlek, in *Volksstimme*, Vienna, August 12, 1973.

24. Author's conversation with Janez Ranzinger, October 30, 1976. In this connection Ranzinger also names Rudi Göbel, a German veteran of the Spanish Civil War. As senior block inmate in Block 5, Göbel had close contact with Ernst Burger at that time.

25. Author's conversation with Isaac Liver, March 3, 1976. Originally from Poland, Liver was deported from France to Auschwitz on a Jewish transport.

26. Garnier erroneously writes Ernst Bruger.

27. Bruno Baum, *Widerstand in Auschwitz: Bericht der internationalen antifaschistischen Lagerleitung* (Resistance in Auschwitz: Report of the International Anti-Fascist Camp Leadership) Berlin-Potsdam, 1949, p. 8 ff. Evidently Baum was poorly informed, for he wrote that Langbein escaped from Bremen, where he had been transferred. "We also heard that he had been arrested again in Berlin, and then we lost track of him." In point of fact, from Bremen I was able to establish contact with Auschwitz through the good offices of Sister Maria, but I never fled to Berlin. The second, expanded edition of Baum's book contains the same statement with some stylistic changes (p. 66 ff.) In a later edition, issued by the same publisher in 1961, the name Langbein was omitted and replaced with "an Austrian" (p. 66 ff.) Between 1957 and 1961, I broke with the Austrian Communist Party.

28. Secret letter from Józef Cyrankiewicz to "Adam," later translated into German by Cyrankiewicz, unpublished (in the author's possession).

29. From its establishment in the spring of 1943 to August 1944, the leadership of the Combat Group consisted of the Poles Józef Cyrankiewicz and Tadeusz Hołuj and the Austrians Ernst Burger and Hermann Langbein. When, in August 1944, preparations were made for an escape in which Burger and Langbein were to be involved, they resigned from the executive committee and were replaced by the Austrian Rudolf Friemel.

30. "Landsberg/Lech, Fliegerhorst," a report by Edwin Tangl about a subcamp of Dachau, transcribed from a tape, unpublished (Dachau Museum). This subcamp contained French inmates almost exclusively.

12. THE POLES

1. Gerhard Harig and Max Mayr write in their report "Die zahlenmässige Entwicklung des Konzentrationslagers Buchenwald [The numerical development of the concentration camp Buchenwald], 1937–1945," composed shortly after

the liberation, unpublished (in the author's possession): "On October 15, 1939, 1,000 Poles and on the next day 1,098 arrived. They were sheltered under the most primitive and most barbaric conditions in tents in the half-finished roll-call area, where they received only half-rations." As a consequence, the number of deaths rose from forty-four between mid-September and mid-October to 283 between mid-October and mid-November.

2. "In that period 17,000 prisoners, predominantly Poles, arrived in the camp. By means of terrorism and murder, SS men and specially selected criminal inmates decimated this big group of prisoners. Some of them were later transported to Flossenbürg, Neuengamme, Dachau, and Gross–Rosen" (*Damals in Sachsenhausen* 1967, 143).

3. In "Geschichte des Konzentrationslagers Neuengamme [History of the concentration camp Neuengamme]," evidently written by Hans Schwarz, unpublished (Wiener Library, London), Polish mass transports in the spring of 1940 are mentioned. We have no exact data about Gross–Rosen, but reports agree that numerous Poles were sent there at that period.

4. The first transport of prisoners of a different nationality (sixty Czechs) did not arrive in Auschwitz until June 6, 1941, when the camp had been in operation for almost a year (Czech 1959–64).

5. Author's conversation with David Rousset, November 16, 1973.

6. In this connection Kautsky speaks of a "gang of mostly young lads" who indulged their cruel instincts in Auschwitz undisturbed by the fact that from time to time the SS "shot large numbers of Polish functionaries or killed them in some other way."

7. Author's conversation with Heribert Kreuzmann, January 27, 1978.

8. Hermann Joseph, "Der Fall [case] 104338," unpublished manuscript, p. 159 ff.

9. Conversation between Dawid Szmulewski and Tzipora Weiss, November 16, 1977.

10. Secret letter from Józef Cyrankiewicz to "Adam," later translated into German by the writer, unpublished (in the author's possession).

11. Bistric names Adam Zacharski, Tadeusz Paczula, and Jurek Czubak, but these certainly were not the only Poles on the staff of the infirmary who rejected anti-Semitic tendencies.

12. Józef Gárliński repeatedly mentions Władysław Dering as an activist and commander of the military organization in the infirmary (Gárliński 1975A, 143). In the Appendix he writes that Dering was tacitly denounced in a London trial (he had sued the American writer Leon Uris for defamation of character, and the court awarded him a contemptuous halfpenny as compensation for his tarnished reputation), but he does not give the reason for this verdict. On the basis of a great deal of testimony, the court concluded that Dering had taken action against Jewish fellow inmates (Gárliński 1975A, 273; Langbein 1972, 257). The charges against him referred to the voluntary assistance he gave SS doctors in medical experiments on Jews. Józef Cyrankiewicz, who may be credited with a good knowledge of Polish internal affairs in Auschwitz, has stated that, far from being a Hitler agent, Dering took an active part in the

Polish resistance, but that he was not much of a surgeon (Cyrankiewicz's conversation with Tzipora Weiss, November 12, 1977). As regards Alfred Stössel, whom Gárliński has also identified as an active member of the Polish military organization, Wiesław Kielar (who calls him Fred Stessel) remembers his excessive zeal and his kowtowing to the camp authorities, but he adds that this Polish senior block inmate's death in the bunker rehabilitated him in the eyes of many (Kielar 1979, 254).

13. Letter to the author from Tadeusz Patzer, May 17, 1976.

14. Author's conversation with Walter Vielhauer, November 21, 1976.

15. Otto Horn, "Ausführlicher Bericht über das Konzentrationslager Buchenwald [Complete report on concentration camp Buchenwald]," unpublished (Documentations Archives of the Austrian Resistance, Vienna).

16. Hans Pointner, "Zur politischen Lage in Sachsenhausen [The political situation in Sachsenhausen]," written in Berlin in July 1945, unpublished (Royal Institute for War Documentation, Amsterdam).

17. Author's conversation with Heinz Junge, November 6, 1973.

18. Unpublished manuscript by J. B. Krokowski (in the author's possession).

19. Letter to the author from Bogdan Suczowiak, November 8, 1975.

20. Letter to the author from Jerzy Kwiatkowski, April 4, 1974.

21. Maria Kuryuszowa, "Die Polinnen im Kampf gegen die biologische Vernichtung im Konzentrationslager Ravensbrück [Polish women in the struggle against biological destruction in concentration camp Ravensbrück]," unpublished (German translation in the author's possession).

22. Urszula Wińska, "Die kulturelle Bildungsarbeit als eigentümliche Form der Widerstandsbewegung der Häftlinge im Konzentrationslager Ravensbrück [Cultural education as a characteristic form of resistance activity of the prisoners in concentration camp Ravensbrück]" unpublished (in the author's possession).

23. U. Wińska, op. cit.

24. Author's conversation with Hans Gasparitsch, November 29, 1976.

25. Cf. note 3.

26. Ewald Gondzik, "Zusammenarbeit der Nationen in deutschen Konzentrationslagern [Collaboration of the nations in German concentration camps]," Hamburg, October 29, 1945, unpublished (Royal Institute, Amsterdam).

27. Letter to the author from Ewald Gondzik, July 11, 1974.

28. Author's conversation with Józef Gárliński, November 10, 1973.

29. Letter from E. Gondzik, op. cit.

30. Letter to the author from Albin Lüdke, November 10, 1973.

31. "Die polnische Geheimorganisation im K. L. Buchenwald [The Polish secret organization in concentration camp Buchenwald]," written on behalf of the Komitet Polski by Stefan Szczepaniak, Pawel Kwoczek, and Władek Nowak, unpublished (Royal Institute, Amsterdam). Szczepaniak, who was elected as chairman of the committee shortly after the liberation, is identified as "president of the association of Poles in Germany" and Nowak as "chairman of the

association of Polish boy scouts in Germany." Nowak was the first Polish senoir block inmate in Buchenwald.

32. Janez Ranzinger, "Wie sich die Jugoslawen mit dem internationalen Komitee im Konzentrationslager Buchenwald verbunden haben [How the Yugoslavians allied themselves with the international committee in concentration camp Buchenwald]," unpublished (in the author's possession). The names he gives are different from those given in the report cited in note 31 and also by Czarnecki.

33. Author's conversation with Janez Ranzinger, October 30, 1976.

34. Mariano Constante, "Les republicains espagnols dans le lutte anti-nazi [The Spanish republicans in the anti-Nazi struggle]," unpublished (in the author's possession). In this connection he gives special mention to Marian, the capo of the construction detail.

35. Stanislaw Nogaj, "Gusen: Tagebuch eines Journalisten [Diary of a journalist]," unpublished (Central Office in the Province Nordrhein-Westfalen for the Compiling of Nazi Mass Crimes in Concentration Camps, Cologne).

36. J. B. Krokowski, op. cit.

37. Author's conversation with Harry Naujoks, November 3, 1973.

38. Author's conversation with Helene Potetz, February 12, 1976.

39. "Die Rettung [The deliverance]," in Österreicherinnen unter Hitler im Frauen-KL Ravensbrück [Austrian women under Hitler in the female concentration camp Ravensbrück], unpublished (in the author's possession).

40. Verdict of the Essen district court, May 8, 1970 (Az:29a Ks 9/66), unpublished.

13. THE RUSSIANS

1. Author's conversation with Julius Schätzle, February 5, 1977.

2. This source also describes the breakout from the camp, in late June 1942, of the surviving Russians, whose situation was hopeless. Thanks to the dark night, only four of the fugitives were shot. The SS killed the fifty remaining Russians in the courtyard of the camp.

3. Notes made by Hermann Langbein in Hannover in late April 1945, unpublished (in the author's possession).

4. Josef Marszalek, "Geneza i poczatki budowy obozu koncentracyjnego na Majdanku [Genesis of the original building of a concentration camp at Majdanek]," in Zeszyty Majdanka No. 1, Lublin, 1965. This article contains a letter to the Reichsführer SS [Himmler] from the Reich minister of transportation and general director of the Reich railroads, dated March 7, 1942: "A barracks camp for 150,000 people is to be built immediately in Lublin. It will initially serve as a prisoner-of-war camp, and at a later date it will be converted into a concentration camp." The Lublin district in which this camp was built is called Majdan Tatarski (Tartar Square) or Majdanek.

5. Author's conversation with Andrzej Kamiński, December 14, 1974.

6. Selbmann writes that this chief capo, Korsikov, prepared an attempt by Rus-

sians to break out but evidently betrayed it to the SS. The Russians were shot, and Korsikov disappeared in the bunker. "Perhaps the SS will ship him off to another camp in order to repeat this treacherous game there. On the other hand, now that he has done his duty, he may be eliminated in the usual way. . . . In any case, the camp won't see him again," (Selbmann 1961, 310).

7. Author's conversation with Helene Potetz, February 12, 1976.
8. Maria Kurcyuszowa, op. cit.
9. Notes by J. B. Krokowski, unpublished (in the author's possession).
10. Author's conversation with Leo Bartimes, November 18, 1973.
11. Otto Horn, op. cit.
12. Hans Pointner, "Zur politischen Lage in Sachsenhausen [The political situation in Sachsenhausen]," written in July 1945, unpublished (Royal Institute for War Documentation, Amsterdam).
13. Author's conversation with Jan van Dijk, November 8, 1973.
14. Author's conversation with Georg Buch, November 22, 1973.
15. Author's conversation with Harry Naujoks, November 3, 1973.
16. Antonius Franciscus van Velsen, "Verslag [Report]," February 8, 1948, unpublished (Royal Institute, Amsterdam).
17. *War Behind Barbed Wire: Reminiscences of Buchenwald Ex-Prisoners of War* (Foreign Languages Publishing House, Moscow, 1959). It has repeatedly been reported that many Russians who had been able to survive Nazi concentration camps were subsequently interned in Soviet camps. Nikolai Simakov, a high Russian officer who, according to all reports, was the head of the Russian resistance groups in Buchenwald, was placed in a Soviet detention camp after the war. (Author's conversation with Eric Fein, December 28, 1976.) Jorge Semprun, formerly a leading official of the Spanish Communist Party and himself interned in Buchenwald, writes that the Soviet prisoners "for the most part went directly from the German camps to Stalin's gulags" (Semprun 1978, 132).
18. W. Biktashov, "Wir haben unseren Tod überlebt [We have survived our death]," manuscript translated from the Russian.
19. In the last days before the liberation the Russians actually constituted the second-largest group. The count on April 26, 1945, was 14,994 Poles and 13,536 Russians, followed by Jews, Germans (including Austrians), and Frenchmen, who numbered 5,706 (Berben 1968, 213).
20. Author's conversation with Albert Guérisse, March 2, 1976.
21. Statement by N. Wijnen, February/March 1948, unpublished (Royal Institute, Amsterdam).
22. A. van Velsen, op. cit.
23. Author's conversation with David Rousset, November 26, 1973.

14. OTHER ETHNIC GROUPS

1. The first Czechs arrived in Mauthausen on May 10, 1939 and were transferred

to Dachau on June 16 (Maršàlek 1974, 93). Sachsenhausen admitted 1,700 Czechs, including 1,200 students at the universities of Prague and Brno, on November 20, 1939 (*Damals in Sachsenhausen* 1967, 141). The first sixty Czechs were deported to Auschwitz on June 6, 1941.

2. The first Belgians and Frenchmen arrived in Mauthausen on May 11, 1942, and larger numbers began to arrive in April 1943 (Maršàlek 1974, 96 ff.). The first Frenchmen were deported to Buchenwald in early 1942 (Buchenwald 1960, 42), and larger numbers of them began to arrive there in June 1943 (Gerhard Harig/ Max Mayr, "Die zahlenmässige Entwicklung des Konzentrationslagers Buchenwald [The numerical development of concentration camp Buchenwald]," unpublished (in the author's possession).

3. Author's conversation with Helene Potetz, February 12, 1976.

4. Author's conversation with Willi Bleicher, November 20, 1976.

5. Author's conversation with David Rousset, November 16, 1976.

6. J. B. Krokowski's unpublished manuscript about Dora (in the author's possession).

7. "Rückblick auf Dachau" Karl Ludwig Schecher's unpublished notes (Dachau Museum).

8. Cf. Langbein 1949, 100 ff., and 1972, 98 ff. For a description of the way the resistance movement in Auschwitz managed to get Jewish doctors placed on the staffs of the prisoners' hospitals.

9. Author's conversation with Ernest Martin, June 11, 1973.

10. Author's conversation with Père Riquet, November 15, 1973.

11. Author's conversation with Juan de Diego, July 9, 1974.

12. Author's conversation with Albert Guérisse, March 2, 1976.

13. "Österreicherinnen unter Hitler im Frauen-KL Ravensbrück [Austrian women under Hitler in the female concentration camp Ravensbrück]," unpublished (in the author's possession).

14. Unpublished report (Royal Institute for War Documentation, Amsterdam).

15. Hans Pointner, op. cit.

16. Otto Horn, op. cit. On the basis of unfounded charges that he had been in the service of the Nazis in Buchenwald, Josef Frank, a top Communist leader and Czech representative on the international camp committee, was sentenced to death in the Slansky Trial of 1952 and executed without any protests from his Communist associates in Buchenwald (Semprun 1978, 161 ff.).

17. Maria Kurcyuszowa, op. cit., p. 18.

18. G. Harig and M. Mayr, op. cit. In September 1943, 1,822 Frenchmen arrived in Buchenwald on two transports, 911 in October, 921 in November, and 5,511 on three transports in January 1944. In all, 21,851 Frenchmen and Belgians were sent to Buchenwald. (The two nations were lumped together in these statistics.)

19. Author's conversation with the Luxembourger Leo Bartimes on November 18, 1973.

20. Author's conversation with the Luxembourger Victor Holper on November 19, 1973.

21. Letter to the author from Wincenty Hain, June 10, 1974.

22. An unsigned "Bericht über die Lage und den Kampf der französischen Schutz-häftlinge im KZ-Lager Buchenwald [Report on the situation and the struggle of the French in protective custody in concentration camp Buchenwald]," has this to say: "The first groups of French prisoners arrived in Buchenwald in early 1942. In the succeeding months the camp admitted around 5,000 Frenchmen from Mauthausen. All these new arrivals were slated for transfer to the subsidiary camp Dora and stayed in Buchenwald for only a short time. In 1944 about 10,000 French prisoners arrived from the Compiègne camp; approximately one-third of these remained in Buchenwald, and all the others were distributed among the satellite camps" (Buchenwald 1960, 420).

23. In the summer of 1943, more than 2,000 Frenchmen arrived in Sachsenhausen. On June 27, 1941, 244 French mine workers were sent there because they had participated in a strike (Damals in Sachsenhausen 1967, 143, 146).

24. Author's conversation with Joseph Rovan, March 2, 1976.

25. Ibid.

26. Author's conversation with Albert Guérisse, March 2, 1976.

27. The Austrian Toni Lehr has called her conduct "fantastic" (in a conversation with the author on September 19, 1975), and Bertl Lauscher, another Austrian, has described her as "very comradely" (in a conversation with the author on December 3, 1975).

28. Author's conversation with Margarete Buber-Neumann, June 21, 1973.

29. Letter to the author from Vratislav Bušek, December 25, 1973.

30. Letter to the author from Drahomír Bárta, March 2, 1980.

31. Author's conversation with David Rousset, November 16, 1973.

32. G. Harig and M. Mayr, op. cit., p. 11.

33. O. Horn, op. cit.

34. Author's conversation with Leo Eitinger, October 28, 1973.

35. Leo Eitinger's unpublished notes about his experiences in Buchenwald, 1945 (in the author's possession).

36. Karl Raddatz, "Die Sonderaktion am 2. August 1944 gegen KPD-Funktionäre im KL Sachsenhausen [Special roundup of KPD officials in concentration camp Sachsenhausen, August 2, 1944]," Berlin, May 20, 1945, unpublished (Royal Institute, Amsterdam).

37. Karl Ludwig Schecher, op. cit.

15. GROUPS IN A SPECIAL POSITION

1. "Bericht über das Konzentrationslager Sachsenhausen [Report on concentration camp Sachsenhausen]," unpublished, (Royal Institute for War Documentation, Amsterdam), p. 27.

2. Author's conversation with Helene Potetz, February 12, 1976.

3. Stanisław Nogaj, "Gusen-Tagebuch eines Journalisten [Diary of a journalist]," unpublished (Central Office in the Province Nordrhein-Westfalen

for the Compiling of Nazi Mass Crimes in Concentration Camps, Cologne),
p. 48.

4. Statement by N. Wijnen, February–March 1948, unpublished (Royal Institute,
   Amsterdam).

5. Author's conversation with Margarete Buber-Neumann, June 21, 1973.

6. Hermine Jursa, "Bericht über das KZ Ravensbrück [Report on concentration
   camp Ravensbrück]," unpublished (Documentations Archives of the Austrian
   Resistance, Vienna).

7. Author's conversation with Margarete Buber-Neumann, June 21, 1973.

8. Otto Horn, op. cit. According to Horn, "in contrast to the method of beating
   inmates to death, the Jehovah's Witnesses were to be brought to their knees by
   petty harassment."

9. Testimony of Wrobel in the Treblinka trial in Düsseldorf on February
   1, 1965. This refusal had no detrimental consequences for the two Jehovah's
   Witnesses.

10. Author's conversation with Helene Potetz, February 12, 1976. Potetz remem-
    bers that thousands of Austrian Gypsies, particularly from the Burgenland
    province and the Laaerberg near Vienna, were brought to Ravensbrück at that
    time.

11. Gerhard Harig and Max Mayr, "Die zahlenmässige Entwicklung des Kon-
    zentrationslagers Buchenwald [Numerical development of the concentration
    camp Buchenwald]," unpublished (in the author's possession).

12. Author's conversation with Jean Pierre Schmit and Leo Bartimes, November
    18, 1973.

13. Author's conversation with Alfred Hammerl and Leo Jansa, November 9, 1976.

14. Author's conversation with Heribert Kreuzmann, January 27, 1978.

15. "Bericht der Österreicher an die Abteilung für psychologische Kriegsführung
    in der amerikanischen Armee [Report of the Austrians on the unit for psycho-
    logical warfare of the American army]," unsigned, evidently written in
    Buchenwald after the liberation, unpublished (Documentations Archives,
    Vienna). An abridged version with minor emendations, signed by Otto Horn
    and Kurt Gardner, has been published under the title Bericht des öster-
    reichischen Komitees über das KZ Buchenwald (Report of the Austrian Com-
    mittee on concentration Camp Buchenwald). The cited passage is omitted
    there (Buchenwald 1960, 399 ff.).

16. A list of the Polish veterans of the Spanish Civil War has been given by David
    Szmulewski (in Revue de l'association des médecins israelites de France No.
    219, Oct. 1973) and by Jozef Sterman (in a letter to the author dated May 1974).
    The Austrian veterans of that war have been identified from memory by
    Heribert Kreuzmann (in a conversation with the author on January 27, 1978)
    and by me. These lists contain the names of veterans of the Spanish Civil War
    and of other nationalities as well, such as Germans, Sudeten Germans, and
    Czechs, but these compilations seem to be even less complete than the lists of
    Polish and Austrian veterans.

17. When this leadership constituted itself in May 1943, I was one of the four

members of the executive committee. When I resigned from it in August 1944, because I was preparing to escape and join the partisans in the vicinity of the camp (and, after the postponement of that flight, was assigned to a transport to Neuengamme), Rudi Friemel, an Austrian veteran of the Spanish Civil War, took my place.

18. In addition to those who will be mentioned in another context, two men who directly collaborated with the leadership of the Combat Group should be named: Josef Farber from Czechoslovakia and Szymon Zajdow from Poland.

19. Conversation between Alter Feinsylberg and Tzipora Weiss, November 17, 1977.

20. Danuta Czech, "Französische Häftlinge des KL Auschwitz [French inmates of the concentration camp Auschwitz]," in *Bulletin des Comité International d'Auschwitz*, Warsaw, August 1975, p. 3. On March 3, 1943, a transport from Drancy brought a hundred prisoners to Auschwitz, where they were assigned to the special detail. "A majority of them had fought against the Germans in the international brigades in Spain and in 1940 as volunteers in the French army. Many of them had been born and raised in Poland.... Those who survived took an active part in the combat groups of the special detail."

21. Unpublished report in the possession of the author. The authors of this report were transferred to Buchenwald after the evacuation of Jawiszowice.

22. Author's conversation with Ludwig Göring, May 8, 1973.

23. Cf. note 21.

24. Author's conversation with Heribert Kreuzmann, January 27, 1978.

25. Hermann Joseph, "Der Fall 104338," unpublished manuscript, p. 82. At that time Joseph himself was registered as a German—that is, "western"—Jew.

26. Author's conversation with Harry Naujoks, November 3, 1973.

27. Author's conversation with Fritz Kleinmann, December 12, 1976. Kleinmann, who had been sent to Auschwitz and Monowitz on the transport from Buchenwald, names the German Stefan Heymann and the Austrians Gustav Herzog, Felix Rausch, and Erich Eisler (who was shot in the fall of 1943 because of his resistance activity).

28. Curt Posener, "Auschwitz—Monowitz," unpublished (in the author's possession).

29. G. Harig and M. Mayr, op. cit. The authors mention ten transports in that period—three with Hungarian Jews from Auschwitz, one each from Graz and Budapest, and three with Polish Jews.

30. Ernst Thape, "Buchenwald—Tagebuch vom 1. April bis 1. Mai 1945 [Diary, April 1–May 1945]," unpublished (in the author's possession).

31. Since Russian Jews in German prisoner-of-war camps frequently took Slavic names in order to escape instant extermination as Jews, it is difficult to establish today which members of the resistance organization were Jewish. Joseph Guri has managed to identify Josef Feldmann (who assumed the name Georgi Pesenko and died on March 10, 1944, in the Dachau prisoners' hospital after having been tortured), Boris Grojsman (Vladimir Moiseyev), Michael

Singer, and Abraham Yasenski (Boris Kelesov)—all of whom were shot on September 4, 1944.

32. "Die polnische Geheimorganisation im K.L. Buchenwald [The Polish secret organization in concentration camp Buchenwald]," undated, evidently written shortly after the liberation, unpublished (in the author's possession). This report, which was signed by the Komitet Polski in liberated Buchenwald, names three representatives of the Polish-Jewish group: Fränkiel, Landau, and Werber.

33. C. Posener, op. cit., p. 37, 54.

34. Hanna Hoffmann, "Aufzeichnungen über den Kinderblock im Theresienstädter Familienlager [Notes on the children's block in Theresienstadt family camp]," unpublished (archives of Yad Vashem, Jerusalem).

35. Conversation between David Szmulewski and Tzipora Weiss, November 16, 1977.

36. The Dutchman Antonius Franciscus van Velsen has described the preparations that he and two Germans, who also were employed in the Gypsy camp, had made to spring into action as soon as the agreed-upon signal came from the Theresienstadt family camp (Van Velsen, "Verslag [Report]," February 5, 1948, unpublished (Royal Institute, Amsterdam), p. 59 ff.

37. Czech (1959–64) gives the names of fourteen prisoners who were shot while trying to escape. Roux (1968) names thirteen of these and spells their names somewhat differently, but the prisoners' numbers are the same.

38. "Bericht über das Konzentrationslager Sachsenhausen [Report on the concentration camp Sachsenhausen]," op. cit., p. 34.

39. Unpublished record of a conversation between Steinberg and Johannes Hüttner on April 29, 1963 (unpublished, Center for Contemporary Jewish Documentation, Paris). Hüttner also names the German Jews who participated in this action.

40. Author's conversation with Ernst Toch, September 3, 1976.

41. Author's conversation conversation with Charlotte Delbo, November 16, 1973.

42. Conversation between Józef Cyrankiewicz and Tzipora Weiss, November 12, 1977.

43. Author's conversation with Alina Brewda, November 11, 1973.

44. Carolus, "21,000 Häftlinge befreit! Die letzten Tage des Konzentrationslagers Buchenwald: Ein Erlebnisbericht nach einigen Tagebuchaufzeichnungen [21,000 Inmates freed! The last days of concentration camp Buchenwald: An eyewitness report on the basis of some diary entries]," Buchenwald, April 14, 1945, unpublished (Documentations Archives, Vienna), p. 5.

45. E. Thape, op. cit., entry of April 5, 1945.

46. Author's conversation with Heinz Schmidt, November 8, 1973.

47. Author's conversation with Albin Lüdke, November 4, 1973.

48. Author's conversation with Kurt Hirsch, March 5, 1976.

49. Author's conversation with Fritz Kleinmann, December 12, 1976.

50. Author's conversation with Albin Lüdke, November 4, 1973.

16. THE SAVING OF LIVES

1. Judgment of the Essen district court against Helmut Bischoff and accomplices, May 8, 1970 (Az.:29a Ks 9/66).

2. David Rousset, "La signification de l'affaire Dodkin-Hessel," in *Les Temps Modernes* (Paris) No. 6, March 1, 1946, p. 1088. He comes to the conclusion that "the questions of power and of choice belong together and constitute the origin of all struggles and all dramas in the world of the concentration camps."

3. "Bericht der Österreicher an die Abteilung für psychologische Kriegsführung in der amerikanischen Armee [Report of the Austrians to the unit for psychological warfare in the American army]," undated and unsigned, written in Buchenwald, unpublished (Documentations Archives of the Austrian Resistance, Vienna), p. 1. Also cf. *Buchenwald* 1960, 350 ff. In both reports Eugen Kogon is mentioned among those who were saved in this way, and Kogon confirmed to me that this assertion is correct.

4. Author's conversation with Ernst Martin, June 11, 1973.

5. Author's conversation with Walter Vielhauer, November 21, 1976.

6. Unpublished manuscript by J. B. Krokowski (in the author's possession).

7. In this book, which takes the form of a novel, Meier calls Mandryckxs Marcel, but there is no doubt about the identity of the two.

8. "Konzentrationslager Sachsenhausen: Die Periode der Sonderkommission (von Ende 1943 bis 1944) [The period of the special commission, from late 1943 to 1944]," Oranienburg, May 1945, unsigned and unpublished (Royal Institute for War Documentation, Amsterdam). The name of the second deputy senior camp inmate was Volck. "Baltic fighter" refers to a person who served in an ultrarightist military formation on the Baltic after World War I.

9. Karl Raddatz, "Die Sonderaktion vom 2. August 1944 gegen KPD-Funktionäre im KL Sachsenhausen [Special roundup of KPD officials in concentration camp Sachsenhausen, from August 2, 1944]," Berlin, May 20, 1945, unpublished (Royal Institute, Amsterdam), p. 3.

10. Rudolf Wunderlich, "Flucht aus dem KZ [Flight from the concentration camp]," unpublished (Documentation Archives, Vienna), p. 116 ff. Wunderlich continues: "At first not all prisoners who received parcels were willing to share with others some of the things they could not use. However, a certain percentage of them did not hesitate to give some of their personal possessions away— especially the comrades from these countries with a leftist organization or orientation."

11. J. B. Krokowski, op. cit.

12. Wim Zwart, "Bergen–Belsen: Solidarität liess überleben! [Solidarity let us survive!]", in *Der Appell. Mitteilungsblatt für ehemalige Häftlinge des KZ Sachsenhausen-Oranienburg* (Dortmund) No. 76, April 6, 1974. Zwart explains this procedure as follows: "The SS even camouflaged its mass murders in the camp because it wanted to avoid anything that could arouse resistance and tried to keep those selected to be murdered unsuspecting until the last moment."

13. Author's conversation with Andrzej Kamiński, December 14, 1974. The two men escaped from Brieg, a satellite camp of Gross–Rosen.

14. "Österreicherinnen unter Hitler im Frauen-KL Ravensbrück [Austrian women under Hitler in the female concentration camp Ravensbrück]," unpublished (in the author's possession); statements by Toni Bruha, p. 18; author's conversation with Helene Potetz, February 12, 1976.

15. Maria Kurcyuszowa, "Die Polinnen im Kampf gegen die biologische Vernichtung im Konzentrationslager Ravensbrück [Polish women in the struggle against biological destruction in concentration camp Ravensbrück]," unpublished (German translation in the author's possession), p. 32.

16. Vincenzo Pappalettera gives the names of two Italians who were saved in that way. Maršàlek does not mention his own participation in this rescue action, but Pappalettera explicitly names him.

17. Ewald Gondzik, "Zusammenarbeit der Nationen in deutschen Konzentrationslagern [Collaboration of the nations in German concentration camps]," Hamburg, October 29, 1945, unpublished (Royal Institute, Amsterdam).

18. Author's conversation with Albert Guérisse, March 2, 1976.

19. Anonymous, secret Dutch report about Buchenwald, unpublished (Royal Institute, Amsterdam).

20. David Rousset, "La signification de l'affaire Dodkins-Hessel," op. cit., p. 1084. Cf. also Hessel 1954, 356 ff., and Kogon 1946, 245 ff. Kogon names forty-three members of secret services of the Western allies, but Rousset and Hessel mention thirty-seven.

21. D. Rousset, op. cit., p. 1085.

22. J. P. Schalker, "Rapport over de toestanden in het proefblok voor vlektyphus (blok 46) in Buchenwald [Report on the situation in the experimental block for typhus—block 46—in Buchenwald]," May 3, 1946, unpublished, (Royal Institute, Amsterdam).

23. D. Rousset, op. cit.

24. Author's conversation with Eugen Kogon, November 11, 1978.

25. Author's conversation with Toni Lehr, September 19, 1975.

26. Ibid. Cf. also "Österreicherinnen unter Hitler im Frauen-KL Ravensbrück [Austrian women under Hitler in the female concentration camp Ravensbrück]," op. cit., and Chapter 14, note 13.

27. T. Lehr, op. cit.; Female Concentration Camp 1973, 207 ff.

28. "Österreicherinnen [Austrian women]", op. cit.

29. Cf. also Antonius Franciscus van Velsen, "Verslag [Report]," February 5, 1948, unpublished (Royal Institute, Amsterdam), p. 46 ff.

30. Letter from Wagner, the head of the German Foreign Office's internal department II, to SS Lieutenant General Dr. Kaltenbrunner, chief of the security police, dated July 5, 1944, and marked "Reich secret."

31. "Bericht der Österreicher [Report of the Austrians]", op. cit., p. 7. This report appears in Buchenwald 1960, 399 ff. under the title "Bericht des österreichischen Komitees über das KZ Buchenwald [Report of the Austrian committee on concentration camp Buchenwald]," and with a few minor

emendations not identified as such. For example, "the measures were often inexplicable" was changed to "some measures often were inexplicable to the uninitiated."

32. Letter from Hans Sündermann to "Walter," Vienna, March 3, 1958, unpublished (in the author's possession).

33. Albert Guérisse gained this impression in Dachau (author's conversation with Guérisse, March 2, 1967).

34. Author's conversation with Hans Gasparitsch, November 20, 1976.

35. Olga Wormser, "Observation," p. 248.

17. AGAINST THE INHUMANITY OF THE SYSTEM

1. Testimony of Harry Naujoks in the Treblinka trial, Düsseldorf, February 1, 1965.

2. It has been confirmed by Karl Feuerer in his "Widerstand [Resistance] in Dora," (in *Frankfurter Rundschau*, 1947), in a letter to the author from Wicenty Hein, June 10, 1974, and in Kiessling 1964, 214 ff.

3. Testimony of Stanislaw Baranowski in the Majdanek trial, Düsseldorf, August 21, 1978, cited after Dietrich Strothmann, "Im Angesicht der Angeklagten [In the presence of the accused]," *Die Zeit*, Hamburg, September 1, 1978.

4. Testimony of Fritz Bringmann in the Treblinka trial, Düsseldorf, February 1, 1965; also *So ging es zu Ende* 1960, 57.

5. Statement by Walther Piller, May 19, 1945, unpublished (Central Office of the Provincial Law Administration, Ludwigsburg).

6. Letter from Tadeusz Patzer to J. B. Krokowski, February 6, 1976, and Krokowski's remarks in a letter to the author.

7. Walter Vielhauer, "Allach 1943: Ein SS-Befehl wird verweigert [Allach 1943: An SS order was disobeyed]," in *Mitteilungsblatt der Lagergemeinschaft Dachau*, Munich, July 1971.

8. W. Vielhauer, op. cit., author's conversation with Karl Wagner, September 19, 1976; letter to the author from Hans Biederer, May 30, 1976.

9. Letter to the author from Karl Wagner, July 19, 1976.

10. Wagner's letter and the author's conversation with Hans Biederer, September 27, 1976.

11. H. Biederer's letter to the author, op. cit.

12. Author's conversation with Franz Freihaut, July 11, 1978.

13. Nuremberg document NO-1554.

14. Author's conversation with Andrzej Kamiński, December 14, 1974.

15. Kornelis Hofman, "Verklaring [Statement]," January 25, 1951, unpublished (Royal Institute for War Documentation, Amsterdam), p. 64.

16. Testimony of the defendant Heinz Petrick in the Majdanek trial, Düsseldorf. Petrick believes that the name of this informer may have been Galbani or Galvani.

17. "Bericht über das Konzentrationslager Sachsenhausen [Report on the concen-

tration camp Sachsenhausen]," signed by twelve former inmates of this camp, undated but evidently written soon after the liberation, unpublished (Royal Institute, Amsterdam), p. 30.

18. Rudolf Wunderlich, "Flucht aus dem KZ [Flight from the concentration camp]," unpublished (Documentatijons Archives for Austrian Resistance, Vienna), p. 115.

19. Karl Raddatz, "Die Sonderaktion vom 2. August 1944 gegen KPD-Funktionäre im KL Sachsenhausen [Special roundup of KPD functionaries in concentration camp Sachsenhausen, August 2, 1944]," Berlin, May 30, 1945, unpublished, (Royal Institute, Amsterdam). Cf. also chapter 9, note 26.

20. K. Raddatz, op. cit. The informers were organized in such a way that "an informer was assigned to every labor detail." One of the chief informers, who attended "stoolie school" in Berlin together with others, was named Calpari.

21. "Konzentrationslager Sachsenhausen: Die Periode der Sonderkommission (von Ende 1943 bis 1944 [Concentration camp Sachsenhausen: The period of the special commission—from late 1943 to 1944]," unsigned, written in May 1945 in Oranienburg, unpublished (Royal Institute, Amsterdam). This report, which was evidently written by a Communist, contains a detailed description of this struggle in all its phases.

22. K. Raddatz, op. cit.

23. "Konzentrationslager Sachsenhausen," op. cit.

24. Ibid.

25. Ibid.

26. Ibid.

27. K. Raddatz, op. cit.

28. "Konzentrationslager Sachsenhausen," op. cit.

29. "Bericht der Österreicher [Report of the Austrians]," op. cit.

30. Otto Horn, "Ausführlicher Bericht über das Konzentrationslager Buchenwald [Complete report on the concentration camp Buchenwald]," unpublished (Documentations Archives, Vienna).

31. Report by N. Wijnen, March 10, 1948, unpublished (Royal Institute, Amsterdam).

32. Letter to the author from Tadeusz Patzer, August 8, 1977.

33. Sworn statement by Stanisław Szmajzner, Rio de Janeiro, February 9, 1961, unpublished (in the author's possession) and testimonies in the Sobibor trial, Hagen, by Thomas Blatt (November 23, 1965), Salomon Paull (December 6, 1965), Mosze Bachir (December 14, 1965), Dov Freiberg (December 21, 1965), Josef Herszmann (January 21, 1966), and Stanisław Szmajzner (January 24, 1966).

34. Author's conversation with Franz Graczoll, October 11, 1975.

35. Stanisław Nogaj, "Gusen–Tagebuch eines Journalisten [Diary of a journalist]," unpublished (Central Office in the Province Nordrhein-Westfalen for the compiling of Nazi Mass Crimes in Concentration Camps, Cologne).

36. According to admission records of Dachau, Johann Meanssarian, a fifty-two-

year-old stateless person, had arrived in the camp "on suspicion of hostile activities against the German Reich."

37. Walter Leitner, "Die letzten Tage im Konzentrationslager Dachau [The last days in concentration camp Dachau]," unpublished (Dachau Museum).

38. Arthur Haulot/Ali Kuci, "Die letzten Tage von Dachau [The last days of Dachau]," unpublished (Dachau Museum).

39. "Bericht über die erste Sitzung des internationalen Häftlingskomitees im befreiten Lager Dachau [Report on the first session of the international inmates' committee in liberated camp Dachau]," unpublished (Dachau Museum).

40. Karl Ludwig Schecher, "Rückblick auf Dachau," unpublished (Dachau Museum).

41. Author's conversation with Albin Lüdke, November 4, 1973.

42. Author's conversation with Heinz Junge, November 6, 1973.

43. "Bericht über Erlebnisse in Berliner Gestapo-Gefängnissen und KZ Buchenwald auf Grund der Mitteilungen des Herrn Ernest Platz, geb. am 15. February 1906 in Brühl/Köln [Report on the experiences in the Berlin Gestapo prison and concentration camp Buchenwald on the basis of information from Mr. Ernest Platz, born February 15, 1906, in Brühl]," unpublished (Wiener Library, London).

44. Oskar Müller, "Zum Problem 'Widerstand und Solidarität' im KL Dachau [The problem 'resistance and solidarity' in concentration camp Dachau]," March 11, 1969, unpublished (Dachau Museum).

45. Author's conversation with Franz Freihaut, July 11, 1978.

46. "Vorläufiger Bericht über die militärische Organisation im Konzentrationslager Buchenwald [Preliminary report on the military organization in concentration camp Buchenwald]," unsigned and unpublished, (Royal Institute, Amsterdam). The same statement may be found almost verbatim in O. Horn, op. cit.

47. Conversation between Alter Feinsylberg and Tzipora Weiss, November 17, 1977.

48. Author's conversation with Heribert Kreuzmann, January 27, 1978.

49. Testimony of Yankel Wiernik at the Treblinka trial, Düsseldorf, January 5, 1965.

50. Stanisław's Kohn's report, which has been published in several languages (Yad Vashem, Jerusalem); letter to the author from Shalom (his new first name) Kohn, January 20, 1976.

51. Testimony of S. Szmajzner, op. cit.

52. Sworn statement by S. Szmajzner, op. cit.

53. Testimony of Herman Posner at the Sobibor trial, Hagen, December 1965.

54. Testimony by Ilona Safran at the Sobibor trial, Hagen, November 8, 1965.

55. Sworn statement by S. Szmajzner, op. cit.

56. Testimony by A. Margulies, op. cit.

57. The name of the nurse in the experiment station, Walter Neff, is not given there. Thanks to Neff, Otto Albl, a veteran of the Spanish Civil War, was able to survive the camp.

58. Author's conversation with Gustl Gattinger, March 5, 1976.

59. K. Feuerer, op. cit.

60. Götz Dieckmann, *Existenzbedingungen und Widerstand im Konzentrationslager Dora–Mittelbau unter dem Aspekt der funktionellen Einbeziehung der SS in das System der faschistischen Kriegswirtschaft* (*Living Conditions and Resistance in Concentration Camp Dora–Mittelbau Under the Aspect of the Functional Inclusion of the SS in the System of the Fascist War Economy*), dissertation, Humboldt University, Berlin, 1968, p. 241.

61. Willi Gardini, "Erinnerungen [memories]," unpublished, p. 67.

62. Letter from Mathias Mai to Emil Peters, May 30, 1948 (in the author's possession).

63. Author's conversation with Pierre Schneider, November 19, 1973.

64. G. Dieckmann, op. cit., p. 243.

65. Court's opinion in the Dora trial, Essen, judgment against Erwin Busta and others, p. 235 (Yad Vashem, Jerusalem).

66. Letter to the author from Tadeusz Patzer, April 15, 1976.

67. Author's conversation with Wincenty Hein, March 18, 1978.

68. Author's conversation with Rudi Gottschalk, February 12, 1977.

69. Author's conversation with Janet Ranzinger, October 30, 1976. Ranzinger, who was in Auschwitz prior to his transfer to Buchenwald and collaborated with the resistance movement there, believes that Wegerer worked with Dr. Hoven in Buchenwald as Hermann Langbein worked in Auschwitz with Dr. Wirths.

70. Transcript of a recorded interview with Edwin Tangl, unpublished (Dachau Museum).

71. Consider those SS doctors who used the unlimited opportunities in the concentration camps to conduct experiments (quite often lethal) on human beings—for example, the Luftwaffe doctor Sigmund Rascher in Dachau and Josef Mengele, Carl Clauberg, and Horst Schumann in Auschwitz. The two last-named physicians did not belong to the SS but applied for permission to conduct such experiments. Consider also the physicians who participated in the murders in the "euthanasia" institutions: Herta Oberheuser in Ravensbrück and Albert Trzebinski in Neuengamme, to name only a few. Detailed information may be found in Mitscherlich/Mielke 1948 and Bayle 1950.

72. Letter from Ewald Gondzik to the author, July 11, 1974.

73. Jean Jaans, "Intervention eines Luxemburgers beim berüchtigten KZ-Kommandanten Kramer [Intervention of a Luxembourger with the infamous concentration camp Commandant Kramer]," in *Rappel*, Luxembourg, March–April 1976, p. 71.

74. Author's conversation with Ernst Martin, June 11, 1973.

75. Author's conversation with Alois Stockinger, December 2, 1975.

76. Author's conversation with Eugen Kogon, December 15, 1977.

77. H. Wijnen, op. cit.

78. Transcript of a recorded interview with Max Günther, unpublished (Dachau Museum).

79. Max Eichhorn, "Dachau," unpublished (Dachau Museum).

80. A Feinsylberg, op. cit.

81. Conversation between Dawid Szmulewski and Tzipora Weiss, November 16, 1977.

82. Judgment in the Sobibor jury trial at the Hagen district court (against Dubois and others), December 20, 1966, p. 103.

83. Testimony of Chaim Engel at the Sobibor trial, Hagen, October 19, 1965.

84. Author's conversation with Albert Guérisse, March 2, 1976.

85. K. L. Schecher, op. cit.

86. W. Leitner, op. cit. According to him, this made it possible to remove Wernicke and Meanssarian from their positions in the last days. Cf. also note 37.

87. Karl Riemer, "Amerikaner helfen [Americans help]," Dachau, May 11, 1945, unpublished (Dachau Museum). Riemer mentions the SS roll-call officer, Pfeiffer, who wanted to escape together with the inmates (Riemer names eight Germans, including himself, and adds "and other comrades"). Cf. also Oskar Müller, "So wurden 33,000 befreit [Thus 33,000 were liberated]," in *Mitteilungsblätter der Lagergemeinschaft Dachau*, April 1965.

88. Author's conversation with Edwin Tangl, February 16, 1977.

89. Stanisław Nogaj, "Gusen—Tagebuch eines Journalisten [Diary of a journalist]," op. cit.: "Some SS men, first and foremost Füssel, opposed this murder. He was a 100 percent Nazi . . . but he had a heart and was against mass murder." Elsewhere Nogaj states that in making overtures to inmates, SS men were motivated by the desire to save their own lives. In this connection Nogaj mentions the SS Captain Beck. The proposal by the Ukrainian guards was turned down as too risky. The SS got wind of their intentions and shot two ringleaders. Nogaj says that afterward many people took credit for frustrating the murderous design (1967, 170 ff.).

90. Camille Scholtes recalls that, in early February 1945, Captain Payrleitner called him in and had a confidential conversation with him. Alfred Payrleitner has confirmed this and added that he used Josef Poltrum to smuggle pistols with ammunition into the camp. (Author's conversation with Alfred Payrleitner, November 18, 1975.) Scholtes also writes that on the evening of May 3, Payrleitner gave him the "special assignment," via Poltrum, to alert the camp to reject the order expected from the camp commandant. According to Jean Majerus, the International Committee decided to disobey the commandant's order after the guards from the Luftwaffe had promised to support the inmates against the SS. "Weapons were appearing everywhere" (*Letzeburger zu Mauthausen* 1970, 210 ff.). Paul Tillard reports that 200 inmates were armed (1945, 73).

91. W. Gardini, op. cit., p. 101 ff.

92. Author's conversation with Eugen Ochs, February 6, 1977.

93. Walter Vielhauer/Karl Wagner, "Erfahrungen, Gedanken und Rückerinnerungen [Experiences, thoughts, and reminiscences]," in *Mitteilungsblatt der Lagergemeinschaft Dachau*, Munich, December 1971.

94. Hermann Joseph, "Der Fall [case] 104338," unpublished manuscript, p. 456.

95. Eugen Kogon, "Das deutsche Volk und die Konzentrationslager [The German

people and the concentration camps]," in *Das jüdische Echo*, XXIV, 1, Vienna, September 1975.

96. Author's conversations with Rudolf Pekar (October 21, 1979) and Alfred Rüssler (October 20, 1979).

97. Author's conversation with Josef Steinkogler, October 20, 1979.

98. Letter to the author from Tomasz Kiryłłow, February 29, 1976.

99. Papa, "Episodes alsaciens [Alsatian episodes]," in *Rappel*, Luxembourg, Sept./Oct. 1975.

100. W. Leitner, op. cit. Two days before the liberation, Georg Scherer, who had been released from Dachau after six years, smuggled into the camp a document that called upon the inmates, in the case of an evacuation (and a big transport was on its way to points unknown on that day), to stop on Schleissheimerstrasse and refuse to go on; "we will see to it that nothing will happen to the prisoners" ("Dachau ehrt einen Unbeugsamen [Dachau honors an uncompromising man]," *Süddeutsche Zeitung*, September 17, 1976).

101. J. A. Brodski, "Die Geschichte der Bruderschaft der Kriegsgefangenen [History of the brotherhood of war prisoners]," *Nowy Mir* No. 8, August 1957.

102. According to Rudolf Wunderlich, "this detail consisted almost exclusively of good German anti-Fascists" (*KZ Sachsenhausen n.d.*, 8). The Luxembourger René Kerschen also mentions these contacts and points out that Wunderlich helped everyone "and, unlike others, not just his own circle." (Author's conversation with R. Kerschen, November 28, 1973.)

103. Thirty-five pages with handwritten notes that Polish prisoners of war had received from the camp and buried were dug up thirty years later in Mecklenburg ("Neue Dokumente aus Ravensbrück [new documents from Ravensbrück]," in *Der neue Mahnruf*, Vienna, December 1975).

104. O. Horn, op. cit.

105. Letter to the author from Tadeusz Patzer, April 15, 1976.

106. G. Dieckmann, op. cit., p. 251.

107. Author's conversation with David Rousset, November 16, 1973.

108. "Die antifaschistische Arbeit der Häftlinge in den Rüstungsbetrieben [The anti-Fascist work of the inmates in the armaments industry]," unsigned and unpublished (Documentations Archives, Vienna).

109. O. Horn, op. cit.

110. Author's conversation with Matilda Brozek, June 16, 1976.

111. Author's conversation with Bertl Lauscher, December 3, 1975. This opportunity was created by the Austrian Anni Vanik, the capo of the prisoners' detail assigned to that plant.

112. This letter is in the archives of the International Search Service in Arolsen. Another letter from the special detail, dated September 20, 1944, and also kept in Arolsen, indicates that the "politically incriminated" Gau and five other inmates were placed in the isolation Block 58.

113. Author's conversation with George Hess, November 21, 1973.

114. R. Wunderlich, op. cit., p. 42, 73. Cf. also the same author's "Illegale Arbeit in Sachsenhausen [Clandestine work in Sachsenhausen]," op. cit., p. 10.

115. Unpublished notes of Sepp Plieseis (in the possession of Peter Kammerstätter, Linz): "The civilian population was on our side . . . and we were able to use these civilians, sometimes girls, to make the SS men gentler." Cf. also Plieseis 1946, 230 ff.
116. Author's conversation with Leo Jansa, November 9, 1976.
117. Cf. also the author's conversation with Eugene Thomé on November 18, 1975, and a letter from Kettner to Thomé, January 7, 1946.
118. Author's conversation with Josef Steinkogler, October 20, 1979.
119. Author's conversation with Edouard Barbel (November 19, 1973) and Eschenbrenner n.d., 67 ff.
120. Declaration by Józef Cyrankiewicz and Stanisław Klodzínski in *Hefte von Auschwitz* No. 1, Auschwitz, 1959.
121. Declaration by Leon Staischak, September 3, 1947, document NO N1-10928, unpublished (Center for Contemporary Jewish Documentation, Paris). The correct spelling of the name is Stasiak.
122. Unpublished declaration by Adolf Dab (Wiener Library, London) and unpublished declaration by Norbert Wollheim, June 3, 1947, document NO NI-9807 (Jewish Documentation, Paris).
123. Author's conversations with Fritz Kleinmann on December 12, 1976, and March 5, 1977.
124. L. Staischak, op. cit. and Smoleń 1960–67, 37.
125. Letter to the author from Karel Bulaty, January 20, 1978.
126. "Bericht der komm. Parteigruppe des K. L. Jawiszowice, [Report of the Communist Party group of concentration camp Jawiszowice]," signed by Martin Andersen (Erich Hoffmann), Heribert Kreuzmann, Christian Klos, and Hermann Axen, unpublished (in the author's possession).
127. Hermann Joseph, op. cit., p. 294.
128. "Ostatni Krąg," *Wydawnictwo literackie*, Krakąw, 1973, p. 25 ff.; letter to the author from Jozef Kret, May 15, 1975.

18. BREAKING OUT OF THE ISOLATION

1. Stanisław Nogaj, "Gusen-Tagebuch [Diary]," unpublished (Central Office in the Province for the compiling of Nazi mass crimes in concentration camps, Cologne).
2. Karl Röder, "Nachtwache [Night Watch]," unpublished (Dachau Museum).
3. Unpublished notes by Sepp Eberl (Dachau Museum).
4. E. Ost, "Abhören von Feindsendern im KZ Dachau [Listening to enemy broadcasts in concentration camp Dachau]," *Rappel*, Luxembourg, July 1973.
5. Author's conversation with Albin Lüdke, November 4, 1973.
6. Josef Mautner, "Die Vorbereitung zum beabsichtigten Putsch im Konzentrationslager Natzweiler [Preparations for an attempted uprising in concentration camp Natzweiler]," London, January 18, 1943, unpublished (in the author's possession).

7. Among other places in Mauthausen, where a French engineer used this opportunity (author's conversation with Père Riquet, November 15, 1973), and in Auschwitz, where the Pole Zbyszek Raynoch did likewise in the SS hospital (Langbein 1949, 170 ff.).
8. Author's conversation with Georg Scherer, April 2, 1979.
9. Author's conversation with Arthur Hansen, November 19, 1973.
10. Author's conversation with Vratuskav Bušek, October 11, 1973.
11. Author's conversation with Harry Naujoks, November 3, 1973.
12. Author's conversation with Emil Peters, November 19, 1973.
13. Author's conversation with Franz Freihaut, July 11, 1978.
14. Letter from Willi Eifler to Hans Schwarz, February 21, 1970 (in the author's possession).
15. K. Röder, op. cit.
16. Letter to the author from Gustl Gattinger, September 23, 1975, and author's conversation with Gattinger on March 5, 1976. Also, note by Albert Theis, December 14, 1969, unpublished (in the author's possession) and author's conversation with Theis on November 20, 1973.
17. Letter to the author from Tadeusz Patzer, April 15, 1976.
18. Unpublished notes of J. B. Krokowski (in the author's possession). Also Deeckmann/Hockmuth n.d., Biermann 1945. Also 78, 9/38 and letter to the author from Wincenty Hein, July 13, 1974.
19. J. B. Krokowski, op. cit.; T. Patzer, op. cit.; Deeckmann/Hockmuth n.d., 78, Kautsky 1961, 309.
20. Verdict of the Essen district court in the criminal trial of Busta and others, Az.: 29a Ks 9/66, p. 237.
21. Otto Horn, op. cit.
22. "Vorläufiger Bericht über die militärische Organisation im Konzentrationslager Buchenwald [Preliminary report on the military organization in concentration camp Buchenwald]," unpublished (Royal Institute for War Documentation, Amsterdam).
23. Letter to the author from Emil Samek, January 9, 1977. Also Maršálek 1974, 263.
24. Karl Raddatz, "Die Sonderaktion vom 2. August 1944 gegen KPD- Funktionäre im KL Sachsenhausen [The special roundup of KPD functionaries in concentration camp Sachsenhausen, August 2, 1944]," written on May 20, 1945 in Berlin, unpublished (Royal Institute, Amsterdam). Raddatz writes that in those days he and Tietz were charged with having made secret transmissions. However, no radio equipment was found at the place indicated by the informer "because the transmitter was still under construction."
25. Author's conversation with Eugeniusz Niedojadlo, September 5, 1975.
26. Conversation between Józef Cyrankiewicz and Tzipora Weiss, November 12, 1977.
27. Jean-Maurice Rubli, "Als ich nach Mauthausen kam [When I arrived at Mauthausen]," *Weltwoche*, February 19, 1975.

28. Author's conversation with Père Riquet, November 15, 1973; Kupfer-Koberwitz 1960, 182.

29. S. Nogaj, op. cit.; Maršálek 1974, 214 ff.

30. Letter to the author from Władysław Plaskura, May 2, 1976; Mołdawa 1967, 143.

31. J. B. Krokowski, op. cit.

32. Author's conversation with Eugen Kogon, June 18, 1973, and letter to the author from the SPD subdistrict Dortmund, December 15, 1978.

33. Irena Strzelecka, "Die ersten Frauentransporte nach dem KL Auschwitz [The first female transports to concentration camp Auschwitz]," in *Informationsbulletin des Comité International d'Auschwitz*, Warsaw, June 1978. Also Gárliński 1975A, 128.

34. Unpublished declaration by Felipe Yébenes-Romo, December 5, 1978 (in the author's possession). Cf. also Francisco Boix's testimony at the Nuremberg trial and Razola/Constante 1969, 103 ff.

35. Florian Zehethofer, "Die Vernichtung 'lebensunwerten Lebens' im Schloss Hartheim [The destruction of 'lives not worth living' in Hartheim castle] 1938–1945," unpublished (Institute for Modern and Contemporary History at the College for Social and Economic Science, Linz), p. 42.

36. Otto Wolken, "Chronik des Quarantänelagers Birkenau [Chronicle of the quarantine camp in Birkenau]," in *Auschwitz: Zeugnisse und Berichte*, ed. by H. G. Adler, Hermann Langbein, and Ella Lingens-Reiner, Frankfurt, 1962, pp. 139 ff.

37. Foreword by Jadwiga Bezwińska and Danuta Czech in *Inmitten des grauenvollen Verbrechens* (In the midst of dreadful crime) (special issue), Auschwitz, 1972, p. 5 ff.

38. Unpublished notes by Hermann Langbein, Hannover, April 22 to 25, 1945 (in the author's possession).

39. Testimony by Leon Staischak, September 3, 1947, document NO NI-10928.

40. J. Jautner, op. cit.; "L'Histoire de la Photo aerienne illustrant notre couverture [History of the aerial photo revealing our cover]," and a copy of the photograph, unpublished (in the author's possession); Eschenbrenner n.d.; author's conversation with Charles Bené, July 13, 1974.

41. Letters to the author from Vítězslav Lederer, December 28, 1967, January 14 and 20, 1968; Kulka 1965, 193; 1968–69. Lederer cautions that Erich Kulka's publications contain "many untruths and errors."

42. Wetzler's book (1964) appeared under the pseudonym Jozef Lánik. Also cf. Vrba/Bestic 1964.

43. Statement of "two young Slovak Jews" who were able to escape from Auschwitz, cited in 362 (published in 1944). Also cf. 392/284f. and Vrba/Bestic 1964, 284 ff., and Rothkirchen 1961.

44. In *German Extermination Camps: Auschwitz and Birkenau*, published in November 1944 by the Executive Office of the President, War Refugee Board, Washington, the number is given as 1,765,000 (p. 33), in "Should I Be My

Brother's Keeper" 1944, 85, as 1,715,000 and in Vrba/Bestic 1964, 285, as 1,760,000.

45. *German Extermination Camps*, op. cit., p. 35 ff.

46. In a conversation with the author of April 16, 1968, Czesław Mordowicz stated that he spoke to the papal legate himself, together with Vrba. Cf. also Vrba/Bestic 1964, 294, and Rothkirchen 1961.

47. On June 25, the Pope sent a telegram to Horthy; three days later Archbishop Spellman (New York) made an appeal to Hungarian Catholics; on June 30, King Gustav of Sweden intervened with Horthy; on July 5, Max Huber, the president of the International Red Cross, directed an inquiry to Horthy; on the same day Eden, the British Foreign Minister, issued a warning to the Hungarian government; on July 9, the Archbishop of Canterbury appealed to the Christians; and on July 14, the American Secretary of State, Cordell Hull, issued a warning to Hungary (Graham n.d.). The name of the Polish major remained unknown. Cf. also Rothkirchen 1961.

48. Testimony of Samuel Rajzman at the Treblinka trial, Düsseldorf, December 1, 1964.

49. Testimony of Jankel Wiernik in the Adolf Eichmann trial, Jerusalem, June 6, 1961; Emanuel Brand, "The Lesson of the Treblinka Trial," in *Yad Vashem Bulletin* No. 17, Jerusalem, December 1965; Novitch 1967, 99 ff.

19. ESCAPES AS LIFESAVERS

1. From an unpublished manuscript written by E. Büge in Sachsenhausen (Archives of the Red Cross International Search Service, Arolsen).

2. In the Dachau Museum.

3. This retaliation was ordered on April 23, June 17 and 24, and July 28, 1941. On each of the first three occasions, ten inmates were left to starve to death, and fifteen inmates were the victims of the last order. (Letter to the author from Kazimierz Smoleń, the director of the Auschwitz Museum, January 20, 1968.)

4. Letter to the author from Falk Pingel, May 15, 1974.

5. Letter to the author from Hans Biederer, May 30, 1976, and author's conversation with Biederer, September 27, 1976.

6. Stanisław Nogaj, op. cit., p. 41f.

7. "Bericht über das Konzentrationslager Sachsenhausen [Report on concentration camp Sachsenhausen]," written in the liberated camp by twelve survivors from ten nations, unpublished (Royal Institute for War Documentation, Amsterdam). In *Damals in Sachsenhausen* 1967, 23, different figures are given: ninety-seven escapees in 1944 and 269 in 1945.

8. Unpublished letter from SS Lieut. Col. Arthur Liebehenschel, head of Section D of the SS Economic Office, June 20, 1943 (Dachau Museum).

9. Letter to the author from Shalom Kohn, January 20, 1976.

10. Declaration by Stanisław Szmajner, February 9, 1961, unpublished (in the author's possession) and Szmajner's testimony at the Sobibor trial, Hagen,

1965–66), in Miriam Novitch, "Le proces de Sobibor à Hagen," unpublished (in the author's possession).

11. Testimony of Kurt Thomas at the Sobibor trial, Hagen, February 1966, unpublished (in the author's possession).

12. Jury judgment at the Hagen district court (December 20, 1966) at the criminal trial of Dubois and others (Ax.: 11 Ks 1/64), unpublished, p. 106.

13. George Pfeffer/Pauline Kleinmaier, "With an Iron Pen," unpublished (in the author's possession), p. 64.

14. Testimony of Mayer Ziss at the Sobibor trial, op. cit., November 1965.

15. Testimony of Mordechai Goldfarb at the Sobibor trial, op. cit., November 1965.

16. Testimony of Ilona Safran at the Sobibor trial, op. cit., November 1965.

17. Testimony of Platkiewicz at the Stangl trial, Düsseldorf, July 8, 1970, unpublished.

18. Testimony of Berek Rojzman at the Stangl trial, op. cit., August 28, 1970.

19. Testimony of Mayer Ziegelmann at the Treblinka trial, Düsseldorf, April 5, 1965, unpublished.

20. Testimony of Leo Lewi at the Treblinka trial, April 12, 1965.

21. Testimony of Sol Weisberg at the Treblinka trial, March 19, 1965.

22. Testimony of Heinrich Poswolski at the Treblinka trial, April 12, 1965.

23. Testimony of Józef Siedlecki at the Treblinka trial, January 15, 1965.

24. Notes by Rudolf Reder, Kraków, 1946.

25. Conversation between Alter Feinsylberg and Tsipora Weiss, November 17, 1977, unpublished.

26. Author's conversation with Josef Meisel, September 6, 1976.

27. Willi Gardini, "Erinnerungen [Reminiscences]," p. 68 ff., unpublished (in the author's possession).

28. Tomasz Kiryłłow, "Mon evasion du Kommando SS-Baubrigade V West à Hesdin [my escape from the detail SS Construction Brigade V West, at Hesdin]," written on January 20, 1976, unpublished (in the author's possession), and letter to the author from Kiryłłow, February 29, 1976.

29. Author's conversation with Andrzej Kamiński, December 14, 1974.

30. Testimony of Georg Rajgrodski at the Treblinka trial, November 30, 1964.

31. Sworn statement by Ignaz Jakobson, written in Cologne, unpublished (in the author's possession).

32. An unpublished manuscript entitled "Flucht aus dem KZ [Flight from the concentration camp]," contains a detailed description of Rudolf Wunderlich's escape and its background (Documentations Archives of the Austrian Resistance, Vienna). That manuscript and Wunderlich's book *Konzentrationslager Sachsenhausen* (Berlin, 1946), p. 316, contain an account of the escape of Jupp and Franzl (Pietschmann and Primus) and its background. Herbert Tschäpe's escape is described in Hermlin 1954, 321 ff., and in Nitzsche 1957, 106 ff. Tschäpe took part in the work of the KPD group, was arrested together with them, and executed on November 27, 1944. The others managed to keep out of the Gestapo's clutches by hiding.

33. Author's conversation with Leo Jansa and Alfred Hammerl (the other two

veterans of the Spanish Civil War who were able to escape in November 1944) on November 9, 1976, and notes made by Agnes Primocic, one of the persons who helped with these escapes, unpublished (Documentations Archive, Vienna).

34. Letter from Kaspar Bachl to Hans Schwarz, November 9, 1966, unpublished (in the author's possession).

35. Letter from Josef Lauscher to Franz Dahlem, March 28, 1972, unpublished (Documentations Archive, Vienna).

36. J. Lauscher, op. cit.

37. Author's conversation with Franz Freihaut, July 11, 1978.

38. Article in an unknown Luxembourg newspaper, June 1964 (in the possession of the author) which reprints photos and personal information about the escapees from the June 14, 1944, bulletin of the criminal investigation division of the German police. That this escape was prepared and undertaken without any connection with the resistance organization in Buchenwald is evidenced by the fact that it is not mentioned in the collection (Buchenwald 1960) that discusses virtually all actions of this organization.

39. Letters to the author from Jerzy Kwiatkowski (July 9, 1974) and from the Red Cross International Search Service (December 3, 1975). According to the latter, Arold was listed as an inmate assigned to the detail German Armaments Works as late as July 15, 1944, a week before the start of the evacuation.

40. Author's conversation with Andrzej Kamiński, December 14, 1974; Mołdawa 1967, 139 ff.

41. Author's conversation with David Rousset, November 16, 1973.

42. Author's conversation with Rudi Gottschalk, February 12, 1977.

43. Testimony of Heinz Petrick at the Majdanek trial, Düsseldorf, February 25, 1976.

44. The "Kalendarium der Ereignisse im Konzentrationslager Auschwitz–Birkenau [Calendar of events in concentration camp Auschwitz–Birkenau]," (Czech 1959–64) has no entry about this mass escape under November 6, 1942, but M. S. Sobotchenii has given that day and mentioned the escape of sixty-nine Russian prisoners of war (1965). Cf. also Sobański 1974, 108 ff., Czech 1959–64, and Rozański 1948, 61 ff.

45. Antonius Franciscus van Velsen, "Verslag [Report]," February 5, 1948, unpublished (Royal Institute, Amsterdam).

46. The Pole Józef Kret, at that time in the penal company, believes that twenty-one attempted to escape, and he agrees with other reports that nine were successful (Kret 1973, 120 ff.; Czech 1959–64; Rozański 1948, 61 ff.).

47. Testimonies at the Sobibor trial by Meyer Ziss (October 18, 1965), Chaim Engel (October 1965), Ilona Safran (November 1965), and the defendant Karl Frenzel (September 1965) as well as statements by Simha Bialowicz and Dov Freiberg (Novitch 1978, 77 ff., 85 ff.). Although others name a Dutch officer as the organizer of that attempt, Engel believes that the initiative was taken by a Dutch journalist.

48. Letter to the author from Karel Bulaty, January 20 and April 7, 1978.

49. Letter to the author from Władysław Smigielski, January 18, 1978.
50. Letter to the author from K. Bulaty, op. cit.
51. The number of those hanged has been given as between nineteen and twenty-nine. Most eyewitnesses agree that there were twenty-six (Piper 1970, 100 ff.).
52. Testimonies at the Treblinka trial by Lindwasser (December 12, 1964), Epstein (December 12, 1964), and Rajchmann (January 14, 1965) as well as Rosenberg's testimony in the Stangl trial (June 26, 1970).
53. Gerhard Harig and Max Mayr, "Die zahlenmässige Entwicklung des Konzentrationslagers Buchenwald [The numerical development of concentration camp Buchenwald]," unpublished (in the author's possession). Cf. also Barthel 1946, 100, Heilig 1948, 169 and Buchenwald 1960, 181 ff.
54. Author's conversation with Hans Maršàlek, June 27, 1978.
55. Thomas Blatt's testimony at the Sobibor trial, November 1965.
56. Blatt's testimony and the testimonies of Philip Bialowitz (October 25, 1965) and Abraham Margulies (November 1965) at the Sobibor trial as well as Simon Honigman's letters to the author (November 1974 and January 16, 1975).
57. Testimony of Walther Piller, deputy officer-in-charge, May 19, 1945, and indictment of the senior public prosecutor, Bonn, July 5, 1962, p. 138. According to a letter to the author from Michael Tregenza (August 19, 1977), the SS man Haas was killed at that time.

20. RESISTANCE AND REBELLION

1. Pierrre Gregoire writes that this attack was made upon the initiative of the Luxembourger Nicky Schaak (1975, Michaux n.d., 116 ff.). In Damals in Sachsenhausen 1676, the entry for February 2 reads as follows: "178 prisoners, including nineteen Luxembourgers, seven British prisoners of war, and sixty Soviet officers shot by the SS."
2. Testimony of Rudolf Höss on March 24, 1946 (Nuremberg document NO-1210) and testimony by Stanislaw Jankowski (Alter Feinsylberg) on May 13, 1945, in Kraków, in "Inmitten des grauenvollen Verbrechens: Handschriften von Mitgliedern des Sonderkommandos [In the midst of dreadful crime: Holograph documents from members of the special detail]," special issue of Hefte von Auschwitz, Auschwitz, 1972, p. 58.
3. Cf. Chapter 6, note 32.
4. Stenographic minutes of the Jaeger staff meeting on May 2, 1944 (Nuremberg document NOKW-389, No. 3017f). Commentator Schaede writes: "I don't know whether this was a systematic action or just a personal vendetta between Russians and Poles." Hans Popp, a former inmate of Flossenbürg, has endeavored to get to the bottom of these incidents: "[In Zwickau] members of the municipal government told me about the 'revolt' in which camp inmates on labor assignments and forced laborers were involved. Inhuman working conditions as well as bad food and housing were the main reason, but another reason was the detection of a clandestine organization.... Most written inquiries

produced no response, and my experience with numerous queries directed to the association of anti-Fascist resistance fighters in Berlin was mostly negative" (letter from Popp to the author, August 15, 1976).

5. Testimony of the Luxembourger Maximilian Baumann in the Flossenbürg trial at Dachau.

6. V. Smirnov, "Der letzte Kampf der zum Tode Verurteilten [The last struggle of those condemned to death]," in "Der Ausbruch der russischen Offiziere und Kommissare aus dem Block 20 des Konzentrationslagers Mauthausen am 2. Februar 1945: Materialsammlung [The breakout of Russian officers from Block 20 of concentration camp Mauthausen on February 2, 1945: Collection of materials]," by Peter Kammerstätter unpublished (in the author's possession). Also, author's conversation with Juan de Diego, July 9, 1974.

7. V. Smirnov, op. cit., and conversation between Adolf Hassmann and Peter Kammerstätter in "Der Ausbruch."

8. "Postenchronik des Postens Schwertberg [Chronicle of the outpost Schwertberg]," unpublished (Mauthausen Museum).

9. V. Smirnov, op. cit., and conversations between Peter Kammerstätter and inhabitants of the environs, including Pastor Josef Radgeb, in "Der Ausbruch"; Maršàlek 1974, 206.

10. V. Smirnov, op. cit.

11. Smirnov 1978, 282. However, Hans Maršàlek gives the names of nine officers who could be identified in the Soviet Union (1974, 206). Numerous officers who had managed to survive the Nazi concentration camps were arrested after returning to the Soviet Union.

12. Conversation between Alter Feinsylberg (or Feinsilber, in Auschwitz known as Stanisław Jankowski) and Tzipora Weiss on November 14, 1977. Feinsylberg states that he was in contact with the resistance movement in the main camp via David Szmulewski, Sioma Lechtman, and others. Józef Cyrankiewicz has confirmed that the Combat Group Auschwitz planned an uprising in cooperation with the underground movement in Upper Silesia (conversation with Tzipora Weiss on November 12, 1977). Both Cyrankiewicz and David Szmulewski have confirmed (in a conversation with Tzipora Weiss on November 15, 1977) that Szmulewski was the liaison between the Combat Group and the special detail.

13. Testimony of Dr. Horst Fischer in March 1966, quoted in Kazimierz Smoleń, "Der Verlauf des Vernichtungsprozesses im KL Auschwitz [The progress of the extermination procedure in concentration camp Auschwitz]," special issue of Hefte von Auschwitz, op. cit., p. 22 ff.

14. Statement by C. S. Bendel, October 1, 1946, unpublished (Center for Contemporary Jewish Documentation, Paris). Bendel says that those who had weapons refused to use these because they realized that the situation was hopeless.

15. Lewental 1972, 179, and author's conversation with Isaac Liver, March 3, 1976.

16. Conversation between Alter Feinsylberg and Tzipora Weiss, op. cit.; S. Jankowski (Feinsylberg), op. cit., p. 68 ff.; conversation with I. Liver, op. cit.; Langbein 1965, 121 ff.

17. Author's conversation with Józef Hulanicki (April 24, 1976) and Czech 1959–64.

18. At that time Gutman evidently did not know about the uprisings in Treblinka and Sobibor or the events in the Auschwitz crematorium on October 23, 1943 (1958, 161).

19. Isaac Kabuli names six Greek officers, but he erroneously gives the date of the uprising as September 4 and gets some detail wrong (1963–64). In the "Kalendarium" (Czech 1959–64) six Poles are named as the organizers, and Salmen Lewental gives the names of seven Poles (1972, 188). Only four names appear in both accounts.

20. Unpublished testimonies of Chaim Engel (October 1965), Mosze Bachir (December 1965), and Josef Herszmann (January 1966) at the Sobibor trial, Hagen. Cf. also Tregenza 1977, 23.

21. Testimony of Eliahu Rosenberg at the trial of Franz Stangl, Düsseldorf, June 26, 1970, unpublished.

22. Testimony of Kalman Teigmann at the Adolf Eichmann trial, Jerusalem, October 19, 1964, unpublished.

23. Testimony of Kurt Franz at the Treblinka trial, Düsseldorf, October 19, 1964, unpublished.

24. Ibid., November 5, 1964.

25. Testimony of August Miete, at the Treblinka trial, November 3, 1964.

26. Testimony of Georg Rajgrodski, at the Treblinka trial, November 30, 1964.

27. According to Richard Glazar, there were about 1,200 inmates in the two camps "in their peak period, fall 1942" (letter to the author, June 8, 1979). In Ruckerl 1977, 212, the figure 500 to 1,000 is given.

28. In Kohn 1945, 6, and Richard Glazar, "Treblinka as Seen and as Described in Writing," unpublished (in the author's possession). I have adopted Glazar's spelling of Želo Bloch's name, for as Bloch's compatriot he is probably the best source. Kohn writes "Captain Zielo."

29. Testimony of Kurt Franz, op. cit., on November 1964 and at the Stangl trial, op. cit., on July 10, 1970 [both in Düsseldorf].

30. Testimony of Eugen Turowski at the Treblinka trial, Düsseldorf, January 4, 1965.

31. Testimony of Arie Kudlik, at the Treblinka trial, January 7, 1965.

32. R. Glazar, op. cit., and Glazar's letter to the author, June 8, 1979; Kohn 1945, 6.

33. Estimates differ somewhat. Samuel Rajzman estimates that there were around 700 inmates (1968, 147). Richard Glazar (op. cit.) believes there were a bit more than 700. Srewczyński speaks of 600 to 700 inmates (testimony at the Stangl trial, August 3, 1970). According to Franz Suchomel, there were about 750 (testimony at the Stangl trial, July 3, 1970). These estimates differ from that of Yankel Wiernik, who spoke of 1,000 inmates—on one occasion of 300 in Camp I and 700 in Camp II (n.d., 36) and on a later occasion of 600 in Camp I and 400 in Camp II (testimony at the Treblinka trial, op. cit., January 5, 1965).

34. According to Yankel Wiernik (n.d., 39), they realized that as the only witnesses they would be murdered, because "only 25 percent" of the pits were still to be

emptied. This is confirmed by Georg Rajgrodski: "Since the pits were almost empty, we pressed for an uprising" (testimony at the Treblinka trial, November 30, 1964).

35. K. Teigmann, op. cit.; Strewczynski, op. cit.; 403.

36. Richard Glazar's letter to the author, June 8, 1979.

37. Unpublished testimony by Richard Glazar at the Treblinka trial (Central Office in the Province Nordrhein-Westfalen for the Compiling of Nazi Mass Crimes in Concentration Camps, Cologne).

38. Testimony of Franz Suchomel at the Stangl trial, op. cit., quoted in the summation of Alfred Spiess, the chief prosecutor, unpublished (in the author's possession).

39. Testimony of Franz Suchomel at the Treblinka trial, op. cit., October 26, 1964.

40. R. Glazar, "Treblinka as Seen and Described," p. 16.

41. K. Teigmann, op. cit.

42. K. Teigmann's estimate is 150 and S. Rajzman's, op. cit., 150 to 200. Franz Suchomel speaks of 500 escapees (testimony at the Treblinka trial on October 26, 1964), while fellow defendants of his estimate that up to 600 were able to break out (Ainsztein 1944, 737).

43. Testimony of Kurt Franz at the Treblinka trial, October 19, 1964.

44. Kohn 1945, 11. When Kohn was informed of Franz's testimony, he said that it could not be correct, and gave the names of four SS men whose dead bodies he saw. "Many others whose names I didn't know were also killed," he wrote me on January 20, 1976. Samuel Rajzman also states that more than twenty Germans were killed (1968, 147).

45. Testimonies of Willi Mentz and August Miete at the Treblinka trial, October 26, 1964.

46. A. Spiess, op. cit.

47. Testimony of Simcha Bialowitz at the Sobibor trial, October 1965, unpublished (in the author's possession).

48. Testimony of Dov Freiberg at the Sobibor trial, December 1965. At the same trial and in the same month Mosze Bachir confirmed this incident. Cf. also Ainsztein 1974, 751.

49. Verdict of the Hagen court in the Sobibor trial, December 20, 1966, unpublished (in the author's possession), p. 102.

50. There are different spellings of Feldhendler's name; I have adopted N. Blumenthal's version (in *Dokumenty i Materialy*, Lodz, 1946).

51. Pečerskij's name is spelled in a variety of ways as well, and I have chosen the one that seems most logical phonetically. Pecherskii's diary has also been published in Nirenstein n.d. The English translations differ somewhat from each other.

52. Testimony of Jakob Boskovitz at the Adolf Eichmann trial, Jerusalem, June 5, 1961, unpublished (in the author's possession). Cf. also Guri 1965, 17 ff.

53. Sworn statement by Stanisław Szmajzer, Rio de Janeiro, February 9, 1961, unpublished (in the author's possession).

54. Moshe Bachir's testimony at the Sobibor trial, December 1965. Cf. also the testimony of Josef Herszmann, January 1966.
55. Pecherskii refers to Feldhendler only by his first name, Baruch (given by Nirenstein as Boruch). In a letter to the author dated October 17, 1964, Pecherskii confirms that this man was Leon Feldfänger (his version of the name) and that he did not learn his last name until after the war.
56. In the above letter. Pecherskii's explanation for the larger numbers given in other accounts is that a member of his committee may have given some information to someone close to him, which caused the latter to consider himself part of the committee. "But I refuse to believe that," adds Pecherskii. He remembers the names of three men (Schlejm, Lejtman, Feldhendler) whom he knew only by their first names (Janek, Józef, Jakub), and of a seventh man, whose first name he had forgotten.
57. Yuri Suhl, op. cit., p. 60.
58. Samuel Lerer's testimony at the Sobibor trial, October 1965.
59. Testimonies of Ilona Safran at the Sobibor trial, November 1965, and Selda Metz (quoted in a broadcast of the Westdeutscher Rundfunk, "Zeugnisse aus der Hölle [Testimonies from Hell]," by Alexander Drozdzyński, February 26, 1970). There Metz states that "we felt that since the Germans no longer had any work for us and we were of no use to them they were going to finish us off one of those days."
60. *Stern*, Hamburg, June 15, 1978, p. 224.
61. J. Boskovitz, op. cit.
62. I. Safran, op. cit.
63. Letter to the author from Aleksander Pecherskii, April 12, 1974, unpublished (in the author's possession).
64. S. Szmajzner's sworn statement, op. cit.; testimony of Harry Cukiermann at the Sobibor trial, November 1965 (he remembers two brief postponements); testimony of Jakob Biskubicz, at the Sobibor trial, November 1965; testimony of Kurt Thomas at the same trial, February 1966.
65. J. Boskovitz, op. cit.
66. S. Smajzner, op. cit.
67. K. Thomas, op. cit.; H. Cukiermann, op. cit.; Rückerl 1977, 196; Pecherskii, 1968, 196. Pecherskii names Ernst Berg as the first SS man who was killed by the rebels. However, since the other survivors and the court, which had the best chance to reconstruct these events on the basis of all available testimonies and documents, have named Niemann as the first SS man to be killed, I have adopted this version.
68. Aleksandr Pecherskii's letter to the author, April 12, 1974. Cf. also the testimony of S. Bialowicz, op. cit.
69. Testimony of Meyer Ziss at the Sobibor trial, October 1965.
70. S. Bialowicz, op. cit.
71. H. Cukiermann, op. cit. Ada Lichtmann (1961–63, 38) has stated that Schwarz (she writes Schwartz) was from Czechoslovakia. Pecherskii does not remember

the name of this man, to whom Feldhendler entrusted this assignment (letter from A.P. to the author, October 17, 1964). It is possible that Schwarz was a German-speaking Jew from Czechoslovakia. Testimony of Erich Bauer at the Sobibor trial, November 1965.

72. S. Bialowicz, op. cit.
73. S. Szmajzner's sworn statement, op. cit.
74. Karl Frenzel's testimony at the Sobibor trial, September 1965.
75. Franz Wolf's testimony at the Sobibor trial, September 1965.
76. S. Bialowitz, op. cit.
77. Aleksandr Pecherskii's letter to the author, April 12, 1974.
78. S. Szmajzner's sworn statement, op. cit.
79. Pecherskii's letter to the author, April 12, 1974 and Pecherskii 1968, 50 ff.
80. E. Bauer, op. cit.
81. K. Frenzel, op. cit.
82. Author's conversation with public prosecutor Eckert, September 25, 1974, and Eckert's letter to the author, November 6, 1974.
83. "Jewish Resistance in Poland: Extracts from a Report Received in London Through Polish Underground Channels from the Jewish National Committee in Poland, dated Warsaw, November 15, 1943," in *Labour Press Service*, March 22, 1944 (Center for Contemporary Jewish Documentation, Paris).

21. SABOTAGE

1. Maria Kurcyuszowa's unpublished manuscript on the struggle of Polish women against biological destruction in Ravensbrück (German translation in the author's possession).
2. Götz Dieckmann, *Existenzbedingungen und Widerstand im Konzentrationslager Dora-Mittelbau unter dem Aspekt der funktionellen Einbeziehung der SS in das System der fachistischen Kriegswirtschaft* (Living conditions and Resistance in Concentration Camp Dora–Mittelbau under the Aspect of functional Inclusion of the SS in the System of the Fascist War Economy), dissertation, Humboldt University, Berlin, 1968, p. 328.
3. Otto Horn, "Ausführlicher Bericht über das Konzentrationslager Buchenwald [Complete report on concentration camp Buchenwald]," unpublished (Documentations Archive of the Austrian Resistance, Vienna).
4. M. Kurcyuszowa, op. cit.
5. Author's conversation with George Hess, November 21, 1973.
6. In "Zum Problem 'Widerstand und Solidarität' im KL Dachau [The problem 'resistance and solidarity' in concentration camp Dachau]," (March 11, 1969, unpublished (Dachau Museum), the German Communist Oskar Müller writes that the use of the gas chamber was prevented by "the excellent resistance organization," and in this connection he gives three names, though, strangely enough, not that of Karl Wagner. Müller's statements have been adopted by others (Berlin 1968, 174), but these do name Wagner. Another German Com-

munist, Gustl Gattinger, a member of the detail that handled the electrical installations in "Barracks X," calls Müller's assertion "a figment of the imagination" (letter to the author, September 23, 1975).

7. Author's conversation with Karl Wagner, September 19, 1973.

8. G. Gattinger, op. cit.

9. Author's conversation with Heinz Junge, November 6, 1973.

10. Author's conversation with Heribert Kreuzmann, January 27, 1978.

11. Author's conversation with Matilda Brozek, June 1, 1976.

12. Author's conversation with Edouard Barbel, November 19, 1973.

13. Author's conversation with Franz Freihaut, July 11, 1978.

14. K. Wagner, op. cit.

15. Author's conversation with Julius Schätzle, February 5, 1977.

16. Author's conversation with J. B. Krikowski, February 27, 1976.

17. Author's conversation with Margarete Buber-Neumann, June 21, 1973.

18. O. Müller, op. cit.

19. Author's conversation with Albin Lüdke, November 4, 1973, and Lüdke's letter to the author, December 8, 1973.

20. "Bericht der kommunistischen Parteigruppe des K. L. Jawiszowice [Report of the Communist Party group at concentration camp Jawiszowice]," May 16, 1954, unpublished (in the author's possession).

21. Author's conversation with J. Telling, November 8, 1973.

22. Letter to the author from Emil Samek, January 9, 1977.

23. Letter from Kettner to Eugène Thomé, January 7, 1946.

24. E. Samek, op. cit.

25. "Die antifachistische Arbeit der Häftlinge in den Rüstungsbetrieben [The anti-fascist work of inmates in the armanents industry]," unsigned, undated, and unpublished manuscript (Documentations Archive, Vienna); Bunzol 1946, 38 ff., and Leihbrand 1945, 42.

26. Verdict of the Essen district court in the criminal trial of Erwin Busta (22 19/66), p. 242, where several testimonies are cited; also Pontoizeau 1847, 123.

27. Author's conversation with Stanisław Kamiński, September 25, 1978.

28. Author's conversation with Józef Gabis, October 21, 1976.

29. Letter from Zygmunt Karwat to J. B. Krokowski, September 28, 1976.

30. Manuscript by J. B. Krokowski, unpublished, (in author's possession) and author's conversation with K., November 2, 1974.

31. Verdict of the Essen district court, op. cit., p. 237. Concerning the problems of memoirs written after the fact, cf. also Bornemann/Broszat 1970, 188 ff.

32. Wincenty Hein, "Sabotage im KZ Dora-Mittelbau," in *Widerstandskämpfer*, July–September 1968, Vienna, p. 60. ff.

33. Author's conversation with J. B. Krokowski, November 2, 1974.

34. W. Hein, op. cit. Jean Michel recalls that the French organization refused to collaborate with German Communists (Michel 1975, 224). Cf. also Bornemann/Broszat 1970, 189.

35. M. Bornemann and M. Broszat write that six Italian officers were shot at that time, but in a letter to the author dated July 13, 1974, Wincenty Hein

states that G. Dieckmann and P. Hochmuth's account of this incident is correct.

36. Letter to the author from Wincenty Hein, June 10, 1974, and author's conversation with Hein, March 18, 1978.
37. Verdict of the Essen district court, op. cit., p. 238 ff.
38. Ibid., p. 250.
39. Ibid., p. 251, 165 ff., 310 ff., 334 ff.
40. Letter to the author from Wincenty Hein, July 13, 1974.
41. At the Essen trial Ernst Sander, a former SS senior squad leader, charged with browbeating prisoners he was interrogating, testified he had blackmailed Češpiva into cooperating with him. Similar rumors circulated among Češpiva's fellow inmates. At the time of the trial Češpiva was no longer alive. (Letter to the author from Tadeusz Patzer, April 15, 1976). In a letter to Krokowski dated November 6, 1976, Patzer emphasizes that no betrayal by Češpiva can be proved. Cf. also the author's conversations with Józef Gabis (October 21, 1976) and Wincenty Hein (March 28, 1978) as well as Hein's letter to the author of February 8, 1976 and J. B. Krokowski's manuscript, op. cit. According to G. Dieckmann and P. Hochmuth, Češpiva was saved by the SS doctor (n.d., 180).
42. Letter to the author from Wincenty Hein, June 10, 1974.
43. Letter to the author from Tadeusz Patzer, April 25, 1976.
44. It has been reported that inmates of Sachsenhausen were executed because of sabotage ("Bericht über das Konzentrationslager Sachsenhausen [Report on concentration camp Sachsenhausen]," signed by twelve survivors of that camp, undated but evidently written shortly after the liberation, unpublished (Royal Institute, Amsterdam), p. 28. Cf. also the author's conversation with Jan van Dijk, November 8, 1973. This Dutchman remembers that two of his compatriots were exectued; cf. also Stein 1946, 179. Two Polish women, Kurcyuszowa, op. cit., and Maria Liberakowa recall executions of Poles and Russians in Ravensbrück (Frauen-KZ Ravensbrück, 204). Vincenzo Pappalettera (1972) mentions the execution of six Russians because of sabotage in Gusen, and Leopold Arthofer has reported the public execution of a Russian in Dachau (1947, 68).

22. RESISTING DEMORALIZATION

1. "Clandestien kransje uit Ravensbrück [Clandestine group from Ravensbrück]," unpublished, (Royal Institute for War Documentation, Amsterdam).
2. "Konzentrationslager Sachsenhausen: Die Periode der Sonderkommission (von Ende 1943 bis 1944) [Concentration camp Sachsenhausen: The period of the special commission, from late 1943 to 1944]," Oranienburg, May 1945, unsigned and unpublished (Royal Institute, Amsterdam), p. 2. This report expressly states that "the general intellectual and spiritual conditions in the camp had improved" under the political senior camp inmates, "comrades Bartsch and Bender."

3. A five-stanza song in German, "gezongen in het concentratiekamp Sachsenhausen Block 17—kerst 1943—onder leiding von Jan van Houdt [sung in the concentration camp Sachsenhausen Block 27—Christmas 1943—under the direction of Jan van Houdt]" (in the author's possession).

4. Author's conversation with Heinz Junge, November 6, 1973.

5. Author's conversation with Georg Buch, November 22, 1973.

6. Stanisław Nogaj, "Gusen—Tagebuch eines Journalisten [Diary of a journalist]," unpublished (German version at the Zentralstelle im Lande Nordrhein-Westfalen für die Bearbeitung von nationalsozialistischen Massenverbrechen in Konzentrationslagern, Cologne), p. 237.

7. Urszula Wińska, "Die kulturelle Bildungsarbeit als eigentümliche Form der Widerstandsbewegung der Häftlinge im Konzentrationslager Ravensbrück [Cultural education as a characteristic form of the resistance movement of inmates in concentration camp Ravensbrück], unpublished, (Royal Institute, Amsterdam).

8. Kornelis Hofman, "Verklaring [Statement], Rotterdam, January 25, 1951, unpublished (Royal Institute, Amsterdam).

9. Author's conversation with Eugen Kogon, June 18, 1973; Thape 1969, 188; letter to the author from Ernst Thape, September 15, 1975.

10. U. Wińska, op. cit. Cf. also Kiedrzyńska 1960, 96.

11. Ewald Gondzik, "Zusammenarbeit der Nationen in deutschen Konzentrationslagern [Collaboration of the nations in German concentration camps]," Hamburg, October 29, 1945, unpublished, (Royal Institute, Amsterdam).

12. Author's conversation with Bertl Lauscher (December 3, 1975) and Kiedrzyńrska 1960, 97.

13. Otto Horn, "Ausführlicher Bericht über das Konzentrationslager Buchenwald [Complete report on concentration camp Buchenwald]," unpublished (Documentations Archives of the Austrian Resistance, Vienna).

14. U. Wińska, op. cit.

15. Karl Raddatz, "Die Sonderaktion vom 2. August 1944 gegen KPD-Funktionäre im KL Sachsenhausen [The special roundup of KPD functionaries in concentration camp Sachsenhausen, August 2, 1944]," Berlin, May 20, 1945, unpublished (Royal Institute, Amsterdam). Schupp was shot, but the report does not say whether it was in this connection.

16. Juan de Diego, "Un SS llamado Bachmayer . . . El minuto del silencio [An SS man called Bachmayer . . . The minute of silence]," in *Hispania*, bull. de la FEDIP, March 1967. Jose Marfil Escabona was the first Spaniard to die in Mauthausen, and Julian Mur Sanchez delivered a memorial address.

17. "Bericht der Österreicher an die Abteilung für psychologische Kriegsführung der amerikanischen Armee [Report of the Austrians to the unit for psychological warfare of the American Army]," unpublished (Documentations Archive, Vienna).

18. Karl Lhotzky, "Der Tod eines Kämpfers [The death of a fighter]," *Arbeiter-Zeitung*, Vienna, October 25, 1974.

19. Author's conversation with Hans Gasparitsch, November 20, 1976.

20. Author's conversation with Rudi Gottschalk, February 12, 1977.

21. Letter to the author from Rosa Jochmann, September 5, 1976.

22. Franz Freihaut, Josef Lauscher, Fritz Lauscher, "KZ Dachau 1941 bis 1945: Die illegale Tätigkeit und Zusammenarbeit mit unseren russischen Genossen [Concentration Camp Dachau, 1941–45: The underground activity and cooperation with our Russian comrades]," unpublished (in the author's possession).

23. Janez Ranzinger, Vekoslav Figar, "Anteil der Jugoslawen an dem antifaschistischen Kampf gegen die Nazis im KZ Buchenwald [Share of the Yugoslavians in the anti-fascist struggle against the Nazis in concentration camp Buchenwald]," undated and unpublished (in the author's possession).

24. Friedman, Hołuj 1946, 131. Kazimierz Smoleń enumerates only eight points, omitting points 7 to 10, which deal with the role of the workers' movement in the struggle for democracy (1960–67, 38).

25. U. Wińska, op. cit.

26. Hety Schmitt-Maass, "Ein KZ—was ist das gewesen? Häftling Nr. 109 292 berichtet [A concentration camp—what was it? Inmate no. 109292 reports]," unpublished, (in author's possession).

27. Author's conversation with Père Riquet, November 15, 1973.

28. Rieman 1947 and Benedicta Maria Kempner, *Priester vor Hitlers Tribunalen* (Priests before Hitler's Tribunals), Munich 1966; Reimund Schnabel, *Die Frommen in der Hölle: Geistliche in Dachau* (The Pious in Hell: Clergymen in Dachau) Frankfurt 1966; Martin Niemöller, . . . zu verkünden ein gnädiges Jahr des Herrn! Sechs Dachauer Predigten (*To proclaim a gracious year of the Lord! Six Dachau Sermons*), Zollikon 1946; Bruno Köhler, *Die Welt braucht viel, viel Liebe: Werner Sylten* (*The world needs much, much love: Werner Sylten*), Eisenach 1978; François Goldschmidt, "Une ordination a Dachau [An ordination in Dachau]," in *Tragédie de la Deportation 1940–1945: Témoignages [testimony] de survivants des camps de concentration allemands, [German]*, ed. by Olga Wormser and Henri Michel, Paris 1954, August 2.

29. K. Hofman, op. cit., p. 50.

30. "Erlebnisse und Beobachtungen des Herrn A. Schweid unter nationalsozialistischer Herrschafft [Experiences, and observations of Mr. A. Schweid under Nazi rule]," unpublished (Wiener Library, London).

31. Curt Posener, "Auschwitz—Monowitz," unpublished (in author's possession).

32. Testimony of Thomas Blatt at the Sobibor trial, Hagen, November 1965, unpublished (in author's possession).

23. THE END IS IN SIGHT

1. Otto Horn "Ausführlicher Bericht über das Konzentrationslager Buchenwald [Complete report on the concentration camp Buchenwald]," unpublished (Documentations Archives of the Austrian Resistance, Vienna). This manuscript contains the quotation from Karl Keim, but Keim omitted it in his report

which he wrote two years later (*Buchenwald* 1960, 499 ff.). Cf. also Siewert 1960–67, 50.

2. O. Horn, op. cit.

3. Author's conversation with Leo Bartimes, November 18, 1973.

4. Author's conversation with Eugen Ochs, February 6, 1977.

5. Author's conversation with Paul Schnabel, February 13, 1977.

6. Author's conversation with J. B. Krokowski (November 2, 1974) and unpublished notes by Krokowski (in the author's possession).

7. Author's recollection and Czech 1959–64.

8. Nicolaas Wassenaar, "Kamp-politie Concentrkamp Oranienburg [Camp police, concentration camp Oranienburg]," June 1946, unpublished (Royal Institute for War Documentation, Amsterdam).

9. Author's conversation with Bertl Lauscher, December 3, 1975.

10. "Österreicherinnen unter Hitler im Frauen KL Ravensbrück [Austrian women under Hitler in the female concentration camp Ravensbrück]," unpublished (Documentations Archives, Vienna).

11. Arthur Haulot and Ali Kuci, "Die letzten acht Tage von Dachau [The last eight days of Dachau]," unpublished (Dachau Museum).

12. Walter Leitner, "Die letzten Tage im Konzentrationslager von Dachau [The last days in the concentration camp of Dachau]," unpublished (Dachau Museum).

13. "Die Geschichte des Konzentrationslagers Neuengamme [History of the concentration camp Neuengamme]," unpublished (Wiener Library, London), p. 26.

14. O. Horn, op. cit.

15. Notes of N. Wijnen, March 10, 1948, unpublished (Royal Institute, Amsterdam).

16. Author's conversation with Hans Gasparitsch, November 20, 1976.

17. Karl Ludwig Schecher, "Rückblick auf Dachau," 1945, unpublished (Dachau Museum). According to documents of the International Search Service in Arolsen, Schecher was born on August 8, 1883.

18. Karl Röder, "Nachtwache—Nachwort [Night watch—afterword]," unpublished (Dachau Museum).

19. Author's conversation with Gustl Gattinger, March 5, 1976.

20. Letter from N. Padt to the Royal Institute for War Documentation, Amsterdam, January 10, 1951, unpublished (Royal Institute).

21. "Bericht über das Konzentrationslager Sachsenhausen [Report on the concentration camp Sachsenhausen]," written by twelve inmates who stayed behind when the camp was evacuated, unpublished (Royal Institute, Amsterdam).

22. Hans Pointner, "Zur politischen Lage in Sachsenhausen [The political situation in Sachsenhausen], Berlin, July 1945 unpublished (Royal Institute, Amsterdam). It must be noted that Max Opitz does not mention this episode in his account of his resistance activities in Sachsenhausen (1969). Opitz was not inducted into the Dirlewanger Unit but remained in Sachsenhausen until the evacuation.

23. Wassenaar, op. cit.

24. Unpublished letter from Mathias Mai to Emil Peters, May 30, 1948 (in author's possession). Mai writes that he "and seventy other prisoners ... became soldiers in the penal batallion [Dirlewanger Unit]." According to Albin Lüdke (conversation with the author, November 4, 1973), these included two Luxembourgers whose names are known. Lüdke remembers that around "eighty Germans with red triangles, longtime prisoners" were added to this unit at that time; they were "never, consulted" Cf. also. *So it went to the end.* 1960, 41 ff.

25. Unpublished notes by Franz Danimann and a letter to the author from Kazimierz Smoleń, director of the Auschwitz Museum, January 20, 1968. The extant documents indicate that, in addition to German criminals, ethnic Germans were able to volunteer for the Dirlewanger Unit as early as June 1943. As regards the information about November 7, 1944, the incomplete documents indicate that seventy-one Germans from the Reich or ethnic Germans as well as one Pole were added to this unit on that day; forty-five of these wore red markings and one a green triangle. What category the other twenty-six belonged in cannot be ascertained from the documents, nor can it be established whether those seventy-two were the only ones involved in that roundup.

26. Letter to the author from Kazimierz Smoleń, director of the Auschwitz Museum, January 20, 1968. Smoleń says that those involved have given different dates.

27. Notes about a conversation between Józef Cyrankiewicz and Tzipora Weiss on November 23, 1977, unpublished (in author's possession).

28. Author's conversation with Heribert Kreuzmann, January 27, 1978. Kreuzmann recalls that, around the middle of 1944, the resistance movement in Jawiszhowice formed groups of five in order to be prepared for the evacuation, but these endeavors were betrayed by a German criminal and had to be abandoned. Cf. also. Strzelecki 1975, 243 ff.

29. "Le sacrifice du reseau 'Alliance' [Sacrifice of the network 'Alliance']," unpublished (in author's possession).

30. O. Horn, op. cit.

31. "Vorläufiger Bericht über die militärische Organisation im Konzentrationslager Buchenwald [Preliminary report on the military organization in concentration camp Buchenwald]," unsigned and unpublished (Royal Institute, Amsterdam).

32. Sakharov gives the name as Ricolle, but according to the French Amicale des déportés et familles de Mauthausen [Association of Deportees and Families of Manthausen], he must have meant Ricol. Cf. also the author's conversation with Emile Valley on September 26, 1979, and Sakharov 1961, 108 ff.

33. Miguel Serra-Grabulosa, "Aspect de la Résistance au camp," in *Mauthausen, bulletin interieur de l'amicale des déportés et familles de Mauthausen*, No. 176, Paris, June 1975, p. 2.

34. Unpublished manuscript by J. B. Krokowski (in author's possession).

35. "Die Geschichte des Konzentrationslagers Neuengamme [History of the concentration camp Neuengamme]," op. cit.

36. Maria Kurcyuszowa, "Die Polinnen im Kampf gegen die biologische Ver-

nichtung im Konzentrationslager Ravensbrück [Polish women in a struggle against biological destruction in concentration camp Ravensbrück]," unpublished (German translation in the possession of the author).

37. Author's conversation with Albert Guérisse on March 2, 1976. At that time Guérisse was elected as the chairman of that organization, whose leadership included representatives of numerous nations and different political ideologies. The German Communist Walter Vielhauer also remembers (conversation with the author, November 21, 1976) that the resistance organization did not begin to work toward the day of decision until the last year.

38. O. Horn, op. cit. Cf. also Buchenwald 1960, 490 and Czarnecki 1968, 54.

39. O. Horn, op. cit. The Pole Wacław Czarnecki gives the same numbers, but he speaks of fifteen Polish groups (1968, 54), while Otto Horn enumerates nine groups of this nationality.

40. Kornelis Hofman, "Verklaring [Statement]," Rotterdam, January 25, 1951, unpublished (Royal Institute, Amsterdam).

41. Author's conversations with Fritz Kleinmann, December 12, 1976, and March 5, 1977.

42. Antonius van Velsen, "Verslag [Report]," Den Helder, North Holland, February 5, 1948, unpublished (Royal Institute, Amsterdam).

43. J. Cyrankiewicz, op. cit.

44. "Vorläufiger Bericht [Preliminary report] über die militärische Organisation im Konzentrationslager Buchenwald," op. cit.: O. Horn, op. cit.

45. Franz Bera, "Meine Tätigkeit im internationalen militärischen Kader im KL Buchenwald [My activities in the international military cadre in concentration camp Buchenwald]," Vienna, June 5, 1945, unpublished, (in the author's possession).

46. Notes made by Leo Eitinger in Buchenwald after his liberation, unpublished (in the author's possession) and author's conversation with Leo Eitinger, October 28, 1973.

47. Erich Fein, "Bericht über Beschaffung von Waffen für die Internationale Widerstandsbewegung [Report on the procurement of weapons for the international resistance movement]," March 24, 1958, unpublished, (Documentations Archives, Vienna).

48. "Vorläufiger Bericht über die militärische Organisation im Konzentrationslager Buchenwald," op. cit.; O. Horn. op. cit.; "Bericht der Österreicher an die Abteilung für psychologische Kriegsführung in der amerikanischen Armee [Report of the Austrians in the unit for psychological warfare in the American Army]," unpublished (Documentations Archives, Vienna).

49. "Vorläufiger Bericht über die militärische Organisation im Konzentrationslager Buchenwald," op. cit., and O. Horn, op. cit. "Die polnische Geheimorganisation im K.L. Buchenwald [The Polish secret organization in concentration camp Buchenwald]," a report signed in the name of the Komitet Polski by Stefan Szczepaniak, Pawel Kwoczek, and Władek Nowak, unpublished (Royal Institute, Amsterdam), lists "over 100 revolvers, eight hand grenades, eighteen carbines, and even two heavy machine guns."

50. F. Bera, op. cit.

51. M. Serra-Grabulosa, op. cit.

52. "La reunion du Comité International de Mauthausen à Barcelona et la mitraillette de Juan Pagès [Reunion of International Committee of Mauthausen at Barcelona and the submachine gun of Juan Pagès]," in *Mauthausen*, No. 196, Paris, June–July 1979, p. 6.

53. Sworn statement by Alfred Payrleitner, Gmunden, August 21, 1945, unpublished (in the author's possession) and author's conversation with A. P., November 18, 1975. Cf. also *Letzeburger zu Mauthausen* 1970, 245 ff.

54. Rudi Wunderlich, "Flucht aus dem KZ [Flight from the concentration camp], unpublished (Documentatins Archives, Vienna), p. 66.

55. Karl Feuerer, "Widerstand in 'Dora' [Resistance in Dora]", *Frankfurter Rundschau*, August 14, 1947. Cf. also Češpiva Giessner Pelný 1964, 53 and "Dora" 1967, 34.

56. "Die Geschichte [History] des Konzentrationslagers Neuengamme," op. cit., p. 26.

24. THE LIBERATION OF THE CONCENTRATION CAMPS

1. Verdict of the Essen district court in the criminal trial of Erwin Busta and others, 22 (19/66), p. 233.

2. Otto Horn, "Ausführlicher Bericht über das Konzentrationslager Buchenwald [complete report on the concentration camp Buchenwald]" unpublished (Documentations Archives of the Austrian Resistance, Vienna). Cf. also Manhès n.d., 41 ff.

3. This first transport is not mentioned in other accountes. However, since this report appears to be have written soon after the liberation (though the year of its publication is not given), I have used it here.

4. Carolus, "21,000 Häftlinge befreit! Die letzten 10 Tage des Konzentratioinslagers Buchenwald: Ein Erlebnisbericht nach eigenen Tagebuchaufzeichnungen [21,000 inmates freed! The last ten days of the concentration camp Buchenwald: A report of experiences according to diary notes]," Buchenwald, April 14, 1945, unpublished (Documentations Archives, Vienna), p. 3 ff. Eugen Ochs writes that camp commandant Pister "[warned] us against foreign prisoners who might attack us Germans." Ochs managed to give some foreign comrades who worked with him in the inmates' kitchen an opportunity to listen to the commandant's speech. "Afterward I told my comrades not to cooperate with the SS; the fronts were as before: the inmates on one side and the SS on the other. They readily accepted this." (Letter to the author from Eugen Ochs, December 15, 1976.)

5. Carolus, op. cit., p. 5.

6. O. Horn, op. cit.

7. Ibid.

8. Ibid., pp. 20, 68, 223; *Buchenwald* 1960, 541 ff.

9. O. Horn, op. cit.' "Bericht der Österreicher an die Abteilung für psychologische Kriegsführung in der amerikanischen Armee [Report of the Austrians to the unit for psychological warfare in the American Army]," unpublished, (Documentations Archives, Vienna), p. 6.

10. Since Bloch is not on this list (cf. *Buchenwald* 1960, 541 ff.), there probably were forty-seven names on it. Walter Bartel regards this figure as erroneous 1976, 303; Kogon 1946, 338).

11. Carolus, op. cit., p. 22; Kogon 1946, 337.

12. Author's conversation with Eugen Kogon, December 10, 1979.

13. Basing himself on the material of the international camp committee, Rudi Jahn writes: "Meanwhile the anti-Fascist leadership decided to smuggle one of the forty-six comrades out of the camp" (*Das war Buchenwald*, n.d., 108). Otto Horn (op. cit.) uses the same words, which indicates that he too was quoting from the material of the international camp committee.

14. A footnote in Teofil Witek's *Der Hilferuf* (Cry for Help) indicates that this text was written by Walter Bartel and Harry Kuhn (*Buchenwald* 1960, 543).

15. "Vorläufiger Bericht über die militärische Organisation im Konzentrationslager Buchenwald [Preliminary report on the military organization in concentration camp Buchenwald]," (unpublsihed (Royal Institute for War Documentation, Amsterdam), p. 8.

16. Carolus, op. cit., p. 22.

17. Unpublished notes made by Leo Eitinger in Buchenwald between February and April 1945 (in the author's possession).

18. Ernst Thape, "Buchenwald-Tagebuch vom 1. April bis 1. Mai 1945 [Diary, April 1–May 1, 1945]," (unpublished (Archives of Friedrich Ebert Stiftung, Bonn– Bad Godesberg).

19. Alois Neumann, "Wie ich gelebt habe [How I lived]," (unpublished German translation from the Czech). Neumann also writes that he was "the only non-Communist" to have been placed on the international committee.

20. O. Horn, op. cit.

21. Gerhard Harig and Max Mayr, "Die zahlenmässige Entwicklung des Konzentrationslagers Buchenwald 1937–1945, bearbeitet auf Grund vollständiger Unterlagen der zuständigen Dienststellen [The numerical development of concentration camp Buchenwald, 1937–1945, compiled on the basis of complete records of the appropriate office]," unpublished (in the author's possession), p. 19. The same figures are given in *Das war Buchenwald* n.d., 38.

22. Carolus, op. cit., p. 22. According to his account of the ethnic composition of the liberated prisoners, on the day after the evacuation the camp still housed 5,000 Russians, 3,000 Frenchmen, 2,000 Poles, 2,000 Czechs, 600 Yugoslavs, "2,000 Germans, mostly Communists," and members of other nations.

23. Leo Eitinger (op. cit.) states that the siren sounded a "special alarm" at ten o'clock. Rudi Jahn reports a first alarm at 10:15 A.M.; at 11:45 we heard the siren warning of enemy action that had hitherto been used only as a test . . . at 12:10 the inmates heard the hateful voice of roll-call officer Hofschulte for the last time: 'All SS men out of the camp!' " (*Das war Buchenwald* n.d., 113 ff) The

Luxembourger Nicholas Spielmann believes that the siren "sounded an alarm for a full five minutes around 11:30" (1970), but Armin Walther states that it sounded at 11:50 (Kautsley 1961, 309). In the "Bericht der Österreicher an die Abteilung für psychologische Kriegsführung in der amerikanischen Armee" (op. cit., p. 6) we read: "At exactly five minutes before 12 o'clock the siren sounded, indicating that the enemy was approaching and ordering the SS men to leave the camp immediately."

24. L. Eitinger, op. cit.

25. O. Horn (op. cit.) does not name Edelmann, but writes that the camp commandant sent for "an anti-Fascist prisoner from the German Reich and the senior camp inmate."

26. Fritz Freudenberg, "Der letzte Tag im KZ Buchenwald am 11. April 1945 [The last day in concentration camp Buchenwald, April 11, 1945]," unpublished (in the author's possession).

27. E. Thape, op. cit.; Bunzol 1946, 44.

28. E. Thape. op. cit.

29. L. Eitinger, op. cit.

30. Carolus, op. cit., p. 19. This incident has also been described by Rudi Jahn (*Das war Buchenwald* n.d., 114) and O. Horn (op. cit.)

31. F. Freudenberg, op. cit.

32. O. Horn, op. cit.

33. L. Eitinger, op. cit.

34. E. Ochs, op. cit.

35. Franz Bera, "Meine Tätigkeit im internationalen militärischen Kader im KL Buchenwald [My activities in the international military cadre in concentration camp Buchenwald]," Vienna, June 5, 1945, unpublished (in the author's possession).

36. E. Thape, op. cit.

37. Carolus, op. cit.

38. *Konzentrationslager Buchenwald: Bericht des internationalen Lagerkomitees Buchenwald* (Concentration Camp Buchenwald: Report of the International Camp Committee), Weimar, n.d., p. 172.

39. Carolus, op. cit., p. 21. He writes that these two inmates "fell in the heat of the action, done in by unfortunate circumstances." Max Mayr recalls that they were the "victims of a sloppy use of weapons rather than of a struggle" (letter to the author, February 13, 1977), while Otto Horn (op. cit.) writes that "bullets hit them in the first tumult of battle."

40. Author's conversation with Eugen Ochs, December 12, 1979.

41. Carolus, op. cit., p. 21.

42. Text of the official report of the headquarters of the Allied Expeditionary Forces to the U.S. War Department, dated April 1945. The figures differ somewhat from those given by Carolus (cf. note 22). Cf. also *Buchenwald* 1960, 554.

43. "Lagerbericht Nr. 1, Buchenwald, den 11. April 1945 [Camp report No. 1, Buchenwald, April 11, 1945], unpublished (Documentations Archives, Vienna), printed in *Buchenwald* 1960, 554 ff. with small changes that are not identified

as such; on p. 558 there is the first order by the American commander, which appoints the senior camp inmate as the commandant. Cf. also Freund 1945, 1940.

44. Bruno Apitz has given a highly embellished description of a fight that culminates in these words: "The combat groups captured one tower after another." Since the author calls his account a novel (Apitz 1958, 508), he may be granted poetic license. This, however, does not apply to assertions like "The concentration camp Buchenwald . . . had liberated itself" (Czarnecki 1968, 56). Documentations by Günter Kühn and Wolfgang Weber use almost the same words: "military self-liberation" (1976, 52) and "self-liberated Buchenwald" (1976, 427). Numerous survivors of Buchenwald have participated in the frequently heated discussions of this subject, including some with exceptional insight into the events. Thus Ernst Thape writes: "The story that the inmates vanquished the SS is a legend. . . . The value of my diary lies in the fact that it does not contain one word about armed resistance. However, the few weapons in the hands of the inmates sufficed to prevent chaos during the vacuum between the departure of the SS and the arrival of the Americans" (letter to the author, March 22, 1977). August Cohn, who was a member of the inner circle of those possessing inside information and appeared on the SS list of forty-six, writes: "Without exception the resistance was passive. . . . All I can say about the Communist propaganda that Buchenwald fought actively is that all weapons concealed in Block 50 [where Cohn was housed—H.L.] were not given to the camp security until the last SS tower guard had left the camp" (letter to the author, March 22, 1977). Eugen Ochs says that there was "no self-liberation whatever" and refers to Karl Barthel's report (1946): "It was printed in the spring of 1946, when self-liberation had not yet been invented" (conversation with the author on February 6, 1977, and letter to him of February 28, 1977). Paul Schnabel, who worked in the infirmary as a doctor, recalls that "the towers were vacated one after another. There was no fighting whatever and I witnessed no self-liberation" (conversation with the author on February 13, 1977). The French physician E. J. Odic also speaks of a "legend"; having worked in the hospital as physician-in-chief immediately after the liberation, he emphasizes that there were no dead or wounded people there (Le Déporté, Paris, June–July 1976, p. 28). Ailleret, who headed a resistance group composed of Frenchmen, Belgians, and Spaniards, also uses the term "legend" in connection with later publications about fights (Le Déporté, op. cit.) His compatriot Christian Pineau remembers that the SS withdrew from the watchtowers without a fight and that therefore it was not necessary to use the weapons which had been distributed (Le Déporté, April 1977, p. 21). In connection with the above-mentioned accounts of the events of April 11, Kurt Hirsch, a German Jew, speaks of subsequent glorifications (conversation with the author on March 5, 1976), and his compatriot Max Mayr, who credits the Communists with "foolhardiness in creating an illegal political camp organization with a military section," emphasizes that "an armed assault on the gate never took place" and also calls the story of self-liberation a legend (letter to the author, May 26,

1976). Walter Bartel, who has occupied key positions both in the Buchenwald resistance organization and in the circle of those who have written the history of that camp in East Germany, is a bit more cautious when he states that the resistance of the SS was weak and was soon broken with force of arms (1976, 308). In a letter dated November 30, 1973, I drew his attention to contradictory statements in the accounts of the events of April 11, 1945, that were written shortly thereafter and those that were published years later, and I requested his expert opinion on the historical basis for various disputed facts. Bartel did not reply, and when I renewed my request at a meeting in Bielefeld on June 4, 1978, he only referred me to the literature on the subject—that is, the conflicting accounts that I had asked him to clarify.

45. Unsigned and undated manuscript unpublished (Royal Institute, Amsterdam), printed in *Damals in Sachsenhausen* 1967, 130, with minor changes that are not identified as such.

46. "Wie war es mit der Befreiung 1945? [How was it at the liberation 1945?]" in *Sachsenhausen-Informationen, Mitteilungsblatt für ehemalige Häftlinge des KZ Sachsenhausen/Oranienburg, deren Angehörige und Hinterbliebene*, No. 69, Dortmund, March 20, 1972.

47. Author's conversation with Heinz Junge, November 6, 1973.

48. Author's conversation with Georg Buch, November 22, 1973.

49. Cf. note. 42. Here, too, unidentified changes were made—for example, instead of "gehen als Bewachungsmannschaft . . . mit [go along as guards]" there is "müssen . . . mitgehen [have to go along]."

50. Bericht über das Konzentrationslager Sachsenhausen [Report about the concentration camp Sachsenhausen]," signed by twelve survivors of the camp, unpublished (Royal Institute, Amsterdam), p. 35.

51. G. Buch, op. cit.

52. "Wie war es mit der Befreiung 1945? [How was it at the liberation?]?" op. cit. Cf. also H. Junge (op. cit), who confirms that both sides avoided a shootout at that time.

53. Cf. note 45.

54. *Der Appell* (The Roll Call), *Mitteilungsblatt der ehemalige Häftlinge des KZ Sachsenhausen/Oranienburg*, No. 79, April 19, 1975.

55. Report by August Duckstein in *Der Appell*.

56. Record of Bruno Furch's interrogation at the Flossenbürg trial in Dachau unpublished (in the possession of Toni Siegert). Cf. also Selbmann 1961, 321 ff.

57. Author's conversation with Franz Freihaut, July 11, 1978.

58. B. Furch, op. cit.

59. F. Freihaut, op. cit.

60. Author's conversation with Albert Hommel, November 18, 1973; Siegert 1979, 486.

61. Arthur Haulot/Ali Kuci, "Die letzten acht Tage von Dachau [The last eight days of Dachau]" unpublished (Dachau Museum).

62. Arthur Haulot, "Kameradschaft im KZ [Comradeship in the concentration camp]," *Süddeutsche Zeitung*, December 11, 1945.

63. Oskar Müller, "So wurden 33,000 befreit! [That is how 33,000 were liberated!]" in *Mitteilungsblätter der Lagergemeinschaft Dachau*, April 1965, p. 10.

64. A. Haulot and A. Kuci, op. cit.

65. Walter Leitner, "Die letzten Tage im Konzentrationslager Dachau [The last days in concentration camp Dachau]," unpublished (Dachau Museum).

66. A. Haulot and A. Kuci, op. cit.; unpublished notes by camp clerk Jan Domagala (Dachau Museum).

67. W. Leitner, op. cit.

68. A. Haulot and A. Kuci, op. cit.

69. Karl Ludwig Schecher, "Rückblick auf Dachau," unpublished (Dachau Museum).

70. O. Müller, op. cit.

71. A. Haulot and A. Kuci, op. cit.

72. O. Müller, op. cit.

73. Karl Riemer, "Amerikaner helfen [Americans help]," Dachau, May 11, 1945, unpublished (Dachau Museum).

74. Richard Titze, "Aufstand gegen die SS in Dachau am 28. April 1945" unpublished (Dachau Museum).

75. Ibid: "Der Aufstand in Dachau [Revolt in Dachau]," in *Dachauer Neueste Nachrichten*, April 28, 1978; author's conversation with Georg Scherer, April 2, 1979.

76. Adolf Maislinger, "Aufstand in Dachau am 28. April 1945 [Revolt in Dachau, April 28, 1945]," Munich, February 18, 1970, unpublished (Dachau Museum); "Befragung Bürger Sch(erer), Dachau 1973—Dachauer Aufstand [Interrogation of Citizen Scherer, Dachau 1973—Dachau revolt]," unpublished, (Dachau Museum).

77. R. Titze, op. cit.; A Maishinger, "Der Aufstand in Dachau, von einem Augenzeugen berichtet [The revolt in Dachau, reported by an eyewitness], in *Münchner Merkur*, May 22, 1970; "Dachauer Aufstand vom 28. April 1945: Personalien der beim Aufstand gefallenen Dachauer Bürger [Particulars of Dachau citizens who were killed in the revolt]," unpublished (Dachau Museum).

78. "Aufstand der Häftlinge vom 28. April 1945 in Dachau [Revolt of the inmates in Dachau, April 28, 1945]," unsigned, presumably by Georg Scherer, unpublished (Dachau Museum). Cf. also "Der Aufstand in Dachau,' op. cit.

79. A. Haulot and A. Kuci, op. cit.

80. Ibid.

81. O. Mller, op. cit.

82. Letter to the author from Jules Jost, March 15, 1980.

83. A. Haulot and A. Kuci, op. cit.

84. "Bericht über die erste Sitzung des internationalen Häftlingskomitees im befreiten Lager Dachau [Report on the first session of the international inmates' committee in liberated camp Dachau]," unpublished (Dachau Museum); author's conversation with Albert Guérisse, March 2, 1976.

85. A. Haulot and A. Kuci, op. cit.; K. L. Schecher, op. cit.

86. K. Riemer, op. cit.

87. "Kameraden! [Comrades!] (an appeal), Dachau, April 29, 1945, unpublished (Dachau Museum).

88. Max Eichhorn, "Dachau, First Week of May 1945," unpublished, (Dachau Museum). The Belgian Charles Baum, who represented the Jews on the international committee, informed Eichhorn on May 5 that Poles had threatened to break up any Jewish religious services that might be held. "That was only one of many ways in which Poles demonstrated their hostility toward Jews," writes Eichhorn.

89. M. Eichhorn, op. cit.

90. Alfred Hübsch, "Die Insel des Standrechts: Geheimaufzeichnungen des Pförtners von Dachau [The island of martial law: Secret reports of the Dachau gatekeeper]," unpublished (Dachau Museum), p. 436 ff.

91. Unpublished notes of Agnes Primocic (in the author's possession).

92. Letter to the author from Albin Lüdke, December 8, 1973.

93. Hans Schwarz, "Die Geschichte des Konzentrationslagers Neuengamme [History of the Concentration Camp Neuengamme]," unpublished (Wiener Library, London).

94. Author's conversation with Albin Lüdke, November 4, 1973.

95. H. Schwarz, op. cit. In his letter to the author dated December 8, 1973, Albin Lüdke expressed doubts about this report.

96. Author's conversation with Fritz Kleinmann, December 12, 1976.

97. Author's conversation with Hans Maršàlek, November 13, 1979. According to his later calculation, around 300 Germans, including sixty political prisoners, were put into uniform at taht time (Maršàlek 1974, II/327).

98. Letter from Ottokar Merinsky, unpublished (in the author's possession). At Eastertime (April 1 and 2) the German inmates of the subsidiary camp Wiener–Neudorf were put into military uniforms and some of them were given arms—"a seriously disturbing sign for us" (Georges Loustaunau-Lacau, in Bernadac 1976, 146).

99. Letter to the author from H. Maršàlek (March 3, 1975) and Jean-Maurice Rubli, "Als ich nach Mauthausen kam [When I arrived in Mauthausen]," in Weltwoche, Zurich, February 19, 1975. Cf. also Maršàlek 1974, 239, and Bouard 1954, 74.

100. J.–M. Rubli, op. cit.

101. Author's conversation with Józef Cyrankiewica, November 16, 1979.

102. Author's conversation with Hans Maršàlek, November 13, 1979.

103. Ibid.

104. Letter to the author from H. Maršàlek, November 25, 1975.

105. Ibid.

106. Ibid.

107. Author's conversation with Juan de Diego, July 9, 1974.

108. Photocopies of seventeen such reports are in the possession of the author. Six of these came from Gusen, five from the Mauthausen post office, two from the mayor's office in Mauthausen, and one from the SS kitchen.

109. From the archives of Colonel Kodré, unpublished (in the author's possession).

110. Here is a news item given to the British news agency Reuters by six Austrians: "American troops occupied the Mauthausen concentration camp on May 5, 1945, liberating 478 Austrians, including nineteen women." In his capacity as secretary-general of the international Mauthausen committee, Dürmayer, one of the six, on August 17, 1979, wrote a letter to the members of that committee in which he opposed tendencies "to give the U.S. army credit for the liberation of the Mauthausen main camp," (unpublished letter in the possession of the author).

111. Letter from O. Merinsky, op. cit.

112. Ibid.; Bernadac 1976, 200 ff.

113. Rudolf Pekar, "Ablauf des Unternehmens, [Course of the enterprise]," Ebensee, May 8, 1945, unpublished (in the author's possession).

114. Letter to the author from R. Pekar, November 26, 1979.

115. Wacław Malecki, "Bestätigung, [Confirmation]," Ebensee, July 4, 1945, unpublished (in the author's possession).

Bibliography

Abada, Roger. 1946. "Organisation de la resistance," in *Témoignages sur Auschwitz*, Paris.

Abt. Harald. 1980. "Mein Glaube an Gott stützte mich," in *Der Wachtturm*, No. 14, Wiesbaden.

Adam, Walter. 1947. *Nacht über Deutschland: Erinnerungen an Dachau*, Vienna.

Adelsberger, Lucie. 1956. *Auschwitz: Ein Tatsachenbericht*, Berlin.

Adler, H. G. 1960. *Theresienstadt 1941–1945: Das Antlitz einer Zwangsgemeinschaft*, Tübingen.

Ahrens, Franz. 1968. *Über Max Reimann: Streiflichter aus dem Leben eines Kommunisten*, Hamburg.

Ainsztein, Reuben. 1974. *Jewish Resistance in Nazi-Occupied Eastern Europe*, London.

Aktenvermerk. 1979. *R. u.—Ein Bericht über die Solidarität und den Widerstand im Konzentrationslager Mauthausen von 1938 bis 1945*, Berlin.

Antelme, Robert. 1945. "L'espèce humaine [The human species]," in Olga Wormser/Henri Michel, eds. *Tragédie de la déportation 1940–1945. Temoignages de survivants des camps de concentration allemands (German)*, Paris.

Antoni, Ernst. 1979. *KZ: Von Dachau bis Auschwitz*, Frankfurt, 1989.

Apitz, Bruno. 1958. *Nackt unter Wölfen*, Halle.

Arndt, Ino. 1970. "Das Frauenkonzentrationslager Ravensbrück," in *Studien zur Geschichte der Konzentrationslager. Schriftenreihe der Vierteljahrshefte für Zeitgeschichte*, Stuttgart.

Arndt, Ino, Wolfgang Scheffler. 1976. "Organisierter Massenmord an Juden in nationalsozialistischen Vernichtungslagern," in *Vierteljahrshefte für Zeitgschichte*, No. 2, Stuttgart.

Aroneanu, Eugene. n.d. *Konzentrationslager: Tatsachenbericht über die an der Menschheit begangenen Verbrechen*, Nuremberg.

Arthofer, Leopold. 1947. *Als Priester im Konzentrationslager: Meine Erlebnisse in Dachau*, Vienna.

Arvet, Henri, F. Boissard. 1954. "Des geôles de la Gestapo de Dijon à l'enfer de Buchenwald et Dora," in Olga Wormser/Henri Michel, eds., *Tragédie de la deportation 1950–1945. Témoignages de survivants de camps de concentration allemands (German)* Paris.

Auerbach, Hellmuth. 1962. "Die Einheit Dirlewanger," in *Vierteljahrshefte für Zeitgeschichte*, No. 3, Stuttgart.

Bakels, Floris B. 1979. *Nacht und Nebel: Der Bericht eines holländischen Christen aus deutschen Gefängnissen und Konzentrationslagern*, Frankfurt.

Bárta, Drahomir. 1966. "K historii ilegáni činnosti a hnuti odporu veznu v kon-

468   BIBLIOGRAPHY

centračnim táboře Ebensee v letech 1944–1945," in *Historie a vojenstvi*, No. 4, Prague.

Bartel, Walter. 1970. *Wehrwirtschaftsführer—Geheimwaffen—KZ: Gutachten über Rolle und Bedeutung des KZ Dora-Mittelbau und die Funktion der SS bei der A4-Produktion*, Frankfurt.

——. 1976. "Die letzten zehn Tage des faschistischen Konzentrationslagers Buchenwald," in *Beiträge zur Geschichte der Arbeiterbewegung*, No. 2, Berlin.

Barthel, Karl. 1946. *Die Welt ohne Erbarmen: Bilder und Skizzen aus dem KZ*, Rudolstadt.

Bartoszewski, Władysław, Zofia Lewin. 1969. *Righteous Among Nations: How Poles Helped the Jews 1939–1945*, London.

Baum, Bruno. 1965. *Croix gammée contre caducée: Les Experiences humaines en Allemagne pendant la deuxième guerre mondiale*, Neustadt.

Bené, Charles. see Eschenbrenner, Marc.

Berben, Paul. 1968. *Histoire du camp de concentration de Dachau (1933–1945)*, Brussels.

Berger, Alexander. 1963. *Kreuz hinter Stacheldraht: Der Leidensweg deutscher Pfarrer*, Bayreuth.

Bernke, Hanns. 1946. *Buchenwald: Eine Erinnerung an Mörder*, Salzburg.

Bernadac, Christian. 1972. *Le camp des femmes: Ravensbrück*, Paris.

——. 1974. *Les 186 marches: Mauthausen*, Paris.

——. 1975. *Le neuvième cercle Mauthausen II*, Paris.

——. 1976. *Des jours san fin Mauthausen III*, Paris.

——. 1979. *L'holocauste oublié: Le massacre des tsiganes* Paris.

Bernard, Jean. 1962. *Pfarrerblock 25487: Ein Bericht*, Munich 1962.

Bestic, Alan. Cf. Vrba, Rudolf.

Besymeński, Lew. 1968. *Sonderakte "Barbarossa": Dokumente, Darstellung, Deutung*, Stuttgart.

Bezaut, Jean. 1978. "L'évasion d'Alex Luntz et de Paul Muller," in *Rappel*, No. 1, Luxembourg.

Bezwińska, Jadwga. Cf. Czech, Danuta.

Biermann, P. 1945. *Streiflicher aus Hinzert, Natzweiler, Buchenwald.* Luxembourg.

Birin, Frère. 1947. *Seize mois de bagne: Buchenwald–Dora.* Epernay.

Birnbaum, Sizanne, 1946. "Malla la Belge," in *Témoignages sur Auschwitz*, Paris.

Blatt, Tuvia. "The Testimony of Tuvia Blatt," in *Yad Vashem Bulletin*, III, Jerusalem.

Böckle, Bärbel. 1978. "Das Arbeits-und Krankenlager Vaihingen," in *Nationalsozialistische Konzentrationslager im Dienst der totalen Kriegsführung: Sieben württembergische Aussenkommandos des Konzentrationslagers Natzweiler/Elsass*, Stuttgart.

Boissard, F. Cf. Arvet, Henri.

Bonifas, Aime. 1968. *Détenu 20801: Deux ans dans les bagnes nazis* Paris.

Bornemann, Manfred Martin Broszat. 1970. "Das KL Dora-Mittelbau," in *Studien zur Geschichte der Konzentrationslager. Schriftenreihe der Vierteljahreshefte für Zeitgeschichte*, Stuttgart.

Bornstein, Ernst Israel. 1967. *Die lange Nacht: Ein Bericht aus sieben Lagern*, Frankfurt.

Bouard, Michel de. 1954. "Mauthausen," in *Revue d'histoire de la deuxième guerre mondiale*, Nos. 7–9, Paris.

_____. 1962. "Gusen," in *Revue d'histoire de la deuxième guerre mondiale*, No. 12, Paris.

Boulanger, Jakob. 1957. *Eine Ziffer über dem Herzen: Erlebnisbericht aus zwölf Jahren Haft*, Berlin.

Brandhuber, Jerzy. 1961. "Die sowjetischen Kriegsgefangenen im Konzentrationslager Auschwitz," in *Hefte von Auschwitz*, No. 4, Auschwitz.

_____. 1962. "Vergessene Erde," in *Hefte von Auschwitz*, No. 5, Auschwitz.

Brausch, Jean. 1970. "Wien-Mödling-Mauthausen und Befreiung," in *Rappel*, Nox. 3–5, Luxembourg.

Brill, Hermann. 1946. *Gegen den Strom*, Offenbach.

Bringmann, Fritz. 1978. *Kindermord am Bullenhuserdamm: SS-Verbrechen in Hamburg 1945: Menschenversuche an Kindern*, Frankfurt.

Brodski, J. A. 1968. Die Lebenden kämpfen: *Die illegale Organisation Brüderliche Zusammenarbeit der Kriegsgefangenen (BSW)*, Berlin.

Brol, Franciszek, Gerard Wloch, Jan Pilecki. 1959. "Das Bunkerbuch des Blocks 11 im Nazi-Konzentrationslager Auschwitz, in *Hefte von Auschwitz*, No. 1, Auschwitz.

Brome, Vincent. 1957. *L'histoire de Pat O'Leary*, Paris.

Broszat, Martin, 1965. "Nationalsozialistische Konzentrationslager 1933–1945," in *Anatomie des SS-Staates*, Olten. See also Bornemann, Manfred.

Brückner, Siegfried/Horn, Michael. 1975. "Die Verbrechen der Politischen Abteilung im Konzentrationslager Auschwitz: Aufbau und Personal der Politischen Abteilung," in *Bulletin des Arbeitskreises "Zweiter Weltkrieg,"* No. 1.

Buber-Neumann, Margarete. 1958. *Als Gefangene bei Stalin und Hitler: Eine Welt im Dunkel*, Stuttgart.

_____. 1963. *Kafkas Freundin Milena*, Munich.

_____. 1976. *Die erloschene Flamme: Schicksale meiner Zeit*, Munich.

Das war Buchenwald: n.d.: Ein Tatsachenbericht. Kollektivarbeit einer Anzahl Buchenwald-Häftlinge aus Leipzig, zusammengestellt und bearbeitet von Rudi Jahn, Leipzig.

Die Wahrheit. 1945. *über das Konzentrationslager Buchenwald, Leipzig, n.d.*

Konzentrationslager Buchenwald. 1945. Geschildert von Buchenwalder Häftlingen, Vienna.

Buchenwald. 1960. Mahnung und Verpflichtung: Dokumente und Berichte, Frankfurt.

Bunzol, Alfred. 1946. *Erlebnisse eines politischen Gefangenen im Konzentrationslager Buchenwald*, Weimar.

Burney, Christoper. 1946. *The Dungeon Democracy*, New York.

Caban, Mikolaj. 1964. *Powrót za rzeki Styks)*, Warsaw.

Carlebach, Emil. 1969. "So wurden die Juden des Lagers Buchenwald gerettet," in *Die Tat*, Frankfurt, April 12.

Češpiva, Jan, Fritz Giessner, Kurt Pelný. 1964. *Geheimwaffen in Kohnstein*, Nordhausen.

Chassaing, Therese. 1946. "27 Avril 1944: Revier de Birkenau, femmes," in *Témoignages sur Auschwitz*, Paris.

Chêne, Evelyn le. 1971. *Mauthausen: The History of a Death Camp*, London.

Choumoff, Pierre Serge. 1972. *Les chambres a gaz de Mauthausen*, Paris.

Ceisielski, Edward. 1968. *Wspomnienia oswiecimskie*, Cracow.

Comité International de la Croix-Rouge, ed. 1947. *Documents sur l'activité de Comité international de la Croix-Rouge en faveur des civils détenus dans les camps de Concentration en Allemagne (1939–1945)*, Geneva.

———. 1969. *Vorläufiges Verzeichnis der Konzentrationslager und deren Aussenkommandos sowie anderer Haftstätten unter dem Reichsführer-SS in Deutschland und deutsch besetzten Gebieten 1933–1945)*, Arolsen.

Constante, Mariano. 1917. *Les années rouges: De Guernica a Mauthausen*.

———. Cf. Razola, Manuel.

Cyrankiewicz, Józef. 1964. "Resistance in Auschwitz," in *Poland*, No. 11, Warsaw.

Czarnecki, Wacław. 1968. "Am Beispiel Buchenwalds: Widerstand in Konzentrationslagern," in *Der Widerstandskämpfer*, Nos. 4-6, Vienna.

Czarnecki, Wacław, Zygmunt Zonik. 1973. *Kryptonim Dora*, Warsaw.

Czech, Danuta. 1959–64. "Kalendarium der Ereignisse in Konzentrationslagern," in *Hefte von Auschwitz*, Nos. 2-8, Auschwitz.

Czech, Danuta, Jadwiga Bezwińska. 1973. "Vorwort zu Aussiedlung von Lejb (Langfus?)," in *Hefte von Auschwitz*, No. 14, Auschwitz.

———. 1975. "Die Rolle des Häftlingskrankenbaulagers im KL Auschwitz II," in *Hefte von Auschwitz*, No. 15, Auschwitz.

Dam, H. G. van, Ralph Giordano. 1962. *KZ-Verbrechen vor deutschen Gerichten: Dokumente aus den Prozessen gegen Sommer (KZ Buchenwald), Sorge, Schubert (KZ Sachsenhausen), Unkelbach (Ghetto in Czenstochau)*, Frankfurt.

Danimann, Franz. 1960–67. "Zwingburg Mauthausen," in *Internationale Hefte der Widerstandsbewegung*, No. 3, Vienna.

Delbo, Charlotte. 1978. *Le convoi du 24 Janvier*, Paris.

Deutschkron, Inge. 1978. *Ich trug den gelben Stern*, Cologne.

Dieckmann, Götz, Peter Hochmuth. n.d. *KZ Dora Mittelbau: Produktionsstätte der V-Waffen, Kampffront gegen faschistischen Terror und Rüstungsproduktion*, Nordhausen.

Dittmar, Peter, Karl Wilhelm, Fricke. 1975. "Zweimal Buchenwald," in *Deutschland-Archiv, Zeitschrift für Fragen der DDR und der Deutschlandpolitik*, No. 5, Cologne.

Drexel, Joseph. 1978. *Rückkehr unerwünscht: Die Reise nach Mauthausen*, Stuttgart.

Drobisch, Klaus. 1962. *Widerstand hinter Stacheldraht: Aus dem antifaschistischen Kampf im KZ Buchenwald*, Berlin.

———. 1968. *Widerstand in Buchenwald*, Frankfurt.

Dronov, Victor. 1959. "Prisoners of the Nazis." in *War Behind Barbed Wire: Reminiscences of Buchenwald Ex-Prisoners of War*, Moscow.

Dubost, Charles. n.d. *Le procès de Nuremberg: L'accusation francaise*, Paris.

Dunin-Wąsowicz, Krzysztof. 1972. *Oboz koncentracyjny Stuttof*, Danzig.

———. 1972. *La réstance dans les camps de concentration nazis*, Warsaw.

———. n.d. *Transporty Warszawskie w Stutthofie*.

Dunin-Wąsowica, Marek, Tadeusz Matusiak. 1979. *Stutthof: Guide informateur*, Stutthof.

Emmerich, Woflgand, ed. n.d. *Proletarische Lebensläufe: Autobiographische Dokumente zur Entstehung der Zweiten Kultur in Deutschland*, Hamburg.

Eschenbrenner, Marc, Charles, Bene. n.d. *Du Stutthof a la France libre*, Raon-l'Etape.

Fels. Maxime. n.d. *Ich sah die Hölle von Dachau und Hitlers Räubernest bei Berchtesgaden*, Colmar.

Feltes, Jupp, Paul Langers, n.d. *Menschenexperimente in Dauchau*, Esch-Alzette.

Fénelon, Fania. 1976–77. *Sursis pour l'orchestre*, Paris. Published in English as *Playing for Time*, New York.

Feuerbach, Walter. n.d. *55 Monate Dachau: Ein Tatsachenbericht*, Lucerne.

Fraenkel, Heinrich, Roger Manvell. 1965. *Himmler: Kleinbürger und Massenmörder*, Berlin.

Fréjafon, G. L. 1954. "Bergen-Belsen, bagne sanatorium," in Olga Wormser, Henri Michel, eds. *Tragédie de la déportation 1940–1945. Témoignages de survivants des camps de concentration allemands*, Paris.

Freund, Julius. 1945. *O Buchenwald*, Klagenfurt.

Fricke, Karl Wilhelm. Cf. Dittmar, Peter.

Frieden, Camille. 1970. "Les derniers jours de la forteresse de Mauthausen," in *Rappel*, Luxembourg.

Friedmann, Filip, Tadeusz Holug. 1946. *Oswiecim*, Warsaw.

Gagern, Friedrich von. 1948. *Der Retter von Mauthausen*, Vienna.

Gárliński, Józef. 1975 *Fighting Auschwitz: The Resistance Movement in the Concentration Camp*, London.

———. 1975. "The Underground Movement in Auschwitz Concentration Camp," in *Resistance in Europe 1939–45*, Middlesex.

Garnier, Eugène. 1946. "Organization de la resistance," in *Témoignages sur Auschwitz*, Paris.

———. 1954. "Ils ont ainsi vecu, 44792, in Olga Wormser/Henri Michel, eds. *Tragédie de la déportation 1940–1945. Témoignages de survivants des camps de concentration allemands*, Paris.

Gaussen, Dominique. 1966. *Le Kapo*, Paris.

Georg, Enno. 1963. *Die wirtschaftlichen Unternehmunger der SS*, Stuttgart.

Geve, Thomas. 1958. *Youth in Chains*, Jerusalem.

Giessner, Fritz, see Češpiva, Jan.

Giordano, Ralph. Cf. Dam, H. G. van.

Glazar, Richard. 1973. *Die Stimme aus Treblinka*.

Goguel, Rudi, 1947. *ES war ein langer Weg: Ein Bericht*, Singen.

———. 1972. *Cap Arcona: Report über den Untergang der Häftlingsflotte in der Lübecker Bucht am 3. Mai. 1945*, Frankfurt.

Goldschmidt, François. 1954. "Le bon dieu au KZ" in Olga Wormser/Henri Michel, eds., *Tragédie de la déportation 1940–1945. Témoignages de survivants des camps de concentration allemands* (German), Paris.

_____. n.d. *Elsässer und Lothringer in Dachau*, n.p., n.d.

Gostner, Erwin, 1945. *1000 Tage im KZ: Ein Erlebnisbericht aus den Konzentrationslagern Dachau, Mauthausen und Gusen*, Innsbruck.

Gradowski, Salmen. 1972. "Handschrift," in *Hefte von Auschwitz*, special issue, Auschwitz.

Graham, Robert A., S.J. n.d. *Pope Pius XII and the Jews of Hungary in 1944*. U.S.A.

Grand, Anselm J. 1946. *Turm A ohne Neuigkeit. Erleben und Bekenntnis eines Österreichers: Ein Komponist, Maler und Schriftsteller schildert das KZ*, Vienna.

Gray, Martin. 1971. *Au nom de tous les miens* (*In the Name of All My Friends*), Paris.

Grégoire, Pierre. 1975. "KL Sachsenhausen im Endkampfe," in *Luxemburger Wort*, Luxembourg, March 7.

Gross, K. A. n.d. *Fünf Minuten vor Zwölf. Des ersten Jahrtausends letzte Tage unter Herrenmenschen und Herdenmenschen: Dachauer Tagebücher des Häftlings 16921*, Munich.

Grossmann, Wassili. 1945. "Die Hölle von Treblinka," in *Die Vernichtungslager Maidanek und Treblinka*, Vienna.

_____. 1955. "Die Hölle von Treblinka," in *Ewiges Gedenken*, Warsaw.

Grüber, Heinrich. 1968. *Erinnerungen aus sieben Jahrzehnten*, Cologne.

Gryń, Edward, Zofia Murawska. n.d. *Das Konzentrationslager Majdanek*, Lublin.

Gun, Nerin E. 1968. *Die Stunde der Amerikaner*.

Guri, Joseph. 1965. "Soviet Jewish Prisoners of War in German Captivity," in *Yad Vashem Bulletin*, XII, Jerusalem.

Gurin, Alexei. 1959. "In the Name of Life," in *War Behind Barbed Wire: Reminiscences of Buchenwald Ex-Prisoners of War*, Moscow.

Gute, Herbert. 1970. *Partisanen ohne Gewehre: Ein Tagebuch aus der Erinnerung*, Berlin.

Gutman, Israel. 1958. "The Jewish Underground in Auschwitz," in *Extermination and Resistance: Historical Records and Source Material*, Kibbuz Lohamei Hagettaot.

_____. 1962. "Der Aufstand des Sonderkommandos," in H. G. Adler/Hermann Langbein/Ella Lingens-Reiner, eds., *Auschwitz: Zeugnisse und Berichte*, Frankfurt.

Gutman, Israel, Livia Rothkirchen. 1976. *The Catastrophe of European Jewry: Antecedents, History, Reflections*, Jerusalem.

Habaru, Omer. 1946. *Les triangles rouges*, Arlon.

Halkin, Léon E. 1965. *Á l'ombre de la mort*, Gembloux.

Hammer, Franz, 1956. *Theodor Neubauer: Ein Kämpfer gegen den Faschismus*, Berlin.

Harcourt, Pierre de. n.d. *The Real Enemy*, London.

Hartung, Hans-Joachim. 1974. *Signale durch den Todeszaun: Historische Repor-*

tage über Bau, Einsatz und Tarnung illegaler Rundfunkempfänger und-sender im Konzentrationslager Buchenwald, Berlin.

Hass, Hanna. 1961–62. "Bergen-Belsen: Das Tagebuch einer Gefangenen," in *Internationale Hefte der Widerstandsbewegung*, No. 7, Vienna.

Hausner, Gideon. 1967. *Die Vernichtung der Juden: Das grösste Verbrechen der Geschichte*, Munich (reprinted 1979).

Hauter, Charles. 1954. "Temoignages Strasbourgeois," in Olga Wormser, Henri Michel, eds. *Tragédie de la deportation 1950–1945. Témoignages de survivants des camps de concentration allemands*, Paris.

Heger, Heinz. 1972. *Die Männer mit dem rosa Winkel: Der Bericht eines Homosexuellen über seine Haft 1939–1945*, Hamburg.

Heiber, Helmut, ed. 1968. *Reichsführer! Briefe an und von Himmler*, Stuttgart.

Heilig, Bruno. 1948. *Menschen am Kreuz*, Berlin.

Heimler, Eugene. 1961. *Uit Nacht en Nevel*. Amsterdam.

Hein, Wincenty. 1969. *Lebens- und Arbeitsbedingungen im Konzentrationslager "Dora-Mittelbau,"* Warsaw.

Hermlin, Stephan. 1975. *Die erste Reihe*, Dortmund.

Hessel, Stephane. 1954. "Entre leur mains," in Olga Wormser, Henri Michel, eds. *Tragédie de la deportation 1940–1945. Témoignages de survivants des camps de concentration allemands*, Paris.

Hill, Mavis M., L. Norman Williams. 1965. *Auschwitz in England: A Record of a Libel Action*, London.

Hochmuth, Peter, see Dieckmann, Götz.

Holoch, Rudi. 1978. "Das Lager Schörzingen in der 'Gruppe Wüste'," in *Nationalsozialistische Konzentrationslager im Dienst der totalen Kriegsführung: Sieben württembergische Aussenkommandos des Konzentrationslagers Natzweiler/Elsass*, Stuttgart.

Holt, Heinrich Eduard vom. 1947. *Weltfahrt ins Herz*, Cologne.

Hołuj, Tadeusz, see Friedmann, Filip.

Horn, Michael, see Brückner, Siegfried.

Höss, Rudolf. 1958. *Kommandant in Auschwitz: Autobiographische Aufzeichnungen*, Stuttgart.

Internationales Komitee vom Roten Kreuz, ed. 1947. *Die Tätigkeit des IKRK zugunsten der in den deutschen Konzentrationslagern inhaftierten Personen (1939–1945)*, 3d ed., Geneva.

Iosem, Leonid. 1959. "Arsenal in Buchenwald," in *War Behind Barbed Wire: Reminiscences of Buchenwald Ex-Prisoners of War*, Moscow.

Iwaszko, Tadeusz. 1964. "Häftlingsfluchten aus dem Konzentrationslager Auschwitz," in *Hefte von Auschwitz*, No. 7, Auschwitz.

———. 1978. "Das Nebenlager 'Fürstengrube'," in *Hefte von Auschwitz*, No. 16, Auschwitz.

Jarosz, Barbara. 1978. "Widerstandsbewegung im Lager und in der Umgebung," in *Auschwitz: Faschistisches Vernichtungslager*," Warsaw.

Joos, Joseph. 1946. *Leben auf Widerruf: Begegnungen und Beobachtungen im KZ Dachau 1941–1945*, Olten.

Julitte, Pierre. 1965. *L'arbre de Goethe*, Paris.

Kabuli, Isaac. 1963–64. "Jews in the Greek Underground," in *In the Dispersion*, Jerusalem.

Kagan, Raya. 1962. "Mala," in H. G. Adler/Hermann Langbein/Ella Lingens-Reiner, eds. *Auschwitz: Zeugnisse und Berichte*, Frankfurt.

———. 1946. "Die Letzten Opfer des Widerstandes," in *Auschwitz*, op. cit.

Kalmar, Rudolf. 1946. *Zeit ohne Gnade*, Vienna.

Karny, Miroslav. 1979. "Das Theresienstädter Familienlager in Birkenau," in *Judaica Bohemiae*, XV/1, Prague.

Kautsky, Benedikt. 1961. *Teufel und Verdammte: Erfahrungen und Erkenntnisse aus sieben Jahren in deutschen Konzentrationslagern*, Vienna.

———. n.d. *Die psychologische Situation des Konzentrationslager-Häftlings*, Zurich.

Kessel, Sim. 1970. *Perdu à Auschwitz*, Paris. 1970.

Keuerleber-Siegle, Barbara. 1978. "Das Lager Echterdingen," in *Nationalsozialistische Konzentrationslager im Dienst der totalen Kriefsführung: Sieben württembergische Aussenkommandos des Konzentrationslagers Natzweiler/Elsass*, Stuttgart.

Kiedrzyńska, Wanda. 1960. "Darstellung aus der Geschichte dds Konzentrationslagers Ravensbrück," in *Internationale Hefte der Widerstandsbewegung*, No. 3, Vienna.

Kielar, Wiesław. 1972–79. *Anus Mundi*, Kraków, Frankfurt.

Kiessling, Wolfgang. 1960. *Ernst Schneller: Lebensbild eines Revolutionärs*, Berlin.

———. 1964. *Stark und voller Hoffnung: Leben und Kampf von Albert Kuntz*, Berlin.

Klingel, Jürgen. 1978. "Das Lager Leonberg," in *Nationalsozialistische Konzentrationslager im Dienst der totalen Kriegsführung: Sieben württembergische Aussenkommandos des Konzentrationslagers Natzweiler/Elsass*, Stuttgart.

Klodziński, Stanisław. 1969. "Verbrecherische pharmakologische Versuche an Häftlingen des Konzentrationslagers Auschwitz," in *Unmenschliche Medizin*, I/2, Warsaw.

———. 1970. "Der Einsatz des polnischen Sanitätsdienstes bei der Rettung des Lebens der Häftlinge im Konzentrationslager Auschwitz," in *Anthologie*, II/2, Warsaw.

Kogon, Eugen. 1946 (and various new editions). *Der SS-Staat: Das System der deutschen Konzentrationslager*, Frankfurt.

Kohn, Stanisław. 1945. *Opstand in Treblinka* (English edition: *The Theory and Practice of Hell*), Amsterdam.

Kolb, Eberhard. 1962. *Bergen–Belsen*, Hannover.

Korschak, Ruzka. 1968. Kinder in Buchenwald, in: *Yalkut moreshet*, Nr. 8, Tel-Aviv.

Kraus, Ota, Erich Kulka. 1957. *Die Todesfabrik*, Berlin.

Kret, Józef. 1971. "Erinnerungen des Häftlings Nr. 20020 an die kulturelle Arbeit im Todeslager Auschwitz," in *Rocznik nauk Pedagogicznych*, XIII, Kraków.

———. *Ostatni Krąg*, Kraków 1973.

Krivsky, Jiri, Marie Krizkova. 1967. Richard: *Unterirdische Fabrik und Konzentrationslager bei Litomerice: Mahnmal Terezin.*

Krüger, Norbert. 1977. "Wenn Sie nicht ins KZ wollen . . . Häftlinge in Bombenräumkommandos," in *aus politik und zeitgeschichte*, Bonn, April 23.

Kuby, Erich, ed. n.d. *Das Ende des Schreckens: Dokumente des Untergangs, Januar bis Mai 1945*, Munich.

Kühn, Günter, Wolfgang Weber. 1976. "Berichte über die illegale militärische Organisation im ehemaligen Konzentrationslager Buchenwald," in *Militärgeschichte*, XV. "Internationaler Charakter, Aufbau und Tätigkeit der illegalen Militärorganisation im Konzentrationslager Buchenwald," idem.

_____. 1976. *Stärker als die Wölfe*, Berlin.

Kuhn, Leo. 1975. "Solidarität," in *Österreichs Beitrag zu seiner Befreiung*, No. 1, Vienna.

Kühnrich, Heinz. 1960. *Der KZ-Staat: Rolle und Entwicklung der faschistischen Konzentrationslager 1933 bis 1945*, Berlin.

Kulka, Erich. 1965. *Terezin*, Prague.

_____. 1968. "Five Escapes from Auschwitz," in Yuri Suhl, ed. *They Fought Back*, New York.

_____. 1968–69. "Auschwitz Condoned: The Abortive Struggle Against the Final Solution," in *The Wiener Library Bulletin*, XXIII/1, London.

Kulka, see also Kraus, Ota.

Kupfer-Koberwitz, Edgar. 1957, 1960. *Die Mächtigen und die Hilflosen: Als Häftling in Dachau*, Stuttgart.

Kwiatkowski, Jerzy. 1966. *485 dni na Majdanku*, Lublin.

Kyung, Nikolai. 1959. "The Invisible Shield," in *War Behind Barbed Wire: Reminiscences of Buchenwald Ex-Prisoners of War*, Moscow.

Lacaze, André. 1978. *Le tunnel*, Paris.

Lafitte, Jean. *Ceux qui vivent*, Paris 1970.

Langbein, Hermann. *Die Stärkeren: Ein Bericht*, Vienna 1949.

_____. "Die Kampfgruppe Auschwitz," in H. G. Adler, Hermann Langbein, Ella Lingens-Reiner, eds. *Auschwitz: Zeugnisse und Berichte*, Frankfurt 1962 and Cologne 1979.

_____. 1965. *Der Auschwitz Prozess: Eine Dokumentation*, Vienna.

_____. 1972. *Menschen in Auschwitz*, Vienna. It would indeed have been normative to have the date follow the place of publication!

_____. ed. "Genozid im 20. Jahrhundert," in *Frankfurter Hefte* 1976/5.

Langers, Paul, see Feltes, Jupp.

Lánik, Jozef. 1964. *Was Dante nicht sah*, Berlin.

Laszlo, Carl. *Ferien am Waldsee: Erinnerungen eines Überlebenden*, Basel 1956.

Lebedyev, Aleksandr Fyodorovich. 1960. *Soldaty malovajny: Sapiski Osvyechimskovo uznuka*, Moscow.

Leibbrand, Robert. 1945. *Buchenwald: Lieber sterben als verraten: Zur Geschichte der deutschen Widerstandsbewegung*, Switzerland.

_____. n.d. *Buchenwald: Ein Tatsachenbericht zur Geschichte der deutschen Widerstandsbewegung*, Stuttgart.

Lenz, Pater. 1956. *Christus in Dachau: Ein religiöses Volksbuch und ein kirchengeschichtliches Zeugnis*, Vienna.

Leroy, Roger, Jean Vieville, Mex Nevers, Roger Linet. n.d. "À propos de l'article sur le 'Reseau Alliance' falsifiant la verité sur le camp du Struthof" (in the author's possession).

Letzeburger zu Mauthausen. 1970. Luxembourg.

Levi, Primo. 1961, 1979. *Ist das ein Mensch? Erinnerungen an Auschwitz*, Frankfurt.

Lévy-Hass, Hanna. 1979. *Vielleicht war das alles erst der Anfang: Tagebuch aus dem KZ Bergen-Belsen 1944–1945*, Berlin.

Lewental, Salmen. 1972. "Gedenkbuch," in *Hefte von Auschwitz*, special issue, Auschwitz.

Lewin, Zofie, see Bartoszewski, Wladyslaw.

Lichtmann, Ada. 1961–63. "I Have Seen with My Own Eyes," in *Yad Vashem Bulletin*, Jerusalem.

Lienau, Heinrich. 1949. *Zwölf Jahre Nacht: Mein Weg durch das "Tausendjährige Reich,"* Flensburg.

Linet, Roger, see Leroy, Roger.

Lorski, Dorota. 1969. "Block 10 in Auschwitz," in *Unmenschliche Medizin*, I/2, Warsaw.

Lusseyran, Jacques. 1963. *Das wiedergefundene Licht*, Stuttgart 1963.

Mader Julius. 1963. *Geheimnis von Huntsville: Die wahre Karriere des Raketenbarons Wernher von Braun*, Berlin 1963.

————. 1973. "Rekonstruktionen: Schüler rekonstruierten die illegalen Sende-und Empfangsanlagen der Häftlinge des ehemaligen KZ Buchenwald," in *Neue Museumskunde*, No. 3, Berlin.

Die Todesfabrik Majdanek. 1946. *Ein dokumentarischer Tatsachenbericht aus dem berüchtigten deutschen Vernichtungslager*, Vienna.

Makowski, Antoni. 1975. "Organisation, Entwicklung und Tätigkeit des Häftlings-Krankenbaus in Monowitz (KL Auschwitz III)," in *Hefte von Auschwitz*, No. 15, Auschwitz.

Manhès, Frédéric H. n.d. *Buchenwald: L'organisation et l'action clandestines des déportés français 1944–1945*, Paris.

Manvell, Roger, see Fraenkel, Heinrich.

Maršàlek, Hans. n.d. *Mauthausen mahnt! Kampf hinter Stacheldraht: Tatsachen, Dokumente und Berichte über das grösste Hitler'sche Vernichtungslager in Österreich*, Vienna.

————. 1974. *Die Geschichte des Konzentrationslagers Mauthausen: Dokumentation*, Vienna. (Wherever the expanded second edition of this book was used in chapter 24, this was indicated by II between the date and the page number).

————. 1978. "Die Brünner Intelligenz im KZ Mauthausen," in *Der neue Mahnruf*, No. 4, Vienna.

Marshall, Bruce. n.d. *The White Rabbit*, London.

Martin-Chauffier, Louis. 1947. *L'homme et la bête* Paris.

Matusiak, Tadeusz. see Dunin-Wąsowicz, Marek.

Maury, Louis. 1955. "Aperçus sur la psychologie et le comportement des ressortissants des diverses nationalités de déportés au camp de concentration de Neuengamme," in *Revue d'histoire de la deuxième guerre mondiale*, No. 17, Paris.

Meier, Heinrich Christian. 1948, *So war es: Das Leben im KZ Neuengamme*, Hamburg.

———. 1949. *Im Frühwind der Freiheit*, Hamburg.

Mersch. P. 1970. "Das Ende," in *Rappel*, No. 5, Luxembourg.

Michaux, Charlotte. n.d. *damals . . . 1939–45*, Luxembourg.

Michel, Henri, see Wormser, Olga.

Michel, Jean. 1975. *Dora*, Paris.

Michelet, Edmond. 1955. *Die Freiheitsstrasse: Dachau 1943–1945*, Stuttgart.

Mielke, Fred, see Mitscherlich, Alexander.

Minney, R. J. 1966. *I Shall Fear No Evil: The Story of Dr. Alina Brewda*, London.

Mirkes, Metty. 1970. "Mauthausen—Differdingen," in *Rappel*, No. 5, Luxembourg.

Mitscherlich, Alexander, Fred Mielke. 1949, 1978. *Wissenschaft ohne Menschlichkeit: Medizinische und eugenetische Irrwege unter Diktatur, Bürokratie und Krieg*, Heidelberg. Revised new edition 1978: *Medizin ohne Menschlichkeit: Dokumente des Nürnberger Ärzteprozesses*, Frankfurt.

Mołdawa, Miecysław. 1967. *Gross-Rosen: Oboz koncentracyjny na Slasku*, Warsaw.

Müller, Filip. 1979. *Sonderbehandlung: Drei Jahre in den Krematorien und Gaskammern von Auschwitz*, Munich.

Murawska, Zofia, see Gryń, Edward.

Nansen, Odd. 1949. *Von Tag zu Tag: Ein Tagebuch*, Hamburg.

Nazirov, Baky. 1949. "Birth of the Battalions," in *War Behind Barbed Wire: Reminiscences of Buchenwald Ex-Prisoners of War*, Moscow.

So ging es zu Ende (How the End Came). 1960. *Neuengamme, Dokumente und Berichte*, Hamburg.

Neuhäusler, Johann. 1960. *Wie war das im KZ Dachau? Ein Versuch, der Wahrheit näherzukommen*, Munich.

Nevers, Max, see Leroy, Roger.

Nirenstein, Albert. n.d. *A Tower From the Enemy*, New York.

Nitzsche, Gerhard. 1957. *Die Saefkow-Jacob-Bästlein-Gruppe: Dokumente und Materialien des illegalen antifaschistischen Kampfes (1942–1945)*, Berlin.

Nogaj, Stanisław. 1967. "Moj udzial w ruchu oporu w obozach koncentracyjnych Dachau i Gusen," in *Pamietamy*, Katowice.

Novitch, Miriam. 1967. *La verité sur Treblinka*, Paris.

———. 1978. *Sobibor, martyre et révolte: Documents et témoignages*, Paris.

Nyiszli, Miklos. 1960. *Auschwitz: A Doctor's Eyewitness Account*, New York.

Odic, C. J. 1972. *Demain Buchenwald*.

Opitz, Max. 1969. "Widerstand im Konzentrationslager Sachsenhausen," im *Im Kampf bewährt*, Berlin.

Opstand in Treblinka, 1945. Sliedrecht.

Ost Eugène. 1970. "Enfin libres! Dachau, le 29 avril 1945," in *Rappel*, Nos. 3–5, Luxembourg.

Oboz koncentracyjny Oswiecim. 1968. *W świetle akt delegatury rzadu RP na kraj*, Auschwitz.

Oswiecim. 1977. *Hitlerowski oboz masowej zaglady*. Warsaw.

Overduin, Jacobus. 1947. *Der Himmel in der Hölle von Dachau*, Zurich.

Pappalettera, Vincenzo. 1972. *Tu passerai per il camino*, Milan.

Paulus, Günter. 1961. *Der Zweite Weltkrieg: Dokumente und Materialien*, Berlin.

Pawlak, Marlis. 1978. *Fritz Henssler: Ein Leben für die Arbeiterbewegung*, Dortmund.

Pawlak, Zacheusz. 1979. *Ich habe überlebt... Ein Häftling berichtet über Majdanek*, Hamburg.

Pecherskii, Aleksandr. 1968. "Revolt in Sobibor," in Yuri Suhl, ed. *They Fought Back*, New York.

Pelný, Kurt, see Cêŝpiva, Jan.

Perk, Willy. 1979. *Hölle im Moor: Zur Geschichte der Emslandlager 1933–1945*, Frankfurt.

Petit, Pierre. 1965–68. "Das war Bergen–Belsen: Schutzhäftling Nr. 2001," in *Rappel*, Luxembourg.

Pilecki, Jan, see Brol, Franciszek.

Piljar, Juri. 1957. *Wir bezwangen den Tod*, Berlin.

Pingel, Falk. 1978. *Häftlinge unter SS-Herrschaft: Widerstand, Selbstbehauptung und Vernichtung im Konzentrationslager*, Hamburg.

Piper, Franciszek. 1970. "Das Nebenlager Neu-Dachs," in *Hefte von Auschwitz*, No. 12, Auschwitz.

———. 1978. "Das Nebenlager Trzebinia," in *Hefte von Auschwitz*, No. 16, Auschwitz.

———. 1978. "Die Sklavenarbeit der Häftlinge," in *Ausgewählte Probleme aus der Geschichte des KL Auschwitz*, Auschwitz.

Plieseis, Sepp. 1946. *Vom Ebro zum Dachstein: Lebenskampf eines österreichischen Arbeiters*, Linz.

———. 1971. *Partisan der Berge: Lebenskampf eines österreichischen Arbeiters*, Berlin.

Poel, Albert van de. 1948. *Ich sah hinter den Vorhang: Ein Holländer erlebt Neuengamme*, Hamburg.

Poller, Walter. 1960. *Arztschreiber in Buchenwald: Bericht des Häftlings 996 aus Block 36*, Offenbach.

Poltawska, Wanda. 1969. " 'Kaninchen' im Konzentrationslager Ravensbrück," in *Unmenschliche Medizin*, I/2, Warsaw.

Pontoizeau, Andrès. 1947. *Dora-la-mort: De la résistance à la libération par Buchenwald et Dora*, Tours.

Presser, J. 1968. *Ashes in the Wind: The Destruction of Dutch Jewry*, London.

Quinn, William W. 1945. *SS-Dachau*.

Rabitsch, Gisela. 1970. "Das KL Mauthausen," in *Studien zur Geschichte der Konzentrationslager*, Stuttgart.

Rajzman, Samuel. 1968. "Uprising in Treblinka," in Yuri Suhl, ed. *They Fought Back*, New York.

Sourire de Ravensbrück. 1945. Paris.

Die Frauen von Ravensbrück. 1961. Berlin.

Frauen-KZ Ravensbrück. 1973. Berlin.

Rassinier, Paul. 1959. *Die Lüge des Odysseus*, Wiesbaden.

Raths, Albert. 1970. "Befreiung von Loiblpass," in *Rappel*, Nos. 305, Luxembourg.

Razola, Manuel/Constante, Mariano. 1969. *Triangle bleu: Les républicains espagnols à Mauthausen*, Paris.

Red Cross, see Comité International de la Croix-Ronzl.

Riemer, Hermann E. 1947. *Sturz ins Dunkel*, Munich.

Riquet, Michel, S.J. 1972. *Chrétiens de France dans l'Europe enchainée: Genèse du secours catholique*, Paris.

Risel, Heinz. 1978. "Das Lager Neckargartach," in *Nationalosozialistische Konzentrationslager im Dienst der totalen Kriegsführung: Sieben württembergische Aussenkommandos des Konzentrationslagers Natzweiler/Elsass*, Stuttgart.

Robinson, Donald B. 1946. "Kommunistische Grausamkeiten in Buchenwald," in *American Mercury*, No. 10.

Rossa, Bohdan. 1959. "Über die Zusammenarbeit tschechischer Studenten und deutscher Antifaschisten im Konzentrationslager Sachsenhausen," in *Niemals vergessen: Aus dem antifaschistischen Widerstandskampf der Studenten Europas*, Berlin.

Rossmann, Erich. 1947. *Ein Leben für Sozialismus und Demokratie*, Stuttgart.

Rothkirchen, Livia. 1961. "Activities of the Jewish Underground in Slovakia," in *Yad Vashem Bulletin*, No. 8/9, Jerusalem. See also Gutman, Israel.

Rousset, David. *L'univers concentrationnaire*, Paris 1946.

————. 1947. *Les jours de notre mort*, Paris.

Roux, Catherine. 1968. *Triangle rouge*, Paris.

Rozánski, Zenon. 1948. *Mützen ab . . . Eine Reportage aus der Strafkompanie des KZ Auschwitz*, Hannover.

Rückerl, Adalbert. 1977. *Nationalsozialistische Vernichtungslager im Spiegel deutscher Strafprozesse: Belzec, Sobibor, Treblinka, Chelmno*. Munich.

Rutkowski, Adam. 1970. "Les évasions de juifs déportés de France du KL Auschwitz-Birkenau," in *Le Monde Juif*, No. 59, Paris.

Sakharov, Valentin. 1961. *Aufstand in Mauthausen*, Berlin.

Damals in Sachsenhausen 1967. Solidaritat und Widerstand im Konzentrationslager Sachsenhausen, Berlin.

KZ Sachsenhausen 1967. Im Auftrage des Hauptausschusses "Opfer des Faschismus" herausgegeben von Lucie Grosser, Berlin.

Sadron, Charles. 1954. "Témoignages strasbourgeois," in Olga Wormser, Henri

Michel, eds. *Tragédie de la déportation 1940–1945. Témoignages de survivants des camps de concentration allemands (German)*, Paris.

Saint-Clair, Simone, 1966. *Ravensbrück: L'enfer des femmes*, Paris 1966.

Salomon, Ernst von. 1960. *Das Schicksal des A.D.: Ein Mann in Schatten der Geschichte*, Hamburg.

Santos, Agustin. 1967. "La évasion del 5 de abril 1942," in *Hispania*, No. 10, Paris.

Sapunov, Yury. 1959. "True to Their Country," in *War Behind Barbed Wire: Reminiscences of Buchenwald Ex-Prisoners of War*, Moscow 1959.

Sauer, Karl. 1974. "Nur 'widerstrebend' und 'nicht zurechnungsfähig'? Der Massenmord im Vernichtungslager Sobibor oder: Was heute nicht mehr wahr sein darf," in *Der Widerstandskämpfer*, XXV, Nos. 1–3, Vienna.

Schabet-Berger, Elke. 1978. "Das Lager Hessental," in *Nationalsozialistische Konzentrationslager im Dienst der totalen Kriegsführung: Sieben württembergische Aussenkommandos des Konzentrationslagers Natzweiler/Elsass*, Stuttgart 1978.

Schätzle, Julius. 1946. *Wir klagen an! Ein Bericht über den Kampf, das Leiden und das Sterben in deutschen Konzentrationslagern: Moor, Dachau, Mauthausen, Neuengamme, "Cap Arcona,"* Stuttgart.

Scheffler, Wolfgang. Cf. Arndt, Ino.

Schifko-Pungartnik, Manfred. 1946. *Leichenträger ans Tor: Bericht aus fünf Jahren Konzentrationslager*, Graz.

Schmidt, Walter A. 1958. *Damit Deutschland lebe: Ein Quellenwerk über den deutschen antifaschistischen Widerstandskampf 1933–1945*, Berlin.

Scholtes, Camille. 1970. "Wir rüsten zum Endkampf in Ebensee," in *Rappel*, Nos. 3–5, Luxembourg.

Schwarberg, Günther. 1979. *Der SS-Arzt und die Kinder: Bericht über den Mord vom Bullenhuser Damm*, Hamburg.

Schwarz, Hans. 1960–67. "Konzentrationslager Neuengamme," in *Internationale Hefte der Widerstandsbewegung*, II/3, Vienna.

Selbmann, Fritz. 1961. *Die lange Nacht*, Halle.

————. 1969. *Alternative—Bilanz—Credo*, Halle.

Semprun, Jorge. 1963. *Le grand voyage*, Paris.

————. 1978. *Federico Sanchez: Eine Autobiographie*, Hamburg.

Seweryn, Tadeusz. 1965. " 'Wisla' na falach eteru," in *Przeglad Lekarski*, XXXI/II, Kraków.

Siegert, Toni. 1979. "Das Konzentrationslager Flossenbürg: Gegründet für sogenannte Asoziale und Kriminelle," in *Bayern in der NS-Zeit*, vol. 2, Munich.

Siewert, Robert. 1960–67. "Widerstand im Konzentrationslager Buchenwald," in *Internationale Hefte der Widerstandsbewegung*, II/3, Vienna.

Simakov, Nikolai. 1959. "Comrades-in-arms," in *War Behind Barbed Wire: Reminiscences of Buchenwald Ex-Prisoners of War*, Moscow.

Simon, Hermann. 1974. *Der deutsche Widerstand 1933–1945*, Bonn.

Simonov, Konstantin. 1945. "Das Vernichtungslager," in *Die Vernichtungslager Majdanek und Treblinka*, Vienna 1945.

————. n.d. *Ich sah das Vernichtungslager*, Berlin.

Sington, Derrick. 1946. *Belsen Uncovered*, London.

Smirnov, Ivan. 1959. "In the Headquarters of the Underground Army," in *War Behind Barbed Wire: Reminiscences of Buchenwald Ex-Prisoners of War*, Moscow.

Smirnov, S. 1978. "Les héros du bloc 20 de la mort," in *Mauthausen*, Bulletin No. 193, Paris.

Smoleń, Kazimierz. 1960–67. "Die Widerstandsbewegung im Konzentrationslager Auschwitz," in *Internationale Hefte der Widerstandsbewegung*, II/3, Vienna.

———. 1977. "Widerstandsbewegung im KL Auschwitz: Historischer Abriss," in *Informationsbulletin des Comité International d'Auschwitz*, Warsaw.

———. 1978. "Das kämpfende Auschwitz," in *Ausgewählte Probleme aus der Geschichte des KL Auschwitz*, Auschwitz.

Snieszko, Tadeusz. Cf. Szymanski, Tadeusz.

Sobański, Tomasz. 1974. *Ucieczki oswiecismkie*, Warsaw.

Sobochenii, M. S. 1965. "Antifashistskoye podpole Osviechma in *Novaya i noveishaya istoriya*, Moscow.

"Soll ich meines Bruders Hüter sein? 1944." *Weitere Dokumente zur juden- und Flüchtlingsnot unserer Tage*, Zurich.

Spielmann, Nicolas. 1970. "Die Befreiung von Buchenwald," in *Rappel*, Luxembourg.

Spitz, Aime. 1970. *Struthof, bagne nazi en Alsace: Mémoires du déporté résistant* "N.N." 4596, Raon-l'Etape.

SS im Einsatz. Eine Dokumentation über die Verbrechen der SS, Berlin.

Stadler, Karl. 1966. "Österreich 1938–1945 im Spiegel der NS-Akten," in *Das einsame Gewissen: Beiträge zur Geschichte Österreichs 1938 bis 1945*, Vienna.

Stein, Gregor. 1946. *Die Cäsur der Entscheidung*, Luxembourg.

Steinbock, Johann. 1946. *Das Ende von Dachau*, Salzburg.

Steiner, Jean-François. 1966. *Treblinka: Die Revolte eines Vernichtungslagers*, Oldenburg.

Strzelecka, Irena. 1973. "Arbeitslager Gleiwitz I," in *Hefte von Auschwitz*, No. 14, Auschwitz.

———. 1973. "Arbeitslager Gleiwitz II," in *Hefte von Auschwitz*, No. 14, Auschwitz.

———. 1974–6. "Die ersten Polen in Auschwitz," in *Bulletin des Comité International d' Auschwitz*, Warsaw.

Strzelecki, Andrzej. 1973. "Arbeitslager Gleiwitz III," in *Hefte von Auschwitz*, No. 14, Auschwitz.

———. 1973. "Arbeitslager Gleiwitz IV," in *Hefte von Auschwitz*, No. 14, Auschwitz.

———. 1975. "Das Nebenlager Jawischowitz," in *Hefte von Auschwitz*, No. 15, Auschwitz.

Suzhowiak, Bogdan. 1973. *Neuengamme: Z dziejow obozu*, Warsaw.

Suhl, Yuri. 1968. "Rosa Robota: Heroine of the Auschwitz Underground," in Yuri Suhl, ed. *They Fought Back*, New York.

Szymanska, Danuta. Cf. Szymanski, Tadeusz.

Szymanski, Tadeusz, Danuta Szymanska, Tadeusz Snieszko. 1970. "Über den

Krankenbau im Zigeunerfamilienlager in Auschwitz-Birkenau," in *Anthologie*, II/2, Warsaw.

Thape, Ernst. 1969. *Von Rot zu Schwarz-Rot-Gold: Lebensweg eines Sozialdemokraten*, Hannover.

Theis, Albert. 1973. "Abhören von Feindsendern im KZ Dachau," in *Rappel*, Nos. 6–7, Luxembourg.

Thomé, Eugène. 1970. "Gusen öffnet seine Tore," in *Rappel*, Nos. 3–5, Luxembourg.

Tillard, Paul. 1945. *Mauthausen*, Paris.

———. 1955. *Die Triumphierenden*, Berlin.

Das Menschenschlachthaus Treblinka. 1946. *Drei Millionen sterben in den Gaskammern*, Vienna.

Tregenza, Michael. 1977. "Belzec Death Camp," in *The Wiener Library Bulletin*, XXX/41/42, London.

Trhlínová, Marie. 1974. "Pracowni komando Litomerice [Warshop detail Litomerice]," in *Terezinske listy* 4.

Ulmann, André. 1945. "Souvenirs de voyage," in Olga Wormser/Henri Michel, eds. *Tragédie de la déportation 1940–1945. Témoignages de survivants des camps de concentration allemands*, Paris.

Vermehren, Isa. 1947. *Reise durch den letzten Akt: Ein Bericht (10. Februar 44–29. Juni 45)*, Hamburg.

Vieville, Jean, see Leroy, Roger.

Vorländer, Herwart, ed. 1978. *Nationalsozialistische Konzentrationslager im Dienst der totalen Kriegsführung: Sieben württembergische Aussenkommandos des Konzentrationslagers Natzweiler/Elsass*, Stuttgart.

Vrba, Rudolf, Alan Bestic. 1964. *Ich kann nicht vergeben*, Munich.

Waffen-SS in der Bundesrepublik. 1978. Frankfurt.

Wagner, Karl. 1979. *Erinnerungen an Neustift: Beitrag zur Geschichte des antifaschistischen Widerstands 1942–1945 in Neustift/Stubai*, Karlsruhe.

Walter-Becker, Monika. 1978. "Das Lager Hailfingen," in *Nationalsozialistische Konzentrationslager*, idem.

Weber, Wolfgang, see Kühn, Günter.

Weinstein, Mala. 1965. "Memories from the Time of the Auschwitz Revolt (Winter 1944)," in *Yad Vashem Bulletin*, No. XVII, Jerusalem.

Weinstock, Rolf. 1948. *Das wahre Gesicht Hitler–Deutschlands: Dachau—Auschwitz—Buchenwald*, Singen.

Weisblum, Giza. 1968. "The Escape and Death of the 'Runner' Mala Zimetbaum," in Yuri Suhl, ed. *They Fought Back*, New York.

Wellers, Georges. 1973. *Le système concentrationnaire nazi*, Paris 1973.

———. *L'étoile jaune a l'heure de Vichy: De Drancy à Auschwitz*, Paris.

Wiernik, Yankiel. n.d. *A Year in Treblinka: An Inmate Who Escaped Tells the Day-to-Day Facts of One Year of His Torturous Experience*, New York.

Wiesel, Elie. n.d. *Die Nacht zu begraben. Elischa*, Munich.

Willenberg, Shmuel. 1961–63. "Revolt in Treblinka," in *Yad Vashem* Bulletin, No. VIII/IX, Jerusalem.

Williams, L. Norman, see Hill, Mavis M.

Włoch, Gerard. Cf. Brol, Franciszek.

Wormser, Olga, Henri Michel eds. 1954. *Tragédie de la déportation 1940–1945. Témoignages de survivants des camps de concentration allemands,* Paris.

Żmij, Józef. 1967. "Nareszcie przyszla wolnosc in *Pamietamy In Memory,* Katowice.

Zyśko, Wojciech. 1972. "Eksterminacyje dzielalnosc Truppenpolizei w dystrykcie Lubielskim w latach 1943–1944 in *Zeszyty Majdanka (Majdanek notebook)* VI, Lublin.

Zywulska, Krystyna. 1979. *Wo vorher Birken waren: Überlebensbericht einer jungen Frau aus Auschwitz-Birkenau,* Munich.

Index